THE
CRICKETERS'
WHO'S WHO
1997

THE CRICKETERS' WHO'S WHO 1997

Introduction by
HUGH MORRIS

Edited by
CHRIS HAWKES

Statistics by
RICHARD LOCKWOOD

Portraits photographed or researched by
BILL SMITH

Queen Anne Press

QUEEN ANNE PRESS
a division of Lennard Associates Limited
Mackerye End, Harpenden, Herts AL5 5DR

Published in association with
The Cricketers' Who's Who Limited

First published in Great Britain 1997

British Library Cataloguing in Publication is available

ISBN 1 85291 579 X

Typeset in Times and Univers Condensed
Editor (for Queen Anne Press): Kirsty Ennever
Quiz compiled by Chris Hawkes and David Thorne
Cover design by Paul Cooper

Printed and bound by
Butler and Tanner Limited, Frome and London

PICTURE ACKNOWLEDGEMENTS

Cover photographs by Allsport

The publishers are grateful to the *Gloucestershire Echo*, Richard Walsh
and Dessie Houston for supplying photographs

Our thanks also go to Allan Miller for his information
on David Boon, Stuart Law, Matthew Hayden and Shaun Young

CONTENTS

THE QUIZ

Throughout this book there are 100 quiz questions –
50 general trivia questions and 50 questions on the
Ashes taken from *Cricket's Ultimate Ashes Test*
by Mike McCann, 1994 (Queen Anne Press)

The answers can be found on page 720

INTRODUCTION

The journey from being described as 'a promising youngster' to becoming 'an old sweat' is becoming shorter and shorter. The demands on form and fitness only allow the best to keep playing beyond their mid-30s, as the pace and pressures of the modern game take their toll.

The game has changed enormously in the 16 years I have been involved with Glamorgan, and as we move towards the new millennium the cricketers who are just starting their careers can expect many more changes and developments. These youngsters will not have a better time to embark upon their cricketing careers: most counties have ploughed large sums of money into upgrading their facilities; others have lavish plans to develop new grounds; the Professional Cricketers' Association is working hard to improve wages and the general welfare of its members, whilst the increased television coverage has significantly raised the profile of the game.

The introduction of four-day championship cricket has been a big step forward, whilst the debate about the presence of overseas players in our domestic game, and the possibility of a two-divisional championship will be decided in the near future. There are many informed pundits who believe that a two-divisional championship will make county cricket a more competitive game, and produce tougher and more mature cricketers for our Test team. I would agree that our first-class game does need restructuring, but rather than having two divisions with promotion and relegation, I would prefer two equal divisions of nine teams, run along the lines of American football. The divisions would be drawn each season at Lord's, with every team playing each other once. In addition, they would play four teams randomly selected from the other division making a league season of 12 matches. At this stage the top four teams in each group would play off in the quarter-finals with the winners progressing through to the semi-finals and final, which would be a five-day game at Lord's. If there were draws during the final knock-out stages, relative run rates, league positions or bonus points could be taken into account. At least this system would prevent the wealthiest clubs buying up the best players, leaving the smaller counties to struggle for survival. The cricket would be competitive throughout, and those counties eliminated at the league stage could play the touring teams with full sides in a meaningful game of cricket.

Most counties would be resigned to cutting their playing staff to around 18 or 19 quality players and this would result in higher salaries. The English Cricket Board may also help by cutting the amount of players a county can register to 25. This would create a real incentive for young players to work hard and would provide them with an opportunity to make an impression in 2nd XI cricket at a much younger age, with a view to establishing themselves in the first team by the age of 20. They would be helped in their quest by counties improving their practice facilities, particularly the grass nets, and by providing the 2nd XIs with good pitches to play on.

There has been a general view that coaching standards have dropped over the past decade, with a few notable exceptions. This seems to have been borne out by the fact that nearly half of the counties employ coaches from overseas. The ECB has recognised this problem and initiated a management trainee programme for coaches and senior players. It has been designed to produce high-quality coaches who will be able to understand and bring out the best in our young players.

David Lloyd has been a keen supporter of this scheme, and has brought enthusiasm and fresh ideas to our Test team. The squad of players who left for this winter's tour of Zimbabwe and New Zealand were as fit and well prepared as any cricket team which has left these shores. There was hardly a stone left unturned as the players went through a series of eye tests, mental training techniques, team building exercises and physical fitness tests as part of their pre-tour preparation. The England manager is compiling a CD-Rom of the fitness levels of all county cricketers which he will be able to access at the touch of a button.

This technology, along with the Coopers and Lybrand and Whyte and Mackay ratings, should ensure that players remain fit and in form if they are to play for England.

Gone are the days when a cricketer's day consisted of eating a full English breakfast, coffee and biscuits at 10.30 am, a large lunch with chips, sandwiches and cakes at tea time, followed by a chicken tikka masala in the evening and all washed down with a gallon of lager!

Test cricket has always been a serious business, but with a growing call for a league table of the Test-playing nations in order to find an official World Champion, players will need to be more dedicated than ever.

There is now a clearer structure in place that allows our youngsters the chance of progressing to our Test team along a path of regular stepping stones. The A team is a particularly important bridge between county and Test cricket which has fostered the current talents of Atherton, Hussain, Knight, Thorpe, Crawley, Croft, Cork, Gough, Irani and Caddick. These players probably had enough ability to play at the highest level anyway, but having toured together they will get on more easily as a team and have first-hand knowledge of some of the challenges thrown up in different countries.

At the other end of the international scale the England U15 team had their first taste of a major competition last summer when they competed in the inaugural World Cup. They had an insight into some of the sacrifices they will need to make if they want to reach the top, when they spent 12 months preparing for the competition. These youngsters and others have the chance of making themselves an exciting and successful career in the game.

I can look back on my career and say that I would not have changed anything; I just wish that I was not becoming 'an old sweat'.

Hugh Morris
Glamorgan CCC and England

THE PLAYERS

Editor's Notes

The cricketers listed in this volume include all those who played for a first-class county at least once last season, in any form of cricket, and all those registered (at the time of going to press) to play for the 18 first-class counties in 1997, even those who have yet to make a first-team appearance. All statistics are complete to the end of the last English season. Figures about 1000 runs and 50 wickets in a season refer to matches in England only. All first-class figures include figures for Test matches which are also extracted and listed separately. One-day 100s and one-day five wickets in an innings are for the English domestic competitions and all one-day Internationals, home and abroad. Career records include 'rebel' tours to South Africa.

The following abbreviations apply: * means not out; All First – all first-class matches; 1-day Int – one-day Internationals; Sunday – Sunday League; NatWest – NatWest Trophy; B&H – Benson & Hedges Cup. The figures for batting and bowling averages refer to the full first-class English list for 1996, followed in brackets by the 1995 figures. Inclusion in the batting averages depends on a minimum of six completed innings, and an average of at least 10 runs; a bowler has to have taken at least 10 wickets. The same qualification has been used for compiling the bowlers' strike rate.

Readers will notice occasional differences in the way the same kind of information is presented. This is because it has been decided to follow the way in which the cricketers themselves have provided the relevant information.

Each year in *The Cricketers' Who's Who,* in addition to those cricketers who are playing during the current season, we also include the biographical and career details of those who played in the previous season but retired at the end of it. The purpose of this is to have, on the record, the full and final cricketing achievements of every player when his career has ended.

A book of this complexity and detail has to be prepared several months in advance of the cricket season, and occasionally there are recent changes in a player's circumstances which cannot be included in time. Many examples of facts and statistics which can quickly become outdated in the period between the actual compilation of the book and its publication, months later, will spring to the reader's mind, and I ask him or her to make the necessary commonsense allowance and adjustments.

Chris Hawkes, March 1997

ADAMS, C. J.   Derbyshire

Name: Christopher John Adams
Role: Right-hand bat, right-arm medium
bowler, slip fielder
Born: 6 May 1970, Whitwell, Derbyshire
Height: 6ft **Weight:** 13st 7lbs
Nickname: Grizzly
County debut: 1988
County cap: 1992
1000 runs in season: 3
1st-Class 50s: 36
1st-Class 100s: 19
1st-Class 200s: 2
1st-Class catches: 155
One-Day 100s: 5
Place in batting averages: 21st av. 52.78
(1995 65th av. 40.59)
Strike rate: (career 90.00)
Parents: John and Eluned (Lyn)
Wife and date of marriage:

Samantha Claire, 26 September 1992
Children: Georgia Louise, 4 October 1993
Family links with cricket: Brother David played 2nd XI cricket for Derbyshire and
Gloucestershire. Father played for Yorkshire Schools and uncle played for Essex 2nd
XI
Education: Tapton House School; Chesterfield Boys Grammar School; Repton School
Qualifications: 6 O-levels, NCA coaching awards
Overseas tours: Repton School to Barbados 1987; England NCA North to N Ireland 1987
Overseas teams played for: Takapuna, New Zealand 1987-88; Te Puke, New Zealand
1989-90; Primrose, Cape Town, South Africa 1991-92
Cricketers particularly admired: Ian Botham, Geoff Palmer, Adrian Kuiper
Other sports followed: Football, golf, rally driving and Formula 1
Relaxations: Mountain biking, golf and squash. 'My daughter, Georgia, is very
interesting but definitely not relaxing.'
Extras: Beat Richard Hutton's 25-year-old record for most runs scored in a season at
Repton. Represented English Schools U15 and U19, MCC Schools U19 and, in 1989,
England YC. Took two catches as 12th man for England v India at Old Trafford in 1990.
Holds county records for the fastest century by a Derbyshire batsman (57 mins) and the
highest score in the Sunday League (141*). Whittingdale Young Player Award 1992
Opinions on cricket: 'I love it.'
Best batting: 239 Derbyshire v Hampshire, Southampton 1996
Best bowling: 4-29 Derbyshire v Lancashire, Derby 1991

1996 Season

	M	Inns	NO	Runs	HS	Avge	100s	50s	Ct	St	O	M	Runs	Wkts	Avge	Best	5wI	10wM
Test																		
All First	20	36	3	1742	239	52.78	6	8	34	-	14	1	44	0	-	-	-	-
1-day Int																		
NatWest	3	3	1	118	68 *	59.00	-	1	-	-								
B & H	5	4	1	202	100 *	67.33	1	1	1	-								
Sunday	14	13	2	295	88 *	26.81	-	1	7	-								

Career Performances

	M	Inns	NO	Runs	HS	Avge	100s	50s	Ct	St	Balls	Runs	Wkts	Avge	Best	5wI	10wM
Test																	
All First	140	228	19	7664	239	36.66	19	36	155	-	1620	1072	18	59.55	4-29	-	-
1-day Int																	
NatWest	15	14	3	582	109 *	52.90	2	3	7	-	18	15	1	15.00	1-15	-	
B & H	27	24	4	606	100 *	30.30	1	4	9	-	24	21	0	-	-	-	
Sunday	109	102	18	2990	141 *	35.59	2	21	56	-	178	181	2	90.50	2-15	-	

AFFORD, J. A. Nottinghamshire

Name: John Andrew Afford
Role: Slow left-arm 'high' bowler,
right-hand bat and 'hopeless fielder'
Born: 12 May 1964, Crowland, Peterborough
Height: 6ft 2in **Weight:** 'A fleshy 14st'
Nickname: Aff, Des
County debut: 1984
County cap: 1990
50 wickets in a season: 5
1st-Class 5 w. in innings: 16
1st-Class 10 w. in match: 2
1st-Class catches: 57
Place in batting averages: 317th av. 3.40
Place in bowling averages: 49th av. 28.84
(1995 104th 47.18)
Strike rate: 68.21 (career 72.45)
Parents: Jill
Wife and date of marriage: Lynn,

1 October 1988
Children: Lily Meagan, 1 June 1991;
Daisy Tallulah, 12 October 1993
Family links with cricket: 'Cousin Nicholas plays in the Pearl Assurance 25-over mid-week inter-departmentals. Both daughters are Trent Bridge juniors and budding cricket nerds'
Education: Spalding Grammar School; Stamford College for Further Education
Qualifications: 5 O-levels, NCA coaching certificate
Off-season: Studying and coaching
Overseas tours: England A to Kenya and Zimbabwe 1989-90; Nottinghamshire to Cape Town 1992-93
Overseas teams played for: Upper Hutt, Taita and Petone, all in Wellington, New Zealand between 1984 and 1991
Cricketers particularly admired: John Childs ('great bowler'), Chris Cairns and Graham Gooch 'for their enviably luxuriant hair'
Young players to look out for: Anurag Singh, Usman Afzaal, Owais Shah
Other sports followed: 'I like football'
Injuries: 'Embarrassingly well all year'
Relaxations: Fishing and watching television
Extras: Hat-trick against Leics 2nd XI in 1989, also took 100 wickets in that season, 47 in 2nd XI and 53 in 1st XI. 'I think I beat Chris Cairns for player of the month once!'
Opinions on cricket: 'Not as hot as last year though a lot more wasps. Red bats look better on the television.'
Best batting: 22* Nottinghamshire v Leicestershire, Trent Bridge 1989
Best bowling: 6-51 Nottinghamshire v Lancashire, Trent Bridge 1996

1996 Season

	M	Inns	NO	Runs	HS	Avge	100s	50s	Ct	St	O	M	Runs	Wkts	Avge	Best	5wI	10wM
Test																		
All First	18	24	14	34	11 *	3.40	-	-	7	-	579.5	165	1471	51	28.84	6-51	2	-
1-day Int																		
NatWest																		
B & H	3	1	1	1	1 *	-	-	-	-	-	28	5	73	4	18.25	3-18	-	
Sunday																		

Career Performances

	M	Inns	NO	Runs	HS	Avge	100s	50s	Ct	St	Balls	Runs	Wkts	Avge	Best	5wI	10wM
Test																	
All First	169	166	72	385	22 *	4.09	-	-	57	-	33690	15397	465	33.11	6-51	16	2
1-day Int																	
NatWest	7	4	3	3	2 *	3.00	-	-	-	-	486	218	6	36.33	3-32	-	
B & H	24	2	2	2	1 *	-	-	-	3	-	1504	943	25	37.72	4-38	-	
Sunday	19	5	3	1	1	0.50	-	-	7	-	690	576	15	38.40	3-33	-	

AFZAAL, U.   Nottinghamshire

Name: Usman Afzaal
Role: Left-hand bat, slow left-arm bowler
Born: 9 June 1977, Rawalpindi, Pakistan
Height: 6ft **Weight:** 11st 7lbs
Nickname: Gulfraz
County debut: 1995
1st-Class 50s: 1
1st-Class catches: 6
Place in batting averages: 165th av. 29.33
(1995 264th av. 13.40)
Strike rate: 88.00 (career 169.50)
Parents: Mohammed and Firdous
Marital status: Single
Family links with cricket: Brother played
for Nottinghamshire U9
Education: Manvers Pierrepont School
Qualifications: NCA coaching certificate
Overseas tours: England U19 to West Indies
1994-95, to Zimbabwe 1995-96

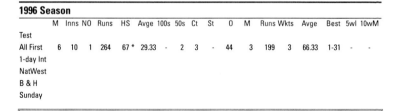

Cricketers particularly admired: Paul Johnson, Phil Tufnell, Mick Newell
Other sports followed: 'Cricket and cricket'
Relaxations: Watching movies and listening to music
Extras: Played for England U15 against South Africa and, in 1994, for England U17
against India
Best batting: 67* Nottinghamshire v Hampshire, Southampton 1996
Best bowling: 2-41 Nottinghamshire v Yorkshire, Trent Bridge 1995

1996 Season

	M	Inns	NO	Runs	HS	Avge	100s	50s	Ct	St	O	M	Runs	Wkts	Avge	Best	5wI	10wM
Test																		
All First	6	10	1	264	67 *	29.33	-	2	3	-	44	3	199	3	66.33	1-31	-	-
1-day Int																		
NatWest																			
B & H																			
Sunday																			

1. Who was the leading run-scorer in the 1996 World Cup?

Career Performances

	M	Inns	NO	Runs	HS	Avge	100s	50s	Ct	St	Balls	Runs	Wkts	Avge	Best	5wI	10wM
Test																	
All First	13	22	3	398	67 *	20.94	-	2	6	-	1356	781	8	97.62	2-41	-	-
1-day Int																	
NatWest	1	1	1	26	26 *	-	-	-	-	-	66	57	0	-		-	-
B & H																	
Sunday	6	2	1	2	2	2.00	-	-	3	-	204	165	8	20.62	2-25	-	

ALDRED, P. Derbyshire

Name: Paul Aldred
Role: Right-hand bat, right-arm medium bowler
Born: 4 February 1969, Chellaston, Derby
Height: 5ft 10in **Weight:** 12st
Nickname: Aldo
County debut: 1995
1st-Class catches: 6
Place in bowling averages: (1995 28th av. 25.00)
Strike rate: 104.87 (career 64.7316)
Parents: Harry and Lynette
Marital status: Single
Family links with cricket: None other than father who played local cricket
Education: Chellaston Primary School; Lady Manners, Bakenall, Derbyshire
Qualifications: 'None worth worrying about!'
Career outside cricket: Building trade – self-employed
Cricketers particularly admired: Ian Botham, Daryll Cullinan, Viv Richards
Other sports played: Golf and rugby, also played hockey for Derbyshire in 1985
Other sports followed: Rugby, golf
Relaxations: Playing sports, a beer with friends in the local pub, long distance running with Karl Krikken
Extras: 'Had the great opportunity to play against New Zealand with the England NCA team in 1994 which was a great day.' Represented Derbyshire U18 and U21 hockey team at the age of 15
Opinions on cricket: 'I think a lot of injuries picked up are due to the amount of cricket played in England. You just don't have time to recover to full fitness. I think the cricket schedule could be lightened a little, at first-class level at least.'

Best batting: 33 Derbyshire v Warwickshire, Edgbaston 1995
33 Derbyshire v Surrey, The Oval 1996
Best bowling: 3-47 Derbyshire v Young Australia, Chesterfield 1995

1996 Season

	M	Inns	NO	Runs	HS	Avge	100s	50s	Ct	St	O	M	Runs	Wkts	Avge	Best	5wI	10wM
Test																		
All First	5	5	2	50	33	16.66	-	-	2	-	139.5	21	537	8	67.12	2-65	-	-
1-day Int																		
NatWest																			
B & H	2	1	0	7	7	7.00	-	-	-	-	9	0	53	2	26.50	2-35	-	
Sunday	9	2	1	16	9	16.00	-	-	3	-	48.5	2	299	8	37.37	4-41	-	

Career Performances

	M	Inns	NO	Runs	HS	Avge	100s	50s	Ct	St	Balls	Runs	Wkts	Avge	Best	5wI	10wM
Test																	
All First	12	17	2	147	33	9.80	-	-	6	-	1489	912	23	39.65	3-47	-	-
1-day Int																	
NatWest																		
B & H	2	1	0	7	7	7.00	-	-	-	-	54	53	2	26.50	2-35	-	
Sunday	17	5	3	34	11 *	17.00	-	-	4	-	532	536	16	33.50	4-41	-	

ALLEYNE, M. W.   Gloucestershire

Name: Mark Wayne Alleyne
Role: Right-hand bat, right-arm medium bowler, cover fielder, occasional wicket-keeper
Born: 23 May 1968, Tottenham
Height: 5ft 11in **Weight:** 13st 7lbs
Nickname: Boo-Boo
County debut: 1986
County cap: 1990
1000 runs in a season: 4
50 wickets in a season: 1
1st-Class 50s: 46
1st-Class 100s: 12
1st-Class 200s: 1
1st-Class 5 w. in innings: 3
1st-Class catches: 156
1st-Class stumpings: 2

One-Day 100s: 3
One-Day 5 w. in innings: 3
Place in batting averages: 137th av. 32.85 (1995 106th av. 33.56)
Place in bowling averages: 20th av. 24.37 (1995 126th av. 42.34)
Strike rate: 50.90 (career 61.18)
Parents: Euclid Clevis and Hyacinth Cordeilla
Marital status: Single
Family links with cricket: Brother played for Gloucestershire 2nd XI and Middlesex YCs. Father played club cricket in Barbados and England
Education: Harrison College, Barbados; Cardinal Pole School, E London
Qualifications: 6 O-levels, NCA Senior Coaching Award, volleyball coaching certificate
Overseas tours: England YC to Sri Lanka 1986-87 and Australia 1987-88
Cricketers particularly admired: Gordon Greenidge, Viv Richards
Other sports followed: Football, volleyball, athletics
Relaxations: Watching films and sport; listening to music
Extras: Youngest player to score a century for Gloucestershire. In 1990 also became the youngest to score a double hundred for the county. Graduate of Haringey Cricket College. Cricket Select Sunday League Player of the Year 1992. Highest Sunday League score for Gloucestershire
Best batting: 256 Gloucestershire v Northamptonshire, Northampton 1990
Best bowling: 5-32 Gloucestershire v Sussex, Bristol 1996

1996 Season

	M	Inns	NO	Runs	HS	Avge	100s	50s	Ct	St	O	M	Runs	Wkts	Avge	Best	5wI	10wM
Test																		
All First	18	30	3	887	149	32.85	1	3	16	-	458.1	123	1316	54	24.37	5-32	2	-
1-day Int																		
NatWest	2	2	0	17	13	8.50	-	-	-	-	9.3	3	26	2	13.00	2-26	-	
B & H	5	4	2	111	75	55.50	-	1	3	-	35	0	168	4	42.00	2-47	-	
Sunday	15	15	3	295	100 *	24.58	1	1	3	-	99.1	3	533	12	44.41	3-52	-	

Career Performances

	M	Inns	NO	Runs	HS	Avge	100s	50s	Ct	St	Balls	Runs	Wkts	Avge	Best	5wI	10wM
Test																	
All First	200	329	33	9180	256	31.01	12	46	156	2	12971	6859	212	32.35	5-32	3	-
1-day Int																	
NatWest	25	21	4	373	73	21.94	-	1	9	-	845	540	19	28.42	5-30	1	
B & H	38	31	6	522	75	20.88	-	1	13	-	1471	1049	33	31.78	5-27	1	
Sunday	160	145	35	3401	134 *	30.91	3	14	55	-	4996	4256	132	32.24	5-28	1	

ALTREE, D. A.   Warwickshire

Name: Darren Anthony Altree
Role: Right-hand bat, left-arm
fast medium bowler
Born: 30 September 1974, Rugby
Height: 5ft 11in
Weight: 12st 7lbs
Nickname: Bobby, Bobster, Dazzler
County debut: 1996
1st-Class catches: 1
Strike rate: 67.00 (career 67.00)
Parents: Tony and Margaret
Marital status: Single
Education: Ashlawn School, Rugby
Career outside cricket: Coil operator for
GEC in Rugby
Overseas tours: Warwickshire U19 to Cape
Town 1992-93
Overseas teams played for: Avendale, Cape
Town 1994-95
Cricketers particularly admired: 'Too many to list'
Young players to look out for: 'Too many to list'
Injuries: Thigh strain, out for two weeks
Relaxations: Watching television and listening to music
Opinions on cricket: 'I have none.'
Best bowling: 3-41 Warwickshire v Pakistan, Edgbaston 1996

1996 Season

	M	Inns	NO	Runs	HS	Avge	100s	50s	Ct	St	O	M	Runs	Wkts	Avge	Best	5wI	10wM
Test																		
All First	3	5	2	0	0 *	0.00	-	-	1	-	67	9	267	6	44.50	3-41	-	-
1-day Int																		
NatWest																			
B & H																			
Sunday																			

2. Who was the leading wicket-taker in the 1996 World Cup?

Career Performances

	M	Inns	NO	Runs	HS	Avge	100s	50s	Ct	St	Balls	Runs	Wkts	Avge	Best	5wI	10wM
Test																	
All First	3	5	2	0	0 *	0.00	-	-	1	-	402	267	6	44.50	3-41	-	-
1-day Int																	
NatWest																		
B & H																		
Sunday																		

AMBROSE, C. E. L. Northamptonshire

Name: Curtly Elconn Lynwall Ambrose
Role: Left-hand bat, right-arm fast bowler, 'like the gully area'
Born: 21 September 1963, Antigua
Height: 6ft 7in **Weight:** 14st
Nickname: Ambie
County debut: 1989
County cap: 1990
Test debut: 1987-88
Tests: 61
One-day internationals: 133
50 wickets in a season: 7
1st-Class 50s: 4
1st-Class 5 w. innings: 40
1st-Class 10 w. in match: 8
1st-Class catches: 71
One-day 5 w. in innings: 4
Place in batting averages: 294th av. 10.54 (1995 169th av. 24.60)
Place in bowling averages: 3rd av. 16.67 (1995 70th av. 29.76)
Strike rate: 39.72 (career 50.94)
Parents: Jasper (deceased) and Hillie
Wife and date of marriage: Bridgette, 6 September 1991
Children: Tanya, May 1990
Family links with cricket: Brother used to play club cricket and had trials for Antigua. Cousin Rolston Otto plays for Antigua and Leeward Islands
Education: Swetes Primary School; All Saints Secondary School
Qualifications: 3 O-levels, 3 A-levels, qualified carpenter
Off-season: Playing for West Indies
Overseas tours: West Indies to England 1988, to Australia 1988-89, to India for Nehru Cup 1989-90, to Pakistan 1990-91, to England 1991, to Pakistan 1991-92, to Australia

for Benson & Hedges World Series and World Cup 1991-92, to Australia and South Africa 1992-93, to Sharjah, India (Hero Cup) and Sri Lanka 1993-94, to New Zealand 1994-95, to England 1995, to Australia 1995-96, to India and Pakistan (World Cup) 1995-96, to Australia 1996-97

Overseas teams played for: Leeward Islands

Cricketers particularly admired: David Gower, Richard Hadlee, Robin Smith and all West Indian Test cricketers

Other sports followed: NBA (American) basketball and tennis

Relaxations: Going to the movies, relaxing on the beach, listening to and playing music (bass guitar)

Extras: A basketball player who only began playing cricket seriously at the age of 17. Took a wicket with his first ball on Championship debut for Northamptonshire against Glamorgan in 1989. Played in two Nat West finals in three years with Northants. Figures of 8 for 45 are the best in Tests for West Indies v England. One of *Wisden*'s Five Cricketers of the Year 1992. Released by Northamptonshire at the end of the 1996 season

Best batting: 78 Northamptonshire v Somerset, Taunton 1994

Best bowling: 8-45 West Indies v England, Bridgetown 1989-90

1996 Season

	M	Inns	NO	Runs	HS	Avge	100s	50s	Ct	St	O	M	Runs	Wkts	Avge	Best	5wI	10wM
Test																		
All First	9	13	2	116	25 *	10.54	-	-	11	-	284.4	80	717	43	16.67	6-26	5	1
1-day Int																		
NatWest	2	1	0	7	7	7.00	-	-	1	-	22	6	39	3	13.00	2-18	-	
B & H	5	1	0	10	10	10.00	-	-	4	-	48.2	4	176	5	35.20	2-40	-	
Sunday	14	5	3	26	11 *	13.00	-	-	6	-	102.2	17	347	17	20.41	3-14	-	

Career Performances

	M	Inns	NO	Runs	HS	Avge	100s	50s	Ct	St	Balls	Runs	Wkts	Avge	Best	5wI	10wM
Test	61	87	19	850	53	12.50	-	1	13	-	14319	5658	266	21.27	8-45	14	3
All First	186	238	58	2671	78	14.83	-	4	71	-	38314	15388	752	20.46	8-45	40	8
1-day Int	133	70	29	449	26 *	10.95	-	-	33	-	7105	4129	184	22.44	5-17	4	
NatWest	21	8	1	96	48	13.71	-	-	7	-	1397	513	32	16.03	4-7	-	
B & H	15	8	4	81	17 *	20.25	-	-	9	-	909	478	25	19.12	4-31	-	
Sunday	59	28	11	227	37	13.35	-	-	14	-	2593	1558	58	26.86	4-20	-	

Name: Mohammed Amjad
Role: Left-hand bat, left-arm leg spin
Born: 23 March 1971, Birmingham
Height: 5ft 6in   **Weight:** 10st
Nickname: Jabbers, Nicknack
County debut: 1996
Parents: Mohammed Ilyas and Amina Bibi
Wife and date of marriage: Abida
Mohammed, April 1993
Family links with cricket: 'Close friends
with Wasim Khan and the late Parvaz Mirza
both of whom were classmates at Small
Heath School'
Education: Regent's Park Junior School;
Small Heath School; Josiah Mason Sixth
Form College
Qualifications: 9 GCSEs, 'also qualified
Muslim hafeez (priest)'

Career outside cricket: Cab driver and Muslim priest in local mosque
Off-season: Intend to play first-class cricket in Pakistan
Cricketers particularly admired: Mushtaq Ahmed, Sachin Tendulkar, Abdul Qadir,
Anil Kumble, Richard Hadlee, Aravinda De Silva
Young players to look out for: Vikram Solanki, Anurag Singh, Wasim Khan
Other sports followed: Football (Aston Villa), squash, table tennis and basketball
Relaxations: Swimming, 'reading the Holy Koran and praying', spending time with
close colleagues and friends
Extras: Took a hat-trick in his only second-class game for Warwickshire in 1989. Has
also played 2nd XI cricket for Somerset
Opinions on cricket: '2nd XI three-day games should be converted to four days to
avoid manufactured declarations and results. Cricket in England is still structured too
rigidly. Young talented cricketers should be thrust into first-class cricket based on their
ability and shouldn't have to wait around in the 2nd XI for a few seasons to "learn their
trade".'
Best batting: 7 Worcestershire v South Africa A, Worcester 1996

3. Which cricketer took a world-record three hat-tricks during the 1996 season?

1996 Season

	M	Inns	NO	Runs	HS	Avge	100s	50s	Ct	St	O	M	Runs	Wkts	Avge	Best	5wI	10wM
Test																		
All First	1	2	0	8	7	4.00	-	-	-	-	4	0	25	0	-		-	--
1-day Int																		
NatWest																		
B & H																		
Sunday																		

Career Performances

	M	Inns	NO	Runs	HS	Avge	100s	50s	Ct	St	Balls	Runs	Wkts	Avge	Best	5wI	10wM
Test																	
All First	1	2	0	8	7	4.00	-	-	-	-	24	25	0	-		-	-
1-day Int																	
NatWest																	
B & H																	
Sunday																	

ANDREW, S. J. W. Essex

Name: Stephen Jon Walter Andrew
Role: Right-hand bat, right-arm
fast-medium bowler
Born: 27 January 1966, London
Height: 6ft 3in **Weight:** 15st
Nickname: Rip
County debut: 1984 (Hampshire), 1990
(Essex)
1st-Class 5 w. in innings: 7
1st-Class catches: 26
One-Day 5 w. in innings: 1
Place in batting averages: 303rd av. 7.62
Place in bowling averages: 124th av. 42.73
Strike rate: 79.46 (career 60.95)
Parents: Jon Trevor and Victoria Julia Maud
Marital status: Single
Education: Hordle House Prep School;
Milton Abbey, Portchester School for Boys
Qualifications: 3 O-levels

Overseas tours: England YC to West Indies 1984-85
Overseas teams played for: Pirates, Durban 1983-84; SAP, Durban 1984-86; Manly,
Sydney 1987-88; Pinetown, Durban 1988-89; Taita, Wellington 1990-91; Parnell,

Auckland, 1991-92, Primrose, Cape Town 1993-94
Cricketers particularly admired: Dennis Lillee ('god')
Other sports followed: Golf, rugby
Relaxations: Music, socialising, films and books
Opinions on cricket: 'The seams should go back to the way they were originally to give those bowlers with the ability more chance of swinging and seaming the ball on the generally flat pitches that we play on.'
Best batting: 35 Essex v Northamptonshire, Chelmsford 1990
Best bowling: 7-47 Essex v Lancashire, Old Trafford 1993

1996 Season

	M	Inns	NO	Runs	HS	Avge	100s	50s	Ct	St	O	M	Runs	Wkts	Avge	Best	5wI	10wM
Test																		
All First	10	14	6	61	13	7.62	-	-	2	-	198.4	47	641	15	42.73	3-67	-	-
1-day Int																		
NatWest	1	0	0	0	0	-	-	-	-	-	7.3	0	52	2	26.00	2-52	-	
B & H																		
Sunday	14	7	3	60	32	15.00	-	-	1	-	87.2	6	423	10	42.30	2-27	-	

Career Performances

	M	Inns	NO	Runs	HS	Avge	100s	50s	Ct	St	Balls	Runs	Wkts	Avge	Best	5wI	10wM
Test																	
All First	129	109	42	472	35	7.04	-	-	26	-	19079	10456	313	33.40	7-47	7	-
1-day Int																	
NatWest	9	2	2	1	1 *	-	-	-	2	-	471	308	11	28.00	2-34	-	
B & H	11	3	3	5	4 *	-	-	-	1	-	654	363	20	18.15	5-24	1	
Sunday	61	20	7	128	32	9.84	-	-	3	-	2384	1988	50	39.76	4-40	-	

4. Who holds the record for fastest hundred in a one-day international?

ARCHER, G. F. — Nottinghamshire

Name: Graeme Francis Archer
Role: Right-hand bat, right-arm
'very medium'
Born: 26 September 1970, Carlisle, Cumbria
Height: 6ft 1in **Weight:** 13st 7lbs
Nickname: Bunka, Archie B
County debut: 1992
County cap: 1995
1000 runs in season: 1
1st-Class 50s: 18
1st-Class 100s: 8
1st-Class catches: 61
Place in batting averages: 60th av. 43.71
(1995 68th av. 40.37)
Strike rate: 54.00 (career 75.00)
Parents: Christopher William and Jean
Elizabeth
Marital status: Single
Family links with cricket: Father played for Carlisle in N Lancashire League; brother Neil plays in the S Cheshire Alliance League
Education: King Edward VI High School; Stafford College
Qualifications: 3 O-levels, City & Guilds and BTEC National Diploma in Leisure Management, NCA Senior Coaching Award
Career outside cricket: 'Not decided'
Off-season: Coaching at Trent Bridge
Overseas teams played for: Hutt Districts, New Zealand 1991-92; Hutt Valley representative side 1991-92, Old Collegians, Christchurch 1994-96
Cricketers particularly admired: Graeme Hick, Ian Botham, Derek Randall, Chris Cairns and Jimmy Adams
Young players to look out for: Usman Afzaal, Noel Gie and Guy Welton
Other sports followed: Badminton, football (Carlisle United) and squash
Injuries: Injury to left index finger, out for three weeks
Relaxations: Music, videos and driving
Extras: Scored 200* in a 15 (8-ball) over match for Walsall U18s. Awarded the A.A.Thompson Fielding Prize by The Cricket Society in 1990. Made 2nd XI debut for Notts in 1987 aged 15. Played for Staffordshire in 1990-91. Rapid Cricketline Player of the Month April/May 1994
Opinions on cricket: 'Good to see the overs reduced to 104. Thirty minutes for tea.'
Best batting: 168 Nottinghamshire v Glamorgan, Worksop 1994
Best bowling: 3-18 Nottinghamshire v Hampshire, Southampton 1996

1996 Season

	M	Inns	NO	Runs	HS	Avge	100s	50s	Ct	St	O	M	Runs	Wkts	Avge	Best	5wI	10wM
Test																		
All First	13	24	3	918	143	43.71	2	5	17	-	27	5	98	3	32.66	3-18	-	-
1-day Int																		
NatWest																		
B & H																		
Sunday	7	6	1	97	47	19.40	-	-	-	-	5	0	19	0	-		-	-

Career Performances

	M	Inns	NO	Runs	HS	Avge	100s	50s	Ct	St	Balls	Runs	Wkts	Avge	Best	5wI	10wM
Test																	
All First	59	104	11	3650	168	39.24	8	18	61	-		675	431	9	47.88	3-18	-	-
1-day Int																	
NatWest	3	2	0	54	39	27.00	-	-	1	-							
B & H	5	4	0	134	74	33.50	-	1	-	-	36	44	0	-		-	-
Sunday	39	34	4	479	53	15.96	-	1	12	-	168	146	6	24.33	2-16	-	

ATHERTON, M. A.　　　　Lancashire

Name: Michael Andrew Atherton
Role: Right-hand bat, leg-break bowler,
county vice-captain
Born: 23 March 1968, Manchester
Height: 6ft **Weight:** 12st 7lbs
Nickname: Athers, Dread
County debut: 1987
County cap: 1989
Test debut: 1989
Tests: 62
One-Day Internationals: 43
1000 runs in a season: 7
1st-Class 50s: 76
1st-Class 100s: 41
1st-Class 5 w. in innings: 3
1st-Class catches: 178
One-Day 100s: 10
Place in batting averages: 82nd av. 38.52
(1995 51st av. 44.10)
Strike rate: 72.00 (career 83.10)
Parents: Alan and Wendy
Marital status: Single

Family links with cricket: Father and brother both play league cricket
Education: Briscoe Lane Primary; Manchester GS; Downing College, Cambridge
Qualifications: 10 O-levels, 3 A-levels; BA (Hons) (Cantab)
Off-season: England tour to Zimbabwe and New Zealand
Overseas tours: England YC to Sri Lanka 1986-87, to Australia 1987-88; England A to Zimbabwe 1989-90; England to Australia and New Zealand 1990-91, to India and Sri Lanka 1992-93, to West Indies 1993-94, to Australia 1994-95, to South Africa 1995-96, to India and Pakistan (World Cup) 1995-96, to Zimbabwe and New Zealand 1996-97
Cricketers particularly admired: Graham Gooch
Other sports followed: Golf, squash, football
Relaxations: 'Decent novels (Heller, Kundera, etc.), good movies, food and wine, travelling, most sports, music'
Extras: In 1987 was first player to score 1000 runs in his debut season since Paul Parker in 1976. Youngest Lancastrian to score a Test century (151 v NZ at Trent Bridge in 1990); second Lancastrian to score a Test century at Old Trafford (138 v India in 1990). First captained England U19 aged 16. Selected for England tour to New Zealand and also England A tour to Bermuda and West Indies in 1991-92 but ruled out of both through injury. Appointed England captain in 1993. Cornhill England Player of the Year 1994. Voted England's Player of the Series against the West Indies in 1995. Hit 185 not out in the second Test against South Africa in Johannesburg in 1995-96 series. The innings lasted 645 minutes and was the fourth longest by an Englishman in Test matches
Best batting: 199 Lancashire v Durham, Gateshead Fell 1992
Best bowling: 6-78 Lancashire v Nottinghamshire, Trent Bridge 1990

1996 Season

	M	Inns	NO	Runs	HS	Avge	100s	50s	Ct	St	O	M	Runs	Wkts	Avge	Best	5wI	10wM
Test	6	10	1	425	160	47.22	1	2	5	-	7	1	20	1	20.00	1-20	-	-
All First	15	26	1	963	160	38.52	1	7	8	-	12	2	35	1	35.00	1-20	-	-
1-day Int	6	6	0	116	65	19.33	-	1	1									
NatWest	5	5	0	245	115	49.00	1	1	1									
B & H	8	8	1	221	121 *	31.57	1	-	7									
Sunday	8	8	2	335	91 *	55.83	-	3	4									

Career Performances

	M	Inns	NO	Runs	HS	Avge	100s	50s	Ct	St	Balls	Runs	Wkts	Avge	Best	5wI	10wM
Test	62	114	3	4627	185 *	41.68	10	29	44	-	408	302	2	151.00	1-20	-	-
All First	223	386	35	15416	199	43.92	41	76	178	-	8975	4726	108	43.75	6-78	3	-
1-day Int	43	43	2	1449	127	35.34	1	11	11	-							
NatWest	20	20	2	780	115	43.33	2	4	7	-	188	154	6	25.66	2-15	-	
B & H	50	49	4	1746	121 *	38.80	3	11	26	-	252	228	7	32.57	4-42	-	
Sunday	73	71	5	2370	111	35.90	4	12	26	-	216	248	7	35.42	3-33	-	

ATHEY, C. W. J.   Sussex

Name: Charles William Jeffrey Athey
Role: Right-hand bat, occasional right-arm medium bowler, occasional wicket-keeper
Born: 27 September 1957, Middlesbrough
Height: 5ft 10in **Weight:** 12st 7lbs
Nickname: Bumper, Wingnut, Ath
County debut: 1976 (Yorkshire), 1984 (Gloucestershire), 1993 (Sussex)
County cap: 1980 (Yorkshire), 1985 (Gloucestershire), 1993 (Sussex)
Benefit: 1990
Test debut: 1980
Tests: 23
One-Day Internationals: 31
1000 runs in a season: 13
1st-Class 50s: 121
1st-Class 100s: 54
1st-Class catches: 420
1st-Class stumpings: 2
One-Day 100s: 11
One-Day 5 w. in innings: 1
Place in batting averages: 135th av. 33.06 (1995 89th av. 35.73)
Strike rate: (career 99.33)
Parents: Peter and Maree
Wife and date of marriage: Janet Linda, 9 October 1982
Family links with cricket: 'Father played league cricket in North Yorkshire and South Durham League for 29 years, 25 of them with Middlesbrough, and has been President of Middlesbrough CC since 1975. Brother-in-law Colin Cook played for Middlesex, other brother-in-law (Martin) plays in Thames Valley League. Father-in-law deeply involved in Middlesex Youth cricket'
Education: Linthorpe Junior; Stainsby Secondary School; Acklam Hall High School
Qualifications: 4 O-levels, some CSEs, NCA coaching certificate
Off-season: Working for Sussex CCC in marketing department
Overseas tours: England YC to West Indies 1975-76; England to West Indies 1980-81, to Australia 1986-87, to Pakistan, Australia and New Zealand 1987-88; England B to Sri Lanka 1985-86; unofficial English XI to South Africa 1989-90; MCC to Bahrain 1994-95; BSI World Cup, India 1994-95
Cricketers particularly admired: 'Too many to mention, but those with enthusiasm for the game'
Young players to look out for: 'Several young players at Sussex'
Other sports followed: Most sports, especially football (Middlesbrough FC)

Injuries: None
Relaxations: Gardening, sport and military history
Extras: Played for Teesside County Schools U16 at age 12. Played for Yorkshire Colts 1974. Played football for Middlesbrough Schools U16 and Junior XI. Offered but declined apprenticeship terms with Middlesbrough FC. Captain of Gloucestershire in 1989. Suspension for playing in South Africa in 1990 was remitted in 1992. 'Scored four hundreds in four innings for Gloucestershire CCC.'
Opinions on cricket: 'Must play county cricket on better wickets.'
Best batting: 184 England B v Sri Lanka XI, Galle 1985-86
Best bowling: 3-3 Gloucestershire v Hampshire, Bristol 1985

1996 Season

	M	Inns	NO	Runs	HS	Avge	100s	50s	Ct	St	O	M	Runs	Wkts	Avge	Best	5wI	10wM
Test																		
All First	18	33	0	1091	111	33.06	3	5	15	-								
1-day Int																		
NatWest	3	3	0	129	57	43.00	-	2	-	-								
B & H	4	4	0	98	55	24.50	-	1	1	-								
Sunday	3	3	0	38	18	12.66	-	-	-	-								

Career Performances

	M	Inns	NO	Runs	HS	Avge	100s	50s	Ct	St	Balls	Runs	Wkts	Avge	Best	5wI	10wM
Test	23	41	1	919	123	22.97	1	4	13	-							
All First	455	763	69	24771	184	35.69	54	121	420	2	4768	2652	48	55.25	3-3	-	-
1-day Int	31	30	3	848	142 *	31.40	2	4	16	-	6	10	0	-	-	-	-
NatWest	49	48	8	1765	115	44.12	2	14	21	-	199	168	1	168.00	1-18	-	
B & H	79	75	11	2430	118	37.96	1	19	34	1	478	364	16	22.75	4-48	-	
Sunday	260	249	22	7252	121 *	31.94	6	46	97	-	913	857	30	28.56	5-35	1	

AUSTIN, I. D.   Lancashire

Name: Ian David Austin
Role: Left-hand bat, right-arm medium bowler
Born: 30 May 1966, Haslingden, Lancs
Height: 5ft 10in **Weight:** 14st 7lbs
Nickname: Oscar, Bully
County debut: 1986
County cap: 1990
1st-Class 50s: 10
1st-Class 100s: 2
1st-Class 5 w. in innings: 5

1st-Class 10 w. in match: 1
1st-Class catches: 20
One-Day 5 w. in innings: 1
Place in batting averages: 35th av. 48.55
(1995 180th av. 22.88)
Place in bowling averages: 53rd av. 29.31
(1995 33rd av. 25.40)
Strike rate: 61.00 (career 67.35)
Parents: Jack and Ursula
Wife and date of marriage:
Alexandra, 27 February 1993
Children: Victoria, 28 January 1995
Family links with cricket: Father opened
batting for Haslingden CC
Education: Haslingden High School
Qualifications: 4 O-levels, NCA coaching
certificate
Career outside cricket: 'Trying to qualify as
a wine taster'
Off-season: Working for local bed firm
Overseas tours: NAYC to Bermuda 1985; Lancashire to Jamaica 1986-87, 1987-88,
to Zimbabwe 1988-89, to Tasmania and Western Australia 1989-90, 1990-91
Overseas teams played for: Maroochydore, Queensland 1987-88, 1991-92;
Randwick, Sydney 1990-91
Cricketers particularly admired: Ian Botham, Hartley Alleyne
Other sports followed: Football (Burnley), golf
Relaxations: Golf, and listening to music
Extras: Holds amateur Lancashire League record for highest individual score (147*).
Broke Lancashire CCC record for most wickets in the Sunday League in 1991. Scored
quickest first-class century in 1991 off authentic bowling (64 balls). Man of the Match
in the 1996 Benson and Hedges final and the NatWest semi-final
Best batting: 115* Lancashire v Derbyshire, Blackpool 1992
Best bowling: 5-23 Lancashire v Middlesex, Old Trafford 1994

1996 Season

	M	Inns	NO	Runs	HS	Avge	100s	50s	Ct	St	O	M	Runs	Wkts	Avge	Best	5wl	10wM
Test																		
All First	10	12	3	437	95 *	48.55	-	3	4	-	223.4	64	645	22	29.31	5-116	1	-
1-day Int																		
NatWest	5	5	1	39	18	9.75	-	-	-	-	49.2	9	169	6	28.16	3-47	-	
B & H	8	6	1	84	39	16.80	-	-	1	-	75	12	266	14	19.00	4-21	-	
Sunday	14	10	3	120	31	17.14	-	-	3	-	110.5	4	496	10	49.60	3-39	-	

Career Performances

	M	Inns	NO	Runs	HS	Avge	100s	50s	Ct	St	Balls	Runs	Wkts	Avge	Best	5wI	10wM
Test																	
All First	88	121	27	2524	115 *	26.85	2	10	20	-	11451	5283	170	31.07	5-23	5	1
1-day Int																	
NatWest	21	15	8	222	57	31.71	-	1	1	-	1365	853	24	35.54	3-32	-	
B & H	45	27	9	411	80	22.83	-	2	9	-	2631	1695	54	31.38	4-8	-	
Sunday	139	84	34	950	48	19.00	-	-	29	-	5773	4447	148	30.04	5-56	1	

AVERIS, J. M. M.   Gloucestershire

Name: James Max Michael Averis
Role: Right-hand bat, right-arm medium-fast bowler
Born: 28 May 1974, Bristol
Height: 6ft **Weight:** 12st 7lb
Nickname: Fish, Chess, Colgate
County debut: 1994 (one-day)
Parents: Michael and Carol
Marital status: Single
Family links with cricket: 'Grandfather and father both played good club cricket'
Education: Bristol Cathedral School, Portsmouth University, Oxford University
Qualifications: 10 GCSEs, 3 A-levels
Career outside cricket: Rugby player
Off-season: Studying at Oxford University and playing rugby for Bristol RFC
Overseas tours: Bristol Schools to Australia 1990-91; Gloucestershire to Zimbabwe 1996; Oxford University RFC to Japan and Australia
Cricketers particularly admired: Courtney Walsh and Ian Botham
Young players to look out for: Jamie Skinner and Dom Hewson
Other sports followed: Rugby (Bristol RFC and Oxford University RFC) and football (Liverpool FC)
Injuries: Cruciate ligament repair
Relaxations: Listening to music, 'going to DTM's'
Extras: Played for Gloucestershire from U16 to U19 and ESCA U19. Bristol RFC U21 tour to South Africa in Spring 1995. Played for Oxford University in the 1996 Varsity Match at Twickenham
Opinions on cricket: 'Second team cricket should be played over four days.'

1996 Season

	M	Inns	NO	Runs	HS	Avge	100s	50s	Ct	St	O	M	Runs	Wkts	Avge	Best	5wI	10wM
Test																		
All First																		
1-day Int																		
NatWest																		
B & H																		
Sunday	2	1	1	1	1*	-	-	-	-	-	14	0	78	4	19.50	2-35	-	

Career Performances

	M	Inns	NO	Runs	HS	Avge	100s	50s	Ct	St	Balls	Runs	Wkts	Avge	Best	5wI	10wM
Test																	
All First																	
1-day Int																	
NatWest																	
B & H																	
Sunday	3	2	2	3	2*	-	-	-	1	-	120	122	4	30.50	2-35	-	

AYMES, A. N.   Hampshire

Name: Adrian Nigel Aymes
Role: Right-hand bat, wicket-keeper
Born: 4 June 1964, Southampton
Height: 6ft **Weight:** 12st 7lbs
Nickname: Aymser, Adi
County debut: 1987
County cap: 1991
1st-Class 50s: 22
1st-Class 100s: 3
1st-Class catches: 286
1st-Class stumpings: 24
Place in batting averages: 73rd av. 40.05
(1995 128th av. 30.00)
Strike rate: (career 42.00)
Parents: Michael and Barbara
Wife and date of marriage: Marie, 12
November 1992
Children: Lucie, 9 November 1994
Family links with cricket: 'Father once walked into a Holt and Haskell Sports Shop'
Education: Shirley Middle; Bellemoor Secondary; Hill College
Qualifications: 4 O-levels, 1 A-level, NCA coaching award
Career outside cricket: Selling cricket equipment and coaching

Overseas tours: Hampshire CCC to Isle of Wight 1992, to Portugal 1993, to Guernsey 1994
Cricketers particularly admired: 'All wicket keepers past and present', Peter Haslop and Kevin Shine
Young players to look out for: John Emburey
Other sports followed: Boxing and non-sport martial arts
Injuries: Cracked thumb, no time off
Relaxations: Watching videos, exercising
Extras: Half century on debut v Surrey; equalled club record of 6 catches in an innings and 10 in a match. Hampshire Exiles Young Player of the Year 1990
Opinions on cricket: 'Great game.'
Best batting: 113 Hampshire v Essex, Southampton 1996
Best bowling: 1-75 Hampshire v Sussex, Southampton 1992

1996 Season

	M	Inns	NO	Runs	HS	Avge	100s	50s	Ct	St	O	M	Runs	Wkts	Avge	Best	5wl	10wM
Test																		
All First	19	32	12	801	113	40.05	2	2	42	3								
1-day Int																		
NatWest	3	1	0	10	10	10.00	-	-	6	-								
B & H	4	3	0	71	38	23.66	-	-	5	-								
Sunday	15	13	3	148	31	14.80	-	-	12	6								

Career Performances

	M	Inns	NO	Runs	HS	Avge	100s	50s	Ct	St	Balls	Runs	Wkts	Avge	Best	5wl	10wM
Test																	
All First	127	189	52	4329	113	31.59	3	22	286	24	42	75	1	75.00	1-75	-	-
1-day Int																	
NatWest	13	4	0	64	34	16.00	-	-	18	2							
B & H	26	13	4	169	38	18.77	-	-	25	7							
Sunday	92	65	29	1020	54	28.33	-	1	89	21							

BAILEY, R. J.   Northamptonshire

Name: Robert John Bailey
Role: Right-hand bat, off-spin bowler, county captain
Born: 28 October 1963, Biddulph, Stoke-on-Trent
Height: 6ft 3in **Weight:** 14st 7lbs
Nickname: Biff, Nose Bag

County debut: 1982
County cap: 1985
Benefit: 1993
Test debut: 1988
Tests: 4
One-Day Internationals: 4
1000 runs in a season: 12
1st-Class 50s: 94
1st-Class 100s: 39
1st-Class 200s: 4
1st-Class 5 w. in innings: 2
1st-Class catches: 222
One-Day 100s: 9
Place in batting averages: 103rd av. 36.10
(1995 76th av. 38.44)
Strike rate: 166.00 (career 82.00)
Parents: Marie, father deceased
Wife and date of marriage: Rachel, 11 April
1987
Children: Harry John, 7 March 1991; Alexandra Joy, 13 November 1993
Family links with cricket: 'Brother professional for Haslington/North Staffs in the
South Cheshire League'
Education: Biddulph High School
Qualifications: 6 CSEs, 1 O-level, NCA advanced cricket coach
Off-season: 'Working for John Liddington wholesale drinks suppliers'
Overseas tours: England to Sharjah 1984-85 and 1986-87, to West Indies 1989-90;
Northants to Durban 1991-92, to Cape Town 1992-93, to Zimbabwe 1994-95;
Singapore Sixes October 1994
Overseas teams played for: Rhodes University, South Africa 1982-83; Uitenhage,
Melbourne 1983-84, 1984-85; Fitzroy, Melbourne, 1985-86; Gosnells, Perth 1987-88
Young players to look out for: David Roberts
Other sports followed: Football (Stoke City)
Injuries: Cartilage damage to left wrist, out for five weeks
Relaxations: Walking and drinking at the local village pub
Extras: Played for Young England v Young Australia 1983. Selected for cancelled tour
of India 1988-89. Youngest Northamptonshire player to score 10,000 runs. Won three
consecutive Man of the Match Awards in the Nat West Trophy in 1995. Took over the
Northamptonshire captaincy for the 1996 season
Best batting: 224* Northamptonshire v Glamorgan, Swansea 1986
Best bowling: 5-54 Northamptonshire v Nottinghamshire, Northampton 1993

1996 Season

	M	Inns	NO	Runs	HS	Avge	100s	50s	Ct	St	O	M	Runs	Wkts	Avge	Best	5wl	10wM
Test																		
All First	12	22	2	722	163	36.10	1	3	8	-	55.2	9	161	2	80.50	1-3	-	-
1-day Int																		
NatWest	2	2	1	27	26 *	27.00	-	-	3	-	4	1	13	0	-		-	-
B & H	7	7	3	425	115 *	106.25	2	2	3	-	11	0	63	0	-		-	-
Sunday	14	14	4	337	70	33.70	-	3	10	-	13	1	87	1	87.00	1-17	-	

Career Performances

	M	Inns	NO	Runs	HS	Avge	100s	50s	Ct	St	Balls	Runs	Wkts	Avge	Best	5wl	10wM
Test	4	8	0	119	43	14.87	-	-	-	-							
All First	300	507	75	18021	224 *	41.71	39	94	222	-	7790	4194	95	44.14	5-54	2	-
1-day Int	4	4	2	137	43 *	68.50	-	-	1	-	36	25	0	-		-	-
NatWest	44	44	12	1529	145	47.78	1	10	15	-	582	340	13	26.15	3-47	-	
B & H	58	55	8	2256	134	48.00	4	16	15	-	360	243	2	121.50	1-22	-	
Sunday	197	186	29	5635	125 *	35.89	4	36	52	-	1168	1108	35	31.65	3-23	-	

BAILEY, T. M. B.   Northamptonshire

Name: Tobin Michael Barnaby Bailey
Role: Right-hand bat, wicket-keeper
Born: 28 August 1976, Kettering
Height: 5ft 10in **Weight:** 12st 6lbs
Nickname: Bill, Mad Dog, Scruff
County debut: 1996
1st-Class catches: 4
Parents: Terry and Penny
Marital status: Single
Family links with cricket: 'Step-dad watches a lot'
Education: Bedford School; Loughborough University
Qualifications: 3 A-levels
Off-season: Studying at Loughborough University
Overseas tours: Bedford to South Africa 1994
Cricketers particularly admired: Jack Russell, Mike Atherton, Alan Knott
Young players to look out for: Michael Davies
Other sports followed: 'Played county hockey and tennis at youth level for Bedfordshire.' Rugby (Bedford RFC) and football (Leicester City FC)

Injuries: 'Pulled calf, missed Minor Counties semi-final in MCC Trophy against Wales'
Relaxations: 'Sleeping in the winter, drinking and spending time with friends'
Extras: Bedfordshire Young Player of the Year in 1995. Northants County League Young Player of the Year in 1995. Holmwoods Schools Cricketer of the Year. Played for England Schools U19 and was a reserve for the England U19 tour to Zimbabwe. Won the BUSA cricket cup with Loughborough in 1996.
Opinions on cricket: 'BBC and ITV should put more games on television. Lunch and tea should be five minutes longer.'
Best batting: 31* Northamptonshire v Lancashire, Northampton 1996

1996 Season

	M	Inns	NO	Runs	HS	Avge	100s	50s	Ct	St	O	M	Runs	Wkts	Avge	Best	5wI	10wM
Test																		
All First	2	2	1	33	31*	33.00	-	-	4	-								
1-day Int																		
NatWest																		
B & H																		
Sunday																		

Career Performances

	M	Inns	NO	Runs	HS	Avge	100s	50s	Ct	St	Balls	Runs	Wkts	Avge	Best	5wI	10wM
Test																	
All First	2	2	1	33	31*	33.00	-	-	4	-							
1-day Int																	
NatWest																	
B & H																	
Sunday																	

5. Who replaced Bobby Simpson as Australia's coach on 1 July 1996?

BAINBRIDGE, P. Durham

Name: Philip Bainbridge
Role: Right-hand bat, right-arm
medium bowler
Born: 16 April 1958, Stoke-on-Trent
Height: 5ft 10in **Weight:** 12st 7lbs
Nickname: Bains, Robbo, Red
County debut: 1977 (Gloucestershire),
1992 (Durham)
County cap: 1981
Benefit: 1989
1000 runs in a season: 9
1st-Class 50s: 94
1st-Class 100s: 24
1st-Class 5 w. in innings: 10
1st-Class catches: 149
One-Day 100s: 1
One-Day 5 w. in innings: 1
Place in batting averages: 119th av. 34.27
(1995 188th 22.00)
Place in bowling averages: (1995 147th av. 77.28)
Strike rate: 105.85 (career 73.77)
Parents: Leonard George and Lilian Rose
Wife and date of marriage: Barbara, 22 September 1979
Children: Neil, 11 January 1984; Laura, 15 January 1985
Family links with cricket: Cousin, Stephen Wilkinson, played for Somerset
Education: Hanley High School; Stoke-on-Trent Sixth Form College; Borough Road
College of Education
Qualifications: 9 O-levels, 2 A-levels, BEd
Career outside cricket: Runs own corporate hospitality company and sports tour
operators – Rhodes Leisure, Bristol. Specialises in sports tours to South Africa
Overseas tours: British Colleges to West Indies 1978; English Counties XI to
Zimbabwe 1984-85; plus other tours to West Indies, Sri Lanka, Holland, South Africa,
Pakistan and Zimbabwe
Overseas teams played for: Alberton, Johannesburg 1980-81, 1982-83
Cricketers particularly admired: Mike Procter
Other sports followed: Rugby union, soccer, golf, American football, boxing
Extras: Played for four 2nd XIs in 1976 – Gloucestershire, Derbyshire,
Northamptonshire and Warwickshire. Played for Young England v Australia 1977.
Scored first century for Stoke-on-Trent aged 14. One of *Wisden*'s Five Cricketers of the
Year 1985. Joined Durham for their first season in first-class cricket after 14 seasons
with Gloucestershire. Played for Leyland CC as professional in 1991 – they won the

Northern League. Player of the Year for Durham 1993. Appointed captain of Durham for 1994 season but handed over captaincy to Mike Roseberry for 1995 season. Retired from first-class cricket at the end of the 1996 season

Opinions on cricket: 'I think the four-day format has worked very well.'
Best batting: 169 Gloucestershire v Yorkshire, Cheltenham 1988
Best bowling: 8-53 Gloucestershire v Somerset, Bristol 1986

1996 Season

	M	Inns	NO	Runs	HS	Avge	100s	50s	Ct	St	O	M	Runs	Wkts	Avge	Best	5wI	10wM
Test																		
All First	11	19	1	617	83	34.27	-	5	10	-	123.3	23	382	7	54.57	2-44	-	-
1-day Int																		
NatWest	2	2	0	35	21	17.50	-	-	-	-	24	4	94	1	94.00	1-21	-	
B & H	2	2	1	39	39	39.00	-	-	-	-	2	0	15	1	15.00	1-15	-	
Sunday	7	7	0	111	34	15.85	-	-	-	-	44.1	1	237	4	59.25	2-26	-	

Career Performances

	M	Inns	NO	Runs	HS	Avge	100s	50s	Ct	St	Balls	Runs	Wkts	Avge	Best	5wI	10wM
Test																	
All First	324	539	73	15707	169	33.70	24	94	149	-	25746	13094	349	37.51	8-53	10	-
1-day Int																	
NatWest	35	31	5	892	89	34.30	-	8	5	-	2035	1187	33	35.96	3-49	-	
B & H	55	51	10	1143	96	27.87	-	6	17	-	2536	1554	48	32.37	4-38	-	
Sunday	213	186	31	3447	106 *	22.23	1	13	48	-	7622	6425	210	30.59	5-22	1	

6. Name the two sets of brothers who played in the same first-class game for the same county in 1996?

BALL, M. C. J. Gloucestershire

Name: Martyn Charles John Ball
Role: Right-hand bat, off-spin bowler, slip fielder
Born: 26 April 1970, Bristol
Height: 5ft 9in **Weight:** 12st 4lbs
Nickname: Benny, Barfo
County debut: 1988
1st-Class 50s: 3
1st-Class 5 w. in innings: 7
1st-Class 10 w. in match: 1
1st-Class catches: 98
Place in batting averages: 273rd av. 13.88
(1995 192nd av. 21.94)
Place in bowling averages: 141st av. 49.15
(1995 99th av. 35.26)
Strike rate: 103.84 (career 74.86)
Parents: Kenneth Charles and Pamela Wendy
Wife and date of marriage: Mona, 28
September 1991

Children: Kristina, 9 May 1990; Alexandra, 2 August 1993
Education: King Edmund Secondary School, Yate; Bath College of Further Education
Qualifications: 6 O-levels, 2 AO-levels
Overseas tours: Gloucestershire to Namibia 1991, to Kenya 1992, to Sri Lanka 1993
Overseas teams played for: North Melbourne, Australia 1988-89; Old Hararians, Zimbabwe 1990-91
Cricketers most admired: Ian Botham, John Emburey, Vic Marks
Other sports followed: All sports except show-jumping
Relaxations: 'Listening to music, watching sport and celebrating a victory for AFC Horton.'
Extras: Played for Young England against New Zealand in 1989. Produced best bowling figures in a match for the Britannic County Championship 1993 season – 14-169 against Somerset
Opinions on cricket: 'Things seem to be moving in the right direction, but I believe that if a club allows a player to run out of contract then he should be a free agent like in any other profession and not be restricted by regulations like those of contested registration.'
Best batting: 71 Gloucestershire v Nottinghamshire, Bristol 1993
Best bowling: 8-46 Gloucestershire v Somerset, Taunton 1993

1996 Season

	M	Inns	NO	Runs	HS	Avge	100s	50s	Ct	St	O	M	Runs	Wkts	Avge	Best	5wI	10wM
Test																		
All First	13	21	4	236	46	13.88	-	-	15	-	225	61	639	13	49.15	3-40	-	-
1-day Int																		
NatWest	2	2	0	35	31	17.50	-	-	3	-	14	3	49	1	49.00	1-24	-	
B & H	2	2	0	25	25	12.50	-	-	2	-	16	1	71	1	71.00	1-17	-	
Sunday	14	12	3	79	24 *	8.77	-	-	6	-	92	2	513	16	32.06	2-16	-	

Career Performances

	M	Inns	NO	Runs	HS	Avge	100s	50s	Ct	St	Balls	Runs	Wkts	Avge	Best	5wI	10wM
Test																	
All First	85	131	25	1644	71	15.50	-	3	98	-	12428	6066	166	36.54	8-46	7	1
1-day Int																	
NatWest	8	4	1	63	31	21.00	-	-	5	-	414	248	9	27.55	3-42	-	
B & H	17	11	1	101	25	10.10	-	-	8	-	882	541	14	38.64	3-26	-	
Sunday	68	47	16	329	28 *	10.61	-	-	20	-	2270	1987	46	43.19	3-24	-	

BARNETT, K. J.　　　　　　　　Derbyshire

Name: Kim John Barnett
Role: Right-hand bat, leg-break bowler
Born: 17 July 1960, Stoke-on-Trent
Height: 6ft **Weight:** 13st 3lbs
Nickname: Barn
County debut: 1979
County cap: 1982
Benefit: 1993 (£37,056)
Test debut: 1988
Tests: 4
One-Day Internationals: 1
1000 runs in a season: 13
1st-Class 50s: 126
1st-Class 100s: 49
1st-Class 200s: 3
1st-Class 5 w. in innings: 3
1st-Class catches: 239
One-Day 100s: 10
One-Day 5 w. in innings: 1
Place in batting averages: 48th av. 45.50 (1995 46th av. 44.67)
Place in bowling averages: 122nd av. 42.25 (1995 119th av. 39.68)
Strike rate: 69.66 (career 74.56)

Parents: Derek and Doreen

Wife: Janet

Children: Michael Nicholas, 24 April 1990; Christina, 11 June 1996

Education: Leek High School, Staffs

Qualifications: 7 O-levels

Career outside cricket: Bank clerk

Overseas tours: English Schools to India 1977-78; England YC to Australia 1978-79; England B to Sri Lanka 1985-86 (vice-captain); unofficial English XI to South Africa 1989-90

Overseas teams played for: Boland 1980-81, 1982-83

Cricketers particularly admired: Eddie Barlow, Gordon Greenidge

Young players to look out for: Vikram Solanki, Andrew Harris and Kevin Dean

Other sports followed: Football, golf, horse racing

Relaxations: Golf and horse racing

Extras: Played for Northamptonshire 2nd XI when aged 15, Staffordshire and Warwickshire 2nd XI. Became youngest captain of a first-class county when appointed in 1983. One of *Wisden*'s Five Cricketers of the Year 1989. Banned from Test cricket after joining tour to South Africa, suspension remitted in 1992. Relinquished captaincy at the end of the 1995 season. Leading century maker and run scorer in all competitions in the history of Derbyshire cricket

Opinions on cricket: 'We will not produce enough bowlers for the Test arena until we produce pitches that encourage the fast bowlers and leg spinners etc., not just for the batsmen.'

Best batting: 239* Derbyshire v Leicestershire, Leicester 1988

Best bowling: 6-28 Derbyshire v Glamorgan, Chesterfield 1991

1996 Season

	M	Inns	NO	Runs	HS	Avge	100s	50s	Ct	St	O	M	Runs	Wkts	Avge	Best	5wI	10wM
Test																		
All First	18	34	2	1456	200 *	45.50	3	9	5	-	139.2	15	507	12	42.25	3-26	-	-
1-day Int																		
NatWest	3	3	0	78	38	26.00	-	-	-	-	11	1	57	5	11.40	5-32	1	
B & H	5	5	0	97	48	19.40	-	-	1	-	6	0	23	1	23.00	1-1	-	
Sunday	16	16	2	649	99	46.35	-	6	6	-	47.2	0	301	13	23.15	3-26	-	

Career Performances

	M	Inns	NO	Runs	HS	Avge	100s	50s	Ct	St	Balls	Runs	Wkts	Avge	Best	5wI	10wM
Test	4	7	0	207	80	29.57	-	2	1	-	36	32	0	-		-	-
All First	399	646	59	23272	239 *	39.64	49	126	239	-	13422	6717	180	37.31	6-28	3	-
1-day Int	1	1	0	84	84	84.00	-	1	-	-							
NatWest	36	35	3	1124	113 *	35.12	1	8	14	-	484	321	21	15.28	6-24	2	
B & H	76	67	4	2270	115	36.03	3	16	30	-	378	242	7	34.57	1-1	-	
Sunday	255	244	39	7092	131 *	34.59	6	39	88	-	1177	1080	36	30.00	3-26	-	

BARWICK, S. R.   Glamorgan

Name: Stephen Royston Barwick
Role: Right-hand bat, right-arm
medium bowler
Born: 6 September 1960, Neath
Height: 6ft 2in **Weight:** 13st
Nickname: Bas
County debut: 1981
County cap: 1987
Benefit: 1995
50 wickets in a season: 2
1st-Class 5 w. in innings: 10
1st-Class 10 w. in match: 1
1st-Class catches: 47
One-Day 5 w. in innings: 5
Place in batting averages: 312th av. 5.66
Place in bowling averages: (1995 144th av.
48.64)
Strike rate: 195.80 (career 80.40)
Parents: Roy and Margaret
Wife and date of marriage: Margaret, 12 December 1987
Children: Michael Warren, 25 September 1990; Katheryn Elizabeth, 17 February
1993; Jessica Margaret, 30 July 1994
Family links with cricket: 'My uncle David played for Glamorgan 2nd XI'
Education: Cwrt Sart Comprehensive; Dwr-y-Felin Comprehensive
Qualifications: 'Commerce, human biology, mathematics, English'
Career outside cricket: Ex-steelworker
Overseas teams played for: Benoni, South Africa
Cricketers particularly admired: Ian Botham, Richard Hadlee
Other sports followed: Football and rugby
Relaxations: 'Sea fishing and the odd pint or two'
Extras: Released by Glamorgan at the end of the 1996 season
Best batting: 30 Glamorgan v Hampshire, Bournemouth 1988
Best bowling: 8-42 Glamorgan v Worcestershire, Worcester 1983

7. Name the only two Yorkshire-born batsmen to have scored
double hundreds against their native county?

	M	Inns	NO	Runs	HS	Avge	100s	50s	Ct	St	O	M	Runs	Wkts	Avge	Best	5wI	10wM
Test																		
All First	7	7	1	34	20 *	5.66	-	-	3	-	163.1	54	391	5	78.20	2-81	-	-
1-day Int																		
NatWest	1	1	0	1	1	1.00	-	-	-	-	12	0	63	0	-		-	-
B & H	6	1	0	0	0	0.00	-	-	1	-	57.5	3	277	6	46.16	2-49	-	
Sunday	15	5	5	7	3 *	-	-	-	1	-	101.5	6	437	15	29.13	4-34		

Career Performances

	M	Inns	NO	Runs	HS	Avge	100s	50s	Ct	St	Balls	Runs	Wkts	Avge	Best	5wI	10wM
Test																	
All First	212	203	74	873	30	6.76	-	-	47	-	36665	16176	456	35.47	8-42	10	1
1-day Int																	
NatWest	30	13	6	24	6	3.42	-	-	4	-	1741	948	41	23.12	5-26	1	
B & H	53	27	14	97	18	7.46	-	-	10	-	2976	1913	63	30.36	4-11	-	
Sunday	181	57	35	228	48 *	10.36	-	-	24	-	7220	5385	201	26.79	6-28	4	

BASE, S. J.   Derbyshire

Name: Simon John Base
Role: Right-hand bat, right-arm fast-medium bowler
Born: 2 January 1960, Maidstone
Height: 6ft 3in **Weight:** 14st 7lbs
Nickname: Basey, Moose Man
County debut: 1986 (Glamorgan), 1988 (Derbyshire)
County cap: 1990
50 wickets in a season: 1
1st-Class 50s: 2
1st-Class 5 w. in innings: 16
1st-Class 10 w. in match: 1
1st-Class catches: 60
Strike rate: 140.00 (career 54.32)
Parents: Christine and Peter (deceased)
Wife and date of marriage:
Louise Anne, 23 September 1989
Children: Christopher Peter Elliot, 15 December 1991
Family links with cricket: Grandfather played, 'brother-in-law pretends he can!'
Education: Fishhoek Primary School; Fishhoek High School, Cape Town, South Africa

Qualifications: High School Matriculation, refrigeration and air conditioning technician
Career outside cricket: Hall-Thermotank in South Africa as a technician, GSPK Electronics, Rhodes Fabrics
Overseas tours: England XI to Holland 1989
Overseas teams played for: Western Province B 1982-83; Boland 1986-89; Border 1989-94 (all South Africa)
Cricketers particularly admired: Graham Gooch, Graeme Pollock, Mike Procter, Richard Hadlee, Malcolm Marshall
Other sports followed: Most other sports
Relaxations: Spending time with family, swimming, windsurfing, 'braaing'
Extras: Suspended from first-class cricket for ten weeks during the 1988 season for a supposed breach of contract, joining Derbyshire when he was still said to be contracted to Glamorgan. The TCCB fined Derbyshire £2000
Best batting: 58 Derbyshire v Yorkshire, Chesterfield 1990
Best bowling: 7-60 Derbyshire v Yorkshire, Chesterfield 1990

1996 Season

	M	Inns	NO	Runs	HS	Avge	100s	50s	Ct	St	O	M	Runs	Wkts	Avge	Best	5wI	10wM
Test																		
All First	1	1	0	1	1	1.00	-	-	-	-	23.2	4	105	1	105.00	1-105	-	-
1-day Int																		
NatWest																		
B & H																			
Sunday	3	0	0	0	0	-	-	-	-	2	-	20	0	106	3	35.33	2-34	-

Career Performances

	M	Inns	NO	Runs	HS	Avge	100s	50s	Ct	St	Balls	Runs	Wkts	Avge	Best	5wI	10wM
Test																	
All First	133	170	35	1526	58	11.30	-	2	60	-	21079	11363	388	29.28	7-60	16	1
1-day Int																	
NatWest	3	2	0	6	4	3.00	-	-	1	-	156	124	3	41.33	2-49	-	
B & H	15	9	3	53	15 *	8.83	-	-	-	-	870	629	15	41.93	3-33	-	
Sunday	92	36	9	184	31	6.81	-	-	26	-	3903	2871	115	24.96	4-14	-	

8. Who holds the record for the highest score against his native county?

BATES, J. J.   Sussex

Name: Justin Jonathan Bates
Role: Right-hand bat, off-spin bowler
Born: 9 April 1976, Farnborough, Hants
Height: 6ft **Weight:** 11st 7lbs
County debut: 1996 (one-day)
Parents: Barry and Sandra
Marital status: Single
Family links with cricket: Father played
club cricket and brother played for Sussex
Young Cricketers
Education: St Mark's Primary School;
Warden Park Secondary School;
Hurstpierpoint College
Qualifications: 8 GCSEs, 3 A-levels, NCA
coaching award
Career outside cricket: Freelance graphic
designer
Off-season: Playing overseas
Overseas tours: Sussex YC to India 1990-91, to Barbados 1992-93,
to Sri Lanka 1994-95
Cricketers particularly admired: Sachin Tendulkar, Eddie Hemmings, Shane Warne
Other sports followed: Golf and rugby
Relaxations: Reading, computing and music
Opinions on cricket: 'Second XI championship cricket should be played over four days
and not three.'

1996 Season

	M	Inns	NO	Runs	HS	Avge	100s	50s	Ct	St	O	M	Runs	Wkts	Avge	Best	5wI	10wM
Test																		
All First																		
1-day Int																		
NatWest																		
B & H																		
Sunday	1	1	0	8	8	8.00	-	-	1	-	3	0	46	0	-		-	-

9. Which batsman collected a 'pair' on the same day in 1996
without his side following on?

Career Performances

	M	Inns	NO	Runs	HS	Avge	100s	50s	Ct	St	Balls	Runs	Wkts	Avge	Best	5wI	10wM
Test																	
All First																	
1-day Int																	
NatWest																	
B & H																	
Sunday	1	1	0	8	8	8.00	-	-	1	-	18	46	0	-	-	-	-

BATES, R. T. Nottinghamshire

Name: Richard Terry Bates
Role: Right-hand bat, off-spin bowler, slip fielder
Born: 17 June 1972, Stamford, Lincs
Height: 6ft 1in **Weight:** 13st 7lbs
Nickname: Blast, Batesy
County debut: 1993
1st-Class 5 w. innings: 1
1st-Class catches: 12
Place in batting averages: 259th av. 16.35
Place in bowling averages: 131st av. 46.14
(1995 108th av. 36.70)
Strike rate: 79.52 (career 85.15)
Parents: Terry and Sue
Marital status: Suzanne, 16 March 1996
Family links with cricket: Father is Director
of Administration and Development for NCA
Education: Bourne Grammar School;
Stamford College for Further Education

Qualifications: 8 GCSEs, BTEC in Business and Finance, NCA Advanced Coach
Career outside cricket: Employed by Notts CCC to coach during the winter
Off-season: Coaching for Notts CCC and keeping fit
Overseas tours: Lincolnshire Colts (U19) to Australia 1989-90
Overseas teams played for: Redwood, New Zealand 1991-92
Cricketers particularly admired: Ian Botham, Derek Randall, Viv Richards,
Paul Johnson, James Hindson
Other sports followed: Football (Liverpool FC)
Injuries: None
Relaxations: Good food, films, 'having a beer with my mates *and* Matthew Dowman'
Best batting: 34 Nottinghamshire v Worcestershire, Worcester 1996
Best bowling: 5-88 Nottinghamshire v Durham, Chester-le-Street 1995

1996 Season

	M	Inns	NO	Runs	HS	Avge	100s	50s	Ct	St	O	M	Runs	Wkts	Avge	Best	5wI	10wM
Test																		
All First	11	15	1	229	34	16.35	-	-	8	-	278.2	46	969	21	46.14	3-42	-	-
1-day Int																		
NatWest	1	1	0	1	1	1.00	-	-	-	-	11	0	56	0	-		-	-
B & H	4	3	0	45	27	15.00	-	-	4	-	37	4	128	7	18.28	3-21	-	
Sunday	16	6	2	58	16	14.50	-	-	9	-	86	1	452	17	26.58	3-30	-	

Career Performances

	M	Inns	NO	Runs	HS	Avge	100s	50s	Ct	St	Balls	Runs	Wkts	Avge	Best	5wI	10wM
Test																	
All First	22	31	5	364	34	14.00	-	-	12	-	3321	1763	39	45.20	5-88	1	-
1-day Int																	
NatWest	1	1	0	1	1	1.00	-	-	-	-	66	56	0	-		-	-
B & H	4	3	0	45	27	15.00	-	-	4	-	222	128	7	18.28	3-21	-	
Sunday	25	10	3	76	16	10.85	-	-	11	-	881	785	27	29.07	3-30	-	

BATTY, G. J.   Yorkshire

Name: Gareth Jon Batty
Role: Right-hand bat, right-arm off-spin bowler
Born: 13 October 1977
Height: 5ft 11in **Weight:** 11st 7lbs
Nickname: Batts, Ginner, Dowie, Chris Evans
County debut: No first-team appearance
Parents: David and Rosemary
Family links with cricket: Father a coach at Yorkshire Academy, brother Jeremy plays for Somerset
Education: Collingworth Primary School; Parkside Middle School; Bingley Grammar School
Qualifications: 9 GCSEs, BTEC in Art Design, NCA Coaching Award
Off-season: England U19 tour to Pakistan
Overseas tours: England U15 to South Africa; England U19 to Zimbabwe 1995-96, to Pakistan 1996-97

Cricketers particularly admired: 'All the Yorkshire staff' and John Emburey
Other sports followed: Rugby league (Bradford Bulls), golf, football
Relaxations: Relaxing with friends, having a couple of drinks and a doner kebab in the local doner house.
Extras: *Daily Telegraph* Under 15 Bowler of the Year 1993
Opinions on cricket: 'A lot of cricket played – possibly a bit too much.'

BATTY, J. D. Somerset

Name: Jeremy David Batty
Role: Right-hand bat, off-spin bowler
Born: 15 May 1971, Bradford
Height: 6ft 1in **Weight:** Variable
Nickname: Nora, Chip, Batts
County debut: 1989 (Yorkshire), 1995 (Somerset)
1st-Class 50s: 2
1st-Class 5 w. in innings: 4
1st-Class catches: 32
Place in batting averages: 261st av. 16.05
Place in bowling averages: 140th av. 49.12
Strike rate: 91.25 (career 76.22)
Parents: David and Rosemary
Marital status: Engaged to Liz
Family links with cricket: Father coach at Yorkshire Academy and played in Bradford League. Brother is on Yorkshire playing staff
Education: Parkside Middle School; Bingley Grammar School; Horsforth College
Qualifications: 5 O-levels, BTEC Diploma in Leisure Studies, coaching certificate
Overseas tours: England YC to Australia 1989-90; Yorkshire CCC to Barbados 1990, to Cape Town 1992-93, to Leeward Islands 1993-94; Sheffield Cricket Lovers to Spain 1991, to Majorca 1992
Overseas teams played for: Sunrise 1989-90, Country Districts 1990-91 (both Zimbabwe); M.O.B., Pietermaritzburg, South Africa 1992-93; Wellington, Cape Town 1993-94; Techs, Cape Town 1994-95
Cricketers particularly admired: John Emburey, Phil Tufnell, Dean Jones, Peter Robinson
Other sports followed: Rugby league, football and hockey
Injuries: Tendonitis in wrist, sprained thumb but 'bit the bullet'
Relaxations: Movies, eating out and 'listening to Peter Robinson'
Extras: Took five wickets on first-class debut v Lancashire in 1989. Yorkshire Young Player of the Year 1991. Whittingdale Bowler of the Month, June 1991. Moved to

Somerset in 1995 and was released at the end of the 1996 season
Opinions on cricket: 'Inspection at 1p.m. after overnight rain. Why change our set-up, it's good as it is.'
Best batting: 51 Yorkshire v Sri Lanka, Headingley 1991
Best bowling: 6-48 Yorkshire v Nottinghamshire, Worksop 1991

1996 Season

	M	Inns	NO	Runs	HS	Avge	100s	50s	Ct	St	O	M	Runs	Wkts	Avge	Best	5wl	10wM
Test																		
All First	16	24	4	321	44	16.05	-	-	4	-	486.4	99	1572	32	49.12	5-85	1	-
1-day Int																		
NatWest																		
B & H	1	1	0	14	14	14.00	-	-	-	-								
Sunday	1	1	0	6	6	6.00	-	-	-	-								

Career Performances

	M	Inns	NO	Runs	HS	Avge	100s	50s	Ct	St	Balls	Runs	Wkts	Avge	Best	5wl	10wM
Test																	
All First	84	97	25	1149	51	15.95	-	2	32	-	13645	7441	179	41.56	6-48	4	-
1-day Int																	
NatWest	3	2	0	7	4	3.50	-	-	1	-	126	97	1	97.00	1-17	-	
B & H	9	4	3	35	19 *	35.00	-	-	2	-	372	220	6	36.66	2-13	-	
Sunday	34	15	6	50	13 *	5.55	-	-	16	-	1470	1161	40	29.02	4-33	-	

BATTY, J. N. Surrey

Name: Jonathan Neil Batty
Role: Right-hand bat, wicket-keeper
Born: 18 April 1974, Chesterfield
Height: 5ft 10in **Weight:** 11st 7lbs
Nickname: Batts, Lizard, Nora, Mutant
County debut: No first-team appearance
1st-Class 50s: 2
1st-Class catches: 11
1st-Class stumpings: 2
Place in batting averages: 158th av. 30.20
Parents: Roger and Gill
Marital status: Single
Family links with cricket: Father played for Nottinghamshire Schools and played a good standard of club cricket
Education: Repton School; Durham University (St Chad's); Keble College, Oxford

Qualifications: 10 GCSEs, 4 A-levels, BSc (Hons) in Natural Sciences, Diploma in Social Studies
Off-season: Getting fit
Overseas tours: Repton School to Holland 1990; MCC to Bangladesh 1996
Cricketers particularly admired: David Gower, Bruce French, Alec Stewart
Young players to look out for: David Roberts, Stephen Peters, Alex Tudor
Other sports followed: Football (Nottingham Forest), rugby union (Leicester Tigers) and squash
Relaxations: Going to the cinema, listening to music and reading
Extras: Oxford Blue in 1996. Has also played Minor Counties cricket for Oxfordshire

Opinions on cricket: 'Four-day Championship games should not be interrupted by the Sunday League. 2nd XI games should be played on 1st XI wickets.'
Best batting: 56 Oxford University v Northamptonshire, The Parks 1996

1996 Season

	M	Inns	NO	Runs	HS	Avge	100s	50s	Ct	St	O	M	Runs	Wkts	Avge	Best	5wI	10wM
Test																		
All First	10	13	3	302	56	30.20	-	2	9	2								
1-day Int																		
NatWest	1	1	0	1	1	1.00	-		-	-								
B & H	5	5	1	61	26 *	15.25	-	-	4	-								
Sunday																			

Career Performances

	M	Inns	NO	Runs	HS	Avge	100s	50s	Ct	St	Balls	Runs	Wkts	Avge	Best	5wI	10wM
Test																	
All First	12	16	4	342	56	28.50	-	2	11	2							
1-day Int																	
NatWest	1	1	0	1	1	1.00	-		-	-							
B & H	10	8	3	83	26 *	16.60	-	-	9	-							
Sunday																		

BELL, M. A. V.   Warwickshire

Name: Michael Anthony Vincent Bell
Role: Right-hand bat, left-arm
fast-medium bowler
Born: 19 December 1967, Birmingham
Height: 6ft 2in **Weight:** 13st 2lbs
Nickname: Belly, Nelly, Breezer
County debut: 1992
1st-Class 5 w. in innings: 3
1st-Class catches: 7
One-Day 5 w. in innings: 2
Strike rate: (career 55.10)
Parents: Vincent and Adelheid
Marital status: Single
Family links with cricket: Father played
cricket mainly for Mitchells & Butler in the
Birmingham League. An uncle played a few
games for Jamaica
Education: Bishop Milner Comprehensive;
Dudley Technical College
Qualifications: 5 O-levels, City and Guilds in Recreation and Leisure Parts 1 & 2
Career outside cricket: Casino croupier, worked with the PE staff at Earls High
School and also worked in the corporate hospitality department at EMP plc for two
years
Overseas tours: BWIA to Barbados and Trinidad & Tobago 1989; John Morris's
Madcap CC to Australia 1992
Overseas teams played for: Swanbourne, Perth 1986-87; Norwood, Melbourne 1989-
90; Phoenix, Perth 1992-93; Sunshine Heights 1993-94
Cricketers particularly admired: Dennis Lillee, Viv Richards, Michael Holding,
Imran Khan, Wasim Akram, Shane Warne
Other sports followed: Any sport played by the best in that particular field
Injuries: Lower back problem, out for most of the season
Relaxations: 'Golf (although I'm no Calvin Peete), good movies and going to a hot
country before winter sets in.'
Opinions on cricket: 'When are the batsmen going to be prevented from taking the
initiative over the bowlers and get limited to, for instance, one extra-cover drive – on the
up – per over ... and when will a cow jump over the moon!'
Best batting: 22* Warwickshire v Gloucestershire, Edgbaston 1993
Best bowling: 7-48 Warwickshire v Gloucestershire, Edgbaston 1993

1996 Season (did not make any first-class or one-day appearances)

Career Performances

	M	Inns	NO	Runs	HS	Avge	100s	50s	Ct	St	Balls	Runs	Wkts	Avge	Best	5wl	10wM
Test																	
All First	17	21	10	79	22 *	7.18	-	-	7	-	2535	1333	46	28.97	7-48	3	-
1-day Int																	
NatWest	1	0	0	0	0	-	-	-	-	-	53	41	2	20.50	2-41	-	
B & H	2	0	0	0	0	-	-	-	1	-	66	34	2	17.00	2-34	-	
Sunday	13	5	2	27	8 *	9.00	-	-	1	-	570	411	22	18.68	5-19	2	

BENJAMIN, J. E. Surrey

Name: Joseph Emmanuel Benjamin
Role: Right-hand bat, right-arm
fast-medium bowler
Born: 2 February 1961, Christchurch,
St Kitts, West Indies
Height: 6ft 2in **Weight:** 12st 7lbs
Nickname: Boggy, Moon Man
County debut: 1988 (Warwickshire), 1992
(Surrey)
County cap: 1993 (Surrey)
Test debut: 1994
Tests: 1
One-day Internationals: 2
50 wickets in a season: 3
1st-Class 5 w. in innings: 16
1st-Class 10 w. in match: 1
1st-Class catches: 23
Place in batting averages: 247th av. 17.62
(1995 269th av. 12.42)
Place in bowling averages: 67th av. 31.20 (1995 30th av. 25.01)
Strike rate: 57.76 (career 57.42)
Parents: Henry and Judith
Marital status: Single
Education: Cayon High School, St Kitts; Mount Pleasant, Highgate, Birmingham
Qualifications: 4 O-levels
Career outside cricket: Landscape gardener, store manager
Overseas teams played for: Prahran, Melbourne 1992-93
Overseas tours: England to Australia 1994-95
Cricketers particularly admired: Imran Khan, Viv Richards, Malcolm Marshall

Other sports followed: Rugby, squash, football

Relaxations: Music, going to the cinema, reading

Extras: Released by Warwickshire at the end of the 1991 season and signed up by Surrey for 1992. Enjoyed his best batting and bowling performances of 1992 on the same day at Guildford. Surrey Player of the Year in 1993

Opinions on cricket: 'The four-day game has been very beneficial to county cricket. It helps batters and bowlers to achieve individual milestones and gives players more time to recover after the game.'

Best batting: 49 Surrey v Essex, The Oval 1995

Best bowling: 6-19 Surrey v Nottinghamshire, The Oval 1993

1996 Season

	M	Inns	NO	Runs	HS	Avge	100s	50s	Ct	St	O	M	Runs	Wkts	Avge	Best	5wI	10wM
Test																		
All First	13	14	6	141	38*	17.62	-	-	1	-	375.3	83	1217	39	31.20	4-17	-	-
1-day Int																		
NatWest	4	1	0	4	4	4.00	-	-	1	-	41.3	5	159	6	26.50	2-35	-	
B & H	1	1	0	3	3	3.00	-	-	-	-	10	2	53	1	53.00	1-53	-	
Sunday	13	3	1	0	0*	0.00	-	-	3	-	82	3	322	17	18.94	3-33	-	

Career Performances

	M	Inns	NO	Runs	HS	Avge	100s	50s	Ct	St	Balls	Runs	Wkts	Avge	Best	5wI	10wM
Test	1	1	0	0	0	0.00	-	-	-	-	168	80	4	20.00	4-42	-	-
All First	105	119	34	943	49	11.09	-	-	23	-	20155	10125	351	28.84	6-19	16	1
1-day Int	2	1	0	0	0	0.00	-	-	-	-	72	47	1	47.00	1-22	-	
NatWest	18	8	3	64	25	12.80	-	-	3	-	1086	652	21	31.04	4-20	-	
B & H	18	4	2	27	20	13.50	-	-	6	-	1110	711	21	33.85	4-27	-	
Sunday	79	33	14	172	24	9.05	-	-	15	-	3459	2574	82	31.39	4-44	-	

BENJAMIN, W. K. M.   Hampshire

Name: Winston Keithroy Matthew Benjamin

Role: Right-hand bat, right-arm fast bowler

Born: 31 December 1964, St John's, Antigua

Height: 6ft 3in

County debut: 1986 (Leicestershire), 1994 (Hampshire)

County cap: 1989 (Leicestershire)

Test debut: 1987-88

Tests: 21

One-Day Internationals: 85

50 wickets in a season: 1
1st-Class 50s: 21
1st-Class 100s: 2
1st-Class 5 w. in innings: 23
1st-Class 10 w. in match: 2
1st-Class catches: 95
One-Day 5 w. in innings: 4
Strike rate: 69.33 (career 56.46)
Education: All Saints School, Antigua
Overseas teams played for: Leeward Islands
1985-95

Overseas tours: West Indies to Australia
1986-87, to Pakistan 1986-87, to India 1987-
88, to Sharjah 1988, to England 1988, to
Australia 1988-89, to Sharjah 1991, to
Australia and New Zealand 1992-93, to
Sharjah, India (Hero Cup) and Sri Lanka
1993-94, to England 1995
Extras: Signed for Hampshire in 1994 after seven years at Leicestershire. During net
practice in 1994 he smashed a ball through the rear window of a Hampshire committee
member's Porsche! Was forced to retire from first-class cricket in 1996 through injury
Best batting: 117 Hampshire v Essex, Southampton 1996
Best bowling: 7-54 Leicestershire v Australia, Leicester 1992

1996 Season

	M	Inns	NO	Runs	HS	Avge	100s	50s	Ct	St	O	M	Runs	Wkts	Avge	Best	5wI	10wM
Test																		
All First	2	4	0	140	117	35.00	1	-	3	-	69.2	13	201	6	33.50	4-96	-	-
1-day Int																		
NatWest	3	3	0	49	41	16.33	-	-	2	-								
B & H	4	4	1	119	58 *	39.66	-	1	3	-	34	6	165	8	20.62	3-26	-	
Sunday	8	8	2	304	104 *	50.66	1	1	2	-	13	0	68	0	-		-	-

Career Performances

	M	Inns	NO	Runs	HS	Avge	100s	50s	Ct	St	Balls	Runs	Wkts	Avge	Best	5wI	10wM
Test	21	26	1	470	85	18.80	-	2	12	-	3694	1648	61	27.01	4-46	-	-
All First	171	213	36	3985	117	22.51	2	21	95	-	26876	12358	476	25.96	7-54	23	2
1-day Int	85	52	12	298	31	7.45	-	-	16	-	4442	3079	100	30.79	5-22	1	
NatWest	19	15	2	125	41	9.61	-	-	6	-	1011	528	22	24.00	5-32	1	
B & H	23	17	4	307	58 *	23.61	-	1	6	-	1319	810	39	20.76	5-17	2	
Sunday	66	50	10	689	104 *	17.22	1	2	11	-	2610	1821	66	27.59	4-19	-	

BETTS, M. M.   Durham

Name: Melvyn Morris Betts
Role: Right-hand bat, right-arm medium-fast
bowler
Born: 26 March 1975, Durham
Height: 5ft 11in **Weight:** 12st 2lbs
Nickname: Betsy, Alpha
County debut: 1993
1st-Class 50s: 1
1st-Class 5 w. in innings: 2
1st-Class catches: 6
Place in batting averages: 253rd av. 17.11
Place in bowling averages: 112th av. 39.84
(1995 145th av. 50.17)
Strike rate: 53.15 (career 57.16)
Parents: Melvyn and Shirley
Marital status: Engaged
Family links with cricket: Father and uncle
played for local club, Sacriston
Education: Fyndoune Comprehensive
Qualifications: 9 GCSEs, plus qualifications in engineering and sports and
recreational studies
Overseas tours: England U19 to Sri Lanka 1993-94
Other sports followed: Football (Newcastle United FC)
Injuries: Achilles, missed six weeks
Relaxations: Football
Extras: Played for England U19 in home series against India in 1994
Opinions on cricket: 'I think that it is getting harder for bowlers due to the reduction in
the seam on the cricket ball and now the one-bouncer-per-over rule.'
Best batting: 57* Durham v Sussex, Hove 1996
Best bowling: 5-68 Durham v Gloucestershire, Chester-le-Street 1996

1996 Season

	M	Inns	NO	Runs	HS	Avge	100s	50s	Ct	St	O	M	Runs	Wkts	Avge	Best	5wI	10wM
Test																		
All First	14	21	3	308	57*	17.11	-	1	4	-	389.5	48	1753	44	39.84	5-68	2	-
1-day Int																		
NatWest	2	2	1	12	11	12.00	-	-	-	-	22	5	120	5	24.00	3-33	-	
B & H	2	0	0	0	0	-	-	-	1	-	9	2	36	2	18.00	2-36	-	
Sunday	8	7	5	28	11	14.00	-	-	1	-	54	0	316	6	52.66	3-26	-	

Career Performances

	M	Inns	NO	Runs	HS	Avge	100s	50s	Ct	St	Balls	Runs	Wkts	Avge	Best	5wl	10wM
Test																	
All First	24	38	9	367	57 *	12.65	-	1	6	-	3544	2625	62	42.33	5-68	2	-
1-day Int																	
NatWest	3	3	1	21	11	10.50	-	-	-	-	204	167	6	27.83	3-33	-	
B & H	2	0	0	0	0	-	-	-	1	-	54	36	2	18.00	2-36	-	
Sunday	17	11	9	61	14 *	30.50	-	-	2	-	709	618	17	36.35	3-26	-	

BEVAN, M. G. — Yorkshire

Name: Michael Gwyl Bevan
Role: Left-hand bat, slow left-arm bowler, county vice-captain
Born: 8 May 1970, Canberra, Australia
County debut: 1995
Test debut: 1994-95
Tests: 6
One-day Internationals: 32
1000 runs in season: 2
1st-Class 50s: 43
1st-Class 100s: 28
1st-Class 200s: 1
1st-Class catches: 63
Place in batting averages: 7th av. 64.47 (1995 13th av. 55.10)
Strike rate: 129.75 (career 124.90)
Marital status: Single
Education: Australian Cricket Academy
Off-season: Playing for New South Wales and Australia
Overseas teams played for: South Australia 1989-90, New South Wales 1990-95
Overseas tours: Australia to Sharjah 1994, to Pakistan 1994-95, to India and Pakistan (World Cup) 1995-96, to South Africa 1996-97
Extras: In 1990-91 he became the first player to score a century in five successive Sheffield Shield matches. Made 82 on his Test debut against Pakistan in Karachi, 1994-95. Played for Rawtenstall in the Lancashire League in 1993 and 1994. Appointed Yorkshire's vice-captain for the 1996 season
Best batting: 203* New South Wales v Western Australia, Sydney 1993-94
Best bowling: 3-6 New South Wales v Wellington, North Sydney 1990-91

1996 Season

	M	Inns	NO	Runs	HS	Avge	100s	50s	Ct	St	O	M	Runs	Wkts	Avge	Best	5wI	10wM
Test																		
All First	12	22	3	1225	160 *	64.47	3	8	6	-	86.3	8	369	4	92.25	3-36	-	-
1-day Int																		
NatWest	4	4	0	222	85	55.50	-	2	-	-	10	1	47	2	23.50	2-47	-	
B & H	6	6	3	397	95 *	132.33	-	5	-	-	5.1	0	25	1	25.00	1-25	-	
Sunday	12	11	2	404	98 *	44.88	-	2	4	-	31	2	165	11	15.00	5-29	1	

Career Performances

	M	Inns	NO	Runs	HS	Avge	100s	50s	Ct	St	Balls	Runs	Wkts	Avge	Best	5wI	10wM
Test	6	10	0	324	91	32.40	-	3	5	-	90	67	1	67.00	1-21	-	-
All First	108	187	30	8432	203 *	53.70	28	43	63	-	2748	1641	22	74.59	3-6	-	-
1-day Int	32	28	14	946	78 *	67.57	-	5	13	-	381	311	8	38.87	2-31	-	
NatWest	8	8	2	388	91 *	64.66	-	4	-	-	114	89	3	29.66	2-47	-	
B & H	10	9	4	544	95 *	108.80	-	7	1	-	31	25	1	25.00	1-25	-	
Sunday	29	27	5	1108	103 *	50.36	2	7	9	-	445	399	23	17.34	5-29	1	

BICKNELL, D. J.   Surrey

Name: Darren John Bicknell
Role: Left-hand opening bat, slow left-arm
Born: 24 June 1967, Guildford
Height: 6ft 4in **Weight:** 14st
Nickname: Denzil
County debut: 1987
County cap: 1990
1000 runs in a season: 6
1st-Class 50s: 58
1st-Class 100s: 28
1st-Class 200s: 2
1st-Class catches: 74
One-Day 100s: 7
Place in batting averages: 117th av. 34.60
(1995 71st av. 39.88)
Place in bowling averages: 16th av. 23.00
Strike rate: 46.62 (career 52.72)
Parents: Vic and Valerie
Wife and date of marriage: Rebecca, 26 September 1992
Children: Lauren Elizabeth, 21 October 1993
Family links with cricket: Brother Martin plays a bit ('actually a lot this year'), dad is a qualified umpire and youngest brother plays club cricket

Education: Robert Haining County Secondary; Guildford County College of Technology
Qualifications: 8 O-levels, 2 A-levels, senior coaching award
Career outside cricket: Marketing and sales for Scottish Courage Ltd
Off-season: Working for Scottish Courage
Overseas tours: Surrey to Sharjah 1988, 1989, to Dubai 1990, to Perth 1995; England A to Zimbabwe and Kenya 1989-90, to Pakistan 1990-91, to Bermuda and West Indies 1991-92
Overseas teams played for: Coburg, Melbourne 1986-87
Cricketers particularly admired: Mark Taylor, Graham Gooch, Mark Butcher
Young players to look out for: Mark Butcher, Adam Hollioake
Other sports followed: Football ('follow West Ham United'), golf (12 handicap)
Injuries: Split webbing, out for two weeks, plus problems with lower back and Achilles, but no time off
Relaxations: Golf, DIY, 'looking after my family'
Extras: Shared county record third-wicket stand of 413 with David Ward v Kent at Canterbury in 1990 – both made career bests. Surrey batsman of the year four times. Hit the fastest hundred of the year in 1990
Opinions on cricket: 'Too much cricket played. Must have two divisions, the best players must play against each other as often as possible.'
Best batting: 235* Surrey v Nottinghamshire, Trent Bridge 1994
Best bowling: 3-7 Surrey v Sussex, Hove 1996

1996 Season

	M	Inns	NO	Runs	HS	Avge	100s	50s	Ct	St	O	M	Runs	Wkts	Avge	Best	5wI	10wM
Test																		
All First	17	31	3	969	129 *	34.60	2	3	9	-	124.2	21	368	16	23.00	3-7	-	-
1-day Int																		
NatWest	2	2	0	53	49	26.50	-	-	-	-								
B & H	5	4	1	108	46	36.00	-	-	3	-								
Sunday	12	12	3	280	52 *	31.11	-	2	4	-								

Career Performances

	M	Inns	NO	Runs	HS	Avge	100s	50s	Ct	St	Balls	Runs	Wkts	Avge	Best	5wI	10wM
Test																	
All First	191	337	34	12102	235 *	39.94	28	58	74	-	1160	751	22	34.13	3-7	-	-
1-day Int																	
NatWest	20	20	4	778	135 *	48.62	1	5	1	-							
B & H	33	32	3	1241	119	42.79	2	9	11	-							
Sunday	92	89	12	2836	125	36.83	4	17	21	-	36	39	2	19.50	1-11	-	

BICKNELL, M. P.   Surrey

Name: Martin Paul Bicknell
Role: Right-hand bat, right-arm
fast-medium bowler
Born: 14 January 1969, Guildford
Height: 6ft 4in **Weight:** 14st 7lbs
Nickname: Bickers
County debut: 1986
County cap: 1989
Test debut: 1993
Tests: 2
One-Day Internationals: 7
50 wickets in a season: 6
1st-Class 50s: 8
1st-Class 5 w. in innings: 26
1st-Class 10 w. in match: 2
1st-Class catches: 55
Place in batting averages: 192nd av. 25.61
(1995 172nd av. 23.66)
Place in bowling averages: 22nd av. 24.74 (1995 26th av. 23.85)
Strike rate: 51.65 (career 54.73)
Parents: Vic and Valerie
Wife and date of marriage: Loraine, 29 September 1995
Children: Eleanor, 31 March 1995; Charlotte, 22 July 1996
Family links with cricket: 'Brother plays, but with no luck'
Education: Robert Haining County Secondary
Qualifications: 2 O-levels, NCA coach
Career outside cricket: Amateur golfer
Off-season: Preparing for benefit year
Overseas tours: England YC to Sri Lanka 1986-87, to Australia 1987-88; England A
to Zimbabwe and Kenya 1989-90, to Bermuda and West Indies 1991-92, to South
Africa 1993-94; England to Australia 1990-91
Cricketers particularly admired: Ian Botham, Dennis Lillee, Richard Hadlee, Jason
Ratcliffe
Young players to look out for: Ben Hollioake
Other sports followed: 'Leeds United and golf'
Injuries: Abductor strain, out for four days
Relaxations: Playing golf and spending time with the family
Extras: Youngest player to play for Surrey since David Smith. His figures of 9 for 45
were the best for the county for 30 years. One of four players on stand-by as reserves for
England's World Cup squad 1991-92. Supporters' Player of the Year 1993
Opinions on cricket: 'There is still too much cricket. Two divisions are a must.'

Best batting: 88 Surrey v Hampshire, Southampton 1992
Best bowling: 9-45 Surrey v Cambridge University, Fenner's 1988

1996 Season

	M	Inns	NO	Runs	HS	Avge	100s	50s	Ct	St	O	M	Runs	Wkts	Avge	Best	5wI	10wM
Test																		
All First	16	18	5	333	59 *	25.61	-	1	2	-	568.1	146	1633	66	24.74	5-17	3	-
1-day Int																		
NatWest	3	1	1	0	0 *	-	-	-	3	-	32	2	115	4	28.75	2-38	-	
B & H	5	1	0	22	22	22.00	-	-	-	-	42	6	198	6	33.00	3-19	-	
Sunday	16	8	5	47	19 *	15.66	-	-	3	-	115	8	535	21	25.47	3-16	-	

Career Performances

	M	Inns	NO	Runs	HS	Avge	100s	50s	Ct	St	Balls	Runs	Wkts	Avge	Best	5wI	10wM
Test	2	4	0	26	14	6.50	-	-	-	-	522	263	4	65.75	3-99	-	-
All First	166	195	53	2674	88	18.83	-	8	55	-	32075	15231	586	25.99	9-45	26	2
1-day Int	7	6	2	96	31 *	24.00	-	-	2	-	413	347	13	26.69	3-55	-	
NatWest	26	13	6	102	66 *	14.57	-	1	13	-	1647	931	35	26.60	4-35	-	
B & H	36	19	3	182	43	11.37	-	-	8	-	2118	1376	54	25.48	4-49	-	
Sunday	123	53	25	378	25	13.50	-	-	29	-	5317	3811	147	25.92	5-12	1	

BIRBECK, S. D.   Durham

Name: Shaun David Birbeck
Role: Left-hand bat, right-arm medium bowler
Born: 26 July 1972, Sunderland
Height: 5ft 11in **Weight:** 14st
Nickname: Birbs
County debut: 1994
1st-Class 50s: 1
1st-Class catches: 2
Strike rate: 63.00 (career 67.80)
Parents: James and Joyce
Marital status: Single
Family links with cricket: Brother Tony played Minor Counties cricket for Durham
Education: Hetton Comprehensive
Qualifications: GCSEs
Off-season: 'Working in some boring factory or going to Australia'
Overseas teams played for: Scarborough, Perth, Western Australia 1992-94

Cricketers particularly admired: Jimmy Adams, Jimmy Daley, Stuart Hutton, Justin Langer, Barrie Welch, David Ligertwood, Lee Welch, Darren Blenkiron
Other sports followed: Football (Sunderland), golf, tennis, ice hockey (Durham Wasps)
Relaxations: Reading and listening to music
Extras: Once ran in the Great North Run. First person to get a hat-trick in Rapid Cricketline Championship for Durham
Opinions on cricket: 'Cricket is a great game so why change it?'
Best batting: 75* Durham v Derbyshire, Chester-le-Street 1995
Best bowling: 3-88 Durham v Sussex, Hove 1996

1996 Season

	M	Inns	NO	Runs	HS	Avge	100s	50s	Ct	St	O	M	Runs	Wkts	Avge	Best	5wI	10wM
Test																		
All First	2	2	0	8	8	4.00	-	-	-	-	42	9	144	4	36.00	3-88	-	-
1-day Int																		
NatWest																		
B & H	2	2	0	9	5	4.50	-	-	-	-	15	0	86	0	-		-	-
Sunday	2	2	0	31	24	15.50	-	-	-	-	11	0	71	2	35.50	1-21	-	

Career Performances

	M	Inns	NO	Runs	HS	Avge	100s	50s	Ct	St	Balls	Runs	Wkts	Avge	Best	5wI	10wM
Test																	
All First	7	9	2	120	75 *	17.14	-	1	2	-	678	428	10	42.80	3-88	-	-
1-day Int																	
NatWest	1	0	0	0	0	-	-	-	-	-	48	27	2	13.50	2-27	-	
B & H	4	3	0	10	5	3.33	-	-	1	-	156	150	3	50.00	3-64	-	
Sunday	12	8	0	88	24	11.00	-	-	1	-	372	346	6	57.66	1-14	-	

---

10. Who won the 1996 European Championship of cricket
and who did they beat in the final?

BISHOP, I. E.   Somerset

Name: Ian Emlyn Bishop
Role: Right-hand bat, right-arm medium-fast
bowler
Born: 26 August 1977, Taunton
Height: 6ft 2in **Weight:** 11st
Nickname: Bish
County debut: 1996
Parents: Brian and Jane
Marital status: Single
Family links with cricket: Both father and
brother play club cricket
Education: Parkfield Primary School,
Taunton; Castle Secondary School, Taunton;
Scat College of Further Education, Taunton
Qualifications: GCSEs
Career outside cricket: None
Off-season: Training
Cricketers particularly admired: Darren
Gough, Chris Lewis, Alec Stewart
Young players to look out for: Andy Harris, Marcus Trescothick
Other sports followed: Football (Liverpool FC)
Injuries: None
Relaxations: Sport and socialising with friends
Best batting: 2 Somerset v Pakistan, Taunton 1996

1996 Season

	M	Inns	NO	Runs	HS	Avge	100s	50s	Ct	St	O	M	Runs	Wkts	Avge	Best	5wI	10wM
Test																		
All First	1	2	0	4	2	2.00	-	-	1	-	7	0	29	0	-	-	-	-
1-day Int																		
NatWest																		
B & H																		
Sunday																		

11. Who won the Gold Award in the 1996 Benson and Hedges final?

Career Performances

	M	Inns	NO	Runs	HS	Avge	100s	50s	Ct	St	Balls	Runs	Wkts	Avge	Best	5wl	10wM
Test																	
All First	1	2	0	4	2	2.00	-	-	1	-		42	29	0	-	-	-
1-day Int																	
NatWest																	
B & H																	
Sunday																	

BLACKWELL, I. D.   Derbyshire

Name: Ian David Blackwell
Role: Left-hand bat, slow left-arm bowler
Born: 10 June 1978, Chesterfield
Height: 6ft 1in **Weight:** 13st 7lbs
Nickname: Blackie
County debut: No first-team appearance
Parents: John and Marilyn
Marital status: Single
Family links with cricket: Father plays
for Derbyshire Over 50s and at local level
Education: Old Hall Primary School;
Manor Community College; Brookfield
Community School
Qualifications: 8 GCSEs, 1 A-level, NCA
coaching course
Career outside cricket: 'Currently
unemployed, but looking for work during the
winter'
Cricketers particularly admired: Dominic Cork and Brian Lara
Young players to look out for: David Sales and Kevin Dean
Other sports followed: Football ('played for Sheffield Wednesday Young Owls')
and golf
Relaxations: Golf and 'visiting Brampton Manor Health and Fitness Club'
Extras: Played for Derbyshire from the age of eight through to the 2nd XI
Opinions on cricket: 'Approve of the influx of Australians into our game, bringing their
superior ideas and knowledge to the county game.'

BLAIN, J. A. R.   Northamptonshire

Name: John Angus Rae Blain
Role: Right-hand bat, right-arm
medium-fast bowler
Born: 4 January 1979
Height: 6ft **Weight:** 11st 7lbs
Nickname: Blainey, Haggis
County debut: No first-team appearance
1st-Class catches: 1
Parents: John and Elma
Marital status: Single
Education: Eastfield Primary School;
Penicuik High School; Jewel and Esk Valley
College
Qualifications: 8 GCSEs, 1 Higher
Off-season: To Malaysia for ICC Tournament
with Scotland
Overseas tours: Scotland U19 to Holland
for International Youth Tournament 1994-95;
Scotland to Denmark for European Championships
Cricketers particularly admired: Curtly Ambrose, John Crawley, Malcolm Marshall,
Jim Love
Other sports followed: Football (schoolboy forms with Hibernian and Falkirk)
Relaxations: Any kind of music, 'particularly dance'
Extras: Youngest ever player to play for Scotland national side at 17 years old. Played
for Scotland in the Benson & Hedges and NatWest competitions. Made his first-class
debut for Scotland against Ireland in 1996
Opinions on cricket: 'Have a blend of youth and experience in a side, but give
youngsters a chance.'

1996 Season

	M	Inns	NO	Runs	HS	Avge	100s	50s	Ct	St	O	M	Runs	Wkts	Avge	Best	5wI	10wM
Test																		
All First	1	0	0	0	0	-	-	-	1	-	22	5	103	0	-	-	-	-
1-day Int																		
NatWest	1	0	0	0	0	-	-	-	1	-	11	0	56	2	28.00	2-56	-	
B & H	2	2	1	14	10 *	14.00	-	-	-	-	9	0	58	1	58.00	1-37	-	
Sunday																		

Career Performances

	M	Inns	NO	Runs	HS	Avge	100s	50s	Ct	St	Balls	Runs	Wkts	Avge	Best	5wl	10wM
Test																	
All First	1	0	0	0	0	-	-	-	1	-	132	103	0	-	-	-	-
1-day Int																	
NatWest	1	0	0	0	0	-	-	-	1	-	66	56	2	28.00	2-56	-	
B & H	2	2	1	14	10 *	14.00	-	-	-	-	54	58	1	58.00	1-37	-	
Sunday																	

BLAKEY, R. J. Yorkshire

Name: Richard John Blakey
Role: Right-hand bat, wicket-keeper
Born: 15 January 1967, Huddersfield
Height: 5ft 10in **Weight:** 11st 4lbs
Nickname: Dick
County debut: 1985
County cap: 1987
Test debut: 1992-93
Tests: 2
One-Day Internationals: 3
1000 runs in a season: 4
1st-Class 50s: 61
1st-Class 100s: 10
1st-Class 200s: 2
1st-Class catches: 468
1st-Class stumpings: 42
One-Day 100s: 3
Place in batting averages: 115th av. 34.95
(1995 231st av. 17.30)
Strike rate: (career 63.00)
Parents: Brian and Pauline
Wife and date of marriage: Michelle, 28 September 1991
Children: Harrison Brad, 22 September 1993
Family links with cricket: Father played local cricket
Education: Woodhouse Primary; Rastrick Grammar School
Qualifications: 4 O-levels, Senior NCA Coach
Career outside cricket: Started own leisure company
Overseas tours: England YC to West Indies 1984-85; Yorkshire to Barbados 1986-87, to Cape Town 1990-91; England A to Zimbabwe and Kenya 1989-90, to Pakistan 1990-91; England to India and Sri Lanka 1992-93
Overseas teams played for: Waverley, Sydney 1985-87; Mt Waverley, Sydney

1987-88; Bionics, Zimbabwe 1989-90

Cricketers particularly admired: Martyn Moxon, Dermot Reeve, Ian Botham, Alan Knott

Other sports followed: All

Relaxations: All sports, particularly golf and squash, eating out, drawing, photography

Extras: Established himself in Huddersfield League. Made record 2nd XI score – 273* v Northamptonshire 1986. Yorkshire's Young Player of the Year 1989. Made Test debut in second Test against India at Madras, February 1993. He was awarded a citation by the International Committee for Fair Play in 1995. He was the only cricketer among the 25 winners worldwide

Opinions on cricket: 'Four-day game is much more enjoyable and the best team wins. National anthem should be played before the start of every international, like football.'

Best batting: 221 England A v Zimbabwe, Bulawayo 1989-90

Best bowling: 1-68 Yorkshire v Nottinghamshire, Sheffield 1986

1996 Season

	M	Inns	NO	Runs	HS	Avge	100s	50s	Ct	St	O	M	Runs	Wkts	Avge	Best	5wl	10wM
Test																		
All First	19	30	6	839	109 *	34.95	1	5	40	4								
1-day Int																		
NatWest	4	3	2	49	33	49.00	-	-	4	-								
B & H	6	4	1	121	80 *	40.33	-	1	4	1								
Sunday	17	12	4	293	61 *	36.62	-	1	13	2								

Career Performances

	M	Inns	NO	Runs	HS	Avge	100s	50s	Ct	St	Balls	Runs	Wkts	Avge	Best	5wl	10wM
Test	2	4	0	7	6	1.75	-	-	2	-							
All First	240	389	59	10684	221	32.37	10	61	468	42	63	68	1	68.00	1-68	-	-
1-day Int	3	2	0	25	25	12.50	-	-	2	1							
NatWest	24	18	4	365	75	26.07	-	2	28	2							
B & H	40	34	5	854	80 *	29.44	-	6	34	2							
Sunday	134	119	23	3824	130 *	39.83	3	23	103	18							

12. Who captained the South Africa A side on their tour to England in 1996?

BLANCHETT, I. N. Middlesex

Name: Ian Neale Blanchett
Role: Right-hand bat, right-arm
fast-medium bowler
Born: 2 February 1975, Melbourne, Australia
Height: 6ft 4in **Weight:** 14st 7lbs
Nickname: Blanchy, Noisy, Ozzy, Terry
('from Viz!')
County debut: No first-team appearance
Parents: Edward Arthur Blanchett and Susan
Anne Billons
Marital status: Single
Family links with cricket: 'Uncle played for
Surrey U19. None other that I know of'
Education: Feltwell Primary, Norfolk;
Methwold High School, Norfolk; Downham
Market High School; Luton University
Qualifications: 8 GCSEs, 2 A-levels, 'in
process of completing a Health
Science/Leisure degree'
Cricketers particularly admired: Richard Hadlee, Ian Botham, Allan Donald,
Graeme Hick
Other sports followed: Football (Norwich City), rugby (Bath and England), snooker,
tennis, American football (San Francisco 49ers)
Injuries: Snapped ligaments in right hand, out for ten weeks
Relaxations: 'Spending time with friends socialising over a few drinks. Listening to
my favourite tunes. Chilling out on my grandfather's boat in Marbella, Spain. Deep-
sea diving'
Extras: Voted Player of the Year four times successively by his club in Norfolk.
Awarded a special achievement prize in the 1994 NAYC Cambridge Festival
Opinions on cricket: 'There could be more involvement of former Test cricketers in the
coaching, development and selection of the national teams. I also feel that the Sunday
League games should not be played in between Championship games, as the adverse
situation sometimes affects both contests.'

BLENKIRON, D. A. Durham

Name: Darren Andrew Blenkiron
Role: Left-hand bat, right-arm
medium bowler
Born: 4 February 1974, Solihull
Height: 5ft 10in **Weight:** 12st 7lbs
Nickname: Blue Dog, Pit Bull
County debut: 1991 (one-day),
1994 (first-class)
1st-Class 50s: 2
1st-Class 100s: 3
1st-Class catches: 7
Place in batting averages: 211th av. 23.82
(1995 146th av. 27.87)
Strike rate: 45.40 (career 53.83)
Parents: William and Margaret
Marital status: Single
Family links with cricket:
Father played for Warwickshire and MCC
Education: Bishop Barrington Comprehensive School
Qualifications: 4 O-levels
Overseas tours: England U19 to Pakistan 1991-92; Durham CCC to
South Africa 1995
Overseas teams played for: Alberton, South Africa 1993-96
Cricketers particularly admired: Graeme Hick, Phil Bainbridge,
Paul Romaines, my father
Other sports followed: Football (Liverpool FC)
Relaxations: Music, socialising
Opinions on cricket: 'Over rate should be reduced, lunches and tea should be extended.'
Best batting: 145 Durham v Glamorgan, Swansea 1995
Best bowling: 4-43 Durham v Glamorgan, Chester-le-Street 1996

1996 Season

	M	Inns	NO	Runs	HS	Avge	100s	50s	Ct	St	O	M	Runs	Wkts	Avge	Best	5wI	10wM
Test																		
All First	9	16	2	328	130	23.42	2	-	4	-	37.5	9	123	5	24.60	4-43	-	-
1-day Int																		
NatWest	1	1	0	25	25	25.00	-	-	-	-	4	0	31	0	-		-	-
B & H																		
Sunday	9	8	1	107	34	15.28	-	-	1	-	8	0	56	0	-		-	-

Career Performances

	M	Inns	NO	Runs	HS	Avge	100s	50s	Ct	St	Balls	Runs	Wkts	Avge	Best	5wI	10wM
Test																	
All First	19	33	3	774	145	25.80	3	2	7	-	323	187	6	31.16	4-43	-	-
1-day Int																	
NatWest	4	4	1	119	56	39.66	-	1	1	-	42	45	0	-	-	-	-
B & H																	
Sunday	20	17	3	277	56	19.78	-	1	3	-	168	192	1	192.00	1-25	-	

BLEWETT, G. S. Middlesex

Name: Gregory Scott Blewett
Role: Right-hand bat, right-arm bowler
Born: 28 October 1971, Adelaide, Australia
Height: 6ft **Weight:** 11st
Nickname: Blewy
County debut: No first-team appearance
Test debut: 1994-95
Tests: 9
One-Day Internationals: 8
1st-Class 50s: 23
1st-Class 100s: 14
1st-Class 200s: 2
Strike rate: (career 78.64)
Parents: Robert and Shirley
Marital status: Single
Family links with cricket: Father captained South Australia
Education: Angaston Primary School, Adelaide; Prince Alfred College, Adelaide
Qualifications: Level 1 cricket coaching
Overseas tours: Australia U19 to England 1991, to Sri Lanka; Australia to New Zealand, to West Indies 1994-95, to South Africa 1996-97
Overseas teams played for: South Australia
Cricketers particularly admired: Steve Waugh, Allan Border
Young players to look out for: Jason Gillespie
Other sports followed: Golf, Aussie rules (Geelong AFL), football (Manchester United), American football (Chicago Bulls)
Relaxations: Spending time with girlfriend
Opinions on cricket: 'Too much one-day cricket for national teams.'
Best batting: 268 South Australia v Victoria, Melbourne 1993-94
Best bowling: 4-39 South Australia v New South Wales, Adelaide 1994-95

1996 (did not make any first-class or one-day appearances)

Career Performances

	M	Inns	NO	Runs	HS	Avge	100s	50s	Ct	St	Balls	Runs	Wkts	Avge	Best	5wl	10wM
Test	9	15	1	468	115	33.42	2	2	11	-	240	122	2	61.00	2-25	-	-
All First	63	111	7	4752	268	45.69	14	23	34	-	3539	1796	45	39.91	4-39	-	-
1-day Int	8	8	0	111	46	13.87	-	-	1	-	263	249	4	62.25	1-30	-	-
NatWest																	
B & H																	
Sunday																	

BODEN, D. J. P. Gloucestershire

Name: David Jonathan Peter Boden
Role: Right-hand bat, right-arm fast bowler
Born: 26 November 1970, Eccleshall, Staffs
Height: 6ft 3in **Weight:** 14st 7lbs
Nickname: Bodie, Horse, Congo
County debut: 1989 (Middlesex),
1992 (Essex), 1995 (Gloucestershire)
1st-Class catches: 6
Strike rate: 222.00 (career 67.00)
Parents: Peter and Mary
Marital status: Single
Family links with cricket: 'Dad is an avid
follower of the game and ferried me
everywhere when I was younger'
Education: Stone Alleynes High School;
Stafford College of Further Education
Qualifications: 3 CSEs, 6 O-levels, BTEC
National Diploma in Business
Studies, NCA coaching certificate, Senior NCA Coach
Overseas teams played for: Waverley, Sydney 1990-95
Cricketers particularly admired: Ian Botham, Don Topley
Other sports followed: Tiddlywinks, rugby, golf, football (Manchester United FC)
Relaxations: Playing golf, listening to music, watching *Pulp Fiction*, relaxing on beach
Extras: Staffordshire Wellington Boot Throwing Champion. Signed by Gloucestershire
for 1995 season after spells with both Middlesex and Essex
Best batting: 5 Essex v Cambridge University, Fenner's 1992; 5 Essex v Middlesex,
Colchester 1993
Best bowling: 4-11 Middlesex v Oxford University, The Parks 1989

1996 Season

	M	Inns	NO	Runs	HS	Avge	100s	50s	Ct	St	O	M	Runs	Wkts	Avge	Best	5wI	10wM
Test																		
All First	2	1	0	1	1	1.00	-	-	1	-	37	5	140	1	140.00	1-50	-	-
1-day Int																		
NatWest																			
B & H																			
Sunday																			

Career Performances

	M	Inns	NO	Runs	HS	Avge	100s	50s	Ct	St	Balls	Runs	Wkts	Avge	Best	5wI	10wM
Test																	
All First	8	5	0	13	5	2.60	-	-	5	-	1005	611	15	40.73	4-11	-	-
1-day Int																	
NatWest	1	0	0	0	0	-	-	-	-	-	72	26	6	4.33	6-26	1	
B & H																	
Sunday	7	5	0	10	5	2.00	-	-	2	-	313	265	7	37.85	3-34	-	

BOILING, J.   Durham

Name: James Boiling
Role: Right-hand bat, right-arm off-spin
bowler, 'wicket-keeper in benefit matches'
Born: 8 April 1968, New Delhi
Height: 6ft 2in **Weight:** 13st 2lbs
Nickname: Bull
County debut: 1988 (Surrey), 1995
(Durham)
1st-Class 50s: 1
1st-Class 5 w. in innings: 4
1st-Class 10 w. in match: 1
1st-Class catches: 57
One-Day 5 w. in innings: 1
Place in batting averages: 285th av. 11.28
(1995 267th av. 12.48)
Place in bowling averages: (1995 150th av.
63.03)
Strike rate: (career 101.91)
Parents: Graham and Geraldine
Wife and date of marriage: Rachel, 7 October 1995
Family links with cricket: 'My father came up with a novel idea for catching practice
in the back garden which involved a golf ball, a washing line, some clothes pegs and

the herbaceous border'

Education: Rutlish School, Merton; Durham University (College of St Hild and Bede)

Qualifications: 10 O-levels, 3 A-levels, BA (Hons) in History, NCA senior coaching award. St. John's Emergency First Aid certificate

Career outside cricket: 'I cannot ever see myself doing anything which does not involve a bat and ball'

Off-season: 'Relaxing in the San Francisco area, with a brief excursion to New Zealand incorporated'

Overseas tours: Surrey Schools to Australia 1985-86; England YC to Australia (Youth World Cup) 1987-88; England A to Australia 1992-93

Overseas teams played for: Bionics, Harare 1991-92; St Augustine, Cape Town 1992-93; Watsonians, California 1996-97

Cricketers particularly admired: 'There is something pleasing in watching Carl Hooper play a late cut'

Young players to look out for: 'My nephew Jonathan is a very promising bowler'

Other sports followed: 'My wife and I watch Newcastle Falcons rugby team in the winter. Rachel is a particular fan of Rob Andrew's kicking'

Injuries: Hypothermia throughout April

Relaxations: 'I like to compare the routes we use to grounds and hotels during the summer and would someday like to produce a definitive guide for cricketers on the subject'

Extras: Believed to be the only player to win a Gold Award against his own county, returning 8-3-9-3 analysis for Combined Universities against Surrey in 1989. Late call-up for England A tour to Australia when Ian Salisbury stayed in India. Moved to Durham from Surrey in 1995

Opinions on cricket: 'I believe that rest days should be reintroduced to Test cricket to enable bodies and minds to recover. There is so much money coming into the game nowadays, what with Sky Television and libel cases and increased sponsorship. Schools cricket is declining and teachers are overburdened. Lots of people seem to think that "things were better in their day". Congratulations to Surrey on their long overdue success. I think we will win The Ashes in 1997, or soon anyway.'

Best batting: 69 Durham v West Indies, Chester-le-Street 1995

Best bowling: 6-84 Surrey v Gloucestershire, Bristol 1992

1996 Season

	M	Inns	NO	Runs	HS	Avge	100s	50s	Ct	St	O	M	Runs	Wkts	Avge	Best	5wI	10wM
Test																		
All First	8	11	4	79	31 *	11.28	-	-	8	-	263.1	85	582	9	64.66	2-69	-	-
1-day Int																		
NatWest	2	1	1	46	46 *	-	-	-	2	-	24	4	93	0	-		-	-
B & H	4	2	1	22	15	22.00	-	-	1	-	29	0	100	5	20.00	2-22	-	
Sunday	12	6	2	62	27	15.50	-	-	1	-	92.2	3	445	13	34.23	3-65	-	

Career Performances

	M	Inns	NO	Runs	HS	Avge	100s	50s	Ct	St	Balls	Runs	Wkts	Avge	Best	5wI	10wM
Test																	
All First	71	99	34	826	69	12.70	-	1	57	-	12790	5708	119	47.96	6-84	4	1
1-day Int																	
NatWest	15	6	2	106	46 *	26.50	-	-	8	-	952	504	13	38.76	4-22	-	
B & H	34	21	13	88	15	11.00	-	-	13	-	1798	1239	29	42.72	3-9	-	
Sunday	83	37	17	251	27	12.55	-	-	31	-	3420	2658	85	31.27	5-24	1	

BOON, D. C. Durham

Name: David Clarence Boon
Role: Right-hand bat, right-arm medium
bowler, county captain
Born: 29 December 1960, Launceston,
Tasmania
County debut: No first-team appearance
Test debut: 1984-85
Tests: 107
One-Day Internationals: 181
1st-Class 50s: 83
1st-Class 100s: 59
1st-Class 200s: 3
1st-Class catches: 224
One-Day 100s: 5
Strike rate: (career 88.45)
Off-season: Playing for Tasmania
Overseas teams played for:
Tasmania, 1978-97

Overseas tours: Young Australia to
Zimbabwe 1982-83; Australia to England 1985, 1989 and 1993, to New Zealand 1985-
86, 1989-90, 1992-93, to India 1986-87, to Pakistan 1988-89, 1994-95, to West Indies
1990-91, 1994-95, to Sri Lanka 1992-93, to South Africa 1993-94, to India and
Pakistan (World Cup) 1986-87
Extras: David Boon first toured England in 1985, and his early struggles to establish his
position in the Test side were overcome when he was paired with Geoff Marsh. They
went on to become Australia's most successful opening pair since Bill Lawry and Bobby
Simpson. Dropped from the Test series for poor form against England in 1986-87, he
came back to win the International Cricketer of the Year the following season. In 1988-
89 he was the leading run-scorer in the series against West Indies, and followed that with
a successful tour of England in 1989. He made his highest Test score against New
Zealand at Perth in 1989-90, but had the rest of the reason ruined by a knee injury. He

recovered to score over 500 runs in successive series against England and India, now batting at No. 3. He returned to opener against the West Indies in 1991-92, scoring 490 runs at an average of over 60. Also one of the world's finest close to the wicket fieldsmen. Retired from Test cricket in 1995-96. Agreed to play for Gloucestershire in the 1995 season, but withdrew through injury and his overseas berth was taken by Javagal Srinath. Has signed a two-year deal with Durham and will be captain for the 1997 season

Best batting: 227 Tasmania v Victoria, Melbourne 1983-84
Best bowling: 1-0 Tasmania v Western Australia, Perth 1995-96

1996 (no first-class or one-day appearances)

Career Performances

	M	Inns	NO	Runs	HS	Avge	100s	50s	Ct	St	Balls	Runs	Wkts	Avge	Best	5wl	10wM
Test	107	190	20	7422	200	43.65	21	32	99	-	36	14	0	-	-	-	-
All First	267	449	43	18881	227	46.33	59	83	224	-	796	478	9	53.11	1-0	-	-
1-day Int	181	177	16	5964	122	37.04	5	37	45	-	12	11	0	-	-	-	-
NatWest																	
B & H																	
Sunday																	

BOSWELL, S. A. J.   Northamptonshire

Name: Scott Antony John Boswell
Role: Right-hand bat, right-arm fast-medium bowler
Born: 11 September 1974, York
Height: 6ft 5in **Weight:** 14st
Nickname: Joey, Bossy, Retro
County debut: 1995 (one-day), 1996 (first-class)
1st-Class catches: 2
Parents: Tony and Judy
Marital status: Single
Education: Pocklington School; Wolverhampton University
Qualifications: 9 GCSEs, 3 A-levels
Off-season: Studying
Overseas teams played for: Hutt Valley, New Zealand 1994-95
Cricketers particularly admired: Dennis Lillee, Richard Hadlee and Kevin Curran

Young players to look out for: David Sales
Other sports followed: Football (York City), rugby union, golf
Relaxations: Watching most sports, playing golf, socialising and spending time with friends and family
Opinions on cricket: 'Overseas players should be allowed in the county championship because they are essential for younger players, like myself, to learn from and to play with and against. Also for the crowds to be able to watch top international players perform. I think most second team cricket should be played at first-class grounds which have been prepared to the quality of first-class cricket.'
Best batting: 2* Northamptonshire v Pakistan, Northampton 1996
Best bowling: 2-52 Northamptonshire v Pakistan, Northampton 1996

1996 Season

	M	Inns	NO	Runs	HS	Avge	100s	50s	Ct	St	O	M	Runs	Wkts	Avge	Best	5wI	10wM
Test																		
All First	3	4	2	5	2*	2.50	-	-	2	-	73.4	9	243	7	34.71	2-52	-	-
1-day Int																		
NatWest																		
B & H	5	5	1	21	14	5.25	-	-	1	-	49.5	2	302	2	151.00	1-61	-	
Sunday																		

Career Performances

	M	Inns	NO	Runs	HS	Avge	100s	50s	Ct	St	Balls	Runs	Wkts	Avge	Best	5wI	10wM
Test																	
All First	3	4	2	5	2*	2.50	-	-	2	-	442	243	7	34.71	2-52	-	-
1-day Int																	
NatWest																	
B & H	6	5	1	21	14	5.25	-	-	1	-	329	308	3	102.66	1-6	-	
Sunday	4	1	0	2	2	2.00	-	-	-	-	138	104	3	34.66	1-20	-	

BOTHAM, L. J. Hampshire

Name: Liam James Botham
Role: Right-hand bat, right-arm fast bowler
Born: 26 August 1977, Doncaster
Height: 6ft 1in **Weight:** 14st
Nickname: Sniffer
County debut: 1996
1st-Class 5 w. in innings: 1
1st-Class catches: 2
Parents: Ian and Kathryn
Marital status: Engaged

Family links with cricket: Father Ian played for England
Education: Cundall Manor Prep School; Rossall School
Qualifications: 6 GCSEs and 2 A-levels
Off-season: Playing rugby for West Hartlepool, coaching for Cundall Manor, keeping fit
Cricketers particularly admired: Malcolm Marshall, Viv Richards, Mark Garaway
Young players to look out for: Ben Hollioake, Dimitri Mascraenhas, David Sales
Other sports followed: Rugby, football (Newcastle United), golf (Ian Woosnam)
Injuries: Bruising of patella ligament, out for two and a half weeks
Relaxations: Fishing, golf, rugby, McClusky's, Paul Whitaker's after dinner speaking

Extras: Played for England U17 v India U17 in 1994. Plays rugby for Lancashire U18. Appeared on *Beadle's About*, as the victim of a practical joke set up by his father. Took five wickets on his Championship debut, including the wicket of Mike Gatting (a feat never achieved by his father). Signed professional rugby union forms with West Hartlepool in December 1996
Opinions on cricket: 'Should not play unless it is over 15ºC. County Championship should be made into two divisions and have promotion and relegation battles, giving teams more to play for in the latter part of the season.'
Best batting: 30* Hampshire v Middlesex, Lord's 1996
Best bowling: 5-67 Hampshire v Middlesex, Lord's 1996

1996 Season

	M	Inns	NO	Runs	HS	Avge	100s	50s	Ct	St	O	M	Runs	Wkts	Avge	Best	5wI	10wM
Test																		
All First	3	3	0	31	30	10.33	-	-	2	-	55	9	268	8	33.50	5-67	1	-
1-day Int																		
NatWest																		
B & H																		
Sunday	1	1	0	1	1	1.00	-	-	-	-	4	0	33	0	-		-	-

Career Performances

	M	Inns	NO	Runs	HS	Avge	100s	50s	Ct	St	Balls	Runs	Wkts	Avge	Best	5wI	10wM
Test																	
All First	3	3	0	31	30	10.33	-	-	2	-	330	268	8	33.50	5-67	1	-
1-day Int																	
NatWest																	
B & H																	
Sunday	1	1	0	1	1	1.00	-	-	-	-	24	33	0	-		-	-

BOVILL, J. N. B. Hampshire

Name: James Noel Bruce Bovill
Role: Right-hand bat, right-arm fast-medium bowler
Born: 2 June 1971, High Wycombe
Height: 6ft **Weight:** 12st 8lbs
Nickname: Jimma, Rigsby
County debut: 1993
1st-Class 5 w. in innings: 4
1st-Class 10 w match: 1
1st-Class catches: 2
Place in batting averages: 302nd av. 7.70
Place in bowling averages: 96th av. 35.26
(1995 50th av. 27.13)
Strike rate: 57.88 (career 53.27)
Parents: Mike and Anne
Marital status: Single
Family links with cricket: Father played for Dorset 1957-60
Education: Sandroyd Preparatory School; Charterhouse; Durham University
Qualifications: 8 O-levels, 3 A-levels, BA (Hons) in Combined Social Sciences
Career outside cricket: 'Still pursuing'
Off-season: Tour to Argentina with the Troubadours
Overseas tours: Hampshire Maniacs to Guernsey and Jersey 1989; Bucks to Zimbabwe 1991-92; Durham University to South Africa 1992-93; MCC to Far East and India 1995-96
Overseas teams played for: Western Province CC, South Africa 1989-90, Tigers Parow, South Africa 1994-95; Durban HS Old Boys 1996
Cricketers particularly admired: Cardigan Connor, Paul Terry, Reg Peacock
Young players to look out for: Jason Laney, David Roberts, Jeremy Snape
Other sports followed: Rugby, football (Notts Forest)

Injuries: Split finger, out for ten days
Relaxations: Travelling, eating out, swimming
Extras: Survived as youngest member of MCC tour party to the Far East. Indoor European Championship winners in Vienna with Durham University in 1994
Opinions on cricket: 'Two divisions are a must. The Cricketers' Association has been a great success.'
Best batting: 31 Hampshire v Worcestershire, Southampton 1995
Best bowling: 6-29 Hampshire v Durham, Stockton 1995

1996 Season

	M	Inns	NO	Runs	HS	Avge	100s	50s	Ct	St	O	M	Runs	Wkts	Avge	Best	5wI	10wM
Test																		
All First	14	19	2	131	29	7.70	-	-	-	-	328	62	1199	34	35.26	5-58	1	-
1-day Int																		
NatWest																		
B & H																		
Sunday	4	1	1	6	6 *	-	-	-	-	-	17.2	0	100	4	25.00	3-45	-	

Career Performances

	M	Inns	NO	Runs	HS	Avge	100s	50s	Ct	St	Balls	Runs	Wkts	Avge	Best	5wI	10wM
Test																	
All First	29	40	14	259	31	9.96	-	-	2	-	4315	2482	81	30.64	6-29	4	1
1-day Int																	
NatWest																	
B & H	7	1	1	14	14 *	-	-	-	1	-	373	249	5	49.80	2-21	-	
Sunday	12	5	2	14	7 *	4.66	-	-	1	-	437	378	10	37.80	3-40	-	

13. Who won the 1996 Lord's Taverners Cricketer Colts Trophy?

BOWEN, M. N. Nottinghamshire

Name: Mark Nicholas Bowen
Role: Right-hand bat, right-arm medium bowler
Born: 6 December 1967, Redcar
Height: 6ft 1in **Weight:** 13st
Nickname: Jim, Bully, Trainspotter
County debut: 1991-92 (Northamptonshire), 1996 (Nottinghamshire)
1st-Class 5 w. in innings: 2
1st-Class catches: 6
Place in batting averages: 293rd av. 10.81
Place in bowling averages: 106th av. 38.81
Strike rate: 66.60 (career 66.22)
Parents: Keith
Marital status: Engaged to Lesley
Family links with cricket: 'Father has always played and still has great interest in the game'
Education: St Mary's, Redcar; Sacred Heart, Redcar; Teesside Polytechnic
Qualifications: 8 O-levels, 3 A-levels, BSc (Hons) in Chemical Engineering
Career outside cricket: Commissioning engineer for British Nuclear Fuels
Overseas tours: Northamptonshire to Durban 1992, to Cape Town 1993; Christians in Sport to Zimbabwe 1994-95
Cricketers particularly admired: Richard Hadlee, Dennis Lillee, Viv Richards, Graham Gooch
Young players to look out for: Paul Franks, David Roberts, David Sales, Usman Afzaal
Other sports followed: Football (Middlesbrough FC), golf, hockey (played for Durham County)
Injuries: Side muscle, out for four weeks during pre-season
Relaxations: Watching television, eating out and a good pint
Extras: Made debut for Northants first team in Natal on 1991-92 tour to South Africa before playing in the 2nd XI. Released by Northamptonshire at the end of the 1995 season and joined Nottinghamshire for the start of the 1996 season
Opinions on cricket: 'Four-day game is a good contest, it allows time for the game to develop and tests the full strength of a side. The surfaces still need to be produced for a balanced contest. Four-day games would allow greater rest between fixtures with time to allow players to work on technical aspects of their game.'
Best batting: 23* Northamptonshire v Durham, Northampton 1993
Best bowling: 5-53 Nottinghamshire v Derbyshire, Derby 1996

1996 Season

	M	Inns	NO	Runs	HS	Avge	100s	50s	Ct	St	O	M	Runs	Wkts	Avge	Best	5wI	10wM
Test																		
All First	13	18	2	173	22	10.81	-	-	3	-	366.2	64	1281	33	38.81	5-53	2	-
1-day Int																		
NatWest	1	1	1	0	0 *	-	-	-	1	-	6	0	42	0	-		-	-
B & H																		
Sunday	13	3	2	45	23 *	45.00	-	-	5	-	88	1	471	13	36.23	3-28	-	

Career Performances

	M	Inns	NO	Runs	HS	Avge	100s	50s	Ct	St	Balls	Runs	Wkts	Avge	Best	5wI	10wM
Test																	
All First	26	32	6	289	23 *	11.11	-	-	6	-	4172	2477	63	39.31	5-53	2	-
1-day Int																	
NatWest	1	1	1	0	0 *	-	-	-	1	-	36	42	0	-		-	-
B & H	1	1	0	0	0	0.00	-	-	-	-	60	39	1	39.00	1-39	-	
Sunday	34	14	7	138	27 *	19.71	-	-	7	-	1332	1119	30	37.30	3-28	-	

BOWLER, P. D. Somerset

Name: Peter Duncan Bowler
Role: Right-hand opening bat, occasional off-spin bowler, wicket-keeper, county captain
Born: 30 July 1963, Plymouth
Height: 6ft 2in **Weight:** 13st
Nickname: Tom
County debut: 1986 (Leicestershire), 1988 (Derbyshire), 1995 (Somerset)
County cap: 1989 (Derbyshire), 1995 (Somerset)
1000 runs in a season: 8
1st-Class 50s: 70
1st-Class 100s: 28
1st-Class 200s: 3
1st-Class catches: 120
1st-Class stumpings: 1
One-Day 100s: 5
Place in batting averages: 70th av. 40.93 (1995 18th av. 53.96)
Strike rate: 63.00 (career 112.33)
Parents: Peter and Etta

Wife and date of marriage: Joanne, 10 October 1992
Children: Peter Robert, 21 September 1993; Rebekah, 25 August 1995
Education: Scots College, Sydney, Australia; Daramalan College, Canberra, Australia
Qualifications: Australian Year 12 certificate
Off-season: With the family in Australia
Cricketers particularly admired: Gus Valence, Rob Jeffery, Bill Carracher, Phil Russell
Young players to look out for: Marcus Trescothick
Other sports followed: Rugby union
Relaxations: Family and reading
Extras: First Leicestershire player to score a first-class century on debut (100* v Hampshire 1986). Moved to Derbyshire at end of 1987 season and scored a hundred on his debut v Cambridge University in 1988. First batsman to 2000 runs in 1992, finishing equal leading run-scorer (2044) with Mike Roseberry of Middlesex. Derbyshire Player of the Year 1992. Signed a five-year contract with Somerset starting in 1995. Took over the Somerset captaincy mid-season after Andy Hayhurst was released
Best batting: 241* Derbyshire v Hampshire, Portsmouth 1992
Best bowling: 3-41 Derbyshire v Leicestershire, Leicester 1991

1996 Season

	M	Inns	NO	Runs	HS	Avge	100s	50s	Ct	St	O	M	Runs	Wkts	Avge	Best	5wI	10wM
Test																		
All First	19	34	4	1228	207	40.93	2	7	5	-	31.3	2	177	3	59.00	2-54	-	-
1-day Int																		
NatWest	3	3	0	115	52	38.33	-	1	-	-								
B & H	5	5	0	74	26	14.80	-	-	1	-	0.3	0	4	0	-	-	-	
Sunday	15	15	1	497	76	35.50	-	5	4	-								

Career Performances

	M	Inns	NO	Runs	HS	Avge	100s	50s	Ct	St	Balls	Runs	Wkts	Avge	Best	5wI	10wM
Test																	
All First	196	342	32	12772	241 *	41.20	28	70	120	1	2696	1756	24	73.16	3-41	-	-
1-day Int																	
NatWest	16	16	0	409	111	25.56	1	2	6	-	36	26	0	-	-	-	
B & H	41	40	1	1205	109	30.89	2	10	19	1	273	158	4	39.50	1-15	-	
Sunday	144	140	15	4347	138 *	34.77	2	36	56	1	242	237	7	33.85	3-31	-	

14. Who won the 1996 Cricketer Cup?

BRIMSON, M. T. Leicestershire

Name: Matthew Thomas Brimson
Role: Right-hand bat, slow left-arm bowler
Born: 1 December 1970, Plumstead, London
Height: 6ft **Weight:** 11st 6lbs
Nickname: Brimmo, Doogie
County debut: 1993
1st-Class 5 w. in innings: 2
1st-Class catches: 1
Place in batting averages: 298th av. 8.50
Place in bowling averages: 70th av. 31.60
(1995 35th av. 25.83)
Strike rate: 61.77 (career 67.94)
Parents: David and Jennifer
Wife and date of marriage: Lyn, 29
December 1993
Children: Poppy Lilian, 14 July 1996
Family links with cricket: Brother played a
little in Kent League and South Thames
League

Education: St Joseph's Preparatory School, Blackheath; Chislehurst and Sidcup
Grammar School, Sidcup; Van Mildert College, Durham University
Qualifications: 8 O-levels, 3 A-levels, BA (Hons) degree in Geography
Off-season: Working for NatWest bank
Overseas tours: Kent Schools U17 to Singapore and New Zealand 1987-88;
Leicestershire to South Africa 1994 and 1995, to Potchefstroom, Western Province,
South Africa 1996
Cricketers particularly admired: Phil Edmonds, Phil Tufnell and Colin Bridge
Other sports followed: Golf, tennis, badminton and football (Charlton Athletic)
Relaxations: Reading, walking, spending time with family
Extras: Was on the Kent staff in 1991, Rapidline 2nd XI Player of the Month, July 1995
Opinions on cricket: 'Second team wickets sometimes leave a lot to be desired, as do
some second team club umpires during the mid-summer months. A 20-over competition,
where one side bats one night and the other the following night, could replace the
NatWest or Benson and Hedges competitions and may attract good size crowds.'
Best batting: 25 Leicestershire v Surrey, Leicester 1995
Best bowling: 5-12 Leicestershire v Sussex, Leicester 1996

1996 Season

	M	Inns	NO	Runs	HS	Avge	100s	50s	Ct	St	O	M	Runs	Wkts	Avge	Best	5wI	10wM
Test																		
All First	12	12	6	51	13 *	8.50	-	-	2	-	360.2	76	1106	35	31.60	5-12	2	
1-day Int																		
NatWest	1	1	0	9	9	9.00	-	-	-	-	10.4	1	34	3	11.33	3-34	-	
B & H	1	0	0	0	0	-	-	-	-	-	10	0	56	1	56.00	1-56	-	
Sunday	5	1	1	4	4 *	-	-	-	-	-	33	0	154	5	30.80	3-23	-	

Career Performances

	M	Inns	NO	Runs	HS	Avge	100s	50s	Ct	St	Balls	Runs	Wkts	Avge	Best	5wI	10wM
Test																	
All First	26	27	12	136	25	9.06	-	-	3	-	3669	1829	54	33.87	5-12	2	-
1-day Int																	
NatWest	1	1	0	9	9	9.00	-	-	-	-	64	34	3	11.33	3-34	-	
B & H	1	0	0	0	0	-	-	-	-	-	60	56	1	56.00	1-56	-	
Sunday	6	1	1	4	4 *	-	-	-	-	-	258	182	6	30.33	3-23	-	

BRINKLEY, J. E.   Worcestershire

Name: James Edward Brinkley
Role: Right-hand bat, right-arm fast-medium bowler
Born: 13 March 1974, Helensburgh, Scotland
Height: 6ft 3in **Weight:** 14st
Nickname: JB
County debut: 1993-94
1st-Class catches: 3
1st-Class 5 w. in innings: 1
Strike rate: (career 65.55)
Parents: Tom and Sharon
Marital status: Single
Family links with cricket: Father played service cricket in the Royal Navy, brother is captain of Worcester University cricket team
Education: Marist College, Canberra; Trinity College, Perth
Qualifications:
West Australian Tertiary Entrance Examinations; Certificate of Fitness Instruction and Gym Management
Career outside cricket: Health and fitness industry

Off-season: Working for Club Athletica
Overseas teams played for: Scarborough, Perth 1990-93; Western Australian U19 1993; Matabeleland, Zimbabwe 1994-95
Cricketers particularly admired: Michael Holding, Courtney Walsh, Stuart Lampitt, Ian Botham
Young players to look out for: Vikram Solanki, Ben Hollioake
Other sports followed: Rugby union (Bath RFC) and golf
Injuries: Torn cartilage in right knee, missed July to September
Relaxations: Watching videos and movies, golf
Extras: Taken a hat-trick in both the 2nd XI Championship and the Bain Clarkson Trophy, against Surrey and Somerset respectively. Coached Zimbabwe Under 19 in South African provincial Coca Cola Cup in 1994
Opinions on cricket: 'I don't think overseas players should be banned as they raise the overall standard and groundsmen should be employed by a central body to try and get pitches of a consistently high quality. What a great game!'
Best batting: 29 Matebeleland v Mashonaland Under-24, Harare 1994-95
Best bowling: 6-35 Matebeleland v Mashonaland Country Districts, Harare South 1994-95

1996 Season

	M	Inns	NO	Runs	HS	Avge	100s	50s	Ct	St	O	M	Runs	Wkts	Avge	Best	5wI	10wM
Test																		
All First																		
1-day Int																		
NatWest																		
B & H	3	0	0	0	0	-	-	-	-	-	25	2	136	4	34.00	2-44	-	
Sunday	2	1	0	0	0	0.00	-	-	-	-	12	1	56	3	18.66	2-26	-	

Career Performances

	M	Inns	NO	Runs	HS	Avge	100s	50s	Ct	St	Balls	Runs	Wkts	Avge	Best	5wI	10wM
Test																	
All First	12	12	4	31	10 *	3.87	-	-	3	-	1747	957	25	38.28	6-98	1	-
1-day Int																	
NatWest																	
B & H	3	0	0	0	0	-	-	-	-	-	150	136	4	34.00	2-44	-	
Sunday	3	1	0	0	0	0.00	-	-	-	-	120	80	3	26.66	2-26	-	

15. Which player achieved the extraordinary feat of taking four
wickets in four balls and against whom in 1996?

BROADHURST, M.   Nottinghamshire

Name: Mark Broadhurst
Role: Right-hand bat, right-arm
fast-medium bowler
Born: 20 June 1974, Barnsley
Height: 6ft **Weight:** 12st
Nickname: Broady, Stanley, Gibby
County debut: 1991 (Yorkshire), 1996
(Nottinghamshire)
Strike rate: (career 65.28)
Parents: Robert and Pamela
Marital status: Single
Family links with cricket: Father played
local league
Education: Worsborough Common Junior
School; Kingstone Comprehensive
Qualifications: 8 GCSEs, City and Guilds
qualification in Leisure and Recreation
Overseas tours: England U19 to New
Zealand 1990-91, to India 1992-93;

NCA YC to Canada 1991; Yorkshire to South Africa 1993
Cricketers particularly admired: Dennis Lillee, Michael Holding, Malcolm
Marshall, Bobby Chapman
Other sports followed: Football (Liverpool FC and Barnsley FC), golf, athletics,
snooker
Relaxations: Reading, music, nightclubs
Extras: Selected for England U19 squad aged 16. Made first-class debut for Yorks at
age 16, becoming the third youngest in Yorkshire history. Contributor to Wombwell
Cricket Society's *Twelfth Man* magazine. Played for England U19 v Australia 1991.
Selected for England U19 tour to Pakistan 1991-92 but forced to drop out through back
injury. Signed by Nottinghamshire in 1995 but was released at the end of the 1996
season
Opinions on cricket: 'I think that the game today is heading in the right direction and
there are great opportunities, but it is still too much of a batsman's game.'
Best batting: 1 Yorkshire v Sri Lanka, Headingley 1991
Best bowling: 3-61 Yorkshire v Oxford University, The Parks 1991

1996 Season

	M	Inns	NO	Runs	HS	Avge	100s	50s	Ct	St	O	M	Runs	Wkts	Avge	Best	5wI	10wM
Test																		
All First	1	0	0	0	0	-	-	-	1	-	7	0	60	0	-		-	-
1-day Int																		
NatWest																		
B & H																		
Sunday																		

Career Performances

	M	Inns	NO	Runs	HS	Avge	100s	50s	Ct	St	Balls	Runs	Wkts	Avge	Best	5wI	10wM
Test																	
All First	6	3	0	7	6	2.33	-	-	1	-	457	291	7	41.57	3-61	-	-
1-day Int																	
NatWest																	
B & H																	
Sunday	1	0	0	0	0	-	-	-	-	-	48	27	0	-		-	-

BROWN, A. D. Surrey

Name: Alistair Duncan Brown
Role: Right-hand bat, occasional
leg-break bowler, occasional wicket-keeper
Born: 11 February 1970, Beckenham
Height: 5ft 10in **Weight:** 12st 6lbs
Nickname: Lordy
County debut: 1992
One-Day Internationals: 3
1000 runs in a season: 3
1st-Class 50s: 21
1st-Class 100s: 11
1st-Class catches: 81
One-Day 100s: 8
Place in batting averages: 202nd av. 24.13
(1995 57th av. 42.16)
Parents: Robert and Ann
Marital status: Single
Family links with cricket: Father played for
Surrey Young Amateurs
Education: Cumnor House School; Caterham School
Qualifications: 5 O-levels, NCA Senior Coach
Career outside cricket: 'Actor, thespian and all round good egg'

Off-season: 'To try and get Nadeem Shahid to come out of his shell whilst helping him with his speech impediment'

Overseas tours: England 6-a-side to Singapore 1993, 1994, 1995

Overseas teams played for: North Perth, Australia 1989-90

Cricketers particularly admired: Ian Botham, Viv Richards

Young players to look out for: Alistair Brown – 'apparently he'll be scoring some runs next year'

Other sports followed: Football (West Ham United), rugby (Harlequins and London Broncos) and golf

Relaxations: 'Watching Jason Ratcliffe bat and listening to Martin Bicknell telling me that Leeds are a good football team'

Extras: Scored three of the eight fastest centuries of the 1992 season (71, 78 & 79 balls). Awarded Man of the Match for 118 against India in the third One-Day International, 'followed by Most Disastrous Season Award' at the end of term prize-giving'

Opinions on cricket: 'Four-day cricket is essential. Over-rate fines should be put back into the game in the form of prize money for the Championship and should be distributed evenly between first and ninth. The three one-day trophies should remain the same.'

Best batting: 187 Surrey v Gloucestershire, The Oval 1995

1996 Season

	M	Inns	NO	Runs	HS	Avge	100s	50s	Ct	St	O	M	Runs	Wkts	Avge	Best	5wI	10wM
Test																		
All First	16	26	3	555	79	24.13	-	5	21	-	6	2	8	0	-	-	-	-
1-day Int	3	3	0	155	118	51.66	1	-	1	-								
NatWest	4	4	0	158	72	39.50	-	1	-	-								
B & H	5	5	1	314	117 *	78.50	1	2	2	-								
Sunday	15	15	1	471	84	33.64	-	3	3	-								

Career Performances

	M	Inns	NO	Runs	HS	Avge	100s	50s	Ct	St	Balls	Runs	Wkts	Avge	Best	5wI	10wM
Test																	
All First	79	129	13	4780	187	41.20	11	21	81	-	228	139	0	-	-	-	-
1-day Int	3	3	0	155	118	51.66	1	-	1	-							
NatWest	13	10	1	314	72	34.88	-	2	2	-							
B & H	22	22	6	731	117 *	45.68	1	3	5	-							
Sunday	93	89	3	2861	142 *	33.26	6	13	25	-							

BROWN, C.   Lancashire

Name: Christopher Brown
Role: Right-hand bat, off-spin bowler
Born: 16 August 1974, Oldham
Height: 6ft 2in **Weight:** 12st
Nickname: Browney, Browneye, Tnuc,
Stick, Scooby, Shaggy
County debut: No first-team appearance
Parents: Paul and Anne
Marital status: Engaged to Gail
Children: Stevie, 10 March 1996
Family links with cricket: Uncle played for
Middletown in the Central Lancashire League
Education: Failsworth High School;
Tameside College of Technology
Qualifications: 5 GCSEs, City and Guilds
qualification in Recreation and Leisure
Off-season: Playing for Inglewood CC,
Taranaki, New Zealand
Overseas teams played for: Cape Town,
South Africa 1992-95

Cricketers particularly admired: Phil Tufnell, Tim May, Greg Matthews, Steve
O'Shaughnessy, Peter Such, Peter Seal
Young players to look out for: Gavin Hamilton, Mark Harvey
Other sports followed: Football (Manchester United), horse racing
Relaxations: 'Playing with my daughter, Stevie'
Extras: Equalled Gary Yates's 32 wickets in a season in 1993 with Lancashire Cricket
Federation. Represented Lancashire Schools U19 1991-92, Lancashire Cricket
Federation 1992-93, Lancashire Cricket Federation Player of the Year 1992, 1993.
Member of the Lancashire Cricket Federation side which won the NAYC
Cambridge/Oxford Festival 1993. Played for NAYC 1993 and Werneth CC in Central
Lancashire League
Opinions on cricket: 'League cricket across the country should be extended from 40 or
50-over "slogs" to two-day cricket. This would produce better players as in South Africa
and abroad. Far too much cricket is being played on the county circuit – results in
average performances – quality not quantity.'

BROWN, D. R. Warwickshire

Name: Douglas Robert Brown
Role: Right-hand bat, right-arm
fast-medium bowler
Born: 29 October 1969, Stirling
Height: 6ft 2in **Weight:** 13st 7lbs
Nickname: Hoots
County debut: 1992
County cap: 1995
1st-Class 50s: 8
1st-Class 5 w. in innings: 2
1st-Class 10 w. in match: 1
1st-Class catches: 25
Place in batting averages: 218th av. 22.36
(1995 143rd av. 28.11)
Place in bowling averages: 94th av. 35.25
(1995 51st av. 27.32)
Strike rate: 61.10 (career 50.51)
Parents: Alastair and Janette
Wife and date of marriage: Brenda,
2 October 1993

Family links with cricket: Both grandfathers played club cricket. 'Siamese twin, Ash, plays a bit!'
Education: Alloa Academy; West London Institute of Higher Education (Borough Road College)
Qualifications: 9 O-Grades, 5 Higher Grades; BEd (Hons) Physical Education
Career outside cricket: PE teacher
Off-season: Coaching in Birmingham, Troubadours to Argentina
Overseas tours: Scotland XI to Pakistan 1988-89
Overseas teams played for: Primrose, Cape Town 1992-93; Uredenburg Salohana, Cape Town 1994; Eastern Suburbs, Wellington 1995-96; Wellington, New Zealand 1995-96
Cricketers particularly admired: 'Everyone that plays for their team and gives it 100%'
Young players to look out for: Darren Altree, Anurag Singh
Other sports followed: Football (Alloa Athletic) and golf
Relaxations: Playing golf, learning to play the guitar
Extras: Played football at Hampden Park for Scotland U18. Played first-class and B & H cricket for Scotland in 1989, and played again for Scotland against Ireland in 1992
Opinions on cricket: 'Great game!'
Best batting: 85 Warwickshire v Essex, Ilford 1995
Best bowling: 6-52 Warwickshire v Kent, Edgbaston 1996

1996 Season

	M	Inns	NO	Runs	HS	Avge	100s	50s	Ct	St	O	M	Runs	Wkts	Avge	Best	5wI	10wM
Test																		
All First	19	32	2	671	76	22.36	-	3	14	-	407.2	81	1410	40	35.25	6-52	2	1
1-day Int																		
NatWest	2	2	0	69	67	34.50	-	1	1	-	17	2	72	0	-		-	-
B & H	7	4	1	85	44	28.33	-	-	3	-	59.3	10	210	6	35.00	2-26	-	
Sunday	17	15	2	314	66	24.15	-	1	6	-	76.3	5	401	15	26.73	4-47	-	

Career Performances

	M	Inns	NO	Runs	HS	Avge	100s	50s	Ct	St	Balls	Runs	Wkts	Avge	Best	5wI	10wM
Test																	
All First	47	73	8	1639	85	25.21	-	8	25	-	6062	3244	120	27.03	6-52	4	2
1-day Int																	
NatWest	6	6	1	170	67	34.00	-	2	1	-	228	176	3	58.66	2-35	-	
B & H	12	7	1	142	44	23.66	-	-	4	-	606	393	12	32.75	3-43	-	
Sunday	42	35	6	555	78 *	19.13	-	2	8	-	1221	946	31	30.51	4-47	-	

BROWN, J. F.   Northamptonshire

Name: Jason F. Brown
Role: Right-hand bat, off-spin bowler
Born: 10 October 1974, Stoke-on-Trent
Height: 6ft 1in   **Weight:** 12st
Nickname: Macey, Brown Fish
County debut: 1996
1st-Class catches: 1
Parents: Peter and Cynthia
Marital status: Engaged to Samantha
Education: St Margaret Ward RC School
Qualifications: 9 O-levels
Off-season: 'Winter nets and keeping fit'
Overseas tours: Kidsgrove League U18 to
Australia 1991
Cricketers particularly admired: John
Emburey
Other sports followed: Football, golf, snooker
Relaxations: Watching videos and listening
to music. Playing and watching all sports, socialising
Extras: Represented Staffordshire at all junior levels and Staffordshire's Minor Counties.
'Once took 10 for 16 in a Kidsgrove League game against Haslington Under 18 playing
for Sandyford Under 18.' Played for Staffordshire in the 1995 NatWest competition

1996 Season

	M	Inns	NO	Runs	HS	Avge	100s	50s	Ct	St	O	M	Runs	Wkts	Avge	Best	5wI	10wM
Test																		
All First	1	1	1	0	0 *	-	-	-	1	-	22	6	64	0	-	-	-	-
1-day Int																		
NatWest																		
B & H																		
Sunday																		

Career Performances

	M	Inns	NO	Runs	HS	Avge	100s	50s	Ct	St	Balls	Runs	Wkts	Avge	Best	5wI	10wM
Test																	
All First	1	1	1	0	0 *	-	-	-	1	-	132	64	0	-	-	-	-
1-day Int																	
NatWest	1	0	0	0	0	-	-	-	-	-	72	72	1	72.00	1-72	-	
B & H																	
Sunday																	

BROWN, K. R.   Middlesex

Name: Keith Robert Brown
Role: Right-hand bat, wicket-keeper
Born: 18 March 1963, Edmonton
Height: 5ft 11in **Weight:** 13st 7lbs
Nickname: Browny, Scarface, Stally
County debut: 1984
County cap: 1990
1000 runs in a season: 2
1st-Class 50s: 52
1st-Class 100s: 12
1st-Class 200s: 1
1st-Class catches: 378
1st-Class stumpings: 25
One-Day 100s: 2
Place in batting averages: 112th av. 35.26
(1995 56th av. 42.17)
Strike rate: (career 53.50)
Parents: Kenneth William and Margaret Sonia
Wife and date of marriage: Marie, 3
November 1984
Children: Zachary, 24 February 1987; Rosanna, 18 December 1989;
Alex, 29 December 1992

Family links with cricket: Brother Gary was on Middlesex staff for three years and then played for Durham. Father is a qualified umpire
Education: Chace Comprehensive School, Enfield
Qualifications: French O-level; NCA Senior Coaching Award; qualified plasterer
Career outside cricket: Plasterer, PE instructor, coach
Off-season: Coaching
Overseas tours: NCA Youth tour to Denmark; Middlesex pre-season tours to La Manga 1985, 1986 and Portugal 1991, 1992, 1993
Overseas teams played for: Sydney University, Australia 1988-89; Motueka Cricket Association, Nelson, New Zealand 1991-92
Cricketers particularly admired: Clive Radley and Derek Randall
Other sports followed: Most sports apart from motor racing
Injuries: Fractured fingers, missed one Sunday League game
Relaxations: 'Long country walks with family and pet greyhound, finishing with a couple of pints in local.'
Extras: Had promising boxing career but gave it up in order to concentrate on cricket. Picked to play rugby for Essex
Opinions on cricket: 'Over rate in Championship cricket too high.'
Best batting: 200* Middlesex v Nottinghamshire, Lord's 1990
Best bowling: 2-7 Middlesex v Gloucestershire, Bristol 1987

1996 Season

	M	Inns	NO	Runs	HS	Avge	100s	50s	Ct	St	O	M	Runs	Wkts	Avge	Best	5wI	10wM
Test																		
All First	18	31	5	917	83	35.26	-	8	60	1								
1-day Int																		
NatWest	2	2	0	36	22	18.00	-	-	2	1								
B & H	5	5	1	82	43	20.50	-	-	2	2								
Sunday	16	14	4	295	74	29.50	-	1	12	5								

Career Performances

	M	Inns	NO	Runs	HS	Avge	100s	50s	Ct	St	Balls	Runs	Wkts	Avge	Best	5wI	10wM
Test																	
All First	211	319	60	9310	200 *	35.94	12	52	378	25	321	276	6	46.00	2-7	-	-
1-day Int																	
NatWest	21	18	3	448	103 *	29.86	1	-	15	6	6	8	0	-	-	-	
B & H	35	32	6	635	75	24.42	-	2	23	7	6	0	0	-	-	-	
Sunday	149	125	37	2646	102	30.06	1	10	90	26	28	29	0	-	-	-	

BROWN, S. J. E.   Durham

Name: Simon John Emmerson Brown
Role: Right-hand bat, left-arm medium pace
bowler, gully fielder
Born: 29 June 1969, Cleadon Village,
Sunderland
Height: 6ft 3in **Weight:** 13st
Nickname: Chubby
County debut: 1987 (Northamptonshire),
1992 (Durham)
Test debut: 1996
Tests: 1
50 wickets in a season: 4
1st-Class 50s: 2
1st-Class 5 w. in innings: 21
1st-Class 10 w. match: 1
1st-Class catches: 34
Place in batting averages: 266th av. 15.53
(1995 273rd av. 11.58)
Place in bowling averages: 39th av. 26.96
(1995 92nd av. 34.22)
Strike rate: 48.77 (career 54.83)
Parents: Ernest and Doreen
Wife and date of marriage: Sarah, 3 October 1992
Education: Boldon Comprehensive, Tyne & Wear; South Tyneside College
Qualifications: 6 O-levels, qualified electrician
Career outside cricket: Electrician
Overseas tours: England YC to Sri Lanka 1986-87, to Australia for Youth World Cup
1987-88; MCC to Bahrain 1994-95
Overseas teams played for: Marist, Christchurch, New Zealand
Cricketers particularly admired: John Lever, Dennis Lillee
Other sports followed: Basketball and golf
Injuries: Damaged tendon in foot, missed one week
Relaxations: Playing basketball and golf
Extras: Offered basketball scholarship in America. Durham supporters' Player of the
Year 1992. Durham Player of the Year 1994. Made his Test debut for England against
Pakistan at Lord's in 1996
Best batting: 69 Durham v Leicestershire, Durham University 1994
Best bowling: 7-70 Durham v Australians, Durham University 1993

1996 Season

	M	Inns	NO	Runs	HS	Avge	100s	50s	Ct	St	O	M	Runs	Wkts	Avge	Best	5wI	10wM
Test	1	2	1	11	10 *	11.00	-	-	1	-	33	4	138	2	69.00	1-60	-	-
All First	19	31	5	404	60	15.53	-	1	5	-	642.1	109	2130	79	26.96	6-77	5	-
1-day Int																		
NatWest	2	2	0	1	1	0.50	-	-	1	-	19	3	68	3	22.66	2-49	-	
B & H	5	2	1	2	2 *	2.00	-	-	1	-	40	6	147	4	36.75	2-28	-	
Sunday	10	8	4	76	18	19.00	-	-	-	-	73	5	367	11	33.36	3-50	-	

Career Performances

	M	Inns	NO	Runs	HS	Avge	100s	50s	Ct	St	Balls	Runs	Wkts	Avge	Best	5wI	10wM
Test	1	2	1	11	10 *	11.00	-	-	1	-	198	138	2	69.00	1-60	-	-
All First	107	148	45	1369	69	13.29	-	2	34	-	18700	10837	341	31.78	7-70	21	1
1-day Int																	
NatWest	9	6	3	12	7 *	4.00	-	-	1	-	580	408	16	25.50	5-22	1	
B & H	15	7	3	30	12	7.50	-	-	1	-	801	496	17	29.17	3-39	-	
Sunday	60	26	11	127	18	8.46	-	-	11	-	2604	2166	66	32.81	4-20	-	

BURNS, M.   Somerset

Name: Michael Burns
Role: Right-hand bat, right-arm medium bowler, wicket-keeper
Born: 6 February 1969, Barrow-in-Furness
Height: 6ft **Weight:** 13st
Nickname: George, Red Hot
County debut: 1991
1st-Class 50s: 4
1st-Class catches: 41
1st-Class stumpings: 5
Place in batting averages: 200th av. 24.64
Parents: Robert and Linda, stepfather Stan
Wife and date of marriage: Carolyn, 9 October 1994
Children: 'Wife Caroline expecting January 1997'
Family links with cricket: 'Grandfather was a great back-garden bowler'
Education: Walney Comprehensive; Barrow College of Further Education
Qualifications: 'Few CSEs, couple of GCEs', qualified fitter at VSEL in Barrow, coaching award

Career outside cricket: 'Signing autographs for DHSS'

Off-season: 'Back home to Barrow, look for a job. Quite busy after Xmas I would think'

Overseas teams played for: Gill College, South Africa 1991-92; Motueka, Nelson, New Zealand 1992-93; Alex CC, Harare

Cricketers particularly admired: Dermot Reeve, Allan Donald, Pop Welch and'Frosty'

Young players to look out for: Tony Frost, Darren Altree

Other sports followed: Rugby league ('had trials for Barrow RLFC and Carlisle RLFC') and golf

Injuries: Shoulder

Relaxations: 'Eating Indians, socialising with friends. One or two pints with Pop Welch'

Extras: Played for Cumberland 1989-90. Had a trial with Glamorgan, went to La Manga with Lancashire junior side 1984. Player of the Tournament at Benson and Hedges Thailand International Cricket Sixes in 1989. Left Warwickshire and has joined Somerset for the 1996 season

Opinions on cricket: 'More should be done to help players in the winter and to help players find work after cricket.'

Best batting: 81 Warwickshire v Nottinghamshire, Edgbaston 1996

1996 Season

	M	Inns	NO	Runs	HS	Avge	100s	50s	Ct	St	O	M	Runs	Wkts	Avge	Best	5wI	10wM
Test																		
All First	8	15	1	345	81	24.64	-	3	16	2	3	0	13	0	-	-	-	-
1-day Int																		
NatWest	2	2	1	37	37 *	37.00	-	-	-	-								
B & H																		
Sunday	12	10	2	179	37	22.37	-	-	8	1								

Career Performances

	M	Inns	NO	Runs	HS	Avge	100s	50s	Ct	St	Balls	Runs	Wkts	Avge	Best	5wI	10wM
Test																		
All First	20	34	2	640	81	20.00	-	4	41	5	60	21	0	-	-	-	-
1-day Int																		
NatWest	2	2	1	37	37 *	37.00	-	-	-	-							
B & H	8	6	0	55	22	9.16	-	-	6	2							
Sunday	31	26	4	337	37	15.31	-	-	28	8							

BUTCHER, G. P.　　　　　　　Glamorgan

Name: Gary Paul Butcher
Role: Right-hand opening bat, right-arm medium bowler
Born: 11 March 1975, Clapham, South London
Height: 5ft 9in **Weight:** 11st
Nickname: Butch, Bouché, The Meatseller, Bob, Billy
County debut: 1994
1st-Class 50s: 5
1st-Class 5 w. in innings: 1
1st-Class catches: 10
Place in batting averages: 123rd av. 33.95
Place in bowling averages: 100th av. 39.33
Strike rate: 56.90 (career 69.43)
Parents: Alan and Elaine
Marital status: Single
Family links with cricket: Father Alan

played for Surrey, Glamorgan and England and is now with Essex; brother Mark plays for Surrey and England A and uncle Ian played for Gloucestershire and Leicestershire
Education: Cumnor House; Trinity School; Riddlesdown Comprehensive; Heath Clark College and 'away trips with Steve Barwick'
Qualifications: 4 GCSEs, BTEC 1st Diploma in Leisure Studies
Career outside cricket: 'Anything that does not involve commuting to London every day. Bar work'
Off-season: 'Going to Sydney to play for Hawkesbury CC. Trying to persuade Grandmother Campbell not to send me on a computer training course'
Overseas tours: England U18 to Denmark 1993; England U19 to Sri Lanka 1993-94; Glamorgan to Portugal 1994, to Zimbabwe 1995, to Pretoria 1996
Cricketers particularly admired: David Gower, Viv Richards, Brian Lara, Curtly Ambrose, Ian Botham, Sachin Tendulkar
Young players to look out for: Alun Evans
Other sports followed: Football ('played one game for Neil Kendrick's side, scored the only goal of the game – an Ian Rush predatory instinct inside the six-yard box – and was never picked again'), gymnastics (Dominique Dawes), and 'the Champers happy hour in Croydon'
Relaxations: 'Playing bass guitar in our band, "The Slide", with Mark, Peter James and Jo Fullman. Spending time with friends. Finding out what Mr F-tastic (Pete James) has been up to'
Extras: Won Glamorgan's Most Improved Player Award 1996, recorded batting and

bowling personal bests during the 1996 season. Appeared on *Gower's Cricket Monthly* with brother Mark

Opinions on cricket: 'Second XI cricket is mostly played on inadequate grounds with the same standard of umpiring. Too much cricket is played, and stop changing the rules. I also think it is only fair that Chris Lewis's agent should send Jo Guest around all the first-class dressing rooms. I feel that it would be good for English cricket on the whole.'

Best batting: 89 Glamorgan v Northamptonshire, Northampton 1996

Best bowling: 7-77 Glamorgan v Gloucestershire, Bristol 1996

1996 Season

	M	Inns	NO	Runs	HS	Avge	100s	50s	Ct	St	O	M	Runs	Wkts	Avge	Best	5wI	10wM
Test																		
All First	14	24	4	679	89	33.95	-	5	8	-	199.1	30	826	21	39.33	7-77	1	-
1-day Int																		
NatWest	1	1	0	48	48	48.00	-	-	-	-	6	1	50	1	50.00	1-50	-	
B & H	2	2	1	12	9	12.00	-	-	-	-	12	0	48	2	24.00	2-21	-	
Sunday	9	7	2	59	20 *	11.80	-	-	1	-	25.2	1	142	6	23.66	4-32	-	

Career Performances

	M	Inns	NO	Runs	HS	Avge	100s	50s	Ct	St	Balls	Runs	Wkts	Avge	Best	5wI	10wM
Test																	
All First	20	33	6	750	89	27.77	-	5	10	-	1597	1093	23	47.52	7-77	1	-
1-day Int																	
NatWest	1	1	0	48	48	48.00	-	-	-	-	36	50	1	50.00	1-50	-	
B & H	5	3	1	12	9	6.00	-	-	-	-	84	60	2	30.00	2-21	-	
Sunday	12	7	2	59	20 *	11.80	-	-	1	-	212	208	8	26.00	4-32	-	

BUTCHER, M. A.　　　　　　　　Surrey

Name: Mark Alan Butcher
Role: Left-hand bat, right-arm medium bowler
Born: 23 August 1972, Croydon
Height: 5ft 11in **Weight:** 12st 7lbs
Nickname: Butch, Baz
County debut: 1991
1000 runs in a season: 2
1st-Class 50s: 27
1st-Class 100s: 6
1st-Class catches: 61
Place in batting averages: 24th av. 51.74 (1995 82nd av. 36.66)
Place in bowling averages: (1995 127th av. 42.50 (1994 125th av. 41.87)
Strike rate: 44.57 (career 66.04)

Parents: Alan and Elaine

Marital status: Engaged to Judy

Family links with cricket: Father Alan played for Glamorgan, Surrey and England and is now with Essex; brother Gary plays for Glamorgan; uncle Ian played for Gloucestershire and Leicestershire

Education: Cumnor House School; Trinity School; Archbishop Tenison's, Croydon

Qualifications: 5 O-levels, senior coaching award

Career outside cricket: Singer, guitar player, female impersonator

Off-season: Touring Australia with England A

Overseas tours: England YC to New Zealand 1990-91; Surrey to Dubai 1990 and 1993, to Perth 1995; England A to Australia 1996-97

Overseas teams played for: South Melbourne, Australia 1993-94; North Perth 1994-95

Cricketers particularly admired: Carl Rackemann, Mark and Steve Waugh, Ian Botham, David Gower, Michael Holding, Jason Ratcliffe for his driving skills ('behind the wheel')

Other sports followed: Football, tennis, rhythmic gymnastics

Relaxations: 'Books, collecting CDs and records, playing guitar and singing in my band with my brother Gary, Peter James and Jo Fullman'

Extras: Played his first game for Surrey against his father's Glamorgan in the Refuge Assurance League at The Oval, the first-ever match of any sort between first-class counties in which a father and son have been in opposition

Opinions on cricket: 'Since introducing four-day cricket, the aim of those involved in producing the directives for pitches and the pitches themselves seems to be to have the game finish as soon as possible. The standard of first-class pitches is extremely poor and if they are not improved, neither will the standard of the players. Surely a hard-fought draw over four days is more beneficial to producing Test cricketers than a game which is over in two days. Secondly, why in England are first-class games played over 110 overs? Nowhere else in the world do cricketers play so many games let alone over so many overs. Fewer overs would produce a better quality of cricket throughout the day.'

Best batting: 167 Surrey v Durham, The Oval 1995

Best bowling: 4-31 Surrey v Worcestershire, The Oval 1994

1996 Season

	M	Inns	NO	Runs	HS	Avge	100s	50s	Ct	St	O	M	Runs	Wkts	Avge	Best	5wI	10wM
Test																		
All First	18	34	3	1604	160	51.74	3	13	21	-	52	7	233	7	33.28	3-23	-	-
1-day Int																		
NatWest	4	4	0	211	91	52.75	-	2	-	-								
B & H	3	2	2	48	42 *	-	-	-	1	-	12	0	74	0	-		-	-
Sunday	6	6	0	145	57	24.16	-	1	3	-	0.4	0	0	0	-		-	-

Career Performances

	M	Inns	NO	Runs	HS	Avge	100s	50s	Ct	St	Balls	Runs	Wkts	Avge	Best	5wI	10wM
Test																	
All First	56	100	10	3697	167	41.07	6	27	61	-	4029	2389	61	39.16	4-31	-	-
1-day Int																	
NatWest	8	8	2	335	91	55.83	-	3	3	-	216	127	3	42.33	2-57	-	
B & H	9	6	2	63	42 *	15.75	-	-	2	-	343	291	6	48.50	3-37	-	
Sunday	42	30	10	454	57	22.70	-	1	11	-	1333	1270	27	47.03	3-23	-	

BYAS, D.   Yorkshire

Name: David Byas
Role: Left-hand bat, right-arm medium bowler, county captain
Born: 26 August 1963, Middledale, Kilham
Height: 6ft 4in **Weight:** 14st 7lbs
Nickname: Bingo, Gadgett
County debut: 1986
County cap: 1991
1000 runs in a season: 4
1st-Class 50s: 55
1st-Class 100s: 17
1st-Class 200s: 1
1st-Class catches: 223
One-Day 100s: 4
Place in batting averages: 152nd av. 31.10 (1995 9th av. 56.26)
Strike rate: (career 91.00)
Parents: Richard and Anne
Wife and date of marriage:
Rachael Elizabeth, 27 October 1990
Children: Olivia Rachael, 16 December 1991; Georgia Elizabeth, 30 December 1993
Family links with cricket: Father played in local leagues

Education: Scarborough College
Qualifications: 1 O-level (Engineering)
Career outside cricket: Partner in family farming business
Off-season: Working on family farm
Overseas teams played for: Papatoetoe, Auckland 1988
Cricketers particularly admired: David Gower, Viv Richards, Ian Botham
Other sports followed: Hockey, motor racing, rugby union
Relaxations: 'Looking after my two active daughters. Dining out with my wife. Gardening.'
Extras: Became youngest captain (aged 21) of Scarborough CC in 1985. Broke John Hampshire's Sunday League record with 702 runs in 1994, which had stood since 1976. Runner-up in the Sunday League averages 1994. Played hockey for England Under 21. Has just completed end of first season as captain of Yorkshire
Best batting: 213 Yorkshire v Worcestershire, Scarborough 1995
Best bowling: 3-55 Yorkshire v Derbyshire, Chesterfield 1990

1996 Season

	M	Inns	NO	Runs	HS	Avge	100s	50s	Ct	St	O	M	Runs	Wkts	Avge	Best	5wI	10wM
Test																		
All First	19	32	2	933	138	31.10	1	5	32	-								
1-day Int																		
NatWest	4	4	1	190	73 *	63.33	-	2	1	-								
B & H	6	6	1	267	116 *	53.40	1	1	3	-								
Sunday	17	16	4	523	111 *	43.58	1	3	6	-								

Career Performances

	M	Inns	NO	Runs	HS	Avge	100s	50s	Ct	St	Balls	Runs	Wkts	Avge	Best	5wI	10wM
Test																	
All First	180	304	28	9913	213	35.91	17	55	223	-	1092	719	12	59.91	3-55	-	-
1-day Int																	
NatWest	20	18	2	608	73 *	38.00	-	6	9	-	18	23	1	23.00	1-23	-	
B & H	30	27	2	791	116 *	31.64	1	3	8	-	283	155	5	31.00	2-38	-	
Sunday	140	135	22	3527	111 *	31.21	3	18	36	-	529	463	19	24.36	3-19	-	

---

16. In 1996 two wicket-keepers were the only century makers in the game between their respective counties. Who were they?

CADDICK, A. R. Somerset

Name: Andrew Richard Caddick
Role: Right-hand bat, right-arm
fast-medium bowler
Born: 21 November 1968, Christchurch,
New Zealand
Height: 6ft 5in **Weight:** 14st 13lbs
Nickname: Kiwi, Doi, Shack, Bean, ('Quite
a few')
County debut: 1991
County cap: 1992
Test debut: 1993
Tests: 9
One-Day Internationals: 5
50 wickets in a season: 4
1st-Class 50s: 4
1st-Class 5 w. in innings: 20
1st-Class 10 w. in match: 8
1st-Class catches: 29
One-Day 5 w. in innings: 3
Place in batting averages: 275th av. 13.26 (1995 103rd av. 33.85)
Place in bowling averages: 43rd av. 27.79 (1995 34th av. 25.54)
Strike rate: 49.65 (50.08)
Parents: Christopher and Audrey
Wife and date of marriage: Sarah, 27 January 1995
Education: Papanui High School, Christchurch, New Zealand
Qualifications: Qualified plasterer and tiler
Career outside cricket: Plasterer and tiler
Off-season: Touring Zimbabwe and New Zealand with England
Overseas tours: New Zealand YC to Australia (Youth World Cup) 1987-88, to
England 1988; England A to Australia 1992-93; England to West Indies 1993-94, to
Zimbabwe and New Zealand 1996-97
Cricketers particularly admired: Dennis Lillee, Richard Hadlee, Robin Smith,
Jimmy Cook
Young players to look out for: Nasser Hussain, Nick Knight, Marcus Trescothick
Other sports followed: 'Mostly all'
Relaxations: Golf
Extras: Rapid Cricketline Player of the Year 1991
Opinions on cricket: 'For a bowler it's a very hard game. We play too much cricket.'
Best batting: 92 Somerset v Worcestershire, Worcester 1995
Best bowling: 9-32 Somerset v Lancashire, Taunton 1993

1996 Season

	M	Inns	NO	Runs	HS	Avge	100s	50s	Ct	St	O	M	Runs	Wkts	Avge	Best	5wI	10wM
Test	1	1	0	4	4	4.00	-	-	-	-	57.2	10	165	6	27.50	3-52	-	-
All First	15	20	5	199	38	13.26	-	-	7	-	604.1	131	2029	73	27.79	7-83	6	3
1-day Int																		
NatWest	3	2	1	9	5 *	9.00	-	-	-	-	33.4	3	119	9	13.22	4-39	-	
B & H	3	1	1	7	7 *	-	-	-	-	-	27	6	124	7	17.71	5-51	1	
Sunday	15	4	1	68	39	22.66	-	-	7	-	111.3	5	530	23	23.04	3-21	-	

Career Performances

	M	Inns	NO	Runs	HS	Avge	100s	50s	Ct	St	Balls	Runs	Wkts	Avge	Best	5wI	10wM
Test	9	15	2	174	29 *	13.38	-	-	4	-	2284	1198	29	41.31	6-65	2	-
All First	79	101	18	1355	92	16.32	-	4	29	-	15878	8564	317	27.01	9-32	20	8
1-day Int	5	3	3	23	20 *	-	-	-	1	-	318	258	6	43.00	3-39	-	
NatWest	12	7	2	21	8	4.20	-	-	2	-	735	401	27	14.85	6-30	2	
B & H	12	9	6	67	28	22.33	-	-	2	-	720	455	16	28.43	5-51	1	
Sunday	48	17	6	179	39	16.27	-	-	8	-	2031	1578	59	26.74	4-18	-	

CAIRNS, C. L. Nottinghamshire

Name: Christopher Lance Cairns
Role: Right-hand bat, right-arm
fast-medium bowler
Born: 13 June 1970, Picton, New Zealand
Height: 6ft 2in **Weight:** 14st
Nickname: Sheep
County debut: 1988
County cap: 1993
Test debut: 1990-91
Tests: 16
One-Day Internationals: 49
1000 runs in a season: 1
50 wickets in a season: 3
1st-Class 50s: 43
1st-Class 100s: 7
1st-Class 5 w. in innings: 15
1st-Class 10 w. in match: 3
1st-Class catches: 61
One-day 100s: 2
One-Day 5 w. in innings: 2
Place in batting averages: 78th av. 39.41 (1995 67th av. 40.37)
Place in bowling averages: 111th av. 39.48 (1995 8th av. 19.90)

Strike rate: 69.32 (career 54.11)
Parents: Lance and Sue
Family links with cricket: Father played for New Zealand, uncle played first-class cricket in New Zealand
Education: Christchurch Boys' High School, New Zealand
Qualifications: 5th and 6th form certificates
Marital status: Single
Off-season: Playing for New Zealand
Overseas tours: New Zealand YC to Australia (Youth World Cup) 1987-88; New Zealand to Australia 1989-90, 1993-94, to India 1995-96, to India and Pakistan (World Cup) 1995-96
Overseas teams played for: Northern Districts 1988-89; Canterbury 1990-95
Cricketers particularly admired: Mick Newell, Richard Hadlee, Dennis Lillee
Other sports followed: Most sports
Extras: Hit the fastest first-class hundred of the 1995 season (in 65 balls versus Cambridge University)
Opinions on cricket: 'Great game.'
Best batting: 120 New Zealand v Zimbabwe, Auckland 1995-96
Best bowling: 8-47 Nottinghamshire v Sussex, Arundel 1995

1996 Season

	M	Inns	NO	Runs	HS	Avge	100s	50s	Ct	St	O	M	Runs	Wkts	Avge	Best	5wI	10wM
Test																		
All First	16	29	5	946	114	39.41	1	6	10	-	427.3	73	1461	37	39.48	6-110	1	-
1-day Int																		
NatWest	1	1	0	5	5	5.00	-	-	-	-	12	1	76	1	76.00	1-76	-	
B & H	1	1	0	21	21	21.00	-	-	-	-	10	0	50	1	50.00	1-50	-	
Sunday	15	12	6	414	66 *	69.00	-	2	-	-	88.5	6	409	25	16.36	5-41	1	

Career Performances

	M	Inns	NO	Runs	HS	Avge	100s	50s	Ct	St	Balls	Runs	Wkts	Avge	Best	5wI	10wM
Test	16	26	0	675	120	25.96	1	4	7	-	3229	1782	51	34.94	6-52	2	-
All First	133	203	24	6318	120	35.29	7	43	61	-	21701	11438	401	28.52	8-47	15	3
1-day Int	49	45	4	1099	103	26.80	1	4	20	-	1989	1559	45	34.64	4-55	-	
NatWest	7	7	1	306	77	51.00	-	3	2	-	482	279	14	19.92	4-18	-	
B & H	12	8	0	112	46	14.00	-	-	3	-	617	454	16	28.37	4-47	-	
Sunday	60	50	10	1655	126 *	41.37	2	9	17	-	2363	1858	86	21.60	6-52	2	

CAMPBELL, C. L.   Durham

Name: Colin Lockey Campbell
Role: Right-hand bat, right-arm
fast-medium bowler
Born: 11 August 1977, Newcastle-upon-Tyne
Height: 6ft 6in **Weight:** 15st
Nickname: Scunner, Big Man, CC
County debut: 1996
Strike rate: (career 92.00)
Parents: Paul and Jacqueline
Marital status: Single
Family links with cricket: 'Mam's not a bad
bowler'
Education: West Lane, Winlayton Primary
School; Blaydon Comprehensive; Blaydon
Comprehensive Sixth Form
Qualifications: 9 GCSEs, 2 A-levels
Off-season: Touring Sri Lanka with Durham
U19
Overseas tours: Durham to South Africa
1995; England U19 to Zimbabwe 1995-96; Durham U19 to Sri Lanka 1996-97
Cricketers particularly admired: Graeme Hick, Allan Donald, Ian Somerville
Young players to look out for: John Graham, Stephen Harmison
Other sports followed: Golf and football (Newcastle United)
Injuries: Trapped tendon in shoulder, out for two weeks
Relaxations: 'Playing golf with Killer (Neil Killeen) and Jason Searle – the bandit
who plays off 24.' Keeping fit and 'socialising with Mark "The Duck" Drake and Ray
"Biffa" Marshall'
Extras: Top of the bowling averages for Blaydon 1st XI for three years and Blaydon
U18 for two years. Once took 6 for 5 and 8 for 3 in successive games for his club. Had
match figures of 9 for 86 on his debut for Durham 2nd XI
Opinions on cricket: 'What a great game, but could make the wickets a little more in
the bowler's favour.'
Best batting: 7 Durham v Gloucestershire, Chester-le-Street 1996
Best bowling: 1-29 Durham v Gloucestershire, Chester-le-Street 1996

---

17. Who was Wasim Akram's 300th Test victim?

1996 Season

	M	Inns	NO	Runs	HS	Avge	100s	50s	Ct	St	O	M	Runs	Wkts	Avge	Best	5wI	10wM
Test																		
All First	1	1	0	7	7	7.00	-	-	-	-	15.2	3	44	1	44.00	1-29	-	-
1-day Int																		
NatWest																			
B & H																			
Sunday	2	1	0	0	0	0.00	-	-	-	-	16	0	89	3	29.66	2-45	-	

Career Performances

	M	Inns	NO	Runs	HS	Avge	100s	50s	Ct	St	Balls	Runs	Wkts	Avge	Best	5wI	10wM
Test																	
All First	1	1	0	7	7	7.00	-	-	-	-	92	44	1	44.00	1-29	-	-
1-day Int																	
NatWest																		
B & H																		
Sunday	2	1	0	0	0	0.00	-	-	-	-	96	89	3	29.66	2-45	-	

CAMPBELL, S. L. Durham

Name: Sherwin Legay Campbell
Role: Right-hand opening bat
Born: 1 November 1970, Bridgetown, Barbados
Height: 5ft 4in
County debut: 1996
Test debut: 1994-95
Tests: 11
One-day Internationals: 26
1000 runs in a season: 2
1st-Class 50s: 22
1st-Class 100s: 10
1st-Class 200s: 1
1st-Class catches: 60
Place in batting averages: 107th av. 35.89 (1995 35th av. 47.11)
Strike rate: 100.00 (career 112.00)
Education: Ellerslie Secondary School, Barbados
Overseas tours: West Indies to New Zealand 1994-95, to England 1995, to Australia 1995-96, to India and Pakistan (World Cup) 1995-96, to Australia 1996-97
Extras: Was the leading run-scorer in first-class games for West Indies on their 1995

tour to England
Best batting: 208 West Indies v New Zealand, Bridgetown 1995-96
Best bowling: 1-38 Durham v Leicestershire, Chester-le-Street 1996

1996 Season

	M	Inns	NO	Runs	HS	Avge	100s	50s	Ct	St	O	M	Runs	Wkts	Avge	Best	5wI	10wM
Test																		
All First	16	29	0	1041	118	35.89	1	7	15	-	16.4	3	60	1	60.00	1-38	-	-
1-day Int																		
NatWest	2	2	0	66	39	33.00	-	-	1	-	1	0	17	0	-		-	-
B & H	2	2	0	27	27	13.50	-	-	1	-								
Sunday	15	15	0	455	77	30.33	-	3	4	-	5.3	0	34	0	-		-	-

Career Performances

	M	Inns	NO	Runs	HS	Avge	100s	50s	Ct	St	Balls		Runs	Wkts	Avge	Best	5wI	10wM
Test	11	18	1	885	208	52.05	1	6	13	-								
All First	58	100	4	3955	208	41.19	10	22	60	-	112		63	1	63.00	1-38	-	-
1-day Int	26	26	0	610	86	23.46	-	2	9	-								
NatWest	2	2	0	66	39	33.00	-	-	1	-	6		17	0	-		-	-
B & H	2	2	0	27	27	13.50	-	-	1	-								
Sunday	15	15	0	455	77	30.33	-	3	4	-	33		34	0	-		-	-

CAPEL, D. J.   Northamptonshire

Name: David John Capel
Role: Right-hand bat, right-arm medium
bowler, all-rounder, slip fielder
Born: 6 February 1963, Northampton
Height: 5ft 11in **Weight:** 12st 8lbs
Nickname: Capes, Fiery
County debut: 1981
County cap: 1986
Benefit: 1994
Test debut: 1987
Tests: 15
One-Day Internationals: 23
1000 runs in a season: 3
50 wickets in a season: 4
1st-Class 50s: 71
1st-Class 100s: 16
1st-Class 5 w. in innings: 14
1st-Class catches: 155

One-Day 100s: 4
Place in batting averages: 168th av. 29.07 (1995 90th av. 35.61)
Place in bowling averages: 84th av. 33.74 (1995 25th av. 23.64)
Strike rate: 59.68 (career 60.32)
Parents: John and Janet
Wife and date of marriage: Debbie, 21 September 1985
Children: Jenny, 21 October 1987; Jordan, 18 May 1993
Family links with cricket: Father and brother Andrew both captained
their local league sides
Education: Roade Primary School; Roade Comprehensive School
Qualifications: 3 O-levels, 4 CSEs, NCA advanced coaching certificate
Off-season: 'Doing some PR and fitness work'
Overseas tours: England to Sharjah 1986-87, to Pakistan 1987-88, to New Zealand
and Australia 1987-88, to India (Nehru Cup) 1989-90, to West Indies 1989-90;
England A to Australia 1992-93; MCC to Bangladesh 1996
Overseas teams played for: Eastern Province, South Africa 1985-87; Petersham-
Marrickville, Sydney 1991-92
Young players to look out for: Graham and Alec Swann, Adam Hollioake
Other sports followed: 'Golf, local rugby and soccer teams'
Injuries: Broken finger, missed the last two games of the season
Relaxations: 'Family, gardening, golf, walking, cycling, coarse fishing, most music',
fast cars
Extras: Only second Northampton-born man to play for England. Two centuries in a
match against Sussex 1989. All-Rounder of the Year 'Wetherall Award' 1989. Broke
Northants records for fourth wicket in Sunday League with K.M. Curran and for fifth
wicket in NatWest Trophy with A.J. Lamb. Record Northants CCC benefit of £192,000
Opinions on cricket: 'I fail to believe that it is necessary to have three one-day
competitions. Surely it could be arranged to have one knock-out competition and one
league competition of 50 overs per side and scrap 40-over cricket. The league format
should be two divisions and have play-offs for a final.'
Best batting: 175 Northmptonshire v Leicestershire, Northampton 1995
Best bowling: 7-44 Northamptonshire v Warwickshire, Edgbaston 1995

1996 Season

	M	Inns	NO	Runs	HS	Avge	100s	50s	Ct	St	O	M	Runs	Wkts	Avge	Best	5wl	10wM
Test																		
All First	16	30	2	814	103	29.07	1	4	13	-	348.1	57	1181	35	33.74	4-60	-	-
1-day Int																		
NatWest	2	2	0	39	35	19.50	-	-	1	-	14.4	0	61	3	20.33	2-45	-	
B & H	7	7	0	254	82	36.28	-	2	2	-	30	1	137	3	45.66	2-37	-	
Sunday	16	13	1	442	112	36.83	1	1	5	-	91	3	431	16	26.93	4-44	-	

Career Performances

	M	Inns	NO	Runs	HS	Avge	100s	50s	Ct	St	Balls	Runs	Wkts	Avge	Best	5wI	10wM
Test	15	25	1	374	98	15.58	-	2	6	-	2000	1064	21	50.66	3-88	-	-
All First	307	470	66	12062	175	29.85	16	71	155	-	32758	17327	543	31.90	7-44	14	-
1-day Int	23	19	2	327	50 *	19.23	-	1	6	-	1038	805	17	47.35	3-38	-	
NatWest	39	34	8	916	101	35.23	1	4	10	-	1702	1120	33	33.93	3-21	-	
B & H	56	50	5	999	97	22.20	-	3	11	-	2422	1545	54	28.61	4-29	-	
Sunday	178	161	33	3902	121	30.48	3	15	44	-	5293	4258	128	33.26	4-30	-	

CARR, J. D. Middlesex

Name: John Donald Carr
Role: Right-hand bat, right-arm medium bowler, county vice-captain
Born: 15 June 1963, St John's Wood
Height: 6ft **Weight:** 12st
Nickname: Carsy, Gold
County debut: 1983
County cap: 1987
1000 runs in a season: 4
1st-Class 50s: 50
1st-Class 100s: 24
1st-Class 200s: 1
1st-Class 5 w. in innings: 3
1st-Class catches: 260
One-day 100s: 2
Place in batting averages: 169th av. 29.00
(1995 32nd 47.73)
Strike rate: (career 98.33)
Parents: Donald and Stella

Wife and date of marriage: Vicky, 5 May 1990
Children: Holly, 14 December 1992; Elinor, 6 August 1994
Family links with cricket: Father played for Derbyshire and England and is now secretary of the TCCB. Uncle, Major Douglas Carr, was secretary of Derbyshire CCC
Education: The Hall, Hampstead; Repton School; Worcester College, Oxford
Qualifications: Degree in Philosophy, Politics and Economics; senior coaching certificate
Career outside cricket: One year with Barclays Bank
Off-season: 'Close to home, working if possible!'
Overseas tours: Oxbridge to Australia and Hong Kong 1985-86; Troubadours to Argentina and Brazil 1990; MCC to Bahrain 1994-95
Overseas teams played for: Sydney University 1985-86; Weston Creek, Canberra

1987-88; Argentina Colts XI 1989-90

Cricketers particularly admired: Allan Border, Curtly Ambrose

Relaxations: Watching and playing a variety of sports – Eton fives, real tennis, golf, squash, football – good food and the cinema

Extras: Retired from first-class cricket at the end of 1990 season and played for Hertfordshire in 1991. Returned to full-time cricket in 1992. Holds the record for the most consecutive runs scored at Lord's without being dismissed (539 runs). Retired at the end of the 1996 season to take up the post of Cricket Operations Manager for the TCCB

Opinions on cricket: 'I feel very strongly that there is a place for overseas players in county cricket. One per county is ideal. English players must be able to learn from playing with and against the world's top players. Overseas players greatly add to the entertainment value of county cricket. I am amazed by proposals to get rid of them.'

Best batting: 261* Middlesex v Gloucestershire, Lord's 1994

Best bowling: 6-61 Middlesex v Gloucestershire, Lord's 1985

1996 Season

	M	Inns	NO	Runs	HS	Avge	100s	50s	Ct	St	O	M	Runs	Wkts	Avge	Best	5wI	10wM
Test																		
All First	17	28	1	783	94	29.00	-	4	28	-								
1-day Int																		
NatWest	2	2	0	64	62	32.00	-	1	3	-								
B & H	5	5	1	219	55	54.75	-	3	2	-	9	1	31	0	-	-	-	-
Sunday	13	13	3	368	106	36.80	1	-	5	-	38	3	184	6	30.66	2-25	-	

Career Performances

	M	Inns	NO	Runs	HS	Avge	100s	50s	Ct	St	Balls	Runs	Wkts	Avge	Best	5wI	10wM
Test																	
All First	212	331	51	10894	261*	38.90	24	50	260	-	6687	2939	68	43.22	6-61	3	-
1-day Int																	
NatWest	22	21	1	521	83	26.05	-	3	9	-	204	93	4	23.25	2-19	-	
B & H	39	38	2	1140	70	31.66	-	8	21	-	806	497	12	41.41	3-22	-	
Sunday	130	120	24	2761	106	28.76	2	10	56	-	1266	999	34	29.38	4-21	-	

CASSAR, M. E.   Derbyshire

Name: Matthew Edward Cassar
Role: Right-hand bat, right-arm fast-medium bowler
Born: 16 October 1972, Sydney, Australia
Height: 6ft **Weight:** 13st
Nickname: Charchie, Oz

County debut: 1994
1st-Class 50s: 1
1st-Class catches: 2
Strike rate: (career 41.12)
Parents: Edward and Joan
Wife and date of marriage: Jane, 5 October 1996
Family links with cricket: Wife, Jane, is the England Ladies wicket-keeper
Education: Punchbowl Primary School, Sydney; Sir Joseph Banks High School, Sydney
Qualifications: School certificate and NCA Coaching Certificate
Off-season: 'Training for next season's pre-season bleep test at Derby! First English Christmas. Playing in Australia after Christmas and working on the sun tan lying on the beach'
Overseas teams played for: Petersham/Marrickville, Sydney 1988-95
Cricketers particularly admired: Jane
Other sports followed: Football (Derby County), golf, racquet ball
Injuries: Stress fracture of left shin, out for eight weeks
Relaxations: Playing social sports, listening to music, watching television, sleeping 'and spending as much time as possible with Jane'
Extras: Played for New South Wales Colts
Opinions on cricket: 'Overseas players are a vital part of the English game. Playing with and against the greatest players in the world can only be to our advantage.'
Best batting: 66 Derbyshire v New Zealanders, Derby 1994
Best bowling: 4-54 Derbyshire v Oxford University, The Parks 1995

1996 Season (did not make any first-class or one-day appearances)

Career Performances

	M	Inns	NO	Runs	HS	Avge	100s	50s	Ct	St	Balls	Runs	Wkts	Avge	Best	5wI	10wM
Test																	
All First	3	4	0	134	66	33.50	-	1	2	-	329	185	8	23.12	4-54	-	-
1-day Int																	
NatWest																	
B & H																	
Sunday																	

CAWDRON, M. J. Gloucestershire

Name: Michael John Cawdron
Role: Left-hand bat, right-arm medium-fast
bowler
Born: 7 October 1974, Luton
Height: 6ft 3in **Weight:** 12st 7lbs
Nickname: Muscles
County debut: 1995 (one-day)
Parents: William and Mandy
Marital status: Single
Family links with cricket: Father and
brother played local village cricket
Education: Cheltenham College
Qualifications: 10 GCSEs, 3 A-Levels, NCA
Coaching Award
Career outside cricket: 'Vocationally
challenged'
Off-season: House hunting in Bristol and
spending Christmas in South Africa
Overseas tours: West of England U14 to Holland; Cheltenham College to Zimbabwe
1992; Gloucestershire YC to Sri Lanka 1993-94; Gloucestershire Gypsies to
Zimbabwe 1994-95
Cricketers particularly admired: David Gower, Richard Hadlee, Reg Williams 'for
his disco antics'
Young players to look out for: Rob Cunliffe
Other sports followed: Rugby, hockey, racquets, clay-pigeon shooting, golf
Relaxations: Cinema, videos, eating and going out with friends
Extras: Winner of the *Daily Telegraph* Regional Bowling Award 1993. Captain of MCC
Schools and ESCA U19, 1993. 'Made 50 off 32 balls on Sunday League debut against
Essex at my old school' (Cheltenham College)
Opinions on cricket: 'Twelve-month contracts would be of great benefit to those
players who do not wish to winter abroad, as work opportunities are not secure, as other
employers are not eager to take on people on such a temporary basis.'

18. Only four bowlers have taken over 200 Test
wickets for Pakistan. Who are they?

1996 Season

	M	Inns	NO	Runs	HS	Avge	100s	50s	Ct	St	O	M	Runs	Wkts	Avge	Best	5wl	10wM
Test																		
All First																		
1-day Int																		
NatWest																		
B & H	1	0	0	0	0	-	-	-	-	-	6	0	48	2	24.00	2-48	-	
Sunday	3	3	1	76	37	38.00	-	-	1	-	13	0	91	2	45.50	1-28	-	

Career Performances

	M	Inns	NO	Runs	HS	Avge	100s	50s	Ct	St	Balls	Runs	Wkts	Avge	Best	5wl	10wM
Test																	
All First																	
1-day Int																	
NatWest																	
B & H	1	0	0	0	0	-	-	-	-	-	36	48	2	24.00	2-48	-	
Sunday	8	6	1	134	50	26.80	-	1	2	-	288	225	3	75.00	1-23	-	

CHAPMAN, C. A.   Yorkshire

Name: Colin Anthony Chapman
Role: Right-hand bat, wicket-keeper
Born: 8 June 1971, Bradford
Height: 5ft 8in **Weight:** 11st 7lbs
Nickname: Chappy
County debut: 1990
1st-Class catches: 5
1st-Class stumpings: 2
Parents: Mick and Joyce
Wife and date of marriage: Amanda, 11 November 1996
Education: Nabwood Middle; Beckfoot Grammar; Bradford & Ilkley Community College
Qualifications: 5 O-levels, BTEC Diploma in Graphic Design, senior coaching certificate
Off-season: 'Getting married and recovering from the 1996 season'
Overseas teams played for: Waitamata, Auckland 1989-91
Overseas tours: Yorkshire CCC to South Africa 1993 and 1995
Cricketers particularly admired: Phil Carrick, Alan Knott, Mark Nicklin
Young players to look out for: Alex Wharf, Alex Morris

Other sports followed: Football (Liverpool FC)
Injuries: Dodgy back, missed two weeks
Relaxations: 'A few beers or a meal out, DIY, playing and watching sport'
Opinions on cricket: 'Too much travelling'
Best batting: 20 Yorkshire v Middlesex, Uxbridge 1990

1996 Season (did not make any first-class or one-day appearances)

Career Performances

	M	Inns	NO	Runs	HS	Avge	100s	50s	Ct	St	Balls	Runs	Wkts	Avge	Best	5wI	10wM
Test																	
All First	4	7	1	72	20	12.00	-	-	5	2							
1-day Int																	
NatWest	1	0	0	0	0	-	-	-	1	-							
B & H																		
Sunday	7	6	3	89	36 *	29.66	-	-	2	-							

CHAPMAN, M. R. J. Worcestershire

Name: Mark Richard James Chapman
Role: Left-hand bat, right-arm medium bowler
Born: 9 September 1977, Keighley
Height: 6ft 2in **Weight:** 13st
Nickname: Chappy
County debut: No first-team appearance
Parents: John and Julie
Marital status: Single
Family links with cricket: Both grandfather and father played local league cricket
Education: Neff Field First School; Brontë Middle School; South Craven School, Sutton; Worcester College
Qualifications: 6 GCSEs, YTS at Yorkshire Cricket School, GNVQ in Business Management and Sport
Off-season: Studying Business Management and Sports Studies at Worcester College
Cricketers particularly admired: Ian Botham, Richard Hadlee, Brian Lara
Other sports followed: Football (Everton FC and Bradford City), has also represented Bradford at football, athletics, rugby and badminton
Injuries: None

Relaxations: All sports
Extras: Holds his school's record for the highest innings. Plays in the Bradford League for Bradford and Bingley. Has represented Yorkshire at U14 level through to U19.
Opinions on cricket: 'There should be more one-day games.'

CHAPMAN, R. J. Worcestershire

Name: Robert James Chapman
Role: Right-hand bat, right-arm fast-medium bowler
Born: 28 July 1972, Nottingham
Height: 6ft 1in **Weight:** 13st 7lbs
Nickname: Berty, Battling Berty, Bobby Chapper Flapper, Charfish
County debut: 1992 (Notts)
1st-Class catches: 3
Place in bowling averages: (1995 152nd av. 70.63)
Strike rate: 40.83 (career 73.52)
Parents: Robert Dennis and Hazel Janice
Marital status: Single
Family links with cricket: Father plays club cricket for Clifton CC, 'sister has a good arm'
Education: South Wilford School; Farnborough School, Clifton, Nottingham; South Nottingham College

Qualifications: 7 O-levels, 2 A-levels
Overseas teams played for: South Barwon, Geelong, Australia 1995-96
Cricketers particularly admired: Allan Donald, Chris Cairns, Andy Pick, Alec Cottingham (Clifton CC)
Other sports followed: Football (Nottingham Forest, Sheffield United)
Injuries: Shin sores, missed four weeks
Relaxations: Nirvana, Pearl Jam, Oasis, U2, Radiohead, The Cure and Pulp. Going to the cinema and concerts
Extras: 'Father (Sammy) played for Nottingham Forest, Notts County and Shrewsbury Town. Brother-in-law Phil Starbuck plays for Huddersfield Town. Released by Nottinghamshire at the end of the 1996 season and has joined Worcestershire for 1997
Opinions on cricket: 'There are plenty of talented players in the country coming through, watch out you Aussies and you Windies (sorry Chris, and of course you Kiwis).'
Best batting: 25 Nottinghamshire v Lancashire, Trent Bridge 1994
Best bowling: 4-109 Nottinghamshire v South Africa A, Trent Bridge 1996

1996 Season

	M	Inns	NO	Runs	HS	Avge	100s	50s	Ct	St	O	M	Runs	Wkts	Avge	Best	5wI	10wM
Test																		
All First	2	1	0	0	0	0.00	-	-	1	-	40.5	4	183	6	30.50	4-109	-	-
1-day Int																		
NatWest																		
B & H																		
Sunday																		

Career Performances

	M	Inns	NO	Runs	HS	Avge	100s	50s	Ct	St	Balls	Runs	Wkts	Avge	Best	5wI	10wM
Test																	
All First	14	16	3	114	25	8.76	-	-	3	-	1691	1224	23	53.21	4-109	-	-
1-day Int																	
NatWest	1	0	0	0	0	-	-	-	-	-	72	40	0	-	-	-	-
B & H																	
Sunday	11	3	2	6	4 *	6.00	-	-	-	-	369	368	7	52.57	2-36	-	

CHAPPLE, G.   Lancashire

Name: Glen Chapple
Role: Right-hand bat, right-arm medium bowler
Born: 23 January 1974, Skipton, Yorkshire
Height: 6ft 2in **Weight:** 12st 7lbs
Nickname: Chappy, Boris, Boomor, Cheeky
County debut: 1992
50 wickets in a season: 2
1st-Class 50s: 1
1st-Class 100s: 1
1st-Class 5 w. in innings: 6
1st-Class catches: 21
One-Day 5 w. in innings: 1
Place in batting averages: 238th av. 19.35 (1995 210th av. 19.46)
Place in bowling averages: 82nd av. 33.38 (1995 91st av. 34.13)
Strike rate: 57.26 (career 56.64)
Parents: Eileen and Michael
Marital status: Single
Family links with cricket: Father played in Lancashire League for Nelson and was a professional for Darwen and Earby

Education: West Craven High School; Nelson and Colne College
Qualifications: 8 GCSEs, 2 A-Levels in Geography and Economics
Off-season: Touring Australia with England A
Overseas tours: England U18 to Canada 1991; England U19 to New Zealand 1990-91, to Pakistan 1991-92, to India 1992-93; England A to India 1994-95, to Australia 1996-97
Cricketers particularly admired: Dennis Lillee, Robin Smith
Other sports followed: Football (Liverpool), golf
Relaxations: 'Watching films, cinema, music, socialising'
Extras: Hit fastest century (21 minutes) against Glamorgan at Old Trafford 1993. Man of the Match in the 1996 NatWest final against Essex after taking 6 for 18
Best batting: 109* Lancashire v Glamorgan, Old Trafford 1993
Best bowling: 6-48 Lancashire v Durham, Stockton 1994

1996 Season

	M	Inns	NO	Runs	HS	Avge	100s	50s	Ct	St	O	M	Runs	Wkts	Avge	Best	5wl	10wM
Test																		
All First	16	23	6	329	37 *	19.35	-	-	2	-	477.1	94	1669	50	33.38	5-64	2	-
1-day Int																		
NatWest	4	3	0	4	4	1.33	-	-	2	-	34.2	1	158	8	19.75	6-18	1	
B & H	6	4	3	20	8	20.00	-	-	-	-	55	2	256	8	32.00	3-31	-	
Sunday	12	8	3	90	43	18.00	-	-	3	-	77	6	387	13	29.76	3-29	-	

Career Performances

	M	Inns	NO	Runs	HS	Avge	100s	50s	Ct	St	Balls	Runs	Wkts	Avge	Best	5wl	10wM
Test																	
All First	61	86	32	1106	109 *	20.48	1	1	21	-	10196	5409	180	30.05	6-48	8	-
1-day Int																	
NatWest	7	4	0	4	4	1.00	-	-	2	-	419	309	11	28.09	6-18	1	
B & H	13	4	3	20	8	20.00	-	-	2	-	720	561	13	43.15	3-31	-	
Sunday	42	15	7	120	43	15.00	-	-	6	-	1566	1200	40	30.00	3-29	-	

CHILDS, J. H. Essex

Name: John Henry Childs
Role: Left-hand bat, slow left-arm bowler
Born: 15 August 1951, Plymouth
Height: 6ft **Weight:** 12st 6lbs
Nickname: Charlie
County debut: 1975 (Glos), 1985 (Essex)
County cap: 1977 (Glos), 1986 (Essex)
Benefit: 1994
Testimonial: 1985
Test debut: 1988
Tests: 2
50 wickets in a season: 9
1st-Class 5 w. in innings: 52
1st-Class 10 w. in match: 8
1st-Class catches: 116
Place in bowling averages: 113th av. 40.26
(1995 36th av. 25.83)
Strike rate: 70.31 (career 68.74)
Parents: Sydney and Barbara (both
deceased)

Wife and date of marriage: Jane Anne, 11 November 1978
Children: Lee Robert, 28 November 1980; Scott Alexander, 21 August 1984
Education: Audley Park Secondary Modern, Torquay
Qualifications: Advanced cricket coach
Off-season: 'Meeting my family (!) and improving my golf'
Cricketers particularly admired: Gary Sobers, Mike Procter
Other sports followed: Football (Tottenham Hotspur)
Injuries: 'Old age'
Relaxations: 'Watching rugby, decorating at home, walking on moors and beaches,
enjoying my family'
Extras: Played for Devon 1973-74. Released by Gloucestershire at end of 1984 and
joined Essex. One of *Wisden*'s Five Cricketers of the Year 1986. Selected for England's
cancelled tour to India 1988-89. Essex Player of the Year 1992. 1,000 first-class wickets.
Retired from first-class cricket at the end of the 1996 season
Best batting: 43 Essex v Hampshire, Chelmsford 1992
Best bowling: 9-56 Gloucestershire v Somerset, Bristol 1981

1996 Season

	M	Inns	NO	Runs	HS	Avge	100s	50s	Ct	St	O	M	Runs	Wkts	Avge	Best	5wl	10wM
Test																		
All First	6	5	3	1	1 *	0.50	-	-	1	-	222.4	56	765	19	40.26	4-99	-	-
1-day Int																		
NatWest																		
B & H																		
Sunday																		

Career Performances

	M	Inns	NO	Runs	HS	Avge	100s	50s	Ct	St	Balls	Runs	Wkts	Avge	Best	5wl	10wM
Test	2	4	4	2	2 *	-	-	-	1	-	516	183	3	61.00	1-13	-	-
All First	381	359	173	1690	43	9.08	-	-	116	-	70669	30600	1028	29.76	9-56	52	8
1-day Int																	
NatWest	11	5	4	35	14 *	35.00	-	-	-	-	718	404	11	36.72	2-15	-	
B & H	23	7	5	25	10	12.50	-	-	6	-	1272	688	21	32.76	3-36	-	
Sunday	84	32	18	117	16 *	8.35	-	-	16	-	3283	2494	64	38.96	4-15	-	

CHILTON, M. J.   Lancashire

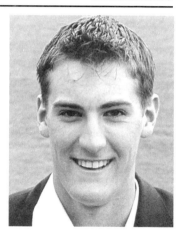

Name: Mark James Chilton
Role: Right-hand bat, right-arm medium bowler
Born: 2 October 1976, Sheffield
Height: 6ft 3in **Weight:** 12st 2lbs
Nickname: Chill, Chilly, Jimmy Chill, Rodney
County debut: No first-team appearance
Parents: Jim and Sue
Marital status: Single
Family links with cricket: Father played local village cricket
Education: Brooklands Primary School; Manchester Grammar School; Durham University
Qualifications: 10 GCSEs, 3 A-levels
Off-season: Studying Business Economics at university
Overseas tours: Manchester Grammar School to Barbados 1993-94, to South Africa 1995-96
Cricketers particularly admired: Michael Atherton, Mark Waugh
Young players to look out for: Ben Hollioake, Owais Shah

Other sports followed: Football (Manchester United), golf, tennis, snooker
Relaxations: Listening to music, watching films, reading
Extras: Represented England U14, U15, U17. Played for North of England v New Zealand U19 in 1996. Awarded England U15 Batsman of the Year in 1992
Opinions on cricket: 'More facilities are needed to practise. In time I would like to see the introduction of day/night matches to England – perhaps they could be linked into the Sunday League.'

CHURCH, M. J. Worcestershire

Name: Matthew John Church
Role: Right-hand bat, right-arm medium bowler
Born: 26 July 1972, Guildford
Height: 6ft 2in **Weight:** 13st
Nickname: Money, Churchy, Loose Unit, Maddy, Larse
County debut: 1994
1st-Class 100s: 1
1st-Class catches: 8
Place in batting averages: 195th av. 25.45 (1995 244th av. 15.75)
Strike rate: 26.11 (career 26.77)
Parents: Anthony and Annette
Marital status: Single
Education: St George's College, Weybridge; Guildford Technical College; Stuart Cricket Academy
Qualifications: 4 GCSEs, 1 A-level ('Thanks Mr Dav and Les')
Off-season: Relaxing, netting, training, working and 'enjoying myself'
Overseas tours: Surrey Young Cricketers to Australia 1989-90; St George's College to Zimbabwe 1990-91
Overseas teams played for: Harmony, Orange Free State 1991-92; North Shore, Geelong 1992-93; Adelaide University 1994-95
Cricketers particularly admired: Ian Glover, Graham Thorpe, Robin Smith, Tim Edwards and Karl Thomas
Other sports followed: All sports
Injuries: Fractured rib, missed three weeks
Extras: Former MCC Young Cricketer, signed by Worcestershire at the beginning of the 1994 season. Sold scorecards at the 1993 Benson & Hedges Cup final and was 12th Man for Worcestershire at the NatWest final the following year. Fielded for England as substitute in 1995 Lord's Test against South Africa. Played for Surrey from U12 to U19.

Released at the end of the 1996 season
Best batting: 152 Worcestershire v Oxford University, The Parks 1996
Best bowling: 4-50 Worcestershire v Oxford University, The Parks 1996

1996 Season

	M	Inns	NO	Runs	HS	Avge	100s	50s	Ct	St	O	M	Runs	Wkts	Avge	Best	5wl	10wM
Test																		
All First	6	11	0	280	152	25.45	1	-	4	-	39.1	5	159	9	17.66	4-50	-	-
1-day Int																		
NatWest	1	1	0	35	35	35.00	-	-	-	-	5	0	34	0	-		-	-
B & H																		
Sunday	3	1	0	11	11	11.00	-	-	-	-	1	0	12	0	-		-	-

Career Performances

	M	Inns	NO	Runs	HS	Avge	100s	50s	Ct	St	Balls	Runs	Wkts	Avge	Best	5wl	10wM
Test																	
All First	14	25	1	471	152	19.62	1	-	8	-	241	163	9	18.11	4-50	-	-
1-day Int																	
NatWest	1	1	0	35	35	35.00	-	-	-	-	30	34	0	-		-	-
B & H	1	0	0	0	0	-	-	-	-	-							
Sunday	14	10	0	73	18	7.30	-	-	7	-	6	12	0	-		-	-

CLARKE, V. P.   Derbyshire

Name: Vincent Paul Clarke
Role: Right-hand bat, leg-break bowler
Born: 11 November 1971, Liverpool
Height: 6ft 3in **Weight:** 15st 10lbs
County debut: 1994 (Somerset), 1995
(Leicestershire)
1st-Class catches: 2
Strike rate: 66.00 (career 92.14)
Parents: Vinnie and Sandra
Marital status: Single
Family links with cricket: Father played
representative schoolboy cricket
Education: Craigie Primary School; Sacred
Heart College, Sorrento; Perth College,
Western Australia
Qualifications: Diploma in Social Training
Overseas teams played for: Wanneroo
District, Perth 1990-94

Cricketers particularly admired: Shane Warne, Ian Botham
Other sports followed: Windsurfing, Aussie Rules football, most sports
Relaxations: Playing the guitar, golf, watching sport
Extras: Brought up in Australia but has English birth qualification. Was in Western Australian Development Squads from U14 to U19. Represented Western Australia at indoor cricket in 1991. Played for Bridgwater and Somerset 2nd XI in 1993. Joined Leicestershire at the start of the 1995 season but was released at the end of the 1996 season. Has joined Derbyshire for the 1997 season
Best batting: 43 Leicestershire v Pakistan, Leicester 1996
Best bowling: 3-72 Leicestershire v Worcestershire, Worcester 1995

1996 Season

	M	Inns	NO	Runs	HS	Avge	100s	50s	Ct	St	O	M	Runs	Wkts	Avge	Best	5wI	10wM
Test																		
All First	1	2	0	43	43	21.50	-	-	1	-	11	1	52	1	52.00	1-42	-	-
1-day Int																		
NatWest																			
B & H																			
Sunday	2	2	0	2	1	1.00	-	-	-	-	6	0	36	1	36.00	1-36	-	

Career Performances

	M	Inns	NO	Runs	HS	Avge	100s	50s	Ct	St	Balls	Runs	Wkts	Avge	Best	5wI	10wM
Test																	
All First	7	13	1	144	43	12.00	-	-	2	-	645	441	7	63.00	3-72	-	-
1-day Int																	
NatWest																		
B & H	1	1	0	22	22	22.00	-	-	-	-							
Sunday	10	10	0	60	26	6.00	-	-	2	-	140	136	3	45.33	1-15	-	

COLLINGWOOD, P. D.   Durham

Name: Paul Davis Collingwood
Role: Right-hand bat, right-arm
medium bowler
Born: 26 May 1976, Shotley Bridge, Tyneside
Height: 5ft 11in **Weight:** 11st 4lbs
Nickname: Colly, Shep
County debut: 1995 (one-day), 1996 (first-class)
1st-Class 50s: 2
1st-Class catches: 6
Place in batting averages: 212th av. 23.20
Strike rate: (career 110.66)

Parents: David and Janet
Marital status: Single
Family links with cricket: Father and brother play in the Tyneside Senior League for Shotley Bridge CC
Education: Benfieldside Junior School; Blackfyne Comprehensive School; Derwentside College
Qualifications: 9 GCSEs and 2 A-levels
Cricketers particularly admired: Dermot Reeve, Graham Thorpe and Ian Botham
Other sports followed: Football (Sunderland AFC) and table tennis
Relaxations: 'I enjoy watching most sports programmes and listening to music. Also going to Sunderland matches home and away'
Opinions on cricket: 'I believe there is far too much cricket played during the season. Surely

if there was less first-class cricket played the standard would improve overall.'
Best batting: 91 Durham v Northamptonshire, Chester-le-Street 1996
Best bowling: 1-13 Durham v Northamptonshire, Chester-le-Street 1996

1996 Season

	M	Inns	NO	Runs	HS	Avge	100s	50s	Ct	St	O	M	Runs	Wkts	Avge	Best	5wI	10wM
Test																		
All First	11	20	0	464	91	23.20	-	2	6	-	55.2	7	181	3	60.33	1-13	-	-
1-day Int																		
NatWest	2	2	0	54	28	27.00	-	-	-	-	2	0	20	0	-		-	-
B & H	5	4	1	42	17	14.00	-	-	1	-	30.1	1	160	5	32.00	3-28	-	
Sunday	14	14	2	268	61 *	22.33	-	2	8	-	12	0	53	1	53.00	1-37	-	

Career Performances

	M	Inns	NO	Runs	HS	Avge	100s	50s	Ct	St	Balls	Runs	Wkts	Avge	Best	5wI	10wM
Test																	
All First	11	20	0	464	91	23.20	-	2	6	-	332	181	3	60.33	1-13	-	-
1-day Int																	
NatWest	2	2	0	54	28	27.00	-	-	-	-	12	20	0	-		-	-
B & H	5	4	1	42	17	14.00	-	-	1	-	181	160	5	32.00	3-28	-	
Sunday	16	16	3	305	61 *	23.46	-	2	8	-	138	106	1	106.00	1-37	-	

CONNOR, C. A.   Hampshire

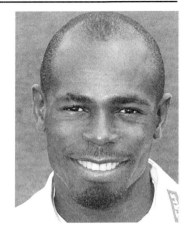

Name: Cardigan Adolphus Connor
Role: Right-hand bat, right-arm
fast-medium bowler
Born: 24 March 1961, The Valley, Anguilla
Height: 5ft 10in **Weight:** 12st 4lbs
Nickname: Cardi
County debut: 1984
County cap: 1988
50 wickets in a season: 5
1st-Class 50s: 2
1st-Class 5 w. in innings: 17
1st-Class 10 w. in match: 4
1st-Class catches: 61
Place in batting averages: 265th av. 15.55
(1995 240th av. 16.00)
Place in bowling averages: 11th av. 21.85
(1995 89th av. 34.10)
Strike rate: 44.40 (career 60.69)
Parents: Ethleen
Wife and date of marriage: Jacqui, 18 March 1995
Education: The Valley Secondary School, Anguilla; Langley College
Qualifications: Engineer
Career outside cricket: Keep-fit instructor and masseur
Overseas teams played for: Merewether DCC, Newcastle, Australia 1983-92; Valley
Secondary School, Anguilla 1992-96
Cricketers particularly admired: Malcolm Marshall, Viv Richards, Kevan James
Young players to look out for: Jason Laney, Dimitri Mascarenhas, Liam Botham
Other sports followed: Football (Arsenal)
Relaxations: Keeping fit
Extras: Played for Buckinghamshire in Minor Counties before joining Hampshire. First
Anguillan-born player to appear in the County Championship
Best batting: 59 Hampshire v Surrey, The Oval 1993
Best bowling: 9-38 Hampshire v Gloucestershire, Southampton 1996

19. Who won the 1996 Minor Counties Championship
and who did they beat in the play-off?

1996 Season

	M	Inns	NO	Runs	HS	Avge	100s	50s	Ct	St	O	M	Runs	Wkts	Avge	Best	5wI	10wM
Test																		
All First	10	12	3	140	42	15.55	-	-	-	-	362.4	99	1071	49	21.85	9-38	2	-
1-day Int																		
NatWest	3	1	1	3	3 *	-	-	-	2	-	32.4	6	103	7	14.71	3-17	-	
B & H	4	3	2	5	4 *	5.00	-	-	-	-	30	0	171	6	28.50	2-22	-	
Sunday	8	3	1	14	14 *	7.00	-	-	2	-	59	2	320	10	32.00	5-25	1	

Career Performances

	M	Inns	NO	Runs	HS	Avge	100s	50s	Ct	St	Balls	Runs	Wkts	Avge	Best	5wI	10wM
Test																	
All First	212	201	51	1780	59	11.86	-	2	61	-	36354	18908	599	31.56	9-38	17	4
1-day Int																	
NatWest	32	7	4	37	13	12.33	-	-	10	-	2078	1233	66	18.68	4-11	-	
B & H	54	14	7	37	11	5.28	-	-	10	-	3031	2002	79	25.34	4-19	-	
Sunday	179	52	16	238	25	6.61	-	-	33	-	7908	5896	222	26.55	5-25	1	

COOPER, K. E.   Gloucestershire

Name: Kevin Edwin Cooper
Role: Left-hand bat, right-arm,
fast-medium bowler
Born: 27 December 1957, Sutton-in-Ashfield
Height: 6ft 1in **Weight:** 13st 2lbs
Nickname: Henry
County debut: 1976 (Nottinghamshire),
1993 (Gloucestershire)
County cap: 1980 (Nottinghamshire),
1995 (Gloucestershire)
Benefit: 1990
50 wickets in a season: 8
1st-Class 50s: 1
1st-Class 5 w. in innings: 26
1st-Class 10 w. in match: 1
1st-Class catches: 93
Place in bowling averages: 4th av. 17.53
(1994 50th av. 28.81)
Strike rate: 46.80 (career 60.57)
Parents: Gerald Edwin and Margaret
Wife and date of marriage: Linda Carol, 14 February 1981
Children: Kelly Louise, 8 April 1982; Tara Amy, 22 November 1984

Family links with cricket: Father played local cricket
Education: Hucknall National Secondary School, Nottingham
Qualifications: Senior coach
Career outside cricket: Sales rep. for Golden Needles
Overseas tours: Derrick Robins U23 to Australasia, 1979-80; Gloucestershire to Sri Lanka, 1993; MCC to Bahrain 1994-95
Overseas teams played for: Nedlands CC, Perth, Australia 1978-79
Cricketers particularly admired: John Snow
Other sports followed: Golf, football (Manchester United)
Relaxations: Golf
Extras: In 1974 took 10-6 in one innings for Hucknall Ramblers against Sutton College in the Mansfield and District League. First bowler to 50 first-class wickets in 1988 season. Took 101 first-class wickets in 1988. Released by Notts at end of 1992 season and released by Gloucestershire at the end of the 1996 season
Best batting: 52 Gloucestershire v Lancashire, Cheltenham 1993
Best bowling: 8-44 Nottinghamshire v Middlesex, Lord's 1984

1996 Season

	M	Inns	NO	Runs	HS	Avge	100s	50s	Ct	St	O	M	Runs	Wkts	Avge	Best	5wI	10wM
Test																		
All First	1	1	0	5	5	5.00	-	-	-	-	39	12	82	5	16.40	4-54	-	-
1-day Int																		
NatWest																		
B & H	4	0	0	0	0	-	-	-	-	-	37	2	183	4	45.75	2-48	-	
Sunday																		

Career Performances

	M	Inns	NO	Runs	HS	Avge	100s	50s	Ct	St	Balls	Runs	Wkts	Avge	Best	5wI	10wM
Test																	
All First	305	330	83	2484	52	10.05	-	1	93	-	49492	22010	817	26.94	8-44	26	1
1-day Int																	
NatWest	27	9	1	50	11	6.25	-	-	7	-	1814	814	41	19.85	4-49	-	
B & H	75	27	17	143	25 *	14.30	-	-	13	-	4363	2415	81	29.81	4-9	-	
Sunday	167	60	21	248	31	6.35	-	-	28	-	6994	5170	141	36.66	4-25	-	

20. Who finished top of the first-class batting averages in 1996?

CORK, D. G.   Derbyshire

Name: Dominic Gerald Cork
Role: Right-hand bat, right-arm, fast-medium bowler, fine leg fielder of bat pad
Born: 7 August 1971, Newcastle-under-Lyme, Staffordshire
Height: 6ft 3in **Weight:** 13st
Nickname: Corky
County debut: 1990
County cap: 1993
Test debut: 1995
Tests: 16
One-Day Internationals: 22
50 wickets in a season: 3
1st-Class 50s: 21
1st-Class 100s: 2
1st-Class 5 w. in innings: 12
1st-Class 10 w. in match: 2
1st-Class catches: 79
Place in batting averages: 124th av. 33.86 (1995 195th av. 21.81)
Place in bowling averages: 79th av. 33.17 (1995 9th av. 20.00)
Strike rate: 62.00 (career 52.70)
Parents: Gerald and Mary
Children: Gregory Theodore Gerald, 29 September 1994
Family links with cricket: 'Father and two brothers play for Betley CC in the North Staffs and South Cheshire League'
Education: St Joseph's College, Stoke-on-Trent; Newcastle College of Further Education
Qualifications: History O-level, leisure and recreation, qualified coach
Career outside cricket: 'None at the moment but I would love to work in the media or in television'
Off-season: Touring Zimbabwe and New Zealand with England
Overseas tours: England YCs to Australia 1989-90; England A to Bermuda and West Indies 1991-92, to Australia 1992-93, to South Africa 1993-94, to India 1994-95; England to South Africa 1995-96, to India and Pakistan (World Cup) 1995-96, to Zimbabwe and New Zealand 1996-97
Overseas teams played for: East Shirley, Christchurch, New Zealand 1990-91
Cricketers particularly admired: Ian Botham, Kim Barnett, 'and particularly Shane Warne'
Young players to look out for: Vikram Solanki, Andrew Harris and Phil DeFreitas ('off-spin')

Other sports followed: Horse racing, football (Stoke 'Premier League soon'), rugby union (England and Bath RFC)

Injuries: Broken left arm ('stay in the crease'), missed four weeks

Relaxations: Gardening ('I love weeding'), listening to music, 'watching Lou Macari rally the mighty men'

Extras: First played cricket for Betley CC in the North Staffs & South Cheshire League. In 1990 he took a wicket in his first over in first-class cricket v New Zealand at Derby and scored a century as nightwatchman for England U19 v Pakistan at Taunton. Played Minor Counties cricket for Staffordshire in 1989 and 1990. Selected for England A in 1991 – his first full season of first-class cricket. The Cricket Association Young Player of 1991. Took eight wickets for 53 runs on 20th birthday. Achieved first-class hat-trick against Kent, 1994. Took seven wickets for 43 runs on Test debut against West Indies at Lord's. Achieved hat-trick against the West Indies at Old Trafford in the fourth Test – the first by an Englishman in Test cricket for thirty years. Won two Man of the Match awards in three Test matches. Voted Player of the Year by the Professional Cricketers' Association for 1995. Finished at the top of the Whyte and Mackay ratings for bowling in 1995. Withdrew from the Zimbabwe leg of England's winter tour through personal reasons, but joined up with the team in New Zealand

Opinions on cricket: 'Counties should be amalgamated together, giving us nine counties. Squads would get stronger and there would be no need for overseas players. England players and fringe players should be contracted to the TCCB and batsmen should stop hitting bowlers for boundaries.'

Best batting: 104 Derbyshire v Gloucestershire, Cheltenham 1993

Best bowling: 9-43 Derbyshire v Northamptonshire, Derby 1995

1996 Season

	M	Inns	NO	Runs	HS	Avge	100s	50s	Ct	St	O	M	Runs	Wkts	Avge	Best	5wI	10wM
Test	6	9	1	95	32 *	11.87	-	-	5	-	251.4	49	803	22	36.50	5-113	1	-
All First	18	29	6	779	101 *	33.86	1	5	12	-	589	121	1891	57	33.17	5-113	1	-
1-day Int	3	1	1	0	0 *	-	-	-	2	-	22	4	102	5	20.40	3-46	-	
NatWest	2	2	0	120	61	60.00	-	2	3	-	24	2	101	0	-	-	-	-
B & H	4	4	1	44	16	14.66	-	-	2	-	33	8	123	6	20.50	5-49	1	
Sunday	9	7	2	74	35	14.80	-	-	5	-	64	2	257	10	25.70	3-41	-	

Career Performances

	M	Inns	NO	Runs	HS	Avge	100s	50s	Ct	St	Balls	Runs	Wkts	Avge	Best	5wI	10wM
Test	16	23	3	361	56 *	18.05	-	1	7	-	3752	1949	67	29.08	7-43	3	-
All First	126	186	27	3896	104	24.50	2	21	79	-	21294	10570	404	26.16	9-43	12	2
1-day Int	22	12	1	92	21	8.36	-	-	5	-	1272	926	34	27.23	3-27	-	
NatWest	11	9	0	274	62	30.44	-	3	3	-	689	414	25	16.56	5-18	2	
B & H	18	14	5	281	92 *	31.22	-	2	8	-	1076	712	20	35.60	5-49	1	
Sunday	66	52	6	800	66	17.39	-	2	26	-	2772	2213	73	30.31	4-44	-	

COSKER, D. A. Glamorgan

Name: Dean Andrew Cosker
Role: Right-hand bat, slow left-arm bowler
Born: 7 January 1978, Weymouth, Dorset
Height: 5ft 11in **Weight:** 12st 7lbs
County debut: 1996
1st-Class catches: 3
Place in bowling averages: 107th av. 38.87
Strike rate: (career 58.37)
Parents: Des and Carol
Marital status: Single
Family links with cricket: 'Grandfather
once launched one into the Bush. Brother has
a little dabble at spin bowling'
Education: Preston Primary School, Yeovil;
Ravenswood Prep School, Devon;
Millfield School
Qualifications: 10 GCSEs, 3 A-levels, Class
3 soccer referee
Career outside cricket: 'Once had auditions
for Bugsy Malone'

Off-season: England U19 tour to Pakistan
Overseas tours: West of England U15 to West Indies 1993-94; Millfield School
to Sri Lanka 1994-95; England U17 to Holland 1995; England U19 to Pakistan 1996-
97
Overseas teams played for: Gordon, Sydney 1996-97
Cricketers particularly admired: Gareth J. Cosker, Matthew Byrne, Tony Cottey,
Steve Barwick 'for his contribution to cricket'
Young players to look out for: Quintin Pickle, Simon Evans
Other sports followed: Soccer (Tottenham Hotspur FC)
Injuries: 'A slight niggle in the left shoulder but very expertly dealt with by Deano
Conway'
Relaxations: 'Spending time with my girlfriend. Trying to learn from the wonderful
game of cricket during the bleak winter months'
Extras: *Daily Telegraph* Regional Bowling Award, England U15 and U17. Played for
U19 TCCB Development of Excellence XI against South Africa U19 in 1995
Opinions on cricket: 'The Sunday League should be 50 overs. Tea should be longer.'
Best batting: 24 Glamorgan v Lancashire, Cardiff 1996
Best bowling: 4-60 Glamorgan v Lancashire, Cardiff 1996

1996 Season

	M	Inns	NO	Runs	HS	Avge	100s	50s	Ct	St	O	M	Runs	Wkts	Avge	Best	5wI	10wM
Test																		
All First	5	6	1	45	24	9.00	-	-	3	-	155.4	38	622	16	38.87	4-60	-	-
1-day Int																		
NatWest																		
B & H																		
Sunday	1	1	0	4	4	4.00	-	-	-	-	8	0	38	2	19.00	2-38	-	

Career Performances

	M	Inns	NO	Runs	HS	Avge	100s	50s	Ct	St	Balls	Runs	Wkts	Avge	Best	5wI	10wM
Test																	
All First	5	6	1	45	24	9.00	-	-	3	-	934	622	16	38.87	4-60	-	-
1-day Int																	
NatWest																	
B & H																	
Sunday	1	1	0	4	4	4.00	-	-	-	-	48	38	2	19.00	2-38	-	

COTTAM, A. C. Somerset

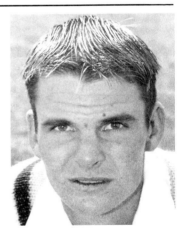

Name: Andrew Colin Cottam
Role: Right-hand bat, slow-left arm bowler
Born: 14 July 1973, Northampton
Height: 6ft 2in **Weight:** 11st
Nickname: Worm, Cotts, Doggers
County debut: 1995
1st-Class catches: 1
Strike rate: 178.00 (career 131.38)
Parents: Bob and Jackie
Marital status: Single
Family links with cricket: Father played for Hampshire, Northants and England and coached at Somerset. Brothers Michael and David played for Devon.
Education: Seaton Primary School; Axminster Secondary School
Qualifications: Qualified cricket coach
Overseas tours: England U18 to Canada 1991; England U19 to Pakistan 1991-92
Other sports followed: Football (Tottenham Hotspur)
Relaxations: Listening to music, 'especially Bob Marley', or watching television
Opinions on cricket: 'Play on uncovered wickets.'

Best batting: 36 Derbyshire v Oxford University, The Parks 1995
Best bowling: 2-5 Derbyshire v Oxford University, The Parks 1995

1996 Season

	M	Inns	NO	Runs	HS	Avge	100s	50s	Ct	St	O	M	Runs	Wkts	Avge	Best	5wI	10wM
Test																		
All First	2	2	0	15	12	7.50	-	-	-	-	89	22	248	3	82.66	2-127	-	-
1-day Int																		
NatWest	1	0	0	0	0	-	-	-	-	-	11	0	47	0	-		-	-
B & H																		
Sunday																		

Career Performances

	M	Inns	NO	Runs	HS	Avge	100s	50s	Ct	St	Balls	Runs	Wkts	Avge	Best	5wI	10wM
Test																	
All First	13	16	1	153	36	10.20	-	-	1	-	1708	819	13	63.00	2-5	-	-
1-day Int																	
NatWest	2	1	0	2	2	2.00	-	-	1	-	138	92	1	92.00	1-45	-	
B & H	1	0	0	0	0	-	-	-	-	-	42	34	0	-		-	-
Sunday	1	0	0	0	0	-	-	-	-	-	36	24	0	-		-	-

COTTEY, P. A. Glamorgan

Name: Phillip Anthony Cottey
Role: Right-hand bat
Born: 2 June 1966, Swansea
Height: 5ft 5in **Weight:** 10st 7lbs
Nickname: Cotts
County debut: 1986
County cap: 1992
1000 runs in season: 6
1st-Class 50s: 52
1st-Class 100s: 19
1st-Class 200s: 1
1st-Class catches: 106
Place in batting averages: 25th av. 51,43
(1995 31st av. 48.83)
Strike rate: 51.00 (career 83.00)
Parents: Bernard John and Ruth
Wife and date of marriage: Gail, 5 October
1992
Children: Lowri Rhiannon, 16 October 1993

Family links with cricket: Father played for Swansea
Education: Bishopston Comprehensive School, Swansea
Qualifications: 9 O-levels, advanced coach
Career outsdide cricket: Cricket Board of Wales Development Officer
Overseas tours: Glamorgan to La Manga, Barbados, Trinidad, Zimbabwe and Cape Town 1987-96
Overseas teams played for: Penrith, Sydney 1986-88; Benoni, Johannesburg 1990-93; Eastern Transvaal 1991-92
Cricketers particularly admired: Ian Botham, Wasim Akram, Stuart Law
Young players to look out for: Alun Evans, Adrian Shaw, Jason Laney
Other sports followed: 'Pro soccer player for Swansea 1982-85. Completed New York Marathon 1995 and running Athens Marathon in 1996. Support Duvant Rugby Club'
Relaxations: 'Golf, long-distance running, watching Premier League football on Sky. Spending time with my daughter, Lowri. I hate a few beers'
Extras: Left school at 16 to play for Swansea City FC for three years as a professional. Three Welsh Youth caps (one as captain). Glamorgan Player of the Year in 1994
Opinions on cricket: 'I don't agree with the ruling of only five fielders on the leg side in one-day cricket. If a bowler is good enough to bowl to a 6/3 field then he should be allowed to do so.'
Best batting: 203 Glamorgan v Leicestershire, Swansea 1996
Best bowling: 4-49 Glamorgan v Leicestershire, Swansea 1996

1996 Season

	M	Inns	NO	Runs	HS	Avge	100s	50s	Ct	St	O	M	Runs	Wkts	Avge	Best	5wI	10wM
Test																		
All First	20	36	6	1543	203	51.43	4	9	16	-	34	3	107	4	26.75	4-49	-	-
1-day Int																		
NatWest	1	1	0	17	17	17.00	-	-	3	-								
B & H	6	4	1	55	29	18.33	-	-	3	-	10	0	49	1	49.00	1-49	-	
Sunday	16	15	3	243	44 *	20.25	-	-	6	-	20.5	1	144	6	24.00	4-56	-	

Career Performances

	M	Inns	NO	Runs	HS	Avge	100s	50s	Ct	St	Balls	Runs	Wkts	Avge	Best	5wI	10wM
Test																	
All First	167	276	42	9132	203	39.02	19	52	106	-	1079	748	13	57.53	4-49	-	-
1-day Int																	
NatWest	19	18	5	347	61 *	26.69	-	2	6	-	102	59	2	29.50	1-11	-	
B & H	25	23	4	417	68	21.94	-	1	8	-	66	50	1	50.00	1-49	-	
Sunday	104	85	17	1630	92 *	23.97	-	8	36	-	323	329	11	29.90	4-56	-	

COUSINS, D. M.   Essex

Name: Darren Mark Cousins
Role: Right-hand bat, right-arm fast-medium
bowler, outfielder
Born: 24 September 1971, Cambridge
Height: 6ft 1in **Weight:** 13st 7lbs
Nickname: Mad Dog, Cuz, Cuzzi, Skuz
County debut: 1993
1st-Class 5 w. in innings: 1
1st-Class catches: 5
Place in batting averages: 280th av. 10.08
Place in bowling averages: 148th av. 53.33
(1994 30th av. 25.92)
Strike rate: 88.00 (career 72.69)
Parents: Dennis Charles and Deanna
Maureen (deceased)
Marital status: Single
Family links with cricket: Father opened the
bowling and was capped for Cambridgeshire
Education: Milton Primary School; Impington Village College
Qualifications: 7 GCSEs
Career outside cricket: Coaching and teaching PE in local secondary school
Off-season: Training and playing and coaching in Australia after Christmas
Overseas teams played for: Gold Coast Dolphins, Queensland 1994-95; Maritzburg
Old Boys, Pietermaritzburg, South Africa 1995–96
Cricketers particularly admired: Neil Foster, Geoff Arnold, Alan Butcher, Keith
Fletcher and 'anyone else who has given me help, advice and guidance during my
career'
Young players to look out for: Robert Rollins, Ashley Cowan, Stephen Peters,
Darren Robinson
Other sports followed: Football (Liverpool, Cambridge United), 'I used to be a
county swimmer and a county footballer but had to give up all other sports due to
glass back syndrome'
Relaxations: 'Socialising. Listening to all types of music from Indie to soul to swing'
Extras: Represented Cambridgeshire at football and swimming and every level at
cricket. Played for a Bull Development Squad against Australia in 1991, taking four
wickets in each innings. Played 2nd XI cricket for Northants and Worcs. Holds the
record for both number of wickets in any single Colts festival (21) and number of
wickets taken in the Hilda Overy Festival overall (74). Awarded 2nd XI cap and Essex
Young Player of the Year, 1994. Essex Cricket Society 2nd XI Player of the Year, 1994.
Leading Essex wicket-taker in Sunday League and top of the bowling averages in 1994.
Underwent third back operation in 22 months and missed his third season of cricket

Opinions on cricket: 'I'd like to play a game sometime.'
Best batting: 18* Essex v Durham, Chelmsford 1995
Best bowling: 6-35 Essex v Cambridge University, Fenner's 1994

1996 Season

	M	Inns	NO	Runs	HS	Avge	100s	50s	Ct	St	O	M	Runs	Wkts	Avge	Best	5wI	10wM
Test																		
All First																		
1-day Int																		
NatWest																		
B & H	2	1	0	10	10	10.00	-	-	-	-	14.4	4	41	1	41.00	1-33	-	
Sunday																		

Career Performances

	M	Inns	NO	Runs	HS	Avge	100s	50s	Ct	St	Balls	Runs	Wkts	Avge	Best	5wI	10wM
Test																	
All First	14	23	5	145	18 *	8.05	-	-	5	-	1890	1086	26	41.76	6-35	1	-
1-day Int																	
NatWest	3	2	1	1	1 *	1.00	-	-	-	-	132	117	1	117.00	1-33	-	
B & H	6	2	1	22	12 *	22.00	-	-	1	-	239	171	2	85.50	1-33	-	
Sunday	28	10	4	17	6	2.83	-	-	2	-	1155	888	37	24.00	3-18	-	

COWAN, A. P.   Essex

Name: Ashley Preston Cowan
Role: Right-hand bat, right-hand
fast-medium bowler
Born: 7 May 1975, Hitchin, Hertfordshire
Height: 6ft 5in **Weight:** 14st
Nickname: Victor, Dic Dic
County debut: 1995
1st-Class 5 w. in innings: 1
1st-Class catches: 7
Place in batting averages: 274th av. 13.42
Place in bowling averages: 104th av. 36.60
Strike rate: 61.40 (career 63.41)
Parents: Jeff and Pam
Marital status: Single
Family links with cricket: 'Father tried to
play in local village team'
Education: Kingshott Prep; Framlingham
College

Qualifications: 5 GCSEs, 1 A-level; Business Vocation Degree
Career outside cricket: Family business
Off-season: 'Playing cricket in South Africa and relaxing'
Overseas teams played for: Zingan CC, Pietermaritzburg, South Africa 1995-97
Cricketers particularly admired: Ian Botham, Graham Dilley, Curtly Ambrose
Young players to look out for: Steve Andrew, Robert Rollins
Other sports followed: Rugby, hockey, golf, football (Newcastle United)
Relaxations: Socialising, playing golf, 'having fun'
Extras: Played rugby and hockey for East of England U18. The youngest person to play for Cambridgeshire. First-class hat-trick at Colchester in 1996. Was the joint leading scorer in the 1996 NatWest final
Opinions on cricket: 'Looking for a younger and more dedicated cricket crowd who will inspire the players through their enthusiasm.'
Best batting: 34 Essex v Sussex, Chelmsford 1996
Best bowling: 5-68 Essex v Gloucestershire, Colchester 1996

1996 Season

	M	Inns	NO	Runs	HS	Avge	100s	50s	Ct	St	O	M	Runs	Wkts	Avge	Best	5wI	10wM
Test																		
All First	15	20	6	188	34	13.42	-	-	6	-	409.2	67	1464	40	36.60	5-68	1	-
1-day Int																		
NatWest	2	1	0	11	11	11.00	-	-	2	-	20	3	77	1	77.00	1-44	-	
B & H	2	0	0	0	0	-	-	-	-	-	19	2	66	1	66.00	1-38	-	
Sunday	9	6	2	48	22 *	12.00	-	-	3	-	47.2	4	217	4	54.25	2-17	-	

Career Performances

	M	Inns	NO	Runs	HS	Avge	100s	50s	Ct	St	Balls	Runs	Wkts	Avge	Best	5wI	10wM
Test																	
All First	17	24	7	235	34	13.82	-	-	7	-	2600	1577	41	38.46	5-68	1	-
1-day Int																	
NatWest	2	1	0	11	11	11.00	-	-	2	-	120	77	1	77.00	1-44	-	
B & H	2	0	0	0	0	-	-	-	-	-	114	66	1	66.00	1-38	-	
Sunday	10	7	3	48	22 *	12.00	-	-	3	-	308	237	4	59.25	2-17	-	

21. Who was the highest-placed Englishman in the
first-class batting 1996 averages?

COWDREY, G. R. Kent

Name: Graham Robert Cowdrey
Role: Right-hand bat, right-arm medium bowler, cover fielder
Born: 27 June 1964, Farnborough, Kent
Height: 5ft 11in **Weight:** 13st 9lbs
Nickname: Van, Mervyn
County debut: 1984
County cap: 1988
1000 runs in season: 3
1st-Class 50s: 45
1st-Class 100s: 16
1st-Class catches: 90
One-Day 100s: 3
Place in batting averages: 151st av. 31.11
(1995 49th av. 44.28)
Strike rate: 69.00 (career 98.00)
Parents: Michael Colin and Penelope Susan
Wife and date of marriage: Maxine, 20
February 1993

Family links with cricket: Father (M.C.) and brother (C.S.) played for, and captained, Kent and England
Education: Wellesley House, Broadstairs; Tonbridge School; Durham University
Qualifications: 8 O-levels, 3 A-levels, farrier
Off-season: Writing for the *Racing Post*
Overseas tours: Christians in Sport to India 1985-86, 1989-90; MCC to West Indies 1991-92
Overseas teams played for: Avendale, Cape Town 1983-84; Mossman, Sydney 1985-86; Randwick, Sydney 1986-87
Cricketers particularly admired: Aravinda De Silva, Nick Cook, Robin Smith
Young players to look out for: Will House, William Haggas
Other sports followed: Horse racing (Giles Bravery), American football (Miami Dolphins), football (Arsenal), rugby (West Hartlepool)
Injuries: 'Savagely axed in the head by Steve Marsh and missed eight weeks'
Relaxations: 'Horse racing – watching wife winning races! Reading – Brian Moore and Jonathan Smith. Music – Van Morrison, Bob Dylan and Paul Brady.'
Extras: Played for England YC. Made 1000 runs for Kent 2nd XI first season on staff, and broke 2nd XI record with 1300 runs in 26 innings in 1985. Plays in contact lenses. Holds Kent record partnership for any wicket with Aravinda De Silva, 382 runs against Derbyshire 1995
Opinions on cricket: 'It's time for everyone, and that includes the media, the players and the county clubs, to become more positive and optimistic about the game in this

country. I feel an underlying depression is quietly destroying the game. If we all enjoy it, success will come'

Best batting: 147 Kent v Gloucestershire, Bristol 1992
Best bowling: 1-5 Kent v Warwickshire, Edgbaston 1988

1996 Season

	M	Inns	NO	Runs	HS	Avge	100s	50s	Ct	St	O	M	Runs	Wkts	Avge	Best	5wI	10wM
Test																		
All First	11	17	0	529	111	31.11	1	3	5	-	11.3	3	42	1	42.00	1-19	-	-
1-day Int																		
NatWest	2	2	0	44	41	22.00	-	-	-	-	1	0	6	0	-		-	-
B & H	6	6	0	67	31	11.16	-	-	4	-	8	0	45	0	-		-	-
Sunday	16	15	1	360	68	25.71	-	3	6	-	6	0	44	1	44.00	1-44	-	

Career Performances

	M	Inns	NO	Runs	HS	Avge	100s	50s	Ct	St	Balls	Runs	Wkts	Avge	Best	5wI	10wM
Test																	
All First	170	269	29	8416	147	35.06	16	45	90	-	1176	841	12	70.08	1-5	-	-
1-day Int																	
NatWest	23	20	4	416	65	26.00	-	1	3	-	303	157	8	19.62	2-4	-	
B & H	48	43	3	864	70 *	21.60	-	5	18	-	202	139	2	69.50	1-8	-	
Sunday	152	135	21	3175	105 *	27.85	3	14	54	-	642	509	22	23.13	4-15	-	

22. Who finished top of the first-class bowling averages in 1996?

COX, D. M. Durham

Name: David Matthew Cox
Role: Left-hand bat, slow left-arm bowler
Born: 2 March 1972, Southall, Middlesex
Height: 5ft 11in **Weight:** 13st
Nickname: Coxy, Cocker
County debut: 1994
1st-Class 50s: 4
1st-Class 5 w. in innings: 2
1st-Class 10 w. in match: 1
1st-Class catches: 3
Place in batting averages: 36th av. 48.22
Place in bowling averages: 88th av. 33.96
(1995 112th av. 38.36)
Strike rate: 70.61 (career 80.63)
Parents: Charles and Georgina
Wife and date of marriage: Hazel Jennifer,
1 October 1994
Family links with cricket: Father played for

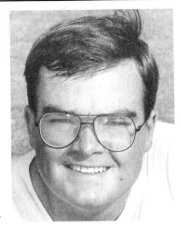

Old Actonians
Education: Lady Margaret Primary School; Greenford High School
Qualifications: 5 GCSEs, cricket coaching certificate, part-qualified plasterer
Career outside cricket: Security officer and plasterer
Off-season: Working for Pinkerton Security
Cricketers particularly admired: Phil Bainbridge, Wayne Larkins and Dean Jones
Other sports followed: Snooker, darts, football (QPR), golf and horse racing
Relaxations: Going to horse racing meetings, eating out with my wife and watching
television
Extras: First Durham player to get over 50 2nd XI Championship wickets in a season
(1995). Player of the Month for Durham CCC in August 1996
Best batting: 95* Durham v Somerset, Weston-super-Mare 1996
Best bowling: 5-97 Durham v Warwickshire, Edgbaston 1996

1996 Season

	M	Inns	NO	Runs	HS	Avge	100s	50s	Ct	St	O	M	Runs	Wkts	Avge	Best	5wI	10wM
Test																		
All First	7	13	4	434	95 *	48.22	-	4	2	-	306	87	883	26	33.96	5-97	2	1
1-day Int																		
NatWest																			
B & H																			
Sunday	3	2	0	7	7	3.50	-	-	1	-	24	0	106	2	53.00	2-34	-	

Career Performances

	M	Inns	NO	Runs	HS	Avge	100s	50s	Ct	St	Balls	Runs	Wkts	Avge	Best	5wl	10wM
Test																	
All First	13	22	5	489	95 *	28.76	-	4	3	-	3064	1650	38	43.42	5-97	2	1
1-day Int																	
NatWest																	
B & H																	
Sunday	6	2	0	7	7	3.50	-	-	1	-	264	195	3	65.00	2-34	-	

CRAWLEY, J. P.   Lancashire

Name: John Paul Crawley
Role: Right-hand bat, occasional wicket-keeper
Born: 21 September 1971, Malden, Essex
Height: 6ft 2in **Weight:** 13st 2lbs
Nickname: Creeps, Jonty, JC
County debut: 1990
Test debut: 1994
Tests: 12
One-day Internationals: 3
1000 runs in a season: 5
1st-Class 50s: 58
1st-Class 100s: 18
1st-Class 200s: 3
1st-Class catches: 100
One-day 100s: 1
Place in batting averages: 29th av. 50.09
(1995 33rd av. 47.48)
Strike rate: (career 78.00)
Parents: Frank and Jean
Marital status: Single
Family links with cricket: Father played in Manchester Association; brother Mark played for Lancashire before moving to Nottinghamshire; other brother Peter plays for Warrington CC and has played for Scottish Universities and Cambridge University; uncle was excellent fast bowler; godfather umpires in Manchester Association
Education: Manchester Grammar School; Trinity College, Cambridge
Qualifications: 10 O-levels, 2 AO-Levels, 3 A-levels, 2 S-levels, BA in History
Off-season: Touring Zimbabwe and New Zealand with England
Overseas tours: England YC to Australia 1989-90, to New Zealand 1990-91; England A to South Africa 1993-94; England to Australia 1994-95, to South Africa 1995-96, to Zimbabwe and New Zealand 1996-97

Overseas teams played for: Midland Guildford, Perth 1990

Cricketers particularly admired: Michael Atherton, Neil Fairbrother, Graham Gooch, Alec Stewart, David Gower, Allan Donald, Ian Salisbury

Other sports followed: Football (Manchester United), golf

Injuries: Pulled hamstring in Durban and again in the English season, missed a total of two months

Relaxations: 'Playing or trying to play the guitar'

Extras: Captained England YC (U19) to New Zealand 1990-91 and played for England YC in three home series v New Zealand 1989, Pakistan 1990 and Australia (as captain) 1991. Made his maiden first-class century for Cambridge University on the same day that brother Mark made his for Notts. First to score 1000 runs in U19 Tests. Scored 286 for England A against Eastern Province at Port Elizabeth in 1994, the highest score by an Englishman on an England or England A tour for almost 30 years. Finished top of the first-class batting averages on England's tour to South Africa in 1995-96 with 336 runs at 67.20, but had to fly home after suffering a hamstring injury whilst fielding in the third Test at Durban. Scored his maiden Test match hundred (106) in the third Test against Pakistan at The Oval in 1996, followed by 112 in England's next Test against Zimbabwe in Bulawayo

Opinions on cricket: 'I think it's good that the four-day schedule has been introduced, and that the Sunday League has been commercialised.'

Best batting: 286 England A v Eastern Province, Port Elizabeth 1993-94

Best bowling: 1-90 Lancashire v Sussex, Hove 1992

1996 Season

	M	Inns	NO	Runs	HS	Avge	100s	50s	Ct	St	O	M	Runs	Wkts	Avge	Best	5wI	10wM
Test	2	3	0	178	106	59.33	1	1	1	-								
All First	15	25	3	1102	112 *	50.09	3	8	6	-								
1-day Int																		
NatWest	4	4	0	141	66	35.25	-	2	-	-								
B & H	6	6	0	208	48	34.66	-	-	2	-								
Sunday	10	10	0	186	52	18.60	-	1	3	-								

Career Performances

	M	Inns	NO	Runs	HS	Avge	100s	50s	Ct	St	Balls	Runs	Wkts	Avge	Best	5wI	10wM
Test	12	19	1	508	106	28.22	1	4	11	-							
All First	128	213	22	9387	286	49.14	18	58	100	-	78	108	1	108.00	1-90	-	-
1-day Int	3	3	0	34	18	11.33	-	-	-	-							
NatWest	9	9	0	238	66	26.44	-	2	2	-							
B & H	25	24	1	918	114	39.91	1	4	7	-							
Sunday	47	45	1	1101	91	25.02	-	8	14	-							

CROFT, R. D. B.   Glamorgan

Name: Robert Damien Bale Croft
Role: Right-hand bat, off-spinner
Born: 25 May 1970, Swansea
Height: 5ft 11in **Weight:** 11st 5lbs
Nickname: Crofty
County debut: 1989
County cap: 1992
Test debut: 1996
Tests: 1
50 wickets in a season: 4
1st-Class 50s: 19
1st-Class 100s: 2
1st-Class 5 w. in innings: 18
1st-Class 10 w. in match: 2
1st-Class catches: 75
Place in batting averages: 184th av. 26.95
(1995 184th av. 22.37)
Place in bowling averages: 76th av. 32.71
(1995 95th av. 34.60)
Strike rate: 75.44 (career 82.13)
Parents: Malcolm and Susan
Family links with cricket: Father and grandfather played local cricket
Education: St John Lloyd Catholic School; Neath Trinity College; West Glamorgan
Institute of Higher Education
Qualifications: 6 O-levels; OND Business Studies; HND Business Studies; NCA
senior coaching certificate
Career outside cricket: Personnel management ('not as yet!')
Off-season: Touring Zimbabwe and New Zealand with England
Overseas tours: England A to Bermuda and West Indies 1991-92, to South Africa
1993-94; England to Zimbabwe and New Zealand 1996-97
Cricketers particularly admired: Alan Jones, Tom Cartwright, Don Shepherd,
John Steele, John Emburey
Other sports followed: Rugby, soccer
Relaxations: Shooting, fishing, driving, music, golf
Extras: Captained England South to victory in International Youth Tournament 1989
and was voted Player of the Tournament. Glamorgan Young Player of the Year 1992.
Made his Test debut in the third Test against Pakistan at The Oval in 1996
Opinions on cricket: 'Enjoyment is of the utmost importance.'
Best batting: 143 Glamorgan v Somerset, Taunton 1995
Best bowling: 8-66 Glamorgan v Warwickshire, Swansea 1992

1996 Season

	M	Inns	NO	Runs	HS	Avge	100s	50s	Ct	St	O	M	Runs	Wkts	Avge	Best	5wl	10wM
Test	1	2	1	11	6	11.00	-	-	1	-	47.4	10	125	2	62.50	2-116	-	-
All First	20	30	6	647	78	26.95	-	5	15	-	955.4	237	2486	76	32.71	6-78	4	-
1-day Int	3	2	0	15	15	7.50	-	-	1	-	28	1	111	5	22.20	2-36	-	
NatWest	1	1	0	9	9	9.00	-	-	1	-	12	1	33	1	33.00	1-33	-	
B & H	6	4	1	24	12	8.00	-	-	-	-	56.5	4	239	11	21.72	4-30	-	
Sunday	12	11	3	302	68	37.75	-	1	2	-	77	4	350	11	31.81	3-21	-	

Career Performances

	M	Inns	NO	Runs	HS	Avge	100s	50s	Ct	St	Balls	Runs	Wkts	Avge	Best	5wl	10wM
Test	1	2	1	11	6	11.00	-	-	1	-	286	125	2	62.50	2-116	-	-
All First	159	233	47	4773	143	25.66	2	19	75	-	33430	15822	407	38.87	8-66	18	2
1-day Int	3	2	0	15	15	7.50	-	-	1	-	168	111	5	22.20	2-36	-	
NatWest	18	14	5	206	50	22.88	-	1	4	-	1048	594	16	37.12	3-30	-	
B & H	19	15	7	238	50 *	29.75	-	1	6	-	1097	669	25	26.76	4-30	-	
Sunday	90	66	22	925	68	21.02	-	2	22	-	3556	2681	82	32.69	6-20	1	

CROWE, C. D.   Leicestershire

Name: Carl Daniel Crowe
Role: Right-hand bat, off-spin bowler
Born: 25 November 1975, Leicester
Height: 6ft **Weight:** 12st 6lbs
Nickname: Strutter, Sheryl
County debut: 1995
1st-Class catches: 1
Parents: Edward Patrick and Jeannette
Marital status: Single
Family links with cricket: Younger brother has played for Leicestershire U15, U16 and U17 and County Colts. Dad manager of Hinckley Town U15s
Education: Lutterworth High School; Lutterworth Grammar School
Qualifications: 11 GCSEs, 2 A-levels, NCA Senior Coach
Off-season: Coaching in England before Christmas, then going to Melbourne, Australia in the New Year
Overseas tours: Leicestershire U19 to South Africa 1993-94; Leicestershire to Holland 1996

Cricketers particularly admired: Les Taylor, Jeff Baxter, Graham Gooch
Young players to look out for: Ian Cox, members of the Leicestershire U12 squad, Ross Blockley
Other sports followed: Try all sports, 'had a hole in one.' 'Support Leicester at everything and follow Spurs'
Relaxations: Cinema, ten-pin bowling and basic yoga
Extras: Played for Leicestershire U12-U19 and Midlands Schools U14-U19. One of the Cricketers of the Festival at Cambridge U19 Festival 1994
Opinions on cricket: 'If the 2nd XI game mirrored the first-class game, i.e. four-day games, similar pitches etc., younger players may find it easier to play at the highest level.'
Best batting: 9 Leicestershire v Warwickshire, Leicester 1995

1996 Season

	M	Inns	NO	Runs	HS	Avge	100s	50s	Ct	St	O	M	Runs	Wkts	Avge	Best	5wI	10wM
Test																		
All First																		
1-day Int																		
NatWest																		
B & H																		
Sunday	1	0	0	0	0	-	-	-	-	-								

Career Performances

	M	Inns	NO	Runs	HS	Avge	100s	50s	Ct	St	Balls	Runs	Wkts	Avge	Best	5wI	10wM
Test																	
All First	1	2	0	10	9	5.00	-	-	1	-	18	4	0	-	-	-	-
1-day Int																	
NatWest																	
B & H																	
Sunday	1	0	0	0	0	-	-	-	-	-							

23. Who was the highest-placed Englishman in the
1996 first-class bowling averages?

CUNLIFFE, R. J.   Gloucestershire

Name: Robert John Cunliffe
Role: Right-hand bat, cover fielder, occasional wicket-keeper
Born: 8 November 1973, Oxford
Height: 5ft 10in **Weight:** 13st
Nickname: 'Too rude to mention'
County debut: 1993 (one-day), 1994 (first-class)
1st-Class 100s: 2
1st-Class 50s: 4
1st-Class catches: 11
One-Day 100s: 2
Place in batting averages: 214th av. 22.90
Parents: Barry and Janet
Marital status: Engaged to Claire
Family links with cricket: 'Dad played in his younger days for his wife's village team and was groundsman for nine years at Banbury Twenty CC'
Education: Banbury School and Banbury Technical College
Qualifications: 'Not too many'
Off-season: Playing for Richmond CC in Australia
Overseas tours: England U19 to India 1992-93
Overseas teams played for: Richmond City CC, Melbourne 1996-97
Cricketers particularly admired: Robin Smith
Young players to look out for: Michael Vaughan
Other sports followed: Football, squash ('not the best'), 'can't watch any sport'
Injuries: Split index finger on right hand. 'Missed a lot of cricket due to my mum in hospital with a brain haemorrhage'
Relaxations: 'Being with Claire'
Extras: Played in England U19 home series against West Indies in 1993
Opinions on cricket: 'Maybe the 2nd XI games should be four days to get used to first-class cricket.'
Best batting: 190* Gloucestershire v Oxford University, The Parks 1995

---

24. 1996 saw four players from one county scoring double centuries. Who were the players and which county do they represent?

1996 Season

	M	Inns	NO	Runs	HS	Avge	100s	50s	Ct	St	O	M	Runs	Wkts	Avge	Best	5wI	10wM
Test																		
All First	6	11	0	252	82	22.90	-	2	1	-								
1-day Int																		
NatWest	1	1	0	37	37	37.00	-	-	-	-								
B & H	5	5	2	353	137 *	117.66	2	1	1	-								
Sunday	3	3	0	71	52	23.66	-	1	2	-								

Career Performances

	M	Inns	NO	Runs	HS	Avge	100s	50s	Ct	St	Balls		Runs	Wkts	Avge	Best	5wI	10wM
Test																		
All First	20	32	4	1018	190 *	36.35	2	4	11	-								
1-day Int																		
NatWest	3	3	0	77	40	25.66	-	-	1	-								
B & H	5	5	2	353	137 *	117.66	2	1	1	-								
Sunday	5	5	0	103	52	20.60	-	1	2	-								

CURRAN, K. M.　　　　　Northamptonshire

Name: Kevin Malcolm Curran
Role: Right-hand bat, right-arm
fast-medium bowler
Born: 7 September 1959, Rusape, Rhodesia
Height: 6ft 2in **Weight:** 14st
Nickname: KC
County debut: 1985 (Glos),
1991 (Northamptonshire)
County cap: 1985 (Glos),
1992 (Northamptonshire)
One-Day Internationals: 11
1000 runs in a season: 6
50 wickets in a season: 5
1st-Class 50s: 70
1st-Class 100s: 23
1st-Class 5 w. in innings: 15
1st-Class 10 w. in match: 4
1st-Class catches: 171
One-day 100s: 1
One-Day 5 w. in innings: 1
Place in batting averages: 14th av. 59.14 (1995 88th av. 35.95)
Place in bowling averages: 152nd av. 58.27 (1995 85th av. 32.48)

Strike rate: 98.18 (career 52.48)
Parents: Kevin and Sylvia
Wife and date of marriage: Sarah, 5 June 1993
Children: Thomas Kevin, 12 March 1995; Benjamin Jack, 7 June 1996
Family links with cricket: Father played for Rhodesia 1947-54. Cousin Patrick Curran played for Rhodesia 1975
Education: Marandellas High School, Zimbabwe
Qualifications: 6 O-levels, 2 M-levels
Career outside cricket: Tobacco buyer/farmer
Overseas tours: Zimbabwe to Sri Lanka 1982 and 1984, to England 1982 and for World Cup 1983, to Pakistan and India for World Cup 1987
Overseas teams played for: Zimbabwe and Natal 1988-92, Boland 1994-95
Other sports followed: Rugby union
Relaxations: 'Game fishing, especially along the North Natal coast, the Mozambique coast, and Magaruque Island'
Extras: First player to take a Sunday League hat-trick, and score 50 in the same match, Gloucestershire v Warwickshire, Edgbaston 1989. Released by Gloucestershire at end of 1990 after he had completed the season's double of 1000 runs and 50 wickets. Chose to join Northamptonshire for the 1991 season after he had been approached by several counties.
Best batting: 150 Northamptonshire v Leicestershire, Leicester 1996
Best bowling: 7-47 Northamptonshire v Yorkshire, Harrogate 1993

1996 Season

	M	Inns	NO	Runs	HS	Avge	100s	50s	Ct	St	O	M	Runs	Wkts	Avge	Best	5wI	10wM
Test																		
All First	15	28	7	1242	150	59.14	2	8	14	-	180	34	641	11	58.27	3-75	-	-
1-day Int																		
NatWest	2	1	0	26	26	26.00	-	-	-	-	16	3	58	3	19.33	3-44	-	
B & H	7	7	1	143	50	23.83	-	1	1	-	58	4	261	4	65.25	1-20	-	
Sunday	17	16	4	456	92 *	38.00	-	3	5	-	66	1	381	15	25.40	3-16	-	

Career Performances

	M	Inns	NO	Runs	HS	Avge	100s	50s	Ct	St	Balls	Runs	Wkts	Avge	Best	5wI	10wM
Test																	
All First	282	441	74	13690	150	37.30	23	70	171	-	29495	15519	562	27.61	7-47	15	4
1-day Int	11	11	0	287	73	26.09	-	2	1	-	506	398	9	44.22	3-65	-	
NatWest	39	33	7	779	78 *	29.96	-	3	11	-	2027	1150	39	29.48	4-34	-	
B & H	47	42	7	906	57	25.88	-	6	8	-	2262	1564	52	30.07	4-38	-	
Sunday	173	163	35	4129	119 *	32.25	1	23	35	-	5397	4401	160	27.50	5-15	1	

CURTIS, T. S. Worcestershire

Name: Timothy Stephen Curtis
Role: Right-hand bat, leg-spin bowler
Born: 15 January 1960, Chislehurst, Kent
Height: 5ft 11in **Weight:** 11st 10lbs
Nickname: TC, Duracell, Professor
County debut: 1979
County cap: 1984
Benefit: 1994 (£129,501)
Test debut: 1988
Tests: 5
1000 runs in a season: 11
1st-Class 50s: 102
1st-Class 100s: 39
1st-Class 200s: 2
1st-Class catches: 180
One-Day 100s: 6
Place in batting averages: 138th av. 32.82

(1995 64th av. 40.70)
Strike rate: 13.50 (career 81.61)
Parents: Bruce and Betty
Wife and date of marriage: Philippa, 21 September 1985
Children: Jennifer May, 9 February 1991; Andrew Stephen Neild, 17 February 1993
Family links with cricket: Father played good club cricket in Bristol and Stafford
Education: Royal Grammar School, Worcester; Durham University; Cambridge University
Qualifications: 12 O-levels, 4 A-levels, BA (Hons) in English,
PCGE in English and Games
Off-season: Teaching at RGS, Worcester
Overseas tours: NCA U19 tour of Canada 1979; 'Worcestershire to most parts of the
cricketing world'
Cricketers particularly admired: 'So many, but watching Hicky from 22 yards has
been awesome'
Young players to look out for: Vikram Solanki, Reuben Spiring, Phil Weston
Other sports followed: Golf, tennis, squash
Injuries: Age
Relaxations: All sports, novels, family life, food and wine
Extras: Captained Durham University to UAU Championship in 1981. Appointed
county captain in 1992. Worcestershire supporters' Player of the Year 1992. A century
against Durham in 1993 meant that he had scored a century against every other first-
class county. Raised £129,501 from his benefit in 1994. Relinquished the captaincy
during the 1995 season. Retired as Chairman of the PCA as from September 1996
Opinions on cricket: 'Four-day cricket is a big success and better still when the start

moves to Wednesday.'

Best batting: 248 Worcestershire v Somerset, Taunton 1991
Best bowling: 2-17 Worcestershire v Oxford University, The Parks 1991

1996 Season

	M	Inns	NO	Runs	HS	Avge	100s	50s	Ct	St	O	M	Runs	Wkts	Avge	Best	5wI	10wM
Test																		
All First	17	31	2	952	118	32.82	2	5	10	-	4.3	0	18	2	9.00	1-1	-	-
1-day Int																		
NatWest	2	2	0	27	15	13.50	-	-	-	-								
B & H	4	4	0	238	67	59.50	-	3	2	-								
Sunday	7	7	1	197	77	32.83	-	1	2	-								

Career Performances

	M	Inns	NO	Runs	HS	Avge	100s	50s	Ct	St	Balls	Runs	Wkts	Avge	Best	5wI	10wM
Test	5	9	0	140	41	15.55	-	-	3	-	18	7	0	-	-	-	-
All First	324	556	66	20083	248	40.98	39	102	180	-	1061	748	13	57.53	2-17	-	-
1-day Int																	
NatWest	40	39	5	1692	136 *	49.76	4	10	11	-	36	31	2	15.50	1-6	-	
B & H	62	62	5	1936	97	33.96	-	18	14	-	2	4	0	-	-	-	
Sunday	187	181	28	6228	124	40.70	2	53	56	-							

DAKIN, J. M. Leicestershire

Name: Jonathan Michael Dakin
Role: Left-hand bat, right-arm medium-fast bowler,
Born: 28 February 1973, Hitchin, Herts
Height: 6ft 5in **Weight:** 15st 5lb
Nickname: J.D., Sidney
County debut: 1993
1st-Class 100s: 1
1st-Class 50s: 2
1st-Class catches: 6
One-Day 100s: 1
Place in batting averages: (1995 135th av. 29.63)
Strike rate: (career 78.54)
Parents: Fred John and Gloria May
Marital status: Single
Family links with cricket: Brother plays club cricket for Wanderers CC in

South Africa
Education: King Edward VII School, Johannesburg, South Africa
Qualifications: Matriculation
Off-season: Playing cricket in Potchefstroom, South Africa
Overseas tours: Rutland Tourists to Jersey 1992
Overseas teams played for: Wanderers, South Africa, 1986-92; Alberts, South Africa 1993; Kaponga CC, New Zealand 1995-96
Cricketers particularly admired: Phil 'Yogi Bear' Simmons, Vince 'Legend' Wells
Young players to look out for: Darren Maddy, Iain Sutcliffe
Other sports followed: Football (Liverpool), rugby (Leicester Tigers) and golf
Injuries: Broken finger and patella operation, out for nine weeks
Extras: Won three Bain Hogg trophies in four years. Scored 193 against Middlesex in the Bain Hogg in 1996. Won the Gold Award against Durham in the 1996 Benson and Hedges. 'I have no calves'
Best batting: 101* Leicestershire v Nottinghamshire, Leicester 1995
Best bowling: 4-45 Leicestershire v Cambridge University, Fenner's 1993

1996 Season

	M	Inns	NO	Runs	HS	Avge	100s	50s	Ct	St	O	M	Runs	Wkts	Avge	Best	5wI	10wM
Test																		
All First																		
1-day Int																		
NatWest	1	1	0	26	26	26.00	-	-	-	-	12	1	63	1	63.00	1-63	-	
B & H	2	2	1	128	108 *	128.00	1	-	-	-								
Sunday	4	4	0	15	8	3.75	-	-	1	-	2.3	0	32	0	-		-	-

Career Performances

	M	Inns	NO	Runs	HS	Avge	100s	50s	Ct	St	Balls	Runs	Wkts	Avge	Best	5wI	10wM
Test																	
All First	11	17	2	360	101 *	24.00	1	2	6	-	864	490	11	44.54	4-45	-	-
1-day Int																	
NatWest	3	3	0	57	26	19.00	-	-	-	-	144	100	1	100.00	1-63	-	
B & H	3	3	1	136	108 *	68.00	1	-	-	-	12	27	0	-	-	-	
Sunday	37	33	4	346	45	11.93	-	-	9	-	870	860	26	33.07	3-23	-	

25. Which player caused a stir after claiming to be the youngest player to play Test cricket in 1996-97, before the validity of his claim was thrown into doubt?

DALE, A. Glamorgan

Name: Adrian Dale
Role: Right-hand bat, right-arm
medium bowler
Born: 24 October 1968, Germiston,
South Africa
Height: 5ft 11in **Weight:** 11st 10lbs
Nickname: Arthur
County debut: 1989
County cap: 1992
1000 runs in a season: 2
1st-Class 50s: 29
1st-Class 100s: 12
1st-Class 200s: 1
1st-Class 5 w. in innings: 1
1st-Class catches: 53
One-day 100s: 1
One-Day 5 w. in innings: 2
Place in batting averages: 170th av. 28.75
(1995 136th av. 29.61)

Place in bowling averages: 109th av. 39.16
Strike rate: 70.58 (career 71.74)
Parents: John and Maureen
Marital status: Single
Family links with cricket: Father played for Glamorgan 2nd XI and Chepstow CC
Education: Pembroke Primary; Chepstow Comprehensive; Swansea University
Qualifications: 9 O-levels, 3 A-levels, BA (Hons) in Economics
Off-season: Playing club cricket in Auckland for Cornwall CC
Overseas tours: Welsh Schools U16 to Australia 1986-87; Combined Universities to
Barbados 1988-89; Glamorgan to Trinidad 1989-90, to Zimbabwe 1990-91, to Trinidad
1991-92, to Cape Town 1992-93; England A to South Africa 1993-94
Overseas teams played for: Bionics, Zimbabwe 1990-91; Cornwall, New Zealand
1991-93, 1995-96
Cricketers particularly admired: Ian Botham, Michael Holding, Mike Gatting
Young players to look out for: Jason Laney, Alun Evans
Other sports followed: Football (Arsenal), athletics, US basketball, rugby league
(Auckland Warriors and Wales), rugby union (Wales), ice hockey (Cardiff Devils)
Injuries: Broken finger, out for four weeks
Relaxations: Eating out, following other sports, travelling
Extras: Played in successful Combined Universities sides of 1989 and 1990. Only
batsman to score two half-centuries against the West Indies tourists in the same match
in 1991. Took a wicket with his first delivery at Lord's. Recorded Glamorgan's best one-

day bowling figures, 6-22 against Durham 1993. Recorded Glamorgan's highest ever partnership, 425, with Viv Richards against Middlesex, 1993

Opinions on cricket: 'Too much cricket. Too much quantity leads to less quality.'

Best batting: 214* Glamorgan v Middlesex, Cardiff 1993

Best bowling: 6-18 Glamorgan v Warwickshire, Cardiff 1993

1996 Season

	M	Inns	NO	Runs	HS	Avge	100s	50s	Ct	St	O	M	Runs	Wkts	Avge	Best	5wI	10wM
Test																		
All First	15	25	1	690	120	28.75	1	4	7	-	141.1	36	470	12	39.16	4-52	-	-
1-day Int																		
NatWest	1	1	0	40	40	40.00	-	-	1	-	6	0	34	1	34.00	1-34	-	
B & H	5	5	1	130	46	32.50	-	-	2	-	30	3	130	7	18.57	5-41	1	
Sunday	14	14	3	358	65 *	32.54	-	2	1	-	64	0	348	9	38.66	2-32	-	

Career Performances

	M	Inns	NO	Runs	HS	Avge	100s	50s	Ct	St	Balls	Runs	Wkts	Avge	Best	5wI	10wM
Test																	
All First	127	213	19	6269	214 *	32.31	12	29	53	-	9470	5097	132	38.61	6-18	1	-
1-day Int																	
NatWest	20	18	2	443	110	27.68	1	1	6	-	934	630	20	31.50	3-54	-	
B & H	25	24	4	510	53	25.50	-	1	8	-	1020	712	28	25.42	5-41	1	
Sunday	101	86	12	2008	67 *	27.13	-	11	25	-	3154	2862	86	33.27	6-22	1	

26. Who holds the record for the highest Test score batting at No.8, and who were the opponents?

DALEY, J. A.   Durham

Name: James Arthur Daley
Role: Right-hand bat
Born: 24 September 1973, Sunderland
Height: 5ft 11in **Weight:** 12st
Nickname: Bebs, Jonty
County debut: 1992
1st-Class 50s: 13
1st-Class 100s: 1
1st-Class catches: 24
Place in batting averages: 188th av. 26.50
(1995 53rd av. 43.50)
Parents: William and Christine
Marital status: Single
Family links with cricket: Brother played
representative cricket for Durham
Education: Hetton Comprehensive
Qualifications: 5 GCSEs
Career outside cricket: Travel agent
Overseas tours: Durham to Zimbabwe,
1991-92; England U19 to India 1992-93; England XI to Holland 1993
Cricketers particularly admired: David Graveney, Wayne Larkins, Jimmy Adams
Other sports followed: Most sports
Relaxations: Socialising, listening to all types of music
Extras: Scored three centuries in 1991 for MCC Young Cricketers at Lord's. Northern
Electric Foundation for Sport award winner 1992
Best batting: 159* Durham v Hampshire, Portsmouth 1994

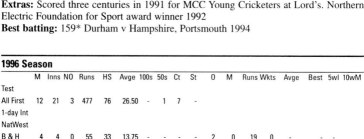

1996 Season

	M	Inns	NO	Runs	HS	Avge	100s	50s	Ct	St	O	M	Runs	Wkts	Avge	Best	5wI	10wM
Test																		
All First	12	21	3	477	76	26.50	-	1	7	-								
1-day Int																		
NatWest																		
B & H	4	4	0	55	33	13.75	-	-	-	-	2	0	19	0	-		-	-
Sunday	5	5	2	104	47	34.66	-	-	2	-	0.1	0	4	0	-		-	-

Career Performances

	M	Inns	NO	Runs	HS	Avge	100s	50s	Ct	St	Balls	Runs	Wkts	Avge	Best	5wI	10wM
Test																	
All First	44	77	8	2178	159 *	31.56	1	13	24	-	12	9	0	-	-	-	-
1-day Int																	
NatWest																	
B & H	6	5	0	72	33	14.40	-	-	-	-	12	19	0	-	-	-	
Sunday	20	18	6	461	98 *	38.41	-	3	5	-	1	4	0	-	-	-	

DALTON, A. J. Glamorgan

Name: Alistair John Dalton
Role: Right-hand bat, right-arm bowler
Born: 27 April 1973, Bridgend
Height: 5ft 8in **Weight:** 11st
Nickname: Ali, Dalts, A.J., Dolly
County debut: 1994
1st-Class 50s: 1
1st-Class catches: 9
Place in batting averages: 186th av. 22.33
(1994 175th av. 23.50)
Parents: John and Christine
Marital status: Single
Family links with cricket: Father captained
Bridgend Town 1st XI for ten years; brother
Simon now plays for the same 1st XI and
used to play for Welsh Schools
Education: Brynteg Comprehensive School;
Millfield School; New College, Cardiff
Qualifications: 8 GCSEs, 3 A-levels, NCA Coach
Career outside cricket: Working for family business
Off-season: Working for father's business DMA Ltd. 'Following Bridgend RFC and
perfecting the "Mike Rayer"'
Overseas tours: Millfield School to Jamaica 1990; Glamorgan Schools to
Singapore/Malaysia 1992; Cardiff Eagles to Cape Town 1994; Glamorgan to Portugal 1994
Overseas teams played for: Paramatta, Sydney 1992-93; Crusaders, Durban 1994-95
Cricketers particularly admired: Tony Cottey, Mark Waugh, Courtney Walsh, Jamie
Bishop, Ollie Slipper, 'my brother Simon', Bobby Shafto
Other sports followed: Rugby (played scrum-half for Millfield 1st XV and follows
Bridgend RFC)
Relaxations: All sports especially rugby, good films, Chinese food, travelling, 'a few
pints with the boys'

Extras: ASW Player of the Month, July 1994. ASW Young Player of the Year, 1994. Glamorgan 2nd XI Player of the Year. ASW Young Player for May and June 1995
Best batting: 51* Glamorgan v South Africans, Pontypridd, 1994

1996 Season

	M	Inns	NO	Runs	HS	Avge	100s	50s	Ct	St	O	M	Runs	Wkts	Avge	Best	5wl	10wM
Test																		
All First	2	3	0	37	17	12.33	-	-	-	-								
1-day Int																		
NatWest																		
B & H																		
Sunday	2	2	0	25	19	12.50	-	-	-	-								

Career Performances

	M	Inns	NO	Runs	HS	Avge	100s	50s	Ct	St	Balls	Runs	Wkts	Avge	Best	5wl	10wM
Test																	
All First	13	23	3	426	51*	21.30	-	1	9	-							
1-day Int																	
NatWest																	
B & H																	
Sunday	2	2	0	25	19	12.50	-	-	-	-							

DAVIES, A. P.   Glamorgan

Name: Andrew Philip Davies
Role: Left-hand bat, right-arm medium-fast bowler
Born: 7 November 1976, Neath
Height: 6ft **Weight:** 12st
County debut: 1995
Strike rate: 156.00 (career 174.00)
Parents: Philip and Anne
Marital status: Single
Family links with cricket: Dad played for Ywysygerwn and B.P. Llandarcy. Mum used to do the teas
Education: Dwr-y-felin Comprehensive School; Christ College, Brecon
Qualifications: 6 GCSEs, 1 A-level
Off-season: Coaching and teaching at Christ College, Brecon
Overseas tours: Wales to Barbados;

Glamorgan to South Africa 1995-96

Overseas teams played for: Marist CC, Whangarei, New Zealand 1995-96

Cricketers particularly admired: Graeme Hick

Young players to look out for: Alun 'face like a clock' Evans – 'hits the ball hard, mainly due to the amount of Big Macs and quarter-pounders he eats'

Other sports followed: Football (had trials at Birmingham City), 'used to be a season ticket holder at Neath RFC, in the days of the great winger Adrian Shaw – he's sadly missed at the Gnoll'

Relaxations: 'Over the last two seasons, my interests have been sadly ruined by the loss of Adrian Shaw on the Neath wing. An influential player whose ability was sorely neglected on the international front'

Extras: Trials at Birmingham City FC. Rugby trials for Wales U17. Welsh U19 Player of the Year 1995

Opinions on cricket: 'Not enough time is actually spent on coaching youngsters, especially in the 2nd XI, because of the amount of cricket played. If a young player has a problem, it is hard to get time to sort the problem out.'

Best batting: 11* Glamorgan v Pakistan, Pontypridd 1996

Best bowling: 1-25 Glamorgan v Oxford University, The Parks 1996

1996 Season

	M	Inns	NO	Runs	HS	Avge	100s	50s	Ct	St	O	M	Runs	Wkts	Avge	Best	5wI	10wM
Test																		
All First	2	2	1	19	11 *	19.00	-	-	-	-	26	5	118	1	118.00	1-25	-	-
1-day Int																		
NatWest																		
B & H																		
Sunday																		

Career Performances

	M	Inns	NO	Runs	HS	Avge	100s	50s	Ct	St	Balls	Runs	Wkts	Avge	Best	5wI	10wM
Test																	
All First	3	2	1	19	11 *	19.00	-	-	-	-	174	135	1	135.00	1-25	-	-
1-day Int																	
NatWest																	
B & H																	
Sunday																	

DAVIES, M. K. Northamptonshire

Name: Michael Kenton Davies
Role: Right-hand bat, slow left-arm bowler
Born: 17 July 1976, Ashby-de-la-Zouch
Height: 6ft **Weight:** 12st
Nickname: Tin Tin, Spacey, Dickie
County debut: No first-team appearance
Parents: Lyndon and Ann
Marital status: Single
Family links with cricket: None
Education: Fairfield Primary School;
Loughborough Grammar School;
Loughborough University
Qualifications: 8 GCSEs and 4 A-levels
Off-season: Studying at university
Cricketers particularly admired:
Phil Tufnell, David Gower
Young players to look out for:
Ben Hollioake, Vikram Solanki, David Sales
Other sports followed: Golf (handicap 8),
football (Derby County) and rugby (Wales and Leicester Tigers)
Relaxations: Clubbing, socialising, sleeping and playing golf
Extras: Leicestershire U19 Player of the Year. 'After leaving school, spent a year travelling around the world and working in a school in Auckland, New Zealand'
Opinions on cricket: '2nd XI games should be increased to four days, and the tea interval should be increased by five or ten minutes.'

DAVIS, R. P. Gloucestershire

Name: Richard Peter Davis
Role: Right-hand bat, slow left-arm bowler
Born: 18 March 1966, Westbrook, Margate
Height: 6ft 4in **Weight:** 14st 4lbs
Nickname: Dicky
County debut: 1986 (Kent), 1994 (Warwickshire), 1996 (Gloucestershire)
County Cap: 1990 (Kent), 1994 (Warwickshire)
50 wickets in a season: 2
1st-Class 50s: 4
1st-Class 5 w. innings: 16
1st-Class 10 w. in a match: 2
1st-Class catches: 146

One-day 5 w. in innings: 1
Place in batting averages: 268th av. 15.40
Place in bowling averages: 130th av. 45.78
Strike rate: 74.43 (career 74.28)
Parents: Brian and Sylvia
Wife and date of marriage: Samantha Jane, 3 March 1990
Family links with cricket: father played club cricket and is an NCA coach; father-in-law, Colin Tomlin, helped with England's fitness training for tours from 1990-93; brother-in-law, Raj Sharma, played for Derbyshire
Education: King Ethelbert's School, Birchington; Thanet Technical College
Qualifications: CSEs, NCA Coaching Certificate
Off-season: Coaching
Overseas tours: Kent Schools to Canada 1983; Kent to Zimbabwe 1992-93; Warwickshire to Zimbabwe 1993-94, to Cape Town 1994-95
Young players to look out for: Vikram Solanki
Other sports followed: Football (Derby County), rugby, squash, golf, badminton
Injuries: Ankle ligaments
Relaxations: Eating out with my wife, Sam, television and reading
Extras: Moved to Warwickshire at the end of the 1993 season after nine years with Kent. Released by Warwickshire at the end of the 1995 season and joined Gloucestershire for the 1996 season
Best batting: 67 Kent v Hampshire, Southampton 1989
Best bowling: 7-64 Kent v Durham, Gateshead Fell 1992

1996 Season

	M	Inns	NO	Runs	HS	Avge	100s	50s	Ct	St	O	M	Runs	Wkts	Avge	Best	5wI	10wM
Test																		
All Firsts	15	22	2	308	43	15.40	-	-	18	-	314.2	70	1053	23	45.78	4-93	-	-
1-day Int																		
NatWest																			
B & H	5	2	0	12	10	6.00	-	-	2	-	41.1	1	194	7	27.71	2-26	-	
Sunday	4	3	1	2	2 *	1.00	-	-	1	-	28	0	179	5	35.80	3-42	-	

Career Performances

	M	Inns	NO	Runs	HS	Avge	100s	50s	Ct	St	Balls	Runs	Wkts	Avge	Best	5wI	10wM
Test																	
All First	160	196	46	2317	67	15.44	-	4	146	-	29552	13936	397	35.10	7-64	16	2
1-day Int																	
NatWest	13	6	1	46	22	9.20	-	-	10	-	729	392	15	26.13	3-19	-	
B & H	23	10	4	57	18 *	9.50	-	-	9	-	1226	828	17	48.70	2-26	-	
Sunday	89	43	17	231	40 *	8.88	-	-	28	-	3392	2629	95	27.67	5-52	1	

DAWOOD, I. Worcestershire

Name: Ismail Dawood
Role: Right-hand bat, wicket-keeper
Born: 23 July 1976, Dewsbury
Nickname: Hectic
County debut: 1994 (Northamptonshire),
1996 (Worcestershire)
1st-Class catches: 3
Parents: Saleem and Rashida
Marital status: Single
Family links with cricket: Grandfather and
father played local league cricket
Education: Batley Grammar School
Qualifications: 8 GCSEs, NCA Coaching
Award
Overseas tours: England U19 to Sri Lanka
1993-94, to West Indies 1994-95
Overseas teams played for: Grafton,
Auckland 1992-93
Cricketers particularly admired:
Mohammed Azharuddin, Allan Border, Ian Healy 'and many others'
Other sports followed: Local soccer team
Relaxations: 'Spending time with family and friends. Eating curries with Michael
Foster'
Extras: Left Northamptonshire at the end of 1995 season and joined Worcestershire in
1996
Opinions on cricket: 'The game should be played in good spirit and enjoyed at all
levels from junior to Test cricket.'
Best batting: 2* Northamptonshire v Somerset, Taunton 1994

1996 Season

	M	Inns	NO	Runs	HS	Avge	100s	50s	Ct	St	O	M	Runs	Wkts	Avge	Best	5wI	10wM
Test																		
All First	1	1	0	1	1	1.00	-	-	3	-								
1-day Int																		
NatWest																		
B & H																		
Sunday																		

Career Performances

	M	Inns	NO	Runs	HS	Avge	100s	50s	Ct	St	Balls	Runs	Wkts	Avge	Best	5wI	10wM
Test																	
All First	2	2	1	3	2*	3.00	-	-	3	-							
1-day Int																	
NatWest																	
B & H																	
Sunday	1	1	0	2	2	2.00	-	-	-	-							

DAWSON, R. I.　　　　　Gloucestershire

Name: Robert Ian Dawson
Role: Right-hand bat, right-arm
medium bowler
Born: 29 March 1970, Exmouth, Devon
Height: 5ft 11in　**Weight:** 12st
Nickname: Daws
County debut: 1991 (one-day),
1992 (first-class)
1000 runs in a season: 1
1st-Class 50s: 11
1st-Class 100s: 2
1st-Class catches: 24
Place in batting averages: 283rd av. 11.75
(1995 173rd av. 23.66)
Parents: Barry and Shirley
Marital status: Single
Family links with cricket: Father and
brother both played club cricket
Education: Millfield School; Newcastle Polytechnic
Qualifications: 8 O-levels, 3 A-levels
Overseas teams played for: Amanzimtoti, South Africa, 1993-94
Cricketers particularly admired: Ian Botham, David Gower, Viv Richards

Other sports followed: Football mainly and most other sports
Relaxations: 'Watching most sports and going down the pub for a pint'
Extras: Played in NatWest for Devon (from 1988), before joining Gloucestershire
Best batting: 127* Gloucestershire v Cambridge University, Bristol 1994
Best bowling: 2-38 Gloucestershire v Derbyshire, Chesterfield 1994

1996 Season

	M	Inns	NO	Runs	HS	Avge	100s	50s	Ct	St	O	M	Runs	Wkts	Avge	Best	5wI	10wM
Test																		
All First	7	13	1	141	21	11.75	-	-	-	-	2.2	0	7	1	7.00	1-3	-	-
1-day Int																		
NatWest	1	1	0	0	0	0.00	-	-	-	-								
B & H	4	4	0	73	33	18.25	-	-	-	-								
Sunday	15	15	1	458	85	32.71	-	4	-	-	1	0	8	0	-		-	-

Career Performances

	M	Inns	NO	Runs	HS	Avge	100s	50s	Ct	St	Balls	Runs	Wkts	Avge	Best	5wI	10wM
Test																	
All First	47	84	7	2046	127 *	26.57	2	11	24	-	290	110	3	36.66	2-38	-	-
1-day Int																	
NatWest	5	4	0	73	60	18.25	-	1	-	-	24	37	1	37.00	1-37	-	
B & H	10	10	0	220	38	22.00	-	-	1	-	18	12	0	-		-	
Sunday	61	55	5	1022	85	20.44	-	4	11	-	86	95	1	95.00	1-19	-	

27. Who was awarded his county cap before England A's
game against Victoria in 1996-97?

DEAN, K. J.   Derbyshire

Name: Kevin James Dean
Role: Left-hand bat, left-arm medium-fast bowler
Born: 16 October 1975, Derby
Height: 6ft 5in **Weight:** 13st 7lbs
Nickname: Deane, Baby Giraffe
County debut: 1996
1st-Class catches: 1
Place in batting averages: 315th av. 4.71
Place in bowling averages: 57th av. 29.43
Strike rate: (career 54.06)
Parents: Kenneth and Dorothy
Marital status: Engaged to Clare
Family links with cricket: None
Education: Waterhouses First School; Leek High School; Leek College
Qualifications: 8 GCSEs, 3 A-levels, 1 AS-level

Career outside cricket: Deputy manager for Ladbrokes
Off-season: Going to Adelaide to play for Sturt
Overseas teams played for: Sturt CC, Adelaide 1996-97
Cricketers particularly admired: Dominic Cork, Wasim Akram, Courtney Walsh
Young players to look out for: Andrew Harris, Vikram Solanki
Other sports followed: Football (Derby County), golf, tennis, horse racing
Injuries: Broken finger, missed two weeks
Relaxations: Horse racing, golf, going to cinema
Extras: A member of the Staffordshire U16 Texaco winning team
Opinions on cricket: 'Come and enjoy Derbyshire's famous lunches and teas.'
Best batting: 12 Derbyshire v Worcestershire, Chesterfield 1996
Best bowling: 3-47 Derbyshire v Nottinghamshire, Derby 1996

1996 Season

	M	Inns	NO	Runs	HS	Avge	100s	50s	Ct	St	O	M	Runs	Wkts	Avge	Best	5wl	10wM
Test																		
All First	8	8	1	33	12	4.71	-	-	1	-	144.1	32	471	16	29.43	3-47	-	-
1-day Int																		
NatWest	3	1	1	0	0 *	-	-	-	1	-	28	1	165	5	33.00	3-52	-	
B & H																		
Sunday	12	1	1	8	8 *	-	-	-	4	-	77	2	359	13	27.61	5-32	1	

Career Performances

	M	Inns	NO	Runs	HS	Avge	100s	50s	Ct	St	Balls	Runs	Wkts	Avge	Best	5wI	10wM
Test																	
All First	8	8	1	33	12	4.71	-	-	1	-	865	471	16	29.43	3-47	-	-
1-day Int																	
NatWest	3	1	1	0	0 *	-	-	-	1	-	168	165	5	33.00	3-52	-	
B & H																	
Sunday	12	1	1	8	8 *	-	-	-	4	-	462	359	13	27.61	5-32	1	

DEFREITAS, P. A. J.   Derbyshire

Name: Phillip Anthony Jason DeFreitas
Role: Right-hand bat, right-arm fast bowler
Born: 18 February 1966, Scotts Head, Dominica
Height: 6ft **Weight:** 13st 7lbs
Nickname: Daffy, Lunchy
County debut: 1985 (Leics), 1989 (Lancs), 1994 (Derbys)
County cap: 1986 (Leics), 1989 (Lancs), 1994 (Derbys)
Test debut: 1986-87
Tests: 44
One-Day Internationals: 101
50 wickets in a season: 9
1st-Class 50s: 35
1st-Class 100s: 6
1st-Class 5 w. in innings: 42
1st-Class 10 w. in match: 3
1st-Class catches: 91
One-Day 5 w. in innings: 6
Place in batting averages: 246th av. 17.90 (1995 200th av. 20.60)
Place in bowling averages: 32nd av. 26.35 (1995 64th av. 29.18)
Strike rate: 51.04 (career 57.61)
Parents: Sybil and Martin
Wife and date of marriage: Nicola, 10 December 1990
Children: Alexandra Elizabeth Jane, 5 August 1991
Family links with cricket: Father played in Windward Islands. All six brothers play
Education: Willesden High School
Qualifications: 2 O-levels
Overseas tours: England YC to West Indies 1984-85; England to Australia 1986-87, to Pakistan, Australia and New Zealand 1987-88, to India and West Indies 1989-90, to

Australia 1990-91, to New Zealand 1991-92, to India and Sri Lanka 1992-93, to Australia 1994-95, to South Africa 1995-96, to India and Pakistan (World Cup) 1995-96
Overseas teams played for: Port Adelaide, South Australia 1985; Mossman, Sydney 1988; Boland, South Africa 1993-94, 1995-96
Cricketers particularly admired: Ian Botham, Graham Gooch, Geoff Boycott, Mike Gatting
Other sports followed: Football (Manchester City) and rugby league (Warrington)
Relaxations: 'Golf, gardening, visiting stately homes, spending spare time with wife and daughter Alexandra'
Extras: Left Leicestershire and joined Lancashire at end of 1988 season. Originally agreed to join unofficial English tour of South Africa 1989-90, but withdrew under pressure. Man of the Match in 1990 NatWest Trophy final. One of *Wisden*'s Five Cricketers of the Year 1992. Man of the Tournament in the Hong Kong Sixes 1993. Left Lancashire at the end of the 1993 season. Player of the Series against New Zealand 1994. He was called up to the England one-day squad in South Africa after spending the winter with Boland and went on to play in the World Cup
Best batting: 113 Leicestershire v Nottinghamshire, Worksop 1988
Best bowling: 7-21 Lancashire v Middlesex, Lord's 1989

1996 Season

	M	Inns	NO	Runs	HS	Avge	100s	50s	Ct	St	O	M	Runs	Wkts	Avge	Best	5wI	10wM
Test																		
All First	14	22	0	394	60	17.90	-	1	12	-	544.3	106	1687	64	26.35	7-101	4	-
1-day Int																		
NatWest	3	2	1	40	23 *	40.00	-	-	1	-	36	9	96	4	24.00	3-31	-	
B & H	5	4	0	68	23	17.00	-	-	-	-	30	3	135	5	27.00	2-20	-	
Sunday	14	12	4	342	72 *	42.75	-	3	4	-	71.4	5	406	9	45.11	3-38	-	

Career Performances

	M	Inns	NO	Runs	HS	Avge	100s	50s	Ct	St	Balls	Runs	Wkts	Avge	Best	5wI	10wM
Test	44	68	5	934	88	14.82	-	4	14	-	9838	4700	140	33.57	7-70	4	-
All First	254	361	34	7140	113	21.83	6	36	91	-	48911	23806	849	28.04	7-21	42	3
1-day Int	101	66	23	690	67	16.04	-	1	26	-	5610	3693	115	32.11	4-35	-	
NatWest	29	20	4	273	69	17.06	-	1	5	-	1829	874	46	19.00	5-13	4	
B & H	50	33	6	549	75 *	20.33	-	2	13	-	2851	1596	76	21.00	5-16	1	
Sunday	142	103	21	1552	72 *	18.92	-	3	25	-	5716	4269	162	26.35	5-26	1	

28. Which former Australian Test player was appointed coach of New Zealand in 1996-97?

Name: Nicholas Alexander Derbyshire
Role: Right-hand bat, right-arm
fast-medium bowler
Born: 11 September 1970, Ramsbottom
Height: 6ft **Weight:** 13st
Nickname: Derbs, Nifty, Trent
County debut: 1994 (Lancashire),
1995 (Essex)
1st-Class catches: 2
Strike rate: 120.00 (career 102.00)
Parents: Desmond and Pauline
Marital status: Single
Family links with cricket: None
Education: Ampleforth College;
University of London
Qualifications: 4 A-levels, BA (Hons)
Career outside cricket: None
Off-season: Playing for Manly,
Sydney, Australia

Overseas tours:
Lancashire to Johannesburg 1991-92
Overseas teams played for: DHS Old Boys, South Africa 1992-93;
Manly, Sydney 1994-96
Cricketers particularly admired: Dennis Lillee, Michael Holding
Other sports followed: Rugby, skiing
Relaxations: 'Chicago Rock Cafe, Chelmsford. Travelling globally'
Extras: Released by Essex at the end of the 1996 season
Opinions on cricket: 'Too much cricket – other countries such as South Africa or Australia play far less and, therefore, are totally ready to play – no niggles, aches and pains or tiredness. There is no sense of monotony for them, whereas in our game it is a perpetual problem, leading to mediocrity on the field.'
Best batting: 17 Essex v Durham, Chelmsford 1995
Best bowling: 1-18 Essex v Cambridge University, Fenner's 1994

29. Who won the one-day Titan Cup in November 1996
and who did they defeat in the final?

1996 Season

	M	Inns	NO	Runs	HS	Avge	100s	50s	Ct	St	O	M	Runs	Wkts	Avge	Best	5wI	10wM
Test																		
All First	1	0	0	0	0	-	-	-	2	-	20	2	87	1	87.00	1-67	-	-
1-day Int																		
NatWest																		
B & H																		
Sunday																		

Career Performances

	M	Inns	NO	Runs	HS	Avge	100s	50s	Ct	St	Balls	Runs	Wkts	Avge	Best	5wI	10wM
Test																	
All First	5	5	1	52	17	13.00	-	-	2	-	510	303	5	60.60	1-18	-	-
1-day Int																	
NatWest																	
B & H	1	0	0	0	0	-	-	-	-	-							
Sunday																	

DIBDEN, R.R.   Hampshire

Name: Richard Rockley Dibden
Role: Right-hand bat, right-arm off-spin bowler
Born: 29 January 1975, Southampton
Height: 6ft **Weight:** 11st 7lbs
Nickname: Dibbers, Rocky, The Vicar
County debut: 1995
Strike rate: 108.00 (career 104.37)
Parents: Keith and Nancy
Marital status: Single
Family links with cricket: 'Dad played competitive club cricket'
Education: Mountbatten School, Romsey; Loughborough University
Qualifications: 10 GCSEs, 4 A-levels, degree ('hopefully 2:1'), NCA coaching award
Career outside cricket: Student
Off-season: 'University for now. Tours to South Africa. Australia later'
Overseas tours: Hampshire 2nd XI to Denmark 1996
Overseas teams played for: Techs, South Africa 1994
Cricketers particularly admired: David Gower, Malcolm Marshall

Young players to look out for: Gul Khan, David Sales
Other sports followed: Football (Southampton FC –'European Champions in the year 2005')
Relaxations: 'Pint of Guinness with the lads' and golf
Extras: *Daily Telegraph* Under-15 Bowling Award winner
Opinions on cricket: 'Tea should be extended to thirty minutes. Great idea to have Academy-type tour during the winter for future England players.'
Best batting: 1 British Universities v India, Fenner's 1996
Best bowling: 2-36 Hampshire v Yorkshire, Scarborough 1995

1996 Season

	M	Inns	NO	Runs	HS	Avge	100s	50s	Ct	St	O	M	Runs	Wkts	Avge	Best	5wI	10wM
Test																		
All First	1	1	0	1	1	1.00	-	-	-	-	36	1	164	2	82.00	2-148	-	-
1-day Int																		
NatWest																		
B & H																		
Sunday																		

Career Performances

	M	Inns	NO	Runs	HS	Avge	100s	50s	Ct	St	Balls	Runs	Wkts	Avge	Best	5wI	10wM
Test																	
All First	5	8	2	1	1	0.16	-	-	-	-	835	592	8	74.00	2-36	-	-
1-day Int																	
NatWest																	
B & H																	
Sunday																	

DIMOND, M. Somerset

Name: Matthew Dimond
Role: Right-hand bat, right-arm fast bowler
Born: 24 September 1975, Taunton
Height: 6ft 1in **Weight:** 12st
Nickname: Dougie Howser MD, Dominic
County debut: 1994
1st-Class catches: 4
Parents: Roger and Gill
Marital status: Single
Family links with cricket: Father and brother play for local club
Education: Castle School, Taunton; Richard Huish Sixth Form College, Taunton
Qualifications: 8 GCSEs, 3 A-levels

Off-season: Working as a sales rep for Shell
Overseas tours: West of England U15 to Trinidad and Tobago, 1991-92; Somerset Youth to Holland, 1992; England U19 to West Indies 1994-95
Cricketers particularly admired: Allan Donald, Andy Caddick, Graham Gooch
Young players to look out for: Chris Silverwood, Andrew Harris, Owais Shah
Other sports followed: Football (Yeovil Town and Southampton), golf, American football (Kansas City)
Injuries: Knee ligament damage, out for four weeks
Relaxations: 'Spending time with my girlfriend, Rachel, enjoying nights out with my college friends, IB, JB and AW'
Opinions on cricket: 'I feel that all 2nd XI games should be played on county grounds and treated in the same way as a first-class game – by reducing the overs from 110 to 100/104 in a day.'
Best batting: 26 Somerset v Derbyshire, Derby 1995
Best bowling: 4-73 Somerset v Yorkshire, Bradford 1994

1996 Season

	M	Inns	NO	Runs	HS	Avge	100s	50s	Ct	St	O	M	Runs	Wkts	Avge	Best	5wl	10wM
Test																		
All First																		
1-day Int																		
NatWest																		
B & H	1	0	0	0	0	-	-	-	-	-	3	0	26	0	-		-	-
Sunday																		

Career Performances

	M	Inns	NO	Runs	HS	Avge	100s	50s	Ct	St	Balls	Runs	Wkts	Avge	Best	5wl	10wM
Test																	
All First	4	4	1	67	26	22.33	-	-	4	-	417	286	6	47.66	4-73	-	-
1-day Int																	
NatWest																	
B & H	1	0	0	0	0	-	-	-	-	-	18	26	0	-		-	-
Sunday	3	0	0	0	0	-	-	-	-	-	60	76	0	-		-	-

DOBSON, A. M.　　　Northamptonshire

Name: Andrew Michael Dobson
Role: Left-hand bat, right-hand medium-fast
bowler
Born: 6 April 1980, Scunthorpe
Height: 6ft **Weight:** 11st 11lbs
County debut: No first-team appearance
Nickname: Dobbo
Parents: David and Susan
Marital status: Single
Family links with cricket: 'My father played
second-class cricket for a while and brother
plays to a high level'
Education: Bottesford School; Frederick
Gough Comprehensive; Oundle School
Qualifications: 10 GCSEs, NCA coaching
award
Off-season: At school
Cricketers particularly admired: Ian
Botham, Richard Hadlee, Nasser Hussain
Young players to look out for: Joe Tucker
Other sports followed: Football (Tottenham Hotspur and Scunthorpe United) and
rugby (Northampton Saints)
Relaxations: Playing other sports, listening to music, spending time with friends
Extras: Played for England at U14, U15 and U17 level. Was the best bowler in North
region at U15 level in 1995
Opinions on cricket: 'The game is possibly a little too sedate. It does not have
enough competition, publicity or marketing.'

D'OLIVEIRA, D. B.　　　Worcestershire

Name: Damian Basil D'Oliveira
Role: Right-hand bat, off-spin bowler, slip or boundary fielder
Born: 19 October 1960, Cape Town,
South Africa
Height: 'half an inch taller than Steve Rhodes' **Weight:** 11st 10lbs
Nickname: Dolly
County debut: 1982
County cap: 1985
Benefit: 1993 (£153,030 in joint benefit with Martin Weston)

1000 runs in a season: 4
1st-Class 50s: 46
1st-Class 100s: 10
1st-Class 200s: 1
1st-Class catches: 205
One-Day 100s: 1
Place in batting averages: (1993 186th av. 21.37)
Strike rate: (career 81.61)
Parents: Basil and Naomi
Wife and date of marriage: Tracey Michele, 26 September 1983
Children: Marcus Damian, 27 April 1986; Dominic James, 29 April 1988; Brett Louis, 28 February 1992
Family links with cricket: Father played for Worcestershire and England
Education: St George's RC Primary School; Blessed Edward Oldcorne Secondary School
Qualifications: 3 O-levels, 5 CSEs, advanced coach
Overseas tours: English Counties to Zimbabwe 1984-85
Overseas teams played for: West Perth, Australia 1980-81; East Christchurch, Shirley 1982-83, 1983-84
Cricketers particularly admired: Greg Chappell, Viv Richards, Dennis Lillee, Malcolm Marshall, Richard Hadlee
Other sports followed: 'Most sport, but not horse racing, also follow Manchester City because father supports United'
Relaxations: Watching films, television, eating out, and playing with the kids
Extras: Captains the Second XI and is Worcestershire's official coach
Best batting: 237 Worcestershire v Oxford University, The Parks 1991
Best bowling: 4-67 Worcestershire v Oxford University, Worcester 1994

1996 Season (did not make any first-class or one-day appearances)

Career Performances

	M	Inns	NO	Runs	HS	Avge	100s	50s	Ct	St	Balls	Runs	Wkts	Avge	Best	5wI	10wM
Test																	
All First	234	366	22	9504	237	27.62	10	46	205	-	4489	2479	55	45.07	4-67	-	-
1-day Int																	
NatWest	27	26	4	588	99	26.72	-	3	3	-	264	155	8	19.37	2-17	-	
B & H	51	46	4	818	66	19.47	-	4	20	-	234	150	5	30.00	3-12	-	
Sunday	175	154	17	3210	103	23.43	1	11	44	-	360	323	11	29.36	3-23	-	

DONALD, A. A.   Warwickshire

Name: Allan Anthony Donald
Role: Right-hand bat, right-arm fast bowler
Born: 20 October 1966, Bloemfontein, South Africa
Height: 6ft 3in **Weight:** 14st
County debut: 1987
County cap: 1989
Test debut: 1991-92
Tests: 25
One-Day Internationals: 61
50 wickets in a season: 4
1st-Class 5 w. in innings: 46
1st-Class 10 w. in match: 7
1st-Class catches: 84
One-Day 5 w. in innings: 6
Place in batting averages: 229th av. 16.07
Place in bowling averages: 1st av. 16.07
(1994 68th av. 31.00)
Strike rate: (career 48.32)
Parents: Stuart and Francine
Wife and date of marriage: Tina, 21 September 1991
Family links with cricket: Father and uncle played club cricket
Education: Grey College High School; Technical High School, Bloemfontein
Qualifications: Matriculation
Off-season: Playing for South Africa
Overseas tours: South Africa to India 1991-92, to Australia and New Zealand (World Cup) 1991-92, to West Indies 1991-92, to Sri Lanka 1992-93, to Australia 1992-93, to England 1994, to New Zealand 1994-95, to Zimbabwe 1995-96, to India and Pakistan (World Cup) 1995-96, to India 1996-97
Overseas teams played for: Orange Free State, South Africa 1985-96
Cricketers particularly admired: Richard Hadlee, Malcolm Marshall, Gladstone Small, Andy Lloyd, Eddie Barlow
Other sports followed: Rugby, golf, tennis
Relaxations: 'Listening to music, having a barbecue, playing golf and having a few beers with my friends'
Extras: Played for South African XI v Australian XI in 1986-87 and v English XI in 1989-90. Retained by Warwickshire for 1991 season ahead of Tom Moody. Toured with South Africa on first-ever visit to India and to West Indies in 1991-92. One of *Wisden*'s Five Cricketers of the Year 1992. Accepted the appointment of fitness coach for Warwickshire for the 1996 season. Took his 100th Test wicket against England in Johannesburg 1995-96. Voted Man of the Series against England finishing with 19

wickets at an average of 26.15. Back for Warwickshire in 1997 after spending a year as fitness coach
Best batting: 46* Orange Free State v Western Province, Cape Town 1990-91
Best bowling: 8-37 Orange Free State v Transvaal, Johannesburg 1986-87

1996 Season (did not make any first-class or one-day appearances)

Career Performances

	M	Inns	NO	Runs	HS	Avge	100s	50s	Ct	St	Balls	Runs	Wkts	Avge	Best	5wl	10wM
Test	25	32	17	233	33	15.53	-	-	6	-	5781	2836	114	24.87	8-71	6	2
All First	221	252	99	1872	46 *	12.23	-	-	86	-	40445	19369	837	23.14	8-37	46	7
1-day Int	50	17	9	29	7 *	3.62	-	-	5	-	2660	1764	67	26.32	5-29	1	
NatWest	24	7	4	28	14 *	9.33	-	-	3	-	1516	800	58	13.79	5-12	4	
B & H	20	11	5	59	23 *	9.83	-	-	3	-	1201	837	30	27.90	4-28	-	
Sunday	57	22	10	134	18 *	11.16	-	-	12	-	2594	1738	72	24.13	6-15	1	

DOWMAN, M. P.   Nottinghamshire

Name: Matthew Peter Dowman
Role: Left-hand bat, right-arm medium bowler
Born: 10 May 1974, Grantham, Lincs
Height: 5ft 10in **Weight:** 11st
Nickname: Doomer, Rid Rod
County debut: 1993 (one-day), 1994 (first-class)
1st-Class 50s: 2
1st-Class 100s: 3
1st-Class catches: 11
Place in batting averages: 203rd av. 24.07 (1995 99th av. 34.25)
Strike rate: 108.00 (career 159.00)
Parents: Clive Stuart and Jackie Anne
Marital status: Single
Family links with cricket: Dad played for Grantham Town. Three brothers also play for Grantham, two of them representing Lincolnshire Schools and Lincolnshire U19
Education: St Hugh's Comprehensive; Grantham College
Qualifications: Senior coach
Off-season: Having a holiday
Overseas tours: England U19 to India 1992-93; Lincolnshire U16 to Zimbabwe 1988-89; Nottinghamshire to Cape Town 1992-93; also to Guernsey for Tim Robinson's

benefit 1992

Overseas teams played for: South Burwon, Geelong, Melbourne 1995-96

Cricketers particularly admired: Robin Smith, Mike Gatting, Malcolm Marshall, Jimmy Adams

Young players to look out for: Owais Shah, Noel Gie

Other sports followed: Golf, 'follow Notts Forest and County and Lincoln City'

Injuries: Side strain, out for two weeks

Relaxations: Watching films, playing golf, listening to music

Extras: Played for England U19 in home series against West Indies in 1993, scoring 267 in second 'Test'. Played in winning Midlands team at ESCA Festival 1989. Most runs in a season for Lincolnshire Schools and holds record for most runs in Lincolnshire Schools career

Best batting: 107 Nottinghamshire v Oxford University, The Parks 1995
107 Nottinghamshire v Surrey, Trent Bridge 1996

Best bowling: 2-43 Nottinghamshire v Leicestershire, Trent Bridge 1996

1996 Season

	M	Inns	NO	Runs	HS	Avge	100s	50s	Ct	St	O	M	Runs	Wkts	Avge	Best	5wI	10wM
Test																		
All First	9	14	0	337	107	24.07	1	-	4	-	36	10	122	2	61.00	2-43	-	-
1-day Int																		
NatWest																		
B & H	3	2	1	33	19 *	33.00	-	-	1	-	19.2	1	86	5	17.20	3-21	-	
Sunday	11	11	1	254	74 *	25.40	-	1	2	-	27	1	172	5	34.40	2-34	-	

Career Performances

	M	Inns	NO	Runs	HS	Avge	100s	50s	Ct	St	Balls	Runs	Wkts	Avge	Best	5wI	10wM
Test																	
All First	21	37	2	996	107	28.45	3	2	11	-	318	197	2	98.50	2-43	-	-
1-day Int																	
NatWest																	
B & H	7	4	2	39	19 *	19.50	-	-	3	-	116	86	5	17.20	3-21	-	
Sunday	24	24	2	416	74 *	18.90	-	2	5	-	264	270	7	38.57	2-34	-	

DRAKES, V. C. — Sussex

Name: Vasbert Conniel Drakes

Role: Right-hand bat, right-arm fast bowler

Born: 5 August 1969, St Michael's, Barbados

Height: 6ft 2in **Weight:** 12st

County debut: 1996

One-day Internationals: 5

1st-Class 50s: 6
1st-Class 100s: 4
1st-Class catches: 8
1st-Class 5 w. innings: 5
One-Day 5 w. in innings: 1
Place in batting averages: 183rd av. 27.41
(1995 255th av. 14.75)
Place in bowling averages: 83rd av. 30.16
(1995 29th av. 25.00)
Strike rate: 54.54 (career 50.47)
Parents: Leon and Caroline
Marital status: Engaged
Family links with cricket: 'Sir Francis
Drake is the famous bowler in the family –
the only bowler to receive a knighthood.
Introduced cricket to Barbados on an away
day'

Education: St Lucy Secondary and College
School, Barbados
Qualifications: NCA Coach
Career outside cricket: Electrician
Off-season: Playing in South Africa for Border
Overseas tours: Barbados U19 to UK 1987; Barbados U21 to UK 1990; Barbados to
South Africa 1992; West Indies to England 1995
Overseas teams played for: Barbados 1991-95; Border, South Africa 1996-97
Cricketers particularly admired: Desmond Haynes, Malcolm Marshall 'and all
successful fast bowlers throughout the world'
Young players to look out for: Ben Hurley (Barbados) and Danny Law
Other sports followed: Tennis, golf, basketball, football (Arsenal) and volleyball
Relaxations: Listening to music, 'spending time with Mrs Washing-up'
Extras: Was called up to the West Indies squad as a replacement for Winston Benjamin
on the 1995 tour to England. Played for West Indies in one-day international series
against Australia in 1994-95. Once took 9 for 2 for Lamhey CC
Opinions on cricket: 'Too many wickets are prepared for batsmen. Make the four-day
game more interesting and more competitive and have less cricket so that the players
would be more enthusiastic all season.'
Best batting: 180* Barbados v Leeward Islands, Anguilla 1994-95
Best bowling: 7-47 Barbados v Guyana, Bridgetown 1994-95

---

30. Name the four current players who have scored a first-class
century against all counties bar their own?

1996 Season

	M	Inns	NO	Runs	HS	Avge	100s	50s	Ct	St	O	M	Runs	Wkts	Avge	Best	5wI	10wM
Test																		
All First	15	27	3	649	145 *	27.04	2	4	1	-	454.3	79	1675	50	33.50	5-47	2	-
1-day Int																		
NatWest	3	3	1	89	35	44.50	-	-	-	-	30.3	5	102	6	17.00	2-19	-	
B & H	4	3	1	55	26	27.50	-	-	-	-	35	6	143	7	20.42	5-19	1	
Sunday	14	12	2	165	37	16.50	-	-	2	-	103.2	3	580	17	34.11	4-50	-	

Career Performances

	M	Inns	NO	Runs	HS	Avge	100s	50s	Ct	St	Balls	Runs	Wkts	Avge	Best	5wI	10wM
Test																	
All First	46	74	12	1700	180 *	27.41	4	6	8	-	7268	4344	144	30.16	7-47	5	-
1-day Int	5	2	0	25	16	12.50	-	-	1	-	239	204	3	68.00	1-36	-	
NatWest	3	3	1	89	35	44.50	-	-	-	-	183	102	6	17.00	2-19	-	
B & H	4	3	1	55	26	27.50	-	-	-	-	210	143	7	20.42	5-19	1	
Sunday	14	12	2	165	37	16.50	-	-	2	-	620	580	17	34.11	4-50	-	

DUTCH, K. P.   Middlesex

Name: Keith Peter Dutch
Role: Right-hand bat, off-spin bowler
Born: 21 March 1973, Harrow, Middlesex
Height: 5ft 9in **Weight:** 11st 6lbs
Nickname: Dutchy, Double, Zoro
County debut: 1993
1st-Class catches: 6
Strike rate: 46.00 (career 84.00)
Parents: Alan and Ann
Marital status: Single
Family links with cricket: Father is a qualified coach
Education: Nower Hill High School, Pinner; Weald College, Harrow
Qualifications: 5 GCSEs and 1 AS-level
Off-season: 'Looking to go abroad for a short time. Working for EMP Publishing on *Ian Botham's definitive guide to The Ashes 1997*'
Overseas teams played for: Worcester United, South Africa 1992-93; Geelong City, Australia, 1994
Cricketers particularly admired: Mark Ramprakash, John Emburey

Young players to look out for: Owais Shah, David Nash, Stephen Peters
Other sports followed: Football (Arsenal FC)
Relaxations: Music, pubs, clubbing
Extras: On MCC groundstaff for one year before becoming a contracted player. Rapid Cricketline 2nd XI Player of the Year 1993, Middlesex 2nd XI Player of the Year 1995. In 1996 scored over 1,000 2nd XI Championship runs and took 65 wickets. During this time he achieved highest-ever batting total and bowling figures by a Middlesex player in the history of the 2nd XI Championship with 261 against Somerset and 15 for 157 against Leicestershire – each was the fourth highest in the championship record books
Opinions on cricket: '2nd XI games should be over four days and the one-day matches should be 50 overs. Could the first-class championship be split into two divisions?'
Best batting: 27 Middlesex v Nottinghamshire, Trent Bridge 1996
Best bowling: 3-25 Middlesex v Somerset, Uxbridge 1996

1996 Season

	M	Inns	NO	Runs	HS	Avge	100s	50s	Ct	St	O	M	Runs	Wkts	Avge	Best	5wI	10wM
Test																		
All First	3	4	0	39	27	9.75	-	-	2	-	23	4	85	3	28.33	3-25	-	-
1-day Int																		
NatWest																		
B & H	1	1	0	13	13	13.00	-	-	-	-	5	0	33	0	-		-	-
Sunday	9	8	1	34	12	4.85	-	-	4	-	26.1	0	149	7	21.28	3-10	-	

Career Performances

	M	Inns	NO	Runs	HS	Avge	100s	50s	Ct	St	Balls	Runs	Wkts	Avge	Best	5wI	10wM
Test																	
All First	5	4	0	39	27	9.75	-	-	6	-	252	127	3	42.33	3-25	-	-
1-day Int																	
NatWest																	
B & H	1	1	0	13	13	13.00	-	-	-	-	30	33	0	-		-	-
Sunday	12	10	2	67	21 *	8.37	-	-	5	-	229	206	7	29.42	3-10	-	

EALHAM, M. A.   Kent

Name: Mark Alan Ealham
Role: Right-hand bat, right-arm
medium bowler
Born: 27 August 1969, Willesborough, Kent
Height: 5ft 10in **Weight:** 13st 9lbs
Nickname: Ealy, Skater
County debut: 1989
County cap: 1992
Test debut: 1996
Tests: 2
One-Day Internationals: 2
1st-Class 50s: 25
1st-Class 100s: 1
1st-Class 5 w. in innings: 8
1st-Class catches: 32
One-Day 5 w. in innings: 1
One-Day 100s: 1
Place in batting averages: 141st av. 32.52
(1995 134th av. 29.70)

Place in bowling averages: 9th av. 21.17 (1995 113th av. 38.36)
Strike rate: 51.27 (career 59.64)
Parents: Alan and Sue
Wife and date of marriage: Kirsty, 24 February 1996
Family links with cricket: Father played county cricket for Kent
Education: Stour Valley Secondary School
Qualifications: 9 CSEs
Off-season: England A tour to Australia
Overseas tours: England A to Australia 1996-97
Overseas teams played for: South Perth, Australia 1992-93; University, Perth,
Australia 1993-94
Cricketers particularly admired: Ian Botham, Viv Richards, Robin Smith, Paul
Blackmore and Albert 'for his F and G'
Other sports followed: Football (Manchester United) and most other sports
Injuries: Rib muscle strain, missed four weeks
Relaxations: Playing golf and snooker, watching films
Extras: Scored fastest Sunday League century off 44 balls. Made his Test debut against
India in the third Test at Trent Bridge in 1996
Best batting: 121 Kent v Nottinghamshire, Trent Bridge 1995
Best bowling: 8-36 Kent v Warwickshire, Edgbaston 1996

1996 Season

	M	Inns	NO	Runs	HS	Avge	100s	50s	Ct	St	O	M	Runs	Wkts	Avge	Best	5wI	10wM
Test	2	3	0	81	51	27.00	-	1	1	-	80	22	192	7	27.42	4-21	-	-
All First	14	23	4	618	74	32.52	-	5	7	-	401.4	130	995	47	21.17	8-36	3	1
1-day Int	2	1	0	40	40	40.00	-	-	-	-	6	0	23	0	-		-	-
NatWest	2	2	0	61	51	30.50	-	1	1	-	20	3	46	3	15.33	2-11	-	
B & H	6	6	1	211	75	42.20	-	2	-	-	51	0	236	10	23.60	4-50	-	
Sunday	11	11	2	303	89*	33.66	-	4	1	-	72	3	363	5	72.60	3-21	-	

Career Performances

	M	Inns	NO	Runs	HS	Avge	100s	50s	Ct	St	Balls	Runs	Wkts	Avge	Best	5wI	10wM
Test	2	3	0	81	51	27.00	-	1	1	-	480	192	7	27.42	4-21	-	-
All First	85	137	18	3497	121	29.38	1	25	32	-	11572	5696	194	29.36	8-36	8	1
1-day Int	2	1	0	40	40	40.00	-	-	-	-	36	23	0	-		-	-
NatWest	13	13	4	252	58*	28.00	-	2	4	-	695	342	15	22.80	4-10	-	
B & H	26	23	5	433	75	24.05	-	3	9	-	1403	911	39	23.35	4-29	-	
Sunday	93	75	22	1334	112	25.16	1	5	21	-	3649	2807	86	32.63	6-53	1	

ECCLESTONE, S. C.   Somerset

Name: Simon Charles Ecclestone
Role: Left-hand bat, right-arm
fast-medium bowler
Born: 16 July 1971, Great Dunmow, Essex
Height: 6ft 3in **Weight:** 14st 7lbs
Nickname: Major
County debut: 1994
1st-Class 50s: 7
1st-Class catches: 6
One-Day 100s: 2
Place in batting averages: 177th av. 27.83
(1995 34th av. 47.20)
Place in bowling averages: (1995 96th av.
34.81)
Strike rate: (career 73.36)
Parents: Jonathan and Pippa
Marital status: Single
Family links with cricket: Brother Giles
played for Essex and Cambridgeshire
Education: Bryanston School; Durham University; Keble College, Oxford
Qualifications: 9 O-levels, 3 A-levels, BA (Hons) Social Sciences, Dip Soc (Oxon)
Off-season: Playing in Australia

Overseas tours: Bryanston to West Indies 1989; Durham University to South Africa 1992-93

Cricketers particularly admired: David Gower

Other sports followed: Rugby and all other sports

Injuries: Knee injury

Relaxations: 'Continuous cycle of cooking it, eating it, drinking it and getting rid of the evidence'

Extras: Played for Essex from U11 to U19/2nd XI and for ESCA U19 v New Zealand 1989; captained Durham University, played for Cambridgeshire, Blue for Oxford University 1994, '"brother of" first *Daily Telegraph* Fantasy League winner'

Best batting: 94 Somerset v Kent, Canterbury 1996

Best bowling: 4-66 Oxford University v Surrey, The Oval 1994

1996 Season

	M	Inns	NO	Runs	HS	Avge	100s	50s	Ct	St	O	M	Runs	Wkts	Avge	Best	5wI	10wM
Test																		
All First	8	13	1	334	94	27.83	-	3	2	-								
1-day Int																		
NatWest	3	3	0	106	52	35.33	-	1	-	-								
B & H	4	4	1	270	112 *	90.00	1	2	1	-	8	0	31	0	-	-	-	-
Sunday	13	13	0	347	130	26.69	1	1	4	-	8	1	49	1	49.00	1-49	-

Career Performances

	M	Inns	NO	Runs	HS	Avge	100s	50s	Ct	St	Balls	Runs	Wkts	Avge	Best	5wI	10wM
Test																	
All First	28	44	7	1140	94	30.81	-	7	6	-	2421	1208	33	36.60	4-66	-	-
1-day Int																	
NatWest	5	5	0	107	52	21.40	-	1	-	-	66	53	0	-	-	-	-
B & H	9	8	2	335	112 *	55.83	1	2	3	-	210	155	3	51.66	2-44	-	-
Sunday	30	30	3	761	130	28.18	1	2	6	-	590	593	18	32.94	4-31	-	-

EDMOND, M. D.   Warwickshire

Name: Michael Dennis Edmond

Role: Right-hand bat, right-arm medium-fast bowler

Born: 30 July 1969, Barrow-in-Furness

Weight: 14st 7lbs

Nickname: Eddo, Aus

County debut: 1996

Strike rate: (career 101.00)

Parents: Tom and Carol

Marital status: Single

Children: Ryen
Family links with cricket: 'My brother plays'
Education: Briar Road Public School, Campbelltown, NSW; Airds High School, Campbelltown, NSW
Qualifications: Level 0 coach in Australia
Career outside cricket: Barman
Off-season: 'I intend to get fit and work on my overall game, to play indoor cricket for Stumps in Birmingham'
Overseas teams played for: Campbelltown, Sydney 1988-93; Fairfield, Sydney 1994
Cricketers particularly admired: Ian Botham, Viv Richards, Len Pascoe
Young players to look out for: 'All with an ambition to play for England'
Other sports followed: Indoor cricket

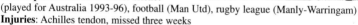

(played for Australia 1993-96), football (Man Utd), rugby league (Manly-Warringam)
Injuries: Achilles tendon, missed three weeks
Relaxations: Spending time with friends, going out and listening to music
Opinions on cricket: 'Only being my first full county season, I have enjoyed it very much. Possibly there are one or two too many counties playing and they should merge with the nearest county and thus reduce the length of the season.'
Best batting: 8* Warwickshire v Middlesex, Lord's 1996
Best bowling: 1-6 Warwickshire v Middlesex, Lord's 1996

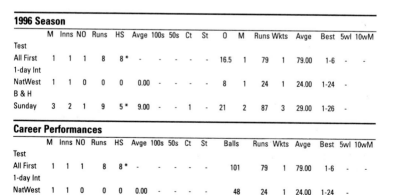

1996 Season

	M	Inns	NO	Runs	HS	Avge	100s	50s	Ct	St	O	M	Runs	Wkts	Avge	Best	5wI	10wM
Test																		
All First	1	1	1	8	8 *	-	-	-	-	-	16.5	1	79	1	79.00	1-6	-	-
1-day Int																		
NatWest	1	1	0	0	0	0.00	-	-	-	-	8	1	24	1	24.00	1-24	-	
B & H																		
Sunday	3	2	1	9	5 *	9.00	-	-	1	-	21	2	87	3	29.00	1-26	-	

Career Performances

	M	Inns	NO	Runs	HS	Avge	100s	50s	Ct	St	Balls	Runs	Wkts	Avge	Best	5wI	10wM
Test																	
All First	1	1	1	8	8 *	-	-	-	-	-	101	79	1	79.00	1-6	-	-
1-day Int																	
NatWest	1	1	0	0	0	0.00	-	-	-	-	48	24	1	24.00	1-24	-	
B & H																	
Sunday	3	2	1	9	5 *	9.00	-	-	1	-	126	87	3	29.00	1-26	-	

EDWARDS, A. D. Sussex

Name: Alexander David Edwards
Role: Right-hand bat, right-arm
fast-medium bowler
Born: 2 August 1975, Cuckfield, Sussex
Height: 6ft **Weight:** 12st 9lbs
Nickname: Al, Steads, Elvis
County debut: 1994 (one-day), 1995 (first-class)
1st-Class catches: 2
Strike rate: (career 120.00)
Parents: Richard John and Angela Janet
Marital status: Single
Family links with cricket: 'Parents drove
me everywhere to play or practise cricket and
have been absolutely wonderful'
Education: Felbridge Primary; Imberhorne
Comprehensive; Loughborough University
Qualifications: 10 GCSEs, 4 A-levels
Career outside cricket: Studying at
Loughborough

Off-season: Completing degree course at Loughborough University
Overseas tours: Sussex U18 to India 1990-91; England U18 to South Africa 1992-93,
to Denmark 1993
Cricketers particularly admired: Dennis Lillee, Michael Holding, Viv Richards,
Stan Berry and Pat Cale 'for their tremendous support, belief and encouragement'
Other sports followed: Football (Liverpool FC)
Relaxations: Snooker, swimming, training, listening to a variety of music, watching
sports on television
Extras: Lord's Taverners U15 Young Cricketer of the Year 1991 and a *Cricketer*
magazine Young Cricketer of the Month in the same year. Played for England U19
against India U19 in 1994
Opinions on cricket: 'Second XI cricket should mirror the first-class game, e.g. same
grounds, practice facilities and duration of matches in the championship (four days).
This would help young players to make the transition from 2nd XI to first-class cricket.
Young players should be given ample opportunity to prove themselves in first-class
cricket. They shouldn't be afraid of initial failure.'
Best batting: 22 Sussex v Young Australia, Hove 1995
Best bowling: 3-83 Sussex v Young Australia, Hove 1995

1996 Season

	M	Inns	NO	Runs	HS	Avge	100s	50s	Ct	St	O	M	Runs	Wkts	Avge	Best	5wI	10wM
Test																		
All First	1	0	0	0	0	-	-	-	-	-	13	2	64	0	-	-	-	-
1-day Int																		
NatWest																		
B & H																		
Sunday																		

Career Performances

	M	Inns	NO	Runs	HS	Avge	100s	50s	Ct	St	Balls	Runs	Wkts	Avge	Best	5wI	10wM
Test																	
All First	3	3	0	38	22	12.66	-	-	2	-	360	310	3	103.33	3-83	-	-
1-day Int																	
NatWest																	
B & H	5	4	1	21	7 *	7.00	-	-	5	-	324	232	5	46.40	2-51	-	
Sunday	1	0	0	0	0	-	-	-	-	-	30	24	0	-	-	-	-

EDWARDS, G. J. M. Glamorgan

Name: Gareth John Maldwyn Edwards
Role: Right-hand bat, off-spin bowler
Born: 13 November 1976, St Asaph, Wales
Height: 6ft 3in **Weight:** 11st 8lbs
Nickname: Legs
County debut: No first-team appearance
Parents: Roger and Manon
Marital status: Single
Family links with cricket: Father played
for Ruthin CC for 25 years
Education: Ysgol Brynhyfryd, Ruthin, North
Wales; University College, London
Qualifications: 12 GCSEs, 3 A-levels; in
final year of Geography degree course
Off-season: 'Concentrating on my studies to
secure a good degree.' Indoor nets
Overseas tours: England U19 to Zimbabwe
1995-96
Cricketers particularly admired: Russell P.
Jones, Eldine Baptiste
Young players to look out for: Alun Evans, Alex Morris
Other sports followed: Rugby (Ruthin RFC), football (Clydesbank FC), tennis, golf
Injuries: Stress fracture of left foot, missed the last eleven weeks of the season

Relaxations: Music, cinema, quizzes, crosswords
Extras: North Wales Young Cricketer of the Year 1993, Denbighshire Young Cricketer of the Year 1993. Played for Welsh Schools at U13, U14, U15, U16 and U19 levels. Played for TCCB Development of Excellence XI v India U19 in 1994 and v South Africa U19 in 1995
Opinions on cricket: 'Uncovered wickets might encourage the finger spinners and even out a game which tends to favour the batsmen. There is too much cricket being played, but the solution is not easy.'

ELLIS, S. W. K. Worcestershire

Name: Scott William Kenneth Ellis
Role: Right-hand bat, right-arm fast-medium bowler
Born: 3 October 1975, Newcastle-under-Lyme
Height: 6ft 3in **Weight:** 14st
Nickname: Llama, Sewts, Sinjun
County debut: 1996
1st-Class catches: 7
1st-Class 5 w. innings: 1
Place in batting averages: 295th av. 10.50
Place in bowling averages: 139th av. 49.00
Strike rate: 72.85 (career 64.73)
Parents: Tony and Valerie Anne
Marital status: Single
Education: Shrewsbury School; Warwick University
Qualifications: 9 GCSEs, 3 A-levels
Off-season: Studying ancient history and philosophy at university
Overseas tours: England U19 to West Indies 1994-95
Cricketers particularly admired: Robin Smith, Courtney Walsh
Other sports followed: Football
Injuries: Recovering from stress fracture to back received at the end of the 1995 season
Relaxations: Listening to music, reading
Extras: Played for England U18 against India U19 in 1994. Made first-class debut for Combined Universities against West Indies in 1995
Opinions on cricket: 'Play too much. Not enough time to practise.'
Best batting: 15 Worcestershire v Middlesex, Lord's 1996
Best bowling: 5-59 Combined Universities v West Indies, The Parks 1995

1996 Season

	M	Inns	NO	Runs	HS	Avge	100s	50s	Ct	St	O	M	Runs	Wkts	Avge	Best	5wI	10wM
Test																		
All First	9	10	4	63	15	10.50	-	-	6	-	170	27	686	14	49.00	3-29	-	-
1-day Int																		
NatWest	1	1	1	0	0*	-	-	-	-	-	7	0	34	2	17.00	2-34	-	
B & H	1	1	0	4	4	4.00	-	-	-	-	9	0	50	1	50.00	1-50	-	
Sunday	6	1	0	1	1	1.00	-	-	2	-	26	1	141	4	35.25	2-35	-	

Career Performances

	M	Inns	NO	Runs	HS	Avge	100s	50s	Ct	St	Balls	Runs	Wkts	Avge	Best	5wI	10wM
Test																	
All First	10	11	4	63	15	9.00	-	-	7	-	1230	832	19	43.78	5-59	1	-
1-day Int																	
NatWest	1	1	1	0	0*	-	-	-	-	-	42	34	2	17.00	2-34	-	
B & H	1	1	0	4	4	4.00	-	-	-	-	54	50	1	50.00	1-50	-	
Sunday	6	1	0	1	1	1.00	-	-	2	-	156	141	4	35.25	2-35	-	

ELWORTHY, S.   Lancashire

Name: Steven Elworthy
Role: Right-hand bat, right-arm
fast-medium bowler
Born: 23 February 1965, Zimbabwe
Height: 6ft 4in **Weight:** 13st 9lbs
County debut: 1996
1st-Class 50s: 6
1st-Class 5 w. in innings: 8
1st-Class 10 w. in innings: 1
1st-Class catches: 25
Place in batting averages: 230th av. 20.57
Place in bowling averages: 119th av. 41.60
Strike rate: 66.03 (career 54.26)
Education: Wits University, South Africa
Qualifications: O- and M-levels, TED
Matriculation, degree in Electrical
Engineering, National Higher Diploma
Off-season: Playing for Northern Transvaal
Overseas teams played for: Northern
Transvaal 1988-1996
Extras: Represented Zimbabwe at cricket, tennis, swimming, rugby, football at junior level before leaving to complete his education in South Africa. Represented Transvaal in

1987, but in 1988 started two years of national service and moved to Northern Transvaal whom he has represented since 1988, and was voted Player of the Year for 1993-94 and 1994-95. He played for Bishop Auckland in the North Yorkshire/South Durham league in 1989 and for Rishton in the Lancashire league in 1991. He has also represented South Africa 'A'

Best batting: 88 Lancashire v Yorkshire, Old Trafford 1996
Best bowling: 7-65 Northern Transvaal v Natal, Durban 1994-95

1996 Season

	M	Inns	NO	Runs	HS	Avge	100s	50s	Ct	St	O	M	Runs	Wkts	Avge	Best	5wI	10wM
Test																		
All First	12	16	2	288	88	20.57	-	1	5	-	308.1	43	1165	28	41.60	4-80	-	-
1-day Int																		
NatWest	2	2	1	13	8	13.00	-	-	-	-	18	4	50	5	10.00	4-40	-	
B & H	5	3	0	26	13	8.66	-	-	-	-	47	4	204	10	20.40	4-14	-	
Sunday	14	9	2	59	15	8.42	-	-	4	-	94	5	477	11	43.36	2-33	-	

Career Performances

	M	Inns	NO	Runs	HS	Avge	100s	50s	Ct	St	Balls	Runs	Wkts	Avge	Best	5wI	10wM
Test																	
All First	71	114	20	1910	88	20.31	-	6	25	-	12644	7090	233	30.42	7-65	8	1
1-day Int																	
NatWest	2	2	1	13	8	13.00	-	-	-	-	108	50	5	10.00	4-40	-	
B & H	5	3	0	26	13	8.66	-	-	-	-	282	204	10	20.40	4-14	-	
Sunday	14	9	2	59	15	8.42	-	-	4	-	564	477	11	43.36	2-33	-	

EMBUREY, J. E.   Northamptonshire

Name: John Ernest Emburey
Role: Right-hand bat, off-spin bowler
Born: 20 August 1952, Peckham
Height: 6ft 2in **Weight:** 14st
Nickname: Embers, Ern
County debut: 1973 (Middlesex), 1996 (Northamptonshire)
County cap: 1977
Benefit: 1986
Testimonial: 1995
Test debut: 1978
Tests: 64
One-Day Internationals: 61
50 wickets in a season: 17
1st-Class 50s: 55

1st-Class 100s: 7
1st-Class 5 w. in innings: 72
1st-Class 10 w. in match: 12
1st-Class catches: 458
One-Day 5 w. in innings: 3
Place in batting averages: 220th av. 22.22
(1995 205th av. 20.36)
Place in bowling averages: 105th av. 38.59
(1995 23rd av. 22.98)
Strike rate: 88.07 (career 69.97)
Parents: John (deceased) and Rose
Wife and date of marriage: Susie, 20
September 1980
Children: Clare, 1 March 1983; Chloë, 31
October 1985
Education: Peckham Manor Secondary
School
Qualifications: O-levels, advanced cricket
coaching certificate
Overseas tours: England to Australia 1978-79, to Australia and India 1979-80,
to West Indies 1980-81, to India and Sri Lanka 1981-82, to West Indies 1985-86,
to Australia 1986-87, to Pakistan, Australia and New Zealand 1987-88, to India 1992-
93; unofficial English XI to South Africa 1981-82 and 1989-90
Overseas teams played for: Prahran, Melbourne 1977-78; St Kilda, Melbourne 1984-
85; Western Province 1982-84
Cricketers particularly admired: Ken Barrington, Alan Knott
Other sports followed: Golf
Relaxations: Reading, golf
Extras: Played for Surrey YC 1969-70. Phil Edmonds of Middlesex and England was
the best man at his wedding. Middlesex vice-captain 1983-93. One of *Wisden*'s Five
Cricketers of the Year 1983. Captain of England v West Indies for two Tests in 1988.
Banned from Test cricket for three years for touring South Africa in 1981-82, and for
five more for touring in 1989-90, suspension remitted in 1992. Published autobiography
Emburey in 1988. In the match against Somerset at Lord's in 1992 he became only the
9th player to take 1,000 wickets for Middlesex. Middlesex Player of the Year 1993.
Manager of the England A tour to Pakistan 1995-96. Left Middlesex at the end of the
1995 season to join Northamptonshire as the club's Chief Coach
Opinions on cricket: 'Young players seem very uptight. They should relax and enjoy
the game. The less pressure you put yourself under, the easier it will become. Good
players don't become bad players, bad players can become good players. They just have
to work a little harder.'
Best batting: 133 Middlesex v Essex, Chelmsford 1983
Best bowling: 8-40 Middlesex v Hampshire, Lord's 1993

1996 Season

	M	Inns	NO	Runs	HS	Avge	100s	50s	Ct	St	O	M	Runs	Wkts	Avge	Best	5wI	10wM
Test																		
All First	11	13	4	200	67 *	22.22	-	1	6	-	396.2	94	1042	27	38.59	4-48	-	-
1-day Int																		
NatWest	2	1	0	46	46	46.00	-	-	-	-	20.3	4	52	6	8.66	3-14	-	
B & H	6	3	2	17	9 *	17.00	-	-	3	-	53.5	3	203	8	25.37	4-24	-	
Sunday	16	6	3	23	8 *	7.66	-	-	5	-	107	7	439	17	25.82	2-15	-	

Career Performances

	M	Inns	NO	Runs	HS	Avge	100s	50s	Ct	St	Balls	Runs	Wkts	Avge	Best	5wI	10wM
Test	64	96	20	1713	75	22.53	-	10	34	-	15391	5646	147	38.40	7-78	6	-
All First	510	641	130	11982	133	23.44	7	55	458	-	112241	41699	1604	25.99	8-40	72	12
1-day Int	61	45	10	501	34	14.31	-	-	19	-	3425	2346	76	30.86	4-37	-	
NatWest	59	37	11	519	46	19.96	-	-	21	-	3938	1824	70	26.05	3-11	-	
B & H	87	59	18	646	50	15.75	-	1	42	-	4672	2479	92	26.94	5-37	1	
Sunday	266	172	60	1876	50	16.75	-	1	82	-	11345	8285	355	23.33	5-23	2	

EVANS, A. W. Glamorgan

Name: Alun Wyn Evans
Role: Right-hand bat, right-arm medium bowler
Height: 5ft 8in **Weight:** 11st 10lbs
Born: 20 August 1975, Glanammen, Dyfed
County debut: 1996
1st-Class 50s: 1
1st-Class catches: 5
Place in batting averages: 90th av. 37.60
Parents: Gareth and Lynfa
Marital status: Single
Family links with cricket: Father formerly with Ammanford CC. Brother played Welsh Schools at all ages and now plays for Ammanford
Education: Fishguard County High School; Neath Tertiary College
Qualifications: 11 GCSEs, BTEC National Diploma in Sports Science
Off-season: Playing in New Zealand
Overseas tours: Welsh Schools U17 to Australia 1992-93
Overseas teams played for: Marist, Whangarei 1995-96

Cricketers particularly admired: Brian Lara, Wasim Akram
Young players to look out for: Ricky Fay
Other sports followed: Rugby, football (Tottenham Hotspur FC)
Injuries: Ankle ligaments, out for two weeks
Relaxations: Music, reading magazines
Extras: Welsh Schools Player of the Year 1994, MCC Young Cricketer 1995. Balconiers 2nd XI Player of the Year. ASW Young Player of the Year.
Opinions on cricket: 'In the Second XI Championship, I think the extra hour rule that has been brought in is out of order.'
Best batting: 71* Glamorgan v Oxford University, The Parks 1996

1996 Season

	M	Inns	NO	Runs	HS	Avge	100s	50s	Ct	St	O	M	Runs	Wkts	Avge	Best	5wI	10wM
Test																		
All First	7	13	3	376	71 *	37.60	-	2	5	-								
1-day Int																		
NatWest																		
B & H																		
Sunday	6	6	2	99	50 *	24.75	-	1	2	-								

Career Performances

	M	Inns	NO	Runs	HS	Avge	100s	50s	Ct	St	Balls	Runs	Wkts	Avge	Best	5wI	10wM
Test																	
All First	7	13	3	376	71 *	37.60	-	2	5	-							
1-day Int																	
NatWest																	
B & H																	
Sunday	6	6	2	99	50 *	24.75	-	1	2	-							

31. Who holds the record for the most 'ducks' in Test match cricket?

EVANS, K. P.   Nottinghamshire

Name: Kevin Paul Evans
Role: Right-hand bat, right-arm
medium bowler
Born: 10 September 1963, Calverton,
Nottingham
Height: 6ft 2in **Weight:** 13st
Nickname: Ghost, Texas
County debut: 1984
County cap: 1990
1st-Class 50s: 21
1st-Class 100s: 3
1st-Class 5 w. in innings: 6
1st-Class catches: 102
One-day 5 w. innings: 2
Place in batting averages: 145th av. 32.13
(1995 174th av. 23.63)
Place in bowling averages: 114th av. 40.56
(1995 125th av. 42.14)

Strike rate: 82.53 (career 70.26)
Parents: Eric and Eileen
Wife and date of marriage: Sandra, 19 March 1988
Family links with cricket: Brother Russell played for Nottinghamshire and still plays
for Minor Counties and Lincolnshire. Father played local cricket
Education: William Lee Primary; Colonel Frank Seely Comprehensive, Calverton
Qualifications: 10 O-levels, 3 A-levels, qualified coach
Off-season: Coaching at Trent Bridge
Overseas teams played for: Wanuiomata, New Zealand 1989-91
Cricketers particularly admired: Richard Hadlee, Clive Rice
Young players to look out for: Wasim Khan, Richard Kettleborough
Other sports followed: Football (Leeds United), tennis, squash
Injuries: Side muscle strain and hip muscle strain, missed a total of four weeks
Relaxations: Listening to music, reading, DIY, gardening
Extras: With brother, Russell, first brothers to bat together for Nottinghamshire in first-
class cricket for 50 years. Kept wicket for the first time in the Championship match
against Essex at Colchester in 1992. Second Notts cricketer to bowl Sunday League hat-
trick v Glamorgan at Trent Bridge, Mark Saxelby was the other
Opinions on cricket: 'Four-day format is very good but there is too much variety in the
pitches. Sunday League is back to its best (40 overs).'
Best batting: 104 Nottinghamshire v Surrey, Trent Bridge 1992
                 104 Nottinghamshire v Sussex, Trent Bridge 1994
Best bowling: 6-67 Nottinghamshire v Yorkshire, Trent Bridge 1993

1996 Season

	M	Inns	NO	Runs	HS	Avge	100s	50s	Ct	St	O	M	Runs	Wkts	Avge	Best	5wI	10wM
Test																		
All First	14	18	3	482	71	32.13	-	4	3	-	412.4	99	1217	30	40.56	5-30	2	-
1-day Int																		
NatWest	1	1	0	10	10	10.00	-	-	-	-	12	1	57	2	28.50	2-57	-	
B & H	3	1	0	8	8	8.00	-	-	-	-	27	2	97	2	48.50	1-29	-	
Sunday	14	4	1	14	5	4.66	-	-	6	-	100.5	7	419	15	27.93	3-38	-	

Career Performances

	M	Inns	NO	Runs	HS	Avge	100s	50s	Ct	St	Balls	Runs	Wkts	Avge	Best	5wI	10wM
Test																	
All First	136	189	43	3861	104	26.44	3	21	102	-	20306	10015	289	34.65	6-67	6	-
1-day Int																	
NatWest	19	14	2	115	21	9.58	-	-	6	-	1162	646	26	24.84	6-10	1	
B & H	30	19	5	223	47	15.92	-	-	8	-	1676	1134	41	27.65	4-19	-	
Sunday	121	71	29	702	30	16.71	-	-	23	-	4940	4177	129	32.37	5-29	1	

EVANS, M. R. Middlesex

Name: Matthew Robert Evans
Role: Right-hand bat, right-arm medium-fast bowler
Born: 27 November 1974, Gravesend, Kent
Height: 6ft 4in **Weight:** 13st 4lbs
Nickname: Shenley
County debut: No first-team appearance
Parents: Tony and Penny
Marital status: Single
Family links with cricket: 'Father plays club cricket in the Hertfordshire league and is a playing member of the MCC. Mother and sister are improving their garden cricket skills'
Education: Aldwickbury School, Harpenden; Bedford School; Loughborough University
Qualifications: 10 GCSEs, 3 A-levels, 2nd year BSc student, NCA senior cricket coach
Off-season: Studying, training and relaxing
Overseas tours: Middlesex pre-season to Portugal 1996
Cricketers particularly admired: Sir Richard Hadlee
Young players to look out for: David Nash, Toby Bailey

Other sports followed: Rugby (Wasps RFC) and 'an interest in all others'
Relaxations: Cinema, theatre, 'joining the night train', eating, playing other sports
Extras: Played rugby for East Midlands U18 and county hockey U18. Completed a hat-trick against Durham University in the UAU semi-final. As captain of Bedford School received the Henry Grierson trophy from Brian Johnston. Played for Hertfordshire U19 for three years, two as captain. Played Minor Counties cricket for Hertfordshire from 1994-95. Played for British Universities in the Benson & Hedges Cup in 1996
Opinions on cricket: 'All people, players and coaches must be encouraged to play aggressive, competitive, positive cricket and not just go through the motions.'

1996 Season

	M	Inns	NO	Runs	HS	Avge	100s	50s	Ct	St	O	M	Runs	Wkts	Avge	Best	5wl	10wM
Test																		
All First																		
1-day Int																		
NatWest																		
B & H	4	4	2	34	16 *	17.00	-	-	2	-	35	1	245	6	40.83	3-64	-	
Sunday																		

Career Performances

	M	Inns	NO	Runs	HS	Avge	100s	50s	Ct	St	Balls	Runs	Wkts	Avge	Best	5wl	10wM
Test																	
All First																	
1-day Int																	
NatWest																	
B & H	4	4	2	34	16 *	17.00	-	-	2	-	210	245	6	40.83	3-64	-	
Sunday																	

FAIRBROTHER, N. H.   Lancashire

Name: Neil Harvey Fairbrother
Role: Left-hand bat, left-arm medium bowler
Born: 9 September 1963, Warrington, Cheshire
Height: 5ft 8in **Weight:** 11st 4lbs
Nickname: Harvey
County debut: 1982
County cap: 1985
Benefit: 1995
Test debut: 1987
Tests: 10
One-Day Internationals: 56
1000 runs in a season: 10

1st-Class 50s: 89
1st-Class 100s: 35
1st-Class 200s: 3
1st-Class 300s: 1
1st-Class catches: 201
One-Day 100s: 6
Place in batting averages: 20th av. 53.40
(1995 125th av. 30.10)
Strike rate: (career 134.60)
Parents: Les and Barbara
Wife and date of marriage: Audrey, 23
September 1988
Children: Rachael Elizabeth, 4 April 1991;
Sam, 3 April 1994
Family links with cricket: Father and two
uncles played local league cricket
Education: St Margaret's Church of England
School, Oxford; Lymn Grammar School
Qualifications: 5 O-levels
Overseas tours: England to Sharjah 1986-87, to India and Pakistan (World Cup)1987,
Australia and New Zealand 1987-88; England A to Pakistan 1990-91; England to New
Zealand 1991-92, to India 1992-93, to Australia 1994-95, to South Africa 1995-96, to
India and Pakistan (World Cup) 1995-96
Cricketers particularly admired: Clive Lloyd, Allan Border, David Gower
Other sports followed: Football, rugby union, rugby league
Relaxations: Music and playing sport
Extras: 'I was named after the Australian cricketer Neil Harvey, who was my mum's
favourite cricketer.' Played for England YC v Australia 1983. His innings of 366 in 1990
was the third highest score ever made in the County Championship, the second highest
first-class score by a Lancashire batsman and the best at The Oval. Appointed
Lancashire captain for 1992 but resigned in 1993. Called up to join England tour party
as a replacement in Australia 1994-95 but was immediately injured in a collision with
Steven Rhodes while fielding and forced to return home. Played in the one-day series
between England and South Africa and represented England in the World Cup
Opinions on cricket: 'There is too much cricket. The game has to be made more
entertaining.'
Best batting: 366 Lancashire v Surrey, The Oval 1990
Best bowling: 2-91 Lancashire v Nottinghamshire, Old Trafford 1987

---

32. Which player achieved the notable feat of dismissing
three England captains in one week during 1996?

1996 Season

	M	Inns	NO	Runs	HS	Avge	100s	50s	Ct	St	O	M	Runs	Wkts	Avge	Best	5wI	10wM
Test																		
All First	12	20	0	1068	204	53.40	2		8	10	-							
1-day Int																		
NatWest	5	5	0	103	46	20.60	-	-	6	-	5	0	28	1	28.00	1-28	-	
B & H	8	8	3	360	80 *	72.00	-	4	4	-								
Sunday	15	14	4	408	93	40.80	-	3	8	-								

Career Performances

	M	Inns	NO	Runs	HS	Avge	100s	50s	Ct	St	Balls	Runs	Wkts	Avge	Best	5wI	10wM
Test	10	15	1	219	83	15.64	-	1	4	-	12	9	0	-	-	-	-
All First	287	459	66	16295	366	41.46	35	89	201	-	673	440	5	88.00	2-91	-	-
1-day Int	56	54	13	1539	113	37.53	1	11	24	-	6	9	0	-			
NatWest	34	33	5	1254	93 *	44.78	-	9	18	-	48	44	1	44.00	1-28		
B & H	64	61	19	2225	116 *	52.97	1	17	32	-	54	67	1	67.00	1-17	-	
Sunday	185	171	40	5006	116 *	38.21	4	30	57	-	48	48	1	48.00	1-33	-	

FAY, R. A.   Middlesex

Name: Richard Anthony Fay
Role: Right-hand bat, right-arm
medium-fast bowler
Born: 14 May 1974, Kilburn, London
Height: 6ft 4in **Weight:** 14st 7lbs
Nickname: Ginga, Red, Bestey
County debut: 1995
1st-Class catches: 5
Place in batting averages: 306th av. 7.40
Place in bowling averages: 101st av. 36.16
Strike rate: 69.67 (career 70.25)
Parents: James Peter and Margaret Christine
Marital status: 'girlfriend named Julie'
Family links with cricket: Father played
Combined Services. Great uncle was
Maurice Tait
Education: Kilburn Park; Brondesbury and
Kilburn, Queen's Park Community School;
City of Westminster College
Qualifications: 4 GCSEs, BTEC in Business Studies, BTEC in Design and
Realisation
Cricketers particularly admired: Angus Fraser, Simon Marcus, Darren Wyrill, Matt

Church, Clive Radley, Chris Sketchley, Ian Kidd
Other sports followed: Football (Chelsea and 'play for Brondesbury CC'),
badminton, pool and table tennis
Injuries: Twisted ankle, out for four days
Relaxations: Going to the pub and having a quiet drink with my mates. Spending time
with my girlfriend
Extras: Best league performance of nine wickets for 45 runs against Wembley CC.
MCC YC 1992-95
Opinions on cricket: 'I don't think that the day should be 110 overs. I think that it should
be 90 or 100 overs at the most so that lunch and tea intervals could be made longer'
Best batting: 26 Middlesex v Glamorgan, Lord's 1996
Best bowling: 4-53 Middlesex v Glamorgan, Lord's 1996

1996 Season

	M	Inns	NO	Runs	HS	Avge	100s	50s	Ct	St	O	M	Runs	Wkts	Avge	Best	5wI	10wM
Test																		
All First	15	24	2	163	26	7.40	-	-	5	-	360	84	1121	31	36.16	4-53	-	-
1-day Int																		
NatWest	2	1	0	0	0	0.00	-	-	2	-	17	0	63	3	21.00	2-43	-	
B & H	4	2	0	1	1	0.50	-	-	1	-	34	4	123	3	41.00	1-13	-	
Sunday	14	4	3	2	1 *	2.00	-	-	2	-	98	8	451	16	28.18	4-33	-	

Career Performances

	M	Inns	NO	Runs	HS	Avge	100s	50s	Ct	St	Balls	Runs	Wkts	Avge	Best	5wI	10wM
Test																	
All First	16	25	3	164	26	7.45	-	-	5	-	2178	1146	31	36.96	4-53	-	-
1-day Int																	
NatWest	2	1	0	0	0	0.00	-	-	2	-	102	63	3	21.00	2-43	-	
B & H	4	2	0	1	1	0.50	-	-	1	-	204	123	3	41.00	1-13	-	
Sunday	20	8	5	36	12 *	12.00	-	-	2	-	810	606	19	31.89	4-33	-	

33. Who took four wickets in four balls on his county debut
in the Benson and Hedges Cup in 1996?

FELTHAM, M. A. Middlesex

Name: Mark Andrew Feltham
Role: Right-hand bat, right-arm
medium bowler
Born: 26 June 1963, London
Height: 6ft 2in **Weight:** 14st 2lbs
Nickname: Felts, Boff, Coldstream
County debut: 1983 (Surrey), 1993
(Middlesex)
County cap: 1990 (Surrey), 1995
(Middlesex)
50 wickets in a season: 1
1st-Class 50s: 9
1st-Class 100s: 1
1st-Class 5 w. in innings: 8
1st-Class catches: 67
One-Day 5 w. in innings: 3
Place in batting averages: (1995 277th av.

10.45)
Place in bowling averages: (1995 48th av. 27.00)
Strike rate: 85.50 (career 61.76)
Parents: Leonard William and Patricia Louise
Wife and date of marriage: Debra Elizabeth, 22 September 1990
Children: Zoë Elizabeth, 23 June 1992; Harrison Leonard Walter, 20 August 1995
Family links with cricket: 'Brother James plays in the Thames Valley League. Mum
is on Allan Lamb's benefit committee'
Education: Roehampton Church School; Tiffin Boys' School
Qualifications: 7 O-levels; advanced cricket coach
Career outside cricket: Sports marketing, promotion and sponsorship
Off-season: Mike Gatting benefit tour to Ireland. 'Looking for that special job'
Overseas teams played for: Glenwood Old Boys, Durban, South Africa 1983-84, 1986-87
Cricketers particularly admired: Ian Botham, Sylvester Clarke and 'all good pros'
Other sports followed: Football, American football and most others
Injuries: Knee and back, missed a total of 13 weeks
Extras: 'I write a weekly column in *Wandsworth Borough News*. Dismissed both Clive
Rice and Richard Hadlee in their last innings in county cricket.' Released by Surrey at
the end of 1992 season and signed by Middlesex for 1993. Writes monthly column in
Cricket World magazine. Retired from first-class cricket at the end of the 1996 season
Opinions on cricket: 'Just because it's Australian doesn't mean it's best.'
Best batting: 101 Surrey v Middlesex, The Oval 1990
Best bowling: 6-41 Middlesex v West Indies, Lord's 1995

1996 Season

	M	Inns	NO	Runs	HS	Avge	100s	50s	Ct	St	O	M	Runs	Wkts	Avge	Best	5wI	10wM
Test																		
All First	3	5	1	14	13 *	3.50	-	-	-	-	57	14	185	4	46.25	3-62	-	-
1-day Int																		
NatWest																		
B & H	1	1	0	12	12	12.00	-	-	2	-	10	0	63	1	63.00	1-63	-	
Sunday	4	4	0	32	12	8.00	-	-	-	-	27	4	138	6	23.00	3-30	-	

Career Performances

	M	Inns	NO	Runs	HS	Avge	100s	50s	Ct	St	Balls	Runs	Wkts	Avge	Best	5wI	10wM
Test																	
All First	160	197	48	3199	101	21.46	1	9	67	-	23965	12279	388	31.64	6-41	8	-
1-day Int																	
NatWest	19	14	4	168	37	16.80	-	-	3	-	1060	749	19	39.42	2-23	-	
B & H	39	25	5	271	37	13.55	-	-	13	-	2127	1417	58	24.43	5-28	2	
Sunday	132	91	24	1145	75	17.08	-	3	33	-	5099	4311	124	34.76	5-51	1	

FISHER, I. D.   *Yorkshire*

Name: Ian Douglas Fisher
Role: Left-hand bat, slow left-arm bowler
Born: 31 March 1976, Bradford
Height: 5ft 11in   **Weight:** 13st 6lbs
Nickname: Fish
County debut: 1996
1st-Class 5 w. in innings: 1
Strike rate: 54.00 (career 34.45)
Parents: Geoff and Linda
Marital status: Single
Family links with cricket: Father played club cricket
Education: Parkside Middle School; Beckfoot Grammar School; Thomas Danby College
Qualifications: 8 GCSEs, City and Guilds Sports and Leisure course, NCA coaching award, Sports Leaders Award
Career outside cricket: Rep for a petrol company
Off-season: Resting, training and working
Overseas tours: Yorkshire to Zimbabwe 1996
Overseas teams played for: Somerset West, South Africa 1994-95

Cricketers particularly admired: Phil Tufnell, Brian Lara, Allan Donald
Young players to look out for: Alex Wharf, Owais Shah, Alex Morris
Other sports followed: Football (Leeds United)
Injuries: Torn cartilage in left knee, missed the last month of the season
Relaxations: Music. television and socialising
Extras: Played England U17 and Yorkshire Schools U15, U16 and Yorkshire U19
Opinions on cricket: 'Two league system would raise the standard of the domestic game. Second teams should play the four-day game.'
Best bowling: 5-35 Yorkshire v Lancashire, Old Trafford 1996

1996 Season

	M	Inns	NO	Runs	HS	Avge	100s	50s	Ct	St	O	M	Runs	Wkts	Avge	Best	5wI	10wM
Test																		
All First	1	1	1	0	0 *	-	-	-	-	-	9	2	29	1	29.00	1-29	-	-
1-day Int																		
NatWest																		
B & H																		
Sunday																		

Career Performances

	M	Inns	NO	Runs	HS	Avge	100s	50s	Ct	St	Balls	Runs	Wkts	Avge	Best	5wI	10wM
Test																	
All First	3	1	1	0	0 *	-	-	-	-	-	390	182	11	16.54	5-35	1	-
1-day Int																	
NatWest																	
B & H																	
Sunday																	

FLANAGAN, I. N. Essex

Name: Ian Nicholas Flanagan
Role: Left-hand bat, off-break bowler
Born: 5 June 1980, Colchester
Height: 6ft **Weight:** 12st
Nickname: Bud, Flanners
County debut: No first-team appearance
Parents: Roy and Anita
Marital status: Single
Family links with cricket: Father played cricket for Colchester and East Essex for a number of years
Education: Millfield County Primary School; The Colne Community School; The Sixth Form College, Colchester

Qualifications: 10 GCSEs
Off-season: Studying and touring Pakistan with England U19
Overseas tours: England U19 to Pakistan 1996-97
Cricketers particularly admired: Paul Franks, Nasser Hussain, Carl Hooper
Young players to look out for: Stephen Peters, Jonathan Powell, Paul Franks
Other sports followed: Rugby, football (Tottenham Hotspur, Colchester United)
Injuries: None
Relaxations: Films, music, going out, cinema
Extras: Also played for England U17

FLEMING, M. V.   Kent

Name: Matthew Valentine Fleming
Role: Right-hand bat, right-arm medium bowler
Born: 12 December 1964, Macclesfield
Height: 5ft 11ins **Weight:** 12st 6lbs
Nickname: Jazzer, Swan Vesta
County debut: 1988
County cap: 1990
1st-Class 50s: 32
1st-Class 100s: 8
1st-Class catches: 55
One-Day 100s: 1
Place in batting averages: 156th av. 30.53 (1995 130th av. 29.80)
Place in bowling averages: 37th av. 26.88
Strike rate: 56.16 (career 86.61)
Parents: Valentine and Elizabeth
Wife and date of marriage: Caroline, 23 September 1989

Children: Hannah, 9 October 1992; Victoria, 16 June 1994
Family links with cricket: Great-grandfather C.F. Leslie played for England in 1880s; father played for Eton 2nd XI; mother opened the bowling for Heathfield School
Education: St Aubyns School, Rottingdean; Eton College
Qualifications: 8 O-levels, 3 A-levels, commissioned Royal Green Jackets in 1985

Career outside cricket: 'Unemployable'

Off-season: 'Not entirely sure'

Overseas tours: 'Never selected for anything'

Overseas teams played for: Avendale, Cape Town 1983-84

Cricketers particularly admired: 'All who play to win yet with a smile'

Young players to look out for: Matthew Walker, Ben Phillips

Other sports followed: Football (Arsenal), golf

Relaxations: Fishing, shooting, stalking, building bonfires

Extras: Ex-army officer in the Royal Green Jackets. First two scoring shots in Championship cricket were sixes. Vice-chairman of the Professional Cricketers' Association. Out twice before lunch batting at number three for Kent against West Indies in 1995

Opinions on cricket: 'The NatWest competition should go. Benson and Hedges format for world one-day cricket should become the premier one-day competition.'

Best batting: 116 Kent v West Indies, Canterbury 1991
116 Kent v Derbyshire, Derby 1996

Best bowling: 4-31 Kent v Gloucestershire, Tunbridge Wells 1993

1996 Season

	M	Inns	NO	Runs	HS	Avge	100s	50s	Ct	St	O	M	Runs	Wkts	Avge	Best	5wI	10wM
Test																		
All First	18	30	2	855	116	30.53	2	3	9	-	168.3	32	484	18	26.88	3-6	-	-
1-day Int																		
NatWest	2	2	0	7	4	3.50	-	-	1	-	6	0	24	0	-	-	-	-
B & H	6	6	0	203	72	33.83	-	1	2	-	47.4	3	234	5	46.80	2-53	-	
Sunday	17	17	1	496	112	31.00	1	3	1	-	104	0	650	29	22.41	4-13	-	

Career Performances

	M	Inns	NO	Runs	HS	Avge	100s	50s	Ct	St	Balls	Runs	Wkts	Avge	Best	5wI	10wM
Test																	
All First	131	213	23	5899	116	31.04	8	32	55	-	11779	5581	136	41.03	4-31	-	-
1-day Int																	
NatWest	17	17	1	285	53	17.81	-	1	10	-	621	406	17	23.88	3-28	-	
B & H	34	31	2	755	72	26.03	-	4	9	-	1676	1192	41	29.07	3-18	-	
Sunday	123	115	13	2514	112	24.64	1	12	34	-	4534	4037	148	27.27	4-13	-	

34. Name the player who took part in the Test series between England and Zimbabwe in 1996-97 will assume the role of coach for Oxford University in 1997?

FLINTOFF, A. Lancashire

Name: Andrew Flintoff
Role: Right-hand bat, right-arm medium bowler
Born: 6 December 1977, Preston
Height: 6ft 4in **Weight:** 13st 10lb
County debut: 1995
1st-Class catches: 3
Parents: Colin and Susan
Family links with cricket: Brother Chris and father both play local league cricket
Education: Greenlands County Primary; Ribbleton Hall High School
Qualifications: 9 GCSEs
Off-season: Touring Pakistan with England U19
Overseas tours: England Schools U15 to South Africa 1993; England U19 to West Indies 1994-95, to Zimbabwe 1995-96, to Pakistan 1996-97

Cricketers particularly admired: Jason Gallian, John Crawley, Stephen Titchard, Warren Hegg
Other sports followed: Football (Preston North End and Liverpool FC)
Injuries: Bad back, 'did not bowl for two months'
Relaxations: Listening to music and sleeping
Extras: Won a *Daily Telegraph* regional award for batting. Represented England U14 to U19 and played for U17 against India in 1994. Captained the England U19 tour to Pakistan
Opinions on cricket: 'Cricket should be promoted more in state schools.'
Best batting: 7 Lancashire v Middlesex, Portsmouth 1995

1996 Season

	M	Inns	NO	Runs	HS	Avge	100s	50s	Ct	St	O	M	Runs	Wkts	Avge	Best	5wl	10wM
Test																		
All First	1	1	0	2	2	2.00	-	-	1	-								
1-day Int																		
NatWest																		
B & H																		
Sunday	1	1	0	2	2	2.00	-	-	-	-								

Career Performances

	M	Inns	NO	Runs	HS	Avge	100s	50s	Ct	St	Balls	Runs	Wkts	Avge	Best	5wl	10wM
Test																	
All First	2	3	0	9	7	3.00	-	-	3	-	66	39	0	-	-	-	-
1-day Int																	
NatWest																	
B & H	1	0	0	0	0	-	-	-	-	-	36	10	1	10.00	1-10	-	
Sunday	3	3	0	36	22	12.00	-	-	-	-							

FOLLETT, D.   Northamptonshire

Name: David Follett
Role: Right-hand bowler, right-arm medium-fast bowler
Born: 14 October 1968, Hanley, Stoke-on-Trent
Height: 6ft 2in **Weight:** 12st 12lbs
Nickname: Foll
County debut: 1995 (Middlesex)
1st-Class 5 w. in innings: 3
1st-Class 10 w. in match: 1
1st-Class catches: 1
Place in bowling averages: 29th av. 25.60
Strike rate: 38.43 (career 44.33)
Parents: Gordon and Sandra
Wife and date of marriage: Victoria Jane, 5 October 1996
Family links with cricket: Father played club cricket for Burslem
Education: Moorland Road High School, Burslem, Stoke-on-Trent; Stoke-on-Trent Tech College
Qualifications: Engineer
Career outside cricket: Engineer
Overseas teams played for: Australian Capital Territory 1994; Queenbeyan, New South Wales, Australia, 1994-95
Cricketers particularly admired: Imran Khan, Richard Hadlee
Other sports followed: Football (Port Vale)
Injuries: Leg injury, missed three months
Relaxations: Swimming, current affairs, dog walking, running, football
Extras: Played for Staffordshire in the Minor Counties before joining Middlesex. Was first team Player of the Month for April and May in 1996. Took 8 for 22 in the Championship game against Durham. Has moved to Northamptonshire for the 1996

season
Best batting: 17 Middlesex v Yorkshire, Lord's 1996
Best bowling: 8-22 Middlesex v Durham, Chester-le-Street 1996

1996 Season

	M	Inns	NO	Runs	HS	Avge	100s	50s	Ct	St	O	M	Runs	Wkts	Avge	Best	5wI	10wM
Test																		
All First	6	6	5	22	17	22.00	-	-	2	-	147.2	26	589	23	25.60	8-22	3	1
1-day Int																		
NatWest																		
B & H	4	1	0	0	0	0.00	-	-	-	-	29	3	133	2	66.50	1-11	-	
Sunday	2	0	0	0	0	-	-	-	1	-	16	0	95	3	31.66	2-47	-	

Career Performances

	M	Inns	NO	Runs	HS	Avge	100s	50s	Ct	St	Balls	Runs	Wkts	Avge	Best	5wI	10wM
Test																	
All First	7	8	6	27	17	13.50	-	-	3	-	1064	684	24	28.50	8-22	3	1
1-day Int																	
NatWest																	
B & H	7	2	0	4	4	2.00	-	-	-	-	318	233	6	38.83	2-44	-	
Sunday	3	0	0	0	0	-	-	-	2	-	138	122	5	24.40	2-27	-	

FORD, J. A.   Kent

Name: James Anthony Ford
Role: Right-hand bat, slow left-arm bowler
Born: 30 March 1976, Penbury, Kent
Height: 5ft 9in **Weight:** 12st 4lbs
Nickname: Fordy, Didge
County debut: 1996
1st-Class catches: 1
Parents: Anthony and Linda
Marital status: Single
Family links with cricket: Father is a keen
follower
Education: Sevenoaks Prep School;
Tonbridge School; University of Durham
Qualifications: 11 GCSEs, 3 A-levels
Off-season: Studying Combined Social
Sciences at university
Overseas tours: Tonbridge School to
Australia 1992-93

Cricketers particularly admired: Viv Richards, Malcolm Marshall, Steve Waugh
Young players to look out for: Anurag Singh, Tim Hodgson
Other sports followed: Football (Tottenham Hotspur), hockey (plays for Durham University and England Students), 'all sports'
Relaxations: Socialising and playing sport
Extras: Member of the 1996 British Universities squad. Played for HMC Schools
Opinions on cricket: 'We play too much cricket. As batsmen know they will have three innings per week they are perhaps not as hungry as their Australian counterparts who play far less.'

1996 Season

	M	Inns	NO	Runs	HS	Avge	100s	50s	Ct	St	O	M	Runs	Wkts	Avge	Best	5wl	10wM
Test																		
All First	1	0	0	0	0	-	-	-	1	-	11.1	1	54	0	-	-	-	-
1-day Int																		
NatWest																		
B & H																		
Sunday																		

Career Performances

	M	Inns	NO	Runs	HS	Avge	100s	50s	Ct	St	Balls	Runs	Wkts	Avge	Best	5wl	10wM
Test																		
All First	1	0	0	0	0	-	-	-	1	-	67	54	0	-	-	-	-
1-day Int																		
NatWest																		
B & H																		
Sunday																		

FORDHAM, A.   Northamptonshire

Name: Alan Fordham
Role: Right-hand bat, occasional right-arm medium bowler, county vice-captain
Born: 9 November 1964, Bedford
Height: 6ft 1in **Weight:** 13st
Nickname: Forders
County debut: 1986
County cap: 1990
1000 runs in a season: 5
1st-Class 50s: 48
1st-Class 100s: 25
1st-Class 200s: 1

1st-Class catches: 107
One-Day 100s: 6
Place in batting averages: 130th av. 33.46
(1995 84th av. 36.60)
Strike rate: (career 101.00)
Parents: Clifford and Ruth
Wife and date of marriage: Clare, 1996
Family links with cricket: Brother John
played school and college cricket
Education: Bedford Modern School; Durham
University
Qualifications: 9 O-levels, 3 A-levels, BSc
(Hons) Chemistry, NCA senior coaching award
Career outside cricket: 'Still groping in the
dark'
Off-season: Coaching and playing in Cape
Town
Overseas tours: Bedford Modern to
Barbados 1983; Gentlemen of Leicestershire to Jersey and Guernsey 1987;
International Ambassadors XI/Christians in Sport to India 1989-90, to Zimbabwe
1994-95; MCC to Leeward Islands 1991-92, to Bangladesh 1995-96;
Northamptonshire to Natal 1991-92; Singapore Sixes 1995
Overseas teams played for: Richmond, Melbourne 1983-84; Camberwell, Melbourne
1987-88; Curtin University, Perth, Western Australia 1988; Nirman Schools XI,
Dhaka, Bangladesh 1989-90; Montrose, Cape Town, South Africa 1992-93 and 1996-
97
Cricketers particularly admired: Allan Lamb, Bob Willis, Mike Brearley
Young players to look out for: Alun Evans, Michael Davies
Other sports followed: Rugby union (Bedford RFC) and football (Aston Villa)
Injuries: Broken thumb, missed two weeks
Relaxations: Television, music, travel
Extras: Has appeared for Bedfordshire in Minor Counties Championship. Played for
Combined Universities in B&H Cup 1987. Shared county third-wicket record stand of
393 with Allan Lamb v Yorkshire at Headingley in 1990. First white man to have played
league cricket in Bangladesh. Treasurer of the Professional Cricketers' Association
Opinions on cricket: 'Pitch quality remains a huge concern. The health of county
cricket depends on the surfaces we play on to a great extent, so if pitches are sub-
standard then English and ultimately England cricket will under-achieve, I'm sure no
one wants that.'
Best batting: 206* Northamptonshire v Yorkshire, Headingley 1990
Best bowling: 1-0 Northamptonshire v West Indies, Northampton 1995

1996 Season

	M	Inns	NO	Runs	HS	Avge	100s	50s	Ct	St	O	M	Runs	Wkts	Avge	Best	5wI	10wM
Test																		
All First	10	18	3	502	144 *	33.46	1	2	8	-								
1-day Int																		
NatWest	1	1	0	27	27	27.00	-	-	1	-								
B & H	5	5	0	29	14	5.80	-	-	2	-								
Sunday	6	5	0	71	43	14.20	-	-	4	-								

Career Performances

	M	Inns	NO	Runs	HS	Avge	100s	50s	Ct	St	Balls	Runs	Wkts	Avge	Best	5wI	10wM
Test																	
All First	158	280	22	10266	206 *	39.79	25	48	107	-	404	289	4	72.25	1-0	-	-
1-day Int																	
NatWest	24	24	1	1158	132 *	50.34	3	6	4	-	21	6	1	6.00	1-3	-	
B & H	27	26	1	732	108	29.28	2	4	6	-							
Sunday	107	100	1	2617	111	26.43	1	17	29	-	6	10	0	-	-	-	-

FOSTER, M. J.   Durham

Name: Michael James Foster
Role: Right-hand bat, right arm medium-fast bowler
Born: 17 September 1972, Leeds
Height: 6ft 2in **Weight:** 15st
Nickname: The Bear, Jodie, Bluto
County debut: 1996 (Durham)
1st-Class 50s: 1
1st-Class catches: 6
One-Day 100s: 1
Place in batting averages: 286th av. 11.16
Strike rate: 70.12 (career 63.57)
Parents: Paul and Maggie
Marital status: Single
Family links with cricket: 'All the family have played, even my sister'
Education: Park High School; New College, Pontefract
Qualifications: 7 GCSEs, 2 A-levels
Off-season: 'Mending my back'
Overseas tours: England U19 to Pakistan 1992; Yorkshire to West Indies
Overseas teams played for: Fremantle, Perth, Western Australia; Queenstown, New

Zealand; Ringswood, Melbourne, Australia
Cricketers particularly admired: The Waugh brothers
Other sports followed: Rugby, squash, football (Newcastle United)
Injuries: 'Spondeoslythesis of the back'
Relaxations: Training, walking Tax, my dog, and drinking
Extras: 'Have played at three counties already, am setting my sights on the record'
Opinions on cricket: 'Should be more professional in our preparations and approach like the Aussies and South Africans.'
Best batting: 63* Yorkshire v Oxford University, The Parks 1994
Best bowling: 4-21 Durham v Middlesex, Lord's 1996

1996 Season

	M	Inns	NO	Runs	HS	Avge	100s	50s	Ct	St	O	M	Runs	Wkts	Avge	Best	5wI	10wM
Test																		
All First	3	6	0	67	25	11.16	-	-	-	-	93.3	15	311	8	38.87	4-21	--	
1-day Int																		
NatWest																		
B & H	5	5	2	105	52	35.00	-	1	-	-	39.2	1	183	4	45.75	2-52	-	
Sunday	4	4	0	96	44	24.00	-	-	-	-	28	1	146	3	48.66	2-57	-	

Career Performances

	M	Inns	NO	Runs	HS	Avge	100s	50s	Ct	St	Balls	Runs	Wkts	Avge	Best	5wI	10wM
Test																	
All First	8	13	1	232	63 *	19.33	-	1	6	-	890	461	14	32.92	4-21	-	-
1-day Int																	
NatWest																	
B & H	5	5	2	105	52	35.00	-	1	-	-	236	183	4	45.75	2-52	-	
Sunday	28	21	2	309	118	16.26	1	-	7	-	690	640	12	53.33	2-30	-	

35. Name the New Zealand women's all-rounder who made the headlines by catching England captain Michael Atherton during a benefit match for Danny Morrison in 1996-97?

FRANCIS, S. R. G.   Hampshire

Name: Simon Richard George Francis
Role: Right-hand bat, right-arm
medium-fast bowler
Born: 15 August 1978, Bromley
Height: 6ft 2in **Weight:** 13st
Nickname: Drakie
County debut: No first-team appearance
Parents: Daniel and Linda
Marital status: Single
Family links with cricket: Father and
grandfather both played club cricket. Brother
played for England U15 in the Lombard
World Cup
Education: Yardley Court, Tonbridge; King
Edward VI, Southampton; Durham University
Qualifications: 10 GCSEs, 3 A-levels
Off-season: At university
Overseas tours: England U17 to Holland for
International Youth Tournament 1995

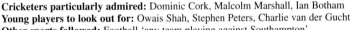

Cricketers particularly admired: Dominic Cork, Malcolm Marshall, Ian Botham
Young players to look out for: Owais Shah, Stephen Peters, Charlie van der Gucht
Other sports followed: Football 'any team playing against Southampton'
Injuries: Lower back, missed first three months of the season
Relaxations: 'Listening to music, partying and going out with the lads for a few
bevvies, women'
Extras: *Daily Telegraph* West Region Bowling Award U15
Opinions on cricket: 'Ask me again when I've played first-class cricket. Not been in
the game long enough.'

FRANKS, P. J.   Nottinghamshire

Name: Paul John Franks
Role: Left-hand bat, right-arm fast-medium bowler
Born: 3 February 1979, Mansfield
Height: 6ft 2in **Weight:** 12st 7lbs
Nickname: Pike, Franksie
County debut: 1996
Strike rate: (career 82.00)
Parents: John and Patricia

Marital status: Single
Family links with cricket: Father played local league cricket for thirty years
Education: Walter D'Ayncourt Primary School; Southwell Minster; West Notts College
Qualifications: 7 GCSEs, NCA coaching award
Off-season: Playing overseas
Overseas tours: England U19 to Pakistan 1996-97
Cricketers particularly admired: Allan Donald, Curtly Ambrose
Other sports followed: Football (Manchester United), golf (Nick Faldo)
Relaxations: Playing golf and travelling
Opinions on cricket: 'An interest from a wider range of sponsors is needed to ensure that the game continues to develop as it needs to.'

Best bowling: 2-65 Nottinghamshire v Hampshire, Southampton 1996

1996 Season

	M	Inns	NO	Runs	HS	Avge	100s	50s	Ct	St	O	M	Runs	Wkts	Avge	Best	5wl	10wM
Test																		
All First	1	0	0	0	0	-	-	-	-	-	41	14	102	3	34.00	2-65	--	
1-day Int																		
NatWest																		
B & H																		
Sunday																		

Career Performances

	M	Inns	NO	Runs	HS	Avge	100s	50s	Ct	St	Balls	Runs	Wkts	Avge	Best	5wl	10wM
Test																	
All First	1	0	0	0	0	-	-	-	-	-	246	102	3	34.00	2-65	-	-
1-day Int																	
NatWest																	
B & H																	
Sunday																	

FRASER, A. R. C. Middlesex

Name: Angus Robert Charles Fraser
Role: Right-hand bat, right-arm medium-fast bowler, outfielder 'specialist'
Born: 8 August 1965, Billinge, Lancashire
Height: 6ft 6in **Weight:** 15st 10lbs
Nickname: Gus, Soup
County debut: 1984
County cap: 1988
Test debut: 1989
Tests: 32
One-Day Internationals: 33
50 wickets in a season: 6
1st-Class 50s: 1
1st-Class 5 w. in innings: 24
1st-Class 10 w. in match: 3
1st-Class catches: 38
Place in batting averages: 292nd av. 10.81
Place in bowling averages: 81st av. 33.38
(1995 63rd av. 29.14)

Strike rate: 72.57 (career 61.93)
Parents: Don and Irene
Wife: Denise
Children: Alexander Charles Mitchell; Bethan Louise
Family links with cricket: Brother Alastair played for Middlesex and Essex. Parents are keen followers
Education: Weald First School; Gayton High School, Harrow; Orange Senior High School, Edgware
Qualifications: 7 O-levels, qualified cricket coach
Career outside cricket: 'Worked for Whittingdale Holding Ltd. 1991-93 when injured. Television work for Sky TV and write for *The Daily Telegraph*'
Off-season: 'At home, doing whatever comes my way and getting fit for next summer'
Overseas tours: Thames Valley Gentlemen to Barbados 1985; Middlesex to La Manga 1985 and 1986, to Portugal 1991-93; England to India (Nehru Cup) 1989-90, to West Indies 1989-90, to Australia 1990-91, to West Indies 1993-94, to Australia 1994-95, to South Africa 1995-96
Overseas teams played for: Plimmerton, Wellington 1985-86 and 1987-88; Western Suburbs, Sydney 1988-89 and 1994-95
Cricketers particularly admired: Richard Hadlee, Allan Border, Graham Gooch and Curtly Ambrose
Young players to look out for: Mike Gatting and John Emburey

Other sports followed: 'Follow Liverpool FC keenly. Enjoy watching rugby internationals at my local rugby club, Harrow'

Injuries: 'Fit all year again, although ego took a bit of a pounding at times'

Relaxations: 'Watching Liverpool FC, Harrow RFC and internationals. Watch most sport to the annoyance of my wife, Denise. Didn't have much time to relax last summer as the batsmen didn't bat for long enough'

Extras: Middlesex Player of the Year 1988 and 1989. Took a hat-trick in the Benson and Hedges Cup in 1989. Selected for England tour to New Zealand 1991-92 but ruled out by injury. Originally left out of England tour party to Australia 1994-95 but called up when Martin McCague was injured. Took his 100th Test wicket (Brian Lara) against West Indies in 1995. Finished 2nd in the Whyte and Mackay bowling ratings for 1995. *Wisden* Cricketer of the Year 1996. Awarded benefit by Middlesex for 1997

Opinions on cricket: 'Keep overseas players in the game. Something needs to be done about left-arm spinners bowling over the wicket, I don't know what though. The way that players are treated over public statements and the fact that they are vetted so tightly is scandalous. We are treated like children. Hell, I'm 31, I've got a mortgage, two children, I can vote but I can't say what I feel about the game in case I upset a few people. Agree with a two division County Championship to make the county game more competitive. The wickets in 1996 were a fair contest.'

Best batting: 92 Middlesex v Surrey, The Oval 1990

Best bowling: 8-75 England v West Indies, Bridgetown, 1994

1996 Season

	M	Inns	NO	Runs	HS	Avge	100s	50s	Ct	St	O	M	Runs	Wkts	Avge	Best	5wI	10wM
Test																		
All First	18	28	6	238	33	10.81	-	-	3	-	592.4	138	1636	49	33.38	5-55	2	1
1-day Int																		
NatWest	2	2	1	18	16	18.00	-	-	-	-	14	1	47	2	23.50	1-8	-	
B & H	5	4	3	23	10 *	23.00	-	-	-	-	43	11	149	4	37.25	2-27	-	
Sunday	16	7	2	54	16 *	10.80	-	-	2	-	126	9	569	14	40.64	2-20	-	

Career Performances

	M	Inns	NO	Runs	HS	Avge	100s	50s	Ct	St	Balls	Runs	Wkts	Avge	Best	5wI	10wM
Test	32	46	10	265	29	7.36	-	-	7	-	7967	3509	119	29.48	8-75	8	-
All Firsts	201	235	57	1931	92	10.84	-	1	38	-	38695	16746	613	27.31	8-75	24	3
1-day Int	33	14	6	80	38 *	10.00	-	-	1	-	1876	1132	38	29.78	4-22	-	
NatWest	25	9	7	56	19	28.00	-	-	3	-	1623	824	38	21.68	4-34	-	
B & H	35	18	9	65	13 *	7.22	-	-	7	-	2073	1199	45	26.64	4-49	-	
Sunday	131	49	22	301	30 *	11.14	-	-	19	-	5744	3847	131	29.36	5-32	1	

FROST, A.   Warwickshire

Name: Anthony Frost
Role: Right-hand bat, wicket-keeper
Born: 17 November 1975, Stoke-on-Trent
Height: 5ft 10in **Weight:** 10st 6lbs
County debut: No first-team apppearance
Parents: Ivan and Christine
Marital status: Single
Family links with cricket: Father played for
Staffordshire
Education: James Brinkley High School;
Stoke-on-Trent College
Qualifications: 5 GCSEs
Off-season: Training
Overseas tours: Kidsgrove U18 to Australia
1990-91
Cricketers particularly admired: Ashley
Giles 'could be described as a legend', 'Pop'
Welch and George Burns 'in the JT bracket'
Other sports followed: Football, golf
Relaxations: Listening to music, watching films, reading aircraft magazines
Extras: Has represented Staffordshire at all levels from U11 to U19. Won Texaco U16
competition with Staffordshire in 1992. Played for Development of Excellence XI U17
v South Africa and U18 v West Indies and U19 v India
Opinions on cricket: 'A lot of people are too critical. If they spent more time building
up the players' confidence instead of putting the player down then they may get better
results. '

FULTON, D. P.   Kent

Name: David Paul Fulton
Role: Right-hand bat, 'The most versatile bowler on the circuit. Also the worst'
Born: 15 November 1971, Lewisham
Height: 6ft 2in **Weight:** 12st
Nickname: Raver, Tav
County debut: 1992
1st-Class 50s: 12
1st-Class 100s: 3
1st-Class catches: 67
Place in batting averages: 150th av. 31.55 (1995 107th av.33.46)

Strike rate: 66.00 (career 67.00)
Parents: John and Ann
Marital status: Single
Family links with cricket: 'Dad plays for village side. Anyone who has watched him will realise my tendency to aim consistently through mid-wicket is hereditary'
Education: Otford County Primary; The Judd School, Tonbridge; University of Kent
Qualifications: 10 GCSEs, 3 A-levels, BA (Hons) Politics and International Relations, senior cricket coach, rugby coach, gym instructor
Career outside cricket: Personal trainer. 'Eventually a diplomat'
Off-season: Working as a personal trainer. 'Attempting to run a student dating agency at the University of Kent'
Overseas tours: Kent Schools U17 to Singapore and New Zealand
Overseas teams played for: Avendale, Cape Town 1993-94; Victoria, Cape Town 1994-95, University of WA, Perth 1995-96
Cricketers particularly admired: Gordon Greenidge, Graham Gooch, Viv Richards, Robin Smith, Curtly Ambrose, Courtney Walsh, Ian Bishop, Steve Waugh
Young players to look out for: Ben Phillips, 'The Musketeers at Kent'
Other sports followed: Rugby (Harlequins) and football (Nottingham Forest), tennis, table tennis ('top 10 in UK as a junior'), chess (England junior), boxing
Relaxations: 'Pursuing money-making schemes.' Clubs, pubs, golf and working out
Extras: 'Helped Dean Headley's hat-trick against Derbyshire by catching Kim Barnett and Chris Adams. Was the last person to catch the great Viv Richards in a first-class match. Opened the batting and the bowling against South Africa in their first county game. Once scored 2000 runs without being dismissed against my little sister in the back garden'
Opinions on cricket: 'As one of the game's deepest thinkers I could be here all day – suffice it to say that it is a game which should be enjoyed more because in the whole scheme of things it seems rather daft to me.'
Best batting: 134* Kent v Oxford University, Canterbury 1996
Best bowling: 1-37 Kent v Oxford University, Canterbury 1996

36. Who, in 1997, became the youngest player to score 3000 Test runs and whose record did he beat?

1996 Season

	M	Inns	NO	Runs	HS	Avge	100s	50s	Ct	St	O	M	Runs	Wkts	Avge	Best	5wl	10wM
Test																		
All First	17	30	3	852	134 *	31.55	1	5	25	-	11	1	65	1	65.00	1-37	-	-
1-day Int																		
NatWest																			
B & H																			
Sunday	2	2	0	18	18	9.00	-	-	1	-								

Career Performances

	M	Inns	NO	Runs	HS	Avge	100s	50s	Ct	St	Balls	Runs	Wkts	Avge	Best	5wl	10wM
Test																	
All First	43	77	5	2152	134 *	29.88	3	12	67	-	67	65	1	65.00	1-37	-	-
1-day Int																	
NatWest	3	3	0	41	19	13.66	-	-	-	-	6	9	0	-		-	-
B & H	1	1	0	25	25	25.00	-	-	1	-							
Sunday	9	9	0	77	29	8.55	-	-	4	-							

GALLIAN, J. E. R.   Lancashire

Name: Jason Edward Riche Gallian
Role: Right-hand bat, right-arm
medium bowler
Born: 25 June 1971, Manly, NSW, Australia
Height: 6ft **Weight:** 13st
Nickname: Gally
County debut: 1990
Test debut: 1995
Tests: 3
1000 runs in a season: 2
1st-Class 50s: 21
1st-Class 100s: 11
1st-Class 300s: 1
1st-Class 5 w. in innings: 1
1st-Class catches: 50
One-Day 100s: 3
One-Day 5 w. in innings: 1
Place in batting averages: 54th av. 44.46
(1995 80th av. 37.40)
Place in bowling averages: 100th av. 36.00 (1995 87th av.33.31)
Strike rate: 56.50 (career 68.55)
Parents: Ray and Marilyn

Marital status: Single
Family links with cricket: Father played for Stockport
Education: The Pittwater House Schools, Australia; Oxford University
Qualifications: Higher School Certificate, Diploma in Social Studies
(Keble College, Oxford)
Off-season: Touring Australia with England A
Overseas tours: Australia U20 to West Indies 1989-90; England A to India 1994-95, to Pakistan 1995-96, to Australia 1996-97; England to South Africa 1995-96
Overseas teams played for: NSW and Australia U19 1988-89; NSW Colts and NSW 2nd XI 1990-91; Australia U20 and U21 1991-92; Manly 1993-94
Cricketers particularly admired: Desmond Haynes, Mike Gatting
Other sports followed: Rugby league and union, football
Injuries: Broken finger, out for six weeks
Relaxations: Listening to music, playing golf
Extras: Played for Oxford University in 1992 and for Combined Universities in the B&H Cup. Captained Oxford University 1993. Was called up to the England squad in South Africa in 1995-96 as a replacement for the injured John Crawley and played in the fourth Test at Port Elizabeth. He was dogged by finger injuries throughout the England A tour to Australia in 1996-97
Best batting: 312 Lancashire v Derbyshire, Old Trafford 1996
Best bowling: 6-115 Lancashire v Surrey, Southport 1996

1996 Season

	M	Inns	NO	Runs	HS	Avge	100s	50s	Ct	St	O	M	Runs	Wkts	Avge	Best	5wI	10wM
Test																		
All First	15	29	3	1156	312	44.46	3	3	10	-	150.4	28	576	16	36.00	6-115	1	-
1-day Int																		
NatWest	4	4	0	102	35	25.50	-	-	3	-	4	0	11	1	11.00	1-11	-	
B & H	6	6	0	115	61	19.16	-	1	2	-	14	2	61	4	15.25	3-30	-	
Sunday	13	13	1	333	85	27.75	-	2	7	-	29.1	1	187	5	37.40	2-34	-	

Career Performances

	M	Inns	NO	Runs	HS	Avge	100s	50s	Ct	St	Balls	Runs	Wkts	Avge	Best	5wI	10wM
Test	3	6	0	74	28	12.33	-	-	1	-	84	62	0	-	-	-	-
All First	79	138	10	5184	312	40.50	11	25	50	-	5073	2922	74	39.48	6-115	1	-
1-day Int																	
NatWest	7	7	1	211	101 *	35.16	1	-	3	-	78	51	1	51.00	1-11	-	
B & H	20	19	1	612	134	34.00	2	3	3	-	407	323	12	26.91	5-15	1	
Sunday	36	35	4	978	85	31.54	-	7	13	-	526	509	22	23.13	2-10	-	

GARAWAY, M. Hampshire

Name: Mark Garaway
Role: Right-hand bat, wicket-keeper
Born: 20 July 1973, Swindon, Wilts
Height: 5ft 7in **Weight:** 11st 8lbs
Nickname: Wolf
County debut: 1996
1st-Class catches: 4
1st-Class stumpings: 1
Parents: Michael and Valerie Anne
Marital status: Single
Family links with cricket: 'Grandfather kept
wicket for 40 years for Glamorgan. Father
regularly outscores and outclasses me at club
level for Ventnor 1st XI. Sister captains
Ventnor U14'
Education: Carhampton Primary, Somerset;
Ventnor Middle and Sandown High School,
Isle of Wight, 'Ventnor CC, the Astoria
(Hermanus, SA)'

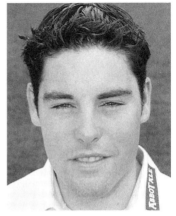

Qualifications: 10 O-levels, 3 A-levels, NCA cricket coach
Career outside cricket: Civil engineer
Off-season: Working and playing in Hermanus, South Africa for three months before
returning to coach cricket in Hampshire and the Isle of Wight
Overseas tours: Isle of Wight U14 and U17 to Jersey and Guernsey 1988-91; Ventnor
to Winchester 1994; Hampshire to Val de Lobo 1994
Overseas teams played for: Worcester, Boland, South Africa 1991-93; Hermanus,
South Africa 1993, 1995-97; 'Ventnor, Isle of Wight 1982-94'
Cricketers particularly admired: Ian Botham, Robin Smith, Jeff Hose, Gary Yates and
Simon Rodney
Young players to look out for: Jason Laney, Dimitri Mascarenhas, Adam Hope
Other sports followed: Football (Swindon Town – 'somebody has to keep Jason Laney
company').
Injuries: Bruised retina, missed the last game of the season
Relaxations: 'Music, sun bathing, video watching, regular socialising and the odd bit of
training'
Extras: Represented England at U15, U17 and U19 level. Played for Isle of Wight at
U16, U17, U21 and senior level in the same season. Spent two years (1991 and 1992) as
MCC Young Professional. Hampshire Schools Wicketkeepers Award 1988. Andrew
Swallow Memorial Cup 1987. Wight Waters Sports Award 1989-91
Opinions on cricket: 'People are generally too hasty in criticising English cricket,
mostly after poor performances in a Test or one-day international. A more positive and

patient public and media will greatly increase the chances of a cricketing revival in this country. Equally, a more long-term plan by cricketing hierarchy in terms of the development of the county championship (two divisions?), selection for the England team and the coaches, managers and selectors that run them will, in my opinion, assist in the quest of returning English cricket to its rightful position.'

Best batting: 44 Hampshire v Cambridge University, Fenner's 1996

1996 Season

	M	Inns	NO	Runs	HS	Avge	100s	50s	Ct	St	O	M	Runs	Wkts	Avge	Best	5wI	10wM
Test																		
All First	1	1	0	44	44	44.00	-	-	4	1								
1-day Int																		
NatWest																		
B & H																		
Sunday																		

Career Performances

	M	Inns	NO	Runs	HS	Avge	100s	50s	Ct	St	Balls	Runs	Wkts	Avge	Best	5wI	10wM
Test																		
All First	1	1	0	44	44	44.00	-	-	4	1								
1-day Int																		
NatWest																		
B & H																		
Sunday																		

37. Which former Test player will succeed Les Lenham
as coach of the British Universities XI in 1997?

GATTING, M. W. Middlesex

Name: Michael William Gatting
Role: Right-hand bat, right-arm medium bowler, slip fielder
Born: 6 June 1957, Kingsbury, Middlesex
Height: 5ft 10in **Weight:** 15st 7lbs
Nickname: Gatt, Jabba
County debut: 1975
County cap: 1977
Benefit: 1988 (£205,000)
Test debut: 1977-78
Tests: 79
One-Day Internationals: 92
1000 runs in a season: 17
1st-Class 50s: 170
1st-Class 100s: 90
1st-Class 200s: 9
1st-Class 5 w. in innings: 2
1st-Class catches: 451
One-Day 100s: 12

Place in batting averages: 104th av. 36.04 (1995 16th av. 54.23)
Strike rate: (career 64.03)
Parents: Bill and Vera
Wife and date of marriage: Elaine, 9 September 1980
Children: Andrew, 21 January 1983; James, 11 July 1986
Family links with cricket: Father used to play club cricket. Brother Steve played for Middlesex 2nd XI
Education: Wykeham Primary School; John Kelly Boys' High School
Qualifications: 4 O-levels
Off-season: Travelling with the England A side as coach
Overseas tours: England to New Zealand and Pakistan 1977-78, to West Indies 1980-81, to India and Sri Lanka 1981-82, to New Zealand and Pakistan 1983-84, to India 1984-85, to West Indies 1985-86, to Australia 1986-87, to India and Pakistan (World Cup), Australia and New Zealand 1987-88; unofficial English XI to South Africa 1989-90; England to India and Sri Lanka 1992-93, to Australia 1994-95
Cricketers particularly admired: Gary Sobers, Len Hutton
Young players to look out for: Andrew Harris, Owais Shah, Vikram Solanki, David Nash, James Hewitt
Other sports followed: Football, golf, tennis, swimming, indoor cricket, rugby
Injuries: Knee surgery for torn ligament and a virus, missed a total of five weeks
Relaxations: Golf, swimming, reading, music
Extras: Awarded OBE in Queen's Birthday Honours 1987 for services to cricket.

Captain of Middlesex since 1983. Captain of England from 1986 to 1988. Published autobiography *Leading From the Front* in 1988. Won a bronze medal for ballroom dancing at the Neasden Ritz. Played football for Edgware Town as a teenager. Started as a goalkeeper, but also played centre-half for Middlesex Schools. Was recommended to West Ham, had a trial with QPR and offered an apprenticeship by Watford. His brother Steve has had a successful football career with Arsenal and Brighton. Mike started his cricket career as wicket-keeper for his school team. He toured West Indies with England Young Cricketers in 1976 and 'to my immense pleasure (and to most other people's total disbelief) I was given the job of opening the bowling in the "Test" matches.' One of *Wisden*'s Five Cricketers of the Year 1983. His finest achievement was as captain of England on victorious tour of Australia, 1986-87, when they won the Ashes, the Perth Challenge Cup and World Series Cup. Was relieved of England captaincy after the First Test against West Indies in 1988. Captain of unofficial English team in South Africa in 1989-90 and was banned from Test cricket for five years; suspension remitted in 1992. Captained Middlesex to Championship title in 1990 and 1993. Retired from Test cricket after the final Test of the 1994-95 series against Australia

Opinions on cricket: 'Four-day cricket has been an eye-opener.'

Best batting: 258 Middlesex v Somerset, Bath 1984

Best bowling: 5-34 Middlesex v Glamorgan, Swansea 1982

1996 Season

	M	Inns	NO	Runs	HS	Avge	100s	50s	Ct	St	O	M	Runs	Wkts	Avge	Best	5wI	10wM
Test																		
All First	16	25	0	901	171	36.04	1	8	10	-	4	0	25	0	-	-	-	-
1-day Int																		
NatWest	2	2	0	77	71	38.50	-	1	-	-								
B & H	5	5	0	83	45	16.60	-	-	4	-								
Sunday	12	12	1	375	90	34.09	-	2	2	-								

Career Performances

	M	Inns	NO	Runs	HS	Avge	100s	50s	Ct	St	Balls	Runs	Wkts	Avge	Best	5wI	10wM
Test	79	138	14	4409	207	35.55	10	21	59	-	752	317	4	79.25	1-14	-	-
All First	515	803	118	34357	258	50.15	90	170	451	-	9989	4648	156	29.79	5-34	2	-
1-day Int	92	88	17	2095	115 *	29.50	1	9	22	-	392	336	10	33.60	3-32	-	
NatWest	61	59	13	2083	132 *	45.28	2	15	24	-	1004	643	19	33.84	2-14	-	
B & H	92	86	18	2859	143 *	42.04	3	18	28	-	1382	940	41	22.92	4-49	-	
Sunday	257	231	29	6507	124 *	32.21	6	39	84	-	3196	2730	90	30.33	4-30	-	

GIBSON, O. D.　　　　　　　　Glamorgan

Name: Ottis Delroy Gibson
Role: Right-hand bat, right-arm fast bowler
Born: 16 March 1969, St James, Barbados
Height: 6ft 2in **Weight:** 13st 3lb
County debut: 1994
Test debut: 1995
Tests: 1
One-day Internationals: 13
50 wickets in a season: 1
1st-Class 50s: 14
1st-Class 100s: 1
1st-Class 5 w. in innings: 12
1st-Class 10 w. in match: 3
1st-Class catches: 30
Place in batting averages: 92nd av. 37.41
(1995 149th av. 27.54)
Place in bowling averages: 144th av. 52.00
(1995 80th av. 31.36)

Strike rate: 76.20 (career 51.64)
Marital status: Single
Education: St Silas Primary; Ellerslie Secondary
Qualifications: 3 O-levels
Overseas tours: West Indies to England 1995, to Australia 1995-96, to India and Pakistan (World Cup) 1995-96
Overseas teams played for: Fremantle, Perth 1989-90; Spartan, Barbados and Barbados 1991-94 ; Border, South Africa 1992-95
Cricketers particularly admired: Malcolm Marshall, Ian Botham, Viv Richards, Brian Lara
Other sports followed: All sports
Extras: Played for Farnworth in the Bolton League 1992 and 1993. South African Player of the Year 1992-93. Has played for West Indies A. Reported to have hit a straight six 150 yards over the pavilion at Buffalo Park, East London (South Africa) and into a car park
Best batting: 101* West Indies v Somerset, Taunton 1995
Best bowling: 7-55 Border v Natal, Durban 1994-95

1996 Season

	M	Inns	NO	Runs	HS	Avge	100s	50s	Ct	St	O	M	Runs	Wkts	Avge	Best	5wI	10wM
Test																		
All First	9	15	3	449	97	37.41	-	3	6	-	254	41	1040	20	52.00	3-43	-	-
1-day Int																		
NatWest																		
B & H	3	1	0	68	68	68.00	-	1	-	-	25	3	126	1	126.00	1-33	-	
Sunday	12	9	1	156	47 *	19.50	-	-	4	-	76.4	5	339	10	33.90	2-18	-	

Career Performances

	M	Inns	NO	Runs	HS	Avge	100s	50s	Ct	St	Balls	Runs	Wkts	Avge	Best	5wI	10wM
Test	1	2	0	43	29	21.50	-	-	-	-	204	132	2	66.00	2-81	-	-
All First	84	121	19	2322	101 *	22.76	1	14	30	-	14770	8565	286	29.94	7-55	12	3
1-day Int	13	10	1	138	52	15.33	-	1	3	-	631	512	29	17.65	5-40	2	
NatWest	3	3	0	68	44	22.66	-	-	1	-	162	116	5	23.20	3-34	-	
B & H	4	2	0	105	68	52.50	-	1	-	-	202	176	3	58.66	2-50	-	
Sunday	29	24	8	362	47 *	22.62	-	-	8	-	1017	785	22	35.68	2-18	-	

GIDDINS, E. S. H.   Warwickshire

Name: Edward Simon Hunter Giddins
Role: Right-hand bat, right-arm
medium-fast bowler
Born: 20 July 1971, Eastbourne
Height: 6ft 4in **Weight:** 13st 7lb
Nickname: Geezer
County debut: 1991
County cap: 1994
50 wickets in a season: 2
1st-Class 5 w. in innings: 13
1st-Class 10 w. in match: 1
1st-Class catches: 12
Place in batting averages: 313th av. 5.50
Place in bowling averages: 24th av. 25.08
(1995 67th av. 29.47)
Strike rate: 45.95 (career 53.46)
Parents: Simon and Pauline
Marital status: Single
Family links with cricket: None
Education: St Bede's Prep School; Eastbourne College
Qualifications: 'Various O and A-levels, national coaching certificate, recorder (grade 2), shorthand and typing 100/60.'

Career outside cricket: None
Off-season: 'Due to an enforced extended close season, I'm in the middle of an intense fitness and strength programme to enable me to be a fitter, stronger person for the sole purpose of being of more benefit to Warwickshire'
Overseas tours: England A to Pakistan 1995-96
Overseas teams played for: Mossman, Sydney 1994-95
Cricketers particularly admired: Derek Randall
Young players to look out for: Alan Wells
Other sports followed: Brighton & Hove Albion FC, 'fingers crossed'
Injuries: Severe earache, out for 20 months
Relaxations: Gym, fitness and mountain biking
Best batting: 34 Sussex v Essex, Hove 1995
Best bowling: 6-47 Sussex v Yorkshire, Eastbourne 1996

1996 Season

	M	Inns	NO	Runs	HS	Avge	100s	50s	Ct	St	O	M	Runs	Wkts	Avge	Best	5wI	10wM
Test																		
All First	14	16	6	55	11	5.50	-	-	-	-	367.4	66	1204	48	25.08	6-47	2	-
1-day Int																		
NatWest	2	2	1	12	10 *	12.00	-	-	-	-	19	1	58	4	14.50	3-24	-	
B & H	3	1	1	0	0 *	-	-	-	1	-	29.4	2	122	1	122.00	1-42	-	
Sunday	6	3	1	3	2	1.50	-	-	-	-	43	2	268	4	67.00	1-23	-	

Career Performances

	M	Inns	NO	Runs	HS	Avge	100s	50s	Ct	St	Balls	Runs	Wkts	Avge	Best	5wI	10wM
Test																	
All First	80	96	39	321	34	5.63	-	-	12	-	13259	7427	248	29.94	6-47	13	1
1-day Int																	
NatWest	10	4	2	25	13	12.50	-	-	-	-	665	393	11	35.72	3-24	-	
B & H	12	3	2	0	0 *	0.00	-	-	3	-	704	468	11	42.54	3-28	-	
Sunday	62	28	11	25	9 *	1.47	-	-	8	-	2604	2255	70	32.21	4-23	-	

GIE, N. A.   Nottinghamshire

Name: Noel Addison Gie
Role: Right-hand bat, right-arm medium bowler
Born: 12 April 1977, Pretoria, South Africa
Height: 6ft **Weight:** 12st 8lbs
County debut: 1995
Place in batting averages: (1995 238th av. 16.33)
Parents: Clive and Lindy

Marital status: Single
Family links with cricket: Father played first-class cricket in South Africa for Western Province, Northern Transvaal and Natal
Education: Fornwood School, Nottingham; Trent College, Nottingham; Nottingham Trent University
Qualificatons: Studying for degree in Business Studies from October 1996, NCA coaching award
Overseas tours: Trent College to Australia 1993-94; England U19 to Zimbabwe 1995-96
Overseas teams played for: Berea Rovers, Durban, South Africa 1995
Cricketers particularly admired: Robin Smith
Other sports followed: Squash, tennis, rugby league
Relaxations: Reading and cycling
Extras: Scored 3,153 runs for the Ist XI during his time at Trent College
Opinions on cricket: 'Counties need to be more competitive i.e. fewer in "top league" and fewer players on full-time staff.'
Best batting: 34 Nottinghamshire v Glamorgan, Cardiff 1995

1996 Season

	M	Inns	NO	Runs	HS	Avge	100s	50s	Ct	St	O	M	Runs	Wkts	Avge	Best	5wI	10wM
Test																		
All First	1	0	0	0	0	-	-	-	-	-								
1-day Int																		
NatWest																		
B & H																		
Sunday																		

Career Performances

	M	Inns	NO	Runs	HS	Avge	100s	50s	Ct	St	Balls	Runs	Wkts	Avge	Best	5wI	10wM
Test																	
All First	4	6	0	98	34	16.33	-	-	-	-							
1-day Int																	
NatWest																	
B & H																	
Sunday																	

GILES, A. F.   Warwickshire

Name: Ashley Fraser Giles
Role: Right-hand bat, slow left-arm bowler
Born: 19 March 1973, Chertsey, Surrey
Height: 6ft 4in **Weight:** 15st 7lbs
Nickname: Splash, Skinny, Melink, Medog,
Savo Melinkovic
County debut: 1993
50 wickets in a season: 1
1st-Class 50s: 4
1st-Class 100s: 1
1st-Class 5 w. innings: 4
1st-Class catches: 11
One-Day 5 w. in innings: 1
Place in batting averages: 132nd av. 33.33
Place in bowling averages: 26th av. 25.23
(1995 17th av. 22.12)
Strike rate: 59.39 (career 59.40)
Parents: Michael and Paula

Marital status: 'Girlfriend Ally'
Family links with cricket: 'Brother Andrew and brother-in-law Nigel play club
cricket. Dad used to slog it. Sister Tracy gets it through'
Education: Kingfield Promary School, Old Woking; George Abbot County Secondary,
Guildford
Qualifications: 9 GCSEs, 2 A-levels, NCA coaching award
Off-season: Touring Australia with England A before Christmas and then playing in
Cape Town
Overseas tours: Surrey U19 to Barbados 1990-91; Warwickshire to Cape Town 1993
and 1996; England A to Australia 1996-97
Overseas teams played for: Vredenburg/Saldanha, South Africa 1992-95; Avendale
CC, Cape Town 1995-96
Cricketers particularly admired: Dermot Reeve, Ian Botham, Phil Tufnell, Allan
Donald and Dougie Brown
Young players to look out for: Darren Altree
Other sports followed: Football (QPR), golf, basketball
Injuries: Back spasms, but no time off
Relaxations: Listening to music, playing golf, socialising, 'getting premiered up with
Dougie and spending valuable time with Ally'
Extras: Surrey Young Cricketer of the Year 1991, NBC Dennis Compton Award for
Warwickshire in 1996. Whyte and Mackay Bowler of the Month for August.
Warwickshire Player of the Year in 1996. Warwickshire Most Improved Player 1996
Opinions on cricket: 'Great game. Should be played harder and marketed better.'

Best batting: 106* Warwickshire v Lancashire, Edgbaston 1996
Best bowling: 6-45 Warwickshire v Durham, Edgbaston 1996

1996 Season

	M	Inns	NO	Runs	HS	Avge	100s	50s	Ct	St	O	M	Runs	Wkts	Avge	Best	5wI	10wM
Test																		
All First	17	27	9	600	106 *	33.33	1	4	11	-	633.3	191	1615	64	25.23	6-45	3	-
1-day Int																		
NatWest	1	1	0	3	3	3.00	-	-	-	-	7	0	44	1	44.00	1-44	-	
B & H	4	2	0	17	9	8.50	-	-	2	-	19	1	105	1	105.00	1-49	-	
Sunday	16	8	2	110	36	18.33	-	-	7	-	79	4	353	22	16.04	5-36	1	

Career Performances

	M	Inns	NO	Runs	HS	Avge	100s	50s	Ct	St	Balls	Runs	Wkts	Avge	Best	5wI	10wM
Test																	
All First	25	36	10	737	106 *	28.34	1	4	11	-	4931	2097	83	25.26	6-45	4	-
1-day Int																	
NatWest	3	2	1	24	21 *	24.00	-	-	-	-	132	83	4	20.75	3-14	-	
B & H	4	2	0	17	9	8.50	-	-	2	-	114	105	1	105.00	1-49	-	
Sunday	19	8	2	110	36	18.33	-	-	9	-	474	353	22	16.04	5-36	1	

GOOCH, G. A. Essex

Name: Graham Alan Gooch
Role: Right-hand bat, right-arm
medium bowler
Born: 23 July 1953, Leytonstone
Height: 6ft **Weight:** 13st
Nickname: Zap, Goochie
County debut: 1973
County cap: 1975
Benefit: 1985 (£153,906)
Testimonial: 1995
Test debut: 1975
Tests: 118
One-Day Internationals: 125
1000 runs in a season: 20
1st-Class 50s: 128
1st-Class 100s: 128
1st-Class 200s: 12
1st-Class 300s: 1
1st-Class 5 w. in innings: 3

1st-Class catches: 543
One-Day 100s: 41
One-Day 5 w. innings: 1
Place in batting averages: 3rd av. 67.03 (1995 24th av. 50.2)
Strike rate: 63.00 (career 76.31)
Parents: Alfred and Rose
Wife and date of marriage: Brenda, 23 October 1976
Children: Hannah; Megan and Sally (twins)
Family links with cricket: Father played local cricket for East Ham Corinthians. Second cousin, Graham Saville, played for Essex CCC and was England U19 team manager
Education: Cannhall School and Norlington Junior High School, Leytonstone; Redbridge Technical College
Qualifications: 6 CSEs; four-year apprenticeship in tool-making
Overseas tours: England YC to West Indies 1971-72; England to Australia 1978-79, to Australia and India 1979-80, to West Indies 1980-81, to India and Sri Lanka 1981-82, to World Cup and Pakistan 1987-88, to India and West Indies 1989-90, to Australia 1990-91, to New Zealand 1991-92, to Australia (World Cup) 1991-92, to India 1992-93, to Australia 1994-95; unofficial English XI to South Africa 1981-82
Overseas teams played for: Western Province, South Africa 1982-84
Cricketers particularly admired: Bob Taylor, a model sportsman; Mike Procter for his enthusiasm; Barry Richards for his ability
Other sports followed: Squash, soccer, golf. Has trained with West Ham United FC
Relaxations: 'Relaxing at home'
Extras: One of *Wisden*'s Five Cricketers of the Year 1979. Captained English rebel team in South Africa in 1982 and was banned from Test cricket for three years. Hit a hole in one at Tollygunge Golf Club during England's tour in India, 1981-82. Appointed Essex captain 1986, but resigned captaincy at end of 1987, being reappointed in 1989 following retirement of Keith Fletcher. Captain of England for last two Tests of 1988 season against West Indies and Sri Lanka in 1988 and chosen to captain England on the cancelled tour of India in 1988-89. Reappointed captain for the tour to India and West Indies in 1989-90, and led England to their first Test victory over West Indies for 16 years. His 333 in the Lord's Test v India was the third highest score ever by an England batsman in a Test match, and by hitting 123 in the second innings he created a record Test aggregate of 456 runs and became the first man to hit a triple century and a century in the same first-class match. His aggregate for the season (2746 runs at 101.70) was the best since 1961 and he was only the fourth batsman to finish an English season with an average better than 100. When he first joined Essex, he was a wicket-keeper and batted at No 11 in his first match. He went on a Young England tour to the West Indies as second wicket-keeper to Andy Stovold of Gloucestershire. Autobiography *Out of the Wilderness* published in 1988; *Test of Fire,* an account of the West Indies tour, published in 1990; *Captaincy* published in 1992. Scored his 100th century in 1993. Resigned as England captain after Australia had retained the Ashes in 1993. Became the 15th player to pass 40,000 runs in first-class cricket. Resigned as Essex captain at end of 1994 season. Retired from Test cricket after final Test of 1994-95 series against

Australia. *Graham Gooch: My Autobiography* written with Frank Keating was published in 1995
Best batting: 333 England v India, Lord's 1990
Best bowling: 7-14 Essex v Worcestershire, Ilford 1982

1996 Season

	M	Inns	NO	Runs	HS	Avge	100s	50s	Ct	St	O	M	Runs	Wkts	Avge	Best	5wI	10wM
Test																		
All First	17	30	1	1944	201	67.03	8	6	18	-	21	7	57	2	28.50	1-20	-	-
1-day Int																		
NatWest	5	5	0	130	50	26.00	-	2	2	-								
B & H	5	5	1	172	100	43.00	1	-	5	-								
Sunday	7	6	0	186	87	31.00	-	1	4	-								

Career Performances

	M	Inns	NO	Runs	HS	Avge	100s	50s	Ct	St	Balls	Runs	Wkts	Avge	Best	5wI	10wM
Test	118	215	6	8900	333	42.58	20	46	103	-	2655	1069	23	46.47	3-39	-	-
All First	570	971	74	44472	333	49.57	128	215	543	-	18773	8454	246	34.36	7-14	3	-
1-day Int	125	122	6	4290	142	36.98	8	23	45	-	2066	1516	36	42.11	3-19	-	
NatWest	57	56	4	2547	144	48.98	6	17	27	-	1655	855	33	25.90	5-8	1	
B & H	111	110	14	5106	198 *	53.18	15	30	68	-	3770	2195	69	31.81	3-24	-	
Sunday	273	267	23	8545	176	35.02	12	58	100	-	2576	4244	143	29.67	4-33	-	

GOODCHILD, D. J.   Middlesex

Name: David John Goodchild
Role: Right-hand bat, right-arm medium bowler
Born: 17 September 1976, Harrow
Height: 6ft 2in **Weight:** 14st 7lbs
County debut: No first-team appearance
Nickname: Golden, G
Parents: John and Brenda
Marital status: Single
Family links with cricket: Father played club cricket
Education: Vaughan First and Middle School; Whitmore High School; Weald College; North London University
Qualifications: 9 GCSEs, 3 A-levels and NCA coaching award
Off-season: Relaxing, training and at

university
Cricketers particularly admired: Graham Gooch, Mike Gatting, Mark Ramprakash
Young players to look out for: Stefan James, Owais Shah
Other sports followed: Football (Arsenal), basketball, badminton, fishing, American football (Miami Dolphins)
Injuries: Dislocated finger, out for two weeks
Relaxations: 'Having a few drinks with my friends. Going to the cinema with my girlfriend Sarah and watching television'
Extras: Holds the top score for Middlesex U11 side (153) and the top total aggregate for that age group (563). Awarded 2nd XI county cap at the end of the 1996 season
Opinions on cricket: 'I think the lunch and tea intervals are too short. We play a lot of cricket and I feel that because of this not enough time is free to be devoted to basic cricket skills i.e. techniques and fielding practices.'

GOODWIN, G. J. A. Essex

Name: Giles Jeremy Anthony Goodwin
Role: Right-hand bat, left-arm bowler
Born: 16 September 1976, Isle of Sheppey
Height: 6ft 3in **Weight:** 13st 7lbs
Nickname: Jazza
County debut: No first-team appearance
Parents: Keith and Susan
Marital status: Single
Family links with cricket: 'Brother talks a good game'
Education: Felsted School; UMIST
Qualifications: 10 GCSEs, 3 A-levels
Off-season: Studying at Manchester University
Overseas tours: Felsted School to Australia 1995-96
Cricketers particularly admired: Phil Tufnell and Stuart Law
Young players to look out for: Stephen Peters
Other sports followed: Rugby (Leicester RFC), golf, squash and tennis
Relaxations: Socialising anywhere in Chelmsford and golf
Extras: Five seasons in Felsted 1st XI. Played England Schools U19, HMC Schools U19 and NCA XI
Opinions on cricket: 'An increased need to divide the championship into two divisions. This would decrease the number of matches and increase the will to win over the whole summer. More and more counties looking to their youth set-up for the next generation of players.'

GOUGH, D.   Yorkshire

Name: Darren Gough
Role: Right-hand bat, right-arm fast bowler
Born: 18 September 1970, Barnsley
Height: 5ft 11in **Weight:** 13st
Nickname: Dazzler
County debut: 1989
County cap: 1993
Test debut: 1994
Tests: 12
One-Day Internationals: 27
50 wickets in a season: 3
1st-Class 50s: 8
1st-Class 100s: 1
1st-Class 5 w. in innings: 13
1st-Class 10 w. in innings: 2
1st-Class catches: 31
One-day 5 w. innings: 2
Place in batting averages: 215th av. 22.77
(1995 219th av. 18.44)
Place in bowling averages: 14th av. 22.91 (1995 43rd av. 26.76)
Strike rate: 51.35 (career 54.26)
Parents: Trevor and Christine
Wife and date of marriage: Anna Marie, 16 October 1993
Children: Liam James, 24 November 1994
Education: St Helens Junior; Priory Comprehensive; Airedale and Wharfdale College (part-time)
Qualifications: 2 O-levels, 5 CSEs, BTEC Leisure, distinction coaching award 1
Off-season: Touring Zimbabwe and New Zealand with England
Overseas tours: England YC to Australia 1989-90; Yorkshire to Barbados 1989-90, to South Africa 1991-92 and 1992-93; England A to South Africa 1993-94; England to Australia 1994-95, to South Africa 1995-96, to India and Pakistan (World Cup) 1995-96, to Zimbabwe and New Zealand 1996-97
Overseas teams played for: East Shirley, Christchurch, New Zealand 1991-92
Cricketers particularly admired: Ian Botham, Martin Crowe, 'my sporting hero is Glenn Hoddle'
Young players to look out for: Michael Vaughan, Anthony McGrath, Chris Silverwood, Richard Green
Other sports followed: Football (Tottenham Hotspur and Barnsley) and golf
Relaxations: Playing golf, 'being at home watching television with a cold beer and playing with my son, Liam'
Extras: England Cornhill Player of the Year 1994. Yorkshire Sports Personality of the Year 1994. Voted Man of the Match in England's third Test match against Australia at

Sydney in 1994-95. Took a hat-trick against Kent in 1995. Named Player of the Year by Cornhill Insurance for 1995 season. Whyte and Mackay Bowler of the Year in 1996
Opinions on cricket: 'Read my book – *My Guide to your Success*'
Best batting: 121 Yorkshire v Warwickshire, Headingley 1996
Best bowling: 7-28 Yorkshire v Lancashire, Headingley 1995

1996 Season

	M	Inns	NO	Runs	HS	Avge	100s	50s	Ct	St	O	M	Runs	Wkts	Avge	Best	5wI	10wM
Test																		
All First	16	25	3	501	121	22.77	1	2	6	-	573.3	142	1535	67	22.91	6-36	2	-
1-day Int	5	2	0	5	5	2.50	-	-	-	-	46	3	193	6	32.16	3-39	-	
NatWest	4	1	0	42	42	42.00	-	-	2	-	45.3	8	147	8	18.37	3-47	-	
B & H	6	3	1	53	48 *	26.50	-	-	3	-	51	6	190	5	38.00	2-39	-	
Sunday	15	11	1	152	30	15.20	-	-	3	-	109.5	6	501	20	25.05	3-31	-	

Career Performances

	M	Inns	NO	Runs	HS	Avge	100s	50s	Ct	St	Balls	Runs	Wkts	Avge	Best	5wI	10wM
Test	12	18	3	319	65	21.26	-	2	7	-	2521	1358	43	31.58	6-49	1	-
All First	118	160	30	2254	121	17.33	1	8	31	-	20620	10780	380	28.36	7-28	13	2
1-day Int	27	18	5	164	45	12.61	-	-	4	-	1492	982	38	25.84	5-44	1	
NatWest	18	9	0	133	42	14.77	-	-	3	-	1153	650	28	23.21	3-31	-	
B & H	18	10	2	90	48 *	11.25	-	-	3	-	942	563	19	29.63	2-21	-	
Sunday	79	50	11	502	72 *	12.87	-	1	16	-	3392	2508	91	27.56	5-13	1	

38. Three England players scored a century in successive Tests in 1996 and 1997. Who were they?

GOULD, I. J. Middlesex

Name: Ian John Gould
Role: Left-hand bat, wicket-keeper
Born: 19 August 1957, Taplow, Berks
Height: 5ft 7in **Weight:** 12st 4lbs
Nickname: Gunner
County debut: 1975 (Middlesex),
1981 (Sussex)
County cap: 1977 (Middlesex),
1981 (Sussex)
Benefit: 1990 (£87,097)
One-Day Internationals: 18
1st-Class 50s scored: 47
1st-Class 100s scored: 4
1st-Class catches: 536
1st-Class stumpings: 67
Parents: George and Doreen
Wife and date of marriage: Joanne, 25
September 1986

Children: Gemma Louise; Michael James Thomas
Education: Westgate Secondary Modern, Slough
Overseas tours: England YC to West Indies 1976; Derrick Robins XI to Canada
1978-79; International XI to Pakistan 1980-81; England to Australia and New Zealand
1982-83; MCC to Namibia
Overseas teams played for: Auckland 1979-80
Extras: Captain of Sussex in 1986 and 1987. Returned to Middlesex as coach in 1993
Best batting: 128 Middlesex v Worcestershire, Worcester 1978
Best bowling: 3-10 Sussex v Surrey, The Oval 1989

1996 Season

	M	Inns	NO	Runs	HS	Avge	100s	50s	Ct	St	O	M	Runs	Wkts	Avge	Best	5wI	10wM
Test																		
All First	1	0	0	0	0	-	-	-	-	-	-							
1-day Int																		
NatWest																		
B & H																		
Sunday																		

Career Performances

	M	Inns	NO	Runs	HS	Avge	100s	50s	Ct	St	Balls	Runs	Wkts	Avge	Best	5wl	10wM
Test																	
All First	298	399	63	8756	128	26.05	4	47	536	67	478	365	7	52.14	3-10	-	-
1-day Int	18	14	2	155	42	12.91	-	-	15	3							
NatWest	33	24	2	443	88	20.13	-	2	26	7							
B & H	62	54	9	761	72	16.91	-	4	55	5	20	16	1	16.00	1-0	-	
Sunday	191	170	27	2907	84 *	20.32	-	14	139	22							

GRAYSON, A. P. Essex

Name: Adrian Paul Grayson
Role: Right-hand bat, slow left-arm
bowler, slip fielder
Born: 31 March 1971, Ripon
Height: 6ft 2in **Weight:** 12st 2lb
Nickname: PG, Laz, Ravi
County debut: 1990 (Yorkshire),
1996 (Essex)
County cap: 1996 (Essex)
1000 runs in a season: 1
1st-Class 50s: 15
1st-Class 100s: 3
1st-Class catches: 55
Place in batting averages: 116th av. 34.77
(1995 222nd av. 18.07)
Place in bowling averages: 121st av. 42.16
Strike rate: 88.16 (career 109.35)
Parents: Adrian and Carol
Wife and date of marriage: Alison, 30 September 1994
Family links with cricket: 'Dad played good league cricket and is also an NCA staff
coach; brother also plays when free from football commitments'
Education: Bedale Comprehensive School
Qualifications: 8 CSEs, BTEC in Leisure, NCA Senior Coaching Award
Off-season: Coaching in local schools and working on my game
Overseas tours: England YC to Australia 1989-90; Yorkshire to Barbados 1989-90, to
Cape Town 1991-92, to Cape Town 1992-93, to Leeward Islands 1993-94, to Cape
Town 1994-95
Overseas teams played for: Petone, Wellington 1991-92 and 1995-96
Cricketers particularly admired: Graham Gooch, Martyn Moxon, Darren Gough
'and all the Essex playing staff'
Young players to look out for: Stephen Peters, Jason Laney

Other sports followed: Football 'turned down apprentice terms with Middlesbrough at 16. Support Leeds United and Leicester City. Brother Simon plays for Leicester'
Relaxations: Playing golf, spending time with my wife
Extras: Played for England YC v New Zealand 1989 and Pakistan 1990. Brother plays football for Leicester City. Scored 1000 runs for first time in 1994. Yorkshire Player of the Year 1994. Released by Yorkshire at end of 1995 but joined Essex for 1996 season. Awarded county cap 1996
Opinions on cricket: 'More cricket should be played in schools. Tea break should be longer. Short run-ups in the Sunday League.'
Best batting: 140 Essex v Middlesex, Lord's 1996
Best bowling: 4-82 Essex v Hampshire, Southampton 1996

1996 Season

	M	Inns	NO	Runs	HS	Avge	100s	50s	Ct	St	O	M	Runs	Wkts	Avge	Best	5wI	10wM
Test																		
All First	17	30	3	939	140	34.77	2	3	19	-	264.3	58	759	18	42.16	4-82	-	-
1-day Int																		
NatWest	5	4	0	31	12	7.75	-	-	-	-	41.5	0	181	9	20.11	3-24	-	
B & H	5	4	2	35	12 *	17.50	-	-	2	-	40	4	156	5	31.20	3-30	-	
Sunday	17	15	3	178	34	14.83	-	-	7	-	96.2	1	601	19	31.63	4-46	-	

Career Performances

	M	Inns	NO	Runs	HS	Avge	100s	50s	Ct	St	Balls	Runs	Wkts	Avge	Best	5wI	10wM
Test																	
All First	69	110	13	2897	140	29.86	3	15	55	-	3390	1605	31	51.77	4-82	-	-
1-day Int																	
NatWest	12	10	0	122	29	12.20	-	-	3	-	557	422	13	32.46	3-24	-	
B & H	14	11	3	152	22 *	19.00	-	-	4	-	402	274	8	34.25	3-30	-	
Sunday	66	50	9	545	55	13.29	-	1	21	-	1820	1652	50	33.04	4-25	-	

---

39. Two Australians topped the Coopers & Lybrand world ratings for both batting and bowling at the start of 1997. Who were they?

GREEN, R. J. Lancashire

Name: Richard James Green
Role: Right-hand bat, right-arm
medium-fast bowler
Born: 13 March 1976, Warrington, Cheshire
Height: 6ft **Weight:** 12st 6lbs
Nickname: Greeny, Slimey, Greendog
County debut: 1995
1st-Class 5 w. in innings: 1
1st-Class catches: 2
Place in batting averages: 277th av. 13.00
Place in bowling averages: 41st av. 27.22
Strike rate: 51.22 (career 49.88)
Parents: Jim and Christina
Marital status: Single
Family links with cricket: Father and
brother played League cricket
Education: Bridgewater County High
School, Warrington; Hartford College

Qualifications: 5 GCSEs, BTEC National Business and Finance
Off-season: NBC cricket scholarship in Cape Town, South Africa
Overseas tours: Lancashire to Jamaica 1996
Overseas teams played for: Pro Waratah, Newcastle, NSW 1994-95
Cricketers particularly admired: David Gower, Warren Hegg
Young players to look out for: David Sales, Chris Brown
Other sports followed: Rugby league (Warrington) and football (Manchester United)
Injuries: Side strain, out for one week
Relaxations: Music, fast cars and socialising
Extras: Cheshire County League's youngest century-maker. Played for England U17
and England U19
Opinions on cricket: 'No breaks between games to work on any technical problems that
creep in during the season. Sunday League cricket should play music. Each batsman has
own song. Also pom-pom girls and crowd competitions etc.'
Best batting: 25* Lancashire v Northamptonshire, Northampton 1996
Best bowling: 6-41 Lancashire v Yorkshire, Old Trafford 1996

1996 Season

	M	Inns	NO	Runs	HS	Avge	100s	50s	Ct	St	O	M	Runs	Wkts	Avge	Best	5wl	10wM
Test																		
All First	7	10	3	91	25 *	13.00	-	-	2	-	187.5	36	599	22	27.22	6-41	1	-
1-day Int																		
NatWest																		
B & H																		
Sunday	5	1	1	0	0 *	-	-	-	-	-	38	1	193	8	24.12	2-23	-	

Career Performances

	M	Inns	NO	Runs	HS	Avge	100s	50s	Ct	St	Balls	Runs	Wkts	Avge	Best	5wl	10wM
Test																	
All First	8	11	3	92	25 *	11.50	-	-	2	-	1247	686	25	27.44	6-41	1	-
1-day Int																	
NatWest																	
B & H																	
Sunday	7	1	1	0	0 *	-	-	-	-	-	306	255	11	23.18	3-38	-	

GREENFIELD, K.   Sussex

Name: Keith Greenfield
Role: Right-hand bat, right-arm off-spin bowler, emergency wicket-keeper
Born: 6 December 1968, Brighton
Height: 6ft **Weight:** 12st 12lbs
Nickname: Grubby, G-Man, Grav
County debut: 1987
1st-Class 50s: 13
1st-Class 100s: 8
1st-Class catches: 53
One-Day 100s: 1
Place in batting averages: 67th av. 41.63 (1995 151st av. 27.51)
Strike rate: (career 150.80)
Parents: Leslie Ernest and Sheila
Wife and date of marriage: Caroline Susannah, 22 February 1992
Family links with cricket: Father keen spectator, father-in-law played club cricket for 20 years and now umpires and spectates
Education: Coldean First and Middle Schools; Falmer High School
Qualifications: 3 O-levels, BTEC National Diploma in Leisure and Management, junior, senior and advanced coaching certificates

Career outside cricket: Cricket coach
Off-season: Coaching at Hove for Sussex
Overseas tours: Sussex U16 to Guernsey 1985; Select XI to Malaga 1993; Sussex to Malaga 1993-94; David Smith Testimonial XI to Malaga 1994; MCC Tour to SE Asia and Far East 1994-95, to Bangladesh 1996
Overseas teams played for: Cornwall, Auckland 1988-90
Cricketers particularly admired: Derek Randall, Ian Botham, Chris Tugwell, Malcolm Eldridge (St Peters), Ray Bierber (Brighton & Hove) and Chris Pickett
Young players to look out for: Giles Haywood, Matthew Prior, James Chadburn, Jonathan Armitage 'all from Sussex Youth teams'
Other sports followed: Liverpool FC and 'a big watcher of golf'
Relaxations: 'Eating out with friends. DIY, music and concerts. Spending time with Caroline and lads at St Peters and Brighton and Hove CC'
Extras: First person taken on Youth Training Scheme to become a professional cricketer at Sussex. Only uncapped player to have captained Sussex at Hove (v Cambridge U), scored century in this game. Captained 2nd XI to Championship title in 1990. Sussex Team Man of the Year 1990, 1993. Joining Bill Athey on a trip to Belarus to take aid to the cancer hospital near Chernobyl
Opinions on cricket: 'As players we seem to be forever rushing around between overs just so that we can manage the current over-rate and not end up with large fines. The over-rate should be reduced to a realistic amount. Teams no longer seem to socialise after matches anywhere near as much as in years gone by, thus taking away an important part of county cricket – making friends from other counties.'
Best batting: 154* Sussex v India, Hove 1996
Best bowling: 2-40 Sussex v Essex, Hove 1993

1996 Season

	M	Inns	NO	Runs	HS	Avge	100s	50s	Ct	St	O	M	Runs	Wkts	Avge	Best	5wI	10wM
Test																		
All First	14	26	4	916	154 *	41.63	3	3	10	-	23	6	52	0	-	-	-	-
1-day Int																		
NatWest	3	3	0	42	32	14.00	-	-	3	-	4	0	23	0	-	-	-	
B & H	4	4	1	89	51 *	29.66	-	1	1	-	8	0	48	0	-	-	-	
Sunday	16	16	1	343	72	22.86	-	2	5	-	21	0	119	5	23.80	2-42	-	

Career Performances

	M	Inns	NO	Runs	HS	Avge	100s	50s	Ct	St	Balls	Runs	Wkts	Avge	Best	5wI	10wM
Test																	
All First	67	114	15	3178	154 *	32.10	8	13	53	-	754	479	5	95.80	2-40	-	-
1-day Int																	
NatWest	11	10	2	208	96 *	26.00	-	1	5	-	282	182	3	60.66	2-35	-	
B & H	18	17	2	395	62	26.33	-	3	7	-	402	327	1	327.00	1-35	-	
Sunday	96	94	8	2208	102	25.67	1	12	31	-	922	916	21	43.61	3-34	-	

GRIFFITH, F. A. Glamorgan

Name: Frank Alexander Griffith
Role: Right-hand bat, right-arm medium bowler
Born: 15 August 1968, Leyton
Height: 6ft **Weight:** 12st
Nickname: Sir Learie
County debut: 1988 (Derbyshire)
1st-Class 50s: 4
1st-Class catches: 28
Place in batting averages: (1995 156th av. 26.66)
Place in bowling averages: (1995 104th av. 36.11)
Strike rate: 162.00 (career 61.78)
Parents: Alex and Daisy
Marital status: Single
Education: William Morris High School, Walthamstow
Qualifications: Food and Nutrition and Art O-levels; NCA coaching certificate
Cricketers particularly admired: Collis King, Franklyn Stephenson
Other sports followed: Table tennis, basketball, football
Relaxations: Listening to music
Extras: Attended Haringey Cricket College. Released by Derbyshire at the end of the 1996 season
Best batting: 81 Derbyshire v Glamorgan, Chesterfield 1992
Best bowling: 4-33 Derbyshire v Leicestershire, Ilkeston 1992

1996 Season

	M	Inns	NO	Runs	HS	Avge	100s	50s	Ct	St	O	M	Runs	Wkts	Avge	Best	5wI	10wM
Test																		
All First	1	0	0	0	0	-	-	-	-	-	27	1	137	1	137.00	1-70	-	-
1-day Int																		
NatWest																		
B & H	4	3	0	33	24	11.00	-	-	-	-	21	0	144	4	36.00	3-63	-	
Sunday	3	2	1	6	6 *	6.00	-	-	-	-	22	0	111	3	37.00	2-36	-	

Career Performances

	M	Inns	NO	Runs	HS	Avge	100s	50s	Ct	St	Balls	Runs	Wkts	Avge	Best	5wI	10wM
Test																	
All First	43	63	9	1087	81	20.12	-	4	28	-	4510	2571	73	35.21	4-33	-	-
1-day Int																	
NatWest	7	4	0	16	8	4.00	-	-	4	-	314	190	5	38.00	1-13	-	
B & H	10	8	1	68	24	9.71	-	-	3	-	380	355	11	32.27	3-63	-	
Sunday	47	33	6	267	31	9.88	-	-	8	-	1807	1597	50	31.94	4-48	-	

GRIFFITHS, S. P. Derbyshire

Name: Stephen Paul Griffiths
Role: Right-hand bat, wicket-keeper
Born: 31 May 1973, Hereford
Height: 5ft 11in **Weight:** 12st
Nickname: 'Too many to name'
County debut: 1995
1st-Class catches: 14
Parents: Paul and Lesley
Marital status: Single
Family links with cricket: 'Father has played a good standard of club cricket for years'
Education: Bathford Primary School; Beechen Cliff School, Bath; Brunel College of Art and Technology
Qualifications: 7 GCSEs, basic coaching award
Career outside cricket: Studying antique furniture restoration and conservation
Off-season: 'Studying at Brunel College of Art and Technology and keeping fit'
Overseas tours: Bath Schools to Zimbabwe and Kenya 1989
Overseas teams played for: CBC Old Boys, Bloemfontein, South Africa 1992-93
Cricketers particularly admired: Jack Russell, Bob Taylor, Alan Knott, Doug C. Storey, Gregg Brown
Young players to look out for: Andrew Harris, Kevin Dean
Other sports followed: Rugby (Bath RFC) and golf
Relaxations: 'Music (listening to and collecting blues, jazz, reggae, Irish, Motown), roaming through flea markets, reading, going to pubs in Bath with friends, spending time with girlfriend Ceri, eating foreign food and doing up old furniture'
Extras: Took six catches on first-class debut against Worcestershire in 1995 (five of them in the first innings). Played for Somerset 2nd XI before joining Derbyshire. Member of Bath CC and Buccaneers CC

Opinions on cricket: 'It is far too easy for young cricketers to slip through the net. The standard of coaching in many schools is very poor and luck plays a big part in being spotted.'

Best batting: 20 Derbyshire v Surrey, Derby 1995

1996 Season (did not make any first-class or one-day appearances)

Career Performances

	M	Inns	NO	Runs	HS	Avge	100s	50s	Ct	St	Balls	Runs	Wkts	Avge	Best	5wI	10wM
Test																	
All First	5	9	0	75	20	8.33	-	-	14	-							
1-day Int																		
NatWest																		
B & H																			
Sunday																			

HABIB, A.   Leicestershire

Name: Aftab Habib
Role: Right-hand bat, right-arm slow-medium bowler
Born: 7 February 1972, Reading, Berks
Height: 5ft 11in **Weight:** 12st
Nickname: Afie, Tabby, Scabby, Habbiby
County debut: 1992 (Middlesex), 1995 (Leicestershire)
1st-Class 50s: 2
1st-Class 100s: 1
1st-Class 200s: 1
1st-Class catches: 10
Place in batting averages: 105th av. 36.00
Parents: Hussain and Tahira
Marital status: Single
Family links with cricket: Cousin of Zahid Sadiq (ex-Surrey and Derbyshire)

Education: Alfred Sutton Primary School; Millfield Junior School; Taunton School
Qualifications: 7 GCSEs, NCA coaching certificate
Career outside cricket: Salesman for Sewards
Off-season: Playing club cricket in New Zealand
Overseas tours: England YC to Australia 1989-90, to New Zealand 1990-91; Berkshire CCC to South Africa 1996

Overseas teams played for: Gloobe Wakatu, Nelson, New Zealand, 1992-93 and 1996-97
Cricketers particularly admired: Desmond Haynes, Javed Miandad, Dean Jones, Mark Waugh, Steve Waugh, Vince Wells, James Whitaker
Young players to look out for: Darren Maddy
Other sports followed: Football ('I support Reading because I was born there, and Liverpool – top class'), squash
Relaxations: Music, cinema, reading magazines
Extras: 2nd XI Seaxe Player of the Year 1992. Released by Middlesex at end of 1994 season. Leicestershire 2nd XI Player of the Year in 1995
Best batting: 215 Leicestershire v Worcestershire, Leicester 1996

1996 Season

	M	Inns	NO	Runs	HS	Avge	100s	50s	Ct	St	O	M	Runs	Wkts	Avge	Best	5wI	10wM
Test																		
All First	16	24	2	792	215	36.00	1	2	10	-								
1-day Int																		
NatWest	1	1	0	35	35	35.00	-	-	-	-								
B & H																		
Sunday	9	7	3	183	99 *	45.75	-	2	3	-	0.1	0	4	0	-		-	-

Career Performances

	M	Inns	NO	Runs	HS	Avge	100s	50s	Ct	St	Balls		Runs	Wkts	Avge	Best	5wI	10wM
Test																		
All First	20	31	5	1041	215	40.03	2	2	10	-								
1-day Int																		
NatWest	2	2	0	38	35	19.00	-	-	-	-								
B & H																		
Sunday	12	10	3	224	99 *	32.00	-	2	3	-	1		4	0	-		-	-

HALL, J. W. Sussex

Name: James William Hall
Role: Right-hand opening batsman
Born: 30 March 1968, Chichester
Height: 6ft 3in **Weight:** 14st
Nickname: Gus
County debut: 1990
County cap: 1992
1000 runs in a season: 2
1st-Class 50s: 30
1st-Class 100s: 6

1st-Class catches: 47
Place in batting averages: 197th av. 25.38
(1995 170th av. 24.40)
Parents: Maurice and Marlene (deceased)
Marital status: Single
Family links with cricket: Father played
club cricket for Chichester Priory Park.
Brother David a very keen supporter
Education: Chichester Boys' High School
Qualifications: 9 O-levels, level 1 and 2
Coaching Awards
Career outside cricket: Coach
Off-season: Coaching at the Scots College in
Sydney, Australia
Overseas tours: Malaga Select XI, Spain,
1993
Overseas teams played for: Southern
Districts, Perth, Western Australia 1986-87;

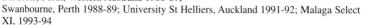

Swanbourne, Perth 1988-89; University St Helliers, Auckland 1991-92; Malaga Select
XI, 1993-94
Cricketers particularly admired: Peter Moores, Alec Stewart, Allan Green,
Robin Smith and 'all those who have played as professional cricketers'
Other sports followed: Football (Brighton & Hove Albion and Carlisle United)
Injuries: Broken left hand, out for four weeks
Relaxations: Music, socialising, 'exploring the Sydney club scene, Brighton's wide
and varied pubs and the occasional all-nighter with a few beers'
Extras: Scored 53 on 1st XI debut v Zimbabwe and scored maiden first-class century in
same week (120* v New Zealand) in 1990, going on to make over 1000 runs in debut
season of first-class cricket. Run out without facing a ball on NatWest debut v
Glamorgan ('thanks Neil'). Whittingdale Young Cricketer of the Month for May 1991.
Scorer of slowest ever Championship 50 v Surrey, The Oval 29 July 1994. Released by
Sussex at the end of the 1996 season
Opinions on cricket: 'The usual – play too much, paid too little, too many overs in a
day, tea too short, wickets too inconsistent – all in all it's a great game that allows us to
travel all over the world and country. All those lucky enough to have played as
professional cricketers should never take it for granted and always enjoy the good days
as the not so good ones will surely turn up.'
Best batting: 140* Sussex v Lancashire, Hove 1992

---

40. Which pair hold the record for the longest Test
match-saving last-wicket stand?

1996 Season

	M	Inns	NO	Runs	HS	Avge	100s	50s	Ct	St	O	M	Runs	Wkts	Avge	Best	5wI	10wM
Test																		
All First	7	13	0	330	93	25.38	-	3	6	-								
1-day Int																		
NatWest	1	1	0	38	38	38.00	-	-	-	-								
B & H																		
Sunday	4	4	0	69	33	17.25	-	-	-	-								

Career Performances

	M	Inns	NO	Runs	HS	Avge	100s	50s	Ct	St	Balls	Runs	Wkts	Avge	Best	5wI	10wM
Test																		
All First	97	175	10	4997	140 *	30.28	6	30	47	-	12	14	0	-	-	-	-	-
1-day Int																		
NatWest	6	6	0	158	70	26.33	-	1	-	-								
B & H	13	13	0	524	81	40.30	-	5	2	-								
Sunday	33	32	0	822	77	25.68	-	6	8	-								

HAMILTON, G. M.   Yorkshire

Name: Gavin Mark Hamilton
Role: Right-hand bat, right-arm fast bowler
Born: 16 September 1974, Broxburn
Height: 6ft 1in **Weight:** 13st
Nickname: Hammy, Scotty, Jock, 'anything Scottish'
County debut: 1994
1st-Class 50s: 1
1st-Class catches: 7
1st-Class 5 w. innings: 1
Strike rate: 76.25 (career 66.34)
Parents: Gavin and Wendy
Marital status: Single
Family links with cricket: Father long-serving player for West Lothian CC. Brother another long-term player for Aberdeenshire CC and opening bat for Scotland
Education: Hurstmere School, Sidcup
Qualifications: 10 GCSEs and 'numerous coaching awards'
Off-season: Playing for Maties University, Stellenbosch in South Africa
Overseas teams played for: Municipals, Orange Free State, South Africa; Wellington, Cape Town, South Africa; Stellenbosch University, Boland, South Africa

Cricketers particularly admired: Craig White, Alan Mullally
Young players to look out for: Danny Law
Other sports followed: Golf, football (Arsenal YTS)
Injuries: 'Waiter's elbow – for most of the season'
Relaxations: Listening to most kinds of music, 'playing golf on a hot day'
Opinions on cricket: 'Nowhere near enough days off. Cricketers should be allowed or forced to come off when it is too cold, it shouldn't have to rain.'
Best batting: 61 Yorkshire v Essex, Headingley 1996
Best bowling: 5-65 Scotland v Ireland, Eglinton 1993

1996 Season

	M	Inns	NO	Runs	HS	Avge	100s	50s	Ct	St	O	M	Runs	Wkts	Avge	Best	5wI	10wM
Test																		
All First	4	5	1	71	61	17.75	-	1	2	-	101.4	12	304	8	38.00	3-65	-	-
1-day Int																		
NatWest																		
B & H																		
Sunday	2	0	0	0	0	-	-	-	-	-	10	2	59	1	59.00	1-26	-	

Career Performances

	M	Inns	NO	Runs	HS	Avge	100s	50s	Ct	St	Balls	Runs	Wkts	Avge	Best	5wI	10wM
Test																	
All First	14	16	5	236	61	21.45	-	1	7	-	2123	1126	32	35.18	5-65	1	-
1-day Int																	
NatWest	2	1	0	2	2	2.00	-	-	1	-	120	86	4	21.50	2-42	-	
B & H	2	1	1	8	8 *	-	-	-	-	-	78	42	0	-	-	-	
Sunday	16	9	2	46	16 *	6.57	-	-	2	-	589	550	20	27.50	4-27	-	

41. Which England player chose the song *Cigarettes and Alcohol* to accompany him to the crease during England's one-day series against New Zealand in 1996-97?

HANCOCK, T. H. C. Gloucestershire

Name: Timothy Harold Coulter Hancock
Role: Right-hand bat, occasional right-arm
medium bowler, short-leg or cover fielder
Born: 20 April 1972, Reading
Height: 5ft 11in **Weight:** 12st 12lb
Nickname: Herbie
County debut: 1991
1st-Class 50s: 19
1st-Class 100s: 3
1st-Class catches: 48
Place in batting averages: 161st av. 29.54
(1995 179th av. 22.91)
Strike rate: (career 68.15)
Parents: John and Jennifer
Marital status: Single
Family links with cricket: 'Dad still plays'
Education: St Edward's, Oxford;
Henley College

Qualifications: 8 GCSEs
Overseas tours: Gloucestershire to Kenya 1991, to Sri Lanka 1993
Overseas teams played for: CBC Old Boys, Bloemfontein 1991-92; Wynnum
Manley, Brisbane 1992-93
Cricketers particularly admired: Ian Botham, Viv Richards
Other sports followed: Rugby union, golf, hockey
Relaxations: Playing golf, watching television,'having a pint or two with friends'
Extras: Played hockey for Oxfordshire U19
Best batting: 123 Gloucestershire v Essex, Chelmsford 1994
Best bowling: 3-10 Gloucestershire v Glamorgan, Abergavenny 1993

1996 Season

	M	Inns	NO	Runs	HS	Avge	100s	50s	Ct	St	O	M	Runs	Wkts	Avge	Best	5wI	10wM
Test																		
All First	15	27	3	709	116	29.54	1	4	11	-	18	4	60	0	-		-	-
1-day Int																		
NatWest	2	2	0	10	10	5.00	-	-	2	-								
B & H	5	5	2	150	71*	50.00	-	1	-	-	13	1	51	4	12.75	3-13	-	
Sunday	10	9	0	95	31	10.55	-	-	3	-	14.5	0	92	4	23.00	2-6	-	

	M	Inns	NO	Runs	HS	Avge	100s	50s	Ct	St	Balls	Runs	Wkts	Avge	Best	5wI	10wM
Test																	
All First	75	134	10	3161	123	25.49	3	19	48	-	886	559	13	43.00	3-10	-	-
1-day Int																	
NatWest	4	4	0	84	45	21.00	-	-	3	-	41	39	2	19.50	2-7	-	
B & H	16	14	2	288	71 *	24.00	-	1	2	-	78	51	4	12.75	3-13	-	
Sunday	53	49	1	652	46	13.58	-	-	20	-	203	213	7	30.42	2-6	-	

HARDEN, R. J.   Somerset

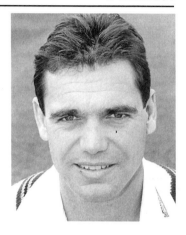

Name: Richard John Harden
Role: Right-hand bat, left-arm medium bowler
Born: 16 August 1965, Bridgwater
Height: 5ft 11in **Weight:** 13st 7lbs
Nickname: Sumo, Curtis
County debut: 1985
County cap: 1989
1000 runs in a season: 6
1st-Class 50s: 64
1st-Class 100s: 26
1st-Class catches: 169
One-Day 100s: 4
Place in batting averages: 109th av. 39.74 (1995 30th av. 49.27)
Strike rate: 48.00 (career 72.70)
Parents: Chris and Anne
Wife and date of marriage: Nicki Rae, 25 September 1992
Family links with cricket: Grandfather played club cricket for Bridgwater
Education: King's College, Taunton
Qualifications: 8 O-levels, 2 A-levels, coaching award
Career outside cricket: Print broker for Pennine Dataforms
Overseas teams played for: Central Districts, New Zealand
Cricketers particularly admired: Viv Richards, Jimmy Cook
Other sports followed: Squash, golf, rugby
Relaxations: 'Love my domestic duties (dusting, Hoovering, etc.) rather than golf. Good food and the odd drink.'
Best batting: 187 Somerset v Nottinghamshire, Taunton 1992
Best bowling: 2-7 Central Districts v Canterbury, Blenheim 1987-88

1996 Season

	M	Inns	NO	Runs	HS	Avge	100s	50s	Ct	St	O	M	Runs	Wkts	Avge	Best	5wl	10wM
Test																		
All First	12	20	1	676	136	35.57	1	5	11	-	8	0	42	1	42.00	1-39	-	-
1-day Int																		
NatWest	2	2	0	34	34	17.00	-	-	1	-								
B & H	5	4	0	57	38	14.25	-	-	-	-								
Sunday	11	11	4	442	90	63.14	-	4	3	-								

Career Performances

	M	Inns	NO	Runs	HS	Avge	100s	50s	Ct	St	Balls	Runs	Wkts	Avge	Best	5wl	10wM
Test																	
All First	222	363	56	12201	187	39.74	26	64	169	-	1454	1011	20	50.55	2-7	-	-
1-day Int																	
NatWest	21	19	2	733	108 *	43.11	3	2	12	-	18	23	0	-	-	-	
B & H	47	45	4	801	76	19.53	-	3	11	-							
Sunday	152	146	26	3886	100 *	32.38	1	23	44	-	1	0	0	-	-	-	

HARRIS, A. J. Derbyshire

Name: Andrew James Harris
Role: Right-hand bat, right-arm fast bowler
Born: 26 June 1973, Ashton-under-Lyne
Height: 6ft **Weight:** 11st 7lbs
Nickname: AJ
County debut: 1994
County cap: 1996
1st-Class 5 w. in innings: 2
1st-Class 10 w. in match: 1
1st-Class catches: 3
Place in batting averages: 301st av. 7.84
Place in bowling averages: 31st av. 26.03
(1995 32nd av. 25.28)
Strike rate: 42.92 (career 41.41)
Parents: Norman and Joyce
Marital status: Single
Education: Tintwistle Primary School;
Hadfield Comprehensive School;
Glossopdale Community College
Qualifications: 6 GCSEs, 1 A-level
Off-season: Touring Australia with England A
Overseas tours: England A to Australia 1996-97

Overseas teams played for: Ginninderra, West Belconnen, Australia 1992-93
Cricketers particularly admired: Kim Barnett, 'Brian Lara – he's top drawer – and Merv Hughes for his effort and determination'
Young players to look out for: Vikram Solanki
Other sports followed: 'Soccer, as my brother plays for Altrincham, but I support the True Blues, Manchester City, and every sport I will view with great determination'
Injuries: Side strain and broken middle finger sustained in the same game against Kent at Derby. Out for three weeks
Relaxations: 'Playing any sport, golf in particular. As relaxing goes, watching television, playing on my Sega, and how could I forget having quite a few beers, although I have never been to the Pink Coconut'
Extras: Awarded county cap in 1996
Best batting: 17 Derbyshire v Glamorgan, Cardiff 1996
Best bowling: 6-40 Derbyshire v Middlesex, Derby 1996

1996 Season

	M	Inns	NO	Runs	HS	Avge	100s	50s	Ct	St	O	M	Runs	Wkts	Avge	Best	5wI	10wM
Test																		
All First	12	16	3	102	17	7.84	-	-	3	-	379.1	76	1380	53	26.03	6-40	2	1
1-day Int																		
NatWest	2	1	1	11	11 *	-	-	-	1	-	21	4	77	3	25.66	3-58	-	
B & H	1	0	0	0	0	-	-	-	1	-	7	0	34	1	34.00	1-34	-	
Sunday	11	3	1	1	1	0.50	-	-	4	-	76	4	358	15	23.86	3-41	-	

Career Performances

	M	Inns	NO	Runs	HS	Avge	100s	50s	Ct	St	Balls	Runs	Wkts	Avge	Best	5wI	10wM
Test																	
All First	18	25	6	160	17	8.42	-	-	3	-	2982	1899	72	26.37	6-40	2	1
1-day Int																	
NatWest	2	1	1	11	11 *	-	-	-	1	-	126	77	3	25.66	3-58	-	
B & H	2	1	0	5	5	5.00	-	-	1	-	108	88	2	44.00	1-34	-	
Sunday	22	5	2	4	2	1.33	-	-	7	-	868	728	30	24.26	3-15	-	

42. Which England player chose the song *How Much Is That Doggy In The Window?* to accompany him to the crease during England's one-day series against New Zealand in 1996-97?

HARRISON, J. C.   Middlesex

Name: Jason Christian Harrison
Role: Right-hand bat, off-spin bowler,
slip fielder
Born: 15 January 1972, Amersham, Bucks
Height: 6ft 3in **Weight:** 13st 10lbs
Nickname: Harry, Big J
County debut: 1994
1st-Class catches: 10
Place in batting averages: 224th av. 18.09
Parents: Paul and Carry (deceased)
Marital status: Single
Education: Great Marlow Senior School;
Bucks College of Further Education
Qualifications: 6 GCSEs, NCA coaching
certificate, City & Guilds apprenticeship in
sheet metal fabrication
Career outside cricket: Sheet metal
fabricator

Off-season: 'Working as a sheet metal fabricator and working hard on my fitness and
game for the 1997 season'
Overseas tours: Middlesex to Portugal 1992, 1993, 1994, 1995; Buckinghamshire to
South Africa 1995-96
Overseas teams played for: Bellville, South Africa 1993-95
Cricketers particularly admired: Malcolm Roberts, Mike Roseberry, Keith Brown,
Jason Pooley
Young players to look out for: Owais Shah, Andy Harris, David Roberts
Other sports followed: Football ('loyal supporter of Wycombe Wanderers')
Injuries: Back spasms, missed one week and broken finger but missed no cricket
Relaxations: Listening to music, spending time with friends, gym work
Extras: Played for Buckinghamshire 1991-96 and for NCA U19 and NAYC in 1991.
Held the record for the highest score in the Thames Valley League (164 not out).Held
Middlesex 2nd XI record with 225. Was out first ball in first-class cricket
Opinions on cricket: 'Four-day cricket seems to be working well. Tea is too short and
should be increased from 20 to 30 minutes. Players should have nine-month contracts to
help prepare themselves for the coming season. All 2nd XI games should be played on
first-class grounds, under first-class conditions.'
Best batting: 46* Middlesex v Cambridge University, Fenner's 1995

1996 Season

	M	Inns	NO	Runs	HS	Avge	100s	50s	Ct	St	O	M	Runs	Wkts	Avge	Best	5wI	10wM
Test																		
All First	7	13	2	199	40	18.09	-	-	10	-								
1-day Int																		
NatWest																		
B & H	1	1	0	24	24	24.00	-	-	-	-								
Sunday																		

Career Performances

	M	Inns	NO	Runs	HS	Avge	100s	50s	Ct	St	Balls	Runs	Wkts	Avge	Best	5wI	10wM
Test																	
All First	10	18	3	298	46 *	19.86	-	-	12	-							
1-day Int																	
NatWest																	
B & H	1	1	0	24	24	24.00	-	-	-	-							
Sunday	4	3	1	17	13 *	8.50	-	-	-	-	6	3	1	3.00	1-3	-	

HART, J. P. Nottinghamshire

Name: Jamie Paul Hart
Role: Right-hand bat, right-arm medium bowler
Born: 31 December 1975, Blackpool
Height: 6ft 2in **Weight:** 13st 8lbs
Nickname: Harty
County debut: 1995 (one-day), 1996 (first-class)
Parents: Paul and Vicky
Marital status: Single
Education: Grosvenor School, Nottingham; Millfield School
Qualifications: 8 GCSEs and 1 A-level
Career outside cricket: Sales
Overseas tours: Millfield School to Sri Lanka 1993
Cricketers particularly admired: Ian Botham, Dermot Reeve
Other sports followed: Football (Leeds United)
Relaxations: Listening to music and reading
Extras: Father played professional football and is now at Leeds United on the coaching staff

Opinions on cricket: 'The different standards of second-class pitches compared with first-class pitches and grounds often make the step-up harder i.e. more often than not one can get more out of a 2nd XI pitch than a first-class one (as a bowler).'

Best batting: 18* Nottinghamshire v Yorkshire, Scarborough 1996

1996 Season

	M	Inns	NO	Runs	HS	Avge	100s	50s	Ct	St	O	M	Runs	Wkts	Avge	Best	5wI	10wM
Test																		
All First	1	2	2	18	18 *	-	-	-	-	-	18	7	51	0	-		-	-
1-day Int																		
NatWest																		
B & H																		
Sunday																		

Career Performances

	M	Inns	NO	Runs	HS	Avge	100s	50s	Ct	St	Balls	Runs	Wkts	Avge	Best	5wI	10wM
Test																	
All First	1	2	2	18	18 *	-	-	-	-	-	108	51	0	-		-	-
1-day Int																	
NatWest																	
B & H																	
Sunday	2	0	0	0	0	-	-	-	-	-	72	87	1	87.00	1-48	-	

HARTLEY, P. J.   Yorkshire

Name: Peter John Hartley
Role: Right-hand bat, right-arm medium-fast bowler
Born: 18 April 1960, Keighley
Height: 6ft **Weight:** 13st 7lbs
Nickname: Jack
County debut: 1982 (Warwickshire), 1985 (Yorkshire)
County cap: 1987 (Yorkshire)
Benefit: 1996
50 wickets in a season: 6
1st-Class 50s: 13
1st-Class 100s: 2
1st-Class 5 w. in innings: 20
1st-Class 10 w. match: 2
1st-Class catches: 59
One-Day 5 w. in innings: 4

Place in batting averages: 217th av. 22.66 (1995 262nd av. 13.47)
Place in bowling averages: 58th av. 29.66 (1995 22nd av. 22.97)
Strike rate: 51.03 (career 54.44)
Parents: Thomas and Molly
Wife and date of marriage: Sharon Louise, 12 March 1988
Children: Megan Grace, 25 April 1992; Courtney, 25 June 1995
Family links with cricket: Father played local league cricket
Education: Hartington/Greenhead Grammar School; Bradford College
Qualifications: City & Guilds in textile design and management, senior Coaching Award
Career outside cricket: Textiles
Off-season: Benefit, golf and time at home
Overseas tours: Yorkshire pre-season tours to Barbados 1986-87, to South Africa 1991-92, 1992-93
Overseas teams played for: Melville, New Zealand 1983-84; Adelaide, Australia 1985-86; Harmony and Orange Free State, South Africa 1988-89
Cricketers particularly admired: Malcolm Marshall, Richard Hadlee
Young players to look out for: Peter Hartley, Nick Faldo, Ernie Els
Other sports followed: Rugby league (Keighley Cougars), football (Chelsea FC)
Relaxations: Golf, walking
Opinions on cricket: 'Underpaid, overworked.'
Best batting: 127* Yorkshire v Lancashire, Old Trafford 1988
Best bowling: 9-41 Yorkshire v Derbyshire, Chesterfield 1995

1996 Season

	M	Inns	NO	Runs	HS	Avge	100s	50s	Ct	St	O	M	Runs	Wkts	Avge	Best	5wI	10wM
Test																		
All First	16	24	3	476	89	22.66	-	3	6	-	459.2	96	1602	54	29.66	6-67	2	1
1-day Int																		
NatWest	4	1	1	1	1 *	-	-	-	1	-	42	7	177	6	29.50	2-22	-	
B & H	6	2	2	25	17 *	-	-	-	2	-	50	7	200	3	66.66	1-27	-	
Sunday	17	11	5	188	52	31.33	-	1	1	-	119	6	533	25	21.32	3-27	-	

Career Performances

	M	Inns	NO	Runs	HS	Avge	100s	50s	Ct	St	Balls	Runs	Wkts	Avge	Best	5wI	10wM
Test																	
All First	189	231	52	3754	127 *	20.97	2	13	59	-	30381	17121	558	30.68	9-41	20	2
1-day Int																	
NatWest	25	15	8	164	52	23.42	-	1	1	-	1583	1027	42	24.45	5-46	1	
B & H	37	20	9	130	29 *	11.81	-	-	11	-	2045	1300	53	24.52	5-43	1	
Sunday	132	90	29	964	52	15.80	-	2	18	-	5687	4308	162	26.59	5-36	2	

HARVEY, M. E.   Lancashire

Name: Mark Edward Harvey
Role: Right-hand bat, off-spin bowler
Born: 26 June 1974, Burnley, Lancs
Height: 5ft 9in **Weight:** 13st
Nickname: Harv, Vadge, Baz
County debut: 1994
1st-Class catches: 1
Parents: David and Wendy
Marital status: Single
Family links with cricket: Brother Jonathan spent four years as MCC young player and was professional for Greenmount CC in the Bolton League, 'father, David, is still playing local club cricket, 50 n.o.'
Education: Worsthorne County Primary; Habergham High School, Burnley; Loughborough University
Qualifications: 8 GCSEs, 3 A-levels, BSc Honours in PE Sports Management and Recreational Management
Career outside cricket: 'None yet!'
Off-season: Playing for Queanbeyan CC in Canberra, Australia
Overseas tours: England U19 to India 1992-93
Overseas teams played for: Queanbeyan CC, Canberra, Australia 1996-97
Cricketers particularly admired: 'David Gower (someone who makes it all look so easy), Dean Jones (exciting both batting and fielding), Mudassar Nazar (an admired professional for many years at Burnley), Les "The Whirlwind" Seal'
Young players to look out for: Andrew Flintoff
Other sports followed: Football (Manchester United, Burnley and Oxford United)
Relaxations: 'I'd love to say that watching Burnley FC was a relaxation, but unfortunately it's very frustrating', watching and reading about Eric Cantona, 'drinking at the Crooked Billet, Workthorne with father and brother'
Extras: Captained England U17, represented England at U17, U18 and U19 levels, represented Lancashire from U13 to U19. In an attempt to produce a result in a rain-affected 2nd XI match v Yorkshire at Todmorden, he bowled an over costing 108 runs from 18 no-balls, all of which went for four without hitting the bat. 'This allowed both teams to contrive a game in five rather than 50 minutes. A claim to fame which earns me never-ending stick at the local pub!' Played for Combined Universities in 1995
Opinions on cricket: 'The increasing introduction of top class, ex-Test playing coaches, and the like, whether foreign or British, can only be a good thing, allowing young players such as myself to benefit from their vast knowledge and experience. Different methods and approaches can only serve to widen our horizons of the game.'

Best batting: 23 Lancashire v Nottinghamshire, Trent Bridge 1994
23 Combined Universities v West Indies, The Parks 1995

1996 Season

	M	Inns	NO	Runs	HS	Avge	100s	50s	Ct	St	O	M	Runs	Wkts	Avge	Best	5wl	10wM
Test																		
All First																		
1-day Int																		
NatWest																		
B & H	2	2	0	6	5	3.00	-	-	1	-								
Sunday																		

Career Performances

	M	Inns	NO	Runs	HS	Avge	100s	50s	Ct	St	Balls	Runs	Wkts	Avge	Best	5wl	10wM
Test																	
All First	3	4	0	67	23	16.75	-	-	1	-							
1-day Int																	
NatWest																	
B & H	4	4	0	9	5	2.25	-	-	3	-							
Sunday																	

HAYDEN, M. L.   Hampshire

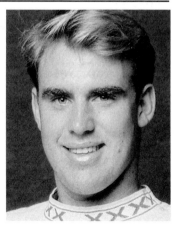

Name: Matthew Lawrence Hayden
Role: Left-hand bat, right-arm medium bowler
Born: 29 October 1971, Kingaroy, Australia
County debut: No first-team appearance
Test debut: 1994
Tests: 1
One-Day Internationals: 13
1st-Class 50s: 30
1st-Class 100s: 21
1st-Class 200s: 2
1st-Class catches: 64
Strike rate: (career 173.00)
Overseas tours: Australia to England 1993, to South Africa 1994, 1996-97
Overseas teams played for: Queensland 1991-1997
Extras: Scored 149 on his first-class debut for Queensland against South Australia and went on to become the youngest Australian to score

1000 runs in his first season. Played in his first Test match in South Africa in 1994 after a sequence of impressive run-scoring in the Sheffield Shield forced his inclusion in the tour squad, but has failed to hold down a regular place in the Test side. Was given another chance after opener Matthew Elliot was injured and played in the Test series against West Indies in 1996-97 and solid performances warranted his inclusion in the squad to tour South Africa. Has played league cricket for Greenmount in the Bolton League, breaking the club record with an aggregate of 1483 runs

Best batting: 234 Queensland v Tasmania, Brisbane 1995-96
Best bowling: 1-24 Australia v Durham, Durham 1993

1996 (made no first-class or one-day appearances)

Career Performances

	M	Inns	NO	Runs	HS	Avge	100s	50s	Ct	St	Balls	Runs	Wkts	Avge	Best	5wl	10wM
Test	1	2	0	20	15	10.00	-	-	1	-							
All First	77	140	17	6971	234	56.67	21	30	64	-	173	116	1	116.00	1-24	-	-
1-day Int	13	12	1	286	67	26.00	-	1	4	-							
NatWest																	
B & H																	
Sunday																	

HAYHURST, A. N.   Somerset

Name: Andrew Neil Hayhurst
Role: Right-hand bat, right-arm medium bowler
Born: 23 November 1962, Davyhulme, Manchester
Height: 6ft **Weight:** 13st 10lbs
Nickname: Bull
County debut: 1985 (Lancashire), 1990 (Somerset)
County cap: 1990 (Somerset)
1000 runs in a season: 3
1st-Class 50s: 40
1st-Class 100s: 14
1st-Class catches: 53
One-Day 5 w. in innings: 1
Place in batting averages: 240th av. 18.66 (1995 95th av. 34.37)
Place in bowling averages: (1995 146th av. 51.90)

Strike rate: 150.00 (career 81.70)
Parents: William and Margaret
Wife and date of marriage: April, 17 February 1990
Children: Myles William David, 30 March 1992
Family links with cricket: Father played club cricket for Worsley. We played in the same side. Grew up in house lived in by Tyldesley brothers (Lancashire and England)
Education: St Mark's Primary School; Worsley Wardley High; Eccles Sixth Form College; Leeds Polytechnic (Carnegie College of PE)
Qualifications: 8 O-levels, 4 A-levels, BA (Hons) Human Movement, advanced cricket coach, qualified financial consultant
Off-season: New job within the game
Overseas tours: Lancashire to Jamaica 1986-87 and 1987-88, to Zimbabwe 1988-89; Somerset to Bahamas 1989-90
Overseas teams played for: South Launceston, Tasmania 1987-89
Cricketers particularly admired: Dermot Reeve, Jimmy Cook, Clive Lloyd, Jack Bond, Andy Caddick
Young players to look out for: Vikram Solanki, Andy Harris
Other sports followed: Football (Manchester United) and rugby league (Salford)
Injuries: Shoulder, missed three weeks
Relaxations: Animals and statistics
Extras: Made 110* on his first-class debut for Somerset and was appointed captain for the 1994 season. His first scoring shot in first-class cricket was a six off the bowling of Kapil Dev whilst opening the batting. Was released by Somerset at the end of the 1996 season
Opinions on cricket: 'The huge gap between 2nd XI and 1st XI needs to be closed. The players are there, it's just the attitude. Four-day cricket has worked.'
Best batting: 172* Somerset v Gloucestershire, Bath 1991
Best bowling: 4-27 Lancashire v Middlesex, Old Trafford 1987

1996 Season

	M	Inns	NO	Runs	HS	Avge	100s	50s	Ct	St	O	M	Runs	Wkts	Avge	Best	5wI	10wM
Test																		
All First	9	13	1	224	96	18.66	-	2	2	-	25	5	91	1	91.00	1-8	-	-
1-day Int																		
NatWest	3	2	0	25	21	12.50	-	-	-	-	8	0	41	0	-	-	-	
B & H	4	3	2	116	67 *	116.00	-	1	1	-	24	4	96	5	19.20	3-29	-	
Sunday	7	5	4	122	60 *	122.00	-	1	-	-	41.3	1	198	10	19.80	3-21	-	

	M	Inns	NO	Runs	HS	Avge	100s	50s	Ct	St	Balls	Runs	Wkts	Avge	Best	5wI	10wM
Test																	
All First	164	263	34	7819	172 *	34.14	14	40	53	-	8906	4961	109	45.51	4-27	-	-
1-day Int																	
NatWest	22	20	4	588	91 *	36.75	-	3	4	-	809	543	24	22.62	5-60	1	
B & H	34	30	5	736	95	29.44	-	6	3	-	1114	770	32	24.06	4-50	-	
Sunday	119	101	24	2233	84	29.00	-	12	16	-	2916	2570	72	35.69	4-37	-	

HAYNES, G. R. Worcestershire

Name: Gavin Richard Haynes
Role: Right-hand bat, right-arm medium bowler
Born: 29 September 1969, Stourbridge
Height: 5ft 10in **Weight:** 12st
Nickname: Splash
County debut: 1991
County cap: 1994
1000 runs in a season: 1
1st-Class 50s: 13
1st-Class 100s: 3
1st-Class catches: 31
One-Day 100s: 1
Place in batting averages: (1995 168th av. 24.56)
Place in bowling averages: (1995 121st av. 40.00)
Strike rate: 77.71 (career 93.91)
Parents: Nicholas and Dorothy
Marital status: Engaged to Joanne
Family links with cricket: Father played club cricket and manages Worcester U14 side. Cousin Peter Haynes played very good club cricket
Education: Gigmill Junior School; High Park Comprehensive; King Edward VI College, Stourbridge
Qualifications: 5 O-levels, 1 A-level, NCA advanced coaching award
Off-season: Coaching in England, resting
Overseas tours: Worcestershire to Zimbabwe and South Africa
Overseas teams played for: Sunrise Sports Club, Zimbabwe 1989-90
Cricketers particularly admired: Ian Botham, Graham Dilley, Graham Gooch, Malcolm Marshall, Viv Richards, Graeme Hick
Young players to look out for: 'The good ones'

Other sports followed: Football (Aston Villa), golf
Injuries: Missed the whole season due to a knee injury
Relaxations: Playing golf, watching television
Extras: Represented England Schools U15. Worcestershire Uncapped Player of the Year 1993
Opinions on cricket: 'Play far too much cricket. Over rates are ridiculous. To keep to 18.5 is unrealistic, teams end up at the end of the season bowling spinners to get the over rate up, simply to keep their fines down.'
Best batting: 158 Worcestershire v Kent, Worcester 1993
Best bowling: 4-33 Worcestershire v Kent, Worcester 1995

1996 Season (did not make any first-class or one-day appearances)

Career Performances

	M	Inns	NO	Runs	HS	Avge	100s	50s	Ct	St	Balls	Runs	Wkts	Avge	Best	5wI	10wM
Test																	
All First	62	95	6	2630	158	29.55	3	13	31	-	3259	1643	35	46.94	4-33	-	-
1-day Int																	
NatWest	8	6	1	277	116 *	55.40	1	1	2	-	264	186	4	46.50	1-9		
B & H	12	10	3	191	65	27.28	-	1	4	-	443	263	12	21.91	3-17		
Sunday	50	40	3	786	83	21.24	-	2	16	-	1378	920	30	30.66	4-21	-	

HAYNES, J. J. Lancashire

Name: Jamie Jonathan Haynes
Role: Right-hand bat, wicket-keeper
Born: 5 July 1974, Bristol
Height: 5ft 10in **Weight:** 12st 3lbs
Nickname: Haynsey, Pterodactyl, Dessy
County debut: 1996
1st-Class stumpings: 1
Parents: Steve Haynes and Moiya Ford
Marital status: Single
Family links with cricket: Dad and uncle both played for Gloucestershire CCC
Education: Garran Primary; St Edmunds College; University of Canberra, Australia
Qualifications: Year 12 Certificate
Career outside cricket: 'Odds and bods during the winter. Managing a bar etc.'
Off-season: Playing club cricket for South Canberra in Australia

Overseas teams played for: Tuggeranong Valley CC, Australia 1995-96; South Canberra CC, Australia 1996-97
Cricketers particularly admired: Warren Hegg, Jack Russell, Graham Lloyd, Paul Evans
Young players to look out for: Richard Green, Andrew Flintoff
Other sports followed: Football (Manchester United, Burnley) and Australian rules (Carlton)
Injuries: 10 stitches in lip but missed no cricket
Relaxations: Shopping, playing golf, going to the movies
Best batting: 16 Lancashire v Middlesex, Old Trafford 1996

1996 Season

	M	Inns	NO	Runs	HS	Avge	100s	50s	Ct	St	O	M	Runs	Wkts	Avge	Best	5wI	10wM
Test																		
All First	1	2	0	26	16	13.00	-	-	-	1								
1-day Int																		
NatWest																		
B & H																		
Sunday	1	0	0	0	0	-	-	-	1	-								

Career Performances

	M	Inns	NO	Runs	HS	Avge	100s	50s	Ct	St	Balls	Runs	Wkts	Avge	Best	5wI	10wM
Test																	
All First	1	2	0	26	16	13.00	-	-	-	1							
1-day Int																	
NatWest																	
B & H																	
Sunday	1	0	0	0	0	-	-	-	1	-							

HAYWOOD, G. R. Sussex

Name: Giles Ronald Haywood
Role: Left-hand bat, right-arm medium bowler
Born: 8 September 1979, Chichester, West Sussex
Height: 6ft 1in **Weight:** 12st
County debut: 1996 (one-day)
Parents: Ronald and Shirley
Family links with cricket: Father and brother currently play club cricket
Education: The Prebendal, Chichester; Lancing College
Qualifications: 11 GCSEs
Career outside cricket: Student
Off-season: At school studying for A-levels (Geography, English, Economics)

Overseas tours: Sussex U19 to Sri Lanka 1995
Cricketers particularly admired: David Gower, Sachin Tendulkar
Young players to look out for: Danny Law, Russell Staves
Other sports followed: Football (Bognor Regis Town FC), hockey and squash
Relaxations: Listening to music, relaxing at home and going out for a drink with friends
Extras: Played for ESCA U15, England U16. Made Sunday League debut at the age of 17
Opinions on cricket: 'Higher player salaries would mean more competition in county sides and ultimately a higher standard of cricket.'

1996 Season

	M	Inns	NO	Runs	HS	Avge	100s	50s	Ct	St	O	M	Runs	Wkts	Avge	Best	5wI	10wM
Test																		
All First																		
1-day Int																		
NatWest																		
B & H																		
Sunday	1	1	0	4	4	4.00	-	-	-	-								

Career Performances

	M	Inns	NO	Runs	HS	Avge	100s	50s	Ct	St	Balls	Runs	Wkts	Avge	Best	5wI	10wM
Test																	
All First																	
1-day Int																	
NatWest																	
B & H																	
Sunday	1	1	0	4	4	4.00	-	-	-	-							

43. Which former Test player became the first living Australian to be commemorated on a postage stamp?

Name: Dean Warren Headley
Role: Right-hand bat, right-arm
medium-fast bowler
Born: 27 January 1970, Stourbridge
Height: 6ft 5in **Weight:** 13st 10lbs
Nickname: Frog
County debut: 1991 (Middlesex),
1993 (Kent)
County cap: 1993 (Kent)
One-Day Internationals: 2
50 wickets in a season: 1
1st-Class 50s: 4
1st-Class 5 w. in innings: 15
1st-Class 10 w. in a match: 1
1st-Class catches: 35
One-Day 5 w. in innings: 2
Place in batting averages: 237th av. 19.46
(1995 257th av. 14.05)
Place in bowling averages: 40th av. 27.19
(1995 59th av. 29.00)
Strike rate: 49.76 (career 57.92)
Parents: Ronald George Alphonso and Gail
Marital status: Single
Family links with cricket: Grandfather (George) and Ron (father) both played for
West Indies
Education: Gigmill Junior School; Oldswinford Hospital School; Royal Grammar
School, Worcester
Qualifications: 7 O-levels
Career outside cricket: 'None yet'
Off-season: England A tour to Australia then work or travel after Christmas
Overseas tours: RGS Worcester to Zimbabwe 1988; Christians in Sport to India
1989-90; England A to Pakistan 1995-96, to Australia 1996-97
Overseas teams played for: Melbourne, Jamaica 1991-92; Primrose CC, South Africa
1993-95
Cricketers particularly admired: Malcolm Marshall, 'my dad', Ian Botham, Gavin
O'Hanlon, Adam Patrick, Min Patel
Young players to look out for: Matthew Walker, Owais Shah, Andrew Harris
Other sports followed: 'Have a go at anything'
Injuries: Hip injury, out for eight weeks
Relaxations: Socialising, watching films, playing golf and eating out
Extras: Took five wickets on debut including a wicket with his first ball in

Championship cricket. Played for Worcestershire 2nd XI 1988-89. Left Middlesex at the end of 1992 season and signed for Kent. Called up as a replacement for the England A tour to Pakistan. Took a record-breaking three hat-tricks during the summer of 1996
Opinions on cricket: 'I am a bowler, I have none.'
Best batting: 91 Middlesex v Leicestershire, Leicester 1992
Best bowling: 8-98 Kent v Derbyshire, Derby 1996

1996 Season

	M	Inns	NO	Runs	HS	Avge	100s	50s	Ct	St	O	M	Runs	Wkts	Avge	Best	5wI	10wM
Test																		
All First	12	16	3	253	63 *	19.46	-	1	4	-	423	69	1387	51	27.19	8-98	2	1
1-day Int	2	1	1	3	3 *	-	-	-	-	-	17	0	84	0	-	-	-	
NatWest	2	0	0	0	0	-	-	-	-	-	18	1	64	3	21.33	2-19	-	
B & H																		
Sunday	6	4	3	50	29 *	50.00	-	-	2	-	39	2	213	6	35.50	2-31	-	

Career Performances

	M	Inns	NO	Runs	HS	Avge	100s	50s	Ct	St	Balls	Runs	Wkts	Avge	Best	5wI	10wM
Test																	
All First	83	106	27	1418	91	17.94	-	4	35	-	14945	7770	258	30.11	8-98	15	1
1-day Int	2	1	1	3	3 *	-	-	-	-	-	102	84	0	-	-	-	
NatWest	11	6	5	50	24 *	50.00	-	-	-	-	661	423	18	23.50	5-20	1	
B & H	15	7	2	57	26	11.40	-	-	4	-	887	565	17	33.23	4-19	-	
Sunday	66	20	11	117	29 *	13.00	-	-	14	-	2777	2257	80	28.21	6-42	1	

44. Who holds the record for the highest Test score by a wicket-keeper?

HEGG, W. K.   Lancashire

Name: Warren Kevin Hegg
Role: Right-hand bat, wicket-keeper
Born: 23 February 1968, Radcliffe,
Lancashire
Height: 5ft 9in **Weight:** 12st 10lbs
Nickname: Chucky
County debut: 1986
1st-Class 50s: 25
1st-Class 100s: 4
1st-Class catches: 485
1st-Class stumpings: 61
Place in batting averages: 91st av. 37.52
(1995 145th av. 27.87)
Parents: Kevin and Glenda
Wife and date of marriage: Joanne, 29
October 1994
Family links with cricket: Father and
brother Martin play in local leagues

Education: Unsworth High School; Stand College, Whitefield
Qualifications: 5 O-levels, 7 CSEs, qualified coach
Off-season: Touring Australia with England A and then working as a cocktail waiter
Overseas tours: NCA North U19 to Bermuda 1985; England YC to Sri Lanka 1986-87, to
Australia (Youth World Cup) 1987-88; England A to Pakistan and Sri Lanka 1990-91, to
Australia 1996-97
Overseas teams played for: Sheffield, Tasmania 1988-90, 1992-93
Cricketers particularly admired: Ian Botham, Alan Knott, Bob Taylor, Gehan Mendis
Young players to look out for: Paddy McKeown, Richard Green, Peter Martin, Ian Austin
Other sports followed: Football (Manchester United), rugby league (Wigan), golf,
fishing, Aussie rules football
Injuries: Groin strain, missed one game
Relaxations: Listening to music, walking on my own, sleep, and 'beating Oscar and
Digger at golf'
Extras: First player to make county debut from Lytham CC. Youngest player for 30
years to score a century for Lancashire, 130 v Northamptonshire in his fourth first-class
game. Eleven victims in match v Derbyshire, equalling world record. Wombwell Cricket
Lovers' Society joint Wicket-keeper of the Year 1993
Best batting: 134 Lancashire v Leicestershire, Old Trafford 1996

1996 Season

	M	Inns	NO	Runs	HS	Avge	100s	50s	Ct	St	O	M	Runs	Wkts	Avge	Best	5wl	10wM
Test																		
All First	17	25	6	713	134	37.52	1	3	50	5								
1-day Int																		
NatWest	5	5	0	94	35	18.80	-	-	6	-								
B & H	7	4	1	130	81	43.33	-	1	16	3								
Sunday	16	12	3	246	47 *	27.33	-	-	8	2								

Career Performances

	M	Inns	NO	Runs	HS	Avge	100s	50s	Ct	St	Balls	Runs	Wkts	Avge	Best	5wl	10wM
Test																	
All First	203	298	58	6198	134	25.82	4	25	485	61	6	7	0	-	-	-	-
1-day Int																	
NatWest	25	15	1	251	35	17.92	-	-	33	2							
B & H	49	19	8	288	81	26.18	-	1	70	5							
Sunday	144	81	39	979	52	23.30	-	1	142	16							

HEMP, D. L.   Warwickshire

Name: David Lloyd Hemp
Role: Left-hand bat, right-arm
medium bowler
Born: 15 November 1970, Bermuda
Height: 6ft **Weight:** 12st 7lbs
Nickname: Hempy, Soc, Mad Dog
County debut: 1991
1000 runs in a season: 1
1st-Class 50s: 22
1st-Class 100s: 6
1st-Class catches: 48
One-Day 100s: 1
Place in batting averages: 96th av. 36.81
(1995 154th av. 27.25)
Strike rate: 31.50 (career 37.80)
Parents: Clive and Elisabeth
Wife and date of marriage: Angie,
16 March 1996
Family links with cricket: Father plays for
Ffynone, brother Tim plays for Swansea and Wales Minor Counties, sister Charlotte
played for Parklands Junior School
Education: Olchfa Comprehensive School; Millfield School; West Glamorgan

Institute of Further Education
Qualifications: 5 O-levels, 2 A-levels, NCA Coaching Award
Career outside cricket: Working in accountancy firm
Off-season: Playing and coaching in Durban, South Africa
Overseas tours: Welsh Schools U19 to Australia 1986-87; Welsh Cricket Association U18 to Barbados 1987; Glamorgan to Trinidad 1990; South Wales Cricket Association to New Zealand and Australia 1991-92; England A to India 1994-95
Overseas teams played for: Hirsh Crusaders, Durban, South Africa 1992-94, 1995-96
Cricketers particularly admired: Viv Richards, David Gower, Keith Arthurton, Mark Waugh
Other sports followed: Football (Swansea City)
Injuries: Four broken ribs, missed ten weeks
Relaxations: Watching football and television, going to movies
Extras: Scored 258* for Wales v MCC 1991. In 1990 scored 104* and 101* for Welsh Schools U19 v Scottish Schools U19 and 120 and 102* v Irish Schools U19. Left Glamorgan at the end of the 1996 season and has joined Warwickshire on a three-year contract
Opinions on cricket: 'All 2nd XI games should be played on county grounds rather than club grounds as the quality of wickets is usually poorer at clubs, also they do not have such good facilities for covering wickets. If third umpires are going to be used in semi-finals and finals then they should be used in all the previous rounds. There is too much cricket being played'
Best batting: 157 Glamorgan v Gloucestershire, Abergavenny 1995
Best bowling: 1-9 Glamorgan v Somerset, Taunton 1995

1996 Season

	M	Inns	NO	Runs	HS	Avge	100s	50s	Ct	St	O	M	Runs	Wkts	Avge	Best	5wI	10wM
Test																		
All First	8	13	2	405	103*	36.81	1	1	3	-	21	2	113	4	28.25	3-23	-	-
1-day Int																		
NatWest																		
B & H	2	1	0	33	33	33.00	-	-	-	-								
Sunday	8	7	1	108	64*	18.00	-	1	4	-	6	0	42	1	42.00	1-14	-	

Career Performances

	M	Inns	NO	Runs	HS	Avge	100s	50s	Ct	St	Balls	Runs	Wkts	Avge	Best	5wI	10wM
Test																	
All First	76	133	12	3877	157	32.04	6	22	48	-	378	330	10	33.00	3-23	-	-
1-day Int																	
NatWest	6	5	0	162	78	32.40	-	1	1	-							
B & H	7	6	0	235	121	39.16	1	1	1	-							
Sunday	47	36	2	577	74	16.97	-	3	25	-	38	43	1	43.00	1-14	-	

HEWITT, J. P.　　　　　　　Middlesex

Name: James Peter Hewitt
Role: Left-hand bat, right-arm
medium-fast bowler
Born: 26 February 1976, London
Height: 6ft 3in **Weight:** 12st 8lbs
Nickname: Hewiey
County debut: 1995 (one-day),
1996 (first-class)
1st-Class 50s: 1
1st-Class catches: 5
Place in batting averages: 172nd av. 28.36
Place in bowling averages: 48th av. 28.27
Strike rate: (career 44.87)
Parents: Mr T.D. Hewitt and Mrs G.J.
Underhay
Marital status: Single
Family links with cricket: Father played
club cricket and had trials with Surrey.
Grandfather played club cricket and had
trials with Surrey
Education: Buckingham School, Hampton; Teddington School, Middlesex; Richmond
College; Kingston College; City of Westminster College
Qualifications: GCSEs; City and Guilds Part I, II and III in Recreation and Leisure;
GNVQ Leisure and Tourism; coaching awards in cricket intermediate and advanced;
squash, basketball, hockey, gymnastics, badminton, football, volleyball and referee
qualification; Community Sports Leadership Award
Career outside cricket: Retail, cricket and coaching
Off-season: Studying at Westminster College
Cricketers particularly admired: Richard Hadlee, David Gower, Curtly Ambrose,
Dominic Cork, Richard Johnson, Philip Hudson
Other sports followed: Athletics ('represented South of England at cross-country'),
football ('played for Chelsea Youth'), badminton, volleyball, rugby (Harlequins)
Relaxations: Watching and playing a number of sports and sports quiz programmes
Extras: 'I was invited back to my old school, Teddington, to present the sports awards
to the pupils – I consider this to be an honour'
Opinions on cricket: 'I am pleased to see the injection of youth into the game at Test
level as well as county. I think the young blood together with the more experienced
players can only be good for the game.'
Best batting: 72 Middlesex v Cambridge University, Fenner's 1996
Best bowling: 3-27 Middlesex v Northamptonshire 1996

1996 Season

	M	Inns	NO	Runs	HS	Avge	100s	50s	Ct	St	O	M	Runs	Wkts	Avge	Best	5wI	10wM
Test																		
All First	10	15	4	312	72	28.36	-	1	5	-	179.3	38	681	24	28.37	3-27	-	-
1-day Int																		
NatWest																		
B & H																		
Sunday	11	5	1	46	16 *	11.50	-	-	5	-	54.3	5	249	10	24.90	3-26	-	

Career Performances

	M	Inns	NO	Runs	HS	Avge	100s	50s	Ct	St	Balls	Runs	Wkts	Avge	Best	5wI	10wM
Test																	
All First	10	15	4	312	72	28.36	-	1	5	-	1077	681	24	28.37	3-27	-	-
1-day Int																	
NatWest																	
B & H																	
Sunday	13	7	2	49	16 *	9.80	-	-	6	-	381	302	12	25.16	3-26	-	

HEWSON, D. R. Gloucestershire

Name: Dominic Robert Hewson
Role: Right-hand bat, right-arm medium bowler
Born: 3 October 1974, Cheltenham
Height: 5ft 10in **Weight:** 13st
Nickname: Chopper, Popa, Con
County debut: 1996
1st-Class 50s: 3
1st-Class catches: 2
Place in batting averages: 207th av. 23.72
Parents: Robert and Julie
Marital status: Single
Children: Peter (aged 6); Debbie (aged 2)
Family links with cricket: Dad played for Upper Fathergill CC near Chopperton
Education: Cheltenham College; University of West of England
Qualifications: 10 GCSEs, 3 A-levels
Off-season: 'Chilling on a beach drinking'
Cricketers particularly admired: Jon Lewis, Jack Russell, Courtney Walsh, Mark Snape
Young players to look out for: Jon Lewis, Dom Hewson, Matt Windows, Rob

Cunliffe, Andrew Symonds

Other sports followed: Rugby, ice hockey, Aussie rules, football

Injuries: 'Continuous headaches in the mornings'

Relaxations: Seeing friends

Extras: Made debut for Gloucestershire 2nd XI in July 1993

Opinions on cricket: 'We play too much cricket and Australians should be banned. Baseball-style fighting should be allowed.'

Best batting: 87 Gloucestershire v Hampshire, Southampton 1996

1996 Season

	M	Inns	NO	Runs	HS	Avge	100s	50s	Ct	St	O	M	Runs	Wkts	Avge	Best	5wl	10wM
Test																		
All First	6	12	1	261	87	23.72	-	3	2	-								
1-day Int																		
NatWest																		
B & H																		
Sunday	1	1	0	3	3	3.00	-	-	-	-								

Career Performances

	M	Inns	NO	Runs	HS	Avge	100s	50s	Ct	St	Balls	Runs	Wkts	Avge	Best	5wl	10wM
Test																	
All First	6	12	1	261	87	23.72	-	3	2	-							
1-day Int																	
NatWest																	
B & H																	
Sunday	1	1	0	3	3	3.00	-	-	-	-							

45. When Alec Stewart scored 173 in the first Test against
New Zealand in Auckland 1996-97 to record the highest Test score by
an English wicket-keeper, whose record did he beat?

HIBBERT, A. J. E.   Essex

Name: Andrew James Edward Hibbert
Role: Right-hand bat, right-arm
medium bowler
Born: 17 December 1974, Harold Wood,
Essex
Height: 6ft **Weight:** 13st 10lbs
Nickname: Buns, Hibby
County debut: 1995
1st-Class 50s: 1
Parents: Tony (deceased) and Thelma
Marital status: Single
Family links with cricket: 'Dad played club
cricket and Mum is an avid cricket follower'
Education: St Edward's C of E
Comprehensive, Romford
Qualifications: 8 GCSEs, NCA Senior
Coaching Award
Off-season: Coaching at Essex CCC indoor
school
Overseas tours: England U18 to Denmark (International Youth Tournament) 1993
Overseas teams played for: University of Newcastle, New South Wales, Australia
1995-96
Cricketers particularly admired: Graham Thorpe, Graham Gooch, Stuart Law
Young players to look out for: Matt Church, Jonathan Powell
Other sports followed: Golf, football (Tottenham Hotspur), snooker
Injuries: Split finger, out for four weeks
Relaxations: Music 'would love to be a DJ'
Extras: Played for Essex from U14 upwards, *Daily Telegraph* (South) Batting Award
1990
Opinions on cricket: 'Pitches and facilities in 2nd XI should mirror those of the first-
class game. All hotel rooms should be like The Mount Somerset in Taunton.'
Best batting: 85 Essex v Cambridge University, Fenner's 1996

1996 Season

	M	Inns	NO	Runs	HS	Avge	100s	50s	Ct	St	O	M	Runs	Wkts	Avge	Best	5wl	10wM
Test																		
All First	2	4	1	103	85	34.33	-	1	-	-								
1-day Int																		
NatWest																		
B & H																		
Sunday	6	6	2	45	25	11.25	-	-	1	-								

Career Performances

	M	Inns	NO	Runs	HS	Avge	100s	50s	Ct	St	Balls	Runs	Wkts	Avge	Best	5wI	10wM
Test																	
All First	3	6	1	134	85	26.80	-	1	-	-							
1-day Int																	
NatWest																	
B & H																	
Sunday	6	6	2	45	25	11.25	-	-	1	-							

HICK, G. A. Worcestershire

Name: Graeme Ashley Hick
Role: Right-hand bat, off-spin bowler
Born: 23 May 1966, Salisbury, Rhodesia
Height: 6ft 3in **Weight:** 14st 7lbs
Nickname: Hicky, Ash
County debut: 1984
County cap: 1986
Test debut: 1991
Tests: 46
One-Day Internationals: 62
1000 runs in a season: 12
1st-Class 50s: 103
1st-Class 100s: 90
1st-Class 200s: 10
1st-Class 400s: 1
1st-Class 5 w. in innings: 5
1st-Class 10 w. in match: 1
1st-Class catches: 395
One-Day 100s: 18
Place in batting averages: 53rd av. 44.46 (1995 28th av. 49.70)
Place in bowling averages: (1995 av. 66.60)
Strike rate: 130.80 (career 89.35)
Parents: John and Eve
Wife and date of marriage: Jackie, 5 October 1991
Children: Lauren Amy, 12 September 1992
Family links with cricket: Father served on Zimbabwe Cricket Union Board of Control since 1984 and played representative cricket in Zimbabwe
Education: Banket Primary; Prince Edward Boys' High School, Zimbabwe
Qualifications: 4 O-levels, NCA coaching award
Overseas tours: Zimbabwe to England (World Cup) 1983, to Sri Lanka 1983-84, to England 1985; England to New Zealand and Australia (World Cup) 1991-92, to India

and Sri Lanka 1992-93, to West Indies 1993-94, to Australia 1994-95, to South Africa 1995-96, to India and Pakistan (World Cup) 1995-96

Overseas teams played for: Old Hararians, Zimbabwe 1982-90; Northern Districts, New Zealand 1987-89; Queensland, Australia 1990-91

Cricketers particularly admired: Duncan Fletcher (Zimbabwe captain) for approach and understanding of the game, David Houghton, Basil D'Oliveira

Other sports followed: Follows Liverpool FC, golf, tennis, squash, hockey

Relaxations: 'Leaning against Steve Rhodes at first-slip'

Extras: Made first century aged six for school team; youngest player participating in 1983 Prudential World Cup (aged 17); youngest player to represent Zimbabwe. Scored 1234 runs in Birmingham League and played for Worcestershire 2nd XI in 1984 – hitting six successive centuries. In 1986, at age 20, he became the youngest player to score 2000 runs in an English season. One of *Wisden*'s Five Cricketers of the Year 1986. In 1988 he made 405* v Somerset at Taunton, the highest individual score in England since 1895, and scored 1000 first-class runs by end of May, hitting a record 410 runs in April. In 1990 became youngest batsman ever to make 50 first-class centuries and scored 645 runs without being dismissed – a record for English cricket. Also in 1990 became the fastest to 10,000 runs in county cricket (179 innings). Qualified as an English player in 1991. Scored first Test century v India in Bombay 1992-93 and was England's leading batsman, bowler and fielder. Published *Hick 'n' Dilley Circus* and *A Champion's Diary*. Also played hockey for Zimbabwe. Finished third in the Whyte and Mackay batting ratings in 1995

Opinions on cricket: 'What a great game.'

Best batting: 405* Worcestershire v Somerset, Taunton 1988

Best bowling: 5-18 Worcestershire v Leicestershire, Worcester 1995

1996 Season

	M	Inns	NO	Runs	HS	Avge	100s	50s	Ct	St	O	M	Runs	Wkts	Avge	Best	5wI	10wM
Test	4	6	0	43	20	7.16	-	-	3	-	32	8	93	1	93.00	1-26	-	-
All First	17	29	1	1245	215	44.46	5	3	19	-	109	25	333	5	66.60	2-43	-	-
1-day Int	3	3	0	123	91	41.00	-	1	2	-								
NatWest	2	2	0	13	13	6.50	-	-	1	-	15	0	64	2	32.00	2-37	-	
B & H	4	4	1	206	95	68.66	-	2	2	-	8	0	61	0	-	-	-	-
Sunday	12	11	3	368	63 *	46.00	-	5	7	-	24	0	101	5	20.20	2-13	-	

Career Performances

	M	Inns	NO	Runs	HS	Avge	100s	50s	Ct	St	Balls	Runs	Wkts	Avge	Best	5wI	10wM
Test	46	80	6	2672	178	36.10	4	15	62	-	2973	1247	22	56.68	4-126	-	-
All First	327	535	53	26895	405 *	55.79	90	103	395	-	17425	8513	195	43.65	5-18	5	1
1-day Int	62	61	7	2105	105 *	38.98	2	16	32	-	840	696	18	38.66	3-41	-	
NatWest	33	33	6	1379	172 *	51.07	3	8	18	-	1095	662	20	33.10	4-54	-	
B & H	53	52	11	2500	127 *	60.97	7	16	34	-	570	423	9	47.00	3-36	-	
Sunday	152	146	28	5579	130	47.27	7	45	37	-	2111	1799	65	27.67	4-21	-	

HINDSON, J. E. Nottinghamshire

Name: James Edward Hindson
Role: Right-hand bat, slow left-arm bowler
Born: 13 September 1973, Huddersfield, Yorkshire
Height: 6ft 1in **Weight:** 12st 4lbs
Nickname: Bullseye
County debut: 1992
50 w. in a season: 1
1st-Class 50s: 1
1st-Class 5 w. in innings: 7
1st-Class 10 w. match: 2
1st-Class catches: 12
Place in batting averages: (1995 263rd av. 13.43)
Place in bowling averages: (1995 90th av. 34.13)
Strike rate: (career 63.98)
Parents: Robert and Gloria
Marital status: Single
Family links with cricket: 'Older brother captain of village side, younger brother also plays'
Education: Robert Sherborne Infants School, Rolleston, Staffs; Ernhale Junior School, Arnold; St Peter's Primary School, East Bridgford; Toot Hill Comprehensive School, Bingham
Qualifications: 10 GCSEs, 3 A-levels, senior cricket coach
Off-season: Playing for Lancaster Park in Christchurch, New Zealand
Overseas tours: England U19 to India 1992-93
Overseas teams played for: Lancaster Park, Christchurch, New Zealand 1995-96
Cricketers particularly admired: Andy Afford, Courtney Walsh
Young players to look out for: Guy Welton
Other sports followed: Ice hockey, football
Injuries: Knee problems, out for ten days
Relaxations: 'Keeping the ball on the island. Not getting hit when batting'
Extras: Took five wickets on first-class debut (eight in the match) v Cambridge University. Converted from right-arm to left-arm bowler at age six, still throws right-handed and bowled left-arm medium until 15 years old. Received 2nd team cap at end of 1993 season
Opinions on cricket: 'Admission for spectators should be cheaper.'
Best batting: 53* Nottinghamshire v Oxford University, The Parks 1995
Best bowling: 5-42 Nottinghamshire v Cambridge University, Trent Bridge 1992

	M	Inns	NO	Runs	HS	Avge	100s	50s	Ct	St	O	M	Runs	Wkts	Avge	Best	5wI	10wM
Test																		
All First	1	0	0	0	0	-	-	-	-	-	3	1	7	0	-	-	-	-
1-day Int																		
NatWest																		
B & H																		
Sunday																		

Career Performances

	M	Inns	NO	Runs	HS	Avge	100s	50s	Ct	St	Balls	Runs	Wkts	Avge	Best	5wI	10wM
Test																	
All First	25	32	5	330	53 *	12.22	-	1	12	-	5247	2758	82	33.63	5-42	7	2
1-day Int																	
NatWest	2	1	1	16	16 *	-	-	-	-	-	120	83	2	41.50	2-57	-	
B & H	1	1	1	41	41 *	-	-	-	-	-	60	69	1	69.00	1-69	-	
Sunday	20	7	3	58	21	14.50	-	-	5	-	768	639	16	39.93	4-19	-	

HODGSON, T. P.   Essex

Name: Timothy Philip Hodgson
Role: Left-hand bat, right-arm mixture
Born: 27 March 1975, Guildford
Height: 5ft 10in **Weight:** 12st 7lbs
Nickname: Hodge, TP, Wiggy
County debut: 1996 (one-day)
Parents: Simon and Victoria
Marital status: Single
Family links with cricket: 'Dad bowls leg-spin off 24 yards. Brother Jamie played for Cambridge University, Mark for Surrey 2s and Charlie for Berkshire U19 and full side'
Education: Milbourne Lodge, Esher; Wellington College, Berkshire; Durham University
Off-season: Student at Durham University and 'watching Southampton's bid to spend yet another season in the top flight, and build a side for the title in the year 2005'
Overseas tours: Wellington College to South Africa
Cricketers particularly admired: Graham Gooch, Jason Sayers and Stuart Kirk 'for his dedication to health and physical fitness'

Other sports followed: Football (Southampton FC and Woking FC), tennis and golf
Relaxations: Watching or playing most sports, spending time at home
Extras: Highest first wicket partnership in second team (366). Played Surrey U12 to U19 and several second team games. Member of Wellington Cricketer Cup winning side in 1995. Member of Durham University's UAU winning side in 1995. Scored the highest ever score on 'The Turf'(Wellington school ground) with 205 not out.
Opinions on cricket: 'Durham University should be granted first-class status and never again be subjected to the traumas of playing Hull University away.'

1996 Season

	M	Inns	NO	Runs	HS	Avge	100s	50s	Ct	St	O	M	Runs	Wkts	Avge	Best	5wl	10wM
Test																		
All First																		
1-day Int																		
NatWest																		
B & H																		
Sunday	4	3	0	27	21	9.00	-	-	-	-								

Career Performances

	M	Inns	NO	Runs	HS	Avge	100s	50s	Ct	St	Balls	Runs	Wkts	Avge	Best	5wl	10wM
Test																	
All First																	
1-day Int																	
NatWest																	
B & H																	
Sunday	4	3	0	27	21	9.00	-	-	-	-							

46. Who holds the record for the number of consecutive
Tests with a score of 50 or over?

HOGGARD, M. J. Yorkshire

Name: Matthew James Hoggard
Role: Right-hand bat, right-arm fast bowler
Born: 31 December 1976, Leeds
Height: 6ft 2in **Weight:** 12st 12lbs
Nickname: Mingh the Merciless, Pontius
Pilate, Ben Hur
County debut: 1996
Strike rate: (career 90.00)
Parents: John and Margaret
Marital status: Single
Education: Pudsey Grangefield; Pudsey
Grangefield Sixth Form
Qualifications: GCSEs and A-levels
Off-season: Playing in South Africa
Overseas tours: England U19 to Zimbabwe
1995-96
Overseas teams played for: Johannesburg
Pirates 1995-97
Cricketers particularly admired: Mark
Nicklin, Chris Simpson, Russell Murry
Other sports followed: Rugby league (Leeds), football, athletics, rugby
Injuries: Groin strain, missed three weeks
Relaxations: Music, dog, 'beer more beer'
Extras: Joined England U19 tour to Zimbabwe as a replacement in 1995-96
Opinions on cricket: 'The season is far too long i.e. five months too long.'
Best batting: 10 Yorkshire v South Africa A, Headingley 1996
Best bowling: 1-41 Yorkshire v South Africa A, Headingley 1996

1996 Season

	M	Inns	NO	Runs	HS	Avge	100s	50s	Ct	St	O	M	Runs	Wkts	Avge	Best	5wI	10wM
Test																		
All First	1	1	0	10	10	10.00	-	-	-	-	15	3	41	1	41.00	1-41	-	-
1-day Int																		
NatWest																		
B & H																		
Sunday																		

Career Performances

	M	Inns	NO	Runs	HS	Avge	100s	50s	Ct	St	Balls	Runs	Wkts	Avge	Best	5wl	10wM
Test																	
All First	1	1	0	10	10	10.00	-	-	-	-	90	41	1	41.00	1-41	-	-
1-day Int																	
NatWest																	
B & H																	
Sunday																	

HOLLIOAKE, A. J.   Surrey

Name: Adam John Hollioake
Role: Right-hand bat, right-arm
fast-medium bowler, county captain
Born: 5 September 1971, Melbourne,
Australia
Height: 5ft 11in **Weight:** 13st 4lbs
Nickname: Smokey, Smokin' Joe, Wolf,
Rock, Rambo, Holly, Strong Dance,
Millionaire, Oaky, The Oak, Hokey Cokey,
Abo, Bong, Stumpy, Raj Maru, Gatt, Judgy
County debut: 1992 (one-day),
1993 (first-class)
County Cap: 1995
One-Day Internationals: 2
1000 runs in a season: 2
1st-Class 50s: 21
1st-Class 100s: 10
1st-Class catches: 46
Place in batting average: 5th av. 66.17 (1995 83rd av. 36.63)
Place in bowling averages: 156th av. 66.08 (1995 94th av. 34.33)
Strike rate: 118.00 (career 78.10)
Parents: John and Daria
Marital status: Single
Family links with cricket: 'Brother Ben tries to play but is far too skinny to really
progress any further'
Education: St Joseph's College, Sydney; St Patrick's College, Ballarat, Australia; St
George's School, Weybridge; Surrey Tutorial College, Guildford
Qualifications: 'Some GCSEs and A-levels'
Off-season: Captaining England A to Australia and 'winning the flag for North Perth
CC'
Overseas tours: School trip to Zimbabwe; Surrey YC to Australia; England YC to

New Zealand 1990-91; England A to Australia 1996-97
Overseas teams played for: Fremantle, Western Australia 1990-91; North Shore, Sydney 1992-93; Geelong, Victoria; North Perth, Western Australia 1995-97
Cricketers particularly admired: Steve Waugh, 'anyone who gives 100 per cent'
Young players to look out for: Alex Tudor
Other sports followed: Rugby, boxing, Aussie rules football, American football, 'chess and mind games'
Injuries: 'Severe blow to the scrotum during the 1996 NatWest quarter-final. Spent fifteen minutes on the floor'
Relaxations: 'Spending time with a gorgeous little Indon'
Extras: Played rugby for London Counties, Middlesex and South of England as well as having a trial for England U18. Scored a century on first-class debut against Derbyshire. Surrey Young Player of the Year 1993. Fastest ever one-day 50 – in 15 balls v Yorkshire. Surrey Supporters' Player of the Year 1996 and Surrey Players' Player of the Year 1996. Captained the England A side on their 1996-97 tour to Australia. His 39 wickets in the Sunday league was a record for the competition
Opinions on cricket: 'Boundaries are too small and outfields are too short – it is too easy to score runs. How come everyone in England knows we are playing too much quantity and not enough quality cricket, but no one has the balls to do anything about it?'
Best batting: 138 Surrey v Leicestershire, The Oval 1994
Best bowling: 4-22 Surrey v Yorkshire, The Oval 1995

1996 Season

	M	Inns	NO	Runs	HS	Avge	100s	50s	Ct	St	O	M	Runs	Wkts	Avge	Best	5wI	10wM
Test																		
All First	17	29	6	1522	129	66.17	5	8	18	-	236	45	793	12	66.08	3-80	-	
1-day Int	2	2	0	28	15	14.00	-	-	-	-	15.3	1	68	8	8.50	4-23	-	
NatWest	4	4	1	140	57	46.66	-	1	3	-	30.4	0	131	5	26.20	2-28	-	
B & H	5	4	0	61	45	15.25	-	-	-	-	29	2	162	4	40.50	4-34	-	
Sunday	15	12	1	291	74	26.45	-	1	3	-	91.1	1	474	39	12.15	5-44	2	

Career Performances

	M	Inns	NO	Runs	HS	Avge	100s	50s	Ct	St	Balls	Runs	Wkts	Avge	Best	5wI	10wM
Test																	
All First	57	93	11	3695	138	45.06	10	21	46	-	4999	2777	64	43.39	4-22	-	-
1-day Int	2	2	0	28	15	14.00	-	-	-	-	93	68	8	8.50	4-23	-	
NatWest	10	8	2	261	60	43.50	-	2	6	-	422	322	14	23.00	4-53	-	
B & H	13	9	1	101	45	12.62	-	-	4	-	450	393	10	39.30	4-34	-	
Sunday	58	49	10	1218	93	31.23	-	6	10	-	2171	2070	89	23.25	5-44	2	

HOLLIOAKE, B. C.   Surrey

Name: Ben Caine Hollioake
Role: Right-hand bat, right-arm
medium-fast bowler
Born: 11 November 1977, Melbourne,
Australia
Height: 6ft 2in **Weight:** 12st 7lbs
Nickname: Bedroom Bully, Big Dog,
Pelican, Snoop, Oaky
County debut: 1996
1st-Class catches: 3
One-Day 5 w. in innings: 1
Place in bowling averages: 25th av. 25.20
Strike rate: (career 39.00)
Parents: John and Daria
Marital status: Single
Family links with cricket: 'Dad played for
Victoria, brother for Surrey and captain of
England A'
Education: Edgarley Hall; Millfield School; Wesley College, Perth, Western Australia;
'Joey Benjamin's house'
Qualifications: 'A couple of GCSEs and NCA coaching award'
Career outside cricket: 'Beach lizard'
Off-season: England U19 tour to Pakistan. Playing grade cricket in Perth, Western
Australia
Overseas tours: Millfield to Zimbabwe 1992; West of England to West Indies 1992;
England U19 to Pakistan 1996-97
Overseas teams played for: Mellville, Perth 1992-95; North Perth 1996-97
Cricketers particularly admired: Waugh brothers, Waqar Younis, Graham Dilley,
'brother and the old man' and Neil 'Lionheart' Sargeant
Young players to look out for: Owais 'Youngster' Shah, Alex Tudor, David Sales
Other sports followed: Rugby 7s, league and union, Aussie rules
Injuries: 'Useless ankle, out for three weeks'
Relaxations: Playing the guitar, surfing, 'making sexy chit-chat with women'
Extras: Played England U14 and U15. Played Western Australia U17 and U19. The
youngest player to take five wickets in a Sunday League game (5 for 10)
Opinions on cricket: 'Youngsters are still not backed enough in the "big" games.'
Best batting: 46 Surrey v Warwickshire, The Oval 1996
Best bowling: 4-74 Surrey v Yorkshire, Middlesbrough 1996

1996 Season

	M	Inns	NO	Runs	HS	Avge	100s	50s	Ct	St	O	M	Runs	Wkts	Avge	Best	5wI	10wM
Test																		
All First	3	4	0	63	46	15.75	-	-	3	-	65	12	252	10	25.20	4-74	-	-
1-day Int																		
NatWest	1	0	0	0	0	-	-	-	2	-	4	0	25	0	-		-	-
B & H	1	0	0	0	0	-	-	-	-	-	7	1	25	1	25.00	1-25	-	
Sunday	11	8	2	70	22 *	11.66	-	-	5	-	58.4	4	268	13	20.61	5-10	1	

Career Performances

	M	Inns	NO	Runs	HS	Avge	100s	50s	Ct	St	Balls	Runs	Wkts	Avge	Best	5wI	10wM
Test																	
All First	3	4	0	63	46	15.75	-	-	3	-	390	252	10	25.20	4-74	-	-
1-day Int																	
NatWest	1	0	0	0	0	-	-	-	2	-	24	25	0	-		-	-
B & H	1	0	0	0	0	-	-	-	-	-	42	25	1	25.00	1-25	-	
Sunday	11	8	2	70	22 *	11.66	-	-	5	-	352	268	13	20.61	5-10	1	

HOLLOWAY, P. C. L.   Somerset

Name: Piran Christopher Laity Holloway
Role: Left-hand bat, wicket-keeper
Born: 1 October 1970, Helston, Cornwall
Height: 5ft 8in **Weight:** 11st 5lbs
Nickname: Oggy, Leg, Piras
County debut: 1988 (Warwickshire),
1994 (Somerset)
1st-Class 50s: 12
1st-Class 100s: 4
1st-Class catches: 42
1st-Class stumpings: 1
Place in batting averages: 108th av. 35.66
(1995 19th av. 53.93)
Parents: Chris and Mary
Marital status: 'Engaged to the lovely Nikki'
Family links with cricket: 'Mum and Dad
are keen'
Education: Nansloe CP School, Helston;
Millfield School; Taunton School;
Loughborough University
Qualifications: 7 O-levels, 2 A-levels, BSc Hons in Sports Science
Off-season: 'Surfing in Bali for two weeks, followed by a tour of Western Australia.

Also playing cricket and coaching for Claremont Nedlands in Perth'

Overseas tours: Millfield School to Barbados 1986; England YC to Australia 1989-90; Warwickshire CCC to Cape Town 1992 and 1993; Somerset CCC to Holland 1994

Overseas teams played for: North Perth, 1993-94; Nedlands, Perth 1994-96; Claremont Nedlands 1996-97

Cricketers particularly admired: 'More I've played the less I've admired anyone'

Other sports followed: Squash, football, rugby, tennis, surfing

Injuries: Bat jar, missed no cricket

Relaxations: Surfing or watching videos

Extras: Joined Somerset for the 1995 season. Won the Jack Hobbs Trophy in 1990, played Young England for three years, was fourth in the county averages in 1991. 1995 Somerset Young Player of the Year

Opinions on cricket: 'Remove the boundary rope as spectators still bend down to pick the ball up behind it, only to find it buried in their head as it deflects off. No amount of experience seems to stop people from doing this and so it is down to us to prevent it – even though it is the highlight of fielding. '

Best batting: 168 Somerset v Middlesex, Uxbridge 1996

1996 Season

	M	Inns	NO	Runs	HS	Avge	100s	50s	Ct	St	O	M	Runs	Wkts	Avge	Best	5wI	10wM
Test																		
All First	10	16	1	535	168	35.66	1	3	7	-	4.4	1	34	0	-	-	--	
1-day Int																		
NatWest																		
B & H																		
Sunday	1	1	1	3	3 *	-	-	-	1	-								

Career Performances

	M	Inns	NO	Runs	HS	Avge	100s	50s	Ct	St	Balls	Runs	Wkts	Avge	Best	5wI	10wM
Test																	
All First	40	65	14	2016	168	39.52	4	12	42	1	40	46	0	-	-	-	-
1-day Int																	
NatWest	4	3	1	68	50 *	34.00	-	1	3	1							
B & H	6	6	1	67	27	13.40	-	-	7	-							
Sunday	43	35	9	502	66	19.30	-	2	25	7							

HOOD, J.   Yorkshire

Name: Jamie Hood
Role: Left-hand bat, right-arm medium-fast bowler
Born: 7 September 1976, Middlesbrough
Height: 6ft 1in **Weight:** 11st 5lbs
Nickname: One Eye
County debut: No first-team appearance
Parents: Ray and Lynne
Marital status: Single
Family links with cricket: 'Dad and brother both play for Redcar 1st XI in the North Yorkshire South Durham League'
Education: Riverdale Primary School; West Redcar Comprehensive
Qualifications: NCA Coaching (level 2)
Off-season: Playing club cricket in Cape Town, South Africa
Overseas teams played for: Edgemead CC, Cape Town, South Africa 1994-95; Mowbray CC, Cape Town, South Africa 1996-97
Cricketers particularly admired: Brian Lara, Allan Donald
Other sports followed: Football (Middlesbrough FC), rugby league (Leeds)
Relaxations: 'Like listening to most kinds of music, especially club music. Eating out at Chinese restaurants'
Extras: Won the national bowling award at U15 level

HOOPER, C. L.   Kent

Name: Carl Llewellyn Hooper
Role: Right-hand bat, off-spin bowler
Born: 15 December 1966, Guyana
Height: 6ft **Weight:** 13st
County debut: 1992
County cap: 1992
Test debut: 1987-88
Tests: 52
One-Day Internationals: 141
1000 runs in a season: 6
1st-Class 50s: 68

1st-Class 100s: 33
1st-Class 200s: 1
1st-Class 5 w. in innings: 10
1st-Class catches: 238
One-Day 100s: 7
One-Day 5 w. in innings: 1
Place in batting averages: 41st av. 44.88
(1995 39th av. 46.21)
Place in bowling averages: 60th av. 30.34
(1995 142nd av. 48.29)
Strike rate: 74.19 (career 80.06)
Off-season: Playing for West Indies
Overseas tours: West Indies to India and
Pakistan 1987-88, to Australia 1988-89, to
Pakistan 1990-91, to England 1991, to
Pakistan and Australia (World Cup) 1991-92,
to Australia and South Africa 1992-93, to
Sharjah, India (Hero Cup) and Sri Lanka

1993-94, to India 1994-95, to England 1995, to Australia 1996-97
Overseas teams played for: Guyana 1984-96
Extras: AXA Equity & Law Award 1993. Withdrew from the West Indies squad for
tours to Australia and the World Cup in 1995-96 through illness. Unable to play the 1997
county season due to touring commitments with the West Indies. his overseas slot was
taken by Zimbabwe's Paul Strang
Best batting: 236* Kent v Glamorgan, Canterbury 1993
Best bowling: 5-33 West Indies v Queensland, Brisbane 1988-89

1996 Season

	M	Inns	NO	Runs	HS	Avge	100s	50s	Ct	St	O	M	Runs	Wkts	Avge	Best	5wI	10wM
Test																		
All First	17	29	2	1287	155	47.66	3	9	33	-	321.3	83	789	26	30.34	4-7	-	-
1-day Int																		
NatWest	2	2	0	28	26	14.00	-	-	-	-	24	0	99	0	-		-	-
B & H	6	6	0	277	98	46.16	-	3	1	-	43	0	197	3	65.66	2-36	-	
Sunday	17	16	1	579	145	38.60	1	4	9	-	97	3	467	10	46.70	3-21	-	

Career Performances

	M	Inns	NO	Runs	HS	Avge	100s	50s	Ct	St	Balls	Runs	Wkts	Avge	Best	5wI	10wM
Test	52	87	7	2548	178 *	31.85	5	12	57	-	6066	2672	51	52.39	5-40	2	-
All First	209	329	32	13330	236 *	44.88	33	68	238	-	27302	12063	341	35.37	5-33	10	-
1-day Int	141	126	29	3270	113 *	33.71	2	19	69	-	5626	4107	129	31.83	4-34	-	
NatWest	11	11	1	423	136 *	42.30	1	1	7	-	651	383	5	76.60	2-12	-	
B & H	12	12	0	454	98	37.83	-	4	4	-	654	385	12	32.08	3-28	-	
Sunday	65	62	7	2482	145	45.12	4	19	34	-	2785	1898	57	33.29	5-41	1	

HOUSE, W. J.   Kent

Name: William John House
Role: Left-hand bat, right-arm
medium bowler
Born: 16 March 1976, Sheffield
Height: 5ft 11in **Weight:** 13st
Nickname: Curry, Wendy, Green, Pent
County debut: No first-team appearances
1st-Class 50s: 2
1st-Class 100s: 2
1st-Class catches: 2
Place in batting averages: 22nd av. 52.60
Strike rate: (career 267.00)
Parents: Bill and Anna
Marital status: Single
Education: British School in the
Netherlands, The Hague; Sevenoaks School;
University of Cambridge (Gonville and
Caius College)
Qualifications: 11 GCSEs, International
Baccalaureate

Off-season: Studying at Cambridge University
Overseas teams played for: Royal Hague CC 1985-89; University CC, Adelaide
1994-95
Cricketers particularly admired: Ian Botham, David Gower
Young players to look out for: Anurag Singh, Umer Rashid
Other sports followed: Rugby (Cambridge University U21 XV), football (Sheffield
Wednesday), golf
Relaxations: Music and history
Extras: Cricket Societies leading all-rounder in schools cricket in 1993. Kent CCC's
Most Improved Player 1996. Cambridge University's Player of the Year 1996
Opinions on cricket: 'Need for a two-divisional championship to ensure meaningful
cricket throughout the season.'
Best batting: 136 Cambridge University v Derbyshire, Fenner's 1996
Best bowling: 1-44 Cambridge University v Essex, Fenner's 1996

1996 Season

	M	Inns	NO	Runs	HS	Avge	100s	50s	Ct	St	O	M	Runs	Wkts	Avge	Best	5wI	10wM
Test																		
All First	8	15	5	526	136	52.60	2	2	2	-	89	8	412	2	206.00	1-44	-	-
1-day Int																		
NatWest																			
B & H	1	1	0	22	22	22.00	-	-	1	-								
Sunday	4	4	1	46	19 *	15.33	-	-	1	-								

Career Performances

	M	Inns	NO	Runs	HS	Avge	100s	50s	Ct	St	Balls	Runs	Wkts	Avge	Best	5wI	10wM
Test																	
All First	8	15	5	526	136	52.60	2	2	2	-	534	412	2	206.00	1-44	-	-
1-day Int																	
NatWest																		
B & H	1	1	0	22	22	22.00	-	-	1	-							
Sunday	4	4	1	46	19 *	15.33	-	-	1	-							

HUGHES, J. G. Northamptonshire

Name: John Gareth Hughes
Role: Right-hand bat, right-arm medium-fast bowler
Born: 3 May 1971, Wellingborough
Height: 6ft 2in **Weight:** 13st 7lbs
Nickname: Yozzer
1st-Class 5 w. in innings: 1
1st-Class catches: 5
Strike rate: 106.00 (career 79.00)
Parents: John and Jennifer
Wife and date of marriage: Helen, 28 September 1996
Family links with cricket: 'My grandad, Dad and brother all play or have played for Little Harrowden, whilst two of my uncles umpire for the same club'
Education: Little Harrowden Primary School; Westfield Boys/Sir Christopher Hatton School, Wellingborough; Sheffield Hallam University
Qualifications: 7 O-levels, 2 A-levels, BEd (Hons) in Physical Education
Career outside cricket: Physical education teacher
Off-season: Supply teaching in Northampton/Wellingborough area

Overseas tours: Northamptonshire CA U15 to Holland 1986; Northamptonshire to Durban 1991-92, to Cape Town 1992-93, to Zimbabwe 1994-95, to Johannesburg 1996
Overseas teams played for: Mana and Wellington B 1994-95
Cricketers particularly admired: Nick Cook, Alan Walker, David Capel, Greg Thomas, Bob Carter, Curtly Ambrose
Other sports followed: 'Football especially, but I enjoy most sports'
Injuries: 'Nothing significant'
Relaxations: Going out for a pint and a meal
Extras: Represented both English Schools and England YC at various age groups. Also represented Northamptonshire at football and basketball at schoolboy level. Grandfather played international football for Wales.
Best batting: 17 Northamptonshire v Hampshire, Southampton 1994
Best bowling: 5-69 Northamptonshire v Hampshire, Southampton 1994

1996 Season

	M	Inns	NO	Runs	HS	Avge	100s	50s	Ct	St	O	M	Runs	Wkts	Avge	Best	5wI	10wM
Test																		
All First	2	3	0	22	8	7.33	-	-	1	-	53	11	221	3	73.66	2-21	-	-
1-day Int																		
NatWest																		
B & H																		
Sunday																		

Career Performances

	M	Inns	NO	Runs	HS	Avge	100s	50s	Ct	St	Balls	Runs	Wkts	Avge	Best	5wI	10wM
Test																	
All First	18	25	1	123	17	5.12	-	-	5	-	2449	1481	31	47.77	5-69	1	-
1-day Int																	
NatWest																	
B & H	4	3	0	11	9	3.66	-	-	1	-	116	106	2	53.00	2-47	-	
Sunday	6	5	2	31	21	10.33	-	-	1	-	174	127	3	42.33	2-39	-	

HUMPHRIES, S.   Sussex

Name: Shaun Humphries
Role: Right-hand bat, right-arm net bowler, wicket-keeper
Born: 11 January 1973, Horsham, West Sussex
Height: 5ft 11in **Weight:** 10st 8lbs
Nickname: Stan, Gooner
County debut: 1993
1st-Class catches: 3
Parents: Peter John and Marilyn Christine

Marital status: Single
Education: The Weald School, Billingshurst; Kingston College of Further Education
Qualifications: 5 GCSEs, BTEC National Diploma in Leisure Studies
Off-season: Watching Arsenal, buying a house, beer and girlfriend Kate
Overseas tours: Sussex U13 to Barbados 1987; Sussex U18 to India 1990-91
Overseas teams played for: Sutherland, Sydney 1994-95
Cricketers particularly admired: Peter Moores, Alec Stewart, John Berry, Geoff Kirkham, Ian Healy
Young players to look out for: Giles Haywood
Other sports followed: 'Away trips with the Gunners', cycling, LA Raiders

Injuries: Torn shoulder muscle, out for three weeks
Relaxations: Music, raves, Kate, 'being in awe of Spurs's trophy cabinet'
Opinions on cricket: 'Second XI cricketers are continually playing in sub-standard conditions, wet wickets, bad light. It must be on a par with first-class cricket.'

1996 Season

	M	Inns	NO	Runs	HS	Avge	100s	50s	Ct	St	O	M	Runs	Wkts	Avge	Best	5wI	10wM
Test																		
All First	1	0	0	0	0	-	-	-	1	-								
1-day Int																		
NatWest																		
B & H																		
Sunday																		

Career Performances

	M	Inns	NO	Runs	HS	Avge	100s	50s	Ct	St	Balls	Runs	Wkts	Avge	Best	5wI	10wM
Test																	
All First	2	0	0	0	0	-	-	-	3	-							
1-day Int																	
NatWest																	
B & H																	
Sunday																	

HUSSAIN, N. Essex

Name: Nasser Hussain
Role: Right-hand bat, declaration bowler, county vice-captain
Born: 28 March 1968, Madras, India
Height: 6ft **Weight:** 12st
Nickname: Nashwani
County debut: 1987
Test debut: 1989-90
Tests: 12
One-Day Internationals: 4
1000 runs in a season: 4
1st-Class 50s: 56
1st-Class 100s: 29
1st-Class catches: 231
One-Day 100s: 3
Place in batting averages: 46th av. 46.20
(1995 14th av. 54.52)
Strike rate: (career 138.00)
Parents: Joe and Shireen

Wife and date of marriage: Karen, 24 September 1993
Family links with cricket: Father played for Madras in Ranji Trophy 1966-67. Brother Mel played for Hampshire, brother Abbas played for Essex 2nd XI
Education: Forest School, Snaresbrook; Durham University
Qualifications: 10 O-levels, 3 A-levels; BSc (Hons) in Natural Sciences; NCA cricket coaching award
Off-season: Touring Zimbabwe and New Zealand with England
Overseas tours: England YC to Sri Lanka 1986-87, to Australia (Youth World Cup) 1987-88; England to India (Nehru Cup) 1989-90, to West Indies 1989-90 and 1993-94, to Zimbabwe and New Zealand 1996-97; England A to Pakistan and Sri Lanka 1990-91, to Bermuda and West Indies 1991-92, to Pakistan 1995-96
Overseas teams played for: Madras 1986-87; Petersham, Sydney 1992-93; Adelaide University 1990; Stellenbosch University, South Africa 1994-95; Primrose, Cape Town; Petersham, Sydney
Cricketers particularly admired: Graham Gooch, Mark Waugh
Young players to look out for: Robert Rollins, Anthony McGrath
Other sports followed: Golf (10 handicap), football (Leeds)
Injuries: Broken finger during Trent Bridge Test, out for three weeks
Relaxations: Listening to music. Listening to Mark Ilott. Watching television
Extras: Played for England Schools U15 for two years (one as captain). Youngest player to play for Essex Schools U11 at the age of eight and U15 at the age of 12. At 15, was considered the best young leg-break bowler in the country. Cricket Writers' Club Young

Cricketer of the Year, 1989. Holds record for third, fourth and fifth wicket partnerships for Essex (with Mark Waugh, Salim Malik and Mike Garnham). Essex Player of the Year 1993. Appointed Essex's vice-captain for 1996. Captained the England A tour to Pakistan in 1995-96. Finished 2nd in the Whyte and Mackay batting ratings in 1995. Appointed vice-captain of England's winter tour to Zimbabwe and New Zealand

Opinions on cricket: 'Too much soft cricket. Quality not quantity. Better one-day wickets, especially in September at Lord's.'

Best batting: 197 Essex v Surrey, The Oval 1990

Best bowling: 1-38 Essex v Worcestershire, Kidderminster 1992

1996 Season

	M	Inns	NO	Runs	HS	Avge	100s	50s	Ct	St	O	M	Runs	Wkts	Avge	Best	5wI	10wM
Test	5	8	1	429	128	61.28	2	1	4	-								
All First	18	31	1	1386	158	46.20	3	7	18	-								
1-day Int																		
NatWest	4	4	0	126	105	31.50	1	-	-	-								
B & H	5	5	2	238	82	79.33	-	3	3	-								
Sunday	10	9	0	389	77	43.22	-	3	4	-								

Career Performances

	M	Inns	NO	Runs	HS	Avge	100s	50s	Ct	St	Balls	Runs	Wkts	Avge	Best	5wI	10wM
Test	12	21	3	713	128	39.61	2	2	7	-							
All First	184	287	34	11443	197	45.22	29	56	231	-	276	307	2	153.50	1-38	-	-
1-day Int	4	4	1	43	16	14.33	-	-	2	-							
NatWest	18	17	1	636	108	39.75	2	2	12	-							
B & H	37	34	7	1154	118	42.74	1	10	15	-							
Sunday	110	99	15	2632	83	31.33	-	17	45	-							

47. Who won the Carlton & United World Series in 1996-97
and who did they beat in the final?

HUTCHISON, P. M.   Yorkshire

Name: Paul Michael Hutchison
Role: Left-hand bat, left-arm fast bowler
Born: 9 June 1977, Leeds
Height: 6ft 3in **Weight:** 11st 10lbs
Nickname: Hutch, Pooch, Warhair
County debut: 1996
1st-Class catches: 1
Strike rate: 133.00 (career 34.25)
Parents: David Hutchison and Rita Laycock
Marital status: Single
Family links with cricket: 'Grandfather
pushed me towards cricket as a five-year-old'
Education: Pudsey Greenside; Pudsey
Crawshaw
Qualifications: 4 GCSEs, community sports
leader award, qualified cricket coach
Overseas tours: England U19 to Zimbabwe
1995-96

Cricketers particularly admired: David
Gower, Darren Gough, Ian Botham, Richard Hadlee
Other sports followed: Football (Leeds United) and rugby league (Leeds)
Relaxations: Spending time with friends, golf, listening to music
Extras: Represented England at U17, U18 and U19 levels. Played for Pudsey St.
Lawrence in the Bradford League. Had a place at the Yorkshire Academy
Opinions on cricket: 'Far too much cricket crammed into a small season. I think that
this destroys quality and increases injury. The game is becoming dull due to easy-paced
wickets. Contracts should be nine or 12 months instead of the present six.'
Best bowling: 4-23 Yorkshire v Mashonaland, Harare 1995-96

1996 Season

	M	Inns	NO	Runs	HS	Avge	100s	50s	Ct	St	O	M	Runs	Wkts	Avge	Best	5wI	10wM
Test																		
All First	1	2	0	0	0	0.00	-	-	1	-	22.1	1	123	1	123.00	1-39	-	-
1-day Int																		
NatWest																		
B & H																		
Sunday																		

Career Performances

	M	Inns	NO	Runs	HS	Avge	100s	50s	Ct	St	Balls	Runs	Wkts	Avge	Best	5wl	10wM
Test																	
All First	3	2	0	0	0	0.00	-	-	1	-	411	287	12	23.91	4-23	-	-
1-day Int																	
NatWest																	
B & H																	
Sunday																	

HUTTON, S.   Durham

Name: Stewart Hutton
Role: Left-hand bat, cover fielder
Born: 30 November 1969, Stockton-on-Tees
Height: 6ft **Weight:** 12st
Nickname: Len
County debut: 1992
1st-Class 50s: 12
1st-Class 100s: 3
1st-Class catches: 33
Place in batting averages: 126th av. 33.83
(1995 141st av. 28.81)
Parents: Leonard and Mavis
Marital status: Single
Education: De Brus Comprehensive;
Cleveland Technical College
Qualifications: 6 O-levels (equivalent),
A-level Economics
Overseas tours:
Durham to Zimbabwe 1991-92
Cricketers particularly admired: Mike Gatting
Other sports followed: Golf, football
Relaxations: Playing golf
Extras: Scored century for Durham on pre-season tour to Zimbabwe in 1991-92. Appeared as 12th man for England in the 4th Test against West Indies at Old Trafford in 1995
Best batting: 172 Durham v Oxford University, The Parks 1996

996 Season

	M	Inns	NO	Runs	HS	Avge	100s	50s	Ct	St	O	M	Runs	Wkts	Avge	Best	5wI	10wM
Test																		
All First	14	26	2	812	172 *	33.83	2	1	6	-								
1-day Int																		
NatWest	2	2	0	18	13	9.00	-	-	1	-								
B & H	1	1	0	36	36	36.00	-	-	-	-								
Sunday	13	13	1	369	81	30.75	-	2	4	-								

Career Performances

	M	Inns	NO	Runs	HS	Avge	100s	50s	Ct	St	Balls	Runs	Wkts	Avge	Best	5wI	10wM
Test																	
All First	58	105	5	2983	172 *	29.83	3	12	33	-	25	18	0	-	-	-	-
1-day Int																	
NatWest	8	8	1	287	125	41.00	1	1	3	-							
B & H	2	2	0	44	36	22.00	-	-	-	-							
Sunday	49	46	5	1031	81	25.14	-	3	13	-							

HYAM, B. J. Essex

Name: Barry James Hyam
Role: Right-hand bat, wicket-keeper
Born: 9 September 1975, Romford, Essex
Height: 5ft 11in **Weight:** 11st 7lbs
Nickname: Bazza
County debut: 1993
1st-Class catches: 3
1st-Class stumpings: 1
Parents: Peter and Gloria
Marital status: Single
Family links with cricket: Brother Matthew plays for Harold Wood, brother Richard plays for Gidea Park, 'Matt also has NCA coaching award. Mum and Dad are keen fans'
Education: Marshalls Park; Havering Sixth Form College; Westminster College
Qualifications: 9 GCSEs, 1 A-level, NCA coaching award
Off-season: Coaching at the Essex indoor cricket school at Chelmsford
Cricketers particularly admired: Graham Gooch, Jack Russell
Young players to look out for: Stephen Peters, Jonathan Powell

Other sports followed: Football (West Ham), hockey and golf
Injuries: Broken left arm, out for six weeks
Relaxations: Playing any sport and socialising with friends
Extras: Made first-class debut on his 18th birthday
Opinions on cricket: 'Second XI should play more four-day cricket to prepare them for first-class cricket. They should also play less friendlies on bad wickets.'
Best batting: 49 Essex v Pakistan, Chelmsford 1996

1996 Season

	M	Inns	NO	Runs	HS	Avge	100s	50s	Ct	St	O	M	Runs	Wkts	Avge	Best	5wI	10wM
Test																		
All First	2	4	0	73	49	18.25	-	-	3	1								
1-day Int																		
NatWest																		
B & H																		
Sunday	1	1	0	0	0	0.00	-	-	-	-								

Career Performances

	M	Inns	NO	Runs	HS	Avge	100s	50s	Ct	St	Balls	Runs	Wkts	Avge	Best	5wI	10wM
Test																	
All First	3	6	0	74	49	12.33	-	-	5	1							
1-day Int																	
NatWest																	
B & H																	
Sunday	1	1	0	0	0	0.00	-	-	-	-							

48. Who was voted Player of the Series in the Carlton & United World Series in 1996-97?

IGGLESDEN, A. P. Kent

Name: Alan Paul Igglesden
Role: Right-hand bat, right-arm fast-medium bowler
Born: 8 October 1964, Farnborough, Kent
Height: 6ft 6in **Weight:** 15st
Nickname: Iggy, Norman
County debut: 1986
Test debut: 1989
Tests: 3
One-Day Internationals: 4
50 w. in season: 4
1st-Class 5 w. in innings: 23
1st-Class 10 w. in match: 4
1st-Class catches: 37
One-Day 5 w. in innings: 2
Place in bowling averages: (1995 45th av. 26.80)
Strike rate: (career 52.27)
Parents: Trevor and Gillian

Family links with cricket: 'Brother Kevin plays for Westerham for whom he has just had a prolific season'
Education: St Mary's Primary School, Westerham; Churchill School, Westerham; 'the Kent dressing-room'
Qualifications: Coaching certificate
Off-season: Coaching
Overseas tours: England A to Kenya and Zimbabwe 1990; England to West Indies 1994; Fred Rumsey's XI to Barbados 1993
Overseas teams played for: Avendale CC, Cape Town 1984-89, Green Point CC, Cape Town 1990-91, Western Province 1986-90; Boland Cricket Union 1991-92
Cricketers particularly admired: Dennis Lillee, Terry Alderman, Carl Hooper, Aravinda De Silva
Young players to look out for: Herschelle Gibbs 'and myself'
Other sports followed: Football (Crystal Palace FC), rugby union and golf
Injuries: Slipped disc, missed all but the last month of the season
Relaxations: Golf, sport on television, cinema and reading
Best batting: 41 Kent v Surrey, Canterbury 1988
Best bowling: 7-28 Boland v Griqualand West, Kimberley 1992-93

1996 season (did not make any first-class or one-day appearances)

Career Performances

	M	Inns	NO	Runs	HS	Avge	100s	50s	Ct	St	Balls	Runs	Wkts	Avge	Best	5wI	10wM
Test	3	5	3	6	3 *	3.00	-	-	1	-	555	329	6	54.83	2-91	-	-
All First	145	158	59	862	41	8.70	-	-	37	-	25247	12748	483	26.39	7-28	23	4
1-day Int	4	3	1	20	18	10.00	-	-	1	-	168	122	2	61.00	2-12	-	
NatWest	14	4	3	23	12 *	23.00	-	-	3	-	728	375	18	20.83	4-29	-	
B & H	25	10	7	43	26 *	14.33	-	-	5	-	1457	892	35	25.48	3-24	-	
Sunday	81	27	17	93	13 *	9.30	-	-	19	-	3696	2437	104	23.43	5-13	2	

ILLINGWORTH, R. K.   Worcestershire

Name: Richard Keith Illingworth
Role: Right-hand bat, slow left-arm bowler
Born: 23 August 1963, Bradford
Height: 6ft **Weight:** 13st
Nickname: Lucy, Harry, Illy
County debut: 1982
County cap: 1986
Test debut: 1991
Tests: 9
One-Day Internationals: 25
50 wickets in a season: 5
1st-Class 50s: 16
1st-Class 100s: 3
1st-Class 5 w. in innings: 26
1st-Class 10 w. in match: 5
1st-Class catches: 141
One-Day 5 w. in innings: 2
Place in batting averages: 143rd av. 32.30
(1995 241st av. 16.00)
Place in bowling averages: 85th av. 33.74 (1995 47th av. 26.93)
Strike rate: 84.37 (career 77.04)
Parents: Keith and Margaret
Wife and date of marriage: Anne, 20 September 1985
Children: Miles, 28 August 1987; Thomas, 20 April 1989
Family links with cricket: Father played Bradford League cricket
Education: Wrose Brow Middle; Salts Grammar School ('same school as the late Jim Laker')
Qualifications: 6 O-levels, senior coaching award
Off-season: 'Working on my benefit awarded for 1997'

Overseas tours: England A to Zimbabwe and Kenya 1989-90, to Pakistan and Sri Lanka 1990-91; England to New Zealand and Australia (World Cup) 1991-92, to South Africa 1995-96, to India and Pakistan (World Cup) 1995-96
Overseas teams played for: Natal 1988-89
Cricketers particularly admired: Ian Botham, Wasim Akram
Young players to look out for: Vikram Solanki, Reuben Spiring and Phillip Weston
Other sports followed: Most sports – football (Leeds United and Aston Villa), golf and rugby
Injuries: Broken right little finger, out for 10 days
Relaxations: Listening to music, most sports and playing golf
Extras: Took 11 for 108 on South African first-class debut for Natal B v Boland 1988. Scored 120 not out as nightwatchman for Worcestershire v Warwickshire 1988 and 106 for England A v Zimbabwe 1989-90. In 1991, v West Indies, became 11th person in history to take a wicket with first ball in Test cricket. Took a hat-trick in Sunday League v Sussex in 1993, the first Worcestershire player to do this in one-day cricket. Won 1993 Dick Lygon award for contribution to Worcestershire CCC
Opinions on cricket: 'Staffs should be cut, to make 2nd XI places more competitive. There seems to be a lot of dead wood playing 2nd XI cricket. There should only be two one-day competitions.'
Best batting: 120* Worcestershire v Warwickshire, Worcester 1987
Best bowling: 7-50 Worcestershire v Oxford University, The Parks 1985

1996 Season

	M	Inns	NO	Runs	HS	Avge	100s	50s	Ct	St	O	M	Runs	Wkts	Avge	Best	5wI	10wM
Test																		
All First	19	23	10	420	66*	32.30	-	1	11	-	717.1	208	1721	51	33.74	6-75	3	-
1-day Int																		
NatWest	2	2	1	31	29*	31.00	-	-	-	-	19	2	72	2	36.00	1-28	-	
B & H	4	2	1	10	8	10.00	-	-	-	-	39	3	158	3	52.66	1-18	-	
Sunday	15	5	3	50	27*	25.00	-	-	3	-	102.2	3	446	19	23.47	3-34	-	

Career Performances

	M	Inns	NO	Runs	HS	Avge	100s	50s	Ct	St	Balls	Runs	Wkts	Avge	Best	5wI	10wM
Test	9	14	7	128	28	18.28	-	-	5	-	1485	615	19	32.36	4-96	-	-
All First	324	362	105	5633	120*	21.91	3	16	141	-	58478	23290	759	30.68	7-50	26	5
1-day Int	25	11	5	68	14	11.33	-	-	8	-	1501	1059	30	35.30	3-33	-	
NatWest	33	16	6	139	29*	13.90	-	-	10	-	1969	1014	28	36.21	4-20	-	
B & H	54	26	15	214	36*	19.45	-	-	12	-	2794	1619	51	31.74	4-27	-	
Sunday	177	79	41	540	31	14.21	-	-	41	-	6802	4894	208	23.52	5-24	2	

ILOTT, M. C.   Essex

Name: Mark Christopher Ilott
Role: Left-hand bat, left-arm
fast-medium bowler
Born: 27 August 1970, Watford
Height: 6ft 1in **Weight:** 13st 4lbs
Nickname: Ramble, Choock
County debut: 1988
County cap: 1993
Test debut: 1993
Tests: 5
50 wickets in a season: 4
1st-Class 50s: 4
1st-Class 5 w. in innings: 21
1st-Class 10 w. in match: 3
1st-Class catches: 31
One-Day 5 w. in innings: 1
Place in batting averages: 264th av. 15.59
(1995 258th av. 14.00)
Place in bowling averages: 80th av. 33.32
(1995 27th av. 24.32)

Strike rate: 66.04 (career 56.18)
Parents: John and Glenys
Wife and date of marriage: Sandra Jane, 14 October 1994
Children: 'Due on 30 September 1996'
Family links with cricket: 'Dad played for years and now umpires in the Minor
Counties. Brother has played for Hertfordshire but his face didn't fit in. Mum has made
many a good tea'
Education: Francis Combe School; 'Essex changing-room'
Qualifications: 6 O-levels, 2 A-levels, 2 AO-levels, coaching qualification, diploma in
Fitness and Nutrition
Career outside cricket: 'A bit of work for a graphic design company called
Centremark of Chelmsford and a bit of PR for Air Packing (Europe)'
Off-season: 'Working for anyone who will have me and changing nappies'
Overseas tours: England A to Sri Lanka 1990-91, to Australia 1992-93, to South
Africa 1993-94, to India 1994-95; England to South Africa 1995-96
Overseas teams played for: East Torrens District, Adelaide 1989-91
Cricketers particularly admired: John Lever, Graham Gooch, Stuart Law
Young players to look out for: Ashley Cowan, Steve Andrew 'need to look out for
him because he could be in a gutter'
Other sports followed: Golf, football (Liverpool) and badminton
Injuries: 'Missed two games with a broken hand from a Glen Chapple beamer. Not

only did he ruin my hand, but later on my NatWest final'

Relaxations: Playing my guitar, playing golf, 'but now I have a baby my relaxation will be anything that doesn't involve sleepless nights and cleaning nappies'

Extras: Youngest player ever to play for Hertfordshire. Missed almost all 1991 season with stress fracture of the back

Opinions on cricket: 'When a bowler has a niggle he should be allowed to run through the crease.'

Best batting: 60 England A v Warwickshire, Edgbaston 1995

Best bowling: 9-19 Essex v Northamptonshire, Luton 1995

1996 Season

	M	Inns	NO	Runs	HS	Avge	100s	50s	Ct	St	O	M	Runs	Wkts	Avge	Best	5wI	10wM
Test																		
All First	17	24	2	343	58	15.59	-	1	4	-	550.2	118	1666	50	33.32	5-53	2	-
1-day Int																		
NatWest	5	3	1	2	2	1.00	-	-	3	-	50	6	215	4	53.75	1-29	-	
B & H	5	1	0	12	12	12.00	-	-	2	-	46	8	151	9	16.77	4-17	-	
Sunday	14	13	3	62	24 *	6.20	-	-	5	-	93	6	402	10	40.20	2-37	-	

Career Performances

	M	Inns	NO	Runs	HS	Avge	100s	50s	Ct	St	Balls	Runs	Wkts	Avge	Best	5wI	10wM
Test	5	6	2	28	15	7.00	-	-	-	-	1042	542	12	45.16	3-48	-	-
All First	124	148	34	1593	60	13.97	-	4	31	-	23877	12062	425	28.38	9-19	21	3
1-day Int																	
NatWest	15	9	4	110	54 *	22.00	-	1	5	-	937	615	16	38.43	2-23	-	
B & H	22	7	1	65	21	10.83	-	-	3	-	1175	631	32	19.71	5-21	1	
Sunday	74	48	15	339	56 *	10.27	-	1	14	-	3176	2325	90	25.83	4-15	-	

49. Who, to date, is the only England player to be fined
for his conduct during a Test match?

INNES, K. J. Northamptonshire

Name: Kevin John Innes
Role: Right-hand bat, right-arm
medium bowler
Born: 24 September 1975, Wellingborough
Height: 5ft 10in **Weight:** 10st 5lbs
Nickname: Ernie, Milkman
County debut: 1994
1st-Class 50s: 1
1st-Class catches: 3
Strike rate: 44.25 (career 51.75)
Parents: Peter and Jane
Marital status: Single
Education: Boothville Middle School;
Weston Favell Upper School, Northampton
Qualifications: 6 GCSEs, 4 O-levels
Overseas tours: England U18 to South
Africa 1992-93; England U19 to Sri Lanka
1993-94

Cricketers particularly admired: Carl
Hooper, Viv Richards
Other sports followed: Snooker, football, golf
Relaxations: Watching and playing most sport, music
Extras: Played for England U19 in home series against India in 1994
Opinions on cricket: 'It is a shame that employment is not found at the end of the
season for a lot more cricketers.'
Best batting: 63 Northamptonshire v Lancashire, Northampton 1996
Best bowling: 4-61 Northamptonshire v Lancashire, Northampton 1996

1996 Season

	M	Inns	NO	Runs	HS	Avge	100s	50s	Ct	St	O	M	Runs	Wkts	Avge	Best	5wI	10wM
Test																		
All First	4	5	0	108	63	21.60	-	1	3	-	59	7	193	8	24.12	4-61	-	-
1-day Int																		
NatWest																			
B & H																			
Sunday	1	0	0	0	0	-	-	-	1	-	6.4	0	57	1	57.00	1-57	-	

Career Performances

	M	Inns	NO	Runs	HS	Avge	100s	50s	Ct	St	Balls	Runs	Wkts	Avge	Best	5wl	10wM
Test																	
All First	5	7	0	108	63	15.42	-	1	3	-	414	226	8	28.25	4-61	-	-
1-day Int																	
NatWest																		
B & H	1	0	0	0	0	-	-	-	-	-	36	25	1	25.00	1-25	-	
Sunday	7	2	0	8	5	4.00	-	-	3	-	232	273	3	91.00	1-35	-	

IRANI, R. C. Essex

Name: Ronald Charles Irani
Role: Right-hand bat, right-arm
medium bowler
Born: 26 October 1971, Leigh, Lancashire
Height: 6ft 4in **Weight:** 13st 10lbs
Nickname: Reggie, Ledge
County debut: 1990 (Lancashire),
1994 (Essex)
County cap: 1994
Test debut: 1996
Tests: 2
One-Day Internationals: 4
1000 runs in a season: 2
1st-Class 50s: 26
1st-Class 100s: 4
1st-Class catches: 31
1st-Class 5 w. innings: 3
One-Day 100s: 2
Place in batting averages: 83rd av. 38.48
(1995 85th av. 36.403)
Place in bowling averages: 45th av. 29.40 (1995 133rd av. 45.25)
Strike rate: 50.42 (career 59.77)
Parents: Jimmy and Anne
Marital status: Single
Family links with cricket: 'Father played local league cricket in Bolton for 30 years;
mother did teas for many years!'
Education: Church Road Primary School; Smithills Comprehensive School
Qualifications: 9 GCSEs
Off-season: Touring Zimbabwe and New Zealand with England
Overseas tours: England YC to Australia 1989-90; England A to Pakistan 1995-96;
England to Zimbabwe and New Zealand 1996-97

Overseas teams played for: Technicol Natal, Durban, South Africa 1992-93; Eden-Roskill, Auckland 1993-94

Cricketers particularly admired: Mark Waugh, Javed Miandad, Wasim Akram, John Crawley, Graham Gooch

Other sports followed: 'Most sports especially football'

Relaxations: Sleeping and watching football

Extras: Played for England U19 in home series v Australia 1991, scoring a century and three 50s in six innings and being named Bull Man of the Series. Made his Test debut in the first Test against India at Edgbaston in 1996

Opinions on cricket: 'Too much cricket played by English county cricket professionals'

Best batting: 119 Essex v Worcestershire, Worcester 1994

Best bowling: 5-27 Essex v Nottinghamshire, Chelmsford 1996

1996 Season

	M	Inns	NO	Runs	HS	Avge	100s	50s	Ct	St	O	M	Runs	Wkts	Avge	Best	5wI	10wM
Test	2	3	0	76	41	25.33	-	-	-	-	21	7	74	2	37.00	1-22	-	-
All First	19	31	4	1039	110 *	38.48	1	7	10	-	395	74	1320	47	28.08	5-27	1	-
1-day Int	4	4	2	62	45 *	31.00	-	-	2	-	14	0	90	1	90.00	1-56	-	
NatWest	5	5	1	240	124	60.00	1	2	2	-	44	9	140	5	28.00	3-25	-	
B & H	5	4	1	134	62 *	44.66	-	1	1	-	40	3	156	9	17.33	4-30	-	
Sunday	12	11	1	311	80	31.10	-	3	4	-	74	2	417	11	37.90	2-23	-	

Career Performances

	M	Inns	NO	Runs	HS	Avge	100s	50s	Ct	St	Balls	Runs	Wkts	Avge	Best	5wI	10wM
Test	2	3	0	76	41	25.33	-	-	-	-	126	74	2	37.00	1-22	-	-
All First	68	109	14	3482	119	36.65	4	26	31	-	6874	3785	115	32.91	5-19	3	-
1-day Int	4	4	2	62	45 *	31.00	-	-	2	-	84	90	1	90.00	1-56	-	
NatWest	9	9	1	293	124	36.62	1	2	2	-	540	367	9	40.77	4-55	-	
B & H	12	8	1	226	62 *	32.28	-	1	2	-	576	413	18	22.94	4-30	-	
Sunday	53	48	3	985	101 *	21.88	1	5	11	-	1569	1281	48	26.68	3-22	-	

JAMES, K. D. Hampshire

Name: Kevan David James
Role: Left-hand bat, left-arm medium bowler
Born: 18 March 1961, Lambeth, South London
Height: 6ft ¹/₂in **Weight:** 13st 8lbs
Nickname: Jambo, Jaimo, Jockey
County debut: 1980 (Middlesex), 1985 (Hampshire)
County cap: 1989
1000 runs in a season: 2
1st-Class 50s: 34
1st-Class 100s: 10
1st-Class 5 w. in innings: 9
1st-Class catches: 65
One-Day 5 w. innings: 2
Place in batting averages: 129th av. 33.54 (1995 216th av. 18.94)
Place in bowling averages: 55th av. 29.40 (1995 134th av. 45.63)
Strike rate: 60.23 (career 64.69)

Parents: David (deceased) and Helen
Wife and date of marriage: Debbie, October 1987
Children: Natalie Ann, 8 October 1992; Naomi Claire, 25 October 1995
Family links with cricket: Late father played club cricket in North London; brother Martin plays for Hertfordshire
Education: Edmonton County High School
Qualifications: 5 O-levels, qualified coach, City and Guilds in Electric Theories
Off-season: 'Working for Southern Electric contracting again, plus a regular feature on BBC Radio Solent'
Overseas tours: England YC to Australia 1978-79, to West Indies 1979-80; England to Hong Kong Sixes 1996
Overseas teams played for: Wellington, New Zealand 1982-83, 1983-84
Cricketers particularly admired: Chris Smith
Young players to look out for: Alex Morris 'I was always looking out for him in Hong Kong but couldn't always find him'
Other sports followed: 'Football but never achieved anything – about the same as cricket'
Injuries: Wear and tear on knee, missed five weeks and missed one week with a broken finger
Relaxations: 'Enjoy my work with local radio. Find it a welcome relaxation during the summer when I am writing my scripts'

Extras: Left Middlesex at end of 1984 season and joined Hampshire. Achieved a world record in 1996 when he became the first player in a first-class match to score a century and take four wickets in four balls in Hampshire's game against India at Southampton
Opinions on cricket: 'Haven't got any at the moment, but will have a load when I've finished playing.'
Best batting: 162 Hampshire v Glamorgan, Cardiff 1989
Best bowling: 6-22 Hampshire v Australia, Southampton 1985

1996 Season

	M	Inns	NO	Runs	HS	Avge	100s	50s	Ct	St	O	M	Runs	Wkts	Avge	Best	5wl	10wM
Test																		
All First	13	23	1	738	118 *	33.54	2	3	6	-	301.1	57	882	30	29.40	5-74	1	-
1-day Int																		
NatWest	3	2	1	3	3	3.00	-	-	1	-	34	3	124	9	13.77	4-42	-	
B & H	1	1	0	56	56	56.00	-	1	1	-	4	0	24	1	24.00	1-24	-	
Sunday	11	9	2	120	37	17.14	-	-	5	-	77	1	404	21	19.23	6-35	1	

Career Performances

	M	Inns	NO	Runs	HS	Avge	100s	50s	Ct	St	Balls	Runs	Wkts	Avge	Best	5wl	10wM
Test																	
All First	195	292	46	7569	162	30.76	10	34	65	-	21349	10819	330	32.78	6-22	9	-
1-day Int																	
NatWest	23	14	3	159	42	14.45	-	-	4	-	1426	896	34	26.35	4-42	-	
B & H	39	27	5	407	56	18.50	-	1	9	-	1897	1252	31	40.38	3-31	-	
Sunday	151	104	31	1533	66	21.00	-	4	43	-	6091	4450	149	29.86	6-35	2	

50. Who was voted England's Man of the Series in the Under-19 Test series with Pakistan in 1996-97?

JAMES, S. P. Glamorgan

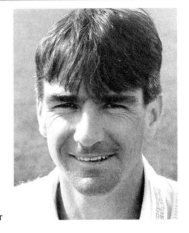

Name: Stephen Peter James
Role: Right-hand opening bat
Born: 7 September 1967, Lydney
Height: 6ft **Weight:** 12st 6lbs
Nickname: Sid, Jamo
County debut: 1985
County cap: 1992
1000 runs in a season: 4
1st-Class 50s: 30
1st-Class 100s: 24
1st-Class 200s: 2
1st-Class catches: 119
One-Day 100s: 5
Place in batting averages: 40th av. 47.72
(1995 66th av. 40.44)
Parents: Peter and Margaret
Marital status: Single
Family links with cricket: Father played for
Gloucestershire 2nd XI. Distant relative of
Dominic Ostler
Education: Monmouth School; University College, Swansea; Cambridge University
Qualifications: BA (Hons) Wales – Classics; BA (Hons) Cantab – Land Economy
Career outside cricket: Journalism
Off-season: Coaching, journalism
Overseas tours: Welsh Schools to Barbados 1984; Monmouth Schools to Sri Lanka
1985; Combined Universities to Barbados 1989; Glamorgan to Trinidad 1989-90, to
Zimbabwe 1990-91, Cape Town 1993-94, to Pretoria 1996
Overseas teams played for: Bionics, Zimbabwe 1990-92; Universals Sports Club,
Zimbabwe 1992-96
Cricketers particularly admired: Michael Atherton, Graham Burgess
Young players to look out for: Alun Evans, Dean Cosker
Other sports followed: Rugby union ('played for Lydney, Gloucestershire and
Cambridge University and was on bench for Varsity Match')
Relaxations: Reading, *Telegraph* crosswords, videos, weight training
Extras: Scored maiden century in only second first-class game. Broke Matthew
Maynard's club record for number of one-day runs in a season in 1995. Also broke Hugh
Morris's club record for number of Sunday League runs in a season
Best batting: 235 Glamorgan v Nottinghamshire, Worksop 1996

	M	Inns	NO	Runs	HS	Avge	100s	50s	Ct	St		O	M	Runs	Wkts	Avge	Best	5wI	10wM
Test																			
All First	20	38	1	1766	235	47.72	7	6	15	-									
1-day Int																			
NatWest	1	1	0	28	28	28.00	-	-	-	-									
B & H	6	6	1	208	121 *	41.60	1	1	4	-									
Sunday	14	14	1	295	91	22.69	-	2	1	-									

Career Performances

	M	Inns	NO	Runs	HS	Avge	100s	50s	Ct	St	Balls	Runs	Wkts	Avge	Best	5wI	10wM
Test																	
All First	149	264	21	8675	235	35.69	24	30	119	-	2	3	0	-	-	-	-
1-day Int																	
NatWest	15	15	1	530	123	37.85	1	3	2	-							
B & H	25	25	1	954	135	39.75	2	8	8	-							
Sunday	78	76	7	2533	107	36.71	2	19	17	-							

JARVIS, P. W. Sussex

Name: Paul William Jarvis
Role: Right-hand bat, right-arm
fast-medium bowler
Born: 29 June 1965, Redcar, North Yorkshire
Height: 5ft 11in **Weight:** 12st 5lbs
Nickname: Jarv, Gnasher
County debut: 1981 (Yorkshire), 1994
(Sussex)
County cap: 1986 (Yorkshire)
Test debut: 1987-88
Tests: 9
One-Day Internationals: 16
50 wickets in a season: 4
1st-Class 50s: 6
1st-Class 5 w. in innings: 20
1st-Class 10 w. in match: 3
1st-Class catches: 54
One-Day 5 w. in innings: 5
Place in batting averages: 210th av. 23.42 (1995 239th av. 16.09)
Place in bowling averages: 64th av. 31.15 (1995 54th av. 27.65)
Strike rate: 53.05 (career 53.35)
Parents: Malcolm and Marjorie

Wife and date of marriage: Wendy Jayne, 3 December 1988
Children: Alexander Michael, 13 June 1989; Isabella Grace, 21 March 1993
Family links with cricket: Father still plays league cricket for Sudbrooke CC in Gwent. Brother plays in Yorkshire (Selby Londesborough)
Education: Bydales Comprehensive School, Marske, Cleveland
Qualifications: 4 O-levels, advanced coaching awards
Career outside cricket: Agent for Adidas eye protection
Off-season: Working for Adidas and coaching
Overseas tours: Yorkshire to St Lucia and Barbados 1987, to South Africa 1991; England to India/Pakistan (World Cup) and Pakistan 1986-87, to Australia and New Zealand 1987-88, to India and Sri Lanka 1992-93; unofficial English XI to South Africa 1989-90
Overseas teams played for: Mossman Middle Harbour, Sydney 1984-85; Avendale, Cape Town 1985-86; Manly Warringah, Sydney 1987; Onslow, Wellington 1994-95
Cricketers particularly admired: Ian Botham, Malcolm Marshall
Young players to look out for: James Kirtley, Danny Law
Other sports followed: Football
Injuries: Stress fracture of left ankle, missed two months
Relaxations: DIY, cooking, golf, fishing, music, eating out, going to the pub
Extras: Youngest player ever to play for Yorkshire in County Championship (16 years, 2 months, 13 days) and youngest player to take hat-trick in Sunday League (1982) and Championship (1985). Played for England YC v West Indies 1982 and Australia 1983. Banned from Test cricket for joining 1989-90 tour of South Africa, suspension remitted in 1992
Opinions on cricket: 'You could write a book on them, but still too much one-day cricket.'
Best batting: 80 Yorkshire v Northamptonshire, Scarborough 1992
Best bowling: 7-55 Yorkshire v Surrey, Headingley 1986

1996 Season

	M	Inns	NO	Runs	HS	Avge	100s	50s	Ct	St	O	M	Runs	Wkts	Avge	Best	5wI	10wM
Test																		
All First	8	11	4	164	35	23.42	-	-	3	-	168	27	592	19	31.15	4-60	-	-
1-day Int																		
NatWest	2	2	1	36	34 *	36.00	-	-	1	-	14	1	53	3	17.66	3-22	-	
B & H	4	3	1	51	38	25.50	-	-	-	-	37	2	158	6	26.33	3-48	-	
Sunday	9	6	2	90	43	22.50	-	-	2	-	63	2	340	15	22.66	3-29	-	

Career Performances

	M	Inns	NO	Runs	HS	Avge	100s	50s	Ct	St	Balls	Runs	Wkts	Avge	Best	5wI	10wM
Test	9	15	2	132	29 *	10.15	-	-	2	-	1912	965	21	45.95	4-107	-	-
All First	190	234	64	2815	80	16.55	-	6	54	-	31531	16695	591	28.24	7-55	20	3
1-day Int	16	8	2	31	16 *	5.16	-	-	1	-	879	672	24	28.00	5-35	1	
NatWest	19	12	3	123	34 *	13.66	-	-	4	-	1213	761	22	34.59	4-41	-	
B & H	40	20	6	192	42	13.71	-	-	4	-	2294	1332	64	20.81	4-34	-	
Sunday	127	72	28	541	43	12.29	-	-	29	-	5364	3971	185	21.46	6-27	4	

JOHNSON, P. Nottinghamshire

Name: Paul Johnson
Role: Right-hand bat, right-arm medium 'occasional' bowler
Born: 24 April 1965, Newark
Height: 'Below average' **Weight:** 'Above average'
Nickname: Johno, Midget, Gus
County debut: 1982
County cap: 1986
Benefit: 1995
1000 runs in a season: 7
1st-Class 50s: 89
1st-Class 100s: 34
1st-Class catches: 176
1st-Class stumpings: 1
One-Day 100s: 10
Place in batting averages: 149th av. 31.61 (1995 96th av. 34.34)
Strike rate: 72.00
Parents: Donald Edward and Joyce
Wife's name and date of marriage: Jackie, 24 December 1993
Children: Ruth, 28 September 1994; Eve, 9 September 1996
Family links with cricket: Father played local cricket and is a qualified coach
Education: Grove Comprehensive School, Newark
Qualifications: 9 CSEs, NCA advanced coach
Overseas tours: England A to Bermuda and West Indies 1991-92
Overseas teams played for: RAU Johannesburg, 1985-86; Hutt District, Wellington, New Zealand 1988-89
Cricketers particularly admired: Clive Rice and Mike Gatting
Young players to look out for: Usman Afzaal, Noel Gie
Other sports followed: Watches ice-hockey (Nottingham Panthers), football

(Nottingham Forest and Notts County)
Relaxations: 'Listening to music, crosswords and reading autobiographies'
Extras: Played for English Schools in 1980-81 and England YC 1982 and 1983. Youngest player ever to join the Nottinghamshire staff. Made 235 for Nottinghamshire 2nd XI, July 1982, aged 17. Won Man of the Match award in his first NatWest game (101* v Staffordshire) in 1985, but missed the final owing to appendicitis. Sunday morning soccer referee in Nottingham. Took over the Nottinghamshire captaincy from Tim Robinson at the start of the 1996 season
Opinions on cricket: 'Who would take any notice?'
Best batting: 187 Nottinghamshire v Lancashire, Old Trafford 1993
Best bowling: 1-9 Nottinghamshire v Oxford University, Trent Bridge 1984

1996 Season

	M	Inns	NO	Runs	HS	Avge	100s	50s	Ct	St	O	M	Runs	Wkts	Avge	Best	5wI	10wM
Test																		
All First	19	33	2	980	109	31.61	2	6	10	-	12	2	51	1	51.00	1-51	-	-
1-day Int																		
NatWest	1	1	0	6	6	6.00	-	-	-	-								
B & H	4	4	2	114	54 *	57.00	-	1	1	-								
Sunday	16	15	5	645	99 *	64.50	-	6	4	-								

Career Performances

	M	Inns	NO	Runs	HS	Avge	100s	50s	Ct	St	Balls	Runs	Wkts	Avge	Best	5wI	10wM
Test																	
All First	284	472	43	15712	187	36.62	34	89	176	1	550	561	6	93.50	1-9	-	-
1-day Int																	
NatWest	29	29	2	769	146	28.48	2	1	7	-	12	16	0	-	-	-	
B & H	50	47	11	1304	104 *	36.22	2	9	15	-							
Sunday	190	179	23	5087	167 *	32.60	6	29	63	-							

JOHNSON, R. L.   Middlesex

Name: Richard Leonard Johnson
Role: Right-hand bat, right-arm fast-medium bowler, outfielder
Born: 29 December 1974, Chertsey, Surrey
Height: 6ft 2in **Weight:** 13st 6lbs
Nickname: Jono, Lenny
County debut: 1992
1st-Class 50s: 1
1st-Class 5 w. in innings: 4
1st-Class 10 w. in match: 2
1st-Class catches: 17

Place in batting averages: 278th av. 12.78
(1995 250th av. 14.90)
Place in bowling averages: 93rd av. 35.12
(1995 10th av. 20.30)
Strike rate: 58.28 (career 53.64)
Parents: Roger and Mary Ann
Marital status: Single
Family links with cricket: Father and
grandfather played club cricket
Education: Sunbury Manor School;
Spelthorne College
Qualifications: 9 GCSEs, A-Level in
Physical Education, NCA Senior Coaching
Award
Overseas tours: England U18 to South
Africa 1992-93; England U19 to South Africa
1993-94; England A to India 1994-95
Cricketers particularly admired: Ian
Botham, Richard Hadlee and Angus Fraser 'for his quality bowling and his dedication
to moaning'
Young players to look out for: David Nash, Owais Shah
Other sports followed: Basketball, soccer, snooker and most other sports
Injuries: Shoulder and knee, missed a total of six weeks
Relaxations: Sport and music
Extras: Plays for Sunbury CC, has represented Middlesex at all levels since U11. Took
10 for 45 v Derbyshire in July 1994, first person to take 10 wickets in an innings since Ian
Thomson (Sussex) in 1964, also most economical figures since Hedley Verity's 10 for 10.
Had to pull out of England's 1995-96 tour to South Africa due to a persistent back injury
Best batting: 50* Middlesex v Cambridge University, Fenner's 1994
Best bowling: 10-45 Middlesex v Derbyshire, Derby 1994

1996 Season

	M	Inns	NO	Runs	HS	Avge	100s	50s	Ct	St	O	M	Runs	Wkts	Avge	Best	5wl	10wM
Test																		
All First	11	20	1	243	37 *	12.78	-	-	1	-	242.5	36	878	25	35.12	5-29	1	-
1-day Int																		
NatWest	2	2	0	17	16	8.50	-	-	-	-	18	1	92	2	46.00	1-29	-	
B & H	3	3	0	18	9	6.00	-	-	1	-	27	2	164	1	164.00	1-66	-	
Sunday	11	7	3	64	29	16.00	-	-	3	-	75.5	1	369	9	41.00	2-24	-	

Career Performances

	M	Inns	NO	Runs	HS	Avge	100s	50s	Ct	St	Balls	Runs	Wkts	Avge	Best	5wI	10wM
Test																	
All First	38	53	7	685	50 *	14.89	-	1	17	-	5794	2988	108	27.66	10-45	4	2
1-day Int																	
NatWest	8	7	2	98	33	19.60	-	-	-	-	444	286	9	31.77	3-33	-	
B & H	6	5	0	19	9	3.80	-	-	1	-	282	226	2	113.00	1-17	-	
Sunday	41	24	10	184	29	13.14	-	-	6	-	1710	1506	38	39.63	4-66	-	

JONES, D. M.   Derbyshire

Name: Dean Mervyn Jones
Role: Right-hand bat, off-spin bowler,
county captain
Born: 24 March 1963, Melbourne, Australia
Height: 6ft 1in **Weight:** 13st 5lbs
Nickname: Deano
County debut: 1992 (Durham),
1996 (Derbys)
Test debut: 1983-84
Tests: 52
One-Day Internationals: 164
1st-Class 50s: 77
1st-Class 100s: 50
1st-Class 200s: 4
1st-Class 300s: 1
1st-Class 5 w. in innings: 1
1st-Class catches: 171
One-Day 100s: 15
Place in batting averages: 23rd av. 51.79
Strike rate: 51.77 (career 99.15)
Parents: Barney and Gaynor
Wife and date of marriage: Jane, 24 April 1986
Children: Phoebe, 26 June 1991; Isabella, 14 April 1996
Family links with cricket: Father was a captain/coach of Carlton, Victoria for 18
years and played district cricket for Victoria
Education: Mt Waverley High School, Victoria
Qualifications: High School Certificate
Career outside cricket: Work for Foxtel cable television and radio
Off-season: Playing in Australia
Overseas tours: Young Australians to Zimbabwe 1983 and 1985; Australia to West
Indies 1984 and 1991, to England 1985 and 1989, to India 1986 and 1987 (World

Cup), to Sharjah 1986 and 1990, to Pakistan 1988, to New Zealand 1989, to USA 1990
Overseas teams played for: Victoria, Australia
Cricketers particularly admired: David Boon, Steve and Mark Waugh, Allan Border, Shane Warne, Ian Healy, Waqar Younis, Wasim Akram
Young players to look out for: Andrew Harris, Chris Adams, Karl Krikken
Other sports followed: Golf, fishing and Aussie rules (Carlton FC)
Injuries: Ankle, rib and fingers but missed no cricket
Relaxations: Watching golf, family, reading and 'walking my Rottweiler, Stanley'
Extras: Played for Durham in their first season as a first-class county in 1992. Appointed captain of Derbyshire for the 1996 season. He is the highest run-scorer in the history of the Sheffield Shield competition
Opinions on cricket: 'Greatest game in the world'
Best batting: 324* Victoria v South Australia, Melbourne 1994-95
Best bowling: 5-112 Derbyshire v Hampshire, Southampton 1996

1996 Season

	M	Inns	NO	Runs	HS	Avge	100s	50s	Ct	St	O	M	Runs	Wkts	Avge	Best	5wl	10wM
Test																		
All First	19	34	5	1502	214 *	51.79	4	7	15	-	77.4	11	321	9	35.66	5-112	1	-
1-day Int																		
NatWest	2	1	1	100	100 *	-	1	-	4	-	0.2	0	0	2	0.00	2-0	-	
B & H	5	5	0	302	142	60.40	1	2	4	-	2	0	18	0	-	-	-	
Sunday	15	15	3	749	118	62.41	4	1	8	-	27.1	0	160	4	40.00	2-15	-	

Career Performances

	M	Inns	NO	Runs	HS	Avge	100s	50s	Ct	St	Balls	Runs	Wkts	Avge	Best	5wl	10wM
Test	52	89	11	3631	216	46.55	11	14	34	-	198	64	1	64.00	1-5	-	-
All First	219	368	40	17281	324 *	52.68	50	77	171	-	2578	1449	26	55.73	5-112	1	-
1-day Int	164	161	25	6068	145	44.61	7	46	54	-	106	81	3	27.00	2-34	-	
NatWest	4	3	1	171	100 *	85.50	1	-	5	-	14	16	2	8.00	2-0	-	
B & H	9	9	0	327	142	36.33	1	2	6	-	54	52	2	26.00	2-34	-	
Sunday	26	25	5	1405	118	70.25	6	6	12	-	200	201	5	40.20	2-15	-	

THE ASHES
51. Which England opening batsman had two non-scoring periods totalling 153 minutes during the Perth Test of 1982-83?

JONES, S. P. Glamorgan

Name: Simon P. Jones
Role: Left-hand bat, right-arm fast bowler
Born: 25 December 1978
Height: 6ft 3in **Weight:** 13st 7lbs
Nickname: Jonsey
County debut: No first-team appearance
Parents: Jeff and Irene
Marital status: Single
Family links with cricket: Father former
Glamorgan and England left-arm fast bowler
Education: Half Way CP School; Coedcar
Comprehensive; Millfield School
Career outside cricket: Student
Cricketers particularly admired: Allan
Donald
Other sports followed: Football (Manchester
United)

JULIAN, B. P. Surrey

Name: Brendon Paul Julian
Role: Right-hand bat, left-arm fast bowler
Born: 10 August 1970, Hamilton,
New Zealand
Height: 6ft 6in **Weight:** 14st 9lbs
Nickname: BJ
County debut: 1996
Test debut: 1993
Tests: 7
One-Day Internationals: 7
50 wickets in a season: 1
1st-Class 50s: 11
1st-Class 100s: 2
1st-Class 5 w. in innings: 17
1st-Class 10 w. in match: 1
1st-Class catches: 55
Place in batting averages: 100th av. 36.14
Place in bowling averages: 50th av. 28.88
Strike rate: 44.03 (career 54.15)

Parents: Graham and Jane
Marital status: Single
Education: Australia and New Zealand
Off-season: Playing in Australia
Overseas tours: Australia U23 to West Indies 1990; Australia to England 1993, to West Indies 1994
Overseas teams played for: Midland Guildford, Perth; Western Australia
Other sports followed: Golf, rugby, football (Chelsea) and Aussie rules (West Coast Eagles)
Relaxations: Videos, drinking coffee on King's Road, movies
Extras: Made his Test debut for Australia on the 1993 Ashes tour. Has played league cricket in England for Nelson and East Lancashire in the Lancashire League
Opinions on cricket: 'Six-and-a-half hours per day is too long'
Best batting: 119 Surrey v Lancashire, Southport 1996
Best bowling: 6-37 Surrey v Northamptonshire, The Oval 1996

1996 Season

	M	Inns	NO	Runs	HS	Avge	100s	50s	Ct	St	O	M	Runs	Wkts	Avge	Best	5wI	10wM
Test																		
All First	16	23	2	759	119	36.14	2	3	9	-	447.4	86	1762	61	28.88	6-37	3	-
1-day Int																		
NatWest	4	3	2	37	23	37.00	-	-	2	-	36.5	1	158	11	14.36	4-46	-	
B & H	5	2	0	29	27	14.50	-	-	4	-	46.1	3	232	7	33.14	3-28	-	
Sunday	15	11	1	167	41	16.70	-	-	5	-	77	1	449	15	29.93	3-5	-	

Career Performances

	M	Inns	NO	Runs	HS	Avge	100s	50s	Ct	St	Balls	Runs	Wkts	Avge	Best	5wI	10wM
Test	7	9	1	128	56 *	16.00	-	1	4	-	1098	599	15	39.93	4-36	-	-
All First	91	127	21	2445	119	23.06	2	11	55	-	15487	8717	286	30.47	6-37	17	1
1-day Int	2	1	0	11	11	11.00	-	-	-	-	126	116	3	38.66	3-50	-	
NatWest	4	3	2	37	23	37.00	-	-	2	-	221	158	11	14.36	4-46	-	
B & H	5	2	0	29	27	14.50	-	-	4	-	277	232	7	33.14	3-28	-	
Sunday	15	11	1	167	41	16.70	-	-	5	-	462	449	15	29.93	3-5	-	

KEECH, M. Hampshire

Name: Matthew Keech
Role: Right-hand bat, right-arm 'military medium' bowler
Born: 21 October 1970, Hampstead
Height: 6ft **Weight:** 13st 4lbs
County debut: 1991 (Middlesex), 1994 (Hampshire)
1st-Class 50s: 10
1st-Class 100s: 1
1st-Class catches: 26
Place in batting averages: 58th av. 44.05
Strike rate: (career 97.71)
Parents: Ron and Brenda
Marital status: Single
Family links with cricket: 'Mother and father like to watch a good game'
Education: Northumberland Park School, Tottenham; 'Middlesex and Hampshire dressing-rooms'

Qualifications: 5 O-levels, NCA coaching certificate
Career outside cricket: Coaching
Off-season: Recovering from wrist operation and coaching for club
Overseas tours: England YC to Australia 1989-90
Overseas teams played for: Mossman, Sydney 1988-89; Lancaster Park, Christchurch NZ 1990-91
Cricketers particularly admired: Mike Gatting, Robin Smith and Tony Middleton
Young players to look out for: Jason Laney, Owais Shah
Other sports followed: Football, golf, squash
Injuries: Displaced bone in right hand. Operation to remove at the end of the season. Missed three weeks
Relaxations: Caffreys, 'avoiding jobs to be done around the house'
Extras: Left Middlesex and moved to Hampshire for 1994 season
Opinions on cricket: 'Format for four days is now right with wickets improving. Surely the third umpire should be present in every round of both the Benson and Hedges and Nat West competitions.'
Best batting: 104 Hampshire v Sussex, Arundel 1996
Best bowling: 2-28 Middlesex v Gloucestershire, Bristol 1993

1996 Season

	M	Inns	NO	Runs	HS	Avge	100s	50s	Ct	St	O	M	Runs	Wkts	Avge	Best	5wl	10wM
Test																		
All First	12	21	3	793	104	44.05	1	7	9	-	18	3	46	0	-		-	-
1-day Int																		
NatWest																		
B & H	1	1	0	0	0	0.00	-	-	3	-								
Sunday	10	10	0	201	37	20.10	-	-	4	-	5.4	0	34	1	34.00	1-26	-	

Career Performances

	M	Inns	NO	Runs	HS	Avge	100s	50s	Ct	St	Balls	Runs	Wkts	Avge	Best	5wl	10wM
Test																	
All First	39	68	7	1618	104	26.52	1	10	26	-	684	332	7	47.42	2-28	-	-
1-day Int																	
NatWest	2	1	0	3	3	3.00	-	-	2	-	60	41	0	-	-	-	
B & H	6	5	0	128	47	25.60	-	-	6	-	66	47	1	47.00	1-37	-	
Sunday	55	50	6	922	98	20.95	-	2	10	-	456	353	7	50.42	2-22	-	

KEEDY, G.   Lancashire

Name: Gary Keedy
Role: Left-hand bat, slow left-arm 'with a few revs on it'
Born: 27 November 1974, Wakefield
Height: 6ft **Weight:** 11st 7lbs
County debut: 1994 (Yorkshire), 1995 (Lancashire)
Nickname: Bod, Seedy, Linus, Binbag
1st-Class catches: 9
Place in batting averages: 280th av. 12.16
Place in bowling averages: 146th av. 52.82 (1995 122nd av. 40.48)
Strike rate: 123.95 (career 97.56)
Parents: Roy and Pat
Marital status: Single
Family links with cricket: Twin brother plays for Castleford in the Yorkshire League
Education: Garforth Comprehensive
Qualifications: 4 GCSEs, junior coaching award
Career outside cricket: 'Self unemployed'
Overseas tours: England U18 to South Africa 1992-93, to Denmark 1994; England U19 to Sri Lanka 1993-94

Overseas teams played for: Frankston, Melbourne 1995-96
Cricketers particularly admired: Shane Warne, Graham Gooch
Other sports followed: Rugby league (Leeds), football (Leeds United)
Extras: Player of the Series for England U19 v West Indies U19 in 1993. Graduate of the Yorkshire Cricket Academy. Played for England U19 in the home series against India in 1994. Signed a three-year contract to play for Lancashire from 1995
Opinions on cricket: 'I reckon that two divisions wouldn't go amiss! Keep the Benson and Hedges and the Nat West but sack the Sunday League.'
Best batting: 26 Lancashire v Essex, Chelmsford 1996
Best bowling: 4-35 Lancashire v Somerset, Taunton 1995

1996 Season

	M	Inns	NO	Runs	HS	Avge	100s	50s	Ct	St	O	M	Runs	Wkts	Avge	Best	5wI	10wM
Test																		
All First	14	14	8	73	26	12.16	-	-	7	-	475.1	131	1215	23	52.82	3-45	-	-
1-day Int																		
NatWest																		
B & H																		
Sunday																		

Career Performances

	M	Inns	NO	Runs	HS	Avge	100s	50s	Ct	St	Balls	Runs	Wkts	Avge	Best	5wI	10wM
Test																	
All First	30	32	20	147	26	12.25	-	-	9	-	6049	2789	62	44.98	4-35	-	-
1-day Int																	
NatWest																	
B & H																	
Sunday	4	0	0	0	0	-	-	-	-	-	144	128	1	128.00	1-40	-	

52. Which Australian bowler took exactly 50 per cent of his Test wickets in Ashes Tests, and turned 35 during his final Test appearance?

KENDALL, W. S.   Hampshire

Name: William Salwey Kendall
Role: Right-hand bat, right-arm medium
bowler, occasional wicket-keeper
Born: 18 December 1973, Wimbledon
Height: 5ft 10in **Weight:** 12st 7lb
Nickname: Villy, Lemon
County debut: 1996
1000 runs in a season: 1
1st-Class 50s: 9
1st-Class 100s: 4
1st-Class catches: 26
Place in batting averages: 18th av. 55.00
(1995 111th av. 32.64)
Strike rate: 57.00 (career 60.00)
Parents: Tom and Sue
Marital status: Single
Family links with cricket: Father played
club cricket with East Horsley, Hampshire

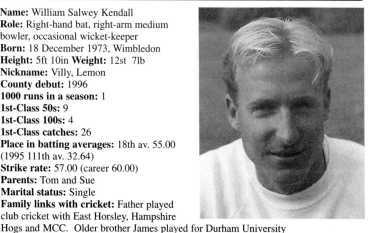

Hogs and MCC. Older brother James played for Durham University
Education: Bradfield College, Berkshire; Keble College, Oxford University
Qualifications: 10 GCSEs, 3 A-levels, 1 AS-level, BA (Hons) Modern History
Career outside cricket: None as yet
Off-season: Gaining work experience with law firm
Overseas tours: Bradfield College to Barbados, 1991
Cricketers particularly admired: Robin Smith, Jonty Rhodes, Graham Thorpe
Other sports followed: Hockey for Oxford University, football (offered terms by
Reading) and golf
Relaxations: Playing or watching sport, socialising with friends, relaxing at home
Extras: Surrey Young Cricketer of the Year 1992. Awarded Gray-Nicolls Trophy for
Schoolboy Cricketer of the Year in memory of Len Newbury 1992. Made first-class
debut for Oxford University in 1994. Played football for Independent Schools 1992.
Offered one-year contract with Reading FC
Best batting: 145* Oxford University v Cambridge University, Lord's 1996
Best bowling: 3-37 Oxford University v Derbyshire, The Parks 1995

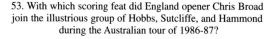

53. With which scoring feat did England opener Chris Broad
join the illustrious group of Hobbs, Sutcliffe, and Hammond
during the Australian tour of 1986-87?

	M	Inns	NO	Runs	HS	Avge	100s	50s	Ct	St	O	M	Runs	Wkts	Avge	Best	5wI	10wM
Test																		
All First	12	23	4	1045	145 *	55.00	3	6	13	-	19	1	82	2	41.00	2-46	-	-
1-day Int																		
NatWest																		
B & H																		
Sunday	8	8	1	130	38 *	18.57	-	-	3	-								

Career Performances

	M	Inns	NO	Runs	HS	Avge	100s	50s	Ct	St	Balls	Runs	Wkts	Avge	Best	5wI	10wM
Test																	
All First	32	49	9	1755	145 *	43.87	4	9	26	-	600	337	10	33.70	3-37	-	-
1-day Int																	
NatWest																	
B & H	3	3	0	54	23	18.00	-	-	-	-							
Sunday	8	8	1	130	38 *	18.57	-	-	3	-							

KENDRICK, N. M. — Glamorgan

Name: Neil Michael Kendrick
Role: Right-hand bat, slow left-arm bowler, gully fielder
Born: 11 November 1967, Bromley
Height: 5ft 10in **Weight:** 12st 7lbs
Nickname: Kendo, Rat, Mers
County debut: 1988 (Surrey), 1995 (Glamorgan)
50 wickets in a season: 1
1st-Class 50s: 4
1st-Class 5 w. in innings: 6
1st-Class 10 w. in match: 1
1st-Class catches: 58
Place in batting averages: (1995 234th av. 17.11)
Place in bowling averages: 118th av. 41.52 (1995 137th av. 46.48)
Strike rate: 83.29 (career 78.82)
Parents: Michael Hall and Anne Patricia
Wife and date of marriage: Caroline Suzanne, 9 November 1996
Family links with cricket: 'Father still tries'
Education: Hayes Primary; Wilson's Grammar School

Qualifications: 7 O-levels, 1 A-level, senior coaching certificate, qualified fitness instructor
Career outside cricket: Running coaching and personal training business
Overseas tours: Surrey U19 to Australia 1985-86; Surrey to Dubai 1988; Glamorgan to Zimbabwe 1995
Cricketers particularly admired: Viv Richards, Ian Botham
Young players to look out for: Ben Hollioake
Other sports followed: Football ('captain of Old Wilsonians and long-time Arsenal supporter')
Injuries: Split webbing, missed two weeks
Relaxations: Music, especially R and B
Extras: Played for Surrey until 1994. Released by Glamorgan at the end of the 1996 season
Opinions on cricket: 'Better coaching and man management of players at first-class level – look to the future and not backwards'
Best batting: 59 Glamorgan v Surrey, The Oval 1995
Best bowling: 7-115 Surrey v Nottinghamshire, The Oval 1993

1996 Season

	M	Inns	NO	Runs	HS	Avge	100s	50s	Ct	St	O	M	Runs	Wkts	Avge	Best	5wI	10wM
Test																		
All First	10	11	6	35	16 *	7.00	-	-	5	-	236	74	706	17	41.52	4-89	-	-
1-day Int																		
NatWest																		
B & H																		
Sunday																		

Career Performances

	M	Inns	NO	Runs	HS	Avge	100s	50s	Ct	St	Balls	Runs	Wkts	Avge	Best	5wI	10wM
Test																	
All First	81	106	30	1206	59	15.86	-	4	58	-	14109	6891	179	38.49	7-115	6	1
1-day Int																	
NatWest	1	0	0	0	0	-	-	-	-	-	72	51	1	51.00	1-51	-	
B & H	2	2	1	25	24	25.00	-	-	1	-	132	98	3	32.66	2-47	-	
Sunday	6	4	3	17	13 *	17.00	-	-	2	-	237	215	4	53.75	2-48	-	

KENLOCK, S. G. Surrey

Name: Stratford Garfield (Mark) Kenlock
Role: Left-hand bat, left-arm medium bowler
Born: 16 April 1965, Jamaica
Height: 6ft **Weight:** 12st
Nickname: Kenny
County debut: 1994
1st-Class catches: 4
Strike rate: (career 100.36)
Parents: Vincent and Lynette
Marital status: Single
Children: Brandon, 13 February 1994
Family links with cricket: Brother plays
league cricket
Education: Stockwell Manor School;
Vauxhall College
Career outside cricket: Engineer
Off-season: Coaching children
Overseas tours: Surrey to Australia 1995

Cricketers particularly admired: Viv Richards, Michael Holding
Other sports followed: Football (Manchester United), American football
Injuries: Split webbing on left hand, out for six weeks
Relaxations: Listening to music (R&B)
Extras: Received 2nd XI cap in 1994 and 2nd XI Bowler of the Year. Won the Gold
Award in the Benson & Hedges Cup for his five for 15 against Ireland in 1995.
Released by Surrey at the end of the 1996 season
Opinions on cricket: 'Four-day cricket is now proving to be better cricket. Sunday
League cricket should remain 40-over game – coloured clothing is good for the game.'
Best batting: 12 Surrey v Northamptonshire, Northampton 1995
Best bowling: 3-104 Surrey v Kent, The Oval 1994

1996 Season

	M	Inns	NO	Runs	HS	Avge	100s	50s	Ct	St	O	M	Runs	Wkts	Avge	Best	5wI	10wM
Test																		
All First	1	2	0	5	5	2.50	-	-	-	-	12	2	40	0	-	-	-	-
1-day Int																		
NatWest																		
B & H																		
Sunday																		

Career Performances

	M	Inns	NO	Runs	HS	Avge	100s	50s	Ct	St	Balls	Runs	Wkts	Avge	Best	5wI	10wM
Test																	
All First	7	10	2	55	12	6.87	-	-	4	-	1104	666	11	60.54	3-104	-	-
1-day Int																	
NatWest																	
B & H	4	0	0	0	0	-	-	-	-	-	210	171	11	15.54	5-15	1	
Sunday	17	5	1	13	9	3.25	-	-	6	-	686	626	19	32.94	4-30	-	

KENNIS, G. J. Surrey

Name: Gregor John Kennis
Role: Right-hand bat, right-arm off-spin bowler
Born: 9 March 1974, Yokohama, Japan
Height: 6ft 2in **Weight:** 12st
Nickname: Nesty
County debut: 1994
1st-Class catches: 3
Parents: Michael and Sally
Marital status: Single
Family links with cricket: 'Dad played for his company side and is now a qualified coach'
Education: Tiffin Boys' School; Stewart Cricket Academy
Qualifications: 9 GCSEs, 1 A-level, NCA senior coach
Career outside cricket: 'Interior designing'
Off-season: Playing in Perth, Western Australia, 'being part of the gathering'
Overseas tours: Surrey U19 to Barbados 1991
Overseas teams played for: Claremont Nedlands, Perth 1995-96; Marist Newman Old Boys CC, Perth 1996-97
Cricketers particularly admired: David Boon, James Bond, Alec Stewart, Neil Stewart, Neil 'what a brave man' Sargeant
Other sports followed: Horse racing and football (West Ham)
Relaxations: Horse racing, drinking with friends
Extras: 1995 Surrey 2nd XI Batsman of the Year. Scored 258 against Leicestershire in 1995, a record for Surrey 2nd XI
Opinions on cricket: 'We should be grateful. We are getting paid for something we enjoy doing, although getting paid more would be good.'
Best batting: 29 Surrey v Kent, Canterbury 1995

1996 Season

	M	Inns	NO	Runs	HS	Avge	100s	50s	Ct	St	O	M	Runs	Wkts	Avge	Best	5wI	10wM
Test																		
All First	1	2	1	3	2 *	3.00	-	-	1	-								
1-day Int																		
NatWest																		
B & H																		
Sunday																		

Career Performances

	M	Inns	NO	Runs	HS	Avge	100s	50s	Ct	St	Balls	Runs	Wkts	Avge	Best	5wI	10wM
Test																	
All First	3	6	1	91	29	18.20	-	-	3	-	18	0	0	-	-	-	-
1-day Int																	
NatWest																	
B & H																	
Sunday	1	1	0	5	5	5.00	-	-	-	-							

KENWAY, D.   Hampshire

Name: Derek Kenway
Role: Right-hand bat, right-arm medium bowler
Born: 12 June 1978, Fareham
Height: 5ft 11in **Weight:** 12st 7lbs
Nickname: Kenners
County debut: No first-team appearance
Parents: Keith and Geraldine
Family links with cricket:
Grandfather played league cricket, father played at school, brother plays for Winchester CC
Education: Botley Primary School; St George's, Southampton
Qualifications: 6 GCSEs, NCA coaching award, qualified snowboard instructor
Off-season: Coaching, training and kickboxing
Overseas tours: West of England U15 to West Indies 1993
Other sports followed: Football, indoor cricket and rugby
Cricketers particularly admired: Mark Waugh, Ian Healy

Young players to look out for: David Sales
Other sports followed: Football (Southampton FC), kickboxing and boxing
Injuries: Split webbing and sore shoulder, but missed no time
Relaxations: Kickboxing, boxing, socialising, spending time with girlfriend
Extras: *Daily Telegraph* Batting Award (West) 1994. Southern League Player of the Year in 1996
Opinions on cricket: 'None.'

KERR, J. I. D. Somerset

Name: Jason Ian Douglas Kerr
Role: Right-hand bat, right-arm
fast-medium bowler
Born: 7 April 1974, Bolton, Lancashire
Height: 6ft 3in **Weight:** 12st 6lbs
Nickname: Norman, Normski, Stretchy
County debut: 1993
1st-Class 50s: 3
1st-Class 5 w. innings: 1
1st-Class catches: 9
Place in batting averages: av. 164th 29.33
(1995 202nd av. 20.52)
Place in bowling averages: 147th av. 53.27
(1995 123rd av. 40.50)
Strike rate: 71.45 (career 60.14)
Parents: Len and Janet
Marital status: Single
Family links with cricket: 'Brother Andy is
becoming a young legend'

Education: Withins High School; Bolton Met College
Qualifications: 5 GCSEs, BTEC National Diploma in Business Studies, cricket coach
Off-season: Playing in Wellington, New Zealand
Overseas tours: England U19 to India 1992-93; Lancashire U19 to Isle of Man
Overseas teams played for: Gordon Districts CC, Sydney, Australia 1994-95; Taita CC, Wellington, New Zealand 1996-97
Cricketers particularly admired: Mushtaq Ahmed, David Gower, Peter Bowler
Young players to look out for: Andy Kerr
Other sports followed: Bolton 'The Great' Wanderers
Injuries: Ripped cartilage on left lower rib, missed four months
Relaxations: Playing golf, socialising, squash, television, swimming, sleeping, listening to music, spending time with friends and girlfriend Emma
Opinions on cricket: 'Cricketers should have 12-month contracts.'
Best batting: 80 Somerset v West Indies, Taunton 1995

Best bowling: 5-82 Somerset v West Indies, Taunton 1995

1996 Season

	M	Inns	NO	Runs	HS	Avge	100s	50s	Ct	St	O	M	Runs	Wkts	Avge	Best	5wI	10wM
Test																		
All First	6	9	3	176	68 *	29.33	-	2	-	-	131	16	586	11	53.27	3-108	-	-
1-day Int																		
NatWest																		
B & H																		
Sunday	5	2	1	12	8	12.00	-	-	1	-	28	0	144	6	24.00	3-27	-	

Career Performances

	M	Inns	NO	Runs	HS	Avge	100s	50s	Ct	St	Balls	Runs	Wkts	Avge	Best	5wI	10wM
Test																	
All First	27	41	8	597	80	18.09	-	3	9	-	3248	2216	54	41.03	5-82	1	-
1-day Int																	
NatWest	2	2	0	3	3	1.50	-	-	-	-	66	74	2	37.00	2-74	-	
B & H	1	0	0	0	0	-	-	-	-	-	48	35	2	17.50	2-35	-	
Sunday	28	18	5	99	17	7.61	-	-	3	-	1106	992	34	29.17	3-27	-	

KERSEY, G. J.   Surrey

Name: Graham James Kersey
Role: Right-hand bat, wicket-keeper
Born: 19 May 1971, Plumstead
County debut: 1991 (Kent), 1993 (Surrey)
County cap: 1996
1st-Class 50s: 9
1st-Class catches: 169
1st-Class stumpings: 12
Place in batting averages: 199th av. 25.12
(1995 137th av. 29.50)
Overseas tours: Kent Schools U17 to
Singapore and New Zealand 1987-88
Overseas teams played for: Eastern Suburbs
District, Brisbane 1989-91, 1993-94;
Windhoek College of Education, Namibia
1992-93; Western Suburbs District, Brisbane
1996-97
Extras: Tragically killed in a car accident in
Australia on New Year's Eve 1996
Best batting: 83 Surrey v Yorkshire, The Oval 1996

1996 Season

	M	Inns	NO	Runs	HS	Avge	100s	50s	Ct	St	O	M	Runs	Wkts	Avge	Best	5wl	10wM
Test																		
All First	15	20	4	402	68 *	25.12	-	3	45	1								
1-day Int																		
NatWest																		
B & H																		
Sunday	7	5	1	41	22 *	10.25	-	-	8	-								

Career Performances

	M	Inns	NO	Runs	HS	Avge	100s	50s	Ct	St	Balls	Runs	Wkts	Avge	Best	5wl	10wM
Test																	
All First	53	82	14	1578	83	23.20	-	9	169	12							
1-day Int																	
NatWest	1	1	0	21	21	21.00	-	-	-	-							
B & H																		
Sunday	28	18	2	260	50	16.25	-	1	30	5							

KETTLEBOROUGH, R. A.   Yorkshire

Name: Richard Allan Kettleborough
Role: Left-hand bat, right-arm medium bowler
Born: 15 March 1973, Sheffield
Height: 5ft 10in **Weight:** 12st
Nickname: Ketts
County debut: 1994
1st-Class 50s: 1
1st-Class 100s: 1
1st-Class catches: 7
Place in batting averages: 121st av. 34.11
Strike rate: 36.00 (career 60.00)
Parents: Allan and Pat
Marital status: Single
Family links with cricket: Father played for Yorkshire and is now coach at Worksop College
Education: Laughton All Saints Junior School; Worksop College; Airedale and Wharfdale College, Leeds
Qualifications: 5 GCSEs, BTEC in Recreational Management, senior coaching award
Career outside cricket: 'Would like to own my own pub'
Off-season: 'Going on holiday to Cape Town'

Overseas tours: Worksop College to Australia 1988-89; England U18 to Canada 1991; Yorkshire CCC to South Africa 1995
Overseas teams played for: Somerset West, Cape Town 1993-94
Cricketers particularly admired: David Gower and 'all the Yorkshire team'
Young players to look out for: Anthony McGrath
Other sports followed: Football (Sheffield Wednesday FC)
Injuries: Pulled hamstring, missed one game
Relaxations: 'Spending time with friends in Sheffield'
Extras: Won the Lord's Taverners U15 award for the Most Promising Young Cricketer in 1988. 2nd XI cap at Yorkshire
Opinions on cricket: 'Not enough time to practise during the season.'
Best batting: 108 Yorkshire v Essex, Headingley 1996
Best bowling: 2-26 Yorkshire v Nottinghamshire, Scarborough 1996

1996 Season

	M	Inns	NO	Runs	HS	Avge	100s	50s	Ct	St	O	M	Runs	Wkts	Avge	Best	5wl	10wM
Test																		
All First	7	9	0	307	108	34.11	1	1	6	-	12	1	40	2	20.00	2-26	-	-
1-day Int																		
NatWest																		
B & H																		
Sunday	4	2	2	23	12 *	-	-	-	4	-								

Career Performances

	M	Inns	NO	Runs	HS	Avge	100s	50s	Ct	St	Balls	Runs	Wkts	Avge	Best	5wl	10wM
Test																	
All First	10	14	2	424	108	35.33	1	2	7	-	120	79	2	39.50	2-26	-	-
1-day Int																	
NatWest																	
B & H																	
Sunday	9	5	3	62	28	31.00	-	-	4	-	66	72	3	24.00	2-43	-	

KEY, R. W. T. Kent

Name: Robert William Trevor Key
Role: Right-hand bat, right-arm fast-medium
bowler, occasional wicket-keeper
Born: 12 May 1979, Dulwich
Height: 6ft 1in **Weight:** 13st 5lbs
Nickname: Keysy, Ronald, Builder
County debut: No first-team appearance
Parents: Trevor and Lynn
Marital status: Single
Family links with cricket: Mother played
for Kent Ladies. Father played club cricket in
Derby. Sister Elizabeth played for her junior
school side
Education: Worsley Bridge Primary School;
Langley Park Boys' School
Qualifications: 7 GCSEs, NCA coaching
award, GNVQ Business
Career outside cricket: Not decided
Off-season: 'Playing hockey for Beckenham, keeping fit and playing abroad'
Overseas tours: Kent U13 to Holland
Overseas teams played for: Green Point CC, Cape Town 1996-97
Cricketers particularly admired: Eddy Stanford, Matt Walker, Jamie Rowe, Steve
Rudduck, David Penfold, Jon Bond, Alan Ealham
Young players to look out for: Simon Evans, James Hockley, Jon Bond, Jamie Rowe,
Ben Phillips, Will House
Other sports followed: Football (Newcastle United), hockey (plays for Beckenham),
basketball (Chicago Bulls), squash, golf, tennis
Relaxations: Going out, socialising and 'playing indoor cricket with David Penfold
and the greatest cheat Steve Rudduck'
Extras: Played for England U17 and England U19 Development XI. Also played for
South England U14 and U19. County tennis player
Opinions on cricket: 'There isn't a lack of talent in the English game, players just lack
the mental toughness needed for the international game.'

KHAN, A. A.

Name: Amer Ali Khan
Role: Right-hand bat, leg-break bowler
Born: 5 November 1969, Lahore, Pakistan
Height: 5ft 10in **Weight:** 12st
Nickname: Aamy, The Chest
County debut: 1995
1st-Class catches: 1
Parents: M. Haneef Khan and Shireen
Haneef
Family links with cricket: Father used to
play club cricket
Education: Muslim Model High School,
Lahore, Pakistan; MAO College, Lahore,
Pakistan
Career outside cricket: 'Cricket is life, the
rest is mere detail'
Off-season: 'Since I have been appointed by
NASA, most of my time will now be taken
up by astronaut training'
Overseas teams played for: Wakatu CC, Nelson, New Zealand 1995
Cricketers particularly admired: Mark Ramprakash, Paul Weekes, Alan Mullally,
Simon Shepherds and 'all cricketers who truly support their team mates'
Young players to look out for: 'I'll be back'
Other sports followed: Bungee jumping, sky diving, deep sea diving, rock climbing
Injuries: Shin splints and broken ankle, missed four months
Relaxations: 'Pumping up the bass in my car. Going to the movies. Reading Ceefax
and changing television channels'
Extras: Released by Middlesex at the end of the 1996 season and has joined Sussex
Opinions on cricket: 'I think that everyone should support the bowler as they do the
batsman. If 20 wickets fall on the first day they report the pitch, and if the pitch is flat
and some team gets 600 runs in the first innings all they say is that the team batted
well. I bet when Lara got his 501 no comment was made about the pitch. I think that
groundsmen should look after the bowler as well. Once in a blue moon we get a
wicket that turns on the first day.'
Best bowling: 4-51 Middlesex v Cambridge University, Fenner's 1996

Career Performances

	M	Inns	NO	Runs	HS	Avge	100s	50s	Ct	St	Balls	Runs	Wkts	Avge	Best	5wI	10wM
Test																	
All First	3	0	0	0	0	-	-	-	1	-	456	142	8	17.75	4-51	-	-
1-day Int																	
NatWest																	
B & H																	
Sunday																	

KHAN, G. A. Derbyshire

Name: Gul Abbass Khan
Role: Right-hand bat, leg-break bowler
Born: 31 December 1973, Gujrat, Pakistan
Height: 5ft 9in **Weight:** 12st
Nickname: Gullie
County debut: 1996
1st-Class 50s: 4
1st-Class 100s: 1
1st-Class catches: 7
Place in batting averages: 87th av. 38.00
Strike rate: (career 58.00)
Parents: Qufait and Shahnaz
Marital status: Single
Family links with cricket: Father played club cricket in Pakistan
Education: Valentine High School; Ipswich School; Swansea University; Keble College, Oxford University
Qualifications: 8 GCSEs, 3 A-levels, BSc (Hons) in Anthropology and Social Studies, Postgraduate Diploma in Social Studies
Off-season: Playing club cricket in Pakistan
Overseas tours: Ipswich School to Australia 1991-92
Overseas teams played for: P&T Gymkhana, Lahore, Pakistan 1993-94
Cricketers particularly admired: Sunil Gavaskar, Javed Miandad, David Gower, Ayaz Lodhi
Young players to look out for: Andrew Alexander, Russell Thompson, Pierre Du Prez
Other sports followed: Football (Manchester United), squash, badminton
Relaxations: Reading, travelling, going out to eat with friends
Extras: *Daily Telegraph* South of England Batting Award 1989 and 1991

Opinions on cricket: 'The issue of ball tampering should be conclusively dealt with by the ICC.'
Best batting: 101* Oxford University v Kent, Canterbury 1996
Best bowling: 2-48 Oxford University v Hampshire, The Parks 1996

1996 Season

	M	Inns	NO	Runs	HS	Avge	100s	50s	Ct	St	O	M	Runs	Wkts	Avge	Best	5wI	10wM
Test																		
All First	13	18	2	608	101 *	38.00	1	4	7	-	29	0	190	3	63.33	2-48	-	-
1-day Int																		
NatWest	1	1	0	15	15	15.00	-	-	1	-								
B & H	5	5	0	232	147	46.40	1	-	1	-								
Sunday	7	6	1	81	27	16.20	-	-	2	-								

Career Performances

	M	Inns	NO	Runs	HS	Avge	100s	50s	Ct	St	Balls	Runs	Wkts	Avge	Best	5wI	10wM
Test																	
All First	13	18	2	608	101 *	38.00	1	4	7	-	174	190	3	63.33	2-48	-	-
1-day Int																	
NatWest	1	1	0	15	15	15.00	-	-	1	-							
B & H	5	5	0	232	147	46.40	1	-	1	-							
Sunday	7	6	1	81	27	16.20	-	-	2	-							

KHAN, W. G. Warwickshire

Name: Wasim Gulzar Khan
Role: Left-hand bat, right-arm
leg-break bowler
Born: 26 February 1971, Birmingham
Height: 6ft 1in **Weight:** 11st 5lbs
Nickname: Wazby, Dog
County debut: 1992 (one-day),
1995 (first-class)
1st-Class 50s: 8
1st-Class 100s: 4
1st-Class catches: 28
Place in batting averages: 180th av. 27.33
(1995 27th av. 49.82)
Parents: Gulzar Khan (deceased)
and Zarina Begum
Marital status: Single
Education: Small Heath Secondary School,

Birmingham; Josiah Mason Sixth Form College, Birmingham
Qualifications: 6 O-levels, 1 A-level, NCA Coaching Award
Off-season: Playing for Petone Riverside, Wellington, New Zealand
Overseas tours: Warwickshire to Cape Town 1993 and 1995
Overseas teams played for: Western Suburbs, Sydney 1990-91; North Perth, Western Australia 1991-93; Albion, Melbourne 1993-95; Petone Riverside, Wellington, New Zealand 1996-97
Cricketers particularly admired: Graham Thorpe, Saeed Anwar, and 'all the Warwickshire team for their competiveness, desire to win and team spirit'
Young players to look out for: Anurag Singh, Darren Altree
Other sports followed: Football (Leeds United), golf, tennis, squash
Relaxations: Listening to music, spending time with family and friends
Extras: Most Promising Young Cricketer 1990. Scored four centuries in a row for Warwickshire U19. Scored 171* v Northants in second trial game for Warwickshire 2nd XI. England Schools U19. Won Oxford/Cambridge U19 Festival 1989, 1990
Opinions on cricket: 'Too much cricket. 2nd XI wickets should be similar in preparation. 2nd XI games should be played on county grounds. Two divisions would be a good idea.'
Best batting: 181 Warwickshire v Hampshire, Southampton 1995

1996 Season

	M	Inns	NO	Runs	HS	Avge	100s	50s	Ct	St	O	M	Runs	Wkts	Avge	Best	5wl	10wM
Test																		
All First	15	28	1	738	130	27.33	3	2	11	-	2.1	1	2	0	-	-	-	-
1-day Int																		
NatWest																		
B & H	1	1	1	0	0 *	-	-	-	1	-								
Sunday	5	5	0	24	9	4.80	-	-	1	-								

Career Performances

	M	Inns	NO	Runs	HS	Avge	100s	50s	Ct	St	Balls	Runs	Wkts	Avge	Best	5wl	10wM
Test																	
All First	28	51	7	1585	181	36.02	4	8	28	-	55	24	0	-	-	-	-
1-day Int																	
NatWest																	
B & H	1	1	1	0	0 *	-	-	-	1	-							
Sunday	7	7	0	32	9	4.57	-	-	2	-							

Name: Neil Killeen
Role: Right-hand bat, right-arm fast-medium bowler
Born: 17 October 1975, Shotley Bridge
Height: 6ft 2 in   **Weight:** 14st 12lbs
Nickname: Killer
County debut: 1995
1st-Class catches: 5
1st-Class 5 w. in innings: 1
Place in batting averages: 306th av. 6.66 (1995 260th av. 13.70)
Place in bowling averages: 102nd av. 36.16 (1995 132nd av. 45.11)
Strike rate: 57.41 (career 64.20)
Parents: Glen and Thora
Marital status: Single
Education: Greencroft Comprehensive School; Derwentside College, University of Teesside
Qualifications: 8 GCSEs, 2 A-levels, cricket coaching award
Off-season: At university doing a sports science degree
Overseas tours: Durham CCC to Zimbabwe 1992; England U19 to West Indies 1994-95
Cricketers particularly admired: Ian Botham, Curtly Ambrose
Other sports followed: Athletics (English Schools javelin) and football
Relaxations: 'Spending time with friends and going out. Listening to music and watching television'
Extras: First Durham bowler to take five wickets in a Sunday League game (5-26 against Northamptonshire in 1995)
Opinions on cricket: 'Too many overs in a day in the first-class game.'
Best batting: 48 Durham v Somerset, Chester-le-Street 1995
Best bowling: 5-118 Durham v Sussex, Hartlepool 1995

---

54. Which batsman scored the winning run for Australia to regain The Ashes at Old Trafford in 1989?

1996 Season

	M	Inns	NO	Runs	HS	Avge	100s	50s	Ct	St	O	M	Runs	Wkts	Avge	Best	5wI	10wM
Test																		
All First	5	7	1	40	32	6.66	-	-	1	-	114.5	22	434	12	36.16	4-57	-	-
1-day Int																		
NatWest	1	0	0	0	0	-	-	-	1	-	12	0	46	1	46.00	1-46	-	
B & H	4	2	0	4	4	2.00	-	-	1	-	28.4	3	153	2	76.50	1-46	-	
Sunday	14	11	2	56	32	6.22	-	-	4	-	103.3	1	570	16	35.62	3-45	-	

Career Performances

	M	Inns	NO	Runs	HS	Avge	100s	50s	Ct	St	Balls	Runs	Wkts	Avge	Best	5wI	10wM
Test																	
All First	12	20	4	177	48	11.06	-	-	5	-	1862	1201	29	41.41	5-118	1	-
1-day Int																	
NatWest	1	0	0	0	0	-	-	-	1	-	72	46	1	46.00	1-46	-	
B & H	9	6	1	18	8	3.60	-	-	2	-	502	387	8	48.37	2-43	-	
Sunday	22	15	3	83	32	6.91	-	-	5	-	961	818	28	29.21	5-26	1	

KIRTLEY, R. J.   Sussex

Name: Robert James Kirtley
Role: Right-hand bat, right-arm
fast-medium bowler
Born: 10 January 1975, Eastbourne
Height: 6ft   **Weight:** 12st
Nickname: Ambi, Hurtler
County debut: 1995
1st-Class 5 w. in innings: 1
1st-Class catches: 7
Place in batting averages: 318th av. 2.75
Place in bowling averages: 44th av. 28.00
Strike rate: 43.03 (career 47.93)
Parents: Bob and Pip
Marital status: Single
Family links with cricket: Brother played
for Sussex Young Cricketers and Eastbourne
Education: St Andrews School, Eastbourne;
Clifton College, Bristol
Qualifications: 9 GCSEs, 2 A-levels, NCA
coaching first level
Off-season: Playing for Old Georgians in Zimbabwe and then in Cape Town with the
NCA scholarship

Overseas tours: Sussex YC to Barbados 1993, to Sri Lanka 1995
Cricketers particularly admired: Curtly Ambrose, Jim Andrew and Darren Gough
Other sports followed: Hockey, golf and football (Brighton & Hove Albion)
Relaxations: Sleeping
Extras: Played in the Mashonaland side which defeated England on their recent tour to Zimbabwe taking seven wickets in the match
Opinions on cricket: 'With hard ground and indoor facilities, the workload of bowlers should be lessened in order to prolong careers and keep bowlers fresh.'
Best batting: 7 Sussex v Derbyshire, Hove 1996
Best bowling: 5-51 TCCB XI v South Africa A, Chester-le-Street 1996

1996 Season

	M	Inns	NO	Runs	HS	Avge	100s	50s	Ct	St	O	M	Runs	Wkts	Avge	Best	5wI	10wM
Test																		
All First	8	12	4	22	7 *	2.75	-	-	5	-	193.4	32	756	27	28.00	5-51	1	-
1-day Int																		
NatWest																		
B & H																		
Sunday	6	2	2	1	1 *	-	-	-	-	-	36	0	185	4	46.25	1-19	-	

Career Performances

	M	Inns	NO	Runs	HS	Avge	100s	50s	Ct	St	Balls	Runs	Wkts	Avge	Best	5wI	10wM
Test																	
All First	10	14	6	25	7 *	3.12	-	-	7	-	1390	859	29	29.62	5-51	1	-
1-day Int																	
NatWest																	
B & H																	
Sunday	9	3	2	3	2	3.00	-	-	-	-	282	254	5	50.80	1-19	-	

KNIGHT, N. V. Warwickshire

Name: Nicholas Verity Knight
Role: Left-hand bat, right-arm medium-fast bowler, close fielder, county vice-captain
Born: 28 November 1969, Watford
Height: 6ft **Weight:** 13st
Nickname: Stitch, Canvas, Fungus
County debut: 1991 (Essex), 1995 (Warwickshire)
County cap: 1994 (Essex), 1995 (Warwickshire)
Test debut: 1995
Tests: 6
One-Day Internationals: 3
1st-Class 50s: 26
1st-Class 100s: 13
1st-Class catches: 123
One-Day 100s: 4
Place in batting averages: 38th av. 47.84 (1995 29th av. 49.27)
Strike rate: (career 112.00)
Parents: John and Rosemary
Marital status: Single
Family links with cricket: Father played for Cambridgeshire, brother plays club cricket for St Giles in Cambridge
Education: St John's School, Cambridge; Felsted Prep; Felsted School; Loughborough University
Qualifications: 9 O-levels, 3 A-levels, BSc (Hons) Sociology, coaching qualification
Off-season: Touring Zimbabwe and New Zealand with England
Overseas tours: Felsted School to Australia 1986-87; England A to India 1994-95, to Pakistan 1995-96; England to Zimbabwe and New Zealand 1996-97
Overseas teams played for: Northern Districts, Sydney 1991-92; East Torrens, Adelaide 1992-94
Relaxations: 'Eating good food and painting'
Extras: Captained English Schools 1987 and 1988, England YC v New Zealand 1989 and Combined Universities 1991. Played hockey for Essex and Young England. Played rugby for Eastern Counties. Won *Daily Telegraph* award 1988; voted Gray-Nicolls Cricketer of the Year 1988, Cricket Society Cricketer of the Year 1989, Essex Young Player of the Year 1991 and Essex U19 Player of the Year. Left Essex at the end of 1994 season to join Warwickshire. Scored successive centuries in the Texaco Trophy against Pakistan in 1996
Opinions on cricket: 'Tea break not long enough and too many overs in a day.'
Best batting: 174 Warwickshire v Kent, Canterbury 1995

Best bowling: 1-61 Essex v Middlesex, Uxbridge 1994

1996 Season

	M	Inns	NO	Runs	HS	Avge	100s	50s	Ct	St	O	M	Runs	Wkts	Avge	Best	5wI	10wM
Test	4	7	0	231	113	33.00	1	1	5	-								
All First	15	28	3	1196	132	47.84	4	5	18	-								
1-day Int	3	3	1	264	125 *	132.00	2	-	2	-								
NatWest	1	1	0	68	68	68.00	-	1	1	-								
B & H	6	5	0	252	104	50.40	1	1	-	-								
Sunday	10	9	1	324	134	40.50	1	1	3									

Career Performances

	M	Inns	NO	Runs	HS	Avge	100s	50s	Ct	St	Balls	Runs	Wkts	Avge	Best	5wI	10wM
Test	6	11	0	320	113	29.09	1	2	10	-							
All First	86	146	17	5215	174	40.42	13	26	123	-	112	105	1	105.00	1-61	-	-
1-day Int	3	3	1	264	125 *	132.00	2	-	2	-							
NatWest	10	10	1	419	151	46.55	1	3	4	-							
B & H	23	20	3	531	104	31.23	1	2	7	-	6	4	0	-	-	-	-
Sunday	67	58	9	1415	134	28.87	1	5	27	-	84	85	2	42.50	1-14	-	

KNOTT, J. A.   Surrey

Name: James Alan Knott
Role: Right-hand bat, leg-spin bowler, wicket-keeper
Born: 14 June 1975
Height: 5ft 6in **Weight:** 11st 5lbs
Nickname: Billy Bunting ('Wolfey to ex-MCC team mates')
County debut: 1995
1st-Class catches: 3
1st-Class stumpings: 1
Parents: Alan and Janet
Marital status: Single
Family links with cricket: 'Dad played a bit'
Education: Herne Church of England Primary School; Dane Court Grammar School; City of Westminster College
Qualifications: 10 GCSEs, 2 A-levels, 2 GNVQ level 3s, basic basketball and cricket coach

Off-season: Playing club cricket in Cape Town
Overseas tours: Canterbury District U15 to Holland
Overseas teams played for: Waverley, Sydney, Australia 1993-94
Cricketers particularly admired: Graham Gooch, David Boon, Mike Atherton and 'I guess my old man helped me out a bit'
Other sports followed: Football (West Ham United)
Injuries: Hamstring strain, missed one week
Relaxations: 'Enjoy movies, horror and science fiction novels, spending time with close friends and a good night out with the Surrey boys'
Extras: 'Shortest ever basketball captain at school.' Has never won a trophy through cricket but has won several through football
Opinions on cricket: 'Need to get youngsters playing a higher standard of cricket earlier. Need to start producing more players of Test calibre and introduce them early to it.'
Best batting: 49* Surrey v South Africa A, The Oval 1996

1996 Season

	M	Inns	NO	Runs	HS	Avge	100s	50s	Ct	St	O	M	Runs	Wkts	Avge	Best	5wI	10wM
Test																		
All First	1	2	1	52	49 *	52.00	-	-	2	1								
1-day Int																		
NatWest																		
B & H																		
Sunday																		

Career Performances

	M	Inns	NO	Runs	HS	Avge	100s	50s	Ct	St	Balls	Runs	Wkts	Avge	Best	5wI	10wM
Test																		
All First	2	2	1	52	49 *	52.00	-	-	3	1								
1-day Int																		
NatWest																		
B & H																		
Sunday																		

KRIKKEN, K. M.   Derbyshire

Name: Karl Matthew Krikken
Role: Right-hand bat, wicket-keeper
Born: 9 April 1969, Bolton
Height: 5ft 10in **Weight:** 12st 7lbs
Nickname: Krikk
County debut: 1987 (one-day), 1989 (first-class)
County cap: 1992
1st-Class 50s: 12
1st-Class 100s: 1
1st-Class catches: 329
1st-Class stumpings: 23
Place in batting averages: 72nd av. 40.09
(1995 157th av. 26.18)
Parents: Brian and Irene
Wife: Leesha
Children: 'At the time of going to press I
should have a little one'

Family links with cricket: Father played for Lancashire and Worcestershire
Education: Horwich Church School; Rivington and Blackrod High School and Sixth
Form College
Qualifications: 6 O-levels, 3 A-levels, cricket coaching certificates
Off-season: Coaching at Derbyshire and 'looking after the missus and bairn'
Overseas tours: Derbyshire to Bermuda 1993, to Torremolinos 1995
Overseas teams played for: CBC Old Boys, Kimberley, South Africa 1988-89; Green
Island, Dunedin, New Zealand 1990-91; United, Cape Town 1992-93; Rivertonians,
Cape Town 1993-94
Cricketers particularly admired: Bob Taylor, Derek Randall, Kim Barnett
Young players to look out for: Andrew Harris
Other sports followed: Football (Wigan FC, Bolton FC), rugby league (Wigan RLFC)
Relaxations: Relaxing at home with Leesha. Walking and good food
Extras: Derbyshire Supporters' Player of the Year 1991 and 1996, Derbyshire Clubman
of the Year 1993
Opinions on cricket: 'It's bloody good.'
Best batting: 104 Derbyshire v Lancashire, Old Trafford 1996

---

55. Which England bowler almost took a hat-trick in
Sydney in 1990-91, dismissing Border and Jones, only
to have Steve Waugh dropped first ball?

1996 Season

	M	Inns	NO	Runs	HS	Avge	100s	50s	Ct	St	O	M	Runs	Wkts	Avge	Best	5wI	10wM
Test																		
All First	19	29	7	882	104	40.09	1	3	64	3								
1-day Int																		
NatWest	3	2	0	69	55	34.50	-	1	3	-								
B & H	5	4	1	35	27	11.66	-	-	3	1								
Sunday	16	13	3	127	27 *	12.70	-	-	12	5								

Career Performances

	M	Inns	NO	Runs	HS	Avge	100s	50s	Ct	St	Balls	Runs	Wkts	Avge	Best	5wI	10wM
Test																	
All First	132	194	42	3499	104	23.01	1	12	329	23	36	40	0	-	-	-	-
1-day Int																	
NatWest	11	7	4	117	55	39.00	-	1	11	-							
B & H	18	12	4	129	37 *	16.12	-	-	22	2							
Sunday	79	50	18	566	44 *	17.68	-	-	87	10							

LACEY, S. J. Derbyshire

Name: Simon James Lacey
Role: Right-hand bat, off-spin bowler
Born: 9 March 1975, Nottingham
Height: 5ft 11in **Weight:** 12st 7lbs
Nickname: Bone 'apparently I'm supposed to be bone idle'
County debut: No first-team appearance
Parents: Phil and Anne
Marital status: Single
Family links with cricket: None
Education: Mundy Street School, Heanor; Aldercar Comprehensive School, Langley Mill; Mill Hill Sixth Form, Ripley
Education: 6 GCSEs, NCA coaching award (level 2)
Career outside cricket: Police force or PE teacher
Off-season: Coaching in local schools
Cricketers particularly admired: Alec Stewart, Kim Barnett
Young players to look out for: Andrew Harris, Anurag Singh
Other sports followed: Football 'a very big fan of the "Rams", Derby County. I also

follow Ilkeston Town who play in the Dr Martens League', snooker, 'I play for South East Derbyshire Snooker Club'

Injuries: 'Blood clot in the patella tendon of my left knee.' Out for six weeks

Relaxations: Listening to music, 'Ocean Colour Scene, Bluetones and Oasis being particular favourites, although I do listen to anything'

Extras: Was a member of the England Junior Volleyball squad in 1991. Captained the NAYC at U19 level against ESCA at Lord's in 1994

Opinions on cricket: 'None in particular.'

LAMPITT, S. R. Worcestershire

Name: Stuart Richard Lampitt
Role: Right-hand bat, right-arm fast-medium bowler
Born: 29 July 1966, Wolverhampton
Height: 5ft 10in **Weight:** 13st 7lb
Nickname: Jed
County debut: 1985
County cap: 1989
50 wickets in a season: 5
1st-Class 50s: 16
1st-Class 100s: 1
1st-Class 5 w. in innings: 12
1st-Class catches: 101
One-Day 5 w. in innings: 3
Place in batting averages: 159th av. 29.90 (1995 159th av. 25.68)
Place in bowling averages: 98th av. 35.53 (1995 55th av. 27.70)
Strike rate: 57.87 (career 55.66)
Parents: Joseph Charles and Muriel Ann
Marital status: Single
Education: Kingswinford Secondary School; Dudley College of Technology
Qualifications: 7 O-levels; Diploma in Business Studies
Career outside cricket: 'None as yet'
Off-season: Coaching
Overseas tours: NCA U19 to Bermuda; Worcestershire to Bahamas 1990, to Zimbabwe 1990-91, to South Africa 1991-92, to Barbados 1996
Overseas teams played for: Mangere, Auckland 1986-88; University CC, Perth 1991-93
Cricketers particularly admired: All first-class cricketers
Other sports followed: Football (Wolves), golf, and most ball sports
Relaxations: Golf and fishing
Extras: Took five wickets and made 42 for Stourbridge in final of the William Younger

Cup at Lord's in 1986. One of the Whittingdale Young Players of the Year 1990. 'Must be the only bowler to be hit for six first ball by Adrian Jones and Phil Tufnell (two master batsmen)'

Opinions on cricket: 'Great game.'
Best batting: 122 Worcestershire v Middlesex, Lord's 1994
Best bowling: 5-32 Worcestershire v Kent, Worcester 1989

1996 Season

	M	Inns	NO	Runs	HS	Avge	100s	50s	Ct	St	O	M	Runs	Wkts	Avge	Best	5wl	10wM
Test																		
All First	19	27	5	658	88	29.90	-	3	15	-	520.5	102	1919	54	35.53	5-58	2	-
1-day Int																		
NatWest	2	2	0	18	13	9.00	-	-	1	-	23	1	91	6	15.16	3-35	-	
B & H	4	2	1	44	25 *	44.00	-	-	1	-	37.2	1	140	7	20.00	4-29	-	
Sunday	16	8	1	129	30	18.42	-	-	5	-	101.4	4	500	19	26.31	4-40	-	

Career Performances

	M	Inns	NO	Runs	HS	Avge	100s	50s	Ct	St	Balls	Runs	Wkts	Avge	Best	5wl	10wM
Test																	
All First	160	205	41	3907	122	23.82	1	16	101	-	21987	11798	395	29.86	5-32	12	-
1-day Int																	
NatWest	20	13	3	135	29	13.50	-	-	6	-	1079	769	33	23.30	5-22	1	
B & H	31	15	5	185	41	18.50	-	-	10	-	1708	1121	57	19.66	6-26	1	
Sunday	123	71	25	909	41 *	19.76	-	-	35	-	4236	3415	132	25.87	5-67	1	

LANEY, J. S. Hampshire

Name: Jason Scott Laney
Role: Right-hand bat, right-arm off-spin
bowler
Born: 24 April 1973, Winchester
Height: 5ft 10in **Weight:** 12st 8lbs
Nickname: Chucky, Hurler, Smiler
County debut: 1993 (one-day),
1995 (first-class)
County cap: 1996
1000 runs in a season: 1
1st-Class 50s: 8
1st-Class 100s: 4
1st-Class catches: 22
One-Day 100s: 1
Place in batting averages: 80th av. 38.76
(1995 139th av. 29.37)
Parents: Geoff and Pam
Marital status: Single
Family links with cricket: Grandfather

played good club cricket and 'parents carted me around whilst playing youth cricket'
Education: Pewsey Vale Comprehensive; St John's, Marlborough; Leeds Metropolitan
University
Qualifications: 8 GCSEs, 2 A-levels, BA (Hons) in Human Movement Studies
Career outside cricket: Coaching abroad
Off-season: Playing for Durban HS Old Boys in South Africa
Overseas tours: England U18 to Canada 1991
Overseas teams played for: Waikatu, New Zealand 1994-95; Matabeleland and Old
Miltonians, Zimbabwe 1995-96; DHS Old Boys, South Africa 1996-97
Cricketers particularly admired: Rupert Cox, Robin Smith, Paul Terry
Young players to look out for: Lee Savident, Will Kendall, Graham Gooch
Other sports followed: Football (Swindon Town), golf
Injuries: Fractured knuckle, out for two to three weeks
Relaxations: 'Watching television, videos, reading, golf, having a beer or two with
friends'
Extras: Hampshire Young Cricketer of the Year 1995. Awarded county cap in 1996.
Only Hampshire cricketer to score a century before lunch on debut in the Nat West
trophy
Opinions on cricket: 'Too much cricket and tea is not long enough. Fielding is very
trying at times – need more rain.'
Best batting: 112 Hampshire v Oxford University, The Parks 1996

1996 Season

	M	Inns	NO	Runs	HS	Avge	100s	50s	Ct	St	O	M	Runs	Wkts	Avge	Best	5wI	10wM
Test																		
All First	17	30	0	1163	112	38.76	4	5	13	-	14	2	61	0	-	-	-	-
1-day Int																		
NatWest	3	3	0	265	153	88.33	1	1	1	-								
B & H	4	4	0	109	41	27.25	-	-	-	-								
Sunday	12	12	0	288	57	24.00	-	1	4	-								

Career Performances

	M	Inns	NO	Runs	HS	Avge	100s	50s	Ct	St	Balls	Runs	Wkts	Avge	Best	5wI	10wM
Test																	
All First	28	51	1	1736	112	34.72	4	8	22	-	102	64	0	-	-	-	-
1-day Int																	
NatWest	3	3	0	265	153	88.33	1	1	1	-							
B & H	4	4	0	109	41	27.25	-	-	-	-							
Sunday	17	17	0	461	57	27.11	-	2	4	-							

LARAMAN, A. W.   Middlesex

Name: Aaron William Laraman
Role: Right-hand bat, right-arm fast bowler
Born: 10 January 1979, Enfield
Height: 6ft 5in **Weight:** 13st
County debut: No first-team appearance
Parents: William and Lynda
Marital status: Single
Education: St Paul's C of E School; Enfield Grammar School
Qualifications: 8 GCSEs
Off-season: Fitness programme supervised by MCC
Overseas tours: England U17 to Holland
Cricketers particularly admired: Viv Richards, Ian Botham
Young players to look out for: Adam Hollioake, Owais Shah
Other sports followed: Football (Arsenal)
Injuries: Left lower leg, was able to bat but not bowl for most of the season
Relaxations: Working out at the gym, watching football, playing golf
Extras: Middlesex Colts county cap. Enfield Grammar School cap at the age of thirteen
Opinions on cricket: 'In the game today, I feel that a high level of fitness is required. The game is becoming much more exciting and much more of a spectator sport.'

LATHWELL, M. N. Somerset

Name: Mark Nicholas Lathwell
Role: Right-hand bat, right-arm medium and off-break bowler
Born: 26 December 1971, Bletchley, Bucks
Height: 5ft 8in **Weight:** 12st
Nickname: Lathers, Rowdy, Trough
County debut: 1991
County cap: 1992
Test debut: 1993
Tests: 2
1000 runs in a season: 4
1st-Class 50s: 37
1st-Class 100s: 11
1st-Class 200s: 1
1st-Class catches: 74
One-Day 100s: 4
Place in batting averages: 59th av. 43.71
(1995 118th av. 31.30)
Strike rate: 46.00 (career 89.33)
Parents: Derek Peter and Valerie
Wife: Lisa

Children and date of birth: Jason, 16 January 1995
Family links with cricket: Brother plays local club cricket; father is a 'retired' club cricketer and now senior coach
Education: Overstone Primary, Wing, Bucks; Southmead Primary, Braunton, North Devon; Braunton Comprehensive
Qualifications: 5 GCSEs
Off-season: Spending time with family and coaching
Overseas tours: England A to Australia 1992-93, to South Africa 1993-94
Cricketers particularly admired: Ian Botham, Graham Gooch
Other sports followed: Snooker, darts
Injuries: Leg muscle strain, missed one week
Relaxations: Cooking and eating
Extras: Spent one season on Lord's groundstaff. Played for England U19 v Australia U19 1991. Young Player of the Year and Somerset Player of the Year 1992. Cricket Writers' Club Young Cricketer of the Year 1993
Opinions on cricket: 'The size of the lunches at most grounds just cannot sustain you all day in the field.'
Best batting: 206 Somerset v Surrey, Bath 1994
Best bowling: 2-21 Somerset v Sussex, Hove 1994

1996 Season

	M	Inns	NO	Runs	HS	Avge	100s	50s	Ct	St	O	M	Runs	Wkts	Avge	Best	5wI	10wM
Test																		
All First	18	32	4	1224	109	43.71	2	7	13	-	7.4	0	27	1	27.00	1-14	-	-
1-day Int																		
NatWest	3	3	0	33	17	11.00	-	-	1	-								
B & H	5	5	0	278	121	55.60	1	2	1	-								
Sunday	15	15	0	414	93	27.60	-	3	3	-								

Career Performances

	M	Inns	NO	Runs	HS	Avge	100s	50s	Ct	St	Balls	Runs	Wkts	Avge	Best	5wI	10wM
Test	2	4	0	78	33	19.50	-	-	-	-							
All First	102	184	8	6282	206	35.69	11	37	74	-	1072	624	12	52.00	2-21	-	-
1-day Int																	
NatWest	14	14	0	416	103	29.71	1	2	4	-	66	23	1	23.00	1-23	-
B & H	16	16	0	718	121	44.87	2	5	3	-	25	50	0	-	-	-
Sunday	75	74	1	1984	117	27.17	1	11	18	-	102	85	0	-	-	-

LAW, D. R. C. Essex

Name: Danny Richard Charles Law
Role: Right-hand bat, right-arm fast bowler
Born: 15 July 1975, Lambeth, London
Height: 6ft 5in **Weight:** 13st 7lbs
Nickname: Decas, Desperate
County debut: 1993
County cap: 1996 (Sussex)
1st-Class 50s: 3
1st-Class 100s: 1
1st-Class 5 w. in innings: 2
1st-Class catches: 6
Place in batting averages: 221st av. 22.10
(1995 214th av. 19.07)
Place in bowling averages: 52nd av. 29.07
Strike rate: 45.80 (career 51.37)
Parents: Richard (deceased) and Claudette
Marital status: 'Attached'
Education: Wolverton Hall School; Steyning
Grammar School
Qualifications: Cricket coach
Overseas tours: Sussex Schools U16 to Jersey 1991; England U18 to South Africa
1992-93, to Denmark 1993; England U19 to Sri Lanka 1993-94

Cricketers particularly admired: Michael Holding, Allan Donald, Courtney Walsh, Franklyn Stephenson, John North, Chris Tugwell
Other sports followed: Most sports
Relaxations: Listening to music, spending time at home
Extras: Left Sussex during the 1996 off-season and has joined Essex on a three-year contract
Opinions on cricket: 'The 2nd XI Championship should be increased from a three-day game to a four-day game so that younger players are used to playing four-day cricket and are not thrown in at the deep end if they progress to first-class cricket.'
Best batting: 115 Sussex v Young Australia, Hove 1995
Best bowling: 5-33 Sussex v Durham, Hove 1996

1996 Season

	M	Inns	NO	Runs	HS	Avge	100s	50s	Ct	St	O	M	Runs	Wkts	Avge	Best	5wI	10wM
Test																		
All First	17	28	0	619	97	22.10	-	3	7	-	320.4	45	1221	42	29.07	5-33	2	-
1-day Int																		
NatWest	3	3	0	25	18	8.33	-	-	1	-	10.3	1	62	1	62.00	1-2	-	
B & H	2	2	0	8	8	4.00	-	-	-	-	16	0	76	1	76.00	1-44	-	
Sunday	16	15	3	370	79 *	30.83	-	1	2	-	98.5	3	566	20	28.30	3-34	-	

Career Performances

	M	Inns	NO	Runs	HS	Avge	100s	50s	Ct	St	Balls	Runs	Wkts	Avge	Best	5wI	10wM
Test																	
All First	28	43	0	878	115	20.41	1	3	13	-	2723	1740	53	32.83	5-33	2	-
1-day Int																	
NatWest	4	3	0	25	18	8.33	-	-	1	-	63	62	1	62.00	1-2	-	
B & H	2	2	0	8	8	4.00	-	-	-	-	96	76	1	76.00	1-44	-	
Sunday	27	23	5	482	79 *	26.77	-	1	6	-	593	566	20	28.30	3-34	-	

56. When did Ian Botham first captain England against Australia?

LAW, S. G.　　　　　　　　　　　　Essex

Name: Stuart Grant Law
Role: Right-hand bat, right-arm medium
bowler
Born: 18 October 1968, Herston, Brisbane,
Australia
Height: 6ft 2in
County debut: 1996
Test debut: 1995-96
Tests: 1
One-Day Internationals: 21
1000 runs in a season: 1
1st-Class 50s: 37
1st-Class 100s: 21
1st-Class 5 w. in innings: 1
1st-Class catches: 101
One-Day 100s: 7
Place in batting averages: 12th av. 61.80
Place in bowling averages: 148th av. 54.28
Strike rate: 89.42 (career 91.70)
Education: Craigslea State High School
Off-season: Playing for Queensland and Australia
Overseas teams played for: Queensland 1988-1997
Overseas tours: Young Australia to England 1995; Australia to India and Pakistan
(World Cup) 1995-96
Extras: Made his first-class debut for Queensland as a 19-year-old scoring 179 in only
his second appearance, still his highest first-class score. Made his Test debut for
Australia against Sri Lanka at Perth in 1995-96 and scored an unbeaten 54. Played in all
17 one-day internationals for Australia in 1995-96
Best batting: 179 Queensland v Tasmania, Brisbane 1988-89
Best bowling: 5-39 Queensland v Tasmania, Brisbane 1995-96

1996 Season

	M	Inns	NO	Runs	HS	Avge	100s	50s	Ct	St	O	M	Runs	Wkts	Avge	Best	5wI	10wM
Test																		
All First	15	26	1	1545	172	61.80	6	5	25	-	208.4	46	760	14	54.28	3-100	-	-
1-day Int																		
NatWest	4	4	0	291	107	72.75	2	1	3	-	23.3	1	110	4	27.50	2-36	-	
B & H	5	5	0	225	116	45.00	1	-	-	-	31.4	1	183	4	45.75	2-57	-	
Sunday	13	13	1	501	120	41.75	3	-	4	-	66.5	3	362	9	40.22	4-40	-	

Career Performances

	M	Inns	NO	Runs	HS	Avge	100s	50s	Ct	St	Balls	Runs	Wkts	Avge	Best	5wl	10wM
Test	1	1	1	54	54 *	-	-	1	1	-	18	9	0	-	-	-	-
All First	106	180	18	7423	179	45.82	21	37	101	-	4952	2387	54	44.20	5-39	1	-
1-day Int	21	20	3	589	110	34.64	1	3	4	-	450	299	6	49.83	2-30	-	
NatWest	4	4	0	291	107	72.75	2	1	3	-	141	110	4	27.50	2-36	-	
B & H	5	5	0	225	116	45.00	1	-	-	-	190	183	4	45.75	2-57	-	
Sunday	13	13	1	501	120	41.75	3	-	4	-	401	362	9	40.22	4-40	-	

LEATHERDALE, D. A. Worcestershire

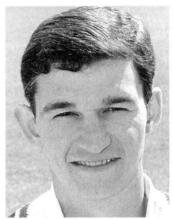

Name: David Anthony Leatherdale
Role: Right-hand bat, right-arm medium bowler, cover fielder
Born: 26 November 1967, Bradford
Height: 5ft 10in **Weight:** 11st
Nickname: Lugsy, Spock
County debut: 1988
County cap: 1994
1st-Class 50s: 27
1st-Class 100s: 6
1st-Class catches: 96
Place in batting averages: 127th av. 33.68 (1995 81st av. 36.67)
Place in bowling averages: 92nd av. 34.90
Strike rate: 57.81 (career 74.90)
Parents: Paul and Rosalyn
Wife's name: Vanessa
Children: Callum Edward, 6 July 1990
Family links with cricket: Father played local cricket; brother plays for East Bierley in Bradford League; brother-in-law played for England YC in 1979
Education: Bolton Royd Primary School; Pudsey Grangefield Secondary School
Qualifications: 8 O-levels, 2 A-levels; NCA coaching award (stage 1)
Off-season: Working as a marketing executive for Worcestershire CCC
Overseas tours: England Indoor to Australia and New Zealand 1994-95
Overseas teams played for: Pretoria Police, South Africa 1987-88
Cricketers particularly admired: Mark Scott, George Batty, Peter Kippax
Other sports followed: Football, American football
Injuries: Broken knuckle, out for two weeks
Relaxations: Golf
Opinions on cricket: '2nd XI wickets need upgrading as many outgrounds are not up

to standard, especially if four-day cricket is extended into the 2nd XI championship.'
Best batting: 157 Worcestershire v Somerset, Worcester 1991
Best bowling: 4-75 Worcestershire v South Africa A, Worcester 1996

1996 Season

	M	Inns	NO	Runs	HS	Avge	100s	50s	Ct	St	O	M	Runs	Wkts	Avge	Best	5wI	10wM
Test																		
All First	11	18	2	539	122	33.68	1	4	8	-	106	21	384	11	34.90	4-75	-	-
1-day Int																		
NatWest																		
B & H	4	4	2	99	66	49.50	-	1	2	-	5	0	23	0	-		-	-
Sunday	14	8	1	122	50	17.42	-	1	6	-	21.5	0	95	7	13.57	4-31	-	

Career Performances

	M	Inns	NO	Runs	HS	Avge	100s	50s	Ct	St	Balls	Runs	Wkts	Avge	Best	5wI	10wM
Test																	
All First	107	166	16	4829	157	32.19	6	27	96	-	1573	905	21	43.09	4-75	-	-
1-day Int																	
NatWest	17	14	1	246	43	18.92	-	-	5	-	64	45	3	15.00	3-14	-	
B & H	19	14	3	216	66	19.63	-	1	4	-	72	62	0	-		-	-
Sunday	96	78	10	1094	62 *	16.08	-	3	47	-	260	202	11	18.36	4-31	-	

LEE, S.   Somerset

Name: Shane Lee
Role: Right-hand bat, right-arm
medium bowler
Height: 6ft 2in **Weight:** 85kg
Born: 8 August 1973, Wollongong,
New South Wales, Australia
County debut: 1996
One-Day Internationals: 8
1000 runs in a season: 1
1st-Class 100s: 8
1st-Class 50s: 12
1st-Class catches: 32
One-Day 100s: 2
Place in batting averages: 11th av. 61.90
Place in bowling averages: 128th av. 44.25
Strike rate: 62.77 (career 71.68)
Parents: Robert and Helen
Marital status: Single

Family links with cricket: Both brothers Brett and Grant play in New South Wales
Education: Balarang Primary School; Oak Flats Senior High School; Wollongong University
Qualifications: High School Certificate and currently studying for a degree in psychology
Off-season: Playing for New South Wales and going to the World Cup with Australia
Overseas tours: Australian Cricket Academy to India and Sri Lanka 1993; Australia U19 to New Zealand; Australia to India and Pakistan (World Cup) 1995-96
Overseas teams played for: New South Wales 1993-96
Extras: Made his debut for New South Wales against Western Australia in 1992-93 season. He was offered a full-time scholarship at the Australian Cricket Academy in 1993 but his university studies prevented him from accepting. He attended on a part-time basis instead. Made his representative debut for Australia in December 1995 in the World Series match against West Indies. Replaced Mushtaq Ahmed as Somerset's overseas player for the 1996 season on a one-year contract
Best batting: 167* Somerset v Worcestershire, Bath 1996
Best bowling: 4-52 Somerset v Sussex, Hove 1996

1996 Season

	M	Inns	NO	Runs	HS	Avge	100s	50s	Ct	St	O	M	Runs	Wkts	Avge	Best	5wl	10wM
Test																		
All First	17	25	4	1300	167 *	61.90	5	5	14	-	418.3	66	1770	40	44.25	4-52	-	-
1-day Int																		
NatWest	3	3	0	122	104	40.66	1	-	1	-	16.5	0	83	0	-		-	-
B & H	5	5	1	63	23	15.75	-	-	2	-	40.2	2	245	6	40.83	3-60	-	
Sunday	16	15	4	442	71 *	40.18	-	5	7	-	115.5	2	618	25	24.72	4-40	-	

Career Performances

	M	Inns	NO	Runs	HS	Avge	100s	50s	Ct	St	Balls	Runs	Wkts	Avge	Best	5wl	10wM
Test																	
All First	41	65	14	2461	167 *	48.25	8	12	32	-	5161	3287	72	45.65	4-20	-	-
1-day Int	8	6	1	61	39	12.20	-	-	5	-	324	207	4	51.75	1-20	-	
NatWest	3	3	0	122	104	40.66	1	-	1	-	101	83	0	-		-	-
B & H	5	5	1	63	23	15.75	-	-	2	-	242	245	6	40.83	3-60	-	
Sunday	16	15	4	442	71 *	40.18	-	5	7	-	695	618	25	24.72	4-40	-	

LENHAM, N. J. Sussex

Name: Neil John Lenham
Role: Right-hand bat, right-arm medium bowler
Born: 17 December 1965, Worthing
Height: 5ft 11in **Weight:** 11st
Nickname: Pin
County debut: 1984
County cap: 1990
1000 runs in a season: 3
1st-Class 50s: 47
1st-Class 100s: 20
1st-Class 200s: 1
1st-Class catches: 71
One-Day 100s: 1
One-Day 5 w. in innings: 1
Place in batting averages: 101st av. 36.12 (1995 73rd av. 39.40)
Strike rate: 112.33 (career 86.59)

Parents: Leslie John and Valerie Anne
Marital status: Single
Family links with cricket: Father played for Sussex and is now one of the NCA's national coaches
Education: Broadwater Manor Prep School; Brighton College
Qualifications: 5 O-levels, 2 A-levels, advanced cricket coach
Off-season: National cricket coach of Namibia
Overseas tours: England YC to West Indies (as captain) 1985
Overseas teams played for: Port Elizabeth, South Africa 1987-88; Brighton, Tasmania 1989-91; United, Namibia 1994-95
Cricketers particularly admired: Ken McEwan, Barry Richards
Young players to look out for: James Kirtley, Danny Law
Other sports followed: Golf, horse racing, rugby and fishing
Injuries: Broken finger ('making a full set'), out for two weeks
Relaxations: Fishing, cooking and drinking wine
Extras: Made debut for England YC in 1983. Broke record for number of runs scored in season at a public school in 1984 (1534 av. 80.74). Youngest player to appear for Sussex 2nd XI at 14 years old. Appointed as Eastbourne's first Cricket Development Officer in 1992
Opinions on cricket: 'Still too much cricket being played. I would like to see the Championship stay as it is and just have two one-day competitions.'
Best batting: 222* Sussex v Kent, Hove 1992
Best bowling: 4-13 Sussex v Durham, Durham University 1993

1996 Season

	M	Inns	NO	Runs	HS	Avge	100s	50s	Ct	St	O	M	Runs	Wkts	Avge	Best	5wI	10wM
Test																		
All First	16	28	3	903	145	36.12	2	5	3	-	56.1	9	146	3	48.66	1-3	-	-
1-day Int																		
NatWest	2	2	0	47	36	23.50	-	-	-	-	7	0	18	1	18.00	1-18	-	
B & H	3	2	0	75	61	37.50	-	1	-	-	1	0	12	0	-		-	-
Sunday	7	5	0	78	43	15.60	-	-	-	-	10	1	49	2	24.50	2-32	-	

Career Performances

	M	Inns	NO	Runs	HS	Avge	100s	50s	Ct	St	Balls	Runs	Wkts	Avge	Best	5wI	10wM
Test																	
All First	185	320	29	9845	222 *	33.83	20	47	71	-	3637	1847	42	43.97	4-13	-	-
1-day Int																	
NatWest	14	13	3	573	129 *	57.30	1	3	-	-	411	240	10	24.00	2-12	-	
B & H	25	23	6	600	82	35.29	-	4	3	-	264	223	4	55.75	1-3	-	
Sunday	94	81	16	1790	86	27.53	-	11	19	-	882	870	29	30.00	5-28	1	

LEWIS, C. C. Surrey

Name: Christopher Clairmonte Lewis
Role: Right-hand bat, right-arm
fast-medium bowler
Born: 14 February 1968, Georgetown,
Guyana
Height: 6ft 2in **Weight:** 13st
Nickname: Carl
County debut: 1987 (Leics), 1992 (Notts),
1996 (Surrey)
County cap: 1990 (Leics), 1992 (Notts)
Test debut: 1990
Tests: 32
One-day Internationals: 51
50 wickets in a season: 2
1st-Class 50s: 27
1st-Class 100s: 7
1st-Class 5w. in innings: 17
1st-Class 10 w. in match: 3
1st-Class catches: 121
One-Day 5 w. in innings: 1
Place in batting averages: 147th av. 31.95
Place in bowling averages: 97th av. 35.48

Strike rate: 65.11 (career 60.08)
Parents: Philip and Patricia
Marital status: Single
Education: Willesden High School
Qualifications: 2 O-levels
Overseas tours: England YC to Australia (Youth World Cup) 1987; England A to Kenya and Zimbabwe 1989-90; England to West Indies 1989-90, to Australia and New Zealand 1990-91, to New Zealand 1991-92, to India and Sri Lanka 1992-93, to West Indies 1993-94, to Australia 1994-95
Cricketers particularly admired: Graham Gooch, Robin Smith
Other sports followed: Snooker, football, darts, American football, basketball
Relaxations: Music, sleeping
Extras: Joined England's tour of West Indies in 1989-90 as a replacement for Ricky Ellcock. Suffers from Raynaud's disease, a problem of blood circulation, and has to spend one night in hospital every two months to have the disease treated. Left Leicestershire at the end of 1991 season and signed for Nottinghamshire. Hit first Test century v India at Madras in 1992-93 tour to India and Sri Lanka. Joined England tour party in Australia following injury to Darren Gough. Suffered a compressed fracture in the ball of his hip joint which prevented him from playing any championship cricket in 1995. Left Nottinghamshire and joined Surrey for the 1996 season
Best batting: 247 Nottinghamshire v Durham, Chester-le-Street 1993
Best bowling: 6-22 Leicestershire v Oxford University, The Parks 1988

1996 Season

	M	Inns	NO	Runs	HS	Avge	100s	50s	Ct	St	O	M	Runs	Wkts	Avge	Best	5wI	10wM
Test	5	7	1	96	31	16.00	-	-	2	-	202.4	43	620	16	38.75	5-72	1	-
All First	14	22	2	639	94	31.95	-	4	15	-	488.2	98	1597	45	35.48	5-25	2	-
1-day Int	3	2	2	33	29 *	-	-	-	-	-	27.1	2	119	4	29.75	4-40	-	
NatWest	2	2	1	49	45 *	49.00	-	-	1	-	22	1	104	5	20.80	3-33	-	
B & H	5	4	3	72	32	72.00	-	-	2	-	47	6	195	9	21.66	3-29	-	
Sunday	8	5	1	168	63	42.00	-	1	4	-	46.1	2	163	11	14.81	3-13	-	

Career Performances

	M	Inns	NO	Runs	HS	Avge	100s	50s	Ct	St	Balls	Runs	Wkts	Avge	Best	5wI	10wM
Test	32	51	3	1105	117	23.02	1	4	25	-	6852	3490	93	37.52	6-111	3	-
All First	148	222	27	6050	247	31.02	7	27	121	-	26917	13396	448	29.90	6-22	17	3
1-day Int	51	38	13	348	33	13.92	-	-	20	-	2513	1854	65	28.52	4-30	-	
NatWest	17	15	1	343	89	24.50	-	2	10	-	942	577	21	27.47	3-24	-	
B & H	28	22	9	392	48 *	30.15	-	-	10	-	1527	1028	41	25.07	5-46	1	
Sunday	89	75	16	1595	93 *	27.03	-	7	25	-	3455	2516	94	26.76	4-13	-	

LEWIS, J.   Gloucestershire

Name: Jonathan Lewis
Role: Right-hand bat,
right-arm medium-fast bowler
Born: 26 August 1975, Aylesbury
Height: 6ft 2in **Weight:** 13st
Nickname: JJ, Nugget, Stupid
County debut: 1995
1st-Class catches: 4
Place in batting averages: 299th av. 8.50
Place in bowling averages: 134th av. 47.00
(1995 3rd av. 17.41)
Strike rate: 92.00 (career 68.73)
Parents: John and Jane
Marital status: Single
Education: Lawn Junior School;
Churchfields Comprehensive School;
Swindon College
Qualifications: 9 GCSEs, BTEC in Leisure
and Hospitality
Career outside cricket: 'Sperm donor'
Off-season: 'Filling up those test tubes'
Overseas tours: Bath Schools to New South Wales, Australia 1993
Overseas teams played for: Marist, Christchurch, New Zealand 1994-95;
Richmond City, Melbourne 1995-96
Cricketers particularly admired: Dom Hewson, Jack Russell, Courtney Walsh, Jon
Summer, Alan Biggins, Paul Rignall
Young players to look out for: Monte Lynch
Other sports followed: Gurning
Injuries: 'Bang on the head, confused all season'
Extras: Was on Northamptonshire staff in 1994 but made no first-team appearance
Opinions on cricket: 'All overseas quick bowlers should be banned from English
cricket. They're not that good, not that fast, and they certainly don't scare me.'
Best batting: 22* Gloucestershire v India, Bristol 1996
Best bowling: 4-34 Gloucestershire v Durham, Bristol 1995

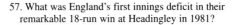

57. What was England's first innings deficit in their
remarkable 18-run win at Headingley in 1981?

1996 Season

	M	Inns	NO	Runs	HS	Avge	100s	50s	Ct	St	O	M	Runs	Wkts	Avge	Best	5wI	10wM
Test																		
All First	10	16	2	119	22 *	8.50	-	-	4	-	276	65	846	18	47.00	3-74	-	-
1-day Int																		
NatWest	2	2	1	7	6 *	7.00	-	-	-	-	16.2	4	46	5	9.20	3-27	-	
B & H	1	0	0	0	0	-	-	-	-	-	10	1	31	3	10.33	3-31	-	
Sunday	14	8	7	26	9 *	26.00	-	-	3	-	90	2	496	11	45.09	2-28	-	

Career Performances

	M	Inns	NO	Runs	HS	Avge	100s	50s	Ct	St	Balls	Runs	Wkts	Avge	Best	5wI	10wM
Test																	
All First	13	19	2	122	22 *	7.17	-	-	4	-	2062	1055	30	35.16	4-34	-	-
1-day Int																	
NatWest	2	2	1	7	6 *	7.00	-	-	-	-	98	46	5	9.20	3-27	-	
B & H	1	0	0	0	0	-	-	-	-	-	60	31	3	10.33	3-31	-	
Sunday	17	9	7	31	9 *	15.50	-	-	3	-	675	590	15	39.33	3-27	-	

LEWIS, J. J. B.   Durham

Name: Jonathan James Benjamin Lewis
Role: Right-hand bat, right-arm
slow-medium net bowler
Born: 21 May 1970, Middlesex
Height: 5ft 9in **Weight:** 11st 5lbs
Nickname: Scrubby, Judgey
County debut: 1990 (Essex)
County cap: 1994
1st-Class 50s: 20
1st-Class 100s: 4
1st-Class catches: 49
Place in batting averages: 190th av. 26.44
(av. 196th av. 21.35)
Parents: Graham Edward and Regina Mary
Marital status: Single
Family links with cricket: Father played
county schools. Uncle is a life-long Somerset
supporter. Sister is right-arm medium-fast
bowler for NorTel
Education: King Edward VI School, Chelmsford; Roehampton Institute of Higher
Education
Qualifications: 5 O-levels, 3 A-levels, BSc (Hons) Sports Science, NCA Senior Coach

Off-season: Playing and coaching Richards Bay, Natal
Overseas teams played for: Old Hararians, Zimbabwe 1991-92; Taita District, New Zealand 1992-93; Eshoue and Zululand 1994-95; Richards Bay 1996-97
Cricketers particularly admired: John Childs, Graham Gooch, Greg Matthews, Keith Fletcher, Mike Garnham and Richard Pearson
Young players to look out for: Ben Hollioake, Colin Campbell
Other sports followed: Soccer, rugby, basketball, 'most sports really'
Injuries: Rotated collarbone, but no time missed
Relaxations: 'Pubs with real ale and Trotters Wine Bar'
Extras: Hit century on first-class debut in Essex's final Championship match of the 1990 season. Has joined Durham for the 1997 season
Opinions on cricket: 'The game continues to lack a Mike Garnham-type personality and is the poorer for it.'
Best batting: 136* Essex v Nottinghamshire, Trent Bridge 1993

1996 Season

	M	Inns	NO	Runs	HS	Avge	100s	50s	Ct	St	O	M	Runs	Wkts	Avge	Best	5wI	10wM
Test																		
All First	6	11	2	238	69	26.44	-	2	11	-	4	0	16	0	-	-	-	-
1-day Int																		
NatWest	1	1	0	12	12	12.00	-	-	-	-								
B & H																		
Sunday	14	11	3	270	61	33.75	-	2	2	-	0.2	0	4	0	-	-	-	

Career Performances

	M	Inns	NO	Runs	HS	Avge	100s	50s	Ct	St	Balls	Runs	Wkts	Avge	Best	5wI	10wM
Test																	
All First	58	101	14	2959	136 *	34.01	4	20	49	-	72	48	0	-	-	-	-
1-day Int																	
NatWest	6	6	1	75	24 *	15.00	-	-	1	-							
B & H	5	5	1	52	19	13.00	-	-	2	-							
Sunday	42	33	8	446	61	17.84	-	2	9	-	2	4	0	-	-	-	

LEWRY, J. D. Sussex

Name: Jason David Lewry
Role: Left-hand bat, left-arm fast-medium
bowler
Born: 2 April 1971, Worthing, West Sussex
Height: 6ft 2in **Weight:** 14st 4lb
Nickname: Urco ('thanks Ath'), Victor
County debut: 1994
County cap: 1996
1st-Class 5 w. innings: 7
1st-Class 10 w. in match: 1
1st-Class catches: 7
Place in batting averages: 284th av. 11.50
(1995 281st av. 10.00)
Place in bowling averages: 15th av. 22.97
(1995 42nd av. 26.53)
Strike rate: 44.19 (career 47.25)
Parents: David and Veronica
Marital status: Single
Family links with cricket: Father coaches
Education: Durrington High School, Worthing; Sixth Form College, Worthing
Qualifications: 6 O-levels, 3 GCSEs, City & Guilds, NCA Award Course
Career outside cricket: Still looking
Off-season: Decorating
Cricketers particularly admired: The Sussex staff, David Gower, Wasim Akram,
Martin Andrews
Young players to look out for: Swing bowlers
Other sports followed: Football (West Ham Utd), golf ('An eagle hole 8, Hill Barn,
Worthing')
Injuries: Trapped nerve in back, missed last month of the season
Relaxations: Golf, eating out, 'watching Naomi cook'
Extras: Selected in a 15-man England indoor cricket squad for the series against South
Africa in England, alongside Mike Gatting and Asif Din, and for the tour of New
Zealand and Australia during 1991-92. The tour was cancelled due to a lack of funds of
the UKICF (UK Indoor Cricket Federation). Diagnosed with a stress fracture of the back
which will cause him to miss the start of the 1997 season
Opinions on cricket: 'Should be an hour for lunch and thirty minutes for tea. The over
rates are too high. There should be two divisions and 2nd XI cricket should be played
over four days. Nightwatchmen should be abolished. The Sunday League should be 20
overs, line and length, hands across the seam, LBW plonker, bring home the bacon!'
Best batting: 34 Sussex v Kent, Hove 1995
Best bowling: 6-43 Sussex v Worcestershire, Eastbourne 1995

1996 Season

	M	Inns	NO	Runs	HS	Avge	100s	50s	Ct	St	O	M	Runs	Wkts	Avge	Best	5wI	10wM
Test																		
All First	10	15	3	138	28 *	11.50	-	-	-	-	302	59	942	41	22.97	6-44	4	1
1-day Int																		
NatWest	2	2	2	8	5 *	-	-	-	-	-	24	0	87	4	21.75	3-45	-	
B & H	1	1	1	8	8 *	-	-	-	-	-	6	0	22	0	-		-	-
Sunday	8	4	1	4	4	1.33	-	-	1	-	50	1	245	11	22.27	3-22	-	

Career Performances

	M	Inns	NO	Runs	HS	Avge	100s	50s	Ct	St	Balls	Runs	Wkts	Avge	Best	5wI	10wM
Test																	
All First	26	40	11	302	34	10.41	-	-	2	-	4489	2504	95	26.35	6-43	7	1
1-day Int																	
NatWest	4	3	3	10	5 *	-	-	-	-	-	252	182	7	26.00	3-45	-	
B & H	4	2	2	22	14 *	-	-	-	-	-	192	174	0	-		-	-
Sunday	22	9	3	22	7 *	3.66	-	-	4	-	868	694	29	23.93	4-29	-	

LIGERTWOOD, D. G. C.   Durham

Name: David George Coutts Ligertwood
Role: Right-hand bat, wicket-keeper
Born: 16 May 1969, Oxford
Height: 5ft 8in **Weight:** 10st
County debut: 1992 (Surrey),
1995 (Durham)
1st-Class 50s: 1
1st-Class catches: 71
1st-Class stumpings: 9
Place in batting averages: 231st av. 20.38
(1995 242nd av. 15.94)
Parents: Andrew and Virginia
Marital status: Single
Family links with cricket: Brother plays
grade cricket
Education: Rose Park Primary School;
Wootton School; St Peter's College,
Adelaide; Magdalen College School, Oxford;
University of South Australia, Adelaide
Qualifications: Matriculation, BA (Juris) LLB, GCLP
Career outside cricket: Lawyer
Off-season: Playing grade cricket in Adelaide

Overseas tours: SPSC tour of England 1986; Durham to South Africa 1995
Overseas teams played for: Adelaide University CC 1986-96
Cricketers particularly admired: Greg Chappell, David Maidment, Darren Webber
Young players to look out for: David Cox, Edward Tolchard
Other sports followed: Aussie rules (Sturt FC), football (Newcastle United), golf, surfing
Relaxations: Golf, surfing, eating, drinking, trainspotting
Extras: Played for Hertfordshire in 1991 NatWest Trophy. Played for Surrey in 1992. Appeared as 12th man for England in the 4th Test against West Indies at Old Trafford in 1995
Opinions on cricket: 'David Cox will revolutionise it.'
Best batting: 56 Durham v Surrey, Stockton 1996

1996 Season

	M	Inns	NO	Runs	HS	Avge	100s	50s	Ct	St	O	M	Runs	Wkts	Avge	Best	5wI	10wM
Test																		
All First	12	23	5	367	56	20.38	-	1	31	5								
1-day Int																		
NatWest	2	2	1	42	30 *	42.00	-	-	2	-								
B & H	1	0	0	0	0	-	-	-	1	1								
Sunday	13	12	2	205	54	20.50	-	1	11	3								

Career Performances

	M	Inns	NO	Runs	HS	Avge	100s	50s	Ct	St	Balls	Runs	Wkts	Avge	Best	5wI	10wM
Test																		
All First	28	51	7	733	56	16.65	-	1	71	9								
1-day Int																		
NatWest	5	4	2	84	37 *	42.00	-	-	4	-								
B & H	2	0	0	0	0	-	-	-	1	1								
Sunday	25	21	5	289	54	18.06	-	1	26	6								

LLONG, N. J. Kent

Name: Nigel James Llong
Role: Left-hand bat, off-spin bowler
Born: 11 February 1969, Ashford, Kent
Height: 6ft **Weight:** 11st 6lb
Nickname: Nidge, Lloyd
County debut: 1991
County cap: 1993
1st-Class 50s: 14
1st-Class 100s: 6
1st-Class 5 w. in innings: 2
1st-Class catches: 48
One-Day 100s: 1
Place in batting averages: 84th av. 38.15
(1995 105th av. 33.62)
Place in bowling averages: 13th av. 22.63
Strike rate: 44.09 (career 63.16)
Parents: Richard and Peggy (deceased)
Wife and date of marriage: Rosemary Ann,
29 February 1996

Family links with cricket: Father and brother played club cricket
Education: Ashford North Secondary School
Qualifications: 6 CSEs, NCA coaching award
Career outside cricket: Groundsman
Off-season: Playing and coaching in Melbourne, Australia
Overseas tours: Kent to Zimbabwe 1992-93
Overseas teams played for: Ashburton, Melbourne 1988-90; Green Point, Cape Town 1990-95
Cricketers particularly admired: David Gower
Other sports followed: Golf and tennis
Injuries: Hamstring strain, out for two weeks
Relaxations: 'Playing golf with my wife. Watching television'
Extras: Kent Supporters Club Young Player of the Year Award 1993
Opinions on cricket: 'TCCB should have total control on pitch preparation. All four-day games should start on Wednesdays.'
Best batting: 130 Kent v Hampshire, Canterbury 1996
Best bowling: 5-21 Kent v Middlesex, Canterbury 1996

1996 Season

	M	Inns	NO	Runs	HS	Avge	100s	50s	Ct	St	O	M	Runs	Wkts	Avge	Best	5wI	10wM
Test																		
All First	14	22	2	763	130	38.15	2	5	12	-	80.5	23	249	11	22.63	5-21	1	-
1-day Int																		
NatWest	2	2	1	152	115 *	152.00	1	-	2	-	9	1	36	3	12.00	3-36	-	
B & H	6	5	1	48	31	12.00	-	-	-	-	10	0	38	2	19.00	2-38	-	
Sunday	17	16	0	231	70	14.43	-	1	9	-	23.1	0	166	5	33.20	2-35	-	

Career Performances

	M	Inns	NO	Runs	HS	Avge	100s	50s	Ct	St	Balls	Runs	Wkts	Avge	Best	5wI	10wM
Test																	
All First	58	90	10	2736	130	34.20	6	14	48	-	1958	1059	31	34.16	5-21	2	-
1-day Int																	
NatWest	5	5	3	193	115 *	96.50	1	-	3	-	78	47	4	11.75	3-36	-	
B & H	9	7	1	54	31	9.00	-	-	1	-	90	69	3	23.00	2-38	-	
Sunday	72	62	15	1003	70	21.34	-	4	22	-	459	449	18	24.94	4-24	-	

LLOYD, G. D.   Lancashire

Name: Graham David Lloyd
Role: Right-hand bat, right-arm medium bowler
Born: 1 July 1969, Accrington
Height: 5ft 7in **Weight:** 13st
Nickname: Bumble
County debut: 1988
County cap: 1992
One-Day Internationals: 2
1000 runs in a season: 3
1st-Class 50s: 43
1st-Class 100s: 14
1st-Class 200s: 1
1st-Class catches: 78
One-Day 100s: 2
Place in batting averages: 31st av. 49.75
(1995 147th av. 27.80)
Strike rate: 12.00 (career 81.50)
Parents: David and Susan
Marital status: Single
Family links with cricket:
Father played for Lancashire and England

Education: Hollins County High School, Accrington
Qualifications: 3 O-levels, NCA coaching certificate
Off-season: 'Working on technique'
Overseas tours: England A to Australia 1992-93; Lancashire CCC to Guernsey 1995
Overseas teams played for: Maroochydore, Queensland 1988-89 and 1991-95
Cricketers particularly admired: Gordon Parsons, David Millns, Nigel Briers
Other sports followed: Football (Manchester United)
Relaxations: 'Eating out and racing'
Extras: His school did not play cricket, so he learnt at Accrington, playing in the same team as his father
Opinions on cricket: 'Bring back timeless cricket (i.e. Test and Championship). Everybody wants to see someone win.'
Best batting: 241 Lancashire v Essex, Chelmsford 1996
Best bowling: 1-4 Lancashire v Warwickshire, Edgbaston 1996

1996 Season

	M	Inns	NO	Runs	HS	Avge	100s	50s	Ct	St	O	M	Runs	Wkts	Avge	Best	5wI	10wM
Test																		
All First	15	25	1	1194	241	49.75	3	4	6	-	2	0	4	1	4.00	1-4	-	-
1-day Int	2	2	1	17	15	17.00	-	-	1	-								
NatWest	5	5	0	186	81	37.20	-	2	3	-	3	0	23	1	23.00	1-23	-	
B & H	8	6	2	119	63 *	29.75	-	1	1	-								
Sunday	16	13	1	434	116	36.16	1	2	3	-	2	0	18	0	-	-	-	-

Career Performances

	M	Inns	NO	Runs	HS	Avge	100s	50s	Ct	St	Balls	Runs	Wkts	Avge	Best	5wI	10wM
Test																	
All First	129	212	22	7236	241	38.08	14	43	78	-	163	190	2	95.00	1-4	-	-
1-day Int	2	2	1	17	15	17.00	-	-	1	-							
NatWest	14	13	0	328	81	25.23	-	2	3	-	18	23	1	23.00	1-23	-	
B & H	30	24	9	521	81 *	34.73	-	3	4	-	18	42	0	-	-	-	
Sunday	111	102	16	2761	116	32.10	2	18	23	-	12	18	0	-	-	-	

LOGAN, R. J.   Northamptonshire

Name: Richard James Logan
Role: Right-hand bat, right-arm bowler
Born: 28 January 1980, Stone
Height: 6ft 1in **Weight:** 12st 7lbs
Nickname: Logie
County debut: No first-team appearance
Parents: Robert and Margaret

Marital status: Single
Family links with cricket: Father plays club cricket for Cannock CC
Education: Walhouse C of E School, Cannock; Wolverhampton Grammar School
Qualifications: 10 GCSEs
Off-season: Studying for A-levels
Cricketers particularly admired: Ian Botham
Other sports followed: Hockey (Cannock – 'also played for Staffordshire from age 9 to present day. Played for Midlands U14 but had to decline Midlands training due to commitment to cricket')
Relaxations: Music, keeping fit and sleeping
Extras: Played for Staffordshire at every level from U11 to U19, and as captain from U13 to U17. Played for Midlands U14 and U15 (both as captain), HMC Schools U15.

1995 *Daily Telegraph*/Lombard U15 Midlands Bowler and Batsman of the Year
Opinions on cricket: 'Although I have no experience in the first-class game, I feel that English cricket would benefit from fewer county games, so that players have a greater appetite to play. For proof, look at Australia!'

LONGLEY, J. I. Durham

Name: Jonathan Ian Longley
Role: Right-hand bat
Born: 12 April 1969, New Brunswick, USA
Height: 5ft 8in **Weight:** 11st 10lbs
County debut: 1989 (Kent), 1994 (Durham)
1st-Class 50s: 8
1st-Class 100s: 2
1st-Class catches: 18
Place in batting averages: (1995 167th av. 24.70)
Parents: Dick and Helen
Marital status: Single
Education: Tonbridge School; Durham University
Qualifications: 9 O-levels, 3 A-levels, BA Sociology
Overseas teams played for: Prospect District, Adelaide 1991-92; Green Point,

Cape Town 1992-93
Cricketers particularly admired: Robin Smith, Gordon Greenidge, Allan Border
Other sports followed: Rugby, golf, squash, tennis
Relaxations: 'Love listening to music (Bob Dylan, Van Morrison and the Rolling Stones). Also love old English pubs, Australian beaches and socialising with friends and family'
Extras: Member of the Combined Universities team which reached the quarter-finals of the B&H Cup in 1989. Moved from Kent to Durham for 1994 season. Retired from first-class cricket at the end of the 1996 season
Best batting: 110 Kent v Cambridge University, Fenner's 1992

1996 Season

	M	Inns	NO	Runs	HS	Avge	100s	50s	Ct	St	O	M	Runs	Wkts	Avge	Best	5wl	10wM
Test																		
All First	2	2	0	6	4	3.00	-	-	-	-								
1-day Int																		
NatWest																		
B & H	4	4	1	119	38 *	39.66	-	-	-	-								
Sunday	3	3	0	44	21	14.66	-	-	1	-								

Career Performances

	M	Inns	NO	Runs	HS	Avge	100s	50s	Ct	St	Balls		Runs	Wkts	Avge	Best	5wl	10wM
Test																		
All First	35	62	3	1381	110	23.40	2	8	18	-	24		47	0	-	-	-	-
1-day Int																		
NatWest	2	2	0	14	9	7.00	-	-	-	-								
B & H	25	25	2	500	57	21.73	-	1	2	-								
Sunday	35	33	3	786	92	26.20	-	6	6	-								

LOYE, M. B.   Northamptonshire

Name: Malachy Bernard Loye
Role: Right-hand bat, off-spin bowler
Born: 27 September 1972, Northampton
Height: 6ft 2in **Weight:** 13st 7lb
Nickname: Mal, Mad Jack, Fruit Bat, Slugs
County debut: 1991
County cap: 1994
1st-Class 50s: 19
1st-Class 100s: 7
1st-Class 200s: 1
1st-Class catches: 46

One-Day 100s: 1
Place in batting averages: 47th av. 45.56
(1995 251st av. 14.88)
Parents: Patrick and Anne
Marital status: Single
Family links with cricket: Father and
brother both played for Cogenhoe CC in
Northampton
Education: Brixworth Primary School;
Moulton Comprehensive School
Qualifications: GCSEs and senior coaching
certificate
Career outside cricket: 'Working hard on
launching a rock and roll career'
Off-season: 'Learning to play the guitar.
Playing football and golf. Trying to earn a
crust'
Overseas tours: England U18 to Canada
1991; England U19 to Pakistan 1991-92; England A to South Africa 1993-94
Overseas teams played for: Riccarton, New Zealand and Canterbury B 1992-93;
Onslow, Wellington, New Zealand 1995-96
Cricketers particularly admired: Gordon Greenidge, Wayne Larkins, Curtly
Ambrose
Young players to look out for: David Roberts, David Sales, Alec Swann, Kevin
Innes, Tobin Bailey
Other sports followed: Football (Liverpool and Northampton Town), golf, basketball
and boxing
Relaxations: Watching films, listening to music, singing and having a good night out
with friends
Extras: Played for England U19 in the home series against Australia U19 in 1991 and
against Sri Lanka U19 1992. Voted Professional Cricket Association's Young Player of
the Year 1993 and Whittingdale Young Player of the Year 1993. Shared a record opening
stand of 375 with Richard Montgomerie versus Yorkshire in 1996
Opinions on cricket: 'Tea time is too short. For such a great game it is so poorly
marketed, which is why we are so far behind other sports. Cricketers should have nine-
month contracts beginning January: this I'm sure will encourage better preparation and
commitment before a season.'
Best batting: 205 Northamptonshire v Yorkshire, Northampton 1996

1996 Season

	M	Inns	NO	Runs	HS	Avge	100s	50s	Ct	St	O	M	Runs	Wkts	Avge	Best	5wI	10wM
Test																		
All First	14	25	2	1048	205	45.56	2	5	5	-								
1-day Int																		
NatWest	2	1	0	2	2	2.00	-	-	-	-								
B & H	6	6	1	168	66	33.60	-	1	4	-								
Sunday	14	13	1	265	58	22.08	-	2	2	-								

Career Performances

	M	Inns	NO	Runs	HS	Avge	100s	50s	Ct	St	Balls	Runs	Wkts	Avge	Best	5wI	10wM
Test																	
All First	74	118	12	3695	205	34.85	7	19	46	-	1	1	0	-	-	-	-
1-day Int																	
NatWest	10	9	3	197	65	32.83	-	1	1	-							
B & H	12	12	3	286	68 *	31.77	-	2	6	-							
Sunday	55	51	6	1349	122	29.97	1	7	11	-							

LUGSDEN, S. Durham

Name: Steven Lugsden
Role: Right-hand bat, right-arm fast bowler
Born: 10 July 1976, Gateshead
Height: 6ft 3in **Weight:** 13st
Nickname: Lugsy, Dynamite, Elwod, Cliff, Keamo
County debut: 1993
1st-Class catches: 1
Place in bowling averages: 18th av. 23.81
Strike rate: 38.45 (career 76.06)
Parents: William and Nora
Marital status: Single
Education: St Edmund Campion RC School, Wrekenton, Gateshead
Qualifications: 7 GCSEs, BTEC Business and Finance
Off-season: Landscape gardening
Overseas tours: England U19 to West Indies 1994-95
Cricketers particularly admired: Dean Jones, Phil Simmons, Michael Foster
Young players to look out for: Steven Lugsden
Other sports followed: Football (Newcastle United)

Injuries: 'Too many to list'
Extras: Youngest player (17 years 27 days) to make first-class debut for Durham. Played against India for England U19 in home series 1994. 'Myself and Neil Killeen once bowled a side out for one run, and that was a leg bye'
Opinions on cricket: 'None.'
Best batting: 9 Durham v Gloucestershire, Chester-le-Street 1996
Best bowling: 3-45 Durham v Lancashire, Chester-le-Street 1996

1996 Season

	M	Inns	NO	Runs	HS	Avge	100s	50s	Ct	St	O	M	Runs	Wkts	Avge	Best	5wl	10wM
Test																		
All First	3	5	1	19	9	4.75	-	-	1	-	70.3	9	262	11	23.81	3-45	-	-
1-day Int																		
NatWest																		
B & H																		
Sunday																		

Career Performances

	M	Inns	NO	Runs	HS	Avge	100s	50s	Ct	St	Balls	Runs	Wkts	Avge	Best	5wl	10wM
Test																	
All First	9	11	4	26	9	3.71	-	-	1	-	1217	759	16	47.43	3-45	-	-
1-day Int																	
NatWest																	
B & H																	
Sunday	1	0	0	0	0	-	-	-	-	-	48	55	1	55.00	1-55	-	

58. Which Australian fast bowler took 7 for 81 in England's first innings at Lord's in 1981, only to miss the final three Tests through injury?

LYE, D.   Middlesex

Name: David Lye
Role: Right-hand bat
Born: 11 April 1979
Height: 5ft 8in **Weight:** 12st 7lbs
County debut: No first-team appearance
Parents: Gerald and Marilyn
Marital status: Single
Family links with cricket: Dad plays
cricket locally
Education: Stockland Primary School;
Honiton Secondary School
Qualifications: 'Going through the stages to
become a coach'
Career outside cricket: 'Left school to play
cricket'
Off-season: 'Help Dad and take part in field
sports as I have most winters'
Cricketers particularly admired: Ian
Botham, Graham Gooch, Allan Border
Other sports followed: Football (Manchester United) and indoor cricket (Honiton)
Relaxations: Field sports
Extras: Devon Young Cricketer of the Year in 1996. Devon U17 Player of the Season
in 1995 and 1996

LYNCH, M. A.   Gloucestershire

Name: Monte Allan Lynch
Role: Right-hand bat, right-arm medium
and off-spin bowler
Born: 21 May 1958, Georgetown, Guyana
Height: 5ft 9in **Weight:** 13st 3lbs
Nickname: Mont
County debut: 1977 (Surrey), 1994 (Glos)
County cap: 1982 (Surrey), 1995 (Glos)
Benefit: 1991 (£107,000)
One-Day Internationals: 3
1000 runs in a season: 10
1st-Class 50s: 85
1st-Class 100s: 39

1st-Class catches: 358
One-Day 100s: 5
Place in batting averages: 155th av. 30.72
(1995 79th av. 38.00)
Strike rate: (career 84.42)
Parents: Lawrence and Doreen Austin
Marital status: Single
Children: Lours, 31 September 1983;
Marissa, 30 July 1989
Family links with cricket: 'Father and most of
family played at some time or another'
Education: Ryden's School, Walton-on-
Thames
Overseas tours: Unofficial West Indies XI to
South Africa 1983-84
Overseas teams played for: Guyana 1982-
83
Other sports followed: Football, table tennis
Extras: When he made 141* for Surrey v Glamorgan at Guildford in August 1982, off
78 balls in 88 minutes, one six hit his captain Roger Knight's car. Joined West Indies
rebels in South Africa 1983-84, although qualified for England. Appeared in all three
one-day internationals v West Indies 1988. Moved to Gloucestershire for 1994 season
Best batting: 172* Surrey v Kent, The Oval 1989
Best bowling: 3-6 Surrey v Glamorgan, Swansea 1981

1996 Season

	M	Inns	NO	Runs	HS	Avge	100s	50s	Ct	St	O	M	Runs	Wkts	Avge	Best	5wI	10wM
Test																		
All First	11	19	1	553	72	30.72	-	5	10	-								
1-day Int																		
NatWest	1	1	0	22	22	22.00	-	-	-	-								
B & H																			
Sunday	11	10	1	242	47	26.88	-	-	1	-								

Career Performances

	M	Inns	NO	Runs	HS	Avge	100s	50s	Ct	St	Balls	Runs	Wkts	Avge	Best	5wI	10wM
Test																	
All First	347	566	63	17860	172 *	35.50	39	85	358	-	2195	1398	26	53.76	3-6	-	-
1-day Int	3	3	0	8	6	2.66	-	-	1	-							
NatWest	41	36	5	889	129	28.67	1	4	19	-	304	179	7	25.57	2-28	-	
B & H	63	58	3	1388	112 *	25.23	2	7	32	-	132	121	0	-	-	-	
Sunday	234	215	27	5237	136	27.85	2	31	80	-	167	205	8	25.62	2-2	-	

MACMILLAN, G. I.　Leicestershire

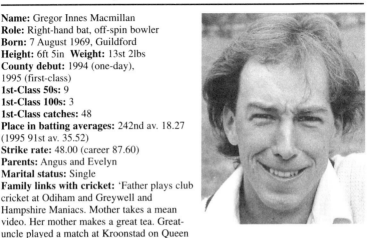

Name: Gregor Innes Macmillan
Role: Right-hand bat, off-spin bowler
Born: 7 August 1969, Guildford
Height: 6ft 5in　**Weight:** 13st 2lbs
County debut: 1994 (one-day),
1995 (first-class)
1st-Class 50s: 9
1st-Class 100s: 3
1st-Class catches: 48
Place in batting averages: 242nd av. 18.27
(1995 91st av. 35.52)
Strike rate: 48.00 (career 87.60)
Parents: Angus and Evelyn
Marital status: Single
Family links with cricket: 'Father plays club
cricket at Odiham and Greywell and
Hampshire Maniacs. Mother takes a mean
video. Her mother makes a great tea. Great-
uncle played a match at Kroonstad on Queen
Victoria's Jubilee Day'
Education: Guildford County School; Charterhouse; Southampton University; Keble
College, Oxford University
Qualifications: 'A few O- and A-levels', BA (Hons) Philosophy and Politics (Soton),
Dip.Soc Admin (Oxon). Currently doing M Litt in Politics at Oxford
Overseas teams played for: Harvinia, Orange Free State 1988-89, 1993-94 'plus the
odd game whenever they ask me'
Cricketers particularly admired: 'Those like Jim Bovill who put up with me without
often complaining. Mickey Carr. Gordon Parsons for being tidy and Richard
Montgomerie for being less tidy than I am'
Other sports followed: Football (Liverpool FC) and 'Scotland at anything except
rugby union and curling'
Extras: Captained Southampton University to the UAU final 1991. Played for Surrey
from U11 to U19. Captain of Oxford University for 1995 season. Played in Oxford's last
two Varsity match victories, plus the winning first one-day match between the two
Universities in 1995. Captained both Oxford and Combined Universities ('a good way
to stay thin'). Scored a century on his championship debut for Leicestershire in 1995
Opinions on cricket: 'You'll have to give me time before I become judgmental. That's
not something you lightly ask a philosopher to do.'
Best batting: 122 Leicestershire v Surrey, Leicester 1995
Best bowling: 3-13 Oxford University v Cambridge University, Lord's 1993

1996 Season

	M	Inns	NO	Runs	HS	Avge	100s	50s	Ct	St	O	M	Runs	Wkts	Avge	Best	5wl	10wM
Test																		
All First	7	12	1	201	41	18.27	-	-	-	-	16	3	59	2	29.50	2-44	-	-
1-day Int																		
NatWest																		
B & H	3	3	0	44	40	14.66	-	-	2	-								
Sunday	11	10	2	186	58	23.25	-	1	3	-	16	1	76	3	25.33	2-37	-	

Career Performances

	M	Inns	NO	Runs	HS	Avge	100s	50s	Ct	St	Balls	Runs	Wkts	Avge	Best	5wl	10wM
Test																	
All First	43	69	8	1749	122	28.67	3	9	48	-	2015	1162	23	50.52	3-13	-	-
1-day Int																	
NatWest	1	1	0	9	9	9.00	-	-	-	-	18	13	1	13.00	1-13	-	
B & H	11	11	1	296	77	29.60	-	2	3	-	89	81	2	40.50	1-18	-	
Sunday	19	18	2	345	58	21.56	-	1	4	-	96	76	3	25.33	2-37	-	

MADDY, D. L.   Leicestershire

Name: Darren Lee Maddy
Role: Right-hand bat, right-arm medium bowler
Born: 23 May 1974, Leicester
Height: 5ft 9in **Weight:** 11st
Nickname: Dazza, Roasting, Stompie
County debut: 1993 (one-day), 1994 (first-class)
County cap: 1996
1st-Class 50s: 4
1st-Class 100s: 1
1st-Class catches: 14
One-Day 100s: 1
Place in batting averages: 120th av. 34.21 (av. 236th av. 16.50)
Strike rate: 54.00 (career 63.00)
Parents: William Arthur and Hilary Jean
Marital status: Single
Family links with cricket: Father and younger brother, Greg, play club cricket
Education: Herrick Junior School, Leicester; Roundhills, Thurmaston; Wreake Valley, Syston

Qualifications: 8 GCSEs
Off-season: Playing for Rhodes University, Grahamstown, South Africa
Overseas tours: Leicestershire to Bloemfontein 1995, to Western Transvaal 1996
Overseas teams played for: Wanderers, Johannesburg 1992-93; Northern Free State, Orange Free State 1993-95; Rhodes University, South Africa 1996-97
Cricketers particularly admired: Brian Lara, Michael Atherton, Richard Hadlee, Viv Richards, 'Babe Ruth' Dakin
Young players to look out for: Iain Sutcliffe, Darren Stevens
Other sports followed: Rugby union (Leicester Tigers), golf, American football, baseball, football (Leicester City and Manchester United)
Relaxations: Scuba diving, bungee jumping, listening to music
Extras: 'Voted having the biggest thighs in Leicester by team-mates.' Set a new 2nd XI Championship run aggregate record (1498) beating the previous one which had stood since 1961. Rapid Cricketline 2nd XI Player of the Year 1994. Awarded county cap in 1996
Opinions on cricket: 'The third umpire should be used in all one-day domestic competitions. The cameras for the third umpire should be in better positions like they are in South Africa. The over-rate fine system is too severe in first-class matches. I don't think that we should recalculate the overs between innings when the fielding side has bowled them slowly.'
Best batting: 131 Leicestershire v Oxford University, The Parks 1995
Best bowling: 2-21 Leicestershire v Lancashire, Old Trafford 1996

1996 Season

	M	Inns	NO	Runs	HS	Avge	100s	50s	Ct	St	O	M	Runs	Wkts	Avge	Best	5wl	10wM
Test																		
All First	20	30	2	958	101 *	34.21	1	4	18	-	36	11	104	4	26.00	2-21	-	-
1-day Int																		
NatWest	2	2	0	13	9	6.50	-	-	-	-	7	0	56	2	28.00	2-56	-	
B & H	5	5	1	163	61	40.75	-	1	-	-	13	2	81	4	20.25	3-32	-	
Sunday	16	13	2	486	106 *	44.18	1	4	2	-	14.2	0	120	0	-	-	-	-

Career Performances

	M	Inns	NO	Runs	HS	Avge	100s	50s	Ct	St	Balls	Runs	Wkts	Avge	Best	5wl	10wM
Test																	
All First	32	53	3	1302	131	26.04	2	4	35	-	252	145	4	36.25	2-21	-	-
1-day Int																	
NatWest	3	3	0	47	34	15.66	-	-	-	-	108	94	4	23.50	2-38	-	
B & H	8	8	1	244	61	34.85	-	2	1	-	78	81	4	20.25	3-32	-	
Sunday	43	35	5	899	106 *	29.96	1	7	19	-	554	555	15	37.00	3-29	-	

MALCOLM, D. E.   Derbyshire

Name: Devon Eugene Malcolm
Role: Right-hand bat, right-arm fast bowler
Born: 22 February 1963, Kingston, Jamaica
Height: 6ft 2in **Weight:** 15st
Nickname: Dude
County debut: 1984
County cap: 1989
Benefit: 1995
Test debut: 1989
Tests: 36
One-Day Internationals: 10
50 wickets in a season: 5
1st-Class 50s: 1
1st-Class 5 w. in innings: 26
1st-Class 10 w. in innings: 5
1st-Class catches: 31
One-Day 5 w. in innings: 1
Place in batting averages: 305th av. 7.43
Place in bowling averages: 71st av. 31.67 (1995 54th av. 29.20)

Strike rate: 46.76 (career 52.68)
Parents: Albert and Brendalee (deceased)
Wife and date of marriage: Jennifer, October 1989
Children: Erica Cian, 11 June 1991; Natile Jade, 25 June 1993
Education: St Elizabeth Technical High School; Richmond College; Derby College of Higher Education
Qualifications: College certificates, O-levels, coaching certificate
Overseas tours: England to West Indies 1989-90, to Australia 1990-91, to India and Sri Lanka 1992-93, to West Indies 1993-94, to Australia 1994-95, to South Africa 1995-96; England A to Bermuda and West Indies 1991-92
Overseas teams played for: Ellerslie, Auckland 1985-87
Cricketers particularly admired: Michael Holding, Richard Hadlee, Malcolm Marshall, Alan Warner, Viv Richards
Other sports followed: Football, boxing
Relaxations: Music and movies, eating
Extras: Played league cricket for Sheffield Works and Sheffield United. Became eligible to play for England in 1987. Took 10 for 137 v West Indies in Port-of-Spain Test, 1989-90. Struck down with chickenpox early in the England tour to Australia 1994-95
Best batting: 51 Derbyshire v Surrey, Derby 1989
Best bowling: 9-57 England v South Africa, The Oval 1994

1996 Season

	M	Inns	NO	Runs	HS	Avge	100s	50s	Ct	St	O	M	Runs	Wkts	Avge	Best	5wI	10wM
Test																		
All First	18	23	7	119	21	7.43	-	-	1	-	639.1	99	2597	82	31.67	6-52	6	2
1-day Int																		
NatWest	1	0	0	0	0	-	-	-	-	-	10	1	49	0	-		-	-
B & H	5	3	2	14	12	14.00	-	-	2	-	41	1	233	5	46.60	3-36	-	
Sunday	2	1	0	42	42	42.00	-	-	-	-	8	0	64	1	64.00	1-64	-	

Career Performances

	M	Inns	NO	Runs	HS	Avge	100s	50s	Ct	St	Balls	Runs	Wkts	Avge	Best	5wI	10wM
Test	36	53	18	224	29	6.40	-	-	5	-	7922	4441	122	36.40	9-57	5	2
All First	213	253	77	1432	51	8.13	-	1	31	-	37826	22486	718	31.31	9-57	26	5
1-day Int	10	5	2	9	4	3.00	-	-	1	-	526	404	16	25.25	3-40	-	
NatWest	18	10	1	29	10 *	3.22	-	-	1	-	1138	752	23	32.69	3-29	-	
B & H	29	14	4	72	15	7.20	-	-	3	-	1638	1204	45	26.75	5-27	1	
Sunday	63	24	10	131	42	9.35	-	-	7	-	2779	2377	86	27.63	4-21	-	

MALLENDER, N. A.   Northamptonshire

Name: Neil Alan Mallender
Role: Right-hand bat, right-arm
fast-medium bowler
Born: 13 August 1961, Kirk Sandall,
Doncaster
Height: 6ft **Weight:** 13st
Nickname: Ghostie
County debut: 1980 (Northamptonshire),
1987 (Somerset)
County cap: 1984 (Northamptonshire),
1987 (Somerset)
Tests: 2
50 wickets in a season: 6
1st-Class 50s: 10
1st-Class 100s: 1
1st-Class 5 w. in innings: 36
1st-Class 10 w. in match: 5
1st-Class catches: 111
One-Day 5 w. in innings: 3
Place in batting averages: 232nd av. 17.28 (1994 129th av. 30.00)
Place in bowling averages: 31st av. 25.11 (1994112th av. 37.62)
Strike rate: 246.00 (career 56.59)

Parents: Ron and Jean
Wife and date of marriage: Caroline, 1 October 1984
Children: Kirstie Jane, 18 May 1988; Dominic James, 21 September 1991
Family links with cricket: Brother Graham used to play good representative cricket before joining the RAF
Education: Beverley Grammar School, East Yorkshire
Qualifications: 7 O-levels, NCA preliminary coaching course
Overseas tours: England YC to West Indies 1979-80
Overseas teams played for: Otago, New Zealand 1983-93; Kalkorai, New Zealand 1983-93
Cricketers particularly admired: Richard Hadlee, Dennis Lillee, Peter Willey
Other sports followed: Golf, rugby league, football
Relaxations: Golf
Extras: Joined Somerset in 1987. Equalled Somerset first-class record for ninth wicket v Sussex at Hove in 1990 – batting with Chris Tavaré. Called up to join England tour squad in New Zealand 1991-92 as cover for injured fast bowlers. On debut for England v Pakistan in 1992 at Headingley, he achieved a new bowling record for a Test debutant at that ground by taking eight wickets in the game. At school opened both the batting and the bowling. Returned to Northamptonshire for 1995 season but was released at the end of the 1996 season
Opinions on cricket: 'Still believe that new ball should be available to be taken after 85 overs in first-class cricket.'
Best batting: 100* Otago v Central Districts, Palmerston North 1991-92
Best bowling: 7-27 Otago v Auckland, Auckland 1984-85

1996 Season

	M	Inns	NO	Runs	HS	Avge	100s	50s	Ct	St	O	M	Runs	Wkts	Avge	Best	5wI	10wM
Test																		
All First	3	3	0	31	13	10.33	-	-	1	-	41	12	137	1	137.00	1-27	-	-
1-day Int																		
NatWest																		
B & H	2	0	0	0	0	-	-	-	-	-	17	1	63	1	63.00	1-30	-	
Sunday	5	1	0	5	5	5.00	-	-	-	-	37	4	158	5	31.60	2-20	-	

Career Performances

	M	Inns	NO	Runs	HS	Avge	100s	50s	Ct	St	Balls	Runs	Wkts	Avge	Best	5wI	10wM
Test	2	3	0	8	4	2.66	-	-	-	-	449	215	10	21.50	5-50	1	-
All First	345	396	122	4709	100 *	17.18	1	10	111	-	53223	24654	937	26.31	7-27	36	5
1-day Int																	
NatWest	31	13	6	63	11 *	9.00	-	-	5	-	1892	889	43	20.67	7-37	1	
B & H	56	26	10	93	16 *	5.81	-	-	14	-	3135	1952	65	30.03	5-53	1	
Sunday	183	82	44	562	31 *	14.78	-	-	31	-	7463	5473	202	27.09	5-34	1	

MARSH, S. A.   Kent

Name: Steven Andrew Marsh
Role: Right-hand bat, wicket-keeper,
county captain
Born: 27 January 1961, Westminster
Height: 5ft 11in **Weight:** 13st
Nickname: Marshy
County debut: 1982
County cap: 1986
Benefit: 1995
1st-Class 50s: 45
1st-Class 100s: 8
1st-Class catches: 557
1st-Class stumpings: 48
Place in batting averages: 228th av. 20.78
(1995 150th av. 27.52)
Parents: Melvyn Graham and Valerie Ann
Wife and date of marriage: Julie, 27
September 1986
Children: Hayley Ann, 15 May 1987;
Christian James Robert, 20 November 1990
Family links with cricket: Father played local cricket for Lordswood. Father-in-law,
Bob Wilson, played for Kent 1954-66
Education: Walderslade Secondary School for Boys; Mid-Kent College of Higher and
Further Education
Qualifications: 6 O-levels, 2 A-levels, OND in Business Studies
Off-season: 'Training and relaxing'
Overseas tours: Fred Rumsey XI to Barbados 1986-87
Overseas teams played for: Avendale CC, Cape Town 1985-86
Cricketers particularly admired: Robin Smith, Graham Cowdrey, Ian Botham
Young players to look out for: Ben Phillips
Other sports followed: Golf
Injuries: Fractured left index finger, missed four weeks
Extras: Appointed Kent vice-captain in 1991. In the match v Middlesex at Lord's in
1991 he held a world record eight catches in an innings and scored 113*. 'Cycling
proficiency'
Opinions on cricket: 'Generally very tedious, brought on by four-day cricket. Unless
of course you watch Kent who will either be bowled out for 150 in a session or score
450 in a day. Now that's what I call cricket. Boredom bores me!'
Best batting: 127 Kent v Essex, Ilford 1996
Best bowling: 2-20 Kent v Warwickshire, Edgbaston 1990

1996 Season

	M	Inns	NO	Runs	HS	Avge	100s	50s	Ct	St	O	M	Runs	Wkts	Avge	Best	5wI	10wM
Test																		
All First	15	24	1	478	127	20.78	1	2	28	6	6	4	5	0	-	-	-	-
1-day Int																		
NatWest	2	1	0	26	26	26.00	-	-	4	1	0.3	0	3	1	3.00	1-3	-	
B & H	6	5	1	81	29	20.25	-	-	10	1								
Sunday	13	10	5	155	32 *	31.00	-	-	5	2								

Career Performances

	M	Inns	NO	Runs	HS	Avge	100s	50s	Ct	St	Balls	Runs	Wkts	Avge	Best	5wI	10wM
Test																	
All First	242	352	57	8175	127	27.71	8	45	557	48	202	240	2	120.00	2-20	-	-
1-day Int																	
NatWest	22	15	3	209	55	17.41	-	1	33	4	3	3	1	3.00	1-3	-	
B & H	51	40	9	505	71	16.29	-	1	61	3							
Sunday	162	117	33	1656	59	19.71	-	4	158	21							

MARTIN, N. D. Middlesex

Name: Neil Donald Martin
Role: Right-hand bat, right-arm fast-medium bowler
Born: 19 August 1979, Enfield
Height: 5ft 10in **Weight:** 11st 7lbs
Nickname: Nelly
County debut: No first-team appearance
Parents: Cliff and Jill
Marital status: Single
Family links with cricket: Father has played club cricket for thirty years at Winchmore Hill and North Mymms
Education: Wheatfields, St Albans; Verulam, St Albans
Qualifications: 9 GCSEs, NCA coaching award
Off-season: Touring Pakistan with England U19 and learning to drive
Overseas tours: England U19 to Pakistan 1996-97
Cricketers particularly admired: Allan Donald, Darren Gough
Other sports followed: Football (Tottenham Hotspur)
Relaxations: Swimming and socialising with friends

MARTIN, P. J.   Lancashire

Name: Peter James Martin
Role: Right-hand bat, right-arm
fast-medium bowler
Born: 15 November 1968, Accrington
Height: 6ft 5in **Weight:** 15st 4lbs
Nickname: Digger, Long John
County debut: 1989
County cap: 1994
Test debut: 1995
Tests: 7
One-Day Internationals: 16
50 wickets in a season: 1
1st-Class 50s: 4
1st-Class 100s: 1
1st-Class 5 w. in innings: 4
1st-Class catches: 30
One-Day 5 w. innings: 1
Place in batting averages: 235th av. 19.85
(1995 208th av. 20.00)

Place in bowling averages: 33rd av. 26.38 (1995 41st av. 26.34)
Strike rate: 58.31 (career 69.11)
Parents: Keith and Catherine Lina
Marital status: Single
Education: Danum School, Doncaster
Qualifications: 6 O-levels, 2 A-levels
Overseas tours: England YC to Australia (Youth World Cup) 1988; 'and various other tours with English Schools and NAYC'; England to South Africa 1995-96, to India and Pakistan (World Cup) 1995-96
Overseas teams played for: Southern Districts, Queensland 1988-89; South Launceston, Tasmania 1989-90; South Canberra, ACT 1990-92
Cricketers particularly admired: 'Too many to mention'
Other sports followed: Football (Manchester United), rugby league (St Helens), golf
Injuries: Ankle ligament damage, missed five to six weeks
Relaxations: Music, painting, golf, cooking, walking, rugby league
Extras: Plays district football and basketball for Doncaster. Played for England A v Sri Lankans 1991. Was originally selected for the England A tour to Pakistan in 1995-96, but was drafted onto the senior tour after the withdrawal of Richard Johnson
Opinions on cricket: 'Should only be six-hour days with 100 overs a day.'
Best batting: 133 Lancashire v Durham, Gateshead Fell 1992
Best bowling: 7-50 Lancashire v Nottinghamshire, Trent Bridge 1996

1996 Season

	M	Inns	NO	Runs	HS	Avge	100s	50s	Ct	St	O	M	Runs	Wkts	Avge	Best	5wI	10wM
Test	1	2	0	27	23	13.50	-	-	-	-	34	10	70	1	70.00	1-70	-	-
All First	13	18	4	278	42	19.85	-	-	1	-	427.4	106	1161	44	26.38	7-50	1	-
1-day Int	4	1	0	6	6	6.00	-	-	1	-	34.2	1	151	6	25.16	3-34	-	
NatWest	5	3	3	11	5 *	-	-	-	-	-	53	12	164	12	13.66	4-36	-	
B & H	6	3	3	8	5 *	-	-	-	3	-	55	5	273	6	45.50	3-43	-	
Sunday	14	5	5	53	35 *	-	-	-	1	-	100	8	502	16	31.37	3-29	-	

Career Performances

	M	Inns	NO	Runs	HS	Avge	100s	50s	Ct	St	Balls	Runs	Wkts	Avge	Best	5wI	10wM
Test	7	11	0	92	29	8.36	-	-	5	-	1338	529	17	31.11	4-60	-	-
All First	117	135	35	2035	133	20.35	1	4	30	-	19559	9072	283	32.05	7-50	4	-
1-day Int	16	10	6	33	6	8.25	-	-	1	-	838	610	25	24.40	4-44	-	
NatWest	12	4	3	27	16	27.00	-	-	1	-	696	383	22	17.40	4-36	-	
B & H	14	4	4	18	10 *	-	-	-	4	-	762	522	14	37.28	3-43	-	
Sunday	65	20	13	132	35 *	18.85	-	-	9	-	2542	1949	71	27.45	5-32	1	

MARTIN-JENKINS, R. S. C.   Sussex

Name: Robin Simon Christopher Martin-Jenkins
Role: Right-hand bat, right-arm medium-fast bowler
Born: 28 October 1975, Guildford
Height: 6ft 6in **Weight:** 13st 7lbs
Nickname: Tucker, Cérise, Crazy MF
County debut: 1995
1st-Class 50s: 1
Strike rate: 348.00 (career 366.00)
Parents: Christopher and Judy
Marital status: Single
Family links with cricket: Father is *Daily Telegraph* cricket correspondent
Education: Cranleigh Prep School, Surrey; Radley College, Oxon; Durham University
Qualifications: 10 GCSEs, 3 A-levels, 1 AS-level, Grade 3 bassoon
Off-season: University and Young Cricketers tour to Sri Lanka
Overseas tours: Radley College to Barbados 1992
Overseas teams played for: Lima, Peru 1995
Cricketers particularly admired: Robin Smith, Angus Fraser, Steve Waugh

Young players to look out for: Raj Rao, Jim Chaplin
Other sports followed: Fives, hockey, tennis, skiing, football (Liverpool FC)
Injuries: Glandular fever, missed two months
Relaxations: Watching television ('Pink Panther, James Bond'), listening to music
Opinions on cricket: 'Tea should definitely be longer – the time could be added on to the end of the day's play. This would eradicate the dizzy spell that bowlers like me suffer from after tea, as the smeggy mix of undigested sandwiches and yoghurt react with one's body.'
Best batting: 50 Sussex v Northamptonshire, Hove 1995
Best bowling: 1-26 Sussex v Cambridge University, Hove 1996

1996 Season

	M	Inns	NO	Runs	HS	Avge	100s	50s	Ct	St	O	M	Runs	Wkts	Avge	Best	5wI	10wM
Test																		
All First	2	1	0	20	20	20.00	-	-	-	-	58	13	158	1	158.00	1-26	-	-
1-day Int																		
NatWest																		
B & H	3	3	0	16	12	5.33	-	-	-	-	27.4	0	136	4	34.00	3-46	-	
Sunday	1	1	0	0	0	0.00	-	-	-	-	1	0	6	0	-	-	-	

Career Performances

	M	Inns	NO	Runs	HS	Avge	100s	50s	Ct	St	Balls	Runs	Wkts	Avge	Best	5wI	10wM
Test																	
All First	4	3	1	70	50	35.00	-	1	-	-	366	169	1	169.00	1-26	-	-
1-day Int																	
NatWest																	
B & H	3	3	0	16	12	5.33	-	-	-	-	166	136	4	34.00	3-46	-	
Sunday	10	6	1	12	10	2.40	-	-	-	-	324	292	5	58.40	2-41	-	

MARU, R. J.   Hampshire

Name: Rajesh Jamnadass Maru
Role: Right-hand bat, slow left-arm bowler, close fielder
Born: 28 October 1962, Nairobi, Kenya
Height: 5ft 6in **Weight:** 11st
Nickname: Raj
County debut: 1980 (Middlesex), 1984 (Hampshire)
County cap: 1986 (Hampshire)
50 wickets in a season: 4
1st-Class 50s: 7
1st-Class 5 w. in innings: 15
1st-Class 10 w. in match: 1

1st-Class catches: 246
Place in batting averages: 198th av. 25.25
Place in bowling averages: 116th av. 40.77
Strike rate: 102.11 (career 74.68)
Parents: Jamnadass and Prabhavati
Wife and date of marriage: Amanda Jane,
21 September 1991
Children: Christopher Patrick, 21 January
1993; Daniel James, 7 January 1996
Family links with cricket: Father played in
Kenya and in England for North London
Polytechnic. Brother Pradip played for
Wembley in the Middlesex League and has
played for Middlesex 2nd XI, Middlesex U19
and for Middlesex Colts & Schools

Education: Rooks Heath High School,
Harrow; Pinner Sixth Form College
Qualifications: NCA advanced coach
Career outside cricket: Cricket coach
Off-season: Coaching for Hampshire CCC
Overseas tours: England YC South to Canada 1979; England YC to West Indies
1979-80; Middlesex to Zimbabwe 1980; Hampshire to Barbados 1987,1988,1990;
Hampshire to Dubai 1989; Barbican International XI to Dubai 1981; MCC to Leeward
Islands 1992, to Far East 1995
Overseas teams played for: Marlborough CA, Blenheim, New Zealand 1985-87
Cricketers particularly admired: David Gower, Bishen Bedi, Richard Hadlee, Phil
Edmonds, John Emburey, Malcolm Marshall, Gordon Greenidge
Young players to look out for: Jason Laney
Other sports followed: Football, rugby (Wasps and England), 'would watch any sport'
Injuries: Hamstring, missed two to three weeks
Relaxations: Spending time with wife and sons, DIY at home
Extras: Played for Middlesex 1980-83; reached 500 first-class wickets in 1995
Opinions on cricket: 'Four-day cricket has been good for the game, but the standard of
wickets have to change. You have to produce good wickets to make the game last the
full four days, or bring back three-day cricket with uncovered pitches.'
Best batting: 74 Hampshire v Gloucestershire, Gloucester 1988
Best bowling: 8-41 Hampshire v Kent, Southampton 1989

---

59. Which was the first Test series of the 1980s
where Australia regained The Ashes?

	M	Inns	NO	Runs	HS	Avge	100s	50s	Ct	St	O	M	Runs	Wkts	Avge	Best	5wI	10wM
Test																		
All First	11	17	5	303	55 *	25.25	-	1	17	-	306.2	101	734	18	40.77	3-50	-	-
1-day Int																		
NatWest																		
B & H	1	1	1	6	6 *	-	-	-	-	-	10	0	43	2	21.50	2-43	-	
Sunday	7	4	3	18	11	18.00	-	-	3	-	43	2	223	2	111.50	2-25	-	

Career Performances

	M	Inns	NO	Runs	HS	Avge	100s	50s	Ct	St	Balls	Runs	Wkts	Avge	Best	5wI	10wM
Test																	
All First	223	225	56	2871	74	16.98	-	7	246	-	38988	17211	522	32.97	8-41	15	1
1-day Int																	
NatWest	14	6	2	44	22	11.00	-	-	12	-	882	531	13	40.84	3-30	-	
B & H	12	4	1	19	9	6.33	-	-	5	-	591	397	12	33.08	3-46	-	
Sunday	64	28	17	169	33 *	15.36	-	-	22	-	2257	1961	48	40.85	3-30	-	

MASCARENHAS, D. A.   Hampshire

Name: Dimitri Adrian Mascarenhas
Role: Right-hand bat, right-arm
medium bowler
Born: 30 October 1977, Chiswick, London
Height: 6ft 2in **Weight:** 11st 7lbs
Nickname: Aussie, Dim, Dimmy, Jeanie
County debut: 1996
1st-Class 5 w. innings: 1
Place in bowling averages: 8th av. 18.56
Strike rate: (career 34.50)
Parents: Malik and Pauline
Marital status: Single
Family links with cricket: Uncle played in
Sri Lanka
Education: Our Lady's Primary, Melbourne;
Trinity College, Perth
Off-season: Playing club cricket in Perth,
Western Australia
Overseas teams played for: Melville CC,
Perth 1991-96

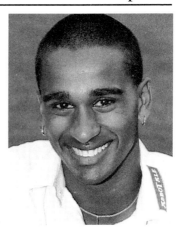

Cricketers particularly admired: Viv Richards, Malcolm Marshall, Dean Jones
Young players to look out for: Ben Hollioake, Jason Laney, Giles White

Other sports followed: Aussie rules (Collingwood)
Relaxations: Golf, tennis and 'occasionally a quiet beer'
Extras: Played for Western Australia at U17 level (as captain) and at U19 level
Opinions on cricket: 'Haven't been in the game long enough to comment'
Best batting: 14 Hampshire v Kent, Canterbury 1996
Best bowling: 6-88 Hampshire v Glamorgan, Southampton 1996

1996 Season

	M	Inns	NO	Runs	HS	Avge	100s	50s	Ct	St	O	M	Runs	Wkts	Avge	Best	5wI	10wM
Test																		
All First	2	3	0	24	14	8.00	-	-	-	-	92	21	297	16	18.56	6-88	1	-
1-day Int																		
NatWest																		
B & H																		
Sunday	3	2	1	7	7 *	7.00	-	-	1	-	21.2	0	124	5	24.80	2-34	-	

Career Performances

	M	Inns	NO	Runs	HS	Avge	100s	50s	Ct	St	Balls	Runs	Wkts	Avge	Best	5wI	10wM
Test																	
All First	2	3	0	24	14	8.00	-	-	-	-	552	297	16	18.56	6-88	1	-
1-day Int																	
NatWest																	
B & H																	
Sunday	3	2	1	7	7 *	7.00	-	-	1	-	128	124	5	24.80	2-34	-	

MASON, T. J. Leicestershire

Name: Timothy James Mason
Role: Right-hand bat, right-arm
off-spin bowler
Born: 12 April 1975, Leicester
Height: 5ft 8in **Weight:** 10st 4lbs
Nickname: Perry, Biffa, Stone
County debut: 1994
1st-Class catches: 3
Parents: Phillip John and Anthea Jane
Marital status: Single
Family links with cricket: Father plays club
cricket and is manager of Leicestershire
Schools U11
Education: Brookvale High School,
Leicester; Denstone College
Qualifications: 9 GCSEs, 3 A-levels
Career outside cricket: Undecided
Off-season: Coaching and playing in the
Western Transvaal in South Africa
Overseas tours: Denstone College to South Africa 1993; England U19 to Sri Lanka 1993-94; Westgold CC to Northern Transvaal 1996
Overseas teams played for: Eastern Freestate, South Africa 1994-95; Westgold CC, Western Transvaal 1995-97
Cricketers particularly admired: Allan Lamb, Malcolm Marshall, Jon Dakin, Darren 'Roasting' Maddy
Young players to look out for: Darren Maddy, Jon Dakin 'and of course myself'
Other sports followed: Rugby union (Leicester Tigers), football (Leicester City)
Injuries: Knee problem, missed two weeks
Relaxations: Going out with friends and girlfriend, Nicole. Listening to music
Extras: Captained Leicestershire Schools at all age levels. 1992 *Daily Telegraph* U19 Midlands Bowler of the Year; 1993 *Daily Telegraph* U19 National Bowler of the Year; 1993 Gray-Nicolls Outstanding Schoolboy Player of the Year. Dislocated shoulder prevented him from going on England U18 tour to South Africa 1992-93. Played in the winning Bain Hogg team in 1996
Opinions on cricket: 'Great game, but 2nd XI grounds have to be better. This will definitely make young players better – especially young bowlers.'
Best batting: 3 Leicestershire v Essex, Leicester 1994
Best bowling: 1-22 Leicestershire v Essex, Leicester 1994

1996 Season

	M	Inns	NO	Runs	HS	Avge	100s	50s	Ct	St	O	M	Runs	Wkts	Avge	Best	5wl	10wM
Test																		
All First																		
1-day Int																		
NatWest																		
B & H	3	2	1	26	19	26.00	-	-	1	-	23	0	97	3	32.33	2-35	-	
Sunday	1	1	0	7	7	7.00	-	-	-	-	4	0	29	0	-	-	-	

Career Performances

	M	Inns	NO	Runs	HS	Avge	100s	50s	Ct	St	Balls	Runs	Wkts	Avge	Best	5wl	10wM
Test																	
All First	2	1	0	3	3	3.00	-	-	3	-	192	101	1	101.00	1-22	-	-
1-day Int																	
NatWest	2	1	0	5	5	5.00	-	-	3	-	144	72	0	-	-	-	
B & H	4	3	2	31	19	31.00	-	-	1	-	204	131	4	32.75	2-35	-	
Sunday	12	4	1	29	17 *	9.66	-	-	1	-	438	388	6	64.66	2-41	-	

MAY, M. R.   Derbyshire

Name: Michael Robert May
Role: Right-hand bat, off-spin bowler
Born: 22 July 1971, Chesterfield
Height: 5ft 9in **Weight:** 14st
Nickname: Hazey, Boonie, Maggie
County debut: 1996
1st-Class 50s: 1
1st-Class catches: 1
Parents: Mick and Christine
Wife and date of marriage: Sasha May, 14 January 1996
Family links with cricket: Brother Paul plays for 2nd XI and Colts for Derbyshire
Education: Duckmanton Primary School; The Bolsover School; North East Derbyshire College
Qualifications: City and Guilds in Recreation and Leisure, NCA cricket coach
Off-season: Playing and coaching in Victoria, Australia
Overseas teams played for: Marist, New Zealand 1988-89; Johannesburg Municipals 1990-92; Sandringham CC, Melbourne 1994-96; St Kilda CC 1996-97

Cricketers particularly admired: Steve Waugh, Ian Botham, Peter Kirsten, Allan Border
Young players to look out for: Andrew Harris, Shawn Craig
Other sports followed: Aussie rules (Essendon) and football (Nottingham Forest)
Relaxations: Watching most sports, reading, music, specnding time with my wife and family
Opinions on cricket: 'Far too much emphasis on one-day cricket in domestic and international cricket.'
Best batting: 63* Derbyshire v South Africa A 1996

1996 Season

	M	Inns	NO	Runs	HS	Avge	100s	50s	Ct	St	O	M	Runs	Wkts	Avge	Best	5wI	10wM
Test																		
All First	3	4	2	160	63 *	80.00	-	1	1	-	3	0	19	0	-	-	-	-
1-day Int																		
NatWest																		
B & H																		
Sunday																		

Career Performances

	M	Inns	NO	Runs	HS	Avge	100s	50s	Ct	St	Balls	Runs	Wkts	Avge	Best	5wI	10wM
Test																		
All First	3	4	2	160	63 *	80.00	-	1	1	-	18	19	0	-	-	-	-
1-day Int																		
NatWest																		
B & H																		
Sunday																		

MAYNARD, M. P.   Glamorgan

Name: Matthew Peter Maynard
Role: Right-hand bat, right-arm medium 'declaration' bowler, cover fielder
Born: 21 March 1966, Oldham, Lancashire
Height: 5ft 11in **Weight:** 13st
Nickname: Ollie
County debut: 1985
County cap: 1987
Benefit: 1996
Test debut: 1988
Tests: 4
One-Day Internationals: 10
1000 runs in a season: 10

1st-Class 50s: 94
1st-Class 100s: 40
1st-Class 200s: 3
1st-Class catches: 251
1st-Class stumpings: 5
One-Day 100s: 9
Place in batting averages: 10th av. 61.92
(1995 44th av. 45.42)
Strike rate: (career 144.16)
Parents: Ken (deceased) and Pat
Wife and date of marriage: Susan, 27
September 1986
Children: Tom, 25 March 1989; Ceri Lloyd,
5 August 1993
Family links with cricket: Father played for
many years for Duckinfield. Brother Charles
plays for St Fagans
Education: Ysgol David Hughes, Menai
Bridge, Anglesey
Qualifications: Cricket coach
Career outside cricket: Marketing executive
Off-season: Playing for Otago in New Zealand
Overseas tours: North Wales XI to Barbados 1982; Glamorgan to Barbados 1982, to
South Africa 1993; unofficial England XI to South Africa 1989-90; HKCC (Australia)
to Bangkok and Hong Kong, 1990; England VI to Hong Kong Sixes 1992 and 1994;
England to West Indies 1993-94
Overseas teams played for: St Joseph's, Whakatane, New Zealand 1986-88;
Gosnells, Perth, Western Australia 1988-89; Papakura and Northern Districts, New
Zealand 1990-92; Morrinsville College and Northern Districts 1991-92; Otago, New
Zealand 1996-97
Cricketers particularly admired: Ian Botham, Viv Richards, David Gower
Young players to look out for: Alun Evans, Dean Cosker, Jason Laney
Other sports followed: Football (Manchester City), golf and squash
Relaxations: Spending time with my wife and family and relaxing
Extras: Scored century on first-class debut v Yorkshire at Swansea in 1985, when he
became the youngest centurion for Glamorgan, and scored 1000 runs in first full season.
In 1987 scored the fastest ever 50 for Glamorgan (14 mins) v Yorkshire and was
youngest player to be awarded Glamorgan cap. Voted Young Cricketer of the Year 1988
by the Cricket Writers' Club. Banned from Test cricket for five years for joining 1989-
90 tour of South Africa, ban remitted 1992. Scored 987 runs in July 1991, including a
century in each innings v Gloucestershire at Cheltenham. Captained Glamorgan for most
of 1992 in Alan Butcher's absence. Second child was born on the morning of the fifth
Test against Australia at Edgbaston 1993 – he had a daughter and a duck on the same
day. Glamorgan's captain for the 1996 season. Awarded benefit for 1996
Opinions on cricket: 'Good to see four-day cricket starting on a Wednesday to lose the

Sunday sandwich. Counties should reduce the size of playing staffs, but increase the salaries of the retained players.'

Best batting: 243 Glamorgan v Hampshire, Southampton 1991

Best bowling: 3-21 Glamorgan v Oxford University, The Parks 1987

1996 Season

	M	Inns	NO	Runs	HS	Avge	100s	50s	Ct	St	O	M	Runs	Wkts	Avge	Best	5wI	10wM
Test																		
All First	17	30	4	1610	214	61.92	6	6	20	-	7.3	4	7	0	-	-	-	-
1-day Int	5	5	0	94	41	18.80	-	-	1	-								
NatWest	1	1	0	4	4	4.00	-	-	-	-								
B & H	6	6	3	396	151 *	132.00	2	1	3	-								
Sunday	14	13	0	363	87	27.92	-	2	10	-	0.2	0	2	0	-	-	-	-

Career Performances

	M	Inns	NO	Runs	HS	Avge	100s	50s	Ct	St	Balls	Runs	Wkts	Avge	Best	5wI	10wM
Test	4	8	0	87	35	10.87	-	-	3	-							
All First	266	442	44	17216	243	43.25	40	94	251	5	865	704	6	117.33	3-21	-	-
1-day Int	10	10	1	153	41	17.00	-	-	2	-							
NatWest	30	29	2	1215	151 *	45.00	2	10	10	-							
B & H	42	42	6	1631	151 *	45.30	4	7	13	-	24	32	0	-	-	-	-
Sunday	163	155	11	4301	122 *	29.86	3	29	60	-	18	29	0	-	-	-	-

McCAGUE, M. J.   Kent

Name: Martin John McCague

Role: Right-hand bat, right-arm fast bowler

Born: 24 May 1969, Larne, Northern Ireland

Height: 6ft 5in **Weight:** 17st

Nickname: Stinger, Pigsy

County debut: 1991

County cap: 1992

Test debut: 1993

Tests: 3

50 wickets in season: 4

1st-Class 50s: 3

1st-Class 5 w. in innings: 20

1st-Class 10 w. in match: 2

1st-Class catches: 55

One-Day 5 w. in innings: 3

Place in batting averages: 239th av. 18.78 (1995 221st av. 18.10)

Place in bowling averages: 23rd av. 24.96 (1995 62nd av. 29.14)
Strike rate: 46.57 (career 50.25)
Parents: Mal and Mary
Marital status: Single
Education: Hedland Senior High School
Qualifications: Electrician
Overseas tours: England A to South Africa 1993-94; England to Australia 1994-95
Overseas teams played for: Western Australia 1990-91
Cricketers particularly admired: Dennis Lillee, Curtly Ambrose
Other sports followed: Football (Crystal Palace and Gillingham)
Injuries: Side strain and knee strain, missed total of three weeks
Relaxations: Golf and snooker
Opinions on cricket: 'Two division championship. Pressure on the teams to perform all year, but who decides which teams start in which divisions?'
Best batting: 63* Kent v Surrey, The Oval 1996
Best bowling: 9-86 Kent v Derbyshire, Derby 1994

1996 Season

	M	Inns	NO	Runs	HS	Avge	100s	50s	Ct	St	O	M	Runs	Wkts	Avge	Best	5wl	10wM
Test																		
All First	18	26	7	357	63 *	18.78	-	1	10	-	590	120	1897	76	24.96	6-51	3	-
1-day Int																		
NatWest	1	1	1	25	25 *	-	-	-	-	-	12	1	49	3	16.33	3-49	-	
B & H	6	4	0	22	17	5.50	-	-	1	-	50.4	4	267	4	66.75	2-30	-	
Sunday	13	7	0	37	16	5.28	-	-	3	-	71	0	457	9	50.77	2-34	-	

Career Performances

	M	Inns	NO	Runs	HS	Avge	100s	50s	Ct	St	Balls	Runs	Wkts	Avge	Best	5wl	10wM
Test	3	5	0	21	11	4.20	-	-	1	-	593	390	6	65.00	4-121	-	-
All First	95	129	30	1501	63 *	15.16	-	3	55	-	17287	9244	344	26.87	9-86	20	2
1-day Int																	
NatWest	11	9	5	96	31 *	24.00	-	-	2	-	642	429	21	20.42	5-26	1	
B & H	22	15	5	145	30	14.50	-	-	7	-	1130	860	29	29.65	5-43	1	
Sunday	65	34	12	211	22 *	9.59	-	-	12	-	2566	2257	95	23.75	5-40	1	

60. Which bowler played only one Test in the 1985 series, becoming the first Yorkshire player to be selected for England since the retirement of Geoff Boycott three years earlier?

McDONALD, S. Warwickshire

Name: Stephen McDonald
Role: Right-hand bat, off-spin bowler
Born: 2 October 1974, Birmingham
Height: 5ft 10in **Weight:** 12st 7lbs
Nickname: Macca, Big Mac,
McDingleburger
County debut: No first-team appearance
Parents: Frank McDonald and Patricia Snookes
Marital status: Single
Education: Uplands Junior School,
Smethwick; Bristnall Hall High School,
Oldbury; Rowley Regis College, Blackheath
Qualifications: 9 GCSEs, 1 A-level, NCA
Junior Cricket Coach
Off-season: Playing and coaching in George,
South Africa
Overseas tours: Warwickshire U19 to South
Africa 1992
Overseas teams played for: George, South
Africa 1996-97
Cricketers particularly admired: David Gower, Tim May
Young players to look out for: Anurag Singh, Darren Altree
Other sports followed: Football (WBA)
Injuries: Back spasm, out for two weeks
Relaxations: Drinking and socialising
Extras: NCA England U14, U15. Bull Development U19. Awarded WSCA colours six
years running
Opinions on cricket: 'I believe the season is too hectic and puts a lot of wear and tear
on the body, maybe the season could be extended or maybe the teams split into two
divisions so that there would be fewer games played. This may also bring more money
into the game.'

McGRATH, A. Yorkshire

Name: Anthony McGrath
Role: Right-hand bat, off-spin bowler
Born: 6 October 1975, Bradford
Height: 6ft 2in **Weight:** 13st 5lbs
Nickname: Mags, Gripper

County debut: 1995
1st-Class 50s: 6
1st-Class 100s: 3
1st-Class catches: 24
Place in batting averages: 144th av. 32.22
(1996 144th av. 28.00)
Parents: Terry and Kath
Marital status: Single
Family links with cricket: Brother Dermot
plays league cricket for East Brierley
Education: St Winefrides; St Blaise;
Yorkshire Martyrs Collegiate School
Qualifications: 9 GCSEs, BTEC in Leisure
Studies
Off-season: England A tour to Australia
Overseas tours: England U19 to West Indies
1994-95; England A to Pakistan 1995-96, to
Australia 1996-97

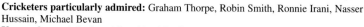

Cricketers particularly admired: Graham Thorpe, Robin Smith, Ronnie Irani, Nasser
Hussain, Michael Bevan
Young players to look out for: Alex Morris
Other sports followed: Football (Manchester United)
Injuries: Gout, missed one game
Relaxations: Watching other sports, listening to music, socialising with friends
Extras: Captained Yorkshire Schools U13, U14, U15 and U16; captained English
Schools U17. Bradford League Young Cricketer of the Year 1992 and 1993. Played for
England U17, and for England U19 in home series against India 1994. Appeared as 12th
man for England in the First Test against West Indies at Headingley in 1995. Scored his
maiden first-class century on the England A tour to Pakistan
Opinions on cricket: 'Too many games are played during the county season. A two
division system would eradicate the problem – less games would be played allowing
more time between games. Also, with promotion and relegation, there would be interest
till the end of the season.'
Best batting: 137 Yorkshire v Hampshire, Harrogate 1996

1996 Season

	M	Inns	NO	Runs	HS	Avge	100s	50s	Ct	St	O	M	Runs	Wkts	Avge	Best	5wI	10wM
Test																		
All First	19	33	2	999	137	32.22	2	5	12	-	7	0	41	0	-	-	-	-
1-day Int																		
NatWest	4	4	1	80	34	26.66	-	-	3	-								
B & H	6	5	0	106	43	21.20	-	-	-	-	2	0	10	2	5.00	2-10	-	
Sunday	16	15	3	255	69	21.25	-	1	3	-								

Career Performances

	M	Inns	NO	Runs	HS	Avge	100s	50s	Ct	St	Balls	Runs	Wkts	Avge	Best	5wl	10wM
Test																	
All First	31	54	3	1552	137	30.43	3	6	24	-	102	64	0	-	-	-	-
1-day Int																	
NatWest	4	4	1	80	34	26.66	-	-	3	-							
B & H	7	6	0	108	43	18.00	-	-	-	-	12	10	2	5.00	2-10	-	
Sunday	18	16	3	327	72	25.15	-	2	5	-							

McKEOWN, P. C.   Lancashire

Name: Patrick Christopher McKeown
Role: Right-hand bat
Born: 1 June 1976, Liverpool
Height: 6ft 3in **Weight:** 13st
Nickname: Paddy
County debut: 1996
1st-Class 50s: 1
1st-Class catches: 1
Parents: Paddy and Cathy
Marital status: Single
Education: St Mary's College, Crosby;
Rossall School (Blackpool)
Qualifications: 7 GCSEs, 3 A-levels
Off-season: Playing grade cricket in Perth
Overseas tours: Rossall School to Australia
1994-95
Overseas teams played for: Subiaco-Floriat,
Perth, Australia 1995-96
Cricketers particularly admired: Graeme Hick and Neil Fairbrother
Other sports followed: Football (Liverpool)
Relaxations: 'Playing most sports, especially football and rugby. I enjoy spending
time on the golf course.'
Extras: Represented England Schools U19, and U18 versus India. Played for Development
of Excellence U19, National Cricket Association U19, Headmasters' Conference U19.
Awarded 2nd XI cap in 1996
Opinions on cricket: 'Tea should be 30 minutes. Players should be on 12-month
contracts to give them more security during the winter.'
Best batting: 64 Lancashire v Warwickshire, Edgbaston 1996

1996 Season

	M	Inns	NO	Runs	HS	Avge	100s	50s	Ct	St	O	M	Runs	Wkts	Avge	Best	5wI	10wM
Test																		
All First	2	2	0	73	64	36.50	-	1	1	-								
1-day Int																		
NatWest																		
B & H																		
Sunday	5	5	0	117	69	23.40	-	1	3	-								

Career Performances

	M	Inns	NO	Runs	HS	Avge	100s	50s	Ct	St	Balls	Runs	Wkts	Avge	Best	5wI	10wM
Test																	
All First	2	2	0	73	64	36.50	-	1	1	-							
1-day Int																	
NatWest																	
B & H																	
Sunday	5	5	0	117	69	23.40	-	1	3	-							

METCALFE, A. A.　　　　Nottinghamshire

Name: Ashley Anthony Metcalfe
Role: Right-hand opening bat,
off-spin bowler
Born: 25 December 1963, Horsforth, Leeds
Height: 5ft 9½in **Weight:** 11st 7lbs
County debut: 1983 (Yorkshire), 1996
(Nottinghamshire)
County cap: 1986 (Yorkshire)
Benefit: 1995
1000 runs in a season: 6
1st-Class 50s: 55
1st-Class 100s: 26
1st-Class 200s: 1
1st-Class catches: 78
One-Day 100s: 4
Place in batting averages: 114th av. 35.04
Strike rate: (career 107.00)
Parents: Tony and Ann
Wife and date of marriage: Diane, 20 April
1986
Children: Zoë, 18 July 1990; Amy, 22 August 1993
Family links with cricket: Father played in local league; father-in-law Ray

389

Illingworth (Yorkshire and England)
Education: Ladderbanks Middle School; Bradford Grammar School; University College, London
Qualifications: 9 O-levels, 3 A-levels, NCA coaching certificate
Career outside cricket: 'Metcalfe & Sidebottom Associates – sports promotion company'
Overseas teams played for: Orange Free State 1988-89
Cricketers particularly admired: Barry Richards, Doug Padgett, Don Wilson, Arnie Sidebottom, Pete Hartley, Paul Jarvis
Other sports followed: Most, particularly golf
Relaxations: 'Relaxing at home with my family'
Extras: Making 122 on first-class debut v Nottinghamshire at Park Avenue in 1983 he became the youngest Yorkshire player to achieve the feat and recorded the highest debut score by a Yorkshireman. Reached 2000 runs for the season in the last match of 1990 with 194* and 107 v Nottinghamshire at Trent Bridge. Released by Yorkshire at the end of the 1995 season and signed for Nottinghamshire for the 1996 season
Best batting: 216* Yorkshire v Middlesex, Headingley 1988
Best bowling: 2-18 Yorkshire v Warwickshire, Scarborough 1987

1996 Season

	M	Inns	NO	Runs	HS	Avge	100s	50s	Ct	St	O	M	Runs	Wkts	Avge	Best	5wI	10wM
Test																		
All First	12	22	0	771	128	35.04	1	3	4	-								
1-day Int																		
NatWest	1	1	0	28	28	28.00	-	-	1	-								
B & H	4	4	0	161	66	40.25	-	2	3	-								
Sunday	12	9	3	225	65	37.50	-	1	4	-								

Career Performances

	M	Inns	NO	Runs	HS	Avge	100s	50s	Ct	St	Balls	Runs	Wkts	Avge	Best	5wI	10wM
Test																	
All First	206	355	20	11663	216 *	34.81	26	55	78	-	428	362	4	90.50	2-18	-	-
1-day Int																	
NatWest	21	21	3	742	127 *	41.22	1	5	5	-	42	44	2	22.00	2-44	-	
B & H	35	35	4	1438	114	46.38	1	10	11	-							
Sunday	152	144	10	3754	116	28.01	2	24	37	-							

METSON, C. P. Glamorgan

Name: Colin Peter Metson
Role: Right-hand bat, wicket-keeper
Born: 2 July 1963, Cuffley, Herts
Height: 5ft 5in **Weight:** 10st 10lbs
Nickname: Meto, Stumpie
County debut: 1981 (Middlesex),
1987 (Glamorgan)
County cap: 1987 (Glamorgan)
1st-Class 50s: 7
1st-Class catches: 557
1st-Class stumpings: 50
Place in batting averages: 304th av. 7.57
(1995 223rd av. 18.07)
Parents: Denis Alwyn and Jean Mary
Wife and date of marriage:
Stephanie Leslie Astrid, 13 October 1991
Family links with cricket: Father captained
Winchmore Hill
Education: Stanborough School, Welwyn
Garden City; Enfield Grammar School; Durham University
Qualifications: 10 O-levels, 5 A-levels, BA (Hons) Economic History, advanced
cricket coach
Career outside cricket: Project co-ordinator with Castle Services
Off-season: Preparing for benefit and Castle Services
Overseas tours: MCC to Bangladesh 1996
Overseas teams played for: Payneham, Adelaide 1986-88; Rostrevor Old Boys,
Adelaide 1987-91
Cricketers particularly admired: Bob Taylor, Rod Marsh, Ian Botham, Mike Gatting
Other sports followed: Football (Tottenham Hotspur FC), golf, rugby (Ebbw Vale
RFC)
Injuries: Trapped nerve behind knee, missed two weeks
Relaxations: Watching sport, videos, good wine, port
Extras: Played for England YC v India YC 1981 and was voted Young Wicket-keeper
of the Year. In 1984 captained Durham University, losing finalists in UAU competition.
Left Middlesex at end of 1986 season. Holds the Glamorgan record for most catches in
an innings (7) and match (9). Played 160 consecutive Championship matches for
Glamorgan, 1987-94. Wombwell Cricket Lovers' Society Wicket-keeper of the Year
1993. Received Man of the Match Award for the first time in his career in the Nat West
quarter-final against Middlesex in 1995, after nine years in the game
Opinions on cricket: 'Cricket must find ways to market itself better, and must give the
sponsors value for money. The 25-point deduction regarding "unfit" pitches should be

more widely used so that the counties will prepare the best possible pitches. Counties should take more interest in the winter and future careers of its players (regarding placements, qualifications, etc). Use of the third umpire in semi-finals as well as the finals. All players should fully support the "new" Professional Cricketers' Association and work together to improve playing standards. The county championship should be split into two equal divisions, similar to American football with the top two teams playing off for the title.'

Best batting: 96 Middlesex v Gloucestershire, Uxbridge 1984

1996 Season

	M	Inns	NO	Runs	HS	Avge	100s	50s	Ct	St	O	M	Runs	Wkts	Avge	Best	5wI	10wM
Test																		
All First	8	11	4	53	18 *	7.57	-	-	14	2								
1-day Int																		
NatWest	1	1	0	1	1	1.00	-	-	1	-								
B & H	6	1	0	4	4	4.00	-	-	10	1								
Sunday	6	2	0	0	0	0.00	-	-	4	1								

Career Performances

	M	Inns	NO	Runs	HS	Avge	100s	50s	Ct	St	Balls	Runs	Wkts	Avge	Best	5wI	10wM
Test																	
All First	230	301	71	4059	96	17.64	-	7	557	50	6	0	0	-	-	-	-
1-day Int																	
NatWest	28	16	2	90	21	6.42	-	-	27	2							
B & H	38	22	4	189	23	10.50	-	-	31	5							
Sunday	156	87	42	647	30 *	14.37	-	-	153	47							

MIKE, G. W.   Nottinghamshire

Name: Gregory Wentworth Mike
Role: Right-hand bat, right-arm
medium-fast bowler
Born: 14 July 1966, Nottingham
Height: 6ft 1in **Weight:** 14st
Nickname: Wenters
County debut: 1989
1st-Class 50s: 6
1st-Class 5 w. in innings: 2
1st-Class catches: 13
Place in batting averages: (1995 171st av. 23.83)
Strike rate: 110.75 (career 65.68)
Parents: Clinton and Kathleen

Marital status: Single
Family links with cricket: Father played
Education: Claremont Comprehensive; Basford College
Qualifications: 5 CSEs, 2 O-levels
Career outside cricket: Youth worker
Overseas tours: Nottinghamshire to Barbados 1987, 1988, 1991
Overseas teams played for: Geelong City, Australia 1990-91; Lancaster Park, New Zealand 1992-93
Cricketers particularly admired: Viv Richards, Ian Botham, Richard Hadlee
Other sports followed: All sports
Relaxations: Listening to music (swing beat, soul and reggae music)
Extras: Released by Notts at the end of the 1996 season
Opinions on cricket: 'Great game.'
Best batting: 66* Nottinghamshire v Oxford University, The Parks 1995
Best bowling: 5-44 Nottinghamshire v Yorkshire, Middlesbrough 1994

1996 Season

	M	Inns	NO	Runs	HS	Avge	100s	50s	Ct	St	O	M	Runs	Wkts	Avge	Best	5wI	10wM
Test																		
All First	3	5	1	25	13 *	6.25	-	-	2	-	73.5	13	312	4	78.00	2-34	-	-
1-day Int																		
NatWest																		
B & H	1	1	1	1	1 *	-	-	-	-	-	8	3	33	1	33.00	1-33	-	
Sunday																		

Career Performances

	M	Inns	NO	Runs	HS	Avge	100s	50s	Ct	St	Balls	Runs	Wkts	Avge	Best	5wI	10wM
Test																	
All First	43	66	12	1019	66 *	18.87	-	6	13	-	5715	3420	87	39.31	5-44	2	-
1-day Int																	
NatWest	2	2	1	8	5 *	8.00	-	-	-	-	108	84	1	84.00	1-71	-	
B & H	11	6	3	65	25 *	21.66	-	-	3	-	633	463	13	35.61	4-44	-	
Sunday	54	35	7	301	51 *	10.75	-	1	11	-	2156	2001	60	33.35	4-41	-	

MILBURN, S. M. Hampshire

Name: Stuart Mark Milburn
Role: Right-hand bat, right-arm
medium-fast bowler
Born: 29 September 1972, Harrogate
Height: 6ft 1in **Weight:** 13st
Nickname: Miller, Mick
County debut: 1992 (Yorkshire), 1996
(Hampshire)
1st-Class 50s: 1
Place in batting averages: 245th av. 18.00
Place in bowling averages: 149th av. 55.23
(1995 11th av. 20.40)
Strike rate: 90.70 (career 76.67)
Parents: Ken and Pam
Wife and date of marriage: Joanne, 30
September 1995
Education: Upper Nidderdale High School,
Pateley Bridge, Harrogate
Qualifications: 7 GCSEs, Diploma in Catering
Overseas teams played for: Somerset West, South Africa 1992-93
Cricketers particularly admired: Ian Botham, Richard Hadlee, Malcolm Marshall
Other sports followed: Golf, snooker
Relaxations: Going to gym, 'staying at home watching a video with a nice cold beer'
Extras: '1995 was the first year that I stayed fit all year. No injuries except food
poisoning when I played at Edgbaston, where I missed one week through illness'
Opinions on cricket: 'I would like to see pitches prepared to keep bowlers interested
instead of declaration pitches, although I think that four-day cricket has improved the
pitches to force a result instead of a declaration on the last day.'
Best batting: 54* Hampshire v India, Southampton 1996
Best bowling: 4-68 Yorkshire v Northamptonshire, Sheffield 1995

1996 Season

	M	Inns	NO	Runs	HS	Avge	100s	50s	Ct	St	O	M	Runs	Wkts	Avge	Best	5wI	10wM
Test																		
All First	10	12	2	180	54 *	18.00	-	1	-	-	257	44	939	17	55.23	3-47	-	-
1-day Int																		
NatWest	2	1	0	27	27	27.00	-	-	-	-	20	0	108	0	-		-	-
B & H	2	1	0	2	2	2.00	-	-	1	-	14.1	6	61	2	30.50	2-7	-	
Sunday	5	2	1	9	8	9.00	-	-	2	-	40	1	199	5	39.80	2-18	-	

Career Performances

	M	Inns	NO	Runs	HS	Avge	100s	50s	Ct	St	Balls	Runs	Wkts	Avge	Best	5wI	10wM
Test																	
All First	16	20	4	202	54 *	12.62	-	1	-	-	2377	1370	31	44.19	4-68	-	-
1-day Int																	
NatWest	2	1	0	27	27	27.00	-	-	-	-	120	108	0	-	-	-	
B & H	2	1	0	2	2	2.00	-	-	1	-	85	61	2	30.50	2-7	-	
Sunday	9	4	2	23	13 *	11.50	-	-	3	-	384	317	7	45.28	2-18	-	

MILLNS, D. J. Leicestershire

Name: David James Millns
Role: Left-hand bat, right-arm fast bowler, slip fielder
Born: 27 February 1965, Clipstone, Nottinghamshire
Height: 6ft 3in **Weight:** 15st
Nickname: Rocket Man, Double D
County debut: 1988 (Nottinghamshire), 1990 (Leicestershire)
County cap: 1991
50 wickets in a season: 4
1st-Class 50s: 5
1st-Class 100s: 1
1st-Class 5 w. in innings: 19
1st-Class 10 w. in match: 3
1st-Class catches: 62
Place in batting averages: 219th av. 22.31 (1995 160th av. 25.58)
Place in bowling averages: 17th av. 23.04 (1995 124th av. 41.68)
Strike rate: 44.84 (career 48.24)
Parents: Bernard and Brenda
Wife and date of marriage: Wanda, 25 September 1993
Family links with cricket: Father and brother Paul played in local Nottinghamshire leagues. Godfather to Gordon Parsons's first child, Alex. Nottinghamshire's Andy Pick married sister Jennie
Education: Samuel Barlow Junior; Garibaldi Comprehensive; North Notts College of Further Education; Nottingham Trent Polytechnic
Qualifications: Senior coach
Career outside cricket: Yet to be decided
Off-season: Playing for Boland Cricket Board in South Africa
Overseas tours: England A to Australia 1992-93; Leicestershire to South Africa 1994

and 1995, to Holland 1994 and 1996

Overseas teams played for: Uitenhage, Port Elizabeth, South Africa 1988-89; Birkenhead, Auckland 1989-91; Tasmania, Australia 1994-95; Boland, South Africa 1996-97

Cricketers particularly admired: Gordon Parsons ('old sod keeps running into the wind for us') and Phil Simmons ('got to be the best all-round cricketer in the world today')

Young players to look out for: Darren Maddy ('ready to open the batting for England now')

Other sports followed: Football (Leicester City), rugby union (Leicester Tigers), golf ('taking money off JJ Whitaker on the golf course gives me great pleasure')

Injuries: Broken left thumb, missed no cricket. Back strain, out for one week

Relaxations: Reading, travelling, driving

Extras: Harold Larwood Bowling Award 1984. Asked to be released by Nottinghamshire at the end of 1989 season and joined Leicestershire in 1990. Finished third in national bowling averages in 1990. Britannic Assurance Player of the Month in August 1991 after taking 9-37 v Derbyshire, the best Leicestershire figures since George Geary's 10-18 v Glamorgan in 1929. Players' representative on Cricketers' Association Executive for Leicestershire. Leicestershire Cricketer of the Year 1992. Leicestershire Bowling Award 1990, 1991, 1992 and 1994

Opinions on cricket: 'To all professionals: enjoy it as it's not forever. To all county clubs: the players are the clubs, they are not here for long, so look after them.'

Best batting: 103 Leicestershire v Essex, Leicester 1996

Best bowling: 9-37 Leicestershire v Derbyshire, Derby 1991

1996 Season

	M	Inns	NO	Runs	HS	Avge	100s	50s	Ct	St	O	M	Runs	Wkts	Avge	Best	5wI	10wM
Test																		
All First	19	20	1	424	103	22.31	1	1	6	-	538.1	133	1659	72	23.04	6-54	2	1
1-day Int																		
NatWest	2	1	0	4	4	4.00	-	-	-	-	16	0	69	0	-		-	-
B & H	2	2	1	40	39 *	40.00	-	-	-	-	16.2	2	71	1	71.00	1-26	-	
Sunday	2	0	0	0	0	-	-	-	1	-	14	1	84	4	21.00	2-37	-	

Career Performances

	M	Inns	NO	Runs	HS	Avge	100s	50s	Ct	St	Balls	Runs	Wkts	Avge	Best	5wI	10wM
Test																	
All First	125	146	48	1813	103	18.50	1	5	62	-	19587	11233	406	27.66	9-37	19	3
1-day Int																	
NatWest	9	3	2	40	29 *	40.00	-	-	2	-	534	342	11	31.09	3-22	-	
B & H	16	9	5	77	39 *	19.25	-	-	2	-	758	540	21	25.71	4-26	-	
Sunday	37	17	8	98	20 *	10.88	-	-	9	-	1404	1256	29	43.31	2-11	-	

MOFFAT, S. P. — Middlesex

Name: Scott Park Moffat
Role: Right-hand bat, off-spin bowler
Born: 1 February 1973, Germiston, South Africa
Height: 6ft **Weight:** 13st 7lbs
Nickname: Access, Fraz
County debut: 1996
Parents: Duncan and Dagny
Marital status: Single
Family links with cricket: Father played league cricket in the Transvaal
Education: Bedfordview, South Africa; Aldenham School, Hertfordshire; Swansea University
Qualifications: 8 GCSEs, 3 A-levels, BSc in Economics, senior coaching award
Career outside cricket: Sports promotion
Off-season: Working for a sports marketing company
Overseas tours: Radlett to India 1995
Overseas teams played for: RAU, Transvaal, South Africa
Cricketers particularly admired: Mike Atherton, Graeme Hick, Angus Fraser, Nick Bothas
Young players to look out for: Owais Shah, Steven Peters
Other sports followed: Golf, football (Tottenham Hotspur)
Injuries: Wrist cartilage, out for three months
Relaxations: Socialising, eating out, reading and fishing
Extras: Played for Hertfordshire since 1992. Represented NAYC in 1992. Won the UAU with Swansea University
Opinions on cricket: 'The 2nd XI team one-day competition (Bain Hogg), should be changed to come in line with the 1st XI one-day i.e. Benson and Hedges format. The present 55-over system seems pointless as it doesn't prepare you properly.'

1996 Season

	M	Inns	NO	Runs	HS	Avge	100s	50s	Ct	St	O	M	Runs	Wkts	Avge	Best	5wI	10wM
Test																		
All First	1	1	0	0	0	0.00	-	-	-	-								
1-day Int																		
NatWest																		
B & H																		
Sunday																		

	M	Inns	NO	Runs	HS	Avge	100s	50s	Ct	St	Balls	Runs	Wkts	Avge	Best	5wl	10wM
Test																	
All First	1	1	0	0	0	0.00	-	-	-	-							
1-day Int																	
NatWest																	
B & H																	
Sunday																	

MOHAMMED AKRAM   Northamptonshire

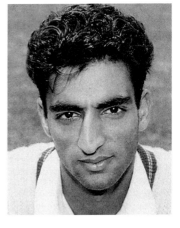

Name: Mohammed Akram Awan
Role: Right-hand bat, right-arm fast bowler
Born: 10 September 1972, Islamabad, Pakistan
Height: 6ft 2in **Weight:** 13st 5lbs
Nickname: Haji, Akee
County debut: No first-team appearance
Place in bowling averages: 86th av. 33.78
Strike rate: 55.00 (career 50.05)
Parents: Mohammed Akber Awan and Zaria Awan
Marital status: Single
Education: Gordon College, Rawalpindi
Career outside cricket: Business and investment
Off-season: Playing for Rawalpindi and Pakistan
Overseas teams played for: Rawalpindi 1992-97
Cricketers particularly admired: Michael Holding, Wasim Akram, Martin Crowe
Young players to look out for: Zahir Ali, Shoaib Akhter, Rob Cunliffe, Shadab Kabir and Mal Loye
Other sports followed: Football (Brazil), squash (Pakistan)
Injuries: Muscular pain under last rib, out for two months
Relaxations: Hunting, music. 'Visit to Swat Valley with my friends or any part of the world with natural scenery. Being with my mother and father'
Opinions on cricket: 'Today's game is very fast and anyone who wants to play has to be super fit. We play too much one-day cricket – Test cricket is the real cricket. I do not agree with the bouncer rule in one-day and Test cricket, it favours the batsmen – the bouncer is one of the beauties of the game.'
Best batting: 24 Rawalpindi v Karachi Blues, Rawalpindi 1993-94

Best bowling: 7-51 Pakistan v Leicestershire, Leicester 1996

1996 Season

	M	Inns	NO	Runs	HS	Avge	100s	50s	Ct	St	O	M	Runs	Wkts	Avge	Best	5wI	10wM
Test	1	0	0	0	0	-	-	-	-	-	22	4	71	1	71.00	1-41	--	
All First	6	5	5	7	4 *	-	-	-	4	-	128.2	21	473	14	33.78	7-51	1-	
1-day Int																		
NatWest																		
B & H																		
Sunday																		

Career Performances

	M	Inns	NO	Runs	HS	Avge	100s	50s	Ct	St	Balls	Runs	Wkts	Avge	Best	5wI	10wM
Test	5	8	2	8	5	1.33	-	-	4	-	919	463	10	46.30	3-39	-	-
All First	21	26	7	113	24	5.94	-	-	12	-	3003	1538	60	25.63	7-51	3	-
1-day Int	7	5	3	11	7 *	5.50	-	-	2	-	342	307	9	34.11	2-36	-	
NatWest																	
B & H																	
Sunday																	

MOLES, A. J. Warwickshire

Name: Andrew James Moles
Role: Right-hand opening bat, right-arm medium bowler
Born: 12 February 1961, Solihull
Height: 5ft 10in **Weight:** 'Above average'
Nickname: Moler
County debut: 1986
County cap: 1987
1000 runs in a season: 6
1st-Class 50s: 87
1st-Class 100s: 28
1st-Class 200s: 4
1st-Class catches: 136
One-Day 100s: 2
Place in batting averages: 102nd av. 36.12
(1996 48th av. 44.37)
Strike rate: (career 84.90)
Parents: Stuart Francis and Gillian Margaret
Wife and date of marriage:
Jacquie, 17 December 1988

Children: Daniel
Family links with cricket: Brother plays club cricket
Education: Finham Park Comprehensive, Coventry; Henley College of Further Education; Butts College of Further Education
Qualifications: 3 O-levels, 4 CSEs, Toolmaker/Standard Room Inspector City & Guilds
Career outside cricket: Selling corporate hospitality
Overseas teams played for: Griqualand West, South Africa 1986-88
Cricketers particularly admired: Dennis Amiss, Fred Gardner, Tom Moody
Other sports followed: Football, golf
Relaxations: Playing golf and spending time with family
Best batting: 230* Griqualand West v Northern Transvaal B, Verwoerdburg 1988-89
Best bowling: 3-21 Warwickshire v Oxford University, The Parks 1987

1996 Season

	M	Inns	NO	Runs	HS	Avge	100s	50s	Ct	St	O	M	Runs	Wkts	Avge	Best	5wI	10wM
Test																		
All First	13	25	0	903	176	36.12	2	4	7	-								
1-day Int																		
NatWest	2	2	0	34	30	17.00	-	-	1	-								
B & H	2	1	0	33	33	33.00	-	-	2	-								
Sunday	8	8	1	110	36	15.71	-	-	1	-								

Career Performances

	M	Inns	NO	Runs	HS	Avge	100s	50s	Ct	St	Balls	Runs	Wkts	Avge	Best	5wI	10wM
Test																	
All First	218	394	37	14670	230 *	41.09	28	87	136	-	3396	1882	40	47.05	3-21	-	-
1-day Int																	
NatWest	31	31	3	996	127	35.57	2	5	5	-	90	81	0	-	-	-	-
B & H	32	30	0	964	89	32.13	-	11	10	-	300	224	4	56.00	1-11	-	
Sunday	99	94	5	2249	96 *	25.26	-	15	26	-	446	415	7	59.28	2-24	-	

MONTGOMERIE, R. R.   Northamptonshire

Name: Richard Robert Montgomerie
Role: Right-hand opening bat, right-arm off-spin bowler
Born: 3 July 1971, Rugby
Height: 5ft 11in **Weight:** 12st
Nickname: Albert, Chesh, Baaaa, Monty
County debut: 1991
County cap: 1995
1000 runs in season: 2

1st-Class 50s: 22
1st-Class 100s: 9
1st-Class catches: 73
Place in batting averages: 86th av. 38.00
(1995 153rd av. 27.47)
Parents: Robert and Gillian
Marital status: Single
Family links with cricket: Father captained
Oxfordshire
Education: Rugby School; Worcester
College, Oxford University
Qualifications: 12 O-levels, 4 A-levels, BA
(Chemistry)
Career outside cricket: Chemist
Off-season: Playing in Australia
Overseas tours: Oxford University to
Namibia 1991
Cricketers particularly admired: Many

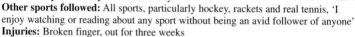

Other sports followed: All sports, particularly hockey, rackets and real tennis, 'I enjoy watching or reading about any sport without being an avid follower of anyone'
Injuries: Broken finger, out for three weeks
Relaxations: Any sport, good television, reading and 'occasionally testing my brain'
Extras: Scored unbeaten 50 in each innings of 1991 Varsity match and was Oxford captain in 1994. Oxford rackets Blue 1990. Captain Combined Universities 1994
Opinions on cricket: 'Four-day cricket should remain as it is.'
Best batting: 192 Northamptonshire v Kent, Canterbury 1995

1996 Season

	M	Inns	NO	Runs	HS	Avge	100s	50s	Ct	St	O	M	Runs	Wkts	Avge	Best	5wl	10wM
Test																		
All First	18	34	3	1178	168	38.00	4	4	17	-								
1-day Int																		
NatWest	2	2	1	77	69 *	77.00	-	1	2	-								
B & H	7	6	2	159	49	39.75	-	-	2	-								
Sunday	13	13	0	371	77	28.53	-	4	1	-								

Career Performances

	M	Inns	NO	Runs	HS	Avge	100s	50s	Ct	St	Balls	Runs	Wkts	Avge	Best	5wl	10wM
Test																	
All First	78	136	13	4171	192	33.91	9	22	73	-	96	65	0	-	-	-	-
1-day Int																	
NatWest	7	7	1	300	109	50.00	1	2	3	-							
B & H	14	13	2	373	75	33.90	-	2	2	-	6	0	0	-	-	-	
Sunday	30	29	0	836	77	28.82	-	8	8	-							

MOODY, T. M. Worcestershire

Name: Thomas Masson Moody
Role: Right-hand bat, right-arm medium
bowler, county captain
Born: 2 October 1965, Adelaide
Height: 6ft 7in **Weight:** 16st
Nickname: Moods, Tex
County debut: 1990 (Warwickshire),
1991 (Worcestershire)
County cap: 1990 (Warwickshire),
1991 (Worcestershire)
Test debut: 1989-90
Tests: 8

One-Day Internationals: 34
1000 runs in a season: 5
1st-Class 50s: 79
1st-Class 100s: 50
1st-Class 200s: 4
1st-Class 5 w. in innings: 5
1st-Class 10 w. in match: 2
1st-Class catches: 230
One-Day 100s: 13
Place in batting averages: 26th av. 50.96 (1995 12th av. 55.17)
Place in bowling averages: 30th av. 25.83
Strike rate: 51.86 (career 70.09)
Parents: John and Janet
Wife and date of marriage: Helen, 3 March 1993
Children: Jackson, 5 March 1995
Family links with cricket: Father played A Grade cricket in South Australia
Education: Guildford Grammar School, Western Australia
Qualifications: HSE
Career outside cricket: Sports shop owner
Off-season: Playing cricket in Australia
Overseas tours: Australia to India/Pakistan (World Cup) 1987, to England 1989, to India 1989-90, to Sri Lanka 1992
Overseas teams played for: Western Australia 1985-96; Midland Guildford, Perth, Western Australia
Cricketers particularly admired: Dennis Lillee, Allan Border, Viv Richards, Rod Marsh
Other sports followed: Aussie rules football (West Coast Eagles), football, golf, tennis
Injuries: Back

Relaxations: Golf, sleeping and films

Extras: Scored 150s in both innings of 1988-89 Sheffield Shield final for Western Australia v Queensland. Hit a century against Warwickshire during Australia's 1989 tour and signed on a one-year contract with them for 1990. Hit centuries in first three first-class matches for Warwickshire, and seven in first eight matches – a unique achievement. Scored the (then) fastest ever first-class century v Glamorgan in 26 minutes – taking advantage of declaration bowling. Reached 1000 first-class runs in first season of county cricket in only 12 innings – another record. Released by Warwickshire at the end of the 1990 season after they had chosen Allan Donald as their one overseas player and was signed by Worcestershire for 1991 when Graeme Hick was no longer considered an overseas player. Not re-signed for 1993 season because he was expected to be touring with the Australian team, although in the event he was not selected. Returned for 1994 season. Scored 180* and shared record unbeaten partnership with Tim Curtis in the semi-final of the NatWest Trophy 1994. Appointed Worcestershire's captain in 1996 after replacing Tim Curtis halfway through the 1995 season. Reclaimed a place in the Australian one-day side for the World Series against West Indies and Pakistan in 1996-97

Opinions on cricket: 'We need more quality not quantity.'

Best batting: 272 Western Australia v Tasmania, Hobart 1994-95

Best bowling: 7-38 Western Australia v Tasmania, Hobart 1995-96

1996 Season

	M	Inns	NO	Runs	HS	Avge	100s	50s	Ct	St	O	M	Runs	Wkts	Avge	Best	5wI	10wM
Test																		
All First	19	31	3	1427	212	50.96	7	4	12	-	319.5	86	956	37	25.83	7-92	3	1
1-day Int																		
NatWest	2	2	0	167	123	83.50	1	-	1	-	23	1	91	1	91.00	1-57	-	
B & H	4	4	1	99	80 *	33.00	-	1	2	-	21	6	90	2	45.00	1-22	-	
Sunday	16	16	2	680	104	48.57	2	2	5	-	108	5	496	20	24.80	4-46	-	

Career Performances

	M	Inns	NO	Runs	HS	Avge	100s	50s	Ct	St	Balls	Runs	Wkts	Avge	Best	5wI	10wM
Test	8	14	0	456	106	32.57	2	3	9	-	432	147	2	73.50	1-17	-	-
All First	235	394	33	16961	272	46.98	50	79	230	-	14860	6669	212	31.45	7-38	5	2
1-day Int	34	32	3	751	89	25.89	-	7	10	-	894	651	16	40.68	3-56	-	
NatWest	13	13	3	742	180 *	74.20	2	3	10	-	511	273	9	30.33	2-33	-	
B & H	29	27	7	1200	110 *	60.00	2	10	11	-	786	460	15	30.66	4-59	-	
Sunday	91	89	10	3693	160	46.74	9	25	26	-	2013	1407	51	27.58	4-46	-	

MOORES, P.   Sussex

Name: Peter Moores
Role: Right-hand bat, wicket-keeper, county captain
Born: 18 December 1962, Macclesfield, Cheshire
Height: 6ft **Weight:** 13st
Nickname: Billy
County debut: 1983 (Worcestershire), 1985 (Sussex)
County cap: 1989
1st-Class 50s: 29
1st-Class 100s: 5
1st-Class catches: 463
1st-Class stumpings: 44
Place in batting averages: 175th av. 27.92 (1995 191st av. 22.00)
Parents: Bernard and Winifred
Wife and date of marriage: Karen Jane, 28 September 1989
Children: Natalie Marie, 4 August 1993

Family links with cricket: Brothers, Anthony, Stephen and Robert, all play club cricket
Education: King Edward VI School, Macclesfield
Qualifications: 7 O-levels, 3 A-levels, advanced cricket coach
Career outside cricket: Coach for Sussex in off-season
Overseas tours: Christians in Sport to India 1989-90; MCC to Namibia 1990-91, to Leeward Islands 1991-92, to Bahrain 1994-95
Overseas teams played for: Orange Free State, South Africa 1988-89
Cricketers particularly admired: Bob Taylor, Alan Knott, Clive Lloyd
Other sports followed: Football, golf
Relaxations: Golf, wine and old films
Extras: On MCC groundstaff in 1982 before joining Worcestershire in latter half of 1982 season. Joined Sussex in 1985 and has been appointed captain for the 1997 season
Opinions on cricket: 'I feel we need to split the Sunday and the four-day game for two reasons: 1. It would prevent injuries in the Sunday game affecting the result in the four-day game. 2. It would benefit players not to have to switch "codes" halfway through a game.'
Best batting: 185 Sussex v Cambridge University, Hove 1996

1996 Season

	M	Inns	NO	Runs	HS	Avge	100s	50s	Ct	St	O	M	Runs	Wkts	Avge	Best	5wI	10wM
Test																		
All First	19	32	4	782	185	27.92	2	1	50	2								
1-day Int																		
NatWest	3	3	0	14	7	4.66	-	-	3	-								
B & H	4	3	0	34	17	11.33	-	-	3	1								
Sunday	15	13	2	268	55	24.36	-	2	9	1								

Career Performances

	M	Inns	NO	Runs	HS	Avge	100s	50s	Ct	St	Balls	Runs	Wkts	Avge	Best	5wI	10wM
Test																	
All First	211	311	37	6724	185	24.54	6	29	463	44	18	16	0	-	-	-	-
1-day Int																	
NatWest	24	17	3	167	26	11.92	-	-	32	2							
B & H	29	22	3	275	76	14.47	-	1	23	3							
Sunday	153	121	36	1745	89 *	20.52	-	7	134	22							

MORGAN, H. J. Somerset

Name: Haydn John Morgan
Role: Right-hand bat, off-spin bowler
Born: 5 July 1973, Torquay
Height: 5ft 9in **Weight:** 11st 11lbs
Nickname: H
County debut: No first-team appearance
Parents: John and Diana
Marital status: Single
Family links with cricket: Father played club cricket and is currently the manager of Torquay CC
Education: Sherwell Valley Primary School; Westlands, Torquay
Qualifications: 10 GCSEs
Career outside cricket: Unsure
Off-season: Playing club cricket in New Zealand
Overseas teams played for: Manawatu-Foxton CC, New Zealand 1993-97; Horowhenua CA, New Zealand 1995-97
Cricketers particularly admired: Alec Stewart, Martin Crowe, Steve Waugh
Other sports followed: 'Follow all sports particularly rugby'

Relaxations: Others sports, television
Extras: Played for NAYC 1991-92. Played for Devon CCC 1995-96. Became the first non-contracted player to score a double hundred for Somerset 2nd XI against Glamorgan in 1996

MORRIS, A. C. Yorkshire

Name: Alexander Corfield Morris
Role: Left-hand bat, right-arm medium bowler
Born: 4 October 1976, Barnsley
Height: 6ft 4in **Weight:** 12st 7lbs
County debut: 1995
1st-Class 50s: 1
1st-Class catches: 8
Place in batting averages: 226th av. 21.00
Strike rate: 46.50 (career 75.60)
Parents: Chris and Janet
Marital status: Single
Education: Wilthorpe Primary School; Holgate School, Barnsley; Barnsley College
Qualifications: 4 GCSEs, BTEC National Diploma in Sports Science, NCA coaching award
Off-season: Playing club cricket in South Africa
Overseas tours: England U19 to West Indies 1994-95, to Zimbabwe 1995-96; England VI to Hong Kong 1996
Cricketers particularly admired: Ian Botham, Martyn Moxon
Young players to look out for: Anthony McGrath, Michael Vaughan
Other sports followed: Football (Barnsley FC)
Injuries: Broken hand, missed one month
Relaxations: Listening to music, relaxing with mates
Extras: Played for Yorkshire U11-U19. Played for England U15 against Barbados and in 1994 for both England U17 and U19 against India. Played junior football with both Barnsley and Rotherham and had trials for Nottingham Forest and Leeds
Opinions on cricket: 'More coloured clothing cricket.'
Best batting: 60 Yorkshire v Lancashire, Old Trafford 1996
Best bowling: 1-11 Yorkshire v Lancashire, Old Trafford 1996

1996 Season

	M	Inns	NO	Runs	HS	Avge	100s	50s	Ct	St	O	M	Runs	Wkts	Avge	Best	5wI	10wM
Test																		
All First	6	9	0	189	60	21.00	-	1	6	-	31	6	116	4	29.00	1-11	-	-
1-day Int																		
NatWest																		
B & H	1	0	0	0	0	-	-	-	1	-	1	0	4	0	-		-	-
Sunday	9	6	1	99	48 *	19.80	-	-	2	-	14	0	81	4	20.25	2-19	-	

Career Performances

	M	Inns	NO	Runs	HS	Avge	100s	50s	Ct	St	Balls	Runs	Wkts	Avge	Best	5wI	10wM
Test																	
All First	9	14	2	245	60	20.41	-	1	8	-	378	219	5	43.80	1-11	-	-
1-day Int																	
NatWest	1	1	1	1	1 *	-	-	-	-	-	48	43	1	43.00	1-43	-	
B & H	1	0	0	0	0	-	-	-	1	-	6	4	0	-		-	
Sunday	13	8	1	106	48 *	15.14	-	-	2	-	198	153	6	25.50	2-19	-	

MORRIS, H. Glamorgan

Name: Hugh Morris
Role: Left-hand bat, right-arm medium bowler
Born: 5 October 1963, Cardiff
Height: 5ft 8in **Weight:** 12st 7lbs
Nickname: Banners
County debut: 1981
County cap: 1986
Benefit: 1994 (£118,837)
Test debut: 1991
Tests: 3
1000 runs in a season: 9
1st-Class 50s: 95
1st-Class 100s: 49
1st-Class 200s: 1
1st-Class catches: 183
One-Day 100s: 13
Place in batting averages: 17th av. 55.53 (1995 21st av. 52.46)
Strike rate: (career 174.00)
Parents: Roger and Anne
Wife: Debra Jane

Children: Bethan Louise; Emily Charlotte
Family links with cricket: Father played club cricket. Brother played junior representative cricket
Education: Llanfair County Primary School; Blundells School; University of Wales Institute, Cardiff
Qualifications: 9 O-levels, 2 A-levels, 1 AO-level, BA (Hons) in Physical Education, advanced cricket coach
Off-season: Doing some television presenting and media work. Working with cricket development officer – coaching in schools
Overseas tours: English Public Schoolboys to West Indies 1980-81, to Sri Lanka 1982-83; England A to Pakistan 1990-91 (called up to join England tour party in Australia), to Bermuda and West Indies 1991-92, to South Africa 1993-94; England to Australia 1990-91; Glamorgan to Holland and Zimbabwe
Overseas teams played for: CBC Old Boys, Pretoria 1985-87
Cricketers particularly admired: Viv Richards, Ian Botham
Young players to look out for: Adam Hollioake
Other sports followed: Rugby ('played first-class rugby for Aberavon and Cardiff Institute and gained a Wales Student cap versus France in 1984'), golf (handicap 11)
Injuries: Virus, out for ten days
Relaxations: Spending time at home with family
Extras: Highest schoolboy cricket average in 1979 (89.71), 1981 (184.60) and 1982 (149.20). Captain of English Schools U19 in 1981 and 1982; played for England YC v West Indies 1982, and captain v Australia 1983. Appointed youngest ever Glamorgan captain 1986, but resigned in 1989 to concentrate on batting. In 1990 scored most runs in a season by a Glamorgan player (2276) and hit most centuries (10). After missing selection for the tour of Australia, appointed captain for England A tour of Pakistan in 1990-91; then, after Gooch had required a hand operation and England had lost the first Test to Australia, he flew out to join the senior tour until the England captain recovered. Glamorgan Player of the Year. Captained the England A tour to South Africa 1993-94 and Wombwell Cricket Lovers' Society Captain of the Year 1993. Played first-class rugby for Aberavon 1984-85 and South Glamorgan Institute, scoring over 150 points. Stood down as Glamorgan captain at the end of the 1995 season
Opinions on cricket: 'The championship should be split into two equal divisions and run along the lines of American football. Each team would play everyone in their division once and four teams from the other division – i.e. 12 games per season and the top two in each group would go into the play-offs with the top two teams playing a five-day final. This system would keep the best players at their clubs.'
Best batting: 202* Glamorgan v Yorkshire, Cardiff 1996
Best bowling: 1-6 Glamorgan v Oxford University, The Parks 1987

1996 Season

	M	Inns	NO	Runs	HS	Avge	100s	50s	Ct	St	O	M	Runs	Wkts	Avge	Best	5wI	10wM
Test																		
All First	18	32	2	1666	202 *	55.53	6	9	14	-								
1-day Int																		
NatWest	1	1	0	32	32	32.00	-	-	-	-								
B & H	6	6	1	285	136 *	57.00	1	-	2	-								
Sunday	12	11	1	372	101 *	37.20	1	2	3	-								

Career Performances

	M	Inns	NO	Runs	HS	Avge	100s	50s	Ct	St	Balls	Runs	Wkts	Avge	Best	5wI	10wM
Test	3	6	0	115	44	19.16	-	-	3	-							
All First	298	516	49	18523	202 *	39.66	49	95	183	-	348	380	2	190.00	1-6	-	-
1-day Int																	
NatWest	32	31	4	1282	154 *	47.48	4	4	10	-	12	12	0	-		-	-
B & H	41	41	3	1192	143 *	31.36	4	3	15	-	18	15	1	15.00	1-14	-	
Sunday	172	166	18	5267	127 *	35.58	5	35	58	-							

MORRIS, J. E.   Durham

Name: John Edward Morris
Role: Right-hand bat, right-arm medium bowler
Born: 1 April 1964, Crewe
Height: 5ft 10in **Weight:** 13st 6lbs
Nickname: Animal
County debut: 1982 (Derbyshire), 1994 (Durham)
County cap: 1986 (Derbyshire)
Test debut: 1990
Tests: 3
One-Day Internationals: 8
1000 runs in a season: 10
1st-Class 50s: 88
1st-Class 100s: 42
1st-Class 200s: 2
1st-Class catches: 127
One-Day 100s: 8
Place in batting averages: 271st av. 14.30 (1995 77th av. 38.14)
Strike rate: (career 141.71)
Parents: George (Eddie) and Jean
Wife and date of marriage: Sally, 30 September 1990

Children: Thomas Edward, 27 June 1991
Family links with cricket: Father played for Crewe for many years as an opening bowler
Education: Shavington Comprehensive School; Dane Bank College of Further Education
Qualifications: O-levels
Off-season: Working for Durham CCC and after-dinner speaking
Overseas tours: England to Australia 1990-91; Romany to South Africa 1993: MCC to Bahrain 1994-95
Overseas teams played for: Umbilo, Durban, South Africa 1982-84; Alex Old Boys, Pietermaritzburg, South Africa 1984-85; Subiaco-Floriat, Western Australia 1986-87; Griqualand West, South Africa 1988-89, 1993-94; Protea, Johannesburg, South Africa 1993
Other sports followed: Golf, football (Derby County)
Relaxations: The golf course and home life
Extras: Youngest player to score a Sunday League century. Left Derbyshire at end of 1993 season
Opinions on cricket: 'I think starting on a Wednesday will make a big difference, due to the fact that you won't be splitting up the championship game with a Sunday League game.'
Best batting: 229 Derbyshire v Gloucestershire, Cheltenham 1993
Best bowling: 1-6 Derbyshire v Cambridge University, Fenner's 1993

1996 Season

	M	Inns	NO	Runs	HS	Avge	100s	50s	Ct	St	O	M	Runs	Wkts	Avge	Best	5wl	10wM
Test																		
All First	17	31	1	429	83	14.30	-	3	9	-	1	0	10	0	-		-	-	-
1-day Int																		
NatWest	2	2	0	133	109	66.50	1	-	-	-								
B & H	5	5	0	235	145	47.00	1	-	3	-								
Sunday	9	9	0	154	46	17.11	-	-	2	-								

Career Performances

	M	Inns	NO	Runs	HS	Avge	100s	50s	Ct	St	Balls	Runs	Wkts	Avge	Best	5wl	10wM
Test	3	5	2	71	32	23.66	-	-	3	-							
All First	296	497	30	17730	229	37.96	42	88	127	-	992	912	7	130.28	1-6	-	-
1-day Int	8	8	1	167	63 *	23.85	-	1	2	-							
NatWest	26	25	3	737	109	33.50	1	4	8	-							
B & H	54	50	6	1379	145	31.34	3	6	12	-	24	14	0	-		-	-
Sunday	182	173	12	4154	134	25.80	4	19	40	-	3	7	0	-		-	-

MORRIS, R. S. M.   Hampshire

Name: Robert Sean Milner Morris
Role: Right-hand bat, off-spin bowler, occasional wicket-keeper
Born: 10 September 1968, Great Horwood, Buckinghamshire
Height: 6ft **Weight:** 12st 7lbs
Nickname: Stowers, The Saint
County debut: 1992
1st-Class 50s: 7
1st-Class 100s: 3
1st-Class catches: 43
Place in batting averages: 222nd av. 21.66 (1995 204th av. 20.44)
Parents: Stuart and Sue
Marital status: Single
Family links with cricket: Great-grandfather played for Worcestershire
Education: Swanbourne House School; Stowe School; Durham University 'and Yung's Bar, Bangkok'
Qualifications: 8 O-levels, 2 A-levels, BA (Dunelm) Sociology
Career outside cricket: 'Beach bumming'
Off-season: Golfing in Malaysia, training in Cape Town
Overseas tours: Stowe to Australia 1982; Combined Universities to Barbados 1990
Overseas teams played for: Midland Guildford, Perth, Western Australia 1987-88; St Albans, Buenos Aires 1991-92; Tigers Parow, Cape Town 1993-94; Western Province, Cape Town 1994-95
Cricketers particularly admired: Bill Whyman, Tim Brooke-Taylor, Kevan James
Other sports followed: Big game fishing ('SA blue marlin record-holder'), rugby (Bath RFC)
Relaxations: 'Beach life and ornithology'
Extras: Captained Durham University hockey and cricket, played hockey for County Durham and the North. Retired from first-class cricket at the end of the 1996 season
Best batting: 174 Hampshire v Nottinghamshire, Basingstoke 1994

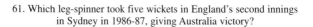

61. Which leg-spinner took five wickets in England's second innings in Sydney in 1986-87, giving Australia victory?

1996 Season

	M	Inns	NO	Runs	HS	Avge	100s	50s	Ct	St	O	M	Runs	Wkts	Avge	Best	5wI	10wM
Test																		
All First	5	9	0	195	112	21.66	1	-	5	-								
1-day Int																		
NatWest																		
B & H	3	3	0	71	39	23.66	-	-	3	-								
Sunday	2	2	0	39	21	19.50	-	-	-	-								

Career Performances

	M	Inns	NO	Runs	HS	Avge	100s	50s	Ct	St	Balls	Runs	Wkts	Avge	Best	5wI	10wM
Test																	
All First	37	67	4	1830	174	29.04	3	7	43	-	4	1	0	-	-	-	-
1-day Int																	
NatWest	3	3	1	86	34 *	43.00	-	-	-	-							
B & H	4	3	0	71	39	23.66	-	-	3	-							
Sunday	20	20	1	520	87	27.36	-	2	5	-							

MOXON, M. D.   *Yorkshire*

Name: Martyn Douglas Moxon
Role: Right-hand bat, right-arm medium bowler
Born: 4 May 1960, Barnsley
Height: 6ft 1in **Weight:** 14st
Nickname: Frog
County debut: 1981
County cap: 1984
Benefit: 1993
Test debut: 1986
Tests: 10
One-Day Internationals: 8
1000 runs in a season: 12
1st-Class 50s: 111
1st-Class 100s: 44
1st-Class 200s: 5
1st-Class catches: 215
One-Day 100s: 7
One-Day 5 w. in innings: 1
Place in batting averages: 61st av. 43.68 (1995 2nd av. 76.33)
Strike rate: (career 94.64)
Parents: Audrey and Derek (deceased)

Wife and date of marriage: Sue, October 1985
Children: Charlotte Louise, 13 March 1990; Jonathan James, 6 May 1993
Family links with cricket: Father and grandfather played local league cricket
Education: Holgate Grammar School, Barnsley
Qualifications: 8 O-levels, 3 A-levels, HNC in Business Studies, advanced cricket coach
Off-season: Coaching in England
Overseas tours: England to India and Australia 1984-85, to Australia and New Zealand 1987-88; England B to Sri Lanka 1985-86; England A to Bermuda and West Indies 1991-92, to Australia 1992-93
Overseas teams played for: Griqualand West, South Africa 1982-83 and 1983-84
Cricketers particularly admired: Viv Richards
Young players to look out for: Anthony McGrath, Michael Vaughan, Chris Silverwood, Matthew Dowman, Vikram Solanki
Other sports followed: Football (supporter of Barnsley FC) and golf
Injuries: Badly bruised right thumb, out for three weeks
Relaxations: Listening to most types of music, having a drink with friends
Extras: Captained Yorkshire Schools U15, North of England U15 and Yorkshire Senior Schools. Played for Wombwell Cricket Lovers' Society U18 side. First Yorkshire player to make centuries in his first two Championship games in Yorkshire, 116 v Essex at Headingley (on debut) and 111 v Derbyshire at Sheffield, and scored 153 in his first innings in a Roses match. Picked for Lord's Test of 1984 v West Indies, but withdrew through injury and had to wait until 1986 to make Test debut. Appointed Yorkshire captain in 1990. Appointed captain of England A team to tour Bermuda and West Indies 1991-92, but played no first-class cricket owing to injury. Wombwell Cricket Lovers' Society Cricketer of the Year 1991. Scored 274* against Worcester which is the highest individual score for Yorkshire since the war. Stood down as Yorkshire captain at the end of the 1995 season
Best batting: 274* Yorkshire v Worcestershire, Worcester 1994
Best bowling: 3-24 Yorkshire v Hampshire, Southampton 1989

1996 Season

	M	Inns	NO	Runs	HS	Avge	100s	50s	Ct	St	O	M	Runs	Wkts	Avge	Best	5wl	10wM
Test																		
All First	14	25	3	961	213	43.68	2	5	5	-								
1-day Int																		
NatWest	4	4	0	247	137	61.75	1	1	-	-								
B & H	5	5	1	123	67	30.75	-	1	2	-								
Sunday	10	10	0	271	72	27.10	-	1	3	-								

Career Performances

	M	Inns	NO	Runs	HS	Avge	100s	50s	Ct	St	Balls	Runs	Wkts	Avge	Best	5wI	10wM
Test	10	17	1	455	99	28.43	-	3	10	-	48	30	0	-	-	-	-
All First	305	523	47	20572	274 *	43.21	44	111	215	-	2650	1481	28	52.89	3-24	-	-
1-day Int	8	8	0	174	70	21.75	-	1	5	-							
NatWest	31	31	6	1208	137	48.32	2	9	12	-	156	85	5	17.00	2-19	-	
B & H	47	47	7	1766	141 *	44.15	2	13	19	-	342	242	9	26.88	5-31	1	
Sunday	149	141	8	4114	129 *	30.93	3	24	46	-	984	868	21	41.33	3-29	-	

MULLALLY, A. D. Leicestershire

Name: Alan David Mullally
Role: Right-hand bat, left-arm fast bowler
Born: 12 July 1969, Southend
Height: 6ft 5in **Weight:** 14st
Nickname: Bob, Bryan, Eric, Spider, 'too many to mention'
County debut: 1988 (Hampshire), 1990 (Leicestershire)
County cap: 1993
Test debut: 1996
Tests: 6
One-Day Internationals: 3
50 wickets in a season: 3
1st-Class 50s: 2
1st-Class 5 w. in innings: 9
1st-Class 10 w. in match: 2
1st-Class catches: 24
Place in batting averages: 229th av. 20.75
Place in bowling averages: 28th av. 25.34
(1995 57th av. 28.81)
Strike rate: 53.90 (career 66.88)
Parents: Michael and Ann
Marital status: Single
Family links with cricket: 'Sister fancied David Gower'
Education: Cannington High School and Primary, Perth, Australia; Wembley and Carlisle Technical College
Qualifications: 'This and that'
Career outside cricket: Musician
Off-season: Touring Zimbabwe and New Zealand with England
Overseas tours: Western Australia to India 1990-91; Leicestershire to Jamaica 1992-93; England to Zimbabwe and New Zealand 1996-97

Overseas teams played for: Western Australia; Victoria; Australian YC
Cricketers particularly admired: Geoff Marsh, Dermot Reeve
Young players to look out for: Darren Maddy
Other sports followed: Australian rules football, basketball, most sports
Relaxations: Music
Extras: English-qualified as he was born in Southend, he made his first-class debut for Western Australia in the 1987-88 Sheffield Shield final, and played for Australian YC 1988-89. Played one match for Hampshire in 1988 before joining Leicestershire
Opinions on cricket: 'Good fun.'
Best batting: 75 Leicestershire v Middlesex, Leicester 1996
Best bowling: 7-72 Leicestershire v Gloucestershire, Leicester 1993

1996 Season

	M	Inns	NO	Runs	HS	Avge	100s	50s	Ct	St	O	M	Runs	Wkts	Avge	Best	5wI	10wM
Test	6	9	4	54	24	10.80	-	-	-	-	279.3	76	675	22	30.68	3-44	-	-
All First	17	17	5	249	75	20.75	-	2	1	-	628.5	166	1774	70	25.34	6-47	3	1
1-day Int	3	1	0	2	2	2.00	-	-	1	-	25	3	127	2	63.50	1-30	-	
NatWest	1	1	1	8	8 *	-	-	-	-	-	11	2	40	2	20.00	2-40	-	
B & H	5	2	1	6	6	6.00	-	-	-	-	50	4	186	6	31.00	2-44	-	
Sunday	5	2	2	0	0 *	-	-	-	-	-	39	5	168	8	21.00	5-15	1	

Career Performances

	M	Inns	NO	Runs	HS	Avge	100s	50s	Ct	St	Balls	Runs	Wkts	Avge	Best	5wI	10wM
Test	6	9	4	54	24	10.80	-	-	-	-	1677	675	22	30.68	3-44	-	-
All First	124	141	36	959	75	9.13	-	2	24	-	22942	10936	343	31.88	7-72	9	2
1-day Int	3	1	0	2	2	2.00	-	-	1	-	150	127	2	63.50	1-30	-	
NatWest	13	7	4	42	19 *	14.00	-	-	2	-	792	438	18	24.33	2-22	-	
B & H	26	10	3	27	11	3.85	-	-	-	-	1450	896	18	49.77	2-30	-	
Sunday	74	33	16	175	38	10.29	-	-	15	-	3263	2456	76	32.31	5-15	1	

62. Which English umpire was threatened by members in front of the Lord's Long Room during the 1980 Centenary Test?

MUNTON, T. A. Warwickshire

Name: Timothy Alan Munton
Role: Right-hand bat, right-arm fast-medium bowler, county captain
Born: 30 July 1965, Melton Mowbray
Height: 6ft 6in **Weight:** 15st 7lbs
Nickname: Harry, Captain Sensible
County debut: 1985
County cap: 1990
Test debut: 1991
Tests: 2
50 wickets in a season: 5
1st-Class 50s: 2
1st-Class 5 w. in innings: 25
1st-Class 10 w. in match: 6
1st-Class catches: 68
One-Day 5 w. in innings: 2
Place in batting averages: 163rd av. 29.50
Place in bowling averages: 66th av. 31.20
(1995 7th av. 19.83)
Strike rate: 69.25 (career 60.02)
Parents: Alan and Brenda
Wife and date of marriage: Helen, 20 September 1986
Children: Camilla Dallas, 13 August 1988; Harrison George Samuel, 17 February 1992
Family links with cricket: Father played for Buckminster CC
Education: Sarson High School; King Edward VII Upper School, Melton Mowbray
Qualifications: CSE grade 1, 9 O-levels, 1 A-level
Overseas tours: England A to Pakistan 1990-91, to Bermuda and West Indies 1991-92, to Pakistan 1995-96
Overseas teams played for: Victoria University, Wellington, New Zealand 1985-86; Witwatersrand University, Johannesburg, South Africa 1986-87
Cricketers particularly admired: Richard Hadlee, David Gower
Other sports followed: Basketball, soccer, golf
Relaxations: 'Playing golf, spending time with my family'
Extras: Appeared for Leicestershire 2nd XI 1982-84. Second highest wicket-taker in 1990 with 78. Called into England A squad to tour Bermuda and West Indies 1991-92 when Dermot Reeve replaced the injured Angus Fraser on the senior tour. Was voted Warwickshire Player of the Season 1990, 1991 and 1994. Missed the first six months of the 1995 season recovering from a back operation. He was flown out to Pakistan as a replacement for the injured Mike Smith on the England A tour, and played in the second 'Test' less than a week after his arrival. Assumed the Warwickshire captaincy after the

retirement of Dermot Reeve in 1996
Best batting: 54 Warwickshire v Worcestershire, Worcester 1992
Best bowling: 8-89 Warwickshire v Middlesex, Edgbaston 1991

1996 Season

	M	Inns	NO	Runs	HS	Avge	100s	50s	Ct	St	O	M	Runs	Wkts	Avge	Best	5wI	10wM
Test																		
All First	12	15	9	177	54 *	29.50	-	2	2	-	404	116	1092	35	31.20	4-41	-	-
1-day Int																		
NatWest	1	1	1	2	2 *	-	-	-	-	-	10	3	28	0	-		-	-
B & H	4	1	1	6	6 *	-	-	-	-	-	32	3	125	3	41.66	2-31	-	
Sunday	9	2	1	6	3 *	6.00	-	-	1	-	62	8	259	9	28.77	3-17	-	

Career Performances

	M	Inns	NO	Runs	HS	Avge	100s	50s	Ct	St	Balls	Runs	Wkts	Avge	Best	5wI	10wM
Test	2	2	1	25	25 *	25.00	-	-	-	-	405	200	4	50.00	2-22	-	-
All First	205	207	86	1339	54 *	11.06	-	2	68	-	35655	15577	594	26.22	8-89	26	6
1-day Int																	
NatWest	32	10	6	11	5	2.75	-	-	5	-	1972	950	35	27.14	3-36	-	
B & H	31	14	9	58	13	11.60	-	-	6	-	1894	1094	36	30.38	4-35	-	
Sunday	142	35	25	128	15 *	12.80	-	-	28	-	6119	3969	141	28.14	5-23	2	

MUSHTAQ AHMED   Somerset

Name: Mushtaq Ahmed
Role: Right-hand bat, leg-break bowler
Born: 28 June 1970, Sahiwal, Pakistan
Height: 5ft 4in **Weight:** 13st
Nickname: Mushy
County debut: 1993
County cap: 1993
Test debut: 1991-92
Tests: 24
One-Day Internationals: 102
50 wickets in a season: 2
1st-Class 50s: 6
1st-Class 5w. in innings: 40
1st-Class 10w. in match: 10
1st-Class catches: 68
Place in batting averages: 270th av. 14.75
(1995 252nd av. 14.80)
Place in bowling averages: 8th av. 21.00

(1995 69th av. 29.69)
Strike rate: 47.56 (career 52.09)
Marital status: Married
Career outside cricket: Banking
Off-season: On tour with Pakistan
Overseas tours: Pakistan to Australia 1989-90, to New Zealand and Australia (World Cup) 1991-92, to England 1992, Australia and South Africa 1992-93, to New Zealand 1993-94, 1995-96, to Sri Lanka 1994, to Australia 1995-96, to New Zealand 1995-96, to India and Sri Lanka (World Cup) 1995-96, to New Zealand and Australia 1996-97
Overseas teams played for: United Bank, Pakistan
Cricketers particularly admired: Viv Richards, Waqar Younis
Other sports followed: Football (Brazil), hockey
Relaxations: Watching videos, eating, spending time with family
Extras: Took 6-81 against England for Punjab Chief Minister's XI 1987. Finished second to Wasim Akram as Pakistan's highest wicket-taker in the World Cup 1991-92 with 16 wickets. Received specialist coaching from Intikhab Alam. Named Somerset Player of the Year 1993. Replaced as overseas player by Shane Lee for the 1996 season due to Pakistan's tour of England, but returns for the 1997 season
Opinions on cricket: 'I like the four-day county championship because it gives spin bowlers a good chance to bowl long spells. One-day cricket is exciting to watch and play in. A good cricketer can play all types of cricket successfully. Most of those against that view have never played it.'
Best batting: 90 Somerset v Sussex, Taunton 1993
Best bowling: 9-93 Multan v Peshawar, Sahiwal 1986-87

1996 Season

	M	Inns	NO	Runs	HS	Avge	100s	50s	Ct	St	O	M	Runs	Wkts	Avge	Best	5wl	10wM
Test	3	5	1	44	20	11.00	-	-	3	-	195	52	447	17	26.29	6-78	2-	
All First	7	9	1	118	38	14.75	-	-	4	-	325	85	861	41	21.00	7-91	5 1	
1-day Int	2	1	1	14	14 *	-	-	-	-	-	20	0	85	2	42.50	2-33	-	
NatWest																		
B & H																		
Sunday																		

Career Performances

	M	Inns	NO	Runs	HS	Avge	100s	50s	Ct	St	Balls	Runs	Wkts	Avge	Best	5wl	10wM
Test	24	37	7	246	27	8.20	-	-	9	-	5706	2607	89	29.29	7-56	5	1
All First	130	165	20	1959	90	13.51	-	6	68	-	30162	14492	579	25.02	9-93	41	11
1-day Int	102	50	19	277	26	8.93	-	-	22	-	5213	3836	116	33.06	4-47	-	
NatWest	7	5	1	82	35	20.50	-	-	1	-	466	252	9	28.00	3-26	-	
B & H	8	6	0	46	21	7.66	-	-	-	-	472	243	10	24.30	4-29	-	
Sunday	34	30	8	236	32	10.72	-	-	2	-	1522	1080	33	32.72	3-17	-	

NASH, D. C.   Middlesex

Name: David Charles Nash
Role: Right-hand bat, wicket-keeper
Born: 19 January 1978, Chertsey, Surrey
Height: 5ft 8in **Weight:** 10st 9lbs
Nickname: Nashy
County debut: 1995 (one-day)
Parents: David and Christine
Marital status: Single
Family links with cricket: 'Father played club cricket, mother is an avid watcher and tea-maker, and brother Glen is a very promising and talented left-hand bat'
Education: Sunbury Manor; Malvern College, Worcestershire
Qualifications: 10 GCSEs, 1 A-level, NCA coach
Career outside cricket: Cricket coach and any other ideas welcome
Off-season: 'Touring Pakistan with England U19, coaching, working on my game, keeping fit and socialising with friends'
Overseas tours: England U15 to South Africa 1993; British Airways Youth Team to West Indies 1993-94; England U19 to Zimbabwe 1995-96, to Pakistan 1996-97
Cricketers particularly admired: Colin Metson, Mark Ramprakash, George Simons and Gareth Rees 'for their big heart and 100% commitment' and Simon Pavitt 'for his avoidance of buying a beer for his team mates'
Young players to look out for: Anthony McGrath, David Sales, Ben Hollioake, 'my younger brother Glen' and Scott Anstiss 'a young player at Sunbury CC'
Other sports followed: Football (Brentford) and most other sports
Injuries: Stitches above eye and concussion, out for four days. 'Severe earache listening to Peter Wellings's theories on the game and life in general'
Relaxations: Watching Brentford play, playing golf, listening to music, going out with friends
Extras: A qualified referee. Represented Middlesex at all ages. Played for England U14, U15, U17 and U18. Once took six wickets in six balls when aged 11 – 'when I could bowl!'. *Daily Telegraph* Southern England Batting Award 1993. Seaxe Young Player of the Year 1993
Opinions on cricket: 'I would like to see 2nd XI matches extended to four days so there is more chance of a result. Also, I would like to see a ruling where counties have to play four players under the age of 24 in the Sunday League, so as to get youngsters introduced to first-team cricket as early as possible. Any other opinions should be left to my good mates "Wello" and Owais Shah because they both seem to know everything.'

1996 Season (did not make any first-class or one-day appearances)

Career Performances

	M	Inns	NO	Runs	HS	Avge	100s	50s	Ct	St	Balls	Runs	Wkts	Avge	Best	5wI	10wM
Test																	
All First																	
1-day Int																	
NatWest																	
B & H																	
Sunday	1	0	0	0	0	-		-	-	2	1						

NASH, D. J. Middlesex

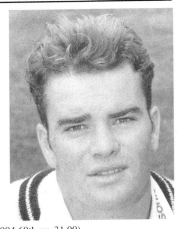

Name: Dion Joseph Nash
Role: Right-hand bat, right arm medium-fast bowler
Born: 20 November 1971, Auckland, New Zealand
Height: 6ft 2in **Weight:** 13st 5lbs
Nickname: Nashi
County debut: 1995
County cap: 1995
Test debut: 1992
Tests: 14
One-Day Internationals: 15
50 w. in a season: 1
1st-Class 50s: 5
1st-Class 5 w. in innings: 7
1st-Class 10 w. in match: 1
1st-Class catches: 30
Place in batting averages: 199th av. 20.61
Place in bowling averages: 61st av. 29.07 (1994 69th av. 31.00)
Strike rate: 60.00 (career 59.49)
Parents: Paul and Joan
Marital status: Single
Education: Pargaville High School; Auckland Grammar School; Otago University
Qualifications: School Certificate, 6th Form Certificate, University Bursary Bachelor of Arts
Career outside cricket: 'Yet to pursue one.'
Overseas tours: New Zealand Youth to India 1991-92; New Zealand to Zimbabwe and Sri Lanka 1992, to England 1994, to South Africa 1994-95, to India 1995-96, to India and Pakistan (World Cup) 1995-96

Cricketers particularly admired: Dennis Lillee, Dean Jones
Other sports followed: Rugby, surfing
Injuries: Persistent back injury caused him to fly home to New Zealand mid-season
Relaxations: Reading, music, all sports
Extras: Suspended from the New Zealand side for three one-day internationals in controversial circumstances along with team-mates Stephen Fleming and Matthew Hart in January 1995. Awarded county cap in August 1995. Was plagued with a back injury throughout the 1996 season and could only play two championship games before being released from his contract to fly back to New Zealand. The injury prevented him from participating in New Zealand's winter series with England
Opinions on cricket: 'More Test cricket should be played as opposed to increasing the number of one-day games.'
Best batting: 67 Middlesex v Essex, Chelmsford 1995
Best bowling: 6-30 New Zealand Academy XI v Northern Districts, Rotorua 1993-94

1996 Season

	M	Inns	NO	Runs	HS	Avge	100s	50s	Ct	St	O	M	Runs	Wkts	Avge	Best	5wI	10wM
Test																		
All First	2	3	1	15	8 *	7.50	-	-	1	-	10	1	44	1	44.00	1-44	-	-
1-day Int																		
NatWest																		
B & H																		
Sunday																		

Career Performances

	M	Inns	NO	Runs	HS	Avge	100s	50s	Ct	St	Balls	Runs	Wkts	Avge	Best	5wI	10wM
Test	14	21	6	236	56	15.73	-	1	7	-	2772	1308	44	29.72	6-76	2	1
All First	67	97	23	1341	67	18.12	-	5	30	-	9995	4859	168	28.92	6-30	7	1
1-day Int	15	11	3	94	40 *	11.75	-	-	4	-	654	541	12	45.08	3-43	-	
NatWest	3	3	0	6	4	2.00	-	-	1	-	120	93	1	93.00	1-36	-	
B & H	6	4	1	97	54	32.33	-	1	3	-	336	223	5	44.60	2-31	-	
Sunday	13	8	0	109	35	13.62	-	-	4	-	510	365	16	22.81	3-34	-	

Name: Keith Newell
Role: Right-hand bat, occasional medium-pace bowler
Born: 25 March 1972, Crawley
Height: 6ft **Weight:** 12st
Nickname: Ede, Wheely
County debut: 1993 (one-day), 1995 (first-class)
1st-Class 50s: 3
1st-Class 100s: 2
1st-Class catches: 4
Place in batting averages: 166th av. 29.25 (1995 138th av. 29.41)
Strike rate: 114.00 (career 366.00)
Parents: Peter Charles and Julie Anne
Marital status: Single
Family links with cricket: Brother Mark is on the Sussex staff. My other brother, Jonathan, plays for Sussex U17 and U19
Education: Gossops Green Junior School; Ifield Community College
Qualifications: 'A few GCSEs', coaching certificate
Career outside cricket: Cricket coach
Off-season: Getting ready for the next season
Overseas teams played for: Zimbabwe Universals 1989-90; Bulawayo Athletic Club 1991-92, 1995-96; Riverside CC, Wellington 1993-94
Cricketers particularly admired: Ian Botham
Young players to look out for: James Kirtley
Other sports followed: Table tennis, football, motor sport
Injuries: Broken hand and swollen knee, missed a total of 5 weeks
Relaxations: Going to the cinema, music
Opinions on cricket: 'Still too much cricket played. Slightly less cricket would help guarantee the players' enthusiasm to get out there and play.'
Best batting: 135 Sussex v West Indies, Hove 1995

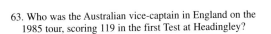

63. Who was the Australian vice-captain in England on the 1985 tour, scoring 119 in the first Test at Headingley?

1996 Season

	M	Inns	NO	Runs	HS	Avge	100s	50s	Ct	St	O	M	Runs	Wkts	Avge	Best	5wl	10wM
Test																		
All First	5	9	1	234	105 *	29.25	1	-	1	-	19	4	66	1	66.00	1-38	-	-
1-day Int																		
NatWest																		
B & H	3	2	0	46	46	23.00	-	-	-	-	13.1	1	57	1	57.00	1-25	-	
Sunday	9	8	1	80	32	11.42	-	-	2	-	7	0	69	1	69.00	1-12	-	

Career Performances

	M	Inns	NO	Runs	HS	Avge	100s	50s	Ct	St	Balls	Runs	Wkts	Avge	Best	5wl	10wM
Test																	
All First	16	30	3	798	135	29.55	2	3	4	-	366	211	1	211.00	1-38	-	-
1-day Int																	
NatWest	2	2	0	100	52	50.00	-	1	-	-							
B & H	4	3	0	81	46	27.00	-	-	-	-	79	57	1	57.00	1-25	-	
Sunday	21	17	2	297	76 *	19.80	-	1	4	-	156	196	1	196.00	1-12	-	

NEWELL, M.   Sussex

Name: Mark Newell
Role: Right-hand bat, right-arm fast-medium bowler
Born: 19 December 1973, Crawley
Height: 6ft 1in **Weight:** 12st
Nickname: Little Ede
County debut: 1996
1st-Class catches: 1
Parents: Peter Charles and Julie Anne
Marital status: Single
Family links with cricket: Brother Keith also on the Sussex staff, younger brother Jonathan plays for Sussex Young Cricketers
Education: Hazelwick Comprehensive; City of Westminster College
Qualifications: 9 GCSEs, GNVQ Advanced Leisure and Tourism, NCA Senior Coaching Award
Career outside cricket: None as yet
Off-season: Playing in Whangarei, New Zealand
Overseas tours: Sussex U18 to India 1990-91; Sussex U19 to Barbados (as captain) 1993-94

Overseas teams played for: Bulawayo Athletic Club, Zimbabwe 1991-92; Marist CC, Whangerei, New Zealand 1996-97

Cricketers particularly admired: Curtly Ambrose, Allan Donald, Allan Border, Graham Gooch

Other sports followed: 'A bit of football every now and then (support West Ham)'

Relaxations: 'Building a nest in the changing-room and sleeping in it.' Films and the film industry

Extras: MCC Young Cricketer in 1994. Was on a sponsored scholarship at Arundel Castle which enabled him and two others to work, play and coach all over Sussex for two years. Played Sussex youth cricket since he was nine years old. 'Bagged them, first-class debut versus Worcestershire – thanks "G"'

Opinions on cricket: 'Four-day cricket in 2nd XI.'

1996 Season

	M	Inns	NO	Runs	HS	Avge	100s	50s	Ct	St	O	M	Runs	Wkts	Avge	Best	5wI	10wM
Test																		
All First	1	2	0	0	0	0.00	-	-	1	-								
1-day Int																		
NatWest																		
B & H																		
Sunday	5	5	1	165	69	41.25	-	1	3	-								

Career Performances

	M	Inns	NO	Runs	HS	Avge	100s	50s	Ct	St	Balls	Runs	Wkts	Avge	Best	5wI	10wM
Test																	
All First	1	2	0	0	0	0.00	-	-	1	-							
1-day Int																	
NatWest																	
B & H																	
Sunday	5	5	1	165	69	41.25	-	1	3	-							

NEWELL, M.   Nottinghamshire

Name: Michael Newell

Role: Right-hand opening bat, leg-break bowler, occasional wicket-keeper

Born: 25 February 1965, Blackburn

Height: 5ft 10in **Weight:** 11st

Nickname: Mugly, Tricky, Animal

County debut: 1984

County cap: 1987

1000 runs in a season: 1

1st-Class 50s: 24

1st-Class 100s: 6
1st-Class 200s: 1
1st-Class catches: 93
1st-Class stumpings: 1
One-Day 100s: 1
Parents: Barry and Janet
Wife and date of marriage: Jayne, 23
September 1989
Children: Elizabeth Rose, 1 September 1993
Family links with cricket: Father chairman
of Notts Unity CC and brother, Paul, is the
captain
Education: West Bridgford Comprehensive
Qualifications: 8 O-levels, 3 A-levels, NCA
advanced coach
Cricketers particularly admired: Matthew
Dowman, Dominic Cork, James Hindson
Other sports followed: Rugby union,
football, darts
Relaxations: 'Feet up, slippers on in front of the television. Spending time with my family.'
Extras: Captain and coach of Nottinghamshire 2nd XI (The Stiffs)
Opinions on cricket: 'There has been a lot of scornful criticism of county cricket and its players from press people who have been too quick to moan. There are a lot of very good players in this country and some excellent young ones. Four-day cricket should lead to a revival in our Test fixtures and should sort out the better players from the average ones.'
Best batting: 203* Nottinghamshire v Derbyshire, Derby 1987
Best bowling: 2-38 Nottinghamshire v Sri Lankans, Trent Bridge 1988

1996 Season (did not make any first-class or one-day appearances)

Career Performances

	M	Inns	NO	Runs	HS	Avge	100s	50s	Ct	St	Balls	Runs	Wkts	Avge	Best	5wI	10wM
Test																	
All First	102	178	26	4636	203 *	30.50	6	24	93	1	363	282	7	40.28	2-38	-	-
1-day Int																	
NatWest	5	5	0	136	60	27.20	-	1	3	-	6	10	0	-		-	-
B & H	10	10	1	205	39	22.77	-	-	2	-							
Sunday	24	21	4	611	109 *	35.94	1	3	8	-							

Name: Philip John Newport
Role: Right-hand bat, right-arm
fast-medium bowler, outfielder
Born: 11 October 1962, High Wycombe
Height: 6ft 2in **Weight:** 13st 7lbs
Nickname: Schnozz, Newps
County debut: 1982
County cap: 1986
Test debut: 1988
Tests: 3
50 wickets in a season: 8
1st-Class 50s: 20
1st-Class 5 w. in innings: 34
1st-Class 10 w. in match: 3
1st-Class catches: 72
One-Day 5 w. in innings: 3
Place in batting averages: 208th av. 23.66

(1995 155th av. 26.93)
Place in bowling averages: 95th av. 35.26 (1995 20th av. 22.47)
Strike rate: 59.21 (career 52.50)
Parents: John and Sheila Diana
Wife and date of marriage: Christine Anne, 26 October 1985
Children: Nathan Alexander, 10 May 1989
Family links with cricket: Brother Stewart is captain of Octopus CC in North London
Education: Royal Grammar School, High Wycombe; Portsmouth University
Qualifications: 8 O-levels, 3 A-levels, BA (Hons) Geography, advanced coaching
qualification
Off-season: Coaching in the Worcester area
Overseas tours: NCA to Denmark 1981; England A to Pakistan 1990-91; England to
Australia 1990-91
Overseas teams played for: Vogeltown, New Plymouth, New Zealand 1986; Boland,
South Africa 1987-88; Ginnenderra and ACT, Australia 1991; Northern Transvaal,
South Africa 1992-93
Other sports followed: American football, basketball, golf, football (QPR)
Injuries: 'Achilles and lower back strain, missed threequarters of the season'
Relaxations: 'Cinema, spending time with my son (improving his golf swing and
cover drive)'
Extras: Had trial as schoolboy for Southampton FC. Played cricket for NAYC England
Schoolboys 1981 and for Buckinghamshire in Minor Counties Championship in 1981
and 1982. Selected for cancelled England tour to India 1988-89 and selected as a
replacement for England's tour to Australia in 1990-91. Winner of Worcestershire's Dick

Lygon Award 1992 and voted Worcestershire Player of the Year 1992 and 1993. Finished 3rd in the Whyte and Mackay bowling ratings in 1995

Opinions on cricket: 'A promotion/relegation system between two divisions (particularly the Sunday League) should maintain a highly competitive edge to all cricket throughout the whole season instead of just to the beginning of August.'

Best batting: 98 Worcestershire v New Zealanders, Worcester 1990

Best bowling: 8-52 Worcestershire v Middlesex, Lord's 1988

1996 Season

	M	Inns	NO	Runs	HS	Avge	100s	50s	Ct	St	O	M	Runs	Wkts	Avge	Best	5wI	10wM
Test																		
All First	6	6	0	142	68	23.66	-	1	1	-	187.3	44	670	19	35.26	6-100	1	-
1-day Int																		
NatWest	2	2	1	15	11	15.00	-	-	1	-	20	3	96	1	96.00	1-60	-	
B & H	1	1	0	15	15	15.00	-	-	-	-	10	0	39	0	-	-	-	-
Sunday	6	0	0	0	0	-	-	-	-	-	35	2	132	5	26.40	3-21	-	

Career Performances

	M	Inns	NO	Runs	HS	Avge	100s	50s	Ct	St	Balls	Runs	Wkts	Avge	Best	5wI	10wM
Test	3	5	1	110	40 *	27.50	-	-	1	-	669	417	10	41.70	4-87	-	-
All First	257	299	87	5344	98	25.20	-	20	72	-	41479	21598	790	27.33	8-52	34	3
1-day Int																	
NatWest	29	15	5	132	25	13.20	-	-	3	-	1557	956	38	25.15	4-30	-	
B & H	47	22	6	164	28	10.25	-	-	9	-	2993	1514	68	22.26	5-22	2	
Sunday	156	67	25	433	26 *	10.30	-	-	32	-	6130	4329	162	26.72	5-32	1	

64. Who was the Kent paceman who played in only two Ashes Tests in the 1980s, taking 17 wickets at 10.80?

NIXON, P. A.   Leicestershire

Name: Paul Andrew Nixon
Role: Left-hand bat, wicket-keeper
Born: 21 October 1970, Carlisle
Height: 5ft 11in **Weight:** 12st 9lbs
Nickname: Nico, Nobby
County debut: 1989
1000 runs in a season: 1
1st-Class 50s: 14
1st-Class 100s: 8
1st-Class catches: 324
1st-Class stumpings: 27
Place in batting averages: 74th av. 40.00
(1995 220th 18.44)
Parents: Brian and Sylvia
Marital status: Single
Family links with cricket: 'Grandad and
father played local league cricket. Mom made
the teas for Edenhall CC, Penrith'

Education: Langwathby Primary; Ullswater High
Qualifications: Coaching certificates
Career outside cricket: 'Partner in "Time to Relax" stress and massage company'
Off-season: Watching football at Leicester, Liverpool and Newcastle
Overseas tours: Cumbria U16 to Denmark 1985; Leicestershire to Holland 1991, to
Montego Bay 1992, to Bloemfontein 1994 and 1995; England A to India 1994-95
Overseas teams played for: Melville and North Fremantle, Perth, Western Australia
1989-92; Mitchells Rain, Cape Town 1993; Primrose CC, Cape Town, South Africa
1995-96
Cricketers particularly admired: David Gower, Alan Knott, Bob Taylor, Jack
Russell
Young players to look out for: Darren Maddy, Aftab Habib
Other sports followed: Football (Carlisle United, Newcastle United and Liverpool FC)
Injuries: 'None, thank God'
Relaxations: 'Walking with Our Jen in Lake District and Scotland'
Extras: Youngest person to score a century against Yorkshire (at U15). Played for
England U15 and played in Minor Counties Championship for Cumberland at 16, MCC
Young Pro in 1988. Took eight catches in debut match v Warwickshire at Hinckley in
1989. Played for Carlisle United and 'once got lost in South African township at
3.30am'. Leicester Young Player of the Year two years running. Second Leicester
wicket-keeper to score 1000 runs in a season. Voted Cumbrian Sports Personality of the
Year 1994-95. Has signed a contract that will keep him at Grace Road until the year 2000
Opinions on cricket: 'Two divisions. Stop advertising boards in front of sightscreens.

Also umpires should wear lighter coloured trousers.'
Best batting: 131 Leicestershire v Hampshire, Leicester 1994

1996 Season

	M	Inns	NO	Runs	HS	Avge	100s	50s	Ct	St	O	M	Runs	Wkts	Avge	Best	5wI	10wM
Test																		
All First	20	27	5	880	106	40.00	3	4	56	6								
1-day Int																		
NatWest	2	2	1	77	39	77.00	-	-	4	2								
B & H	5	5	1	67	26 *	16.75	-	-	3	1								
Sunday	16	13	3	177	32 *	17.70	-	-	11	5								

Career Performances

	M	Inns	NO	Runs	HS	Avge	100s	50s	Ct	St	Balls	Runs	Wkts	Avge	Best	5wI	10wM
Test																	
All First	124	179	39	4029	131	28.77	8	14	324	27							
1-day Int																	
NatWest	14	12	4	204	39	25.50	-	-	16	4							
B & H	12	11	1	125	27	12.50	-	-	6	2							
Sunday	94	77	13	1317	84	20.57	-	6	72	18							

NOON, W. M. Nottinghamshire

Name: Wayne Michael Noon
Role: Right-hand bat, wicket-keeper
Born: 5 February 1971, Grimsby
Height: 5ft 9in **Weight:** 11st 7lbs
Nickname: Noonie
County debut: 1988 (one-day),
1989 (first-class) (Northamptonshire),
1994 (Nottinghamshire)
County cap: 1995 (Nottinghamshire)
1st-Class 50s: 9
1st-Class catches: 129
1st-Class stumpings: 16
Place in batting averages: 241st av. 18.44
(1995 131st av. 29.80)
Parents: Trafford and Rosemary
Marital status: Engaged
Education: Caistor Grammar School
Qualifications: 5 O-levels
Career outside cricket: 'Still looking'

Off-season: 'Staying at home for the first time in ages'
Overseas tours: Lincolnshire U15 to Pakistan 1984; England YC to Australia 1989-90; Rutland tourists to South Africa 1988; Northamptonshire to Durban 1992, to Cape Town 1993
Overseas teams played for: Burnside West, Christchurch, New Zealand 1989-90 and 1993-96; Rivertonians, Cape Town 1993-94; Canterbury, Christchurch 1994-95
Cricketers particularly admired: Ian Botham, Graham Gooch
Young players to look out for: 'Too young myself'
Other sports followed: Football (Lincoln City), horse racing (flat)
Injuries: Thigh, missed two to three weeks
Relaxations: Having a bet. Eating out and having a pint
Extras: Played for England YC v New Zealand YC 1989; captain v Australian YC 1989-90 and Pakistan YC 1990. Was the 1000th player to appear in the Sunday League competition. Broke the Northants record for most 2nd XI hundreds in one season in 1993
Best batting: 75 Nottinghamshire v Northamptonshire, Trent Bridge 1994

1996 Season

	M	Inns	NO	Runs	HS	Avge	100s	50s	Ct	St	O	M	Runs	Wkts	Avge	Best	5wI	10wM
Test																		
All First	13	21	3	332	57	18.44	-	1	30	3	4	1	22	0	-	-	-	-
1-day Int																		
NatWest																		
B & H	4	2	0	11	10	5.50	-	-	2	2								
Sunday	16	5	2	27	12	9.00	-	-	14	2								

Career Performances

	M	Inns	NO	Runs	HS	Avge	100s	50s	Ct	St	Balls	Runs	Wkts	Avge	Best	5wI	10wM
Test																	
All First	62	102	17	1881	75	22.12	-	9	129	16	24	22	0	-	-	-	-
1-day Int																	
NatWest	4	2	0	41	34	20.50	-	-	2	2							
B & H	10	6	1	63	23	12.60	-	-	6	3							
Sunday	61	36	9	332	38	12.29	-	-	45	9							

NOWELL, R. W.   Surrey

Name: Richard William Nowell
Role: Left-hand bat, slow left-arm bowler
Born: 29 December 1975, Croydon
Height: 6ft **Weight:** 12st 7lbs
Nickname: Muesli, Nosebleed, Sid Yobbo, Cockforester
County debut: 1995

1st-Class catches: 5
Place in bowling averages: 118th av. 39.50
Strike rate: 93.00 (career 80.44)
Parents: Bill and June
Marital status: Single
Family links with cricket: 'Father played for Surrey club and ground and once ran out Peter May in a benefit match. Mum fancies David Gower'
Education: Cumnor House Prep School; Trinity School, Croydon
Qualifications: 9 GCSEs, 2 A-levels, coaching certificate
Career outside cricket: 'Potential nightclub owner'
Off-season: Playing in South Africa
Overseas tours: England U18 to South Africa 1992-93
Overseas teams played for: Technikon, Natal 1994-95
Cricketers particularly admired: Graham Kersey, Tim May, Oliver Slipper
Other sports followed: Rugby union and league ('Used to support Arsenal but they have become too exciting to watch lately')
Relaxations: Shopping, 'mixing a few tunes on the decks and a pint of Caffrey's with my mates'
Extras: Played for Surrey from U11 to U19. Played England U15, U17 and U18. Holds record for highest aggregate of runs in school cricket
Opinions on cricket: 'Perhaps the season could be slightly extended to allow for more rest and time to practise. The Sunday League should organise drinking competitions and speakers to liven it up further'
Best batting: 28* Surrey v South Africa A, The Oval 1996
Best bowling: 4-43 Surrey v Nottinghamshire, Guildford 1995

1996 Season

	M	Inns	NO	Runs	HS	Avge	100s	50s	Ct	St	O	M	Runs	Wkts	Avge	Best	5wl	10wM
Test																		
All First	1	2	1	28	28 *	28.00	-	-	-	-	31	5	133	2	66.50	2-76	-	-
1-day Int																		
NatWest																		
B & H																		
Sunday																		

Career Performances

	M	Inns	NO	Runs	HS	Avge	100s	50s	Ct	St	Balls	Runs	Wkts	Avge	Best	5wl	10wM
Test																	
All First	12	22	3	162	28 *	8.52	-	-	5	-	2735	1397	34	41.08	4-43	-	-
1-day Int																	
NatWest	1	1	1	2	2 *	-	-	-	1	-	30	35	0	-		-	-
B & H	2	1	1	15	15 *	-	-	-	1	-	84	47	1	47.00	1-35	-	
Sunday	2	1	0	0	0	0.00	-	-	1	-	48	31	0	-		-	-

O'GORMAN, T. J. G.   Derbyshire

Name: Timothy Joseph Gerard O'Gorman
Role: Right-hand bat, off-spin bowler
Born: 15 May 1967, Woking
Height: 6ft 2in **Weight:** 12st
County debut: 1987
County cap: 1992
1000 runs in a season: 2
1st-Class 50s: 28
1st-Class 100s: 10
1st-Class catches: 76
Place in batting averages: 93rd av. 37.41
(1995 246th av. 15.62)
Strike rate: (career 88.33)
Parents: Brian and Kathleen
Marital status: Single
Family links with cricket: Grandfather Joe
O'Gorman played for Surrey
Education: St George's College, Weybridge;
St Chad's College, Durham University;
College of Law, Guildford
Qualifications: 12 O-levels, 3 A-levels, BA (Hons) Law; Law Society finals
Career outside cricket: Solicitor
Off-season: Working for Ashurst Morris Crisp in the City
Overseas tours: Troubadours to Argentina 1987, to Brazil 1989; Christians in Sport to
Zimbabwe 1994-95
Overseas teams played for: Alexandra, Zimbabwe; Southern Hawkes Bay, New Zealand
Cricketers particularly admired: David Gower, Greg Chappell, Richard Hadlee
Young players to look out for: Vikram Solanki, David Sales, Andrew Harris
Other sports followed: Tennis, golf, hockey, rugby, football
Injuries: Cartilage operation, out for seven weeks
Relaxations: Arts, theatre, music, reading

Extras: Surrey Young Cricketer of the Year 1984. Captained Surrey Young Cricketers for three years. Trials for England schoolboys at hockey
Best batting: 148 Derbyshire v Lancashire, Old Trafford 1991
Best bowling: 1-7 Derbyshire v Cambridge University, Fenner's 1992

1996 Season

	M	Inns	NO	Runs	HS	Avge	100s	50s	Ct	St	O	M	Runs	Wkts	Avge	Best	5wI	10wM
Test																		
All First	11	20	3	636	109 *	37.41	1	6	7	-								
1-day Int																		
NatWest	3	3	1	104	62 *	52.00	-	1	2	-								
B & H																		
Sunday	10	9	3	201	43 *	33.50	-	-	4	-								

Career Performances

	M	Inns	NO	Runs	HS	Avge	100s	50s	Ct	St	Balls	Runs	Wkts	Avge	Best	5wI	10wM
Test																	
All First	117	197	24	5372	148	31.05	10	28	76	-	265	215	3	71.66	1-7	-	-
1-day Int																	
NatWest	10	10	2	268	89	33.50	-	3	3	-							
B & H	25	21	1	404	49	20.20	-	-	6	-	6	1	0	-		-	-
Sunday	92	85	18	1735	69	25.89	-	5	17	-							

ORMOND, J.   Leicestershire

Name: James Ormond
Role: Right-hand bat, right-arm fast-medium bowler
Born: 20 August 1977, Walsgrave, Coventry
Height: 6ft 3in **Weight:** 14st 7lbs
Nickname: Horse, Trigger, Pepé
County debut: 1995
1st-Class catches: 1
Parents: Richard and Margaret
Marital status: Single
Family links with cricket:
Dad played a bit for local club
Education: St Anthony's, Bedworth; St Thomas More, Nuneaton; North Warwickshire College of Further Education
Qualifications: 6 GCSEs
Off-season: Playing overseas

Overseas tours: England U19 to Zimbabwe 1995-96
Cricketers particularly admired: Ian Botham
Young players to look out for: Iain Sutcliffe, Ben Hollioake
Other sports followed: Football (Coventry City)
Injuries: Side strain, out for three weeks
Relaxations: Music and going out
Extras: Played for the Development of Excellence side and England U19 against South Africa U19 in 1995. Was forced to return home after one day of the England U19 tour to Zimbabwe in 1995-96 through injury. Played for England U19 in the summer series against New Zealand U19
Best bowling: 2-65 Leicestershire v Oxford University, The Parks 1995

1996 Season

	M	Inns	NO	Runs	HS	Avge	100s	50s	Ct	St	O	M	Runs	Wkts	Avge	Best	5wI	10wM
Test																		
All First																		
1-day Int																		
NatWest																		
B & H																		
Sunday	3	1	1	2	2 *	-	-	-	-	-	11	0	63	1	63.00	1-32	-	

Career Performances

	M	Inns	NO	Runs	HS	Avge	100s	50s	Ct	St	Balls	Runs	Wkts	Avge	Best	5wI	10wM
Test																	
All First	1	0	0	0	0	-	-	-	1	-	102	65	2	32.50	2-65	-	-
1-day Int																	
NatWest																	
B & H																	
Sunday	4	1	1	2	2 *	-	-	-	-	-	102	104	1	104.00	1-32	-	

65. Who was David Gower's Tiger Moth-flying partner when he buzzed the Carrara ground during England's innings on the 1990-91 tour?

OSTLER, D. P.   Warwickshire

Name: Dominic Piers Ostler
Role: Right-hand bat, right-arm
medium bowler
Born: 15 July 1970, Solihull
Height: 6ft 2in **Weight:** 14st
Nickname: Ossie, Blondie
County debut: 1990
County cap: 1991
1000 runs in a season: 4
1st-Class 50s: 47
1st-Class 100s: 9
1st-Class 200s: 1
1st-Class catches: 149
One-Day 100s: 1
Place in batting averages: 160th av. 29.75
(1995 61st av. 40.95)
Parents: Mike and Ann
Marital status: Single
Family links with cricket: Brother plays for
Knowle and Dorridge

Education: Our Lady of the Wayside; Princethorpe College; Solihull Technical
College
Qualifications: 4 O-levels, City and Guilds Recreation Course
Off-season: Doing up the house and playing golf
Overseas tours: Gladstone Small's Benefit Tour to Barbados, 1992; England A to
Pakistan 1995-96
Overseas teams played for: Avendale CC, South Africa 1991-92
Cricketers particularly admired: Trevor Penney, Gladstone Small, Graeme Welch,
Jason Radcliffe
Young players to look out for: Ashley Giles
Other sports followed: Football (Birmingham City)
Injuries: Cartilage damage, missed two weeks
Relaxations: Taking the dog for a walk
Extras: Played club cricket for Moseley in the Birmingham League; made his
Warwickshire 2nd XI debut in 1989 and was a member of Warwickshire U19 side that
won Esso U19 County Festivals in 1988 and 1989. Has collected winner's medals for
B&H Cup, Britannic Assurance County Championship, NatWest Trophy and Sunday
League
Opinions on cricket: 'The wickets aren't up to standard'
Best batting: 208 Warwickshire v Surrey, Edgbaston 1995

1996 Season

	M	Inns	NO	Runs	HS	Avge	100s	50s	Ct	St	O	M	Runs	Wkts	Avge	Best	5wI	10wM
Test																		
All First	18	32	3	863	90	29.75	-	8	35	-								
1-day Int																		
NatWest	2	2	0	31	20	15.50	-	-	4	-								
B & H	6	5	1	293	86	73.25	-	3	5	-								
Sunday	15	15	1	462	91 *	33.00	-	3	4	-								

Career Performances

	M	Inns	NO	Runs	HS	Avge	100s	50s	Ct	St	Balls	Runs	Wkts	Avge	Best	5wI	10wM
Test																	
All First	132	224	19	7240	208	35.31	9	47	149	-	143	122	0	-	-	-	-
1-day Int																	
NatWest	26	25	3	651	104	29.59	1	3	13	-	9	4	1	4.00	1-4	-	
B & H	24	23	3	923	87	46.15	-	9	12	-							
Sunday	101	94	11	2546	91 *	30.67	-	18	27	-	6	4	0	-	-	-	-

OWEN, J. E. Derbyshire

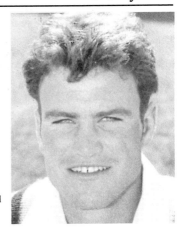

Name: John Edward Owen
Role: Right-hand bat
Born: 7 August 1971, Derby
Height: 5ft 10in **Weight:** 12st
Nickname: Horts 'after grandfather Horton Owen'
County debut: 1995
1st-Class 50s: 4
1st-Class 100s: 2
1st-Class catches: 3
Place in batting averages: 133rd av. 33.26 (1995 164th av. 25.00)
Parents: David Horton and Carole
Marital status: Single
Family links with cricket: Father played in Derbyshire League for Alvaston, Boulton and Spondon and a few times for Derbyshire 2nd XI. Grandfather played for Crewe in the North Staffs South Cheshire league
Education: Springfield Primary School; Spondon School, Derby; Broomfield College
Qualifications: NCA coach, qualified green-keeper
Career outside cricket: 'Don't know yet'

Off-season: Playing for Monte Albert CC in Melbourne, Australia
Cricketers particularly admired: Viv Richards, Brian Lara, Dean Jones, Chris Adams, Kim Barnett
Young players to look out for: Andrew Harris, David Sales
Other sports followed: Football (Derby County), golf, rugby union
Relaxations: Cinema, reading, spending time with family and friends
Opinions on cricket: 'I think we should cut out one of the one-day competitions. The Sunday League is fun and popular with the public so maybe one of the others should go.'
Best batting: 105 Derbyshire v Glamorgan, Cardiff 1996

1996 Season

	M	Inns	NO	Runs	HS	Avge	100s	50s	Ct	St	O	M	Runs	Wkts	Avge	Best	5wI	10wM
Test																		
All First	9	15	0	499	105	33.26	2	2	3	-								
1-day Int																		
NatWest	2	2	0	10	7	5.00	-	-	1	-								
B & H	2	2	0	70	49	35.00	-	-	-	-								
Sunday	7	6	0	95	40	15.83	-	-	2	-								

Career Performances

	M	Inns	NO	Runs	HS	Avge	100s	50s	Ct	St	Balls	Runs	Wkts	Avge	Best	5wI	10wM
Test																	
All First	13	23	0	699	105	30.39	2	4	3	-							
1-day Int																	
NatWest	2	2	0	10	7	5.00	-	-	1	-							
B & H	2	2	0	70	49	35.00	-	-	-	-							
Sunday	11	10	1	186	45	20.66	-	-	2	-							

PARKER, B.   Yorkshire

Name: Bradley Parker
Role: Right-hand bat, right-arm medium
bowler, cover point fielder
Born: 23 June 1970, Mirfield
Height: 5ft 10in **Weight:** 12st 7lbs
Nickname: Nesty, Ceefax, Floyd
County debut: 1992
1st-Class 50s: 5
1st-Class 100s: 1
1st-Class catches: 10
Place in batting averages: 178th av. 23.00
(1994 82nd av. 36.12)
Parents: Diane and David
Marital status: Single
Family links with cricket: Father played
club cricket and Lincolnshire U23
Education: Bingley Grammar School
Qualifications: 'None worth mentioning
from school.' Cricket coaching awards

Off-season: 'Training, and keeping to my strict diet'
Overseas teams played for: Ellerslie, Auckland 1988-90
Cricketers particularly admired: Chris Spence, Alec Stewart, Graham Thorpe
Other sports followed: Rugby league, boxing
Relaxations: Films, eating out, drinking and socialising
Opinions on cricket: 'Far too much cricket played in too short a time.'
Best batting: 127 Yorkshire v Surrey, Scarborough 1994

1996 Season

	M	Inns	NO	Runs	HS	Avge	100s	50s	Ct	St	O	M	Runs	Wkts	Avge	Best	5wI	10wM
Test																		
All First	1	1	0	59	59	59.00	-	1	-	-								
1-day Int																		
NatWest																		
B & H																		
Sunday																		

Career Performances

	M	Inns	NO	Runs	HS	Avge	100s	50s	Ct	St	Balls	Runs	Wkts	Avge	Best	5wI	10wM
Test																	
All First	17	31	3	853	127	30.46	1	5	10	-							
1-day Int																	
NatWest	1	0	0	0	0	-	-	-	-	-							
B & H																	
Sunday	22	19	3	287	36	17.93	-	-	5	-							

PARKIN, O. T.　　　　　　Glamorgan

Name: Owen Thomas Parkin
Role: Right-hand bat, right-arm medium-fast bowler
Born: 24 August 1972, Coventry
Height: 6ft 2in **Weight:** 11st 10lbs
Nickname: Short-term, Residential, Parallel, Parky
County debut: 1994
1st-Class catches: 4
One-Day 5 w. in innings: 1
Place in bowling averages: 126th av. 43.26
Strike rate: 79.29 (career 79.61)
Parents: Vernon Cyrus and Sarah Patricia
Marital status: Single
Family links with cricket: Younger brother Morgan plays for the county in his age group and took a hat-trick last year
Education: Bournemouth Grammar School; Bath University
Qualifications: 9 GCSEs, 4 A-levels, 1 S-level, BSc (Hons) in Mathematics
Career outside cricket: Coaching
Overseas tours: Dorset Youth to Denmark
Overseas teams played for: Kew, Melbourne 1992-93; North Balwyn, Melbourne 1993-94
Cricketers particularly admired: Malcolm Marshall, Richard Hadlee
Other sports followed: Rugby, football (Nottingham Forest), golf
Injuries: 'None!'
Relaxations: General socialising and listening to 'Green Day'
Extras: Played for Dorset in the NatWest Trophy 1992 and 1993. ASW Young Player of the Month July 1994. Took 5 for 28 on debut in Sunday League at Hove – a club record

Opinions on cricket: 'The reverse sweep should be banned – as bowlers you have to tell the batsman which hand you are going to use and which side of the wicket you are going to bowl, yet as a right-hand batsman you play this shot and become a left-hand player whenever you like – it would be a refreshing change to have a rule brought in that was not in favour of the batsman.'

Best batting: 14 Glamorgan v Warwickshire, Edgbaston 1996
Best bowling: 3-22 Glamorgan v Durham, Chester-le-Street 1996

1996 Season

	M	Inns	NO	Runs	HS	Avge	100s	50s	Ct	St	O	M	Runs	Wkts	Avge	Best	5wI	10wM
Test																		
All First	10	12	7	65	14	13.00	-	-	4	-	224.4	47	744	17	43.76	3-22	-	-
1-day Int																		
NatWest	1	1	1	1	1 *	-	-	-	2	-	12	1	23	3	7.66	3-23	-	
B & H																		
Sunday	5	0	0	0	0	-	-	-	-	-	38	5	173	9	19.22	5-28	1	

Career Performances

	M	Inns	NO	Runs	HS	Avge	100s	50s	Ct	St	Balls	Runs	Wkts	Avge	Best	5wI	10wM
Test																	
All First	12	14	9	67	14	13.40	-	-	4	-	1672	914	21	43.52	3-22	-	-
1-day Int																	
NatWest	3	2	1	1	1 *	1.00	-	-	2	-	120	77	3	25.66	3-23	-	
B & H																	
Sunday	5	0	0	0	0	-	-	-	-	-	228	173	9	19.22	5-28	1	

PARSONS, G. J.   Leicestershire

Name: Gordon James Parsons
Role: Left-hand bat, right-arm medium-fast bowler
Born: 17 October 1959, Slough
Height: 6ft 1in **Weight:** 13st ('April') – 14st ('September')
Nickname: Bullhead
County debut: 1978 (Leicestershire), 1986 (Warwickshire)
County cap: 1984 (Leicestershire), 1987 (Warwickshire)
Benefit: 1994
50 wickets in a season: 3
1st-Class 50s: 28
1st-Class 5 w. in innings: 19
1st-Class 10 w. in match: 1
1st-Class catches: 143

Place in batting averages: 260th av. 16.11
(1995 211th av. 19.26)
Place in bowling averages: 75th av. 32.68
(1995 68th av. 29.62)
Strike rate: 70.85 (career 61.00)
Parents: David and Evelyn
Wife and date of marriage: Hester Sophia,
8 February 1991
Children: Alexandra Suzanna, 5 June 1992;
James, 12 December 1995
Family links with cricket: Brothers-in-law,
Hansie and Frans Cronje, both play first-class
cricket in South Africa. Dad played club
cricket 'in the days when bowlers hit a
sixpence five balls in six'
Education: Wexham Primary School;
Woodside County Secondary School, Slough
Qualifications: 5 O-levels
Career outside cricket: Coaching North-West Province in South Africa
Overseas tours: English Schools to India 1977-78; Derrick Robins XI to Australasia
1980; Leicestershire to Zimbabwe 1981, to Jamaica 1993
Overseas teams played for: Maharaja's, Sri Lanka 1979,1987; Boland, South Africa
1982-83; Griqualand West, South Africa 1984-85; Orange Free State, South Africa 1986-92
Cricketers particularly admired: Vince Wells, Graham Lloyd, Andy Moles
Young players to look out for: Darren Maddy
Other sports followed: Golf, football (Reading FC)
Injuries: 'Usual aches and pains that make the body feel like it was hit by a runaway
train'
Relaxations: Family, videos and music
Extras: Played for Leicester 2nd XI from 1976 and for Buckinghamshire in 1977. Left
Leicestershire after 1985 season and joined Warwickshire. Capped by Warwickshire
while in plaster and on crutches. Released at end of 1988 season and returned to his old
county. Justin Benson was best man at his wedding, 'contradiction in terms, though it is!'
Opinions on cricket: 'I don't think that English cricket is as bad as I keep reading. It's
still very strong. The format is about right, but I would like to see the Championship
games finish before the Sunday League. 2nd XI cricket is a worry as the jump between
second-class and first-class cricket is too big.'
Best batting: 76 Boland v Western Province B, Cape Town 1984-85
Best bowling: 9-72 Boland v Transvaal B, Johannesburg 1984-85

---

66. Alan Knott, Bob Taylor and which other wicket-keeper
played for England in the 1981 series?

1996 Season

	M	Inns	NO	Runs	HS	Avge	100s	50s	Ct	St	O	M	Runs	Wkts	Avge	Best	5wI	10wM
Test																		
All First	18	23	5	290	53	16.11	-	2	22	-	555	170	1536	47	32.68	4-21	-	-
1-day Int																		
NatWest	2	1	0	4	4	4.00	-	-	-	-	18	4	46	2	23.00	1-5	-	
B & H	5	3	0	32	19	10.66	-	-	-	-	46	3	187	6	31.16	2-33	-	
Sunday	9	7	4	39	23 *	13.00	-	-	1	-	62	0	316	8	39.50	3-37	-	

Career Performances

	M	Inns	NO	Runs	HS	Avge	100s	50s	Ct	St	Balls	Runs	Wkts	Avge	Best	5wI	10wM
Test																	
All First	330	440	97	6616	76	19.28	-	28	143	-	48499	23861	795	30.01	9-72	19	1
1-day Int																	
NatWest	32	21	6	172	25 *	11.46	-	-	7	-	1784	1097	25	43.88	2-11	-	
B & H	60	34	14	353	63 *	17.65	-	1	11	-	3240	1946	71	27.40	4-12	-	
Sunday	196	123	51	1113	38 *	15.45	-	-	28	-	8089	5987	195	30.70	4-19	-	

PARSONS, K. A.   Somerset

Name: Keith Alan Parsons
Role: Right-hand bat, right-arm medium bowler
Born: 2 May 1973, Taunton
Height: 6ft 1in **Weight:** 13st 6lbs
Nickname: Pilot, Pars, Orv
County debut: 1992
1st-Class 50s: 7
1st-Class 100s: 1
1st-Class catches: 18
Place in batting averages: 167th 117th av. 31.57
Strike rate: 114.00 (career 111.00)
Parents: Alan and Lynne
Marital status: Single
Family links with cricket: Identical twin brother, Kevin, was on the Somerset staff 1992-94 and now plays Minor Counties for Wiltshire. Father played six seasons for Somerset 2nd XI and captained National Civil Service XI
Education: Castle School, Taunton; Richard Huish Sixth Form College, Taunton
Qualifications: 8 GCSEs, 3 A-levels, NCA coaching award

Off-season: Unknown as yet but staying at home for a rest from cricket
Overseas tours: Castle School to Barbados 1989
Overseas teams played for: Kapiti Old Boys, New Zealand 1992-93; Harowhenera, New Zealand 1992-93; Taita District, Wellington, New Zealand 1993-96
Cricketers particularly admired: Viv Richards, Richard Hadlee, Robin Smith
Other sports followed: Rugby union (Bath RFC), football (Nottingham Forest FC), golf
Relaxations: 'All sports'
Extras: Captained two National Cup winning sides – Taunton St Andrews in National U15 Club Championship and Richard Huish College in National U17 School Championship. Represented English Schools at U15 and U19 level. Somerset Young Player of the Year 1993
Opinions on cricket: 'Now that the first-class Championship has been changed to four-day games, in order to improve the Test team and reduce the amount of contrived finishes, shouldn't the next step be to change the 2nd XI competition to a four-day Championship also, to help the younger players, in 2nd XI, become better four-day cricketers?'
Best batting: 105 Somerset v Young Australia, Taunton 1995
Best bowling: 2-11 Somerset v Derbyshire, Derby 1995

1996 (did not make any first-class or one-day appearances)

Career Performances

	M	Inns	NO	Runs	HS	Avge	100s	50s	Ct	St	Balls	Runs	Wkts	Avge	Best	5wl	10wM
Test																	
All First	25	44	4	994	105	24.85	1	7	18	-	660	493	6	82.16	2-11		
1-day Int																	
NatWest	3	3	1	81	48	40.50	-	-	-	-	120	91	2	45.50	2-47		
B & H																	
Sunday	18	18	1	331	52*	19.47	-	1	5	-	324	245	8	30.62	2-16		

67. Which Australian off-spinner took 22 wickets in the 1982-83 Test series?

PATEL, M. M. Kent

Name: Minal Mahesh Patel
Role: Right-hand bat, slow left-arm bowler
Born: 7 August 1970, Bombay, India
Height: 5ft 9in **Weight:** 9st 10lbs
Nickname: Geezer, Diamond, Ho-Chi
County debut: 1989
County cap: 1994
Test debut: 1996
Tests: 2
50 w. in a season: 2
1st-Class 50s: 2
1st-Class 5 w. in innings: 15
1st-Class 10 w. in match: 7
1st-Class catches: 42
Place in batting averages: 267th av. 15.44
(1995 237th av. 16.34)
Place in bowling averages: 135th av. 47.15
(1995 101st av. 35.39)
Strike rate: 106.54 (career 72.69)
Parents: Mahesh and Aruna
Wife and date of marriage: Karuna,
8 October 1995
Family links with cricket: Father played good club cricket in India, Africa and England
Education: Dartford GS; Erith College of Technology; Manchester Polytechnic
Qualifications: 6 O-levels, 3 A-levels, BA (Hons) in Economics
Overseas tours: Dartford GS to Barbados 1988; England A to India 1994-95
Cricketers particularly admired: Derek Underwood, Kapil Dev, Carl Hooper, Aravinda De Silva
Other sports followed: Football (Tottenham Hotspur), American football and basketball
Injuries: Double fracture of right cheekbone, missed two games
Relaxations: Playing golf, listening to music
Extras: Played for English Schools 1988, 1989 and NCA England South 1989. Was voted Kent League Young Player of the Year 1987 while playing for Blackheath. First six overs in NatWest Trophy were all maidens. Whittingdale Young Player of the Year 1994
Opinions on cricket: 'Far too much cricket in the domestic season leads to a "going through the motions" attitude if the county is not competing for trophies. The amount of driving could also lead to a serious accident or injury.'
Best batting: 56 Kent v Leicestershire, Canterbury 1995

Best bowling: 8-96 Kent v Lancashire, Canterbury 1994

1996 Season

	M	Inns	NO	Runs	HS	Avge	100s	50s	Ct	St	O	M	Runs	Wkts	Avge	Best	5wI	10wM
Test	2	2	0	45	27	22.50	-	-	2	-	46	8	180	1	180.00	1-101	-	-
All First	18	23	5	278	33	15.44	-	-	9	-	586	176	1556	33	47.15	6-97	2	1
1-day Int																		
NatWest	2	1	1	5	5 *	-	-	-	3	-	16.2	2	60	2	30.00	1-26	-	
B & H	6	4	4	38	18 *	-	-	-	2	-	36	2	198	4	49.50	2-74	-	
Sunday																		

Career Performances

	M	Inns	NO	Runs	HS	Avge	100s	50s	Ct	St	Balls	Runs	Wkts	Avge	Best	5wI	10wM
Test	2	2	0	45	27	22.50	-	-	2	-	276	180	1	180.00	1-101	-	-
All First	79	112	25	1193	56	13.71	-	2	42	-	18173	8108	250	32.43	8-96	15	7
1-day Int																	
NatWest	6	2	1	9	5 *	9.00	-	-	5	-	386	200	7	28.57	2-29	-	
B & H	10	6	5	39	18 *	39.00	-	-	3	-	456	327	6	54.50	2-29	-	
Sunday	6	2	0	6	5	3.00	-	-	1	-	176	191	6	31.83	3-50	-	

PATTERSON, M. W. Surrey

Name: Mark William Patterson
Role: Right-hand bat, right-arm fast-medium bowler
Born: 2 February 1974, Belfast
Height: 6ft 1in **Weight:** 12st 4lbs
Nickname: Paddy, Pato, Irish
County debut: 1996
1st-Class 5 w. in innings: 1
Strike rate: (career 23.57)
Parents: Billy and Phyllis
Marital status: Single
Family links with cricket: Dad has always played club cricket. Younger brother plays for Ireland as a wicket-keeper batsman and has ambitions to play county cricket
Education: Carnmoney Primary School; Belfast Royal Academy; University of Ulster
Qualifications: 9 GCSEs, 3 A-levels, BA (Hons) in Sport and Leisure Studies
Career outside cricket: Qualified coach in soccer, cricket, rugby, hockey, basketball,

swimming and squash
Off-season: Playing for Burne Yeoman CC in Tasmania
Overseas tours: Ireland U19 to Denmark for International Youth Tournament 1993; Ireland to Denmark for European Championships 1996
Overseas teams played for: Mount Maunganui, Bay of Plenty, New Zealand 1994-95
Cricketers particularly admired: Malcolm Marshall, John Solanky 'our first club professional in Ireland'
Young players to look out for: Alex Tudor, Ben Hollioake
Other sports followed: Soccer (Lingfield, Rangers and Manchester United)
Injuries: 'Just a few niggles'
Relaxations: Drinking with friends, clubbing, dance music, watching Lingfield with my dad and horse racing
Extras: 1993 Irish Young Cricketer of the Year. In 1996 took 6 for 80 against South Africa A – the best ever figures by a Surrey bowler on debut
Opinions on cricket: 'The county championship needs a new image and structure that will make it more appealing to spectators, sponsors and television.'
Best batting: 4 Surrey v South Africa A, The Oval 1996
Best bowling: 6-80 Surrey v South Africa A, The Oval 1996

1996 Season

	M	Inns	NO	Runs	HS	Avge	100s	50s	Ct	St	O	M	Runs	Wkts	Avge	Best	5wI	10wM
Test																		
All First	1	2	0	6	4	3.00	-	-	-	-	27.3	7	124	7	17.71	6-80	1	-
1-day Int																		
NatWest	1	1	0	1	1	1.00	-	-	-	-	11	1	88	1	88.00	1-88	-	
B & H	4	2	1	11	8 *	11.00	-	-	-	-	30	2	208	5	41.60	2-55	-	
Sunday																		

Career Performances

	M	Inns	NO	Runs	HS	Avge	100s	50s	Ct	St	Balls	Runs	Wkts	Avge	Best	5wI	10wM
Test																	
All First	1	2	0	6	4	3.00	-	-	-	-	165	124	7	17.71	6-80	1	-
1-day Int																	
NatWest	2	1	0	1	1	1.00	-	-	-	-	138	154	4	38.50	3-66	-	
B & H	7	5	1	23	9	5.75	-	-	-	-	342	330	10	33.00	3-48	-	
Sunday																	

PEARSON, R. M.   Surrey

Name: Richard Michael Pearson
Role: Right-hand bat, right arm
off-spin bowler
Born: 27 January 1972, Batley, Yorkshire
Height: 6ft 3in **Weight:** 13st 7lbs
Nickname: Batley, Pancho
County debut: 1992 (Northamptonshire),
1994 (Essex), 1996 (Surrey)
1st-Class 5 w. in innings: 2
1st-Class catches: 14
Place in bowling averages: 137th av. 48.67
Strike rate: 91.93 (career 104.12)
Parents: Mike and Carol
Marital status: Single
Family links with cricket: 'Dad played for
Birstall in the Central Yorkshire League.
Mum was a highly esteemed tea lady'
Education: Batley Grammar School; St
John's College, Cambridge
Qualifications: 2 O-levels, 9 GCSEs, 4 A-levels, BA (Hons) in History
Career outside cricket: Starting my own property business in Harrogate
Overseas teams played for: Bulawayo Athletic Club, Zimbabwe 1995-96
Cricketers particularly admired: John Childs, Peter Such, Graham Gooch
Other sports followed: Football (Leeds), rugby league (Batley)
Relaxations: Eating out, music, reading
Extras: Made first-class debut for Cambridge University in 1991 and has played for
Combined Universities in the Benson & Hedges Cup since 1991. Football and cricket Blues
at Cambridge. Moved to Essex for the 1994 season and joined Surrey for the 1996 season
Opinions on cricket: 'Players should be able to move between clubs more freely. If a
contract has expired a player should be a free agent.'
Best batting: 37 Surrey v Sussex, Guildford 1996
Best bowling: 5-108 Cambridge University v Warwickshire, Fenner's 1992

1996 Season

	M	Inns	NO	Runs	HS	Avge	100s	50s	Ct	St	O	M	Runs	Wkts	Avge	Best	5wI	10wM
Test																		
All First	14	14	9	142	37	28.40	-	-	3	-	475	101	1509	31	48.67	5-142	1	-
1-day Int																		
NatWest	4	1	0	11	11	11.00	-	-	-	-	34	1	141	2	70.50	1-39	-	
B & H	5	1	1	12	12 *	-	-	-	-	-	41.5	1	232	4	58.00	3-60	-	
Sunday	14	5	4	12	9 *	12.00	-	-	2	-	67.5	0	389	12	32.41	3-33	-	

Career Performances

	M	Inns	NO	Runs	HS	Avge	100s	50s	Ct	St	Balls	Runs	Wkts	Avge	Best	5wI	10wM
Test																	
All First	50	55	16	474	37	12.15	-	-	14	-	10204	5426	98	55.36	5-108	2	-
1-day Int																	
NatWest	5	1	0	11	11	11.00	-	-	-	-	276	188	3	62.66	1-39	-	
B & H	13	3	2	22	12 *	22.00	-	-	1	-	749	556	11	50.54	3-46	-	
Sunday	29	13	10	46	9 *	15.33	-	-	3	-	901	828	23	36.00	3-33	-	

PEIRCE, M. T. E. Sussex

Name: Michael Toby Edward Peirce
Role: Left-hand bat, slow left-arm bowler
Born: 14 June 1973, Maidenhead
Height: 5ft 10in **Weight:** 11st
Nickname: Beastie
County debut: 1994 (one-day),
1995 (first-class)
1st-Class 50s: 1
1st-Class catches: 6
Place in batting averages: 193rd av. 21.90
Parents: Michael Robert and Katherine Ross
Marital status: Single
Education: Ardingly College; Durham
University
Qualifications: 9 GCSEs, 3 A-levels,
1 S-level
Overseas tours: Sussex Schools U14 to
Barbados 1987; Sussex Schools U18 to India
1990-91; Ardingly College to India 1988-89

Overseas teams played for: Kilbirnie, Wellington, New Zealand 1991-92; Wellington
B, New Zealand 1991-92
Cricketers particularly admired: David Smith, David Gower, Phil Edmonds,
'J. Batty Esq'
Other sports followed: Most
Relaxations: 'Drinks with mates (both of them), music'
Extras: Retired from first-class cricket at the end of the 1995 season, but has re-joined
Sussex for 1997
Best batting: 60 Sussex v Worcestershire, Eastbourne 1995

1996 Season (did not make any first-class or one-day appearances)

Career Performances

	M	Inns	NO	Runs	HS	Avge	100s	50s	Ct	St	Balls	Runs	Wkts	Avge	Best	5wI	10wM
Test																	
All First	7	12	0	243	60	20.25	-	1	6	-	54	30	0	-	-	-	-
1-day Int																	
NatWest																		
B & H	5	5	0	134	44	26.80	-	-	1	-							
Sunday	2	2	0	13	7	6.50	-	-	2	-							

PENBERTHY, A. L.　　　　Northamptonshire

Name: Anthony Leonard Penberthy
Role: Left-hand bat, right-arm medium bowler
Born: 1 September 1969, Troon, Cornwall
Height: 6ft 1in **Weight:** 12st
Nickname: Berth, Penbers, Lennie, Denzil
County debut: 1989
County cap: 1994
1st-Class 50s: 14
1st-Class 100s: 1
1st-Class 5 w. in innings: 3
1st-Class catches: 50
One-Day 5 w. in innings: 1
Place in batting averages: 196th av. 25.40
Place in bowling averages: 72nd av. 31.67
Strike rate: 62.17 (career 64.73)
Parents: Gerald and Wendy
Wife and date of marriage: Rebecca, 9 November 1996
Family links with cricket: Father played in local leagues in Cornwall and is now a qualified umpire instructor
Education: Troon County Primary; Camborne Comprehensive
Qualifications: 3 O-levels, 3 CSEs, coaching certificate
Off-season: Coaching in Bedfordshire
Overseas tours: Druids to Zimbabwe 1988; Northants to Durban 1992, to Cape Town 1993, to Zimbabwe 1995, to Johannesburg 1996
Cricketers particularly admired: Ian Botham, David Gower, Dennis Lillee, Viv Richards, Eldine Baptiste
Young players to look out for: David Sales, David Roberts

Other sports followed: Football (West Ham United), snooker, rugby, golf

Relaxations: Listening to music ('especially Luther Vandross'), watching videos and comedy programmes, 'walking my Irish setter'

Extras: Had football trials for Plymouth Argyle but came to Northampton for cricket trials instead. Took wicket with first ball in first-class cricket – Mark Taylor caught behind, June 1989. Played for England YC v New Zealand YC 1989

Opinions on cricket: 'Short run-ups on Sunday. Lunch and tea intervals are too short. All international one-day cricket should be with a white ball and coloured clothing.'

Best batting: 101* Northamptonshire v Cambridge University, Fenner's 1990

Best bowling: 5-37 Northamptonshire v Glamorgan, Swansea 1993

1996 Season

	M	Inns	NO	Runs	HS	Avge	100s	50s	Ct	St	O	M	Runs	Wkts	Avge	Best	5wl	10wM
Test																		
All First	18	29	4	635	87	25.40	-	3	9	-	352.2	68	1077	34	31.67	5-92	1	-
1-day Int																		
NatWest	2	1	0	79	79	79.00	-	1	-	-	10	3	44	1	44.00	1-17	-	
B & H	7	4	1	91	41	30.33	-	-	3	-	54	4	259	10	25.90	3-38	-	
Sunday	15	11	4	343	80	49.00	-	2	1	-	62	1	387	10	38.70	3-44	-	

Career Performances

	M	Inns	NO	Runs	HS	Avge	100s	50s	Ct	St	Balls	Runs	Wkts	Avge	Best	5wl	10wM
Test																	
All First	88	132	19	2511	101 *	22.22	1	14	50	-	9387	5126	145	35.35	5-37	3	-
1-day Int																	
NatWest	17	10	1	201	79	22.33	-	1	5	-	739	504	12	42.00	2-29	-	
B & H	18	13	2	213	41	19.36	-	-	6	-	858	613	17	36.05	3-38	-	
Sunday	81	59	11	944	80	19.66	-	3	15	-	2601	2366	72	32.86	5-36	1	

PENNETT, D. B.   Nottinghamshire

Name: David Barrington Pennett

Role: Right-hand bat, right-arm fast-medium bowler

Born: 26 October 1969, Leeds

Height: 6ft **Weight:** 12st 7lbs

Nickname: Yorkie, Fiery, SJYT

County debut: 1992

1st-Class 50s: 1

1st-Class 5 w. in innings: 1

1st-Class catches: 7

Place in bowling averages: 154th av. 81.10

Strike rate: 78.00 (career 77.05)

Parents: Barrie and Valerie
Marital status: Engaged
Education: Benton Park Grammar School
Qualifications: 5 O-levels, ASA teacher's certificate (swimming), coaching certificate, senior coaching certificate
Career outside cricket: Modelling, coaching
Off-season: Playing in New Zealand
Overseas tours: Nottinghamshire to Cape Town, South Africa 1992-93
Overseas teams played for: Hamilton Star University, New Zealand 1993-94; Ellerslie, Auckland, New Zealand 1995-96
Cricketers particularly admired: Malcolm Marshall, Ian Botham, Viv Richards
Other sports followed: Football (Manchester United), rugby union (Otley)
Injuries: Ten stitches in knee wounds, missed two weeks
Relaxations: Buying clothes, playing football, mountaineering
Extras: At Yorkshire Cricket Academy in 1990 for two years. Took hat-trick in a Bain Clarkson game for Yorkshire v Nottinghamshire, and one for Nottinghamshire v Herefordshire. Released by Nottinghamshire at the end of the 1996 season
Opinions on cricket: 'A super league should be set up in the counties amateur league programme, playing over two weekends, bringing more people onto the county scene. We should stop criticising our own system too much and belittling the people presently in it. We are quick to judge and slow to praise both on the county and national scene.'
Best batting: 50 Nottinghamshire v Durham, Chester-le-Street 1995
Best bowling: 5-36 Nottinghamshire v Durham, Chester-le-Street 1993

1996 Season

	M	Inns	NO	Runs	HS	Avge	100s	50s	Ct	St	O	M	Runs	Wkts	Avge	Best	5wI	10wM
Test																		
All First	3	4	0	27	10	6.75	-	-	1	-	91	15	376	7	53.71	4-116	-	-
1-day Int																		
NatWest																		
B & H	4	2	1	5	4 *	5.00	-	-	3	-	30	1	175	2	87.50	2-57	-	
Sunday	5	0	0	0	0	-	-	-	1	-	37	0	210	9	23.33	3-49	-	

68. Which Australian batsman scored his only Test century
in his debut match, at The Oval in 1981?

Career Performances

	M	Inns	NO	Runs	HS	Avge	100s	50s	Ct	St	Balls	Runs	Wkts	Avge	Best	5wI	10wM
Test																	
All First	31	31	11	196	50	9.80	-	1	7	-	4623	2697	60	44.95	5-36	1	-
1-day Int																	
NatWest	1	0	0	0	0	-	-	-	-	-	72	22	1	22.00	1-22	-	
B & H	4	2	1	5	4 *	5.00	-	-	3	-	180	175	2	87.50	2-57	-	
Sunday	37	7	5	20	12 *	10.00	-	-	6	-	1512	1307	41	31.87	3-27	-	

PENNEY, T. L. Warwickshire

Name: Trevor Lionel Penney
Role: Right-hand bat, right-arm
leg-break bowler
Born: 12 June 1968, Salisbury, Rhodesia
Height: 6ft **Weight:** 11st
Nickname: TP, Lemon Kop
County debut: 1992
County cap: 1994
1000 runs in a season: 2
1st-Class 50s: 23
1st-Class 100s: 13
1st-Class catches: 56
Place in batting averages: 63rd av. 43.16
(1995 26th av. 49.91)
Strike rate: (career 41.16)
Parents: George and Bets
Wife and date of marriage: Deborah Anne,
19 December 1992
Children: Samantha Anne, 20 August 1995
Family links with cricket: Brother Stephen played for Zimbabwe U25
Education: Blakiston Primary; Prince Edward Boys High School, Zimbabwe
Qualifications: 3 O-levels
Career outside cricket: Tobacco buyer
Off-season: Playing hockey and cricket and coaching cricket in Zimbabwe
Overseas tours: Zimbabwe to Sri Lanka 1987; ICC Associates to Australia (Youth
World Cup); Zimbabwe U20 to England 1984
Overseas teams played for: Old Hararians, Zimbabwe 1983-89 and 1993-94;
Scarborough, Australia 1989-90; Boland, South Africa 1991-92; Avendale, South
Africa 1992-93
Cricketers particularly admired: Colin Bland, Ian Botham, Graeme Hick, Allan
Donald

Other sports followed: Football (Liverpool FC), American football (San Francisco 49ers), golf and tennis

Relaxations: Playing golf and drinking Castle on Lake Kariba. Spending time with my wife and daughter

Extras: Captained the ICC Associates team at the Youth World Cup in 1987-88. Played for Zimbabwe against Sri Lanka in 1987. Played hockey for Zimbabwe from 1984-87 and also made the African team who played Asia in 1987. Qualified to play for England in 1992

Opinions on cricket: 'The four-day game is fine but there is still too much cricket being played, so maybe two divisions should be considered.'

Best batting: 151 Warwickshire v Middlesex, Lord's 1992

Best bowling: 3-18 Mashonaland v Mashonaland U24, Harare 1993-94

1996 Season

	M	Inns	NO	Runs	HS	Avge	100s	50s	Ct	St	O	M	Runs	Wkts	Avge	Best	5wI	10wM
Test																		
All First	19	34	4	1295	134	43.16	3	8	14	-								
1-day Int																		
NatWest	2	2	0	120	90	60.00	-	1	-	-								
B & H	7	5	1	136	50 *	34.00	-	1	-	-								
Sunday	17	16	5	329	75 *	29.90	-	2	9	-								

Career Performances

	M	Inns	NO	Runs	HS	Avge	100s	50s	Ct	St	Balls	Runs	Wkts	Avge	Best	5wI	10wM
Test																	
All First	98	156	29	5484	151	43.18	13	23	56	-	247	183	6	30.50	3-18	-	-
1-day Int																	
NatWest	19	17	4	359	90	27.61	-	2	11	-	10	12	1	12.00	1-8	-	
B & H	17	14	3	261	50 *	23.72	-	1	5	1							
Sunday	75	64	24	1231	83 *	30.77	-	5	32	-	6	2	0	-	-	-	-

PETERS, S. D. Essex

Name: Stephen David Peters
Role: Right-hand bat
Born: 10 December 1976, Harold Wood
Height: 5ft 10in **Weight:** 10st 7lbs
Nickname: Geezer, Pedro, Hot Rod, Rodders
County debut: 1996
1st-Class 100s: 1
1st-Class catches: 5
Place in batting averages: 209th av. 23.66
Parents: Brian and Lesley
Marital status: Single
Family links with cricket: 'Father plays for
Upminster. Mother scores and is a keen
follower of cricket. Sister organises social
events at Upminster CC. Brother-in-law
claims he's quick!'
Education: Upminster Junior School;
Coopers Coburn and Company School

Qualifications: 9 GCSEs
Off-season: Touring Pakistan with England U19
Overseas tours: Essex U14 to Hong Kong; Essex U15 to Barbados; England U19 to
Pakistan 1996-97
Cricketers particularly admired: Graham Gooch and Nasser Hussain 'strange bloke'
Young players to look out for: Ben Hollioake, Alex Tudor
Other sports followed: Football (West Ham United), golf
Relaxations: Music round at DJ Hibbert's and television
Extras: The Sir John Hobbs Jubilee Memorial Prize 1994, a *Daily Telegraph* regional
batting award 1994, represented England at U14, U15, U17 and U19. Essex Young
Player of the Year 1996
Opinions on cricket: 'All 2nd XI games should be played on 1st XI grounds.'
Best batting: 110 Essex v Cambridge University, Fenner's 1996

1996 Season

	M	Inns	NO	Runs	HS	Avge	100s	50s	Ct	St	O	M	Runs	Wkts	Avge	Best	5wI	10wM
Test																		
All First	4	7	1	142	110	23.66	1	-	5	-								
1-day Int																		
NatWest																		
B & H																		
Sunday	1	1	0	1	1	1.00	-	-	-	-								

	M	Inns	NO	Runs	HS	Avge	100s	50s	Ct	St	Balls	Runs	Wkts	Avge	Best	5wl	10wM
Test																	
All First	4	7	1	142	110	23.66	1	-	5	-							
1-day Int																	
NatWest																	
B & H																	
Sunday	1	1	0	1	1	1.00	-	-	-	-							

PHILLIPS, B. J.   Kent

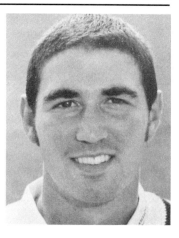

Name: Ben James Phillips
Role: Right-hand bat, right-arm
fast-medium bowler
Born: 30 September 1972, Lewisham
Height: 6ft 6in **Weight:** 15st 6lbs
Nickname: Bustle, Bombhead
County debut: 1996
1st-Class catches: 1
Strike rate: (career 60.00)
Parents: Trevor and Glynnis
Marital status: Single
Family links with cricket: Father and
brother (Danny) play league cricket for
Hayes. 'Mother is clueless about the game
but is good with a washing machine!'
Education: St Josephs Primary, Bromley;
Langley Park School for Boys, Beckenham;
Langley Park Sixth Form
Qualifications: 9 GCSEs and 2 A-levels
Career outside cricket: 'Keeping my options open'
Off-season: Playing and coaching in Cape Town, South Africa
Overseas teams played for: University of Queensland, Australia 1993-94; Cape
Technikon, Cape Town, South Africa 1994-95, 1996-97
Cricketers particularly admired: Mark Waugh, Carl Hooper, Ed Stanford 'the best
No.10 in the country'
Young players to look out for: Robert Key, Matt Walker, Will House
Other sports followed: Basketball (Chicago Bulls), football (West Ham United 'not
that it has done them any good'), golf
Injuries: Torn ligaments in right ankle, missed two weeks
Relaxations: 'Enjoy watching a decent film or listening to music. Slothing it on a
beach somewhere sunny in the off-season'

Extras: Represented England U19 Schools in 1993-94. Holds Langley Park School record for the fastest half century off 11 balls

Opinions on cricket: 'The problem with English cricket is the lack of adequate off-season structure in place to improve playing standards. I would like to see 12-month contracts therefore allowing players to develop aspects of their game during the off-season.'

Best batting: 2 Kent v Sussex, Tunbridge Wells 1996
2 Kent v Nottinghamshire, Tunbridge Wells 1996

Best bowling: 3-34 Kent v Sussex, Tunbridge Wells 1996

1996 Season

	M	Inns	NO	Runs	HS	Avge	100s	50s	Ct	St	O	M	Runs	Wkts	Avge	Best	5wI	10wM
Test																		
All First	3	3	0	5	2	1.66	-	-	1	-	40	12	109	4	27.25	3-34	-	-
1-day Int																		
NatWest																		
B & H																		
Sunday	4	4	1	33	29	11.00	-	-	3	-	20.5	0	112	3	37.33	2-42	-	

Career Performances

	M	Inns	NO	Runs	HS	Avge	100s	50s	Ct	St	Balls	Runs	Wkts	Avge	Best	5wI	10wM
Test																	
All First	3	3	0	5	2	1.66	-	-	1	-	240	109	4	27.25	3-34	-	-
1-day Int																	
NatWest																	
B & H																	
Sunday	4	4	1	33	29	11.00	-	-	3	-	125	112	3	37.33	2-42	-	

PHILLIPS, N. C.   Sussex

Name: Nicholas Charles Phillips
Role: Right-hand bat, off-spin bowler
Born: 10 May 1974, Pembury, Kent
Height: 6ft **Weight:** 11st 4lbs
Nickname: Milky, Spoons, Beastie, Nicky P
County debut: 1994
1st-Class 50s: 3
1st-Class catches: 9
Place in batting averages: (1995 206th av. 20.330
Place in bowling averages: 154th av. 59.84
Strike rate: 103.88 (career 105.65)
Parents: Robert and Joan
Marital status: Single

Family links with cricket: Father plays club cricket for Hastings. Represents Sussex Over 50s and has represented Kent 2nd XI, Kent League XI and has scored over 100 club centuries
Education: Hilden Grange School, Tonbridge; St Thomas's School, Winchelsea; William Parker School, Hastings
Qualifications: 8 GCSEs, NCA coaching award
Off-season: Playing and coaching overseas
Overseas tours: Sussex U18 to India 1990-91
Overseas teams played for: Maris CC, Auckland 1996-97
Cricketers particularly admired: Eddie Hemmings, Derek Randall
Other sports followed: Hockey, football
Relaxations: Spending time with friends and girlfriend. Listening to music. Eating out and socialising with fellow players

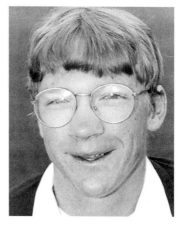

Extras: Represented England U19 in home series against West Indies U19 in 1993. Has played hockey for Sussex U14 and U16
Opinions on cricket: 'It is a good thing that four-day games are being brought into 2nd XI cricket, but this means that the wicket standards should be reviewed as many 2nd XI wickets would not last four days. The NatWest should be scrapped because all one-day cricket around the world is now the 50-over format. Why should we be different?'
Best batting: 53 Sussex v Young Australia, Hove 1995
Best bowling: 3-39 Sussex v Cambridge University 1995

1996 Season

	M	Inns	NO	Runs	HS	Avge	100s	50s	Ct	St	O	M	Runs	Wkts	Avge	Best	5wI	10wM
Test																		
All First	8	12	7	223	45	44.60	-	-	5	-	224	50	778	13	59.84	2-54	-	-
1-day Int																		
NatWest																		
B & H	1	1	0	10	10	10.00	-	-	-	-	5	0	49	0	-	-	-	-
Sunday	5	4	3	55	38 *	55.00	-	-	2	-	21.5	0	162	1	162.00	1-58	-	

Career Performances

	M	Inns	NO	Runs	HS	Avge	100s	50s	Ct	St	Balls	Runs	Wkts	Avge	Best	5wI	10wM
Test																	
All First	16	24	9	443	53	29.53	-	3	9	-	2747	1529	26	58.80	3-39	-	-
1-day Int																	
NatWest																	
B & H	1	1	0	10	10	10.00	-	-	-	-	30	49	0	-	-	-	-
Sunday	14	9	5	79	38 *	19.75	-	-	3	-	425	385	6	64.16	2-19	-	

PICK, R. A.　　　　　　　　　Nottinghamshire

Name: Robert Andrew Pick
Role: Left-hand bat, right-arm
fast-medium bowler
Born: 19 November 1963, Nottingham
Height: 5ft 10in **Weight:** 13st
Nickname: Dad
County debut: 1983
County cap: 1987
50 wickets in a season: 4
1st-Class 50s: 5
1st-Class 5 w. in innings: 16
1st-Class 10 w. in match: 3
1st-Class catches: 50
One-Day 5 w. in innings: 2
Place in batting averages: 300th av. 8.25
(1995 225th av. 17.95)
Place in bowling averages: (1995 81st av.
31.41)
Strike rate: 133.00 (career 60.32)
Parents: Bob and Lillian
Wife and date of marriage:
Jennie Ruth, 8 April 1989
Family links with cricket: Father, uncles and cousins all play local cricket; David
Millns (Leicestershire) is brother-in-law
Education: Alderman Derbyshire Comprehensive; High Pavement College
Qualifications: 7 O-levels, 1 A-level, senior cricket coach
Overseas tours: England A to Pakistan 1990-91, to Bermuda and West Indies 1991-92
Overseas teams played for: Wellington, New Zealand 1989-90
Cricketers particularly admired: Bob White, Mike Hendrick, Mike Harris, Franklyn
Stephenson, Wayne Noon
Other sports followed: Ice hockey (Nottingham Panthers), soccer and American football
Relaxations: 'Spending time with family, fishing, a good pint and a nice feed'
Extras: Played for England YC v Australia YC 1983. Played football for Nottingham
Schoolboys. Took Nottinghamshire's only ever hat-trick in the NatWest against Scotland
in 1995. Awarded benefit for 1996
Opinions on cricket: 'Plenty but no-one who can do anything about them listens.'
Best batting: 65* Nottinghamshire v Northamptonshire, Trent Bridge 1994
Best bowling: 7-128 Nottinghamshire v Leicestershire, Leicester 1990

1996 Season

	M	Inns	NO	Runs	HS	Avge	100s	50s	Ct	St	O	M	Runs	Wkts	Avge	Best	5wI	10wM
Test											-							
All First	6	8	0	66	32	8.25	-	-	1	-	155.1	31	483	7	69.00	3-74	-	-
1-day Int																		
NatWest	1	1	0	1	1	1.00	-	-	1	-	10	0	42	1	42.00	1-42	-	
B & H	1	1	0	7	7	7.00	-	-	-	-	9	1	29	2	14.50	2-29	-	
Sunday	8	3	2	54	32 *	54.00	-	-	4	-	56	1	283	11	25.72	3-31	-	

Career Performances

	M	Inns	NO	Runs	HS	Avge	100s	50s	Ct	St	Balls	Runs	Wkts	Avge	Best	5wI	10wM
Test																	
All First	190	203	54	2227	65 *	14.94	-	5	50	-	29498	16089	489	32.90	7-128	16	3
1-day Int																	
NatWest	28	16	11	121	34 *	24.20	-	-	5	-	1813	1169	47	24.87	5-22	2	
B & H	41	17	11	114	25 *	19.00	-	-	5	-	2443	1708	47	36.34	4-42	-	
Sunday	118	42	19	362	58 *	15.73	-	1	27	-	5151	4308	127	33.92	4-32	-	

PIERSON, A. R. K.   Leicestershire

Name: Adrian Roger Kirshaw Pierson
Role: Right-hand bat, right-arm
off-spin bowler
Born: 21 July 1963, Enfield, Middlesex
Height: 6ft 4in **Weight:** 12st
Nickname: Stick, Skirlogue, Bunny, Bun
County debut: 1985 (Warwickshire), 1993
(Leicestershire)
County cap: 1995 (Leicestershire)
50 w. in a season: 1
1st-Class 50s: 2
1st-Class 5 w. in innings: 12
1st-Class catches: 64
One-Day 5 w. in innings: 1
Place in batting averages: 232nd av. 20.23
(1995 227th av. 17.81)
Place in bowling averages: 99th av. 35.62
(1995 76th av. 30.65)
Strike rate: 68.04 (career 71.24)
Parents: Patrick and Patricia
Wife and date of marriage: Helen Majella, 29 September 1990
Education: Lochinver House Primary School; Kent College, Canterbury; Hatfield

Polytechnic
Qualifications: 8 O-levels, 2 A-levels, senior coaching award
Career outside cricket: Entrepreneur
Off-season: Liaison officer for the World Cricket Masters in India and picture framing
Overseas teams played for: Walmer, South Africa; Manicaland, Zimbabwe
Cricketers particularly admired: John Emburey, Phil Edmonds, Tony Greig, Clive Rice
Young players to look out for: Darren Maddy, Aftab Habib, Matt Brimson
Other sports followed: All sports except horse racing, but especially golf
Injuries: Patella tendonitis and broken finger, missed no cricket
Relaxations: Gardening, music, chess, reading, driving
Extras: On Lord's groundstaff 1984-85 and on Warwickshire staff from 1985-91. First Championship wicket was Viv Richards. Won two Gold Awards in the Benson and Hedges. 'Literally ruffled the Prime Minister in an embarrassing encounter...!?'
Opinions on cricket: 'Scheduled finish time should not be re-adjusted after an innings closes. Generally the pace of the wickets should be improved – bland wickets lead to bland cricket and cricketers. The media should try to talk the game up and find something positive to say – after all, they are earning a living from it.'
Best batting: 58 Leicestershire v Lancashire, Leicester 1993
Best bowling: 8-42 Leicestershire v Warwickshire, Edgbaston 1994

1996 Season

	M	Inns	NO	Runs	HS	Avge	100s	50s	Ct	St	O	M	Runs	Wkts	Avge	Best	5wl	10wM
Test																		
All First	20	23	10	263	44	20.23	-	-	16	-	544.2	108	1710	48	35.62	6-158	2	-
1-day Int																		
NatWest	1	0	0	0	0	-	-	-	-	-	12	2	48	0	-		-	-
B & H	1	1	1	2	2*	-	-	-	-	-	9	0	57	0	-		-	-
Sunday	7	3	0	20	11	6.66	-	-	2	-	30	1	188	5	37.60	3-21	-	

Career Performances

	M	Inns	NO	Runs	HS	Avge	100s	50s	Ct	St	Balls	Runs	Wkts	Avge	Best	5wl	10wM
Test																	
All First	130	162	60	1654	58	16.21	-	2	64	-	20162	10216	283	36.09	8-42	12	-
1-day Int																	
NatWest	11	6	2	33	20*	8.25	-	-	2	-	668	345	9	38.33	3-20	-	
B & H	17	12	8	47	11	11.75	-	-	5	-	866	530	12	44.16	3-34	-	
Sunday	67	35	14	202	29*	9.61	-	-	30	-	2541	2083	61	34.14	5-36	1	

PIGOTT, A. C. S. Surrey

Name: Anthony Charles Shackleton Pigott
Role: Right-hand bat, right-arm
fast-medium bowler, slip fielder
Born: 4 June 1958, London
Height: 6ft 1in **Weight:** 12st 9lbs
Nickname: Lester
County debut: 1978 (Sussex), 1994 (Surrey)
County cap: 1982 (Sussex)
Benefit: 1991 (£60,025)
Test debut: 1983-84
Tests: 1
50 wickets in a season: 5
1st-Class 50s: 20
1st-Class 100s: 1
1st-Class 5 w. in innings: 26
1st-Class 10 w. in match: 2
1st-Class catches: 121
One-Day 5 w. in innings: 3
Place in bowling averages: 75th av. 30.31

(1994 26th av. 25.41)
Strike rate: (career 56.61)
Parents: Tom and Juliet
Marital status: Engaged
Children: Elliot Sebastian, 15 March 1983
Family links with cricket: Father captained village side, mother played at school 'and
claims I got my cricket ability from her'
Education: Holmwood House, Kent; Harrow School
Qualifications: 5 O-levels, 2 A-levels; junior coaching certificate
Career outside cricket: Recently set up sports marketing company
Off-season: Starting new business CML – promoting professional sportsmen. Touring
South Africa with Surrey Vagrants. Touring Sharjah with England over-35s for The Masters
Overseas tours: England to New Zealand 1983-84; MCC to Leeward Islands 1991-
92, to West Africa 1993-94; *Cricket World* to Barbados 1993-94
Overseas teams played for: Wellington, New Zealand 1982-83 and 1983-84
Cricketers particularly admired: Ian Botham, Geoff Arnold, John Snow, Mike Gatting
Other sports followed: Squash, soccer, golf, rugby
Injuries: Hernia, out for three months
Extras: Public schools rackets champion 1975. First three wickets in first-class cricket
were a hat-trick. Had operation on back, April 1981, missing most of season, and was
told by a specialist he would never play cricket again. Postponed wedding to make Test
debut when called into England party on tour of New Zealand 1983-84. Originally going
to Somerset for 1984 season, but remained with Sussex. Was diagnosed as a diabetic

after he lost 11lbs in two weeks in 1987, but recovered to take 74 wickets in 1988 season. Moved to Surrey at end of 1993 season after 18 years with Sussex
Best batting: 104* Sussex v Warwickshire, Edgbaston 1986
Best bowling: 7-74 Sussex v Northamptonshire, Eastbourne 1982

1996 Season

	M	Inns	NO	Runs	HS	Avge	100s	50s	Ct	St	O	M	Runs	Wkts	Avge	Best	5wI	10wM
Test																		
All First																		
1-day Int																		
NatWest	1	1	1	12	12*	-	-	-	1	-	9	1	22	2	11.00	2-22	-	
B & H																		
Sunday																		

Career Performances

	M	Inns	NO	Runs	HS	Avge	100s	50s	Ct	St	Balls	Runs	Wkts	Avge	Best	5wI	10wM
Test	1	2	1	12	8*	12.00	-	-	-	-	102	75	2	37.50	2-75	-	-
All Firsts	260	317	66	4841	104*	19.28	1	20	121	-	38047	20831	672	30.99	7-74	26	2
1-day Int																	
NatWest	33	18	3	185	53	12.33	-	1	9	-	1865	1156	44	26.27	3-4	-	
B & H	44	30	10	289	49*	14.45	-	-	15	-	2428	1680	57	29.47	3-29	-	
Sunday	182	106	41	1145	51*	17.61	-	1	57	-	7398	6038	260	23.22	5-24	3	

PIPER, K. J.   Warwickshire

Name: Keith John Piper
Role: Right-hand bat, wicket-keeper
Born: 18 December 1969, Leicester
Height: 5ft 7in **Weight:** 10st 8lbs
Nickname: Tubbsy, Garden Boy
County debut: 1989
County cap: 1992
1st-Class 50s: 9
1st-Class 100s: 2
1st-Class catches: 348
1st-Class stumpings: 23
Place in batting averages: 223rd av. 21.45
(1995 175th av. 23.41)
Strike rate: (career 28.00)
Parents: John and Charlotte
Marital status: Single
Family links with cricket: Father plays club
cricket in Leicester

Education: Seven Sisters Junior; Somerset Senior
Qualifications: Senior coaching award, basketball coaching award, volleyball coaching award
Overseas tours: Haringey Cricket College to Barbados 1986, to Trinidad 1987, to Jamaica 1988; Warwickshire to La Manga 1989, to St Lucia 1990; England A to India 1994-95, to Pakistan 1995-96
Overseas teams played for: Desmond Haynes's XI, Barbados v Haringey Cricket College
Cricketers particularly admired: Jack Russell, Alec Stewart, Dermot Reeve, Colin Metson
Other sports followed: Snooker, football, tennis
Relaxations: Music, eating
Extras: London Young Cricketer of the Year 1989 and in the last five 1992. Played for England YC 1989. Was batting partner (116*) to Brian Lara when he reached his 501*
Best batting: 116* Warwickshire v Durham, Edgbaston 1994
Best bowling: 1-57 Warwickshire v Nottinghamshire, Edgbaston 1992

1996 Season

	M	Inns	NO	Runs	HS	Avge	100s	50s	Ct	St	O	M	Runs	Wkts	Avge	Best	5wl	10wM
Test																		
All First	13	22	2	429	82	21.45	-	1	21	6								
1-day Int																		
NatWest																		
B & H	7	3	1	12	7	6.00	-	-	12	1								
Sunday	10	6	2	32	12	8.00	-	-	10	4								

Career Performances

	M	Inns	NO	Runs	HS	Avge	100s	50s	Ct	St	Balls	Runs	Wkts	Avge	Best	5wl	10wM
Test																	
All First	130	180	26	3086	116 *	20.03	2	9	348	23	28	57	1	57.00	1-57	-	-
1-day Int																	
NatWest	21	10	5	76	16 *	15.20	-	-	32	2							
B & H	15	10	4	54	11 *	9.00	-	-	20	1							
Sunday	67	38	19	249	30	13.10	-	-	64	17							

POLLARD, P. R.   Nottinghamshire

Name: Paul Raymond Pollard
Role: Left-hand opening bat, right-arm medium bowler
Born: 24 September 1968, Carlton, Nottinghamshire
Height: 5ft 11in **Weight:** 12st
Nickname: Polly, Sugar Ray
County debut: 1987
County cap: 1992
1000 runs in a season: 3
1st-Class 50s: 37
1st-Class 100s: 12
1st-Class catches: 137
One-Day 100s: 4
Place in batting averages: 146th av. 32.04 (1995 132nd av. 29.76)
Strike rate: (career 68.50)
Parents: Eric (deceased) and Mary
Wife's name and date of marriage: Kate, 14 March 1992
Education: Gedling Comprehensive
Off-season: Playing for Harare Sports Club and coaching Zimbabwe B
Overseas teams played for: Southern Districts, Brisbane 1988; North Perth 1990
Cricketers particularly admired: David Gower, Derek Randall, Ian Botham, Graham Gooch
Other sports followed: Football, golf, ice hockey
Relaxations: Watching videos, playing golf and music
Extras: Made debut for Nottinghamshire 2nd XI in 1985. Worked in Nottinghamshire CCC office on a Youth Training Scheme. Shared stands of 222 and 282 with Tim Robinson in the same game v Kent 1989. Youngest player to reach 1000 runs for Nottinghamshire
Opinions on cricket: 'The one bouncer rule should be abolished.'
Best batting: 180 Nottinghamshire v Derbyshire, Trent Bridge 1993
Best bowling: 2-79 Nottinghamshire v Gloucestershire, Bristol 1993

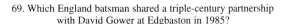

69. Which England batsman shared a triple-century partnership
with David Gower at Edgbaston in 1985?

1996 Season

	M	Inns	NO	Runs	HS	Avge	100s	50s	Ct	St	O	M	Runs	Wkts	Avge	Best	5wl	10wM
Test																		
All First	13	25	2	737	86	32.04	-	6	11	-								
1-day Int																		
NatWest	1	1	0	23	23	23.00	-	-	-	-								
B & H	4	4	1	112	79	37.33	-	1	1	-								
Sunday	14	12	1	384	118	34.90	1	1	7	-								

Career Performances

	M	Inns	NO	Runs	HS	Avge	100s	50s	Ct	St	Balls	Runs	Wkts	Avge	Best	5wl	10wM
Test																	
All First	142	250	15	7667	180	32.62	12	37	137	-	274	268	4	67.00	2-79	-	-
1-day Int																	
NatWest	11	11	1	325	96	32.50	-	2	3	-	18	9	0	-		-	-
B & H	24	23	2	676	104	32.19	1	6	9	-							
Sunday	89	80	9	2537	132 *	35.73	4	12	34	-							

POLLOCK, S. M. Warwickshire

Name: Shaun Maclean Pollock
Role: Right-hand bat, right-arm fast-medium bowler
Born: 16 July 1973, Port Elizabeth, South Africa
Height: 6ft 3in **Weight:** 13st 5lbs
Nickname: Polly
County debut: 1996
County cap: 1996
Test debut: 1995-96
Tests: 5
One-Day Internationals: 18
1st-Class 50s: 4
1st-Class 100s: 2
1st-Class 5 w. in innings: 6
1st-Class 10 w. in match: 1
1st-Class catches: 7
One-Day 5 w. in innings: 2
Place in batting averages: 157th av. 30.30
Place in bowling averages: 46th av. 28.16
Strike rate: 63.80 (career 53.18)
Parents: Peter and Inez
Marital status: Single

Family links with cricket: Father Peter played for Eastern Province and South Africa (1959-71). Uncle Graeme played for Eastern Province, Transvaal and South Africa (1960-86). Father is current convenor of selectors for national teams
Education: Northlands Primary School, Durban, Natal; Northwood, Durban, Natal; Natal University
Qualifications: B Comm
Career outside cricket: None at present
Off-season: Playing for Natal and South Africa
Overseas tours: South Africa Tertiary Team to Kenya and Zimbabwe 1994-95; South Africa U24 to Sri Lanka 1995-96; South Africa to Hong Kong Sixes 1995, to India and Pakistan (World Cup) 1995-96
Cricketers particularly admired: Brian Macmillan, Malcolm Marshall and Clive Rice
Other sports followed: Golf, hockey, tennis, rugby and soccer
Relaxations: Watching sport, spending time with friends and listening to music
Extras: Was voted Player of the Series in the South Africa v England one-day series. Played for Natal Nuffield team and then selected for South Africa Schools in 1991. Made debut for Natal in all three local competitions against Northern Transvaal (same team) at Kingsmead, Durban (same venue)
Best batting: 150* Warwickshire v Glamorgan, Edgbaston 1996
Best bowling: 7-33 Natal v Border, East London 1995-96

1996 Season

	M	Inns	NO	Runs	HS	Avge	100s	50s	Ct	St	O	M	Runs	Wkts	Avge	Best	5wI	10wM
Test																		
All First	13	21	1	606	150 *	30.30	2	1	5	-	446.4	115	1183	42	28.16	6-56	1	-
1-day Int																		
NatWest	2	2	0	40	23	20.00	-	-	-	-	17	2	62	4	15.50	4-37	-	
B & H	7	4	2	98	59 *	49.00	-	1	1	-	64	10	277	15	18.46	6-21	2	
Sunday	14	11	2	273	57	30.33	-	2	3	-	104.3	6	387	25	15.48	3-27	-	

Career Performances

	M	Inns	NO	Runs	HS	Avge	100s	50s	Ct	St	Balls	Runs	Wkts	Avge	Best	5wI	10wM
Test	5	6	1	133	36 *	26.60	-	-	2	-	899	377	16	23.56	5-32	1	-
All First	39	54	9	1339	150 *	29.75	2	4	16	-	7552	3084	142	21.71	7-33	6	1
1-day Int	18	11	6	160	66 *	32.00	-	1	5	-	985	647	26	24.88	4-34	-	
NatWest	2	2	0	40	23	20.00	-	-	-	-	102	62	4	15.50	4-37	-	
B & H	7	4	2	98	59 *	49.00	-	1	1	-	384	277	15	18.46	6-21	2	
Sunday	14	11	2	273	57	30.33	-	2	3	-	627	387	25	15.48	3-27	-	

POOLEY, J. C.   Middlesex

Name: Jason Calvin Pooley
Role: Left-hand bat, right-arm slow bowler
Born: 8 August 1969, Hammersmith
Height: 6ft **Weight:** 12st 7lbs
County debut: 1989
County cap: 1995
1000 runs in a season: 1
1st-Class 50s: 14
1st-Class 100s: 8
1st-Class catches: 60
One-Day 100s: 1
Place in batting averages: 179th av. 27.53
(1995 23rd av. 51.34)
Parents: Dave and Kath
Wife and date of marriage: Justine, 30
September 1995

Family links with cricket: Father and older
brother play club cricket. Younger brother
Gregg has played for Middlesex YC,
Middlesex 2nd XI and Derbyshire 2nd XI
Education: Acton High School
Overseas tours: England A to Pakistan 1995-96
Overseas teams played for: St George's, Sydney 1988-89; Western Suburbs, Sydney 1991-92
Cricketers particularly admired: David Gower, Desmond Haynes, Mark Ramprakash
Other sports followed: 'All sports, support Portsmouth FC'
Relaxations: 'Eating out with my wife Justine'
Extras: Voted Rapid Cricketline 2nd XI Player of the Year in 1989, his first year on the
Middlesex staff. Called up as a late replacement on the England A tour to Pakistan after
the withdrawal of Andrew Symonds
Opinions on cricket: 'Too much cricket played. Sunday League should be 30 overs a
side. Angus Fraser will be able to tell you the rest. He seems to know everything you
want to know.'
Best batting: 138* Middlesex v Cambridge University, Fenner's 1996

1996 Season

	M	Inns	NO	Runs	HS	Avge	100s	50s	Ct	St	O	M	Runs	Wkts	Avge	Best	5wI	10wM
Test																		
All First	18	34	2	881	138 *	27.53	2	4	22	-	4	0	42	0	-	-	-	-
1-day Int																		
NatWest	2	2	0	37	36	18.50	-	-	1	-								
B & H	5	5	0	77	50	15.40	-	1	2	-								
Sunday	15	14	1	283	68	21.76	-	1	6	-								

Career Performances

	M	Inns	NO	Runs	HS	Avge	100s	50s	Ct	St	Balls	Runs	Wkts	Avge	Best	5wI	10wM
Test																	
All First	63	109	11	3192	138 *	32.57	8	14	60	-	60	68	0	-	-	-	-
1-day Int																	
NatWest	5	5	0	79	36	15.80	-	-	1	-							
B & H	14	14	0	269	50	19.21	-	1	5	-							
Sunday	44	42	3	916	109	23.48	1	5	13	-							

POWELL, J. C.   Essex

Name: Jonathan Christopher Powell
Role: Right-hand bat, off-spin bowler
Born: 13 June 1979, Harold Wood
Height: 5ft 11in **Weight:** 10st 7lbs
Nickname: Powelly, Ralphy
County debut: 1996 (one-day)
Parents: Geoff and Joan
Marital status: Single
Family links with cricket: Brother Mark
was on the Essex staff for two years and now
plays Minor Counties cricket for Norfolk.
Father plays local cricket
Education: St Peter's C of E Primary School,
Brentwood; Brentwood County High;
Chelmsford College
Qualifications: 9 GCSEs, NCA coaching
award (level 2)
Off-season: Touring Pakistan with England U19
Overseas tours: Essex U14 to Barbados, to Hong Kong; England U19 to Pakistan
1996-97
Cricketers particularly admired: Graham Gooch, Ronnie Irani, Nasser Hussain
Young players to look out for: Stephen Peters, David Nash
Other sports followed: Football (Arsenal FC) and golf
Injuries: Back injury, out for one week
Relaxations: Watching television and going out
Extras: Winner of the *Daily Telegraph* U15 Bowling Award in 1994
Opinions on cricket: '2nd XI games should be played on first-class grounds.'

1996 Season

	M	Inns	NO	Runs	HS	Avge	100s	50s	Ct	St	O	M	Runs	Wkts	Avge	Best	5wI	10wM
Test																		
All First																		
1-day Int																		
NatWest																		
B & H																		
Sunday	1	0	0	0	0	-	-	-	-	-	8	0	62	2	31.00	2-62	-	

Career Performances

	M	Inns	NO	Runs	HS	Avge	100s	50s	Ct	St	Balls	Runs	Wkts	Avge	Best	5wI	10wM
Test																	
All First																	
1-day Int																	
NatWest																	
B & H																	
Sunday	1	0	0	0	0	-	-	-	-	-	48	62	2	31.00	2-62	-	

POWELL, M. J.   Warwickshire

Name: Michael James Powell
Role: Right-hand bat, right-arm medium bowler
Born: 5 April 1975, Bolton
Height: 5ft 11in **Weight:** 11st 3lbs
Nickname: Arthur
County debut: 1996
1st-Class catches: 2
Place in batting averages: 216th av. 22.75
Strike rate: (career 24.00)
Parents: Terry and Pat
Wife and date of marriage: Sarah, 26 October 1996
Education: Rivington and Blackrod High School, Horwich; Lawrence Sheriff School, Rugby
Qualifications: 6 GCSEs, 2 A-levels, basic coaching award
Career outside cricket: Part-time PE teacher
Off-season: Playing in Cape Town, South Africa
Overseas tours: England U18 (captain) to South Africa 1992-93, to Denmark (captain) 1993; England U19 to Sri Lanka 1993-94

Overseas teams played for: Avendale CC, Cape Town, 1994-95, 1996-97
Cricketers particularly admired: Ian Botham, Graham Gooch, Nick Knight, Andy Moles, Dermot Reeve
Other sports followed: Rugby, football (Manchester United), golf
Relaxations: Golf, spending time with my wife, Sarah
Extras: 2nd XI Player of the Month June 1996. Made his first-class debut against Durham in July 1996. Scored a career-best 210 against Somerset 2nd XI in July 1996
Opinions on cricket: 'Too much cricket.'
Best batting: 39 Warwickshire v Worcestershire, Worcester 1996
Best bowling: 1-18 Warwickshire v Surrey, The Oval 1996

1996 Season

	M	Inns	NO	Runs	HS	Avge	100s	50s	Ct	St	O	M	Runs	Wkts	Avge	Best	5wI	10wM
Test																		
All First	4	8	0	182	39	22.75	-	-	2	-	4	0	18	1	18.00	1-18	-	-
1-day Int																		
NatWest																		
B & H																		
Sunday																		

Career Performances

	M	Inns	NO	Runs	HS	Avge	100s	50s	Ct	St	Balls	Runs	Wkts	Avge	Best	5wI	10wM
Test																	
All First	4	8	0	182	39	22.75	-	-	2	-	24	18	1	18.00	1-18	-	-
1-day Int																	
NatWest																	
B & H																	
Sunday																	

PRATT, A.   Durham

Name: Andrew Pratt
Role: Left-hand bat, wicket-keeper
Born: 4 March 1975, Bishop Auckland
Height: 6ft **Weight:** 11st 3lbs
County debut: No first-team appearance
Parents: Gordon and Brenda
Marital status: Single
Family links with cricket: Brother was with MCC Young Cricketers for four years. Younger brother plays for Durham County Schools and father played in local leagues
Education: Parkside Comprehensive School; Durham New College
Qualications: 9 GCSEs, Advanced Diploma in Information Technology, cricket

coaching certificate
Off-season: Touring Sri Lanka
Cricketers particularly admired: Alan
Knott, Jack Russell
Young players to look out for: Jimmy Daley
Other sports followed: Golf and football
(Middlesbrough FC)
Injuries: Finger injuries but missed no
cricket
Extras: Played for Durham County Schools at
all levels and for the North of England U15.
Played for MCC Young Cricketers for three
years
Opinions on cricket: 'I think that the
English game is very demanding both
physically and mentally. England should take
note of Australia and play less matches,
especially one-day games. I also think that

the better young English players should be given more of a chance to play for their
country.'

PREECE, B. E. A.   Worcestershire

Name: Benjamin Edward Ashley Preece
Role: Right-hand bat, right-arm
fast-medium bowler
Born: 8 November 1976, Birmingham
Height: 6ft 1in **Weight:** 13st 5lbs
Nickname: Brummie ***t
County debut: 1996
1st-Class catches: 1
Strike rate: (career 57.25)
Parents: Christopher and Valerie
Marital status: Single
Family links with cricket: Father played for
school 1st XI
Education: Hourley Grange; Leasures High
Qualifications: 4 GCSEs, senior NCA
coaching award
Off-season: Playing in Western Australia
Cricketers particularly admired:
Phil Newport, Stuart Lampitt
Young players to look out for: Owais Shah, Alec Swann

Other sports followed: Football (Birmingham City FC)
Injuries: Twisted ankle and damaged knee tendons, missed a total of six weeks
Relaxations: 'Training hard and playing hard'
Extras: Played for England U15 and was a reserve for the England U19 tour to Zimbabwe. Took four wickets in four balls in the Bain Hogg Trophy in 1996
Opinions on cricket: 'I feel that 2nd XI games should be played over four days. The pitches should be better prepared. Anything that will help narrow the gulf between 1st and 2nd XI cricket.'
Best batting: 3* Worcestershire v South Africa A, Worcester 1996
Best bowling: 4-79 Worcestershire v South Africa A, Worcester 1996

1996 Season

	M	Inns	NO	Runs	HS	Avge	100s	50s	Ct	St	O	M	Runs	Wkts	Avge	Best	5wI	10wM
Test																		
All Firsts	3	4	2	5	3 *	2.50	-	-	1	-	76.2	3	388	8	48.50	4-79	-	-
1-day Int																		
NatWest																		
B & H																		
Sunday	1	1	1	1	1 *	-	-	-	-	-	2	0	10	1	10.00	1-10	-	

Career Performances

	M	Inns	NO	Runs	HS	Avge	100s	50s	Ct	St	Balls	Runs	Wkts	Avge	Best	5wI	10wM
Test																	
All First	3	4	2	5	3 *	2.50	-	-	1	-	458	388	8	48.50	4-79	-	-
1-day Int																	
NatWest																	
B & H																	
Sunday	1	1	1	1	1 *	-	-	-	-	-	12	10	1	10.00	1-10	-	

PRESTON, N. W.   Kent

Name: Nicholas William Preston
Role: Right-hand bat, right-arm
medium-fast bowler
Born: 22 January 1972, Dartford
Height: 6ft 1in **Weight:** 11st 5lbs
Nickname: North End, Jagback
County debut: 1996
1st-Class catches: 3
Place in batting averages: 297th av. 9.00
Place in bowling averages: 74th av. 32.00
Strike rate: (career 71.36)

Parents: Susan and Geoffrey
Marital status: Single
Family links with cricket: Grandfather played for Leicestershire. Brother plays for Kent youth teams
Education: Gravesend Grammar School; Exeter University
Qualifications:
BSc (Hons) Biology/Geography
Overseas teams played for: Avendale, Cape Town 1993-94; Green Point, Cape Town 1994-95
Cricketers particularly admired: Richard Hadlee, Allan Donald, Carl Hooper
Other sports followed: Rugby, tennis, football, golf
Relaxations: Golf, listening to music, watching movies, spending time with close friends

Extras: Kent League record of five wickets in five balls for Sevenoaks Vine v Midland Bank, 1994
Opinions on cricket: 'All 2nd XI cricket should be played on first-class grounds. Four-day cricket is good, but pitches need to last four days, not two or three. The structure of league cricket needs to be improved, as does the quality of pitches played on.'
Best batting: 17* Kent v Derbyshire, Derby 1996
Best bowling: 4-68 Kent v Yorkshire, Canterbury 1996

1996 Season

	M	Inns	NO	Runs	HS	Avge	100s	50s	Ct	St	O	M	Runs	Wkts	Avge	Best	5wI	10wM
Test																		
All First	8	11	4	63	17 *	9.00	-	-	3	-	130.5	27	352	11	32.00	4-68	-	-
1-day Int																		
NatWest	1	0	0	0	0	-	-	-	1	-	6	2	6	0	-		-	-
B & H																		
Sunday	5	2	1	11	7 *	11.00	-	-	-	-	13	0	83	0	-		-	-

Career Performances

	M	Inns	NO	Runs	HS	Avge	100s	50s	Ct	St	Balls	Runs	Wkts	Avge	Best	5wI	10wM
Test																	
All First	8	11	4	63	17 *	9.00	-	-	3	-	785	352	11	32.00	4-68	-	-
1-day Int																	
NatWest	1	0	0	0	0	-	-	-	1	-	36	6	0	-		-	-
B & H																	
Sunday	5	2	1	11	7 *	11.00	-	-	-	-	78	83	0	-		-	-

PRICE, S. J.   Worcestershire

Name: Stephen James Price
Role: Right-hand bat, off-spin bowler
Born: 30 March 1979, Shrewsbury
Height: 5ft 6in **Weight:** 10st 7lbs
County debut: No first-team appearance
Parents: David and Sue
Marital status: Single
Family links with cricket: None
Education: Hereford Cathedral School
Qualifications: 10 GCSEs, 'currently
studying for A-levels'
Off-season: Studying
Overseas tours: Accompanied father on
Hereford CC to West Indies 1988
Young players to look out for: Stephen
Peters, Paul Franks
Other sports followed: Rugby, football
(Shrewsbury Town) and tennis
Injuries: None

Relaxations: Play rugby in winter
Extras: Played for England U14 and has been in the England squad through to U17
level. Was also in the England U16 rugby squad.
Opinions on cricket: 'Haven't been in the game long enough.'

PRICHARD, P. J.   Essex

Name: Paul John Prichard
Role: Right-hand bat, cover/mid-wicket fielder, county captain
Born: 7 January 1965, Brentwood, Essex
Height: 5ft 10in **Weight:** 13st
Nickname: Pablo
County debut: 1984
County cap: 1986
1000 runs in a season: 7
1st-Class 50s: 77
1st-Class 100s: 26
1st-Class 200s: 2
1st-Class catches: 168
One-Day 100s: 4

Place in batting averages: 154th av. 30.93
(1995 104th av. 33.75)
Strike rate: (career 144.50)
Parents: John and Margaret
Wife's name and date of marriage: Jo-
Anne, 24 November 1991
Children: Danielle Jade, 23 April 1993;
Alexander James, 16 August 1995
Family links with cricket: Father played
club cricket in Essex
Education: Brentwood County High School
Qualifications: NCA coaching certificate
Career outside cricket: Promotions
executive for Ridley's brewery
Off-season: Finishing benefit year and
having back operation
Overseas tours: England A to Australia
1992-93

Overseas teams played for: VOB Cavaliers, Cape Town 1981-82; Sutherland,
Sydney 1984-87; Waverley, Sydney 1987-92
Cricketers particularly admired: Malcolm Marshall, Allan Border, David Gower,
Mark Waugh, Greg Matthews
Young players to look out for: Ashley Cowan, James Kirtley
Other sports followed: Football (West Ham), golf
Injuries: Back, missed three days
Relaxations: Sleeping, being with family, watching West Ham
Extras: Shared county record second wicket partnership of 403 with Graham Gooch v
Leicestershire in 1990. Britannic Assurance Cricketer of the Year 1992. Essex joint
Player of the Year 1993. Appointed Essex captain for 1995. Awarded benefit for 1996
Best batting: 245 Essex v Leicestershire, Chelmsford 1990
Best bowling: 1-28 Essex v Hampshire, Chelmsford 1991

1996 Season

	M	Inns	NO	Runs	HS	Avge	100s	50s	Ct	St	O	M	Runs	Wkts	Avge	Best	5wl	10wM
Test																		
All First	19	31	0	959	108	30.93	1	6	12	-								
1-day Int																		
NatWest	5	5	1	110	33	27.50	-	-	1	-								
B & H	5	4	0	119	82	29.75	-	1	1	-								
Sunday	14	14	0	374	102	26.71	1	1	2	-								

Career Performances

	M	Inns	NO	Runs	HS	Avge	100s	50s	Ct	St	Balls	Runs	Wkts	Avge	Best	5wI	10wM
Test																	
All First	263	427	44	13585	245	35.47	26	77	168	-		289	497	2 248.50	1-28	-	-
1-day Int																	
NatWest	28	27	4	901	94	39.17	-	6	11	-							
B & H	51	48	8	1215	107	30.37	1	7	11	-							
Sunday	157	139	9	3393	107	26.10	3	16	46	-							

PYEMONT, J. P. Sussex

Name: James Patrick Pyemont
Role: Right-hand bat, occasional off-spin bowler
Born: 10 April 1978, Eastbourne
Height: 6ft **Weight:** 11st 11lbs
Nickname: Chucker, Piggy
County debut: No first-team appearance
Parents: Christopher and Pinky
Marital status: Single
Family links with cricket: Father played for Cambridge University (1967) and is now President of Sussex Schools Cricket Association
Education: St Bede's Prep School, Eastbourne; Tonbridge School; 'starting at Trinity Hall, Cambridge in October 1997 to study classics'
Qualifications: 9 GCSEs, 3 A-levels
Off-season: Teaching in Natal, South Africa
Overseas tours: Sussex U19 to Barbados 1993
Cricketers particularly admired: Brian Lara, Sachin Tendulkar. Allan Donald, Shane Warne
Young players to look out for: David Sales
Other sports followed: Football (Brighton & Hove Albion), tennis, hockey - 'anything except horse racing'
Injuries: None
Relaxations: Reading, going to the theatre, cinema
Extras: Schools Cricketer of the Year for 1996. Played for England U18 against New Zealand U19 in 1996
Opinions on cricket: 'None. I haven't been in the game long enough.'

Name: Toby Alexander Radford
Role: Right-hand bat, 'very occasional right-arm off-spin bowler'
Born: 3 December 1971, Caerphilly, Mid Glamorgan
Height: 5ft 10in **Weight:** 10st 4lbs
Nickname: Ronnie, Jockey, Radders
County debut: 1993 (one-day, Middlesex), 1994 (first-class, Middlesex), 1996 (Sussex)
1st-Class 50s: 3
1st-Class catches: 10
Place in batting averages: 281st av. 12.12 (1995 93rd av. 34.85)
Strike rate: (career 6.00)
Parents: Brian and Gillian
Marital status: Single
Family links with cricket: 'Dad is a senior coach and has written articles on cricket in the national press and the book *From the Nursery End* in which he interviewed the county coaches'
Education: Park House School, Newbury; St Bartholomew's School, Newbury; City University, London
Qualifications: 9 O-levels, 3 A-levels, BA (Hons) in Journalism, senior coaching certificate
Career outside cricket: Journalism and coaching
Off-season: Coaching and writing
Overseas tours: England YC to Australia 1989-90, to New Zealand 1990-91
Cricketers particularly admired: Desmond Haynes, Dean Jones, Geoff Boycott
Young players to look out for: Anurag Singh, Umer Rashid
Other sports followed: Football, snooker, speedway, ice hockey, 'boomerang throwing'
Relaxations: Cinema, videos, music (U2), crosswords, eating out, current affairs, writing
Extras: *Daily Telegraph* U15 Batsman of the Year 1987; MCC/Lord's Taverners' Player of the Year at U13, U15 and U19 age-groups. Middlesex Uncapped Player of the Year 1995. Left Middlesex at the end of the 1995 season and joined Sussex in 1996
Opinions on cricket: 'Standard of 2nd XI wickets is generally poor and could be improved.'
Best batting: 69 Middlesex v Essex, Chelmsford 1995
Best bowling: 1-0 Middlesex v Oxford University, The Parks 1995

1996 Season

	M	Inns	NO	Runs	HS	Avge	100s	50s	Ct	St	O	M	Runs	Wkts	Avge	Best	5wI	10wM
Test																		
All First	5	8	0	97	53	12.12	-	1	2	-								
1-day Int																		
NatWest																		
B & H																		
Sunday																		

Career Performances

	M	Inns	NO	Runs	HS	Avge	100s	50s	Ct	St	Balls	Runs	Wkts	Avge	Best	5wI	10wM
Test																	
All First	12	20	4	345	69	21.56	-	3	10	-	6	0	1	0.00	1-0	-	-
1-day Int																	
NatWest	1	1	0	82	82	82.00	-	1	-	-							
B & H																	
Sunday	4	4	1	73	38	24.33	-	-	-	-							

RALPH, J. T.　　　　　　　　　　Worcestershire

Name: James Trevor Ralph
Role: Right-hand bat, leg-break bowler
Born: 9 October 1975, Kidderminster
Height: 5ft 11in **Weight:** 12st 5lbs
Nickname: Ralphy
County debut: 1996
1st-Class catches: 1
Parents: Alan and Mary
Marital status: Single
Family links with cricket: Father plays club cricket
Education: St John's First and Middle School, Kidderminster; Harry Cheshire High School, Kidderminster
Qualifications: 8 GCSEs
Career outside cricket: Postman
Off-season: Relaxing, doing odd jobs, going to the races
Overseas teams played for: North Albany, Western Australia 1994-96
Cricketers particularly admired: Graeme Hick
Young players to look out for: Vikram Solanki
Other sports followed: Hockey, golf, football and horse racing

Injuries: Broken bone in left hand, missed three weeks
Relaxations: Horse racing and going out with friends
Extras: Played for Worcestershire CA and SCA from U11 to U19. Achieved a pair in first-class debut versus South Africa A
Opinions on cricket: 'Too many 2nd XI games are played on inferior pitches which is a disadvantage to young batsmen.'

1996 Season

	M	Inns	NO	Runs	HS	Avge	100s	50s	Ct	St	O	M	Runs	Wkts	Avge	Best	5wI	10wM
Test																		
All First	1	2	0	0	0	0.00	-	-	1	-								
1-day Int																		
NatWest																		
B & H																		
Sunday																		

Career Performances

	M	Inns	NO	Runs	HS	Avge	100s	50s	Ct	St	Balls	Runs	Wkts	Avge	Best	5wI	10wM
Test																	
All First	1	2	0	0	0	0.00	-	-	1	-							
1-day Int																	
NatWest																	
B & H																	
Sunday																	

70. Which two Australian bowlers took a combined 30 wickets
in their first Ashes series in 1986-87?

RAMPRAKASH, M. R. Middlesex

Name: Mark Ravindra Ramprakash
Role: Right-hand bat, right-arm
off-spin bowler
Born: 5 September 1969, Bushey, Herts
Height: 5ft 10in **Weight:** 12st 4lbs
Nickname: Ramps, Bloodaxe
County debut: 1987
County cap: 1990
Test debut: 1991
Tests: 19
One-Day Internationals: 10
1000 runs in a season: 7
1st-Class 50s: 65
1st-Class 100s: 33
1st-Class 200s: 4
1st-Class catches: 111
One-Day 100s: 7
One-Day 5 w. in innings: 1
Place in batting averages: 33rd av. 49.68
(1995 1st av. 77.86)
Strike rate: 62.00 (career 107.06)
Parents: Deonarine and Jennifer
Date of marriage: 24 September 1993
Family links with cricket: Father played club cricket in Guyana
Education: Gayton High School; Harrow Weald Sixth Form College
Qualifications: 6 O-levels, 2 A-levels
Career outside cricket: 'Any ideas welcome'
Overseas tours: England YC to Sri Lanka 1986-87, to Australia (Youth World Cup)
1987-88; England A to Pakistan 1990-91; to West Indies 1991-92, to India (vice
captain) 1994-95; England to New Zealand 1991-92, to West Indies 1993-94, to
Australia 1994-95, to South Africa 1995-96; Lion Cubs to Barbados 1993
Overseas teams played for: Nairobi Jafferys, Kenya 1988; North Melbourne 1989
Cricketers particularly admired: 'All the great all-rounders'
Other sports followed: Snooker, football
Relaxations: 'Being at home with the family, going to movies, eating out'
Extras: Did not begin to play cricket until he was nine years old; played for
Bessborough CC at age 13, played for Middlesex 2nd XI aged 16 and made first-team
debut for Middlesex aged 17. Scored 204* in NCA Guernsey Festival Tournament and
in 1987 made 186* on his debut for Stanmore CC. Voted Best U15 Schoolboy of 1985
by Cricket Society, Best Young Cricketer of 1986 and Most Promising Player of the Year
in 1988. Played for England YC v New Zealand YC in 1989. Man of the Match in

Middlesex's NatWest Trophy final win in 1988, on his debut in the competition. While on tour with England A in India was called up as replacement for Graeme Hick on the senior tour to Australia 1994-95. Finished top of the Whyte and Mackay batting ratings in 1995

Opinions on cricket: 'To lose overseas players would lower playing standards greatly. People should think about the positive things that 99% of them bring to county cricket. Why do the powers-that-be feel that they must constantly tamper with the rules, i.e. bouncers etc?'

Best batting: 235 Middlesex v Yorkshire, Headingley 1995
Best bowling: 3-91 Middlesex v Somerset, Taunton 1995

1996 Season

	M	Inns	NO	Runs	HS	Avge	100s	50s	Ct	St	O	M	Runs	Wkts	Avge	Best	5wI	10wM
Test																		
All First	17	31	2	1441	169	49.68	4	8	7	-	31	4	121	3	40.33	2-26	-	-
1-day Int																		
NatWest	2	2	0	31	30	15.50	-	-	-	-	1	0	2	0	-		-	-
B & H	4	4	0	143	56	35.75	-	2	2	-	15	1	65	3	21.66	3-35	-	
Sunday	14	14	2	515	122	42.91	1	3	4	-	8.5	0	76	2	38.00	1-21	-	

Career Performances

	M	Inns	NO	Runs	HS	Avge	100s	50s	Ct	St	Balls	Runs	Wkts	Avge	Best	5wI	10wM
Test	19	33	1	533	72	16.65	-	2	13	-	265	149	0	-	-	-	-
All First	205	334	43	13144	235	45.16	33	65	111	-	1713	1025	16	64.06	3-91	-	-
1-day Int	10	10	3	184	32	26.28	-	-	5	-	12	14	0	-	-	-	
NatWest	21	20	1	522	104	27.47	1	1	6	-	204	124	6	20.66	2-15	-	
B & H	32	31	7	975	119 *	40.62	2	5	10	-	126	94	3	31.33	3-35	-	
Sunday	118	112	22	3960	147 *	44.00	4	27	36	-	262	281	12	23.41	5-38	1	

71. Mark Taylor's 1989 tour aggregate of 839 runs was surpassed by only two players in the history of Ashes rubbers. Who were they?

RAO, R. K. Sussex

Name: Rajesh Krishnakant Rao
Role: Right-hand bat, right-arm leg-spin bowler
Born: 9 December 1974, London
Height: 5ft 10in **Weight:** 12st 7lbs
Nickname: Harry, Mayo, Chairman
County debut: 1996
Parents: Krishnakant and Meena
Marital status: Single
Family links with cricket: Dad played for Ugandan national side. Brother Rishi has represented Middlesex regional sides. All uncles and cousins are cricket fanatics
Education: Lyon Park Primary School; Alperton High School; City of Westminster College; University of Brighton
Qualifications: 5 GCSEs, GNVQ Advanced Leisure and Tourism, BSc Sports Science, basic coaching award
Career outside cricket: Student
Off-season: Studying
Overseas tours: Sussex to Portugal 1996
Cricketers particularly admired: My Dad, Sachin Tendulkar, Shane Warne, Sunil Gavaskar, Kapil Dev
Young players to look out for: 'Too many to mention'
Other sports followed: Football (Liverpool and Bedmont Eagles), tennis, snooker, badminton
Injuries: Stomach virus, out for two weeks
Relaxations: Spending time with family and friends. Listening to music (soul, swing and rap), going on holiday
Extras: Played for England at all youth levels up to age 18. MCC Lord's Taverners Player of the Year 1989 (at Under 14)
Opinions on cricket: 'Standards of 2nd XI grounds and pitches must improve in order for younger players to be better prepared to first team introduction. All second team Championship matches should be four days instead of three. The golden hour rule should be abolished.'
Best batting: 38 Sussex v Somerset, Hove 1996

1996 Season

	M	Inns	NO	Runs	HS	Avge	100s	50s	Ct	St	O	M	Runs	Wkts	Avge	Best	5wI	10wM
Test																		
All First	2	3	1	87	38	43.50	-	-	-	-	5	3	7	0	-		-	-	-
1-day Int																		
NatWest																		
B & H																		
Sunday	11	11	1	293	91	29.30	-	3	4	-	9	0	48	3	16.00	3-31	-	

Career Performances

	M	Inns	NO	Runs	HS	Avge	100s	50s	Ct	St	Balls	Runs	Wkts	Avge	Best	5wI	10wM
Test																	
All First	2	3	1	87	38	43.50	-	-	-	-	30	7	0	-		-	-	-
1-day Int																	
NatWest																	
B & H																	
Sunday	11	11	1	293	91	29.30	-	3	4	-	54	48	3	16.00	3-31	-	

RASHID, U. B. A.   Middlesex

Name: Umer Bin Abdul Rashid
Role: Left-hand bat, slow left-arm bowler
Born: 6 February 1976, Southampton
Height: 6ft 3in **Weight:** 12st 7lbs
Nickname: Umie, Looney, Bin
County debut: 1995 (one-day), 1996 (first-class)
Parents: Mirza and Sebea
Marital status: Single
Education: Southfield Combined First and Middle School; Ealing Green High; Ealing Tertiary College; South Bank University
Qualifications: 7 GCSEs, 2 A-levels, 'currently studying for BA (Hons) in Business Studies'
Off-season: 'Studying at university and keeping fit. Working on my game'
Cricketers particularly admired: Carl Hooper, Aamir Sohail
Young players to look out for: Vikram Solanki, Owais Shah, David Nash, David Sales, Anurag Singh
Other sports followed: Football (Southampton FC), Formula One
Relaxations: 'Chilling out with family and friends, playing Nintendo and computer

games. A keen reader of books by John Grisham'

Extras: Lord's Taverners' Cricketer of the Year 1994-95. Played England U19 against South Africa in 1995. Played for the Combined Universities side in the B & H Cup

Opinions on cricket: 'I think that a two-tier league system should be introduced to improve the intensity and the standard of cricket. This will allow all of the best players to play with each other and thus prepare them for international cricket.'

Best batting: 9 Middlesex v Gloucestershire, Lord's 1996

1996 Season

	M	Inns	NO	Runs	HS	Avge	100s	50s	Ct	St	O	M	Runs	Wkts	Avge	Best	5wI	10wM
Test																		
All First	1	2	0	15	9	7.50	-	-	-	-	6	1	17	0	-		-	-
1-day Int																		
NatWest																		
B & H	4	4	1	81	29	27.00	-	-	1	-	34.3	3	146	3	48.66	2-57	-	
Sunday	3	1	0	0	0	0.00	-	-	-	-	14	0	117	3	39.00	2-57	-	

Career Performances

	M	Inns	NO	Runs	HS	Avge	100s	50s	Ct	St	Balls	Runs	Wkts	Avge	Best	5wI	10wM
Test																	
All First	1	2	0	15	9	7.50	-	-	-	-	36	17	0	-		-	-
1-day Int																	
NatWest																	
B & H	7	6	2	96	29	24.00	-	-	1	-	405	300	5	60.00	2-57	-	
Sunday	7	4	0	14	8	3.50	-	-	-	-	240	235	7	33.57	2-34	-	

RATCLIFFE, J. D.   Surrey

Name: Jason David Ratcliffe
Role: Right-hand opening bat, right-arm medium/off-spin bowler, slip fielder
Born: 19 June 1969, Solihull
Height: 6ft 4in **Weight:** 14st 7lbs
Nickname: Ratters, Fridge
County debut: 1988 (Warwickshire),
1995 (Surrey)
1st-Class 50s: 30
1st-Class 100s: 3
1st-Class catches: 55
One-Day 100s: 1
Place in batting averages: 136th av. 32.93 (1995 113th av. 32.35)
Strike rate: 50.40 (career 66.11)
Parents: David and Sheila

Wife and date of marriage: Andrea, 7 January 1995

Family links with cricket: Father (D.P. Ratcliffe) played for Warwickshire 1956-62

Education: Meadow Green Primary School; Sharmans Cross Secondary School; Solihull Sixth Form College

Qualifications: 6 O-levels; NCA staff coach

Career outside cricket: Sports PR and marketing

Off-season: Working in London

Overseas tours: NCA (South) to Ireland 1988; Warwickshire to South Africa 1991-92

Overseas teams played for: West End, Kimberley, South Africa 1987-88; Belmont, Newcastle, NSW 1990-91; Penrith, Sydney 1992-94

Cricketers particularly admired: Nadeem Shahid

Young players to look out for: Ben Hollioake

Other sports followed: Football, tennis, golf

Injuries: Broken thumb, did not miss any cricket

Relaxations: Music, reading, eating out

Extras: Scored a century against Boland on Warwickshire tour to South Africa 1991-92. Released by Warwickshire at end of 1994 season and signed for Surrey

Best batting: 127* Warwickshire v Cambridge University, Fenner's 1989

Best bowling: 2-26 Surrey v Yorkshire, Middlesbrough 1996

1996 Season

	M	Inns	NO	Runs	HS	Avge	100s	50s	Ct	St	O	M	Runs	Wkts	Avge	Best	5wl	10wM
Test																		
All First	9	16	1	494	69	32.93	-	4	5	-	42	7	166	5	33.20	2-26	-	-
1-day Int																		
NatWest																			
B & H																			
Sunday	2	2	1	60	42	60.00	-	-	1	-								

Career Performances

	M	Inns	NO	Runs	HS	Avge	100s	50s	Ct	St	Balls	Runs	Wkts	Avge	Best	5wl	10wM
Test																	
All First	96	177	9	4907	127 *	29.20	3	30	55	-	595	401	9	44.55	2-26	-	-
1-day Int																	
NatWest	9	9	1	337	105	42.12	1	2	1	-	30	20	0	-	-	-
B & H	2	2	0	43	29	21.50	-	-	-	-							
Sunday	21	20	3	277	42	16.29	-	-	6	-	163	179	5	35.80	2-11	-

RAWNSLEY, M.   Worcestershire

Name: Matthew Rawnsley
Role: Right-hand bat, slow left-arm bowler
Born: 8 June 1976, Birmingham
Height: 6ft 4in   **Weight:** 13st 7lbs
County debut: 1996
1st-Class catches: 1
Strike rate: (career 91.20)
Parents: Christopher (deceased) and June
Marital status: Single
Education: Bourneville School,
Birmingham; Shenley Court School,
Birmingham
Qualifications: 9 GCSEs and 3 A-levels
Off-season: Playing in New Zealand
Overseas teams played for: Kumeu,
Auckland 1995-96
Other sports followed: Rugby (plays for Old
Griffonians)

Relaxations: Listening to music, reading, keeping fit, circuit training
Best batting: 4* Worcestershire v Sussex, Worcester 1996
Best bowling: 1-4 Worcestershire v Sussex, Worcester 1996

1996 Season

	M	Inns	NO	Runs	HS	Avge	100s	50s	Ct	St	O	M	Runs	Wkts	Avge	Best	5wI	10wM
Test																		
All First	4	1	1	4	4 *	-	-	-	1	-	76	18	219	5	43.80	1-4	-	-
1-day Int																		
NatWest																		
B & H																		
Sunday	3	3	0	11	7	3.66	-	-	-	-	12.5	1	69	0	-		-	-

Career Performances

	M	Inns	NO	Runs	HS	Avge	100s	50s	Ct	St	Balls	Runs	Wkts	Avge	Best	5wI	10wM
Test																	
All Firs	4	1	1	4	4 *	-	-	-	1	-	456	219	5	43.80	1-4	-	-
1-day Int																	
NatWest																	
B & H																	
Sunday	3	3	0	11	7	3.66	-	-	-	-	77	69	0	-		-	-

READ, C. M. W.

Gloucestershire

Name: Christopher Mark Wells Read
Role: Right-hand bat, wicket-keeper
Born: 10 August 1978, Paignton, Devon
Height: 5ft 8in **Weight:** 10st 7lbs
Nickname: Readie
County debut: No first-team appearance
Parents: Geoffrey and Caroline
Family links with cricket: Father played club cricket and is a very keen supporter
Education: Roselands Primary School; Torquay Boys' Grammar School; University of Bath
Qualifications: 9 GCSEs, 4 A-levels, NCA coaching award
Off-season: England U19 tour to Pakistan and studying at university
Overseas tours: West of England U13 to Holland 1991; West of England U15 to West Indies 1992-93; England U17 to Holland (International Youth tournament) 1995; England U19 to Pakistan 1996-97
Cricketers particularly admired: Alan Knott, Jack Russell, Graham Thorpe
Young players to look out for: David Sales
Other sports followed: Football (Everton), rugby union (Bath), hockey
Relaxations: Listening to music, sleeping, going out with friends
Extras: Represented Devon in Minor Counties Championship and NatWest in 1995 and 1996. Played for England U18 against New Zealand U19 in 1996. Has also played hockey for Devon U18 and U21 and for West of England U17
Opinions on cricket: '2nd XI games should be extended to four days to prepare players better for the jump to the 1st XI. More 2nd XI games should be played on county pitches. Tea should last 30 minutes.'

REEVE, D. A.   Somerset

Name: Dermot Alexander Reeve
Role: Right-hand bat, right-arm
medium-fast bowler
Born: 2 April 1963, Hong Kong
Height: 6ft **Weight:** 11st 11lbs
Nickname: Legend
County debut: 1983 (Sussex), 1988
(Warwickshire)
County cap: 1986 (Sussex), 1989
(Warwickshire)
Tests: 3
One-Day Internationals: 29
1000 runs in a season: 2
50 wickets in a season: 2
1st-Class 50s: 52
1st-Class 100s: 7
1st-Class 200s: 1
1st-Class 5 w. in innings: 8
1st-Class catches: 200

One-Day 100s: 1
One-Day 5 w. in innings: 1
Place in batting averages: 28th av. 50.14 (1995 86th av. 36.22)
Place in bowling averages: (1995 2nd av. 17.39)
Strike rate: 68.66 (career 64.76)
Parents: Alexander James and Monica
Marital status: Divorced
Children: Emily Kaye, 14 September 1988
Family links with cricket: Brother Mark still plays club cricket. Dad used to play and
mother took over as scorer during the England tour to India and Sri Lanka 1992-93
when Clem Driver was taken ill
Education: King George V School, Kowloon, Hong Kong
Qualifications: 7 O-levels
Off-season: 'Doing some after-dinner speaking and then visiting my daughter in
Australia. Lots of sitting on the beach and golf.'
Overseas teams played for: Hong Kong
Cricketers particularly admired: 'John Barclay (enthusiasm), Wasim Akram (talent),
Tim Munton (commitment), Malcolm Marshall (power with grace), Alec Stewart
(timing), Ray Alikhan (guts), Graham Gooch and Mike Gatting (dedication), Allan
Donald'
Other sports followed: Football (Manchester United)
Injuries: Back strain, missed ten days

Relaxations: Swimming, golf, eating out, music, movies and popcorn
Extras: Formerly on Lord's groundstaff. Represented Hong Kong in ICC Trophy June 1982. Hong Kong Cricketer of the Year 1980-81 and Hong Kong's Cricket Sports Personality of the Year 1981. Twice Western Australian CA Cricketer of the Year. Man of the Match in 1986 NatWest final for Sussex and 1989 final for Warwickshire. Originally selected for England A tour to Bermuda and West Indies 1991-92 but promoted to senior tour to New Zealand when Angus Fraser was ruled out by injury. Appointed Warwickshire captain for 1993 and was voted their Player of the Year 1993 after leading them to victory in the NatWest Trophy. On the Sky Sports commentary team for the England tour of Australia 1994-95. Now holds the record for the number of Man of the Match Awards in the NatWest final with three. During his three years as Warwickshire captain, they have won six trophies. Played for England in the one-day series against South Africa and called up to the England squad for the World Cup in India and Pakistan as a replacement for the injured Craig White. Awarded benefit for 1996. Was forced to retire from first-class cricket during the 1996 season due to an arthritic hip and has joined Somerset as first team coach for 1997. His book *Dermot Reeve's Winning Ways* was published in 1996
Best batting: 202* Warwickshire v Northamptonshire, Northampton 1990
Best bowling: 7-37 Sussex v Lancashire, Lytham 1987

1996 Season

	M	Inns	NO	Runs	HS	Avge	100s	50s	Ct	St	O	M	Runs	Wkts	Avge	Best	5wI	10wM
Test																		
All First	5	8	1	351	168 *	50.14	1	-	7	-	103	32	195	9	21.66	5-37	1	-
1-day Int																		
NatWest																			
B & H	7	4	1	96	27	32.00	-	-	7	-	63.5	7	218	13	16.76	4-23	-	
Sunday	5	4	1	10	5	3.33	-	-	2	-	34.4	2	138	8	17.25	3-22	-	

Career Performances

	M	Inns	NO	Runs	HS	Avge	100s	50s	Ct	St	Balls	Runs	Wkts	Avge	Best	5wI	10wM
Test	3	5	0	124	59	24.80	-	1	1	-	149	60	2	30.00	1-4	-	-
All First	241	322	77	8541	202 *	34.86	7	52	200	-	29533	12232	456	26.82	7-37	8	-
1-day Int	29	21	9	291	35	24.25	-	-	12	-	1147	820	20	41.00	3-20	-	
NatWest	43	33	12	784	81 *	37.33	-	4	16	-	2452	1247	49	25.44	4-20	-	
B & H	44	35	13	567	80	25.77	-	1	16	-	2291	1548	55	28.14	4-23	-	
Sunday	172	127	33	2352	100	25.02	1	9	49	-	6065	4522	164	27.57	5-23	1	

REMY, C. C.

Name: Carlos Charles Remy
Role: Right-hand bat, right-arm fast-medium bowler
Born: 24 July 1968, Castries, St Lucia
Height: 5ft 10in **Weight:** 11st
Nickname: Dredd
County debut: 1989
1st-Class 50s: 2
1st-Class catches: 7
Strike rate: (career 86.15)
Parents: Mary Annette
Marital status: Single
Family links with cricket: Stepfather played club cricket for STC in Morrant League
Education: St William of York School, London
Qualifications: 1 O-level, 3 CSEs, NCA coaching certificate

Career outside cricket: 'Doing any job'
Overseas tours: Haringey Cricket College to West Indies 1988, 1989
Overseas teams played for: Bionics, Harare 1989-90; Parnell, Auckland 1990-91
Cricketers particularly admired: Franklyn Stephenson, Robin Smith, Allan Border, Malcolm Marshall
Other sports followed: Football and rugby
Relaxations: Listening to music (soul, swing, rap and ragga), dancing
Extras: 'Scored my very first hundred for Sussex in my first game for the 2nd XI.' Joined Leicestershire in 1996 but was released at the end of the season
Best batting: 60 Sussex v Northamptonshire, Northampton 1994
Best bowling: 4-63 Sussex v Cambridge University, Hove 1990

1996 Season

	M	Inns	NO	Runs	HS	Avge	100s	50s	Ct	St	O	M	Runs	Wkts	Avge	Best	5wI	10wM
Test																		
All First	1	0	0	0	0	-	-	-	-	-								
1-day Int																		
NatWest	1	1	1	0	0 *	-	-	-	-	-	12	1	65	0	-		-	-
B & H	1	1	1	1	1 *	-	-	-	-	-	3	0	29	0	-		-	-
Sunday	13	10	1	67	17*	7.44	-	-	3	-	63	2	331	11	30.09	2-9	-	

Career Performances

	M	Inns	NO	Runs	HS	Avge	100s	50s	Ct	St	Balls	Runs	Wkts	Avge	Best	5wI	10wM
Test																	
All First	22	29	3	480	60	18.46	-	2	7	-	1637	1051	19	55.31	4-63	-	-
1-day Int																	
NatWest	2	2	1	1	1	1.00	-	-	-	-	132	95	0	-	-	-	-
B & H	3	3	1	11	7	5.50	-	-	-	-	78	66	0	-	-	-	-
Sunday	41	32	3	218	19	7.51	-	-	10	-	1372	1143	40	28.57	4-31	-	

RENSHAW, S. J. Hampshire

Name: Simon John Renshaw
Role: Right-hand bat, right-arm fast bowler
Born: 6 March 1974, Bebington, Wirral
Height: 6ft 3in **Weight:** 14st 8lbs
Nickname: Toady
County debut: 1996
1st-Class catches: 3
Place in bowling averages: 143rd av. 49.53
Strike rate: 82.73 (career 87.11)
Parents: Michael and Barbara
Marital status: Single
Family links with cricket: Father and brother play in local league competitions
Education: Birkenhead Prep School; Birkenhead; Leeds University
Qualifications: 9 GCSEs, 4 A-levels, BSc in Microbiology
Career outside cricket: 'None yet but expected to be in microbiology'
Off-season: 'Gaining a stone in weight in Melbourne'
Overseas teams played for: Mulgrave, Melbourne 1995-96; Ashwood, Melbourne 1996-97
Cricketers particularly admired: Ian Botham, Viv Richards
Young players to look out for: David Sales
Other sports followed: Football (Everton) and snooker
Injuries: Tendonitis by the shin, missed one week
Relaxations: Music, films and reading
Extras: Was captain of the Birkenhead U17 side that won the Barclays Knock-out Cup in 1991. Captain of Birkenhead 1st XI in 1992. Represented North of England Schools and MCC Schools. Played for Cheshire in the Minor Counties and for Cheshire U25 in the Bain Hogg Trophy in 1995. Captain of Cheshire U19 at the Cambridge Festival and

was voted Cheshire Young Player of the Year. Best performance in the Minor Counties was 7 for 19 against Shropshire. Played for the Combined Universities in the Benson and Hedges Cup and against West Indies at The Parks. Priestley Cup Final Winner with Farsley in 1995

Opinions on cricket: 'Current County Championship is stagnating. Two divisions with promotion and relegation would increase interest. There should be a greater liaison between minor counties and major ones. There is no structured development plan for any boy who lives outside the major county catchment area, which means that many players of county standard are ignored.'

Best batting: 9* Hampshire v Leicestershire, Leicester 1996
Best bowling: 4-56 Hampshire v Leicestershire, Leicester 1996

1996 Season

	M	Inns	NO	Runs	HS	Avge	100s	50s	Ct	St	O	M	Runs	Wkts	Avge	Best	5wI	10wM
Test																		
All First	7	7	5	10	9 *	5.00	-	-	3	-	206.5	51	743	15	49.53	4-56	-	-
1-day Int																		
NatWest	1	1	0	4	4	4.00	-	-	-	-	5	0	25	0	-		-	-
B & H																		
Sunday	5	2	2	7	6 *	-	-	-	-	-	23	0	109	3	36.33	2-18	-	

Career Performances

	M	Inns	NO	Runs	HS	Avge	100s	50s	Ct	St	Balls	Runs	Wkts	Avge	Best	5wI	10wM
Test																	
All First	8	8	5	10	9 *	3.33	-	-	3	-	1481	934	17	54.94	4-56	-	-
1-day Int																	
NatWest	2	2	0	5	4	2.50	-	-	-	-	72	45	2	22.50	2-20	-	
B & H	5	2	1	0	0 *	0.00	-	-	1	-	294	210	5	42.00	2-34	-	
Sunday	5	2	2	7	6 *	-	-	-	-	-	138	109	3	36.33	2-18	-	

RHODES, S. J.   Worcestershire

Name: Steven John Rhodes
Role: Right-hand bat, wicket-keeper, county vice-captain
Born: 17 June 1964, Bradford
Height: 5ft 8in **Weight:** 12st
Nickname: Bumpy
County debut: 1981 (Yorkshire), 1985 (Worcestershire)
County cap: 1986 (Worcestershire)
Benefit: 1996
Test debut: 1994
Tests: 11

One-Day Internationals: 9
1000 runs in a season: 1
1st-Class 50s: 53
1st-Class 100s: 9
1st-Class catches: 774
1st-Class stumpings: 104
Place in batting averages: 79th av. 39.12
(1995 63rd av. 40.72)
Parents: William Ernest and Norma Kathleen
Wife and date of marriage: Judy Ann, 6
March 1993
Children: Holly Jade, 20 August 1985;
George Harry, 26 October 1993; Lily Amber,
3 March 1995
Family links with cricket: Father played for
Nottinghamshire 1959-64
Education: Bradford Moor Junior School;
Lapage St Middle; Carlton-Bolling
Comprehensive, Bradford
Qualifications: 4 O-levels, coaching certificate
Career outside cricket: Labourer; trainee sports shop manager
Overseas tours: England A to Sri Lanka 1986-86; England A to Zimbabwe and Kenya
1989-90, to Pakistan 1990-91, to West Indies 1991-92, to South Africa 1993-94;
England to Australia 1994-95
Overseas teams played for: Past Bros, Bundaberg, Queensland; Avis Vogeltown,
New Plymouth, New Zealand; Melville, Perth, Australia
Cricketers particularly admired: Graeme Hick, Richard Hadlee
Other sports followed: Rugby league, horse racing and golf
Injuries: 'Niggles'
Relaxations: Keeping and breeding tropical fish ('very therapeutic')
Extras: Played for England YC v Australia YC in 1983 and holds record for most
victims in an innings for England YC. Youngest wicket-keeper to play for Yorkshire.
Released by Yorkshire to join Worcestershire at end of 1984 season. Selected for
cancelled England tour to India 1988-89 and was one of four players put on stand-by as
reserves for 1992 World Cup squad. Writes a weekly cricket column for a Birmingham
newspaper. One of the *Wisden* Cricketers of the Year for 1994. Awarded benefit for 1996
Opinions on cricket: 'How England Test bowlers can stay fresh in between Test
matches is beyond me. They bowl their hearts out in a Test and then go straight into five
tough days county cricket. The next day they report to the next Test venue for another
gruelling match. No wonder we can't sustain the same high level in the second
consecutive bowling day of a Test. Don't ask me how we achieve the perfect answer to
the problem. Extending the four-foot rule to six feet would be worth experimenting with,
to help spinners on flat pitches.'
Best batting: 122* Worcestershire v Young Australia, Worcester 1995

1996 Season

	M	Inns	NO	Runs	HS	Avge	100s	50s	Ct	St	O	M	Runs	Wkts	Avge	Best	5wI	10wM
Test																		
All First	19	29	5	939	110	39.12	1	8	40	8								
1-day Int																		
NatWest	2	2	0	15	8	7.50	-	-	2	1								
B & H	4	2	0	12	8	6.00	-	-	3	-								
Sunday	16	8	3	75	27 *	15.00	-	-	14	5								

Career Performances

	M	Inns	NO	Runs	HS	Avge	100s	50s	Ct	St	Balls	Runs	Wkts	Avge	Best	5wI	10wM
Test	11	17	5	294	65 *	24.50	-	1	46	3							
All First	309	425	120	10185	122 *	33.39	9	53	774	104	6	30	0	-	-	-	-
1-day Int	9	8	2	107	56	17.83	-	1	9	2							
NatWest	37	28	9	387	61	20.36	-	2	45	7							
B & H	57	40	7	481	51 *	14.57	-	1	79	9							
Sunday	182	112	27	1574	48 *	18.51	-	-	186	55							

RIDGEWAY, P. M. Lancashire

Name: Paul Matthew Ridgeway
Role: Right-hand bat, right-arm
fast-medium bowler
Born: 13 February 1977, Airedale, Yorkshire
Height: 6ft 3in **Weight:** 17st
County debut: No first-team appearance
Parents: Peter and Judith
Marital status: Single
Family links with cricket: Father is first
cousin to Don Wilson (Yorkshire and
England)
Education: Hellifield Primary School; Settle
High School
Qualifications: GCSEs, BTEC Business and
Finance
Career outside cricket: Working for Turner
Construction
Cricketers particularly admired: Ian Austin
Young players to look out for: D Welch
Other sports followed: Rugby league
Injuries: Groin, out for two weeks
Relaxations: Music, going to the gym

RIPLEY, D.   Northamptonshire

Name: David Ripley
Role: Right-hand bat, wicket-keeper
Born: 13 September 1966, Leeds
Height: 5ft 11in **Weight:** 11st 11lbs
Nickname: Rips, Spud, Porn Star
County debut: 1984
County cap: 1987
1st-Class 50s: 15
1st-Class 100s: 6
1st-Class catches: 496
1st-Class stumpings: 67
Place in batting averages: 30th av. 49.77
Strike rate: (career 30.00)
Parents: Arthur and Brenda
Wife and date of marriage: Jackie, 24
September 1988

Children: Joe David, 11 October 1989;
George William, 5 March 1994
Education: Woodlesford Primary; Royds
High, Leeds
Qualifications: 5 O-levels, NCA advanced coach
Career outside cricket: Youth development coaching for Northants
Off-season: Coaching at Northants CCC and 'working on my benefit'
Overseas tours: England YC to West Indies 1984-85; Northants to Durban, South
Africa 1991-92, to Cape Town 1992-93, to Zimbabwe 1994-95, to Johannesburg 1996
Overseas teams played for: Marists and Poverty Bay, New Zealand 1985-87
Cricketers particularly admired: Alan Knott, Bob Taylor 'and many other keepers',
Clive Radley, Ian Botham, Geoff Boycott, Dennis Lillee
Young players to look out for: David Sales, Michael Davies
Other sports followed: Football (Leeds United), rugby league (Castleford), golf
Injuries: Broken finger, out for three weeks
Relaxations: 'Eating out, and sampling different bitters'
Extras: Finished top of wicket-keepers' dismissals list for 1988 and 1992 and was voted
Wombwell Cricket Lovers' Society Best Wicket-keeper 1992. Played for England YC v
Sri Lanka 1986
Opinions on cricket: 'Four-day cricket is working well. I would like to see short run-
ups on Sundays as there are too many low-scoring games.'
Best batting: 134* Northamptonshire v Yorkshire, Scarborough 1986
Best bowling: 2-89 Northamptonshire v Essex, Ilford 1987

1996 Season

	M	Inns	NO	Runs	HS	Avge	100s	50s	Ct	St	O	M	Runs	Wkts	Avge	Best	5wI	10wM
Test																		
All First	11	16	7	448	88 *	49.77	-	3	23	-								
1-day Int																		
NatWest																		
B & H																		
Sunday	7	1	1	0	0 *	-	-	-	8	-								

Career Performances

	M	Inns	NO	Runs	HS	Avge	100s	50s	Ct	St	Balls	Runs	Wkts	Avge	Best	5wI	10wM
Test																	
All First	230	299	81	5477	134 *	25.12	6	15	496	67	60	103	2	51.50	2-89	-	-
1-day Int																	
NatWest	35	20	9	130	27 *	11.81	-	-	36	3							
B & H	37	25	9	305	36 *	19.06	-	-	37	4							
Sunday	134	80	36	832	52 *	18.90	-	1	95	13							

ROBERTS, A. R.   Northamptonshire

Name: Andrew Richard Roberts
Role: Right-hand bat, leg-break bowler
Born: 16 April 1971, Kettering
Height: 5ft 5in **Weight:** 10st 7lbs
Nickname: Reggie
County debut: 1989
1st-Class 50s: 2
1st-Class 5 w. in innings: 1
1st-Class catches: 23
Place in batting averages: 248th av. 17.62
Place in bowling averages: 145th av. 52.70
Strike rate: 103.70 (career 86.00)
Parents: David and Shirley
Marital status: Engaged to Kirsty
Family links with cricket: Father (Dave) played a few games for Northants 2nd XI; brother Tim won the Lord's Taverners U13 award in 1991, played Midlands Schools U14 and England Schoolboys U15
Education: Bishop Stopford Comprehensive, Kettering
Qualifications: 3 O-levels, 5 CSEs, Carpentry and Joinery City & Guilds
Career outside cricket: Carpentry and joinery

Overseas tours: Northamptonshire to Durban, South Africa 1991-92, to Cape Town, South Africa 1992-93

Overseas teams played for: Woolston Working Men's Club, Christchurch, New Zealand 1989-91; Eastern Suburbs, Wellington 1993-95

Cricketers particularly admired: Richard Williams, Wayne Larkins, Dennis Lillee

Other sports followed: Rugby (Northampton Saints RFC) and golf

Injuries: Shoulder prevented throwing

Relaxations: 'Music, sleeping, eating, a good pint of bitter!'

Extras: Played for England YC v Pakistan YC 1990. Named the Rapid Cricketline Second XI Championship Player of the Year in 1995. Released by Northants at the end of the 1996 season

Opinions on cricket: 'In favour of uncovered wickets, which would produce better technique and more exciting cricket.'

Best batting: 62 Northamptonshire v Nottinghamshire, Trent Bridge 1992

Best bowling: 6-72 Northamptonshire v Lancashire, Lytham 1991

1996 Season

	M	Inns	NO	Runs	HS	Avge	100s	50s	Ct	St	O	M	Runs	Wkts	Avge	Best	5wI	10wM
Test																		
All First	6	8	0	141	39	17.62	-	-	1	-	172.5	44	527	10	52.70	3-57	-	-
1-day Int																		
NatWest																		
B & H																		
Sunday																		

Career Performances

	M	Inns	NO	Runs	HS	Avge	100s	50s	Ct	St	Balls	Runs	Wkts	Avge	Best	5wI	10wM
Test																	
All First	61	83	18	1173	62	18.04	-	2	23	-	9203	4829	107	45.13	6-72	1	-
1-day Int																	
NatWest	1	0	0	0	0	-	-	-	1	-	72	23	1	23.00	1-23	-	
B & H																	
Sunday	11	5	0	42	20	8.40	-	-	4	-	263	251	10	25.10	3-26	-	

72. Which England batsman was dismissed 'handled ball' in the 1993 series?

ROBERTS, D. J. Northamptonshire

Name: David James Roberts
Role: Right-hand bat
Born: 29 December 1976, Truro, Cornwall
Height: 6ft **Weight:** 12st
Nickname: Robo
County debut: 1996
1st-Class 50s: 2
Place in batting averages: 99th av. 36.28
Parents: Dennis and Pam
Marital status: Single
Family links with cricket: Cousin, Chris
Bullen, played for Surrey. Father played
cricket for local club and is also a youth
coach. Mother is a keen supporter!
Education: Mullion County Primary;
Mullion Comprehensive
Qualifications: 9 GCSEs, senior cricket
coach
Career outside cricket: Helping on the family farm
Off-season: Touring Zimbabwe with England U19 and working on farm
Overseas tours: West of England to Barbados, Trinidad and Tobago 1990-91 and
1991-92 (captain)
Cricketers particularly admired: Mal Loye
Other sports followed: Football (Manchester United), NBA basketball and all sports
Relaxations: Watching television, listening to music, playing football
Extras: Played for English Schools since the age of 14, including matches against South
Africa in 1992. Represented England U17 against India U17 in 1994
Opinions on cricket: 'Tea is too short, should be increased from 10 minutes to 30
minutes. Second team cricket should be played at first-class grounds instead of club
grounds.'
Best batting: 73 Northamptonshire v Essex, Chelmsford 1996

1996 Season

	M	Inns	NO	Runs	HS	Avge	100s	50s	Ct	St	O	M	Runs	Wkts	Avge	Best	5wI	10wM
Test																		
All Firss	4	7	0	254	73	36.28	-	2	-	-								
1-day Int																		
NatWest																		
B & H																		
Sunday																		

Career Performances

	M	Inns	NO	Runs	HS	Avge	100s	50s	Ct	St		Balls		Runs	Wkts	Avge	Best	5wI	10wM
Test																			
All First	4	7	0	254	73	36.28	-	2	-	-									
1-day Int																			
NatWest																			
B & H																			
Sunday																			

ROBERTS, G. M. Derbyshire

Name: Glenn Martin Roberts
Role: Left-hand bat, slow left-arm bowler
Born: 4 October 1973, Huddersfield
Height: 5ft 10in **Weight:** 11st 11lbs
Nickname: Glenda, Robbo, Alf, Julia
County debut: 1996
1st-Class 50s: 1
1st-Class catches: 1
Strike rate: (career 216.00)
Parents: Tony and Margaret
Marital status: Single
Family links with cricket: 'Major influence
was my grandfather who played Huddersfield
League cricket. My parents took me
everywhere to play and support me'
Education: King James's School; Greenhead
College, Huddersfield; Carnegie College,
Leeds Metropolitan University
Qualifications: 8 GCSEs, 4 A-levels, BEd
(Hons) Physical Education, FA Teaching Certificate, NCA advanced coach
Off-season: Final year of PE degree
Cricketers particularly admired: Craig Norris (Eastern Transvaal), Chris Pickles
(ex-Yorkshire)
Young players to look out for: Andrew Harris, Kevin Dean, Anthony McGrath,
Gavin Hamilton
Other sports followed: Football (goalkeeper) and rugby league (Huddersfield)
Relaxations: Jogging, fitness, gym work, socialising
Extras: Played for Yorkshire from U14 to U19 and captained the U16s and the U19s.
Was a member of the Yorkshire Academy for two years. Scored a fifty batting at No.9
on his Championship debut for Derbyshire and featured in a Derbyshire record, eighth
wicket stand of 118 with Karl Krikken

Opinions on cricket: 'Introduce fitness trainers, sports psychologists, dieticians, nutritionists and other specialists to raise standards of performance of county and international players. Optional schemes for players to obtain professional qualifications during the off-season e.g. sports coaching, PE teaching, etc.'
Best batting: 52 Derbyshire v Somerset, Taunton 1996
Best bowling: 1-55 Derbyshire v Somerset, Taunton 1996

1996 Season

	M	Inns	NO	Runs	HS	Avge	100s	50s	Ct	St	O	M	Runs	Wkts	Avge	Best	5wI	10wM
Test																		
All First	1	1	0	52	52	52.00	-	1	1	-	36	18	73	1	73.00	1-55	-	-
1-day Int																		
NatWest																		
B & H																		
Sunday	5	2	2	6	6 *	-	-	-	2	-	38	1	198	6	33.00	2-28	-	

Career Performances

	M	Inns	NO	Runs	HS	Avge	100s	50s	Ct	St	Balls	Runs	Wkts	Avge	Best	5wI	10wM
Test																	
All First	1	1	0	52	52	52.00	-	1	1	-	216	73	1	73.00	1-55	-	-
1-day Int																	
NatWest																	
B & H																	
Sunday	5	2	2	6	6 *	-	-	-	2	-	228	198	6	33.00	2-28	-	

ROBINSON, D. D. J.   Essex

Name: Darren David John Robinson
Role: Right-hand opening bat, occasional right-arm medium bowler
Born: 2 March 1973, Braintree, Essex
Height: 5ft 11in **Weight:** 14st
Nickname: Pie shop 'or any other name that Fletch might call me'
County debut: 1993
1st-Class 50s: 10
1st-Class 100s: 2
1st-Class catches: 34
Place in batting averages: 113th av. 35.14 (1995 189th av. 22.25)
Parents: David and Dorothy
Marital status: Engaged to Alyssa Jarvi ('she's bloody lovely'), date set for September 1998
Family links with cricket: Father plays club cricket for Halstead
Education: Tabor High School, Braintree; Chelmsford College of Further Education

Qualifications: 5 GCSEs, BTEC National Diploma in Building and Construction
Career outside cricket: Civil engineering and surveying
Off-season: 'Playing golf, relaxing, bit of work, going to the theatre, saving for house, forgetting to water the house plants'
Overseas tours: England U18 to Canada 1991; England U19 to Pakistan 1991-92
Overseas teams played for: Waverley, Sydney 1992-94; Eden Roshill CC, Auckland 1995-96
Cricketers particularly admired: Stuart Law ('drinking ability'), Graham Gooch
Young players to look out for: Stephen Peters, Jonathan Powell
Other sports followed: Golf, football, rugby, swimming
Injuries: Broken finger, out for three weeks
Relaxations: Reading crime novels, music, eating out, pubs
Extras: *Daily Telegraph* batting award 1988 and International Youth Tournament in Canada batting award 1991
Opinions on cricket: 'Cricket's a great game when everything is going well, but a pain in the arse when it's not.'
Best batting: 123 Essex v Gloucestershire, Cheltenham 1995

1996 Season

	M	Inns	NO	Runs	HS	Avge	100s	50s	Ct	St	O	M	Runs	Wkts	Avge	Best	5wl	10wM
Test																		
All First	12	23	2	738	97	35.14	-	8	6	-	5	0	24	0	-	-	-	-
1-day Int																		
NatWest	5	5	0	63	39	12.60	-	-	2	-								
B & H	5	5	1	93	36	23.25	-	-	1	-								
Sunday	14	14	1	432	80	33.23	-	3	1	-								

Career Performances

	M	Inns	NO	Runs	HS	Avge	100s	50s	Ct	St	Balls	Runs	Wkts	Avge	Best	5wl	10wM
Test																	
All First	32	60	2	1600	123	27.58	2	10	34	-	36	31	0	-	-	-	-
1-day Int																	
NatWest	7	7	0	128	55	18.28	-	1	3	-							
B & H	10	9	2	192	36	27.42	-	-	2	-							
Sunday	32	32	4	673	80	24.03	-	3	7	-	12	19	0	-	-	-	

ROBINSON, P. E. Leicestershire

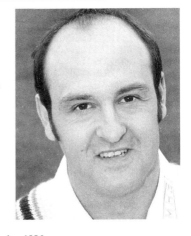

Name: Phillip Edward Robinson
Role: Right-hand bat, left-arm 'declaration' bowler
Born: 3 August 1963, Keighley, West Yorkshire
Height: 5ft 9in **Weight:** 13st 10lbs
Nickname: Roundbat, Brigadier, F.B., Skip, Robbo, Red
County debut: 1984 (Yorkshire), 1992 (Leicestershire)
County cap: 1988 (Yorkshire)
1000 runs in a season: 3
1st-Class 50s: 51
1st-Class 100s: 7
1st-Class catches: 130
One-Day 100s: 1
Place in batting averages: (1994 40th av. 43.57)
Parents: Keith and Lesley
Wife and date of marriage: Jane, 19 September 1986
Family links with cricket: Father and brother played in Bradford League. Dad now an umpire
Education: Long Lee Primary; Hartington Middle; Greenhead Comprehensive
Qualifications: 2 O-levels
Off-season: Coaching in Leicester indoor school
Overseas tours: Southland CC to Tasmania 1987; Yorkshire to St Lucia and Barbados 1988; Leicestershire to Jamaica 1993, to South Africa 1994-95
Overseas teams played for: Southland, New Zealand 1987; Eastern Southland cricket coach 1987; Eden Roskill, Auckland 1989-90; Riverside, Wellington 1990-91
Cricketers particularly admired: Geoff Boycott, Richard Hadlee, Michael Holding
Other sports followed: Football (Manchester United), rugby league (Keighley Cougars)
Relaxations: War-gaming, eating out
Extras: Made the highest score by a Yorkshire 2nd XI player with 233 in 1983. Scored most runs by an overseas player in the Auckland Cricket League for Eden Roskill 1989-90 (1200 runs). Hit the fastest televised 50 in the Sunday League (19 balls) v Derbyshire at Chesterfield 1991. Released by Yorkshire at his own request at the end of the 1991 season. Played for Cumberland in 1992 and could play only limited-overs for Leicestershire in 1992 (apart from one match) but on full contract from 1993. Captain of Leicestershire 2nd XI. Led the team to Bain Hogg win in 1995
Opinions on cricket: 'Cricket should be played on uncovered pitches over three days. Alternatively, four-day games should be played Wednesday to Saturday, with the Sunday League game after. Also, second-class cricket should be played Wednesday to Friday to

allow the younger players to work with the senior players during the season.'
Best batting: 189 Yorkshire v Lancashire, Scarborough 1991
Best bowling: 1-10 Yorkshire v Somerset, Scarborough 1990

1996 Season

	M	Inns	NO	Runs	HS	Avge	100s	50s	Ct	St	O	M	Runs	Wkts	Avge	Best	5wI	10wM
Test																		
All First																		
1-day Int																		
NatWest																		
B & H	3	3	0	45	40	15.00	-	-	-	-								
Sunday																		

Career Performances

	M	Inns	NO	Runs	HS	Avge	100s	50s	Ct	St	Balls	Runs	Wkts	Avge	Best	5wI	10wM
Test																	
All First	159	261	35	7617	189	33.70	7	51	130	-	296	329	3	109.66	1-10	-	-
1-day Int																	
NatWest	17	13	0	421	73	32.38	-	3	5	-							
B & H	33	29	4	684	73 *	27.36	-	4	12	-							
Sunday	145	140	14	3111	104	24.69	1	14	59	-							

ROBINSON, R.   Yorkshire

Name: Ryan Robinson
Role: Right-hand bat, right-arm medium bowler
Born: 19 October 1976, Huddersfield
Height: 6ft 1in   **Weight:** 11st 10lbs
Nickname: Robbo
County debut: No first-team appearance
Parents: Peter and Jennifer
Marital status: Single
Family links with cricket: Cousin, Alan Walker, plays for Durham CCC. Father still playing in local league after 30 years
Education: Emley First School; Kirkburton Middle School; Shelley High School and Sixth Form College
Qualifications: 9 GCSEs
Off-season: Playing cricket abroad
Overseas teams played for: Darling CC,

South Africa 1996-97
Cricketers particularly admired: Chris Silverwood
Young players to look out for: Alex Wharf
Other sports followed: Football (Liverpool FC – 'had schoolboy forms with Hull FC')
Injuries: Back problems 'only stopped me from bowling'
Relaxations: 'Interested in becoming a DJ, mixing house. I admire Stu Allen and any life resident'
Opinions on cricket: 'Should be made more interesting. There are too many drawn games.'

ROBINSON, R. T.   Nottinghamshire

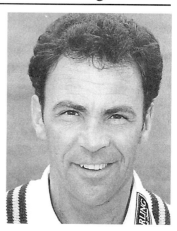

Name: Robert Timothy Robinson
Role: Right-hand opening bat, right-arm medium bowler
Born: 21 November 1958, Sutton-in-Ashfield, Nottinghamshire
Height: 6ft **Weight:** 12st 7lbs
Nickname: Robbo, Chop
County debut: 1978
County cap: 1983
Benefit: 1992 (£90,040)
Test debut: 1984-85
Tests: 29
One-Day Internationals: 26
1000 runs in a season: 14
1st-Class 50s: 128
1st-Class 100s: 61
1st-Class 200s: 3
1st-Class catches: 234
One-Day 100s: 9
Place in batting averages: 50th av. 44.89 (1995 17th av. 54.00)
Strike rate: (career 64.75)
Parents: Eddy and Christine
Wife and date of marriage: Patricia, 2 November 1985
Children: Philip Thomas; Alex James
Family links with cricket: Father, uncle, cousin and brother all played local cricket
Education: Dunstable Grammar School; High Pavement College, Nottingham; Sheffield University
Qualifications: BA (Hons) in Accountancy and Financial Management
Career outside cricket: Owns two sports shops
Overseas tours: England to India and Australia 1984-85, to West Indies 1985-86, to

504

India and Pakistan (World Cup) 1987-88, to New Zealand 1987-88; unofficial English XI to South Africa 1989-90
Cricketers particularly admired: Geoffrey Boycott
Other sports followed: Golf, squash
Relaxations: Spending time with family
Extras: Played for Northamptonshire 2nd XI in 1974-75 and for Nottinghamshire 2nd XI in 1977. Had soccer trials with Portsmouth, Chelsea and QPR. One of *Wisden*'s Five Cricketers of the Year 1985. Banned from Test cricket for joining 1989-90 tour of South Africa, remitted in 1992. Handed over captaincy to Paul Johnson in 1995 to give more time to business
Best batting: 220* Nottinghamshire v Yorkshire, Trent Bridge 1990
Best bowling: 1-22 Nottinghamshire v Northamptonshire, Northampton 1982

1996 Season

	M	Inns	NO	Runs	HS	Avge	100s	50s	Ct	St	O	M	Runs	Wkts	Avge	Best	5wI	10wM
Test																		
All First	17	31	2	1302	184	44.89	3	6	8	-	1	0	4	0	-		-	-	-
1-day Int																		
NatWest	1	1	0	35	35	35.00	-	-	1	-								
B & H	4	4	0	88	52	22.00	-	1	-	-								
Sunday	14	14	2	602	90	50.16	-	6	2	-								

Career Performances

	M	Inns	NO	Runs	HS	Avge	100s	50s	Ct	St	Balls	Runs	Wkts	Avge	Best	5wI	10wM
Test	29	49	5	1601	175	36.38	4	6	8	-	6	0	0	-	-	-	-
All First	384	668	78	25667	220 *	43.50	61	128	234	-	259	289	4	72.25	1-22	-	-
1-day Int	26	26	0	597	83	22.96	-	3	6	-							
NatWest	38	38	2	1501	139	41.69	2	7	16	-							
B & H	71	69	9	2495	120	41.58	3	18	16	-							
Sunday	222	216	26	6328	119 *	33.30	4	42	70	-							

74. Who captained England during the 1989 series?

ROLLINS, A. S. Derbyshire

Name: Adrian Stewart Rollins
Role: Right-hand bat, right-arm medium
bowler, occasional wicket-keeper
Born: 8 February 1972, Barking, Essex
Height: 6ft 5in **Weight:** 16st 7lbs
Nickname: Rollie
County debut: 1993
County cap: 1995
1000 runs in a season: 2
1st-Class 50s: 18
1st-Class 100s: 5
1st-Class 200s: 1
1st-Class catches: 50
1st-Class stumpings: 1
One-Day 100s: 1
Place in batting averages: 110th av. 35.51
(1995 100th av. 34.21)
Strike rate: (career 72.00)
Parents: Marva
Marital status: Engaged to Debbie
Family links with cricket: Brother Robert on Essex staff. Brother Gary is trialling for
various counties
Education: Little Ilford Comprehensive School, Manor Park, London
Qualifications: 10 GCSEs, 4 A-levels, NCA coaching award, Diploma in Sports Psychology
Off-season: Coaching for Derbyshire in schools
Overseas tours: London Federation of Boys Clubs to Barbados 1987
Overseas teams played for: Kaponga, New Zealand 1993-94
Cricketers particularly admired: Gordon Greenidge, Kim Barnett, Desmond
Haynes, Phillip DeFreitas, Viv Richards, Michael Holding
Young players to look out for: Robert Rollins, Vikram Solanki
Other sports followed: Basketball and football (West Ham United)
Injuries: Back injury, missed two weeks
Relaxations: Listening to music
Extras: Made Championship debut on same day as brother. Became 500th first-class
player for Derbyshire, for whom he was named Young Player of the Year 1993. Was the
100th Derbyshire player to score a hundred. Holds record for the highest score by a
Derbyshire opener to carry his bat and his 200 not out against Gloucestershire was the
longest innings by a Derbyshire player. He became the youngest English qualified
Derbyshire double centurion. Voted Derbyshire Player of the Year for 1995
Opinions on cricket: 'Something is not right in the professional cricket game today.
Rugby union turns professional and players are on £50,000 to £200,000-a-year
contracts. The grounds are no greater in rugby than in cricket, so where is our money?

Pay the players.'
Best batting: 200* Derbyshire v Gloucestershire, Bristol 1995
Best bowling: 1-19 Derbyshire v Essex, Chelmsford 1995

1996 Season

	M	Inns	NO	Runs	HS	Avge	100s	50s	Ct	St	O	M	Runs	Wkts	Avge	Best	5wl	10wM
Test																		
All First	19	36	5	1101	131	35.51	3	5	11	-	5	0	50	0	-		-	-
1-day Int																		
NatWest																		
B & H	2	2	0	61	42	30.50	-	-	-	-								
Sunday	5	3	0	6	4	2.00	-	-	1	-								

Career Performances

	M	Inns	NO	Runs	HS	Avge	100s	50s	Ct	St	Balls	Runs	Wkts	Avge	Best	5wl	10wM
Test																	
All First	59	111	12	3296	200 *	33.29	5	18	50	1	72	101	1	101.00	1-19	-	-
1-day Int																	
NatWest	4	4	0	64	56	16.00	-	1	3	-							
B & H	6	6	0	159	70	26.50	-	1	2	-							
Sunday	37	31	2	527	126 *	18.17	1	1	18	-							

ROLLINS, R. J.   Essex

Name: Robert John Rollins
Role: Right-hand bat, wicket-keeper
Born: 30 January 1974, Plaistow, London
Height: 5ft 9in **Weight:** 13st 4lbs
Nickname: Rollie
County debut: 1992
County cap: 1995
1st-Class 50s: 7
1st-Class 100s: 1
1st-Class catches: 115
1st-Class stumpings: 18
Place in batting averages: 205th av. 23.96
(1995 161st av. 25.28)
Parents: Marva
Marital status: Engaged to Joanne
Family links with cricket: 'Brother Adrian
plays for Derbyshire and brother Gary is
captain of the London Cricket College.

Uncle, Keith Hurst, is captain of Hainault and Clayhill where Gary and myself still play'

Education: Little Ilford Comprehensive School

Qualifications: 6 GCSEs

Off-season: Playing in Natal, South Africa

Overseas tours: England U18 to Canada 1991; England U19 to Pakistan 1991-92, to India 1992-93

Overseas teams played for: MOB Pietermaritzburg, South Africa 1995-96

Cricketers particularly admired: Keith Hurst, Alan Knott, Keith Fletcher

Other sports followed: 'West Ham from the comfort of an armchair'

Extras: Named Essex Young Player of the Year 1992 and awarded his 2nd XI cap in September of that year. Made Championship debut on the same day as his brother Adrian. Both kept wicket in the same Sunday League game.

Opinions on cricket: 'Four-day cricket is enjoyable.'

Best batting: 133* Essex v Glamorgan, Swansea 1995

1996 Season

	M	Inns	NO	Runs	HS	Avge	100s	50s	Ct	St	O	M	Runs	Wkts	Avge	Best	5wI	10wM
Test																		
All First	21	34	4	719	74 *	23.96	-	3	56	6								
1-day Int																		
NatWest	5	5	3	134	54 *	67.00	-	2	2	2								
B & H	5	2	1	3	3	3.00	-	-	4	-								
Sunday	16	15	2	204	32	15.69	-	-	9	2								

Career Performances

	M	Inns	NO	Runs	HS	Avge	100s	50s	Ct	St	Balls	Runs	Wkts	Avge	Best	5wI	10wM
Test																	
All First	45	76	8	1570	133 *	23.08	1	7	115	18							
1-day Int																	
NatWest	7	7	3	163	54 *	40.75	-	2	2	3							
B & H	8	3	1	3	3	1.50	-	-	7	-							
Sunday	43	35	9	319	32	12.26	-	-	42	6							

ROSE, G. D.   Somerset

Name: Graham David Rose

Role: Right-hand bat, right-arm fast-medium bowler, first slip

Born: 12 April 1964, Tottenham

Height: 6ft 4in **Weight:** 15st

Nickname: Hagar

County debut: 1985 (Middlesex), 1987 (Somerset)
County cap: 1988 (Somerset)
Benefit: 1996
1000 runs in a season: 1
50 wickets in a season: 3
1st-Class 50s: 32
1st-Class 100s: 6
1st-Class 5 w. in innings: 11
1st-Class 10 w. in match: 1
1st-Class catches: 100
One-Day 100s: 2
Place in batting averages: 193rd av. 25.50 (1995 122nd av. 30.84)
Place in bowling averages: 19th av. 24.36 (1995 103rd av. 35.94)
Strike rate: 47.20 (career 56.20)
Parents: William and Edna

Wife and date of marriage: Teresa Julie, 19 September 1987
Children: Georgina Charlotte, 6 December 1990
Family links with cricket: Father and brothers have played club cricket
Education: Northumberland Park School, Tottenham
Qualifications: 6 O-levels, 4 A-levels, NCA coaching certificate
Off-season: Working for Samson Computer Supplies
Overseas teams played for: Carey Park, Bunbury, Western Australia 1984-85; Fremantle, Perth 1986-87; Paarl, Cape Town 1988-89
Cricketers particularly admired: Richard Hadlee, Jimmy Cook, Mushtaq Ahmed
Young players to look out for: Vikram Solanki, Andrew Harris
Other sports followed: Football, rugby, golf
Injuries: Left thigh strain, missed last three championship matches
Relaxations: Wine, music, gardening, playing golf and 'my daughter, Georgina'
Extras: Played for England YC v Australia YC 1983. Took 6-41 on Middlesex debut in 1985, then scored 95 on debut for Somerset in 1987. Completed double of 1000 runs and 50 wickets in first-class cricket in 1990 and scored fastest recorded centuries in NatWest Trophy (v Devon) and Sunday League (v Glamorgan)
Opinions on cricket: 'Reluctantly I am coming round to the idea of a two-divisional County Championship, but on a parallel basis as in American football. I think that it is time we did away with one of the one-day competitions with the remaining one being 50 overs per side. We should also do away with leg-byes – what purpose do they serve?'
Best batting: 138 Somerset v Sussex, Taunton 1993
Best bowling: 7-47 Somerset v Nottinghamshire, Taunton 1996

1996 Season

	M	Inns	NO	Runs	HS	Avge	100s	50s	Ct	St	O	M	Runs	Wkts	Avge	Best	5wI	10wM
Test																		
All First	15	21	5	408	93 *	25.50	-	2	8	-	393.2	98	1218	50	24.36	7-47	3	1
1-day Int																		
NatWest	3	3	2	21	12 *	21.00	-	-	-	-	36	5	151	4	37.75	3-61	-	
B & H	5	5	0	50	37	10.00	-	-	2	-	44	6	183	5	36.60	2-42	-	
Sunday	15	13	4	183	54	20.33	-	1	6	-	111	4	535	11	48.63	3-33	-	

Career Performances

	M	Inns	NO	Runs	HS	Avge	100s	50s	Ct	St	Balls	Runs	Wkts	Avge	Best	5wI	10wM
Test																	
All First	186	258	45	6318	138	29.66	6	32	100	-	24731	13186	440	29.96	7-47	11	1
1-day Int																	
NatWest	20	18	3	329	110	21.93	1	1	3	-	1061	698	21	33.23	3-11	-	
B & H	45	39	4	768	79	21.94	-	4	9	-	2496	1616	55	29.38	4-21	-	
Sunday	150	131	23	3049	148	28.23	1	17	39	-	5720	4367	140	31.19	4-26	-	

ROSEBERRY, M. A. Durham

Name: Michael Anthony Roseberry
Role: Right-hand bat, right-arm medium-fast bowler
Born: 28 November 1966, Houghton-le-Spring, Sunderland
Height: 6ft 2in **Weight:** 14st 7lbs
Nickname: Micky
County debut: 1985 (Middlesex), 1995 (Durham)
County cap: 1990 (Middlesex)
1000 runs in a season: 4
1st-Class 50s: 51
1st-Class 100s: 19
1st-Class catches: 141
One-Day 100s: 6
Place in batting averages: 186th av. 26.57 (1995 165th av. 24.77)
Strike rate: (career 127.75)
Parents: Matthew and Jean
Wife and date of marriage: Helen Louise, 22 February 1991
Children: Jordan Louise, 29 May 1992; Lauren Ella, 19 February 1994
Family links with cricket: Brother Andrew played for Glamorgan and Leicestershire;

father is director of Durham CCC

Education: Tonstall Preparatory School, Sunderland; Durham School

Qualifications: 5 O-levels, 1 A-level, advanced cricket coach

Career outside cricket: 'Coaching cricket. Director in our business'

Off-season: Playing club cricket in Johannesburg

Overseas tours: England YC to West Indies 1984-85; England A to Australia 1992-93; England XI and Lord's Taverners to Hong Kong 'on numerous occasions'; MCC to West Africa 1993-94; Durham CCC to South Africa 1994-95

Overseas teams played for: Fremantle, Western Australia 1986; Melville, Perth 1988; Alberton, Johannesburg 1994-96

Cricketers particularly admired: 'Desmond Haynes for the obvious and his generosity on the golf course'

Other sports followed: 'Played rugby union at a good level when at school representing Durham County at all levels except the senior side. Follow golf and very loyal supporter of Sunderland FC'

Injuries: Broken knuckle and knee trouble, out for between four and six weeks

Relaxations: 'Eating out and spending time with my family which is limited during the summer'

Extras: Won Lord's Taverners/MCC Cricketer of the Year 1983, Cricket Society award for Best Young Cricketer of the Year 1984 and twice won Cricket Society award for best all-rounder in schools cricket. Played in Durham League as a professional while still at school. At age 16, playing for Durham School v St Bees, he hit 216 in 160 minutes. In 1992 scored 2044 runs in 1992 – joint highest in first-class cricket with Peter Bowler and was named Middlesex Player of the Year and Lucozade Player of the Year. Left Middlesex at end of 1994 to return to his native Durham as captain for the 1995 season but relinquished the captaincy during the 1996 season

Opinions on cricket: 'Four-day cricket is a winner, but as clubs and captains we must improve the pitches.'

Best batting: 185 Middlesex v Leicestershire, Lord's 1993

Best bowling: 1-1 Middlesex v Sussex, Hove 1988

1996 Season

	M	Inns	NO	Runs	HS	Avge	100s	50s	Ct	St	O	M	Runs	Wkts	Avge	Best	5wI	10wM
Test																		
All First	17	30	2	744	145 *	26.57	1	3	6	-								
1-day Int																		
NatWest	1	1	0	100	100	100.00	1	-	1	-								
B & H	5	5	1	130	57	32.50	-	2	2	-								
Sunday	11	10	3	272	65	38.85	-	2	5	-								

Career Performances

	M	Inns	NO	Runs	HS	Avge	100s	50s	Ct	St	Balls	Runs	Wkts	Avge	Best	5wI	10wM
Test																	
All First	192	324	36	10106	185	35.09	19	51	141	-	511	406	4	101.50	1-1	-	-
1-day Int																	
NatWest	16	16	0	680	121	42.50	3	1	7	-	36	42	1	42.00	1-22	-	
B & H	27	25	2	638	84	27.73	-	6	7	-	6	2	0	-	-	-	-
Sunday	111	106	10	3024	119 *	31.50	3	21	42	-	4	7	0	-	-	-	-

RUSSELL, R. C. · Gloucestershire

Name: Robert Charles Russell
Role: Left-hand bat, wicket-keeper,
county captain
Born: 15 August 1963, Stroud
Height: 5ft 8¹/₂in **Weight:** 9st 9lbs
Nickname: Jack
County debut: 1981
County cap: 1985
Benefit: 1994
Test debut: 1988
Tests: 49
One-Day Internationals: 37
1st-Class 50s: 61
1st-Class 100s: 6
1st-Class catches: 838
1st-Class stumpings: 104
One-Day 100s: 1
Place in batting averages: 118th av. 34.82
(1995 47th av. 44.40)
Strike rate: (career 38.00)
Parents: John and Jennifer
Wife and date of marriage: Aileen Ann, 6 March 1985
Children: Stepson, Marcus Anthony 1980; Elizabeth Ann, March 1988; Victoria,
1989; Charles David, 1991
Education: Uplands County Primary School; Archway Comprehensive School; Bristol
Polytechnic ('walked out after two months of accountancy course. Couldn't
understand the sociology and economics – wanted to play cricket instead')
Qualifications: 7 O-levels, 2 A-levels
Career outside cricket: Professional artist
Off-season: Touring Zimbabwe and New Zealand with England. Working on new
commissions and exhibitions at Jack Russell Gallery, 41 High Street, Chipping

Sodbury. Working on autobiography and new book of sketches.

Overseas tours: England to Pakistan 1987-88, to India and West Indies 1989-90, to Australia 1990-91, to New Zealand 1991-92, to West Indies 1993-94, to Australia 1994-95, to South Africa 1995-96, to Pakistan and India (World Cup) 1995-96, to Zimbabwe and New Zealand 1996-97; England A to Australia 1992-93

Cricketers particularly admired: Alan Knott, Bob Taylor, Ian Botham, Rodney Marsh 'and other greats'

Young players to look out for: Andrew Symonds, Rob Cunliffe, Robert Rollins, Keith Piper, Paul Nixon

Other sports followed: Football (Tottenham Hotspur), rugby (England), snooker, 'anything competitive'

Relaxations: Playing cricket and painting pictures. 'I love comedians and comedies. Life is too short, you need to laugh as much as you can'

Extras: Spotted at age nine by Gloucestershire coach, Graham Wiltshire. Youngest Gloucestershire wicket-keeper (17 years 307 days) and set record for most dismissals in a match on first-class debut: 8 (7 caught, 1 stumped) for Gloucestershire v Sri Lankans at Bristol, 1981. Hat-trick of catches v Surrey at The Oval 1986. Represented England YC v West Indies YC in 1982. Was chosen as England's Man of the Test Series, England v Australia 1989 and was one of *Wisden*'s Five Cricketers of the Year 1990. Appointed vice-captain to Martyn Moxon on the England A tour to Australia 1992-93. Called up as stand-by wicket-keeper for the England tour to Australia 1994-95 when Alec Stewart broke his finger for the second time on the tour. Had a three-week exhibition of his drawings in Bristol 1988 and published a book of his work entitled *A Cricketer's Art*. Co-author with Christopher Martin-Jenkins of *Sketches of a Season*, published in 1989. Commissioned by Dean of Gloucester to do a drawing of Gloucester Cathedral to raise funds for 900th Anniversary. Still turns out for his original club, Stroud CC, whenever he can. Runs six miles a day to keep fit and drinks up to 20 cups of tea a day. Keen military enthusiast 'We must never forget'. His paintings are sold and displayed in museums and private collections all around the world, Loves England. 'To me, it's the greatest place of all to play and paint'. Broke Bob Taylor's long-standing world record for the number of dismissals in a Test match with 11 in the second Test v South Africa at Johannesburg 1995-96

Opinions on cricket: 'England can win again – provided we all genuinely believe it and want it badly enough. If we plan, *encourage* and work hard enough, English cricket can go back to the top of the tree. We'll need some vision to make sure we get ahead.'

Best batting: 128* England v Australia, Old Trafford 1989

Best bowling: 1-4 Gloucestershire v West Indians, Bristol 1991

1996 Season

	M	Inns	NO	Runs	HS	Avge	100s	50s	Ct	St	O	M	Runs	Wkts	Avge	Best	5wI	10wM
Test	5	7	1	213	124	35.50	1	-	17	-								
All First	19	30	5	858	124	34.32	1	7	48	3								
1-day Int																		
NatWest	2	2	0	30	27	15.00	-	-	4	-								
B & H	5	2	0	32	24	16.00	-	-	3	2								
Sunday	11	11	2	158	59	17.55	-	1	5	1								

Career Performances

	M	Inns	NO	Runs	HS	Avge	100s	50s	Ct	St	Balls	Runs	Wkts	Avge	Best	5wI	10wM
Test	49	77	15	1807	128 *	29.14	2	6	141	11							
All First	347	505	111	11824	129 *	30.01	6	61	838	104	38	53	1	53.00	1-4	-	-
1-day Int	37	28	7	381	30	18.14	-	1	39	6							
NatWest	36	25	7	434	59 *	24.11	-	1	47	8							
B & H	56	40	15	633	51	25.32	-	1	54	10							
Sunday	182	138	33	2443	108	23.26	1	9	146	27							

SAGGERS, M. J.   Durham

Name: Martin John Saggers
Role: Right-hand bat, right-arm fast-medium
Born: 23 May 1972, King's Lynn
Height: 6ft 2in   **Weight:** 13st 11lbs
Nickname: Saggs, Pony, Wibs
County debut: 1996
1st-Class 5 w. in innings: 1
Place in batting averages: 229th av. 11.12
Place in bowling averages: 90th av. 34.07
Strike rate: (career 46.61)
Parents: Brian and Edna
Marital status: Single
Education: Roseberry Avenue Primary
School; Gaywood Junior School; Springwood
High School; Springwood Sixth Form
College; University of Huddersfield
Qualifications: 10 GCSEs, 2 A-levels, 1 AO-
level, BA (Hons) Architectural Studies

Career outside cricket: Architectural technician/consultant
Off-season: Playing club cricket in South Africa
Overseas teams played for: Randburg CC, Johannesburg, South Africa 1996-97
Cricketers particularly admired: Graham Dilley, Malcolm Marshall. Allan Donald

Other sports followed: Football (Tottenham Hotspur), golf, motorsport (British Touring Car Championship), squash, snooker
Injuries: Side strain, missed four weeks and twisted ankle, missed one week
Relaxations: Listening to loud music, Egyptology, watching the television
Opinions on cricket: 'It's becoming more of a batsman's game i.e. only one bouncer per batsman per over, no LBW if it pitches outside leg, no ball if above shoulder height in one-day cricket, anything down the leg side is a wide in one-day cricket.'
Best batting: 18 Durham v Somerset, Weston-super-Mare 1996
Best bowling: 6-65 Durham v Glamorgan, Chester-le-Street 1996

1996 Season

	M	Inns	NO	Runs	HS	Avge	100s	50s	Ct	St	O	M	Runs	Wkts	Avge	Best	5wI	10wM
Test																		
All First	5	9	1	89	18	11.12	-	-	-	-	101	12	443	13	34.07	6-65	1	-
1-day Int																		
NatWest	1	1	0	0	0	0.00	-	-	-	-	10	1	56	0	-	-	-	-
B & H	5	5	3	58	34 *	29.00	-	-	2	-	41	2	247	5	49.40	2-49	-	
Sunday	3	1	0	13	13	13.00	-	-	-	-	20	0	59	3	19.66	2-24	-	

Career Performances

	M	Inns	NO	Runs	HS	Avge	100s	50s	Ct	St	Balls	Runs	Wkts	Avge	Best	5wI	10wM
Test																	
All First	5	9	1	89	18	11.12	-	-	-	-	606	443	13	34.07	6-65	1	-
1-day Int																	
NatWest	1	1	0	0	0	0.00	-	-	-	-	60	56	0	-	-	-	-
B & H	5	5	3	58	34 *	29.00	-	-	2	-	246	247	5	49.40	2-49	-	
Sunday	3	1	0	13	13	13.00	-	-	-	-	120	59	3	19.66	2-24	-	

75. Which Australian wicket-keeper of the 1980s joined the 'nineties club' - narrowly missing out on an Ashes Test century?

Name: David John Sales
Role: Right-hand bat, right-arm occasional bowler
Born: 3 December 1977, Carshalton, Surrey
Height: 6ft **Weight:** 13st
Nickname: Jumble
County debut: 1994 (one-day), 1996 (first-class)
1st-Class 200s: 1
1st-Class catches: 4
Place in batting averages: 75th av. 40.00
Parents: John and Daphne
Marital status: Single
Family links with cricket: Father played club cricket
Education: Cumnor House Prep School, Croydon; Caterham Boys' School
Qualifications: 7 GCSEs, cricket coach
Off-season: Touring Pakistan with England U19

Overseas tours: England U15 to South Africa 1993; England U19 to West Indies 1994-95, to Zimbabwe 1995-96, to Pakistan 1996-97
Cricketers particularly admired: Graham Gooch
Young players to look out for: Owais Shah
Other sports followed: Football (Crystal Palace), golf
Injuries: Torn tendon in left shoulder, missed five weeks at the beginning of the season
Relaxations: Golf and fishing
Extras: Youngest batsman to score a 50 in the Sunday League. The first Englishman to score a double century on his championship debut and the youngest ever to score a double century.
Best batting: 210* Northamptonshire v Worcestershire, Kidderminster 1996

1996 Season

	M	Inns	NO	Runs	HS	Avge	100s	50s	Ct	St	O	M	Runs	Wkts	Avge	Best	5wI	10wM
Test																		
All First	4	8	1	280	210 *	40.00	1	-	4	-								
1-day Int																		
NatWest																		
B & H																		
Sunday	3	2	1	6	6	6.00	-	-	1	-								

	M	Inns	NO	Runs	HS	Avge	100s	50s	Ct	St	Balls	Runs	Wkts	Avge	Best	5wl	10wM
Test																	
All First	4	8	1	280	210 *	40.00	1	-	4	-							
1-day Int																	
NatWest																	
B & H																	
Sunday	8	6	3	116	70 *	38.66	-	1	2	-							

SALISBURY, I. D. K.   Surrey

Name: Ian David Kenneth Salisbury
Role: Right-hand bat, leg-break
Born: 21 January 1970, Northampton
Height: 5ft 11in **Weight:** 12st
Nickname: Sals
County debut: 1989 (Sussex)
County cap: 1991 (Sussex)
Test debut: 1992
Tests: 9
One-Day Internationals: 4
50 wickets in a season: 4
1st-Class 50s: 10
1st-Class 5 w. in innings: 24
1st-Class 10 w. in match: 4
1st-Class catches: 124
One-Day 5 w. in innings: 1
Place in batting averages: 227th av. 20.81
(1995 190th av. 22.18)
Place in bowling averages: 51st av. 28.96
(1995 79th av. 31.00)
Strike rate: 58.26 (career 66.65)
Parents: Dave and Margaret
Wife and date of marriage: Emma Louise, 25 September 1993
Family links with cricket: 'Dad is vice-president of my first club, Brixworth'
Education: Moulton Comprehensive, Northampton
Qualifications: 7 O-levels, NCA coaching certificate
Off-season: 'Resting and house husband (man of the 90s)'
Overseas tours: England A to Pakistan 1990-91, to Bermuda and West Indies 1991-92, to India 1994-95, to Pakistan 1995-96; England to India and Sri Lanka 1992-93, to West Indies 1993-94; World Masters XI v Indian Masters XI Nov 1996 ('Masters aged 26?')

Cricketers particularly admired: 'Any that keep performing day in, day out, for both country and county'
Young players to look out for: Ben Hollioake, Owais Shah, Vasbert Drakes
Other sports followed: Most sports
Injuries: Twisted back, out for three weeks
Relaxations: 'Spending time with wife, Emma, meeting friends and relaxing with them and eating out – with good wine'
Extras: Picked to play two Tests for England against Pakistan in 1992, 'proudest moments of my career'. Originally selected for England A tour to Australia 1992-93 but was asked to stay on in India and played in the first two Tests of the series. In 1992 was named Young Player of the Year by both the Wombwell Cricket Lovers and the Cricket Writers. One of *Wisden*'s Five Cricketers of the Year 1993. Left Sussex during the off-season and has joined Surrey for 1997
Opinions on cricket: 'Players should be asked for their opinion on changes in the game, before authorities make the changes themselves.'
Best batting: 83 Sussex v Glamorgan, Hove 1996
Best bowling: 8-75 Sussex v Essex, Chelmsford 1996

1996 Season

	M	Inns	NO	Runs	HS	Avge	100s	50s	Ct	St	O	M	Runs	Wkts	Avge	Best	5wI	10wM
Test	2	4	1	50	40	16.66	-	-	-	-	61.2	8	221	2	110.50	1-42	-	-
All First	18	30	3	562	83	20.81	-	3	8	-	505	109	1506	52	28.96	8-75	3	1
1-day Int																		
NatWest	3	3	0	64	33	21.33	-	-	2	-	29	4	65	4	16.25	2-23	-	
B & H	3	2	0	26	19	13.00	-	-	3	-	30	1	152	5	30.40	2-50	-	
Sunday	12	11	2	138	42	15.33	-	-	4	-	92	2	468	8	58.50	2-37	-	

Career Performances

	M	Inns	NO	Runs	HS	Avge	100s	50s	Ct	St	Balls	Runs	Wkts	Avge	Best	5wI	10wM
Test	9	17	2	255	50	17.00	-	1	3	-	1773	1154	18	64.11	4-163	-	-
All First	165	217	48	3176	86	18.79	-	10	124	-	30998	16349	479	34.13	8-75	24	4
1-day Int	4	2	1	7	5	7.00	-	-	1	-	186	177	5	35.40	3-41	-	
NatWest	17	12	3	97	33	10.77	-	-	5	-	1068	594	18	33.00	3-28	-	
B & H	18	11	4	98	19	14.00	-	-	8	-	1065	735	23	31.95	3-40	-	
Sunday	92	60	16	580	48 *	13.18	-	-	27	-	3558	2914	84	34.69	5-30	1	

SAVIDENT, L.   Hampshire

Name: Lee Savident
Role: Right-hand bat, right-arm medium bowler
Born: 22 October 1976, Guernsey

Height: 6ft 5in **Weight:** 15st 7lbs
County debut: No first-team appearance
Parents: Nev and Sue
Marital status: Single
Family links with cricket: None
Education: Castel Primary School;
Guernsey Grammar School; Guernsey
College of Further Education
Career outside cricket: Student
Off-season: Studying at college
Cricketers particularly admired: Robin
Smith, Graeme Hick, Allan Donald
Other sports followed: Football (Tottenham
Hotspur), basketball (Orlando Magic) and golf
Injuries: Knee injury, out for three weeks
Relaxations: Playing golf, watching
television
Extras: Currently holds two Hampshire U16
records. The most runs in a season (679 in 14 matches) and the highest partnership (173
with Lee Nurse against Jersey)
Opinions on cricket: 'Clubs should look forward and place more emphasis on coaching
people at a young age, to further develop the level of ability as a country.'

SCHOFIELD, C. J. Yorkshire

Name: Christopher John Schofield
Role: Right-hand bat, leg-break bowler
Born: 21 March 1976, Barnsley
Height: 5ft 7in **Weight:** 10st 3lbs
Nickname: Scoff, Linford, Munchkin
County debut: 1996
Parents: John and Pat
Marital status: Single
Family links with cricket: Father played
local league cricket
Education: Kingstone School
Qualifications: 6 GCSEs, City and Guilds
Sport and Leisure
Off-season: Training and relaxing
Overseas tours: England U19 to Sri Lanka
1993-94, to West Indies 1994-95
Cricketers particularly admired: Carlisle
Best, Desmond Haynes, Viv Richards, Brian

Lara, Richie Richardson
Other sports followed: Football, rugby league
Extras: Played Yorkshire U11 to U15, Yorkshire Cricket Association U16 and U19, Yorkshire Cricket Academy and England U19 in home series against India 1994
Opinions on cricket: 'Cricket needs to be made more attractive to public, e.g. televised county cricket leading to more sponsorship.'
Best batting: 25 Yorkshire v Lancashire, Old Trafford 1996

1996 Season

	M	Inns	NO	Runs	HS	Avge	100s	50s	Ct	St	O	M	Runs	Wkts	Avge	Best	5wI	10wM
Test																		
All First	1	1	0	25	25	25.00	-	-	-	-								
1-day Int																		
NatWest																		
B & H																		
Sunday																		

Career Performances

	M	Inns	NO	Runs	HS	Avge	100s	50s	Ct	St	Balls	Runs	Wkts	Avge	Best	5wI	10wM
Test																	
All First	1	1	0	25	25	25.00	-	-	-	-							
1-day Int																	
NatWest																	
B & H																	
Sunday																	

SCOTT, C. W.   Durham

Name: Christopher Wilmot Scott
Role: Right-hand bat, wicket-keeper
Born: 23 January 1964, Lincoln
Height: 5ft 8in **Weight:** 'Increasing'
Nickname: George
County debut: 1981 (Nottinghamshire), 1992 (Durham)
County cap: 1988 (Nottinghamshire)
1st-Class 50s: 16
1st-Class 100s: 2
1st-Class catches: 283
1st-Class stumpings: 17
Place in batting averages: 213th av. 23.11 (1995 158th av. 25.91)
Parents: Kenneth and Kathleen
Marital status: Girlfriend Susan

Family links with cricket: Family linked to Collingham CC in Notts. Youngest brother plays for Sudbourne Hall CC
Education: Thorpe-on-the-Hill Primary School; Robert Pattinson Comprehensive, North Hykeham, Lincoln
Qualifications: O-levels, advanced cricket coach
Career outside cricket: None
Off-season: 'Hoping to get involved in coaching development'
Overseas tours: Durham to Zimbabwe 1991-92, to South Africa 1995
Overseas teams played for: Poverty Bay, New Zealand 1983-84; Queensland University 1985-86, 1987-88; Rotorua, New Zealand 1989-90
Cricketers particularly admired: Simon Brown and all wicket-keepers 'it's not an easy job'
Young players to look out for: Jon Longley 'to see where he's gone'
Other sports followed: 'I have played lots of football and rugby – now it's just the occasional round of golf and a bit of skiing'
Injuries: Groin strain, out for two weeks
Relaxations: 'The usual stuff and a nice pint'
Extras: One of the youngest players to make Championship debut for Nottinghamshire – 17 years 157 days. Equalled the Nottinghamshire record for most catches in a match with ten against Derbyshire in 1988. Left Nottinghamshire at end of 1991 season to join Durham. Only wicket-keeper to manage ten catches in a match for two different counties. 1996 was his last season in county cricket
Opinions on cricket: 'More training and courses should be made available to prepare cricketers for life after cricket.'
Best batting: 108 Durham v Surrey, Darlington 1994

1996 Season

	M	Inns	NO	Runs	HS	Avge	100s	50s	Ct	St	O	M	Runs	Wkts	Avge	Best	5wI	10wM
Test																		
All First	7	10	1	208	59	23.11	-	2	20	-								
1-day Int																		
NatWest																		
B & H	4	2	1	36	27 *	36.00	-	-	3	-								
Sunday	3	3	0	26	17	8.66	-	-	2	1								

Career Performances

	M	Inns	NO	Runs	HS	Avge	100s	50s	Ct	St	Balls	Runs	Wkts	Avge	Best	5wI	10wM
Test																	
All First	129	176	31	3228	108	22.26	2	16	283	17	26	40	0	-	-	-	-
1-day Int																	
NatWest	7	1	0	2	2	2.00	-	-	7	-							
B & H	14	11	2	86	27 *	9.55	-	-	12	-							
Sunday	52	33	10	357	45	15.52	-	-	48	8							

SEARLE, J. P.   Durham

Name: Jason Paul Searle
Role: Right-hand bat, off-spin bowler
Born: 16 May 1976, Chittenham
Height: 5ft 8in **Weight:** 11st
Nickname: Shaggy, Village, Dumb, Elf
County debut: 1994
Parents: Paul and Chris
Marital status: Single
Family links with cricket: Father played for
Chippenham and Wiltshire
Education: John Bentley School, Calne;
Wiltshire and Swindon Building College
Qualifications: Bricklayer, farmer, 'gigolo'
Off-season: Farmer and playing football
Overseas tours: England U19 to West Indies
1994-95; Durham to South Africa
Cricketers particularly admired: Steve
Lugsden, Martin Robinson
Young players to look out for: 'Me'
Other sports followed: Football (Manchester United)
Injuries: 'Broken nose and a black eye'
Relaxations: 'Music and the fairer sex'
Opinions on cricket: 'Teams should have to play two spinners. Change it to a winter
sport'
Best batting: 5* Durham v Lancashire, Stockton 1994
Best bowling: 2-126 Durham v Surrey, The Oval 1995

1996 Season (did not make any first-class or one-day appearances)

Career Performances

	M	Inns	NO	Runs	HS	Avge	100s	50s	Ct	St	Balls	Runs	Wkts	Avge	Best	5wI	10wM
Test																	
All First	2	4	3	7	5 *	7.00	-	-	-	-	222	133	2	66.50	2-126	-	-
1-day Int																	
NatWest																	
B & H	1	0	0	0	0	-	-	-	-	-							
Sunday	1	0	0	0	0	-	-	-	-	-	12	19	0	-		-	-

SHADFORD, D. J. Lancashire

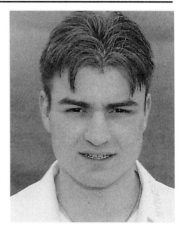

Name: Darren James Shadford
Role: Right-hand bat, right-arm
medium fast bowler
Born: 4 March 1975, Oldham, Lancashire
Height: 6ft 2in **Weight:** 14st
Nickname: Shaddy, Dead Beat
and 'many others'
County debut: 1994 (one-day),
 1995 (first-class)
Parents: Ken and Sue
Marital status: Single
Family links with cricket: Father and
brother play club cricket for Oldham
Education: Roundthorn Primary School;
Breeze Hill High School; Oldham College of
Technology
Qualifications: Information Technology,
BTEC in Business and Finance. 'No O's, no
A's, but not bothered'
Career outside cricket: Travelling the world
Off-season: 'Training mostly, and seeing the world with my girlfriend, Diane'
Overseas tours: Lancashire to Jamaica 1995-96
Overseas teams played for: Sandgate CC, Brisbane 1994-95
Cricketers particularly admired: Paul Thompson, Neil Holt
Young players to look out for: Chris Hall ('spins it more than CB'), 'Chinny' Chilton
and 'Professor' Paul Ridgeway
Other sports followed: Football (Manchester United), kabadi, crown green bowling,
lacrosse (Heaton Mersey)
Injuries: Broken bone in foot, missed ten weeks

Relaxations: 'Socialising, music, bird watching, train spotting, stamp collecting, collecting autographs from players around the counties'
Extras: Represented Oldham at cricket, football and athletics
Opinions on cricket: 'Make the balls bigger and the bats wider.'
Best batting: 1 Lancashire v Essex, Old Trafford 1995
Best bowling: 2-40 Lancashire v Surrey, The Oval 1995

1996 Season (did not make any first-class or one-day appearances)

Career Performances

	M	Inns	NO	Runs	HS	Avge	100s	50s	Ct	St	Balls	Runs	Wkts	Avge	Best	5wl	10wM
Test																	
All First	2	2	1	1	1	1.00	-	-	-	-	179	107	3	35.66	2-40	-	-
1-day Int																	
NatWest																		
B & H																		
Sunday	3	0	0	0	0	-	-	-	1	-	48	42	0	-	-	-	

SHAH, O. A.   Middlesex

Name: Owais Alam Shah
Role: Right-hand bat, off-spin bowler
Born: 22 October 1978, Karachi, Pakistan
Height: 6ft 1in **Weight:** 12st 7lbs
Nickname: Ace
County debut: 1995 (one-day), 1996 (first-class)
1st-Class 50s: 2
1st-Class catches: 2
Place in batting averages: 189th av. 26.50
Strike rate: (career 30.00)
Parents: Jamshed and Mehjabeen
Marital status: Single
Family links with cricket: Father played for his college side
Education: Berkley's Junior School; Isleworth and Syon School; Lampton School; National Westminster University
Qualifications: 7 GCSEs

Off-season: 'Touring Australia with England A and then carrying on with A-levels'
Overseas tours: England U19 to Zimbabwe 1995-96; England A to Australia 1996-97
Cricketers particularly admired: Viv Richards, Mark Waugh, Waqar Younis

Young players to look out for: David Sales, Stephen Peters, Anurag Singh, Ricky Fay, James Hewitt
Other sports followed: Table tennis, snooker and pool
Relaxations: Chilling out with friends, going to the cinema, listening to music
Extras: Middlesex Sports Federation Award winner. Man of the Series in U17 Test series against India 1994. Played for Middlesex U13, Ken Barrington Trophy (National Champions) and Middlesex U15, county competition winners, as captain. Scored record 232 for England U15 against England U16. Man of the Series for England U17 against India U17. Awarded 2nd XI cap in 1996
Opinions on cricket: 'Cricketers should play more county cricket than school cricket (i.e. David Nash).'
Best batting: 75 Middlesex v Somerset, Uxbridge 1996
Best bowling: 1-24 Middlesex v Somerset, Uxbridge 1996

1996 Season

	M	Inns	NO	Runs	HS	Avge	100s	50s	Ct	St	O	M	Runs	Wkts	Avge	Best	5wI	10wM
Test																		
All First	5	9	1	212	75	26.50	-	2	2	-	5	0	24	1	24.00	1-24	-	-
1-day Int																		
NatWest	1	1	0	11	11	11.00	-	-	-	-								
B & H	3	3	1	52	42 *	26.00	-	-	-	-								
Sunday	11	8	2	161	38	26.83	-	-	4	-	1.1	0	4	1	4.00	1-4	-	

Career Performances

	M	Inns	NO	Runs	HS	Avge	100s	50s	Ct	St	Balls	Runs	Wkts	Avge	Best	5wI	10wM
Test																	
All First	5	9	1	212	75	26.50	-	2	2	-	30	24	1	24.00	1-24	-	-
1-day Int																	
NatWest	1	1	0	11	11	11.00	-	-	-	-							
B & H	3	3	1	52	42 *	26.00	-	-	-	-							
Sunday	16	13	3	247	64	24.70	-	1	5	-	7	4	1	4.00	1-4	-	

76. The now-BBC commentator Jonathan Agnew played in just one Ashes Test in 1995. How many wickets did he take?

Name: Nadeem Shahid
Role: Right-hand bat, leg-spin bowler
Born: 23 April 1969, Karachi
Height: 6ft **Weight:** 12st
Nickname: Nad, Gonads, National Hero,
Maggie, 'far too many to mention'
County debut: 1989 (Essex), 1995 (Surrey)
1000 runs in a season: 1
1st-Class 50s: 23
1st-Class 100s: 5
1st-Class catches: 85
One-Day 100s: 1
Place in batting averages: 131st av. 33.43
(1995 74th av. 39.13)
Strike rate: 85.16 (career 70.34)
Parents: Ahmed and Salma
Marital status: Single
Family links with cricket: Brother plays in
the local Two Counties League for Felixstowe
Education: Stoke High; Northgate High; Ipswich School; Plymouth Polytechnic
Qualifications: 6 O-levels, 1 A-level, coaching certificate
Off-season: 'Playing indoor cricket for Ipswich. Getting my golf handicap down. Being amused and entertained by Ed Giddins, helping Adam Hollioake not to be too sensitive, helping Jason Ratcliffe to mellow out'
Overseas tours: Ipswich School to Barbados (Sir Garfield Sobers Trophy) 1987; England (South) to N Ireland (Youth World Tournament) 1988
Overseas teams played for: Gosnells, Perth, Western Australia 1989-91; Fairfield, Sydney 1992-93
Cricketers particularly admired: Ian Botham, Shane Warne, Graham Thorpe and Nasser Hussain
Young players to look out for: Ben Hollioake, Alex Tudor
Other sports followed: Golf, tennis, badminton, squash, most ball sports
Injuries: Hangovers, but missed no cricket
Relaxations: 'Wrestling Adam Hollioake in the dressing-room and winning. Watching Brendan Julian throwing the flying fish. Socialising with all the Surrey players, watching movies, dining out and searching for the meaning of life with Ed Giddins. Listening to Joey Benjamin'
Extras: Youngest Suffolk player aged 17. Played for HMC, MCC Schools, ESCA U19, NCA Young Cricketers (Lord's and International Youth tournament in Belfast), England U25 and at every level for Suffolk. TSB Young Player of the Year 1987, winner of the *Daily Telegraph* Bowling Award 1987 and 1988, Cricket Society's All-rounder of the

Year 1988 and Laidlaw Young Player of the Year for Essex 1993. Essex Society Player of the Year 1993. Released by Essex at end of 1994 season and signed for Surrey. Member of the Surrey Sunday League-winning side of 1996

Opinions on cricket: 'Players should be allowed to have fun on the field, and be allowed to express themselves in order to bring the best out of them. Players can and should work a lot harder at their game. I favour the two-divisional system in order to improve the standard of English cricket. It would allow players more time off the field and more time to work on skills, fitness etc. All first-class cricketers should be presented with a gold card which would allow them into any night club.'

Best batting: 139 Surrey v Yorkshire, The Oval 1995
Best bowling: 3-91 Essex v Surrey, The Oval 1990

1996 Season

	M	Inns	NO	Runs	HS	Avge	100s	50s	Ct	St	O	M	Runs	Wkts	Avge	Best	5wI	10wM
Test																		
All First	11	19	3	535	101	33.43	1	4	6	-	85.1	13	285	6	47.50	3-93	-	-
1-day Int																		
NatWest	1	1	0	25	25	25.00	-	-	-	-								
B & H																			
Sunday	12	11	1	327	58	32.70	-	1	4	-	1	0	18	0	-		-	-

Career Performances

	M	Inns	NO	Runs	HS	Avge	100s	50s	Ct	St	Balls	Runs	Wkts	Avge	Best	5wI	10wM
Test																	
All First	91	143	21	3997	139	32.76	5	23	85	-	2884	1913	41	46.65	3-91	-	-
1-day Int																	
NatWest	7	5	1	151	85 *	37.75	-	1	5	-	18	0	1	0.00	1-0	-	
B & H	12	6	1	116	65 *	23.20	-	1	1	-	150	131	1	131.00	1-59	-	
Sunday	68	57	9	1210	101	25.20	1	2	23	-	36	43	0	-		-	-

77. Ian Botham scored 138 runs in the Brisbane Test of 1986-87, with one over off Merv Hughes realising an Ashes record. How many?

SHAW, A. D.   Glamorgan

Name: Adrian David Shaw
Role: Right-hand bat, wicket-keeper
Born: 17 February 1972, Neath
Height: 5ft 11in **Weight:** 12st 10lbs
Nickname: Shawsy, Gloves, Teflon,
Cymbals, Dale, Barrymore
County debut: 1992 (one-day), 1994 (first-class)
1st-Class 50s: 2
1st-Class catches: 9
1st-Class stumpings: 5
Place in batting averages: 258th av. 16.52
Parents: David Colin and Christina
Marital status: Single
Family links with cricket: 'Mum thinks
Mark Ramprakash is "handsome". Apart from
that absolutely none… Grandad saw a game
once'

Education: Llangatwe Comprehensive;
Neath Tertiary College, 'Wallabies, Market Tavern and very often on Saturday nights.
Very enlightening!'
Qualifications: 9 O-levels, 3 A-levels, cricket coaching awards, 'degree from the
school of life – James Williams'
Career outside cricket: 'Currently making a living from the government i.e.
unemployed'
Off-season: 'Spending as much time as possible with my lovely girlfriend Jo-anna in
that wonderful north west city of Liverpool, where she lives. May occasionally
socialise and have just the one Budweiser'
Overseas tours: Welsh Schools to Barbados 1988; England YC to New Zealand 1990-91
Overseas teams played for: Welkom, Orange Free State 1995-96
Cricketers particularly admired: James Williams 'dedication personified'
Young players to look out for: Matthew Condé, Scott Bater, Lyndon Joshua. 'Watch
this space'
Other sports followed: Rugby (played for Neath RFC, Welsh Youth and Wales U21
squads), football (Leeds), rugby league (Warrington) 'and contrary to what Anthony
Cottey and Robert Croftmay believe, I do actually support Wales'
Relaxations: 'There is nothing like a good chat on a rainy day with Cotts and Crofty.
They always value my moderate opinions on things very highly. Thanks boys!'
Extras: One of youngest players (18 years 7 days) to play first-class rugby for Neath.
Only current county cricketer playing first-class rugby. Played for Neath against
Swansea six days after playing against Zimbabwe for Glamorgan, and had the 'pleasure'

of marking Scott Gibbs. Neath RFC Back of the Year 1993-94. Hopes to become the first player for a number of years to play against South Africa in two sports when Neath play them. 'Hoping to be awarded Glamorgan 2nd XI's first benefit after 10 years in the "Stiffs"!' Voted Glamorgan 2nd XI Player of the Year and Glamorgan Young Player of the Year in 1995. 2nd XI Player of the Month, June 1996

Opinions on cricket: 'Despite continually pushing me to the point of a nervous breakdown, I still enjoy it. Can anyone please explain to me how? By the way, if you are reading, Alun Evans of the *Western Mail*, why do you hate me so much? It's not my fault ET kidnapped Colin!!'

Best batting: 74 Glamorgan v Surrey, Cardiff 1996

1996 Season

	M	Inns	NO	Runs	HS	Avge	100s	50s	Ct	St	O	M	Runs	Wkts	Avge	Best	5wl	10wM
Test																		
All First	13	18	1	281	74	16.52	-	2	28	5								
1-day Int																		
NatWest																		
B & H																		
Sunday	10	7	3	105	36 *	26.25	-	-	3	4								

Career Performances

	M	Inns	NO	Runs	HS	Avge	100s	50s	Ct	St	Balls		Runs	Wkts	Avge	Best	5wl	10wM
Test																		
All First	18	25	3	319	74	14.50	-	2	37	7								
1-day Int																		
NatWest																		
B & H																		
Sunday	12	7	3	105	36 *	26.25	-	-	3	4								

78. Who are the two Australians whose only Test against England was the Bicentenary Test of 1988?

SHEERAZ, K. P. Gloucestershire

Name: Kamran Pashah Sheeraz
Role: Right-hand bat, right-arm medium-fast bowler
Born: 28 December 1973, Wellington, Shropshire
Height: 5ft 11in **Weight:** 13st 7lbs
County debut: 1994
1st-Class 5 w. in innings: 2
1st-Class 10 w. in match: 1
1st-Class catches: 4
Place in bowling averages: (1995 109th av. 37.00)
Strike rate: 234.00 (career 62.03)
Parents: Mohammed and Shamim
Wife and date of marriage: Shamim, 25 March 1996

Family links with cricket: Brother, Humeran, a county youth player. Cousin, Ali, plays for Berkshire Colts
Education: Licensed Victuallers School, Ascot; East Berks College of Further Education; University of East London
Qualifications: GCSE and BTEC National Diploma (Business and Finance), advanced cricket coach
Off-season: Working for family business
Overseas teams played for: RDCA Rawalpindi, Pakistan
Cricketers particularly admired: Imran Khan, Dennis Lillee, Courtney Walsh
Young players to look out for: Rob Cunliffe, Matt Windows, Dom Hewson
Other sports followed: Football (Liverpool and Slough Town)
Injuries: Finger infection, out for eight weeks
Relaxations: Reading, music, working out and spending time with family and loved ones
Extras: Toured Australia 1991-92 with Berkshire Youth XI and attended Bull Development of Excellence at Lilleshall 1992. Received Texaco (U16) outstanding bowling award (seven wickets in innings) from Ted Dexter. Represented Bedfordshire in Minor Counties Championship. Senior NABC 67kg Boxing Champion. England Amateur Boxing International
Opinions on cricket: 'Too much cricket is played in the first-class season. Players should be given more time to recover to prevent injuries'
Best batting: 3* Gloucestershire v India, Bristol 1996
Best bowling: 6-67 Gloucestershire v West Indies, Bristol 1995

1996 Season

	M	Inns	NO	Runs	HS	Avge	100s	50s	Ct	St	O	M	Runs	Wkts	Avge	Best	5wI	10wM
Test																		
All First	1	1	1	3	3 *	-	-	-	-	-	39	6	142	1	142.00	1-41	-	-
1-day Int																		
NatWest																			
B & H																				
Sunday																				

Career Performances

	M	Inns	NO	Runs	HS	Avge	100s	50s	Ct	St	Balls	Runs	Wkts	Avge	Best	5wI	10wM
Test																	
All First	11	14	7	12	3 *	1.71	-	-	4	-	1675	1064	27	39.40	6-67	2	1
1-day Int																	
NatWest																		
B & H																		
Sunday	12	5	3	26	14 *	13.00	-	-	2	-	492	399	9	44.33	2-20	-	

SHERIYAR, A.   Worcestershire

Name: Alamgir Sheriyar
Role: Right-hand bat, left-arm fast bowler
Born: 15 November 1973, Birmingham
Height: 6ft 1in **Weight:** 13st
Nickname: Sheri
County debut: 1993 (one-day, Leics),
1994 (first-class, Leics), 1996
(Worcestershire)
1st-Class 5 w. in innings: 3
1st-Class 10 w. in match: 1
1st-Class catches: 5
Place in batting averages: 311th av. 6.33
Place in bowling averages: 129th av. 44.89
(1995 53rd av. 27.25)
Strike rate: 74.59 (career 58.20)
Parents: Mohammed Zaman (deceased) and
Safia Sultana
Marital status: Single
Family links with cricket: Brothers play a bit
Education: George Dixon Secondary School, Birmingham; Joseph Chamberlain Sixth
Form College, Birmingham; Oxford Brookes University
Qualifications: 6 O-levels, studying for BEng (Hons) Combined Engineering

Overseas tours: Leicestershire to South Africa 1995; Worcestershire to Barbados 1996

Cricketers particularly admired: Wasim Akram

Other sports followed: Football, basketball

Relaxations: Time at home, music

Extras: Played for English Schools U17 and has also played in the Indoor National League. Became only the second player to take a hat-trick on his first-class debut. Asked to be released by Leicestershire at the end of the 1995 season and joined Worcestershire for 1996

Opinions on cricket: 'It's a batsman's game.'

Best batting: 19 Leicestershire v West Indies, Leicester 1995

Best bowling: 6-30 Leicestershire v Young Australia, Leicester 1995

1996 Season

	M	Inns	NO	Runs	HS	Avge	100s	50s	Ct	St	O	M	Runs	Wkts	Avge	Best	5wl	10wM
Test																		
All First	16	15	9	38	13	6.33	-	-	4	-	460	78	1661	37	44.89	6-99	1	-
1-day Int																		
NatWest	1	1	0	10	10	10.00	-	-	-	-	5	0	35	0	-		-	-
B & H	3	1	1	1	1*	-	-	-	-	-	25.1	3	108	5	21.60	3-40	-	
Sunday	14	5	4	35	19	35.00	-	-	2	-	65	3	373	9	41.44	4-27	-	

Career Performances

	M	Inns	NO	Runs	HS	Avge	100s	50s	Ct	St	Balls	Runs	Wkts	Avge	Best	5wl	10wM
Test																	
All First	28	30	12	125	19	6.94	-	-	7	-	4482	2860	77	37.14	6-30	3	1
1-day Int																	
NatWest	1	1	0	10	10	10.00	-	-	-	-	30	35	0	-		-	-
B & H	3	1	1	1	1*	-	-	-	-	-	151	108	5	21.60	3-40	-	
Sunday	17	6	5	35	19	35.00	-	-	2	-	468	446	9	49.55	4-27	-	

SHINE, K. J.   Somerset

Name: Kevin James Shine

Role: Right-hand bat, right-arm fast bowler

Born: 22 February 1969, Bracknell, Berks

Height: 6ft 3in **Weight:** 15st

Nickname: Kenny, Shiney, Wookie, Polish ('courtesy of Robbo')

County debut: 1989 (Hampshire), 1994 (Middlesex), 1996 (Somerset)

1st-Class 5 w. in innings: 9

1st-Class 10 w. in match: 1

1st-Class catches: 16
Place in batting averages: 289th av. 11.00
Place in bowling averages: 91st av. 34.54
Strike rate: 47.50 (career 57.31)
Parents: Joe and Clair
Marital status: Single
Education: Winnersh County Primary;
Maiden Erlegh Comprehensive
Qualifications: 5 O-levels, 'gave up A-levels
to pursue a cricket career', NCA Advanced
coach, qualified free weight training
instructor
Career outside cricket: Cricket coach.
Director of Coaching for Berkshire Indoor
Cricket Centre
Off-season: Coaching and weight training
instructor
Overseas teams played for: Merewether,
Newcastle, NSW 1990
Cricketers particularly admired: Malcolm Marshall, Bob Cottam ('great bowling
coach'), Adi Aymes, SS, CCM, Paul Farbrace ('for his continued commitment to diet
and fitness even after retirement')
Young players to look out for: Jason Laney
Other sports followed: Football (Reading)
Injuries: Severed ankle ligaments, out for four weeks
Relaxations: 'Constructive arguments with the "Posh Boy", and also watching him
display his boxing skills'
Extras: Took 8-47 including a hat-trick against Lancashire at Old Trafford in May 1992.
Has written (with Jason Harris) a weekly column for the *Reading Chronicle.* 'Told I was
released by Middlesex four days before major surgery on left ankle.' Joined Somerset
for the 1996 season
Opinions on cricket: 'It's still too easy for the batters.'
Best batting: 40 Somerset v Surrey, Taunton 1996
Best bowling: 8-47 Hampshire v Lancashire, Old Trafford 1992

1996 Season

	M	Inns	NO	Runs	HS	Avge	100s	50s	Ct	St	O	M	Runs	Wkts	Avge	Best	5wI	10wM
Test																		
All First	12	15	4	121	40	11.00	-	-	5	-	276.3	44	1209	35	34.54	6-95	2	-
1-day Int																		
NatWest																			
B & H	3	1	1	38	38 *	-	-	-	-	-	19	2	162	2	81.00	2-57	-	
Sunday	3	1	1	1	1 *	-	-	-	1	-	19	0	103	5	20.60	4-31	-	

Career Performances

	M	Inns	NO	Runs	HS	Avge	100s	50s	Ct	St	Balls	Runs	Wkts	Avge	Best	5wl	10wM
Test																	
All First	81	71	30	424	40	10.34	-	-	16	-	10890	7094	190	37.33	8-47	9	1
1-day Int																	
NatWest	2	0	0	0	0	-	-	-	-	-	129	92	3	30.66	3-31	-	
B & H	7	2	1	38	38 *	38.00	-	-	-	-	308	329	6	54.83	4-68	-	
Sunday	18	4	4	5	2 *	-	-	-	2	-	731	664	20	33.20	4-31	-	

SIDEBOTTOM, R. J.   Yorkshire

Name: Ryan Jay Sidebottom
Role: Left-hand bat, left-arm fast-medium bowler
Born: 15 January 1978, Huddersfield
Height: 6ft 3in **Weight:** 12st 7lbs
Nickname: Red Pup, Gigsy, Medusa
County debut: No first-team appearance
Parents: Arnie and Gillian
Marital status: Single
Family links with cricket: Father played for Yorkshire and England
Education: Almondbury Primary, Huddersfield; King James Grammar School, Huddersfield
Qualifications: 5 GCSEs
Off-season: Coaching at the Yorkshire Cricket School and promoting the game at schools around the county
Overseas tours: England U17 to Holland 1995
Cricketers particularly admired: Allan Donald, Darren Gough, Craig White, Bradley Parker
Young players to look out for: Chris Silverwood, Matthew Thewlis, John Inglis
Other sports followed: Football (Huddersfield Town FC), rugby league (Leeds)
Relaxations: Listening to music, sleeping, watching videos

SILVERWOOD, C. E. W.   Yorkshire

Name: Christopher Eric Wilfred Silverwood
Role: Right-hand bat, right-arm
fast-medium bowler
Born: 5 March 1975, Pontefract
Height: 6ft 1in **Weight:** 12st 9lbs
Nickname: Spoon, Silvers, Tarby
County debut: 1993
Test debut: 1996-97
1st-Class 50s: 1
1st-Class 5 w. in innings: 3
1st-Class catches: 11
Place in batting averages: 290th av. 11.00
(1995 247th av. 15.14)
Place in bowling averages: 63rd av. 30.68
(1995 97th av. 35.00)
Strike rate: 51.63 (career 53.03)
Parents: Brenda Millicent
Marital status: Engaged to Emma
Education: Gibson Lane School, Kippax; Garforth Comprehensive
Qualifications: 8 GCSEs, City and Guilds in Leisure and Recreation
Off-season: Touring Zimbabwe and New Zealand with England
Overseas tours: England to Zimbabwe and New Zealand 1996-97
Overseas teams played for: Wellington, Cape Town 1993-94, 1995-96
Cricketers particularly admired: Ian Botham, Allan Donald
Other sports followed: Rugby league (Castleford), karate
Injuries: Stress fracture of back
Relaxations: Listening to music, watching videos, 'riding my motorbike'
Extras: Black belt in karate. Attended the Yorkshire Cricket Academy. Represented Yorkshire at athletics. Played for England U19 in the home series against India in 1994. Made his Test debut against Zimbabwe in the first Test at Bulawayo
Best batting: 50 Yorkshire v Lancashire, Old Trafford 1995
Best bowling: 5-62 Yorkshire v Surrey, The Oval 1995

1996 Season

	M	Inns	NO	Runs	HS	Avge	100s	50s	Ct	St	O	M	Runs	Wkts	Avge	Best	5wI	10wM
Test																		
All First	16	24	6	198	45 *	11.00	-	-	6	-	404.3	79	1442	47	30.68	5-72	2	-
1-day Int																		
NatWest	4	1	1	0	0 *	-	-	-	3	-	36	6	131	3	43.66	3-45	-	
B & H	4	1	0	1	1	1.00	-	-	2	-	37.4	5	158	11	14.36	5-28	1	
Sunday	16	7	5	35	14 *	17.50	-	-	-	-	108	9	485	17	28.52	4-26	-	

Career Performances

	M	Inns	NO	Runs	HS	Avge	100s	50s	Ct	St	Balls	Runs	Wkts	Avge	Best	5wI	10wM
Test																	
All First	34	50	12	439	50	11.55	-	1	11	-	5038	3076	95	32.37	5-62	3	-
1-day Int																	
NatWest	5	2	2	8	8 *	-	-	-	3	-	282	169	4	42.25	3-45	-	
B & H	5	2	0	3	2	1.50	-	-	2	-	268	177	12	14.75	5-28	1	
Sunday	33	14	9	65	14 *	13.00	-	-	2	-	1323	997	43	23.18	4-26	-	

SIMMONS, P. V. Leicestershire

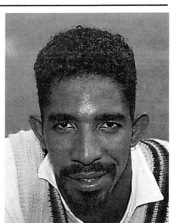

Name: Philip Verant Simmons
Role: Right-hand bat, right-arm
medium bowler, county vice-captain
Born: 18 April 1963, Port-of-Spain, Trinidad
County debut: 1994
Test debut: 1988
Tests: 24
One-Day Internationals: 117
1000 runs in a season: 1
50 wickets in a season: 1
1st-Class 50s: 54
1st-Class 100s: 20
1st-Class 200s: 2
1st-Class 5w. in innings: 4
1st-Class catches: 188
One-Day 100s: 8
One-Day 5 w. in innings: 1
Place in batting averages: 16th av. 56.54
Place in bowling averages: 5th av. 18.23
Strike rate: 39.07 (career 62.38)
Overseas tours: West Indies YC to England 1982; West Indies B to Zimbabwe 1983
and 1986; West Indies to India and Pakistan (World Cup) 1987-88, to England 1988, to
Sharjah and India (Nehru Cup) 1989-90, to Sharjah 1991-92, to Australia and South
Africa 1992-93, to Sharjah, India (Hero Cup) and Sri Lanka 1993-94, to India 1994-
95, to England 1995, to Australia 1995-95, to India and Pakistan (World Cup) 1995-
96, to Australia 1996-97
Overseas teams played for: Crompton, Trinidad; Trinidad and Tobago 1983-95
Extras: Suffered a bad head injury on West Indies tour to England in 1988. Appointed
captain of Trinidad in 1989. Scored record 261 on his debut for Leicestershire in 1994
Best batting: 261 Leicestershire v Northamptonshire, Leicester 1994
Best bowling: 6-14 Leicestershire v Durham, Chester-le-Street 1996

1996 Season

	M	Inns	NO	Runs	HS	Avge	100s	50s	Ct	St	O	M	Runs	Wkts	Avge	Best	5wI	10wM
Test																		
All First	17	24	2	1244	171	56.54	4	7	35	-	364.4	87	1021	56	18.23	6-14	3	-
1-day Int																		
NatWest	2	2	0	109	82	54.50	-	1	1	-	13	0	54	3	18.00	2-34	-	
B & H	2	2	0	15	11	7.50	-	-	1	-	12	0	63	0	-	-	-	
Sunday	16	16	1	815	139	54.33	2	5	8	-	94.1	0	480	14	34.28	5-37	1	

Career Performances

	M	Inns	NO	Runs	HS	Avge	100s	50s	Ct	St	Balls	Runs	Wkts	Avge	Best	5wI	10wM
Test	24	44	2	1000	110	23.80	1	4	23	-	474	181	3	60.33	2-34	-	-
All First	160	274	12	9877	261	37.69	20	54	188	-	9296	4330	149	29.06	6-14	4	-
1-day Int	117	115	7	3242	122	30.01	5	17	50	-	2950	2121	61	34.77	4-3	-	
NatWest	6	6	0	193	82	32.16	-	1	3	-	312	243	8	30.37	3-31	-	
B & H	4	4	0	136	64	34.00	-	2	2	-	162	134	1	134.00	1-29	-	
Sunday	33	33	1	1475	140	46.09	3	10	15	-	1103	924	31	29.80	5-37	1	

SINGH, A.   Warwickshire

Name: Anurag Singh
Role: Right-hand bat, off-spin bowler
Born: 9 September 1975, Kanpur, India
Height: 5ft 10in **Weight:** 11st
Nickname: Ragga, Ragi, Ragstar, Rood
County debut: 1995
1st-Class 50s: 1
1st-Class 100s: 2
1st-Class catches: 7
One-Day 100s: 1
Place in batting averages: 106th av. 35.90
Parents: Vijay and Rajul
Marital status: Single
Education: King Edward's School, Birmingham; Gonville and Caius College, Cambridge
Qualifications: 12 GCSEs, 4 A-levels
Off-season: Studying at Cambridge University

Overseas tours: England U19 to West Indies 1994-95; Warwickshire U21 to South Africa; Warwickshire CCC to South Africa
Cricketers particularly admired: Trevor Penney, Graeme Welch, Brian Lara, Allan

Donald, Mohammed Azharuddin

Young players to look out for: Darren Altree, Vikram Solanki

Other sports followed: Football (Wimbledon FC and Aston Villa)

Relaxations: 'Spending time with my family. Going out with friends and girlfriend, Louise'

Extras: Broke school record for number of runs in a season (1102). *Daily Telegraph* regional award for batting (twice) and bowling (once). Tiger Smith Memorial Award for Warwickshire Most Promising Young Cricketer 1994, Coney Edmonds Trophy for Warwickshire Best U19 Cricketer 1994, Lord's Taverners Trophy for Best Young Cricketer 1994, Gray-Nicolls Len Newberry Award for ESCA U19 Best Player 1994. Scored two centuries for England U19 against India U19 in 1994. Scored one century against West Indies U20 and was Man of the Series 1994-95. Scored 128 for Warwickshire 2nd XI v Gloucestershire 2nd XI in 1994. Awarded 2nd XI cap in 1995

Opinions on cricket: 'Have not played enough to give any valued judged opinions.'

Best batting: 157 Cambridge University v Sussex, Hove 1996

1996 Season

	M	Inns	NO	Runs	HS	Avge	100s	50s	Ct	St	O	M	Runs	Wkts	Avge	Best	5wI	10wM
Test																		
All First	12	22	2	718	157	35.90	2	1	6	-	4	0	14	0	-		-	-	-
1-day Int																		
NatWest																		
B & H	5	5	0	260	123	52.00	1	1	1	-								
Sunday	1	1	0	2	2	2.00	-	-	-	-								

Career Performances

	M	Inns	NO	Runs	HS	Avge	100s	50s	Ct	St	Balls	Runs	Wkts	Avge	Best	5wI	10wM
Test																	
All First	13	24	2	730	157	33.18	2	1	7	-	24	14	0	-		-	-	-
1-day Int																	
NatWest																	
B & H	5	5	0	260	123	52.00	1	1	1	-							
Sunday	1	1	0	2	2	2.00	-	-	-	-							

SLADE, N. D.   Worcestershire

Name: Neil Douglas Slade

Role: Right-hand bat, off-spin bowler

Born: 16 July 1975, Worcester

Height: 5ft 11in **Weight:** 12st

Nickname: Sladey, Tuffers

County debut: No first-team appearances

Parents: Douglas and Marilyn
Marital status: Single
Family links with cricket: Father Douglas
played for Worcestershire
Education: Ridgeway Middle School,
Redditch; The Abbey High, Redditch;
Worcester Sixth Form College
Qualifications: 10 GCSEs and 2 A-levels
Career outside cricket: Running farm,
journalism and teaching
Off-season: Working on farm and in the
Radio Wyvern news room
Cricketers particularly admired: Robert
Croft, Graeme Hick
Young players to look out for: Vikram Solanki
Other sports followed: Football (Manchester
City) and golf
Relaxations: Drawing, working on the farm,
listening to music
Extras: Played for Worcestershire CA and Worcestershire U19. Voted the
Kidderminster Player of the Year in 1996 in the Birmingham League
Opinions on cricket: 'I haven't been in the game long enough.'

SMALL, G. C. Warwickshire

Name: Gladstone Cleophas Small
Role: Right-hand bat, right-arm
fast-medium bowler
Born: 18 October 1961, St George, Barbados
Height: 5ft 11in **Weight:** 12st
Nickname: Gladys, Glad, Stoney
County debut: 1980
County cap: 1982
Benefit: 1992 (£129,500)
Test debut: 1986
Tests: 17
One-Day Internationals: 53
50 wickets in a season: 6
1st-Class 50s: 7
1st-Class 5 w. in innings: 29
1st-Class 10 w. in match: 2
1st-Class catches: 94
One-Day 5 w. in innings: 2

Place in bowling averages: 47th av. 28.21 (1995 72nd av. 29.82)
Strike rate: 51.78 (career 58.02)
Parents: Chelston and Gladys
Wife and date of marriage: Lois, 19 September 1987
Children: Zak, Marcus and Zoe
Family links with cricket: Cousin Milton Small toured England with West Indies in 1988
Education: Moseley School; Hall Green Technical College, Birmingham
Qualifications: 2 O-levels, NCA senior coaching badge
Career outside cricket: Sports marketing consultant
Off-season: Studying Business Studies at Crewe and Alsager faculty
Overseas tours: England YC to New Zealand 1979-80; England to Australia 1986-87, to India and Pakistan (World Cup) 1987-88, to India and West Indies 1989-90, to Australia 1990-91, to Australia and New Zealand (World Cup) 1991-92; Warwickshire to Cape Town, to Zimbabwe, to Trinidad
Overseas teams played for: Balwyn, Melbourne 1982-83, 1984-85; West Torrens, Adelaide 1985-86; South Australia 1985-86
Cricketers particularly admired: Malcolm Marshall, Richard Hadlee, Allan Donald, Brian Lara, Robin Smith
Other sports followed: Golf, tennis, football (Aston Villa FC)
Relaxations: 'Home with family, tending my vegetable garden, wining and dining with friends'
Extras: Was called up for England Test squad v Pakistan at Edgbaston, July 1982, but did not play. Bowled 18-ball over v Middlesex in August 1982, with 11 no-balls. Grandfather watched him take eight wickets in the Barbados Test v West Indies in 1989-90 on his return to the land of his birth. Was Andy Lloyd's best man
Opinions on cricket: 'Counties having to bowl more than 18 overs per hour is one of the major reasons why we can't produce any bowler able to bowl fast consistently. By the time that they have reached fast bowling maturity they have long become line and length medium pacers. Please install a law to assist the bowlers.'
Best batting: 70 Warwickshire v Lancashire, Old Trafford 1988
Best bowling: 7-15 Warwickshire v Nottinghamshire, Edgbaston 1988

1996 Season

	M	Inns	NO	Runs	HS	Avge	100s	50s	Ct	St	O	M	Runs	Wkts	Avge	Best	5wl	10wM
Test																		
All First	7	9	5	55	23 *	13.75	-	-	2	-	164	35	536	19	28.21	4-41	-	-
1-day Int																		
NatWest	2	2	1	14	9	14.00	-	-	2	-	20.5	3	87	4	21.75	2-26	-	
B & H	2	1	0	1	1	1.00	-	-	-	-	9	0	25	3	8.33	3-25	-	
Sunday	12	6	3	37	15 *	12.33	-	-	2	-	78	6	312	15	20.80	4-14	-	

	M	Inns	NO	Runs	HS	Avge	100s	50s	Ct	St	Balls	Runs	Wkts	Avge	Best	5wI	10wM
Test	17	24	7	263	59	15.47	-	1	9	-	3927	1871	55	34.01	5-48	2	-
All First	312	400	96	4396	70	14.46	-	7	94	-	49267	24234	849	28.54	7-15	29	2
1-day Int	53	24	9	98	18 *	6.53	-	-	7	-	2793	1942	58	33.48	4-31	-	
NatWest	43	28	8	220	33	11.00	-	-	8	-	2604	1370	48	28.54	3-22	-	
B & H	58	35	9	169	22	6.50	-	-	11	-	3290	1889	64	29.51	4-22	-	
Sunday	176	82	29	418	40 *	7.88	-	-	37	-	7431	5462	219	24.94	5-29	2	

SMITH, A. M. Gloucestershire

Name: Andrew Michael Smith
Role: Right-hand bat, left-arm
medium bowler
Born: 1 October 1967, Dewsbury,
West Yorks
Height: 5ft 9in **Weight:** 12st
Nickname: Smudge, Ronnie, Piano Man
County debut: 1991
50 w. in a season: 2
1st-Class 50s: 2
1st-Class 5 w. in innings: 8
1st-Class 10 w. in match: 1
1st-Class catches: 11
Place in batting averages: 257th av. 16.54
Place in bowling averages: 38th av. 26.91
(1995 14th av. 21.61)
Strike rate: 48.75 (career 56.88)
Parents: Hugh and Margaret
Wife and date of marriage: Sarah, 2 October 1993
Children: William James, 9 October 1994
Family links with cricket: Father, uncle and brother all play or played club cricket in Yorkshire
Education: Queen Elizabeth Grammar School, Wakefield; Exeter University
Qualification: 10 O-levels, 4 A-levels, BA (Hons) French and German
Off-season: Coaching
Overseas tours: Queen Elizabeth Grammar School to Holland 1985; Bradford Junior Cricket League to Barbados 1986; Exeter University to Barbados 1987;
Gloucestershire to Kenya 1990, to Sri Lanka 1992-93, to Zimbabwe 1996; England A to Pakistan 1995-96
Overseas teams played for: Waimea, New Zealand 1990; WTTU, New Zealand 1991
Cricketers particularly admired: Richard Hadlee, Allan Lamb, Wasim Akram

Young players to look out for: Rob Cunliffe
Other sports followed: Football (Leeds United)
Injuries: Sore back, out for two weeks
Relaxations: Crosswords, reading
Extras: Played for English Schools U19, NAYC and represented Combined Universities in the B&H Cup in 1988 and 1990. Persistent side strain forced him to fly home from the England A tour of Pakistan in 1995-96
Opinions on cricket: 'Why, at international level, do we produce pitches that suit our opposition? Why do we give them a choice of balls if they win the toss? Why do we chop and change players so much? Our opposition are bewildered at our team selection. We should make it hard for teams to play here instead of pampering them. We get few favours when we go overseas. Time to get tough.'
Best batting: 55* Gloucestershire v Nottinghamshire, Trent Bridge 1996
Best bowling: 8-73 Gloucestershire v Middlesex, Lord's 1996

1996 Season

	M	Inns	NO	Runs	HS		Avge	100s	50s	Ct	St	O	M	Runs	Wkts	Avge	Best	5wI	10wM
Test																			
All First	16	25	3	364	55	*	16.54	-	1	2	-	487.3	114	1615	60	26.91	8-73	3	1
1-day Int																			
NatWest	2	2	1	25	13		25.00	-	-	-	-	16	2	49	5	9.80	3-21	-	
B & H	5	2	1	7	7		7.00	-	-	3	-	47.1	7	213	8	26.62	3-23	-	
Sunday	14	8	4	79	26	*	19.75	-	-	2	-	96	7	446	18	24.77	3-16	-	

Career Performances

	M	Inns	NO	Runs	HS		Avge	100s	50s	Ct	St	Balls	Runs	Wkts	Avge	Best	5wI	10wM
Test																		
All First	74	89	15	879	55	*	11.87	-	2	11	-	11932	6452	216	29.87	8-73	8	2
1-day Int																		
NatWest	13	6	4	40	13		20.00	-	-	3	-	703	428	14	30.57	3-21	-	
B & H	27	18	9	76	15	*	8.44	-	-	7	-	1538	1067	35	30.48	6-39	1	
Sunday	80	40	24	215	26	*	13.43	-	-	12	-	3111	2528	85	29.74	4-38	-	

SMITH, A. W.   Surrey

Name: Andrew William Smith
Role: Right-hand bat, right-arm
off-spin bowler
Born: 30 May 1969, Sutton, Surrey
Height: 5ft 10in **Weight:** 11st
Nickname: Smithy, Smudge, Furball
County debut: 1992 (one-day),

1993 (first-class)
1st-Class 50s: 6
1st-Class 100s: 1
1st-Class 200s: 1
1st-Class 5 w. in innings: 1
1st-Class catches: 12
Place in batting averages: (1995 197th av. 20.92)
Place in bowling averages: (1995 151st av. 64.70)
Strike rate: (career 89.23)
Parents: Ben and Gwen
Marital status: Single
Family links with cricket: Father played for Surrey 1960-69
Education: Cheam Boys Church of England School; Sutton Manor High School
Qualifications: 7 O-levels, senior NCA coach
Career outside cricket: Painter and decorator
Off-season: 'Working (hopefully) and gaining experience in a career outside cricket'
Overseas teams played for: Richmond, Adelaide 1989-91; North Perth CC, Australia 1995
Cricketers particularly admired: Tim May, John Emburey, Michael Slater
Other sports followed: Football (West Ham United), baseball (Toronto Blue Jays), American football (Washington Redskins)
Injuries: Tendon injury to right index finger, missed five games
Relaxations: 'All sports, riding my new bicycle, sleeping and tasting red wine'
Extras: In 1992 took catch with first touch on first-team debut in Seeboard Trophy 1992 and was named 2nd XI Bowler of the Year. In 1993 received Man of the Match award in his first NatWest game against Leicestershire and was Surrey Fielder of the Year. 'Richard Blakey almost cleared The Oval pavilion (top tier) off my bowling in the Sunday League game in August.' Released at the end of the 1996 season
Opinions on cricket: 'Play far too much so no time to spend in the nets and work on skills.'
Best batting: 202* Surrey v Oxford University, The Oval 1994
Best bowling: 5-103 Surrey v Somerset, Bath 1994

1996 Season

	M	Inns	NO	Runs	HS	Avge	100s	50s	Ct	St	O	M	Runs	Wkts	Avge	Best	5wI	10wM
Test																		
All First	1	2	0	23	16	11.50	-	-	-	-	7	0	61	0	-	-	-	-
1-day Int																		
NatWest																		
B & H																		
Sunday																		

Career Performances

	M	Inns	NO	Runs	HS	Avge	100s	50s	Ct	St	Balls	Runs	Wkts	Avge	Best	5wl	10wM
Test																	
All First	38	59	7	1379	202 *	26.51	1	6	12	-	3837	2435	43	56.62	5-103	1	-
1-day Int																	
NatWest	2	0	0	0	0	-	-	-	-	-	120	56	3	18.66	3-25	-	
B & H	2	1	1	15	15 *	-	-	-	1	-	84	61	3	20.33	2-38	-	
Sunday	31	24	6	496	58	27.55	-	2	15	-	438	457	9	50.77	3-36	-	

SMITH, B. F. Leicestershire

Name: Benjamin Francis Smith
Role: Right-hand bat, right-arm medium bowler
Born: 3 April 1972, Corby
Height: 5ft 8in **Weight:** 10st 7lbs
Nickname: Smudge, Ferret, Sabba
County debut: 1990
County cap: 1995
1000 runs in a season: 1
1st-Class 50s: 21
1st-Class 100s: 5
1st-Class catches: 38
One-Day 100s: 1
Place in batting averages: 39th av. 47.80
(1995 121st av. 30.84)
Strike rate: (career 112.50)
Parents: Keith and Janet
Marital status: Single
Family links with cricket: Both uncles played for English Schools and Leicestershire Young Amateurs. Father and grandfather played local league cricket
Education: Tugby Primary; Kibworth High; Robert Smyth, Market Harborough
Qualifications: 5 O-levels, ESB distinction
Off-season: Playing club cricket in Western Transvaal, South Africa
Overseas tours: England YC to New Zealand 1990-91; Rutland Tourists to South Africa 1992
Overseas teams played for: Alexandria, Zimbabwe 1990; Bankstown Canterbury, Sydney 1993-96
Cricketers particularly admired: David Gower
Other sports followed: Football (Leicester City)
Relaxations: Eating out, going to cinema, playing golf, listening to good music
Extras: Played tennis for Leicestershire aged 12. Young Cricketer of the Year 1991

Best batting: 190 Leicestershire v Glamorgan, Swansea 1996
Best bowling: 1-5 Leicestershire v Essex, Ilford 1991

1996 Season

	M	Inns	NO	Runs	HS	Avge	100s	50s	Ct	St	O	M	Runs	Wkts	Avge	Best	5wl	10wM
Test																		
All First	20	29	3	1243	190	47.80	3	4	5	-								
1-day Int																		
NatWest	1	1	0	5	5	5.00	-	-	-	-								
B & H	5	5	0	161	61	32.20	-	2	3	-								
Sunday	15	15	1	320	80	22.85	-	1	5	-								

Career Performances

	M	Inns	NO	Runs	HS	Avge	100s	50s	Ct	St	Balls	Runs	Wkts	Avge	Best	5wl	10wM
Test																	
All First	95	146	20	4070	190	32.30	5	21	38	-	225	190	2	95.00	1-5	-	-
1-day Int																	
NatWest	8	7	1	166	63 *	27.66	-	1	2	-							
B & H	17	15	0	346	61	23.06	-	2	8	-							
Sunday	84	82	10	1922	115	26.69	1	6	19	-	18	15	0	-		-	-

SMITH, E. T.   Kent

Name: Edward Thomas Smith
Role: Right-hand bat, right-arm
medium bowler
Born: 19 July 1977, Pembury, Kent
Height: 6ft 2in **Weight:** 13st
Nickname: Jazzer
County debut: 1996
1st-Class 50s: 4
1st-Class 100s: 2
1st-Class catches: 1
Place in batting averages: 37th av. 48.00
Parents: Jonathan and Gillie
Marital status: Single
Family links with cricket: Father Jonathan
wrote *Good Enough?* with Chris Cowdrey
Education: Tonbridge School; Peterhouse,
Cambridge University
Qualifications: 11 GCSEs, 3 A-levels
Off-season: Student

Cricketers particularly admired: Greg Chappell, Martin Crowe, Graham Cowdrey amd Michael Slater
Young players to look out for: Will House, Anurag Singh, Owais Shah
Other sports followed: Football (Arsenal FC)
Injuries: None
Relaxations: Reading, theatre, cinema, socialising
Extras: Scored a century on his first-class debut against Glamorgan (101) and in doing so became the youngest player to score a century on debut for Cambridge University. He is also the first person to score 50 or more in each of his first five first-class games. Cambridge Blue in 1996. Played for England U19 against New Zealand U19 in 1996
Opinions on cricket: 'Cricket is not 50 per cent head, 50 per cent heart and nothing to do with technique. English players should have greater ambition in their own performance – technical and temperamental. The system encourages them to settle for enough; which is not enough at the highest level.'
Best batting: 101 Cambridge University v Glamorgan, Fenner's 1996

1996 Season

	M	Inns	NO	Runs	HS	Avge	100s	50s	Ct	St	O	M	Runs	Wkts	Avge	Best	5wl	10wM
Test																		
All First	7	12	0	576	101	48.00	2	4	1	-								
1-day Int																		
NatWest																		
B & H																		
Sunday																		

Career Performances

	M	Inns	NO	Runs	HS	Avge	100s	50s	Ct	St	Balls	Runs	Wkts	Avge	Best	5wl	10wM
Test																	
All First	7	12	0	576	101	48.00	2	4	1	-							
1-day Int																	
NatWest																	
B & H																	
Sunday																	

SMITH, N. M. K.   Warwickshire

Name: Neil Michael Knight Smith
Role: Right-hand bat, off-spin bowler
Born: 27 July 1967, Solihull
Height: 6ft **Weight:** 13st 7lbs
Nickname: Gurt
County debut: 1987

County cap: 1993
One-Day Internationals: 7
1st-Class 50s: 15
1st-Class 100s: 1
1st-Class 5 w. in innings: 15
1st-Class catches: 37
One-Day 5 w. in innings: 3
Place in batting averages: 181st av. 27.21
(1995 158th av. 25.58)
Place in bowling averages: 77th av. 32.95
(1995 98th av. 35.25)
Strike rate: 67.90 (career 74.47)
Parents: Mike (M.J.K.) and Diana
Wife and date of marriage: Rachel, 4
December 1993
Family links with cricket: Father captained
Warwickshire and England
Education: Warwick School
Qualifications: 3 O-levels (Maths, English, French), cricket coach Grade 1
Career outside cricket: Sports teacher
Overseas tours: England to South Africa 1995-96, to India and Pakistan (World Cup) 1995-96
Overseas teams played for: Phoenix, Perth, Western Australia 1988-89
Cricketers particularly admired: David Gower, Ian Botham, Allan Donald
Other sports followed: Golf, rugby and football
Relaxations: Sport, family and music
Extras: Played for England in the one-day series against South Africa in 1995-96 and was then selected for the squad to play in the World Cup in India and Pakistan
Opinions on cricket: 'Visiting teams should be given the option of batting or bowling to try to stop doctoring of pitches by the home side.'
Best batting: 161 Warwickshire v Yorkshire, Headingley 1989
Best bowling: 7-42 Warwickshire v Lancashire, Edgbaston 1994

1996 Season

	M	Inns	NO	Runs	HS	Avge	100s	50s	Ct	St	O	M	Runs	Wkts	Avge	Best	5wI	10wM
Test																		
All First	16	27	4	626	74	27.21	-	3	11	-	486.4	115	1417	43	32.95	5-76	3	-
1-day Int	2	2	0	28	17	14.00	-	-	-	-	6	0	39	0	-	-	-	
NatWest	2	2	0	44	30	22.00	-	-	-	-	21	3	90	3	30.00	3-40	-	
B & H	7	6	0	196	80	32.66	-	2	1	-	32	1	167	6	27.83	2-37	-	
Sunday	15	15	2	533	111 *	41.00	1	3	2	-	72	2	338	7	48.28	1-19	-	

Career Performances

	M	Inns	NO	Runs	HS	Avge	100s	50s	Ct	St	Balls	Runs	Wkts	Avge	Best	5wI	10wM
Test																	
All First	112	160	22	3442	161	24.94	1	15	37	-	18023	9034	242	37.33	7-42	15	-
1-day Int	7	6	1	100	31	20.00	-	-	1	-	261	190	6	31.66	3-29	-	
NatWest	27	23	6	394	65	23.17	-	2	9	-	1264	756	35	21.60	5-17	1	
B & H	24	18	2	336	80	21.00	-	2	5	-	895	682	24	28.41	3-29	-	
Sunday	122	96	18	1896	111 *	24.30	1	10	40	-	4116	3191	120	26.59	6-33	2	

SMITH, P. A.   Warwickshire

Name: Paul Andrew Smith
Role: Right-hand bat, right-arm
fast-medium bowler
Born: 15 April 1964, Newcastle-on-Tyne
Height: 6ft 2in **Weight:** 12st 7lbs
Nickname: Smithy, Jim
County debut: 1982
County cap: 1986
Benefit: 1995
1000 runs in a season: 2
1st-Class 50s: 48
1st-Class 100s: 4
1st-Class 5 w. in innings: 7
1st-Class catches: 60
One-Day 5 w. in innings: 3
Strike rate: 97.00 (career 56.35)
Parents: Ken and Joy
Wife and date of marriage: Caroline,
31 July 1987
Children: Oliver James, 5 February 1988; Michael Paul, 1993
Family links with cricket: Father played for Leicestershire. Both brothers played for
Warwickshire
Education: Heaton Grammar School, Newcastle
Qualifications: 5 O-levels, car restoration qualifications
Overseas tours: Warwickshire to La Manga 1989, to Trinidad and Tobago 1991, to
Cape Town 1992-93, to Zimbabwe 1993-94
Overseas teams played for: Florida, Johannesburg 1982-83; Belgrano, Buenos Aires
1983-84; Carlton, Melbourne 1984-85; St Augustine's, Cape Town 1992-93
Cricketers particularly admired: Ian Botham
Other sports followed: None
Relaxations: Classic cars, American cars, music, reading, family, working out in the

gym at Edgbaston

Extras: Along with Andy Moles set a new world record for most consecutive opening partnerships of over 50. In 1989 scored 140 v Worcestershire, during which scored 100 out of partnership of 123 with Dermot Reeve. Took a hat-trick against Northamptonshire in 1989 and in 1990 took another against Sussex, bowling in Tim Munton's boots – two sizes too big. Warwickshire's most successful Sunday League all-rounder and has been in the winning team in two NatWest finals. Retired from first-class cricket at the end of the 1996 season

Opinions on cricket: 'Four-day cricket is better than three-day, but wickets around the country must improve. Coloured clothing has been good value. Umpires should decide Man of the Match awards.'

Best batting: 140 Warwickshire v Worcestershire, Worcester 1989

Best bowling: 6-91 Warwickshire v Derbyshire, Edgbaston 1992

1996 Season

	M	Inns	NO	Runs	HS	Avge	100s	50s	Ct	St	O	M	Runs	Wkts	Avge	Best	5wl	10wM
Test																		
All First	2	2	0	23	21	11.50	-	-	1	-	32.2	7	88	2	44.00	1-12	-	-
1-day Int																		
NatWest	1	1	0	1	1	1.00	-	-	-	-	5	0	30	2	15.00	2-30	-	
B & H	6	5	1	134	45	33.50	-	-	1	-	25	0	153	3	51.00	2-56	-	
Sunday	8	7	1	72	25	12.00	-	-	1	-	23.4	0	163	4	40.75	3-27	-	

Career Performances

	M	Inns	NO	Runs	HS	Avge	100s	50s	Ct	St	Balls	Runs	Wkts	Avge	Best	5wl	10wM
Test																	
All First	221	351	42	8173	140	26.44	4	48	60	-	15949	10109	283	35.72	6-91	7	-
1-day Int																	
NatWest	35	33	5	642	79	22.92	-	5	3	-	1459	1058	35	30.22	4-37	-	
B & H	49	44	6	792	74	20.84	-	1	7	-	1472	1105	36	30.69	3-28	-	
Sunday	181	153	27	2934	93 *	23.28	-	9	33	-	5012	4447	161	27.62	5-36	3	

79. Which Lancashire seamer made his debut in the fifth Test of 1981, scoring his maiden first-class 50 batting at No.10?

Name: Robin Arnold Smith
Role: Right-hand bat, slip fielder
Born: 13 September 1963, Durban,
South Africa
Height: 6ft **Weight:** 15st
Nickname: The Judge
County debut: 1982
County cap: 1985
Benefit: 1996
Test debut: 1988
Tests: 62
One-Day Internationals: 71
1000 runs in a season: 10
1st-Class 50s: 103
1st-Class 100s: 51
1st-Class 200s: 1
1st-Class catches: 188
One-Day 100s: 23
Place in batting averages: 36th av. 48.13

(1995 20th av. 53.19)
Strike rate: (career 77.00)
Parents: John and Joy
Wife and date of marriage: Katherine, 21 September 1988
Children: Harrison Arnold, 4 December 1991; Margaux Elizabeth, 28 July 1994
Family links with cricket: Grandfather played for Natal in Currie Cup. Brother Chris
played for Natal, Hampshire and England
Education: Northlands Boys High, Durban
Qualifications: Matriculation, '62 England caps'
Career outside cricket: Director of Masuri Helmets and Judge Tours
Overseas tours: England to India and West Indies 1989-90, to Australia 1990-91, to
Australia and New Zealand (World Cup) 1991-92, to India and Sri Lanka 1992-93, to
West Indies 1993-94, to South Africa 1995-96, to India and Pakistan (World Cup)
1995-96
Overseas teams played for: Natal, South Africa 1980-84; Perth, Western Australia
1984-85 (grade cricket)
Cricketers particularly admired: Malcolm Marshall, Brian Lara, Graeme Hick,
Graham Gooch, Allan Lamb
Other sports followed: Soccer, athletics, rugby, golf, racing
Relaxations: 'Reading (Leslie Thomas in particular), trout fishing, assembling a good
wine cellar, keeping fit and spending as much time as possible with my lovely wife
Katherine and my children'
Extras: Played rugby for Natal Schools and for Romsey RFC as a full-back. Held 19

school athletics records and two South African schools records in shot putt and 100-metre hurdles. One of *Wisden*'s Five Cricketers of the Year 1990. First child was born while he was on tour in Australia

Opinions on cricket: 'I enjoy playing cricket for Hampshire and particularly enjoy the camaraderie of the county circuit.'

Best batting: 209* Hampshire v Essex, Southampton 1987

Best bowling: 2-11 Hampshire v Surrey, Southampton 1985

1996 Season

	M	Inns	NO	Runs	HS	Avge	100s	50s	Ct	St	O	M	Runs	Wkts	Avge	Best	5wl	10wM
Test																		
All First	17	31	2	1396	179	48.13	3	8	1	-								
1-day Int																		
NatWest	3	3	0	188	158	62.66	1	-	1	-								
B & H	4	4	0	165	123	41.25	1	-	2	-								
Sunday	14	14	2	551	122 *	45.91	1	2	3	-								

Career Performances

	M	Inns	NO	Runs	HS	Avge	100s	50s	Ct	St	Balls	Runs	Wkts	Avge	Best	5wl	10wM
Test	62	112	15	4236	175	43.67	9	28	39	-	24	6	0	-	-	-	-
All First	319	545	77	20727	209 *	44.28	51	103	188	-	924	693	12	57.75	2-11	-	-
1-day Int	71	70	8	2419	167 *	39.01	4	15	26	-							
NatWest	33	33	10	1709	158	74.30	5	8	20	-	17	13	2	6.50	2-13	-	
B & H	47	44	8	1939	155 *	53.86	5	8	21	-	6	2	0	-	-	-	
Sunday	140	134	16	5002	131	42.38	9	32	60	-	2	0	1	0.00	1-0	-	

80. Who were the two Australian wicket-keepers during the 1986-87 series?

SNAPE, J. N.   Northamptonshire

Name: Jeremy Nicholas Snape
Role: Right-hand bat, off-spin bowler
Born: 27 April 1973, Stoke-on-Trent,
Staffordshire
Height: 5ft 8in **Weight:** 12st
Nickname: Snapey, Coot, Jez
County debut: 1992
1st-Class 50s: 4
1st-Class 5 w. in innings: 1
1st-Class catches: 25
Place in batting averages: 224th av. 21.30
(1995 148th av. 27.76)
Place in bowling averages: 127th av. 44.04
(1995 116th av. 39.31)
Strike rate: 81.78 (career 79.58)
Parents: Keith and Barbara
Marital status: Single
Family links with cricket: Brother Jonathan
plays local club cricket in North Staffs and

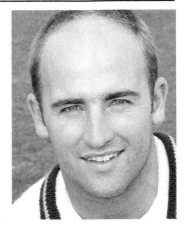

South Cheshire League for Kidsgrove, 'Dad only umpired once as he was the only
person to appeal for a caught behind – off my bowling in the U13'
Education: Denstone College; Durham University
Qualifications: 8 GCSEs, 3 A-levels, studying for BSc (Hons) Natural Science
Career outside cricket: 'Open to suggestions'
Off-season: Playing club cricket in Cape Town, South Africa
Overseas tours: England U18 to Canada 1991 (captain); England U19 to Pakistan
1991-92; Durham University to South Africa 1993; Northamptonshire to Cape Town
1993; Christians in Sport to Zimbabwe 1994-95; Durham University to Vienna (Indoor
European Championships) 1994; Troubadours to South Africa 1997
Overseas teams played for: Petone, Wellington, New Zealand 1994-95; Wainuiamata,
Wellington, New Zealand 1995-96
Cricketers particularly admired: Allan Lamb, Carl Hooper, Anil Kumble
Other sports followed: Golf, rugby union, shove ha'penny, white-water rafting,
Bangalore kabadi team, yarding
Relaxations: Good food and drink, listening to music, travelling
Extras: Sir Jack Hobbs award (U15 Schoolboy 1988), Gold Award winner for
Combined Universities v Worcestershire 1992 (3-34) at The Parks. Player of the
Tournament at European Indoor 6-a-side Championships
Opinions on cricket: 'Definitely in favour of four-day cricket as it induces a more
disciplined approach, although I equally enjoy the challenges of one-day cricket.
Counties should work harder to maximise the potential of their individual players while

encouraging the teamwork essential to competition.'
Best batting: 87 Northamptonshire v Mashonaland Select XI, Harare 1994-95
Best bowling: 5-65 Northamptonshire v Durham, Northampton 1995

1996 Season

	M	Inns	NO	Runs	HS	Avge	100s	50s	Ct	St	O	M	Runs	Wkts	Avge	Best	5wI	10wM
Test																		
All First	10	16	3	277	64	21.30	-	1	3	-	313.3	62	1013	23	44.04	4-42	-	-
1-day Int																		
NatWest																		
B & H	1	0	0	0	0	-	-	-	-	-	9	0	38	0	-	-	-	-
Sunday	6	2	0	6	6	3.00	-	-	3	-	24	2	108	4	27.00	2-18	-	

Career Performances

	M	Inns	NO	Runs	HS	Avge	100s	50s	Ct	St	Balls	Runs	Wkts	Avge	Best	5wI	10wM
Test																	
All First	28	40	8	833	87	26.03	-	4	25	-	3979	2207	50	44.14	5-65	1	-
1-day Int																	
NatWest	5	4	2	40	21	20.00	-	-	2	-	145	117	4	29.25	2-44	-	
B & H	9	8	3	165	52	33.00	-	1	3	-	546	358	10	35.80	3-35	-	
Sunday	30	17	8	147	31 *	16.33	-	-	9	-	870	707	25	28.28	3-25	-	

SOLANKI, V. S.   Worcestershire

Name: Vikram Singh Solanki
Role: Right-hand bat, off-spin bowler
Born: 1 April 1976, Udaipur, India
Height: 6ft **Weight:** 11st 7lbs
County debut: 1993 (one-day),
1995 (first-class)
1st-Class 50s: 6
1st-Class 5 w. in innings: 3
1st-Class 10 w. in match: 1
1st-Class catches: 17
Place in batting averages: 77th av. 39.42
(1995 218th av. 18.75)
Place in bowling averages: 73rd av. 31.96
Strike rate: 47.85 (career 60.66)
Parents: Vijay and Florabell
Marital status: Single
Family links with cricket: Father played in
India

Education: Regis School, Wolverhampton
Qualifications: 9 GCSEs, 3 A-levels
Overseas tours: England U18 to South Africa 1992-93, to Denmark 1993; England U19 to West Indies 1994-95
Cricketers particularly admired: Sachin Tendulkar, Graeme Hick, Anthony McGrath and 'anyone who has made the grade at Test level'
Other sports followed: 'Enjoy playing most sports'
Relaxations: 'Spending time with friends and family'
Opinions on cricket: 'Four-day cricket seems to be working. However, there may be an argument for a two-league system as this would improve the standard of the game in general and also provide players with more time to practise.'
Best batting: 90 Worcestershire v Surrey, The Oval 1996
Best bowling: 5-69 Worcestershire v Middlesex, Lord's 1996

1996 Season

	M	Inns	NO	Runs	HS	Avge	100s	50s	Ct	St	O	M	Runs	Wkts	Avge	Best	5wI	10wM
Test																		
All First	14	24	3	828	90	39.42	-	6	9	-	215.2	37	863	27	31.96	5-69	3	1
1-day Int																		
NatWest	2	2	0	59	50	29.50	-	1	1	-								
B & H																		
Sunday	14	8	2	124	55	20.66	-	1	5	-	15	0	91	3	30.33	1-19	-	

Career Performances

	M	Inns	NO	Runs	HS	Avge	100s	50s	Ct	St	Balls	Runs	Wkts	Avge	Best	5wI	10wM
Test																	
All First	20	33	4	978	90	33.72	-	6	17	-	1820	1222	30	40.73	5-69	3	1
1-day Int																	
NatWest	4	3	0	88	50	29.33	-	1	1	-	120	91	1	91.00	1-48	-	
B & H																	
Sunday	24	15	4	179	55	16.27	-	1	7	-	108	123	3	41.00	1-19	-	

SPEAK, N. J.   Durham

Name: Nicholas Jason Speak
Role: Right-hand opening bat, off-spin bowler
Born: 21 October 1966, Manchester
Height: 6ft **Weight:** 12st 7lbs
Nickname: Judge, Pod
County debut: 1986-87 (Lancashire)
County cap: 1992
1000 runs in a season: 3

1st-Class 50s: 43
1st-Class 100s: 12
1st-Class 200s: 1
1st-Class catches: 84
One-Day 100s: 1
Place in batting averages: 122nd av. 34.05
(1995 109th av. 32.82)
Strike rate: (career 72.50)
Parents: John and Irene
Wife and date of marriage: Michelle, 11
March 1993
Family links with cricket: Father and uncle
were league professionals in Lancashire and
Yorkshire
Education: Parrs Wood High School; Sixth
Form College, Didsbury, Manchester
Qualifications: 5 O-levels, NCA coaching
certificate
Career outside cricket: Yarra Leisure, coaching in Melbourne
Off-season: Playing for Hawthorne in Melbourne
Overseas tours: Lancashire to Jamaica 1986-87, to Zimbabwe 1989, to Perth
1990-91, to Johannesburg 1992
Overseas teams played for: South Canberra 1988-89; North Canberra 1991-93;
Hawthorn, Melbourne 1994-96
Cricketers particularly admired: Mark Waugh, Shane Warne
Other sports followed: Most sports – Manchester City FC
Relaxations: Chardonnay, cold lager, Indian food, and 'constructive arguments with
G.D. Lloyd', spending time at home with our new addition
Extras: Scored century for Australian Capital Territories v England A at Canberra 1992-93.
Released by Lancashire at the end of the 1996 season and has joined Durham for 1997
Opinions on cricket: 'Tea should be ten minutes longer.'
Best batting: 232 Lancashire v Leicestershire, Leicester 1992
Best bowling: 1-0 Lancashire v Warwickshire, Old Trafford 1991

1996 Season

	M	Inns	NO	Runs	HS	Avge	100s	50s	Ct	St	O	M	Runs	Wkts	Avge	Best	5wI	10wM
Test																		
All First	12	21	4	579	138 *	34.05	1	3	10	-	6	0	27	0	-	-	-	-
1-day Int																		
NatWest	1	1	0	83	83	83.00	-	1	-	-	4	0	31	0	-		-	-
B & H	4	4	1	147	79 *	49.00	-	1	-	-								
Sunday	8	7	1	158	39 *	26.33	-	-	3	-								

Career Performances

	M	Inns	NO	Runs	HS	Avge	100s	50s	Ct	St	Balls	Runs	Wkts	Avge	Best	5wI	10wM
Test																	
All First	123	214	21	7398	232	38.33	12	43	84	-	145	164	2	82.00	1-0	-	-
1-day Int																	
NatWest	7	7	0	219	83	31.28	-	2	2	-	24	31	0	-		-	-
B & H	16	15	2	426	82	32.76	-	3	-	-							
Sunday	68	62	7	1483	102 *	26.96	1	6	13	-							

SPEIGHT, M. P. Durham

Name: Martin Peter Speight
Role: Right-hand bat, reserve wicket-keeper
Born: 24 October 1967, Walsall
Height: 5ft 10in **Weight:** 12st 7lbs
Nickname: Sprog, Hoover, Ginger, Speighty, Grumpy
County debut: 1986
County cap: 1991
1000 runs in a season: 2
1st-Class 50s: 35
1st-Class 100s: 13
1st-Class catches: 100
One-Day 100s: 3
Place in batting averages: 182nd av. 27.05
Strike rate: (career 10.50)
Parents: Peter John and Valerie
Marital status: Engaged to Lisa Montague
Education: Hassocks Infants School; The
Windmills School, Hassocks; Hurstpierpoint

College Junior and Senior Schools; Durham University (St Chad's College)
Qualifications: 13 O-levels, 3 A-levels, BA (Hons) Archaeology/Ancient History
Career outside cricket: Artist
Off-season: Decorating house, painting commissions and coaching
Overseas tours: NCA U19 to Bermuda 1984; Hurstpierpoint to India 1986; England
YC to Sri Lanka 1986-87
Overseas teams played for: Karori, Wellington, New Zealand 1989-90; University
CC, Wellington 1990-93; North City, Wellington 1995-96; Wellington CA 1989-90,
1992-93, 1995-96
Cricketers particularly admired: Martin Crowe, Viv Richards, Paul Parker
Young players to look out for: Danny Law, Jason Laney
Other sports followed: Golf, rugby (Wellington Hurricanes), hockey

Injuries: Back strain, missed two weeks. Ruptured ankle ligaments, missed four weeks

Relaxations: Painting (oils and watercolours), pastel and paint drawing, DIY, wine, eating out at nice restaurants with fiancée, classical and modern music, *Telegraph* crosswords

Extras: Member of Durham University UAU winning side 1987; played for Combined Universities in B&H Cup 1987 and 1988; Sussex Most Promising Player 1989. Fastest first-class 100 in 1993 against Lancashire and fastest 50-overs 100 v Somerset at Taunton 1993 (off 48 balls) which still stands as the second fastest Sunday League 100 ever. Has won two Gold Awards in the Benson and Hedges competition. Painted an oil painting of the maiden first-class game at Arundel Castle between Sussex and Hampshire which was later auctioned to raise £1200 for the Sussex YC tour to India 1990-91, and of which a limited edition has also been printed and sold. Has done paintings of Hove, Southampton and The Oval for the benefits of Messrs Pigott, Parks and Greig. Member of Durham University's men's hockey team to Barbados 1988. Book of his paintings *A Cricketer's View*, a collection of 54 paintings and commentary, published in 1995. Various commissions and a print of Abergavenny CC to be published in 1997. Has joined Durham for the 1997 season

Opinions on cricket: 'Too much cricket played with an obvious effect on players.'

Best batting: 184 Sussex v Nottinghamshire, Eastbourne 1993

Best bowling: 1-2 Sussex v Middlesex, Hove 1988

1996 Season

	M	Inns	NO	Runs	HS	Avge	100s	50s	Ct	St	O	M	Runs	Wkts	Avge	Best	5wl	10wM
Test																		
All First	11	21	2	514	122 *	27.05	1	3	9	-								
1-day Int																		
NatWest	3	3	0	77	41	25.66	-	-	1	-								
B & H	4	4	0	88	64	22.00	-	1	-	-								
Sunday	10	9	0	309	117	34.33	1	1	4	-								

Career Performances

	M	Inns	NO	Runs	HS	Avge	100s	50s	Ct	St	Balls	Runs	Wkts	Avge	Best	5wl	10wM
Test																	
All First	123	206	15	6814	184	35.67	13	35	100	-	21	32	2	16.00	1-2	-	-
1-day Int																	
NatWest	16	15	1	350	50	25.00	-	1	4	-							
B & H	31	29	0	656	83	22.62	-	3	20	1							
Sunday	96	87	5	2475	126	30.18	3	12	29	1							

SPENDLOVE, B. L.   Derbyshire

Name: Benjamin Lee Spendlove
Role: Right-hand bat, right-arm medium
bowler, occasional wicket-keeper
Born: 4 October 1978, Derby
Height: 6ft 2in **Weight:** 13st
Nickname: Dylan
Parents: Lee and Chris
Marital status: Single
Family links with cricket: Father ex-cricket
professional for Trent College
Education: Harrington Primary School;
Trent College
Off-season: Playing for Gold Coast CC in
Australia
Overseas tours: England U17 to Holland
(International Youth Tournament)
Overseas teams played for: Gold Coast CC,
Queensland, Australia 1996-97
Cricketers particularly admired: David Gower, Robin Smith, Alec Stewart
Young players to look out for: Stephen Peters, Jeff Pfaff (Queensland)
Other sports followed: Rugby union (Leicester Tigers), football (Derby County)
Injuries: Broken finger and quad strain, missed total of five weeks
Relaxations: Music
Extras: Played for England at U15 and U17 level
Opinions on cricket: 'More money and support should be given to schools cricket.
Schools cricket should have a more competitive format. Maybe a little more faith should
be shown in selections at international level.'

SPIRING, K. R.   Worcestershire

Name: Karl Reuben Spiring
Role: Right-hand opening bat
Born: 13 November 1974, Southport
Height: 5ft 10in **Weight:** 12st
Nickname: Ginga
County debut: 1993 (one-day), 1994 (first-class)
1000 runs in a season: 1
1st-Class 50s: 9
1st-Class 100s: 3
1st-Class catches: 12

Place in batting averages: 66th av. 41.69
Parents: Peter and June
Marital status: Single
Education: Monmouth School; Durham University
Qualifications: 9 GCSEs, 3 A-levels, NCA Senior Coach
Off-season: Playing and coaching in Perth, Australia
Overseas tours: Worcestershire to Barbados 1996
Overseas teams played for: Fremantle/Mosman Park Pirates, Perth, Western Australia 1995-97
Cricketers particularly admired: 'Phil Weston's off-field activities'
Young players to look out for: Vikram Solanki, Phil Weston
Other sports followed: Rugby, football ('but certainly don't support Sunderland as Wesso supports them')

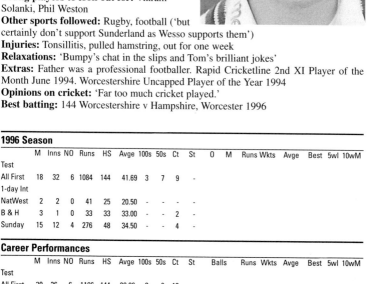

Injuries: Tonsillitis, pulled hamstring, out for one week
Relaxations: 'Bumpy's chat in the slips and Tom's brilliant jokes'
Extras: Father was a professional footballer. Rapid Cricketline 2nd XI Player of the Month June 1994. Worcestershire Uncapped Player of the Year 1994
Opinions on cricket: 'Far too much cricket played.'
Best batting: 144 Worcestershire v Hampshire, Worcester 1996

1996 Season

	M	Inns	NO	Runs	HS	Avge	100s	50s	Ct	St	O	M	Runs	Wkts	Avge	Best	5wI	10wM
Test																		
All First	18	32	6	1084	144	41.69	3	7	9	-								
1-day Int																		
NatWest	2	2	0	41	25	20.50	-	-	-	-								
B & H	3	1	0	33	33	33.00	-	-	2	-								
Sunday	15	12	4	276	48	34.50	-	-	4	-								

Career Performances

	M	Inns	NO	Runs	HS	Avge	100s	50s	Ct	St	Balls	Runs	Wkts	Avge	Best	5wI	10wM
Test																	
All First	20	36	6	1196	144	39.86	3	9	12	-							
1-day Int																	
NatWest	2	2	0	41	25	20.50	-	-	-	-							
B & H	7	5	0	120	35	24.00	-	-	3	-							
Sunday	16	13	4	283	48	31.44	-	-	4	-							

Name: Edward John Stanford
Role: Left-hand bat, left-arm spinner
Born: 21 January 1971, Dartford
Height: 5ft 10in **Weight:** 12st
Nickname: Teddy, Oist
County debut: 1995
1st-Class catches: 2
Strike rate: 81.00 (career 109.00)
Parents: Paul and Pam
Family links with cricket: Father played
club cricket for Dartford CC
Education: Downs Secondary School,
Dartford
Qualifications: 'Too many to mention at
school'
Career outside cricket: 'Had several.
Banker. Groundsman'
Off-season: Edes office removals. 'Moving
those hard-working civil servants around
London, while Bill the boss sits on his backside all day'
Overseas tours: Kent Schools U17 to Singapore and New Zealand 1988
Overseas teams played for: Petersham, Sydney 1990-91
Cricketers particularly admired: Graham Cowdrey ('lot of time'), Matthew Walker
('the greatest')
Young players to look out for: Matthew Walker 'the greatest man to walk the planet'
Other sports followed: Golf, snooker ('Min Patel complete bandit at both!'), football
(Charlton Athletic)
Relaxations: Jack Daniels and Coke, William Hill, Corals
Extras: Headed a ball for six in debut against Essex in the Bain Clarkson Championship
1993 ('Totally misjudged a top edge whilst fielding at fine leg, the ball struck me on the
forehead and carried a further 20 yards to go for six!'). 'Once got Matt Walker out in the
nets'
Opinions on cricket: '2nd XI fixtures should be played on better wickets and last four
days. Matt Walker should bat right-handed to give everyone a chance.'
Best batting: 10* Kent v Durham, Maidstone 1996
Best bowling: 3-84 Kent v Leicestershire, Leicester 1996

1996 Season

	M	Inns	NO	Runs	HS	Avge	100s	50s	Ct	St	O	M	Runs	Wkts	Avge	Best	5wI	10wM
Test																		
All First	2	3	3	12	10 *	-	-	-	1	-	67.3	22	158	5	31.60	3-84	-	-
1-day Int																		
NatWest																			
B & H																			
Sunday																			

Career Performances

	M	Inns	NO	Runs	HS	Avge	100s	50s	Ct	St	Balls	Runs	Wkts	Avge	Best	5wI	10wM
Test																	
All First	4	5	4	16	10 *	16.00	-	-	2	-	872	378	8	47.25	3-84	-	-
1-day Int																	
NatWest																		
B & H																		
Sunday																		

STEELE, M. V.   Northamptonshire

Name: Mark Vincent Steele
Role: Left-hand bat, right-arm fast-medium bowler
Born: 13 November 1976, Kettering
Height: 6ft **Weight:** 13st 5lbs
Nickname: Stan
County debut: No first-team appearance
Parents: David and Carol
Marital status: Single
Family links with cricket: Father played cricket for Northants and England. Father's brother, J.F. Steele, played for Leicestershire and managed Glamorgan, father's cousin, Brian Crump, played for Northants
Education: Wellingborough School; Tresham College, Kettering
Qualifications: 6 GCSEs, GNVQ in Advanced Business
Off-season: Playing cricket in Cape Town, South Africa
Cricketers particularly admired: Dennis Lillee
Other sports followed: Football, table tennis

Relaxations: 'Having a couple of sherbets with friends'
Extras: MCC U13 Young Cricketer of the Year 1984. Played for Midlands Schools from U15 upwards and played for England U16 in 1993. Wellingborough scholarship in 1991. Public School Batsman of the Year 1993

STEMP, R. D.   Yorkshire

Name: Richard David Stemp
Role: Right-hand bat, slow left-arm bowler
Born: 11 December 1967, Erdington, Birmingham
Height: 6ft **Weight:** 12st 4lbs
Nickname: Stempy, Sherriff, Badger
County debut: 1990 (Worcestershire), 1993 (Yorkshire)
County cap: 1996 (Yorkshire)
1st-Class 50s: 2
1st-Class 5 w. in innings: 11
1st-Class 10 w. in match: 1
1st-Class catches: 46
Place in batting averages: 250th av. 17.33
Place in bowling averages: 103rd av. 36.59 (1995 135th av. 45.92)
Strike rate: 80.85 (career 81.02)
Parents: Arnold and Rita Homer
Marital status: Single
Family links with cricket: Father played Birmingham League cricket for Old Hill
Education: Britannia High School, Rowley Regis
Qualifications: NCA coaching award
Off-season: Playing club cricket in Canberra, Australia
Overseas tours: England A to India 1994-95, to Pakistan 1995-96
Overseas teams played for: Pretoria Technikon 1988-89
Cricketers particularly admired: Ian Botham, Phil Tufnell
Other sports followed: Indoor cricket, American football (New England Patriots)
Relaxations: Ornithology, music, driving
Extras: Played for England indoor cricket team v Australia in ManuLife 'Test' series 1990. Moved to Yorkshire at end of 1992 season (first English non-Yorkshireman to be signed for the county). Included in England Test squad against New Zealand in 1994
Opinions on cricket: 'Groundsmen should prepare cricket wickets, not wickets made for corporate hospitality. Is not being given run out as much human judgement as LBW or caught behind? If we are using television to check and decide on run out, why not all decisions?'
Best batting: 65 Yorkshire v Durham, Chester-le-Street 1996

Best bowling: 6-37 Yorkshire v Durham, Durham University 1994

1996 Season

	M	Inns	NO	Runs	HS	Avge	100s	50s	Ct	St	O	M	Runs	Wkts	Avge	Best	5wI	10wM
Test																		
All First	19	24	9	260	65	17.33	-	2	8	-	566	165	1537	42	36.59	5-38	2	-
1-day Int																		
NatWest	4	0	0	0	0	-	-	-	-	-	48	3	176	9	19.55	4-45	-	
B & H	6	1	0	1	1	1.00	-	-	-	-	57	3	248	6	41.33	2-33	-	
Sunday	16	2	0	18	11	9.00	-	-	7	-	107.3	5	484	19	25.47	4-25	-	

Career Performances

	M	Inns	NO	Runs	HS	Avge	100s	50s	Ct	St	Balls	Runs	Wkts	Avge	Best	5wI	10wM
Test																	
All First	107	125	38	1138	65	13.08	-	2	46	-	20256	8488	250	33.95	6-37	11	1
1-day Int																	
NatWest	7	1	1	1	1 *	-	-	-	1	-	462	280	10	28.00	4-45	-	
B & H	13	3	1	1	1	0.50	-	-	-	-	732	484	10	48.40	2-28	-	
Sunday	46	13	4	95	23 *	10.55	-	-	12	-	1743	1411	46	30.67	4-25	-	

STEPHENSON, J. P.   Hampshire

Name: John Patrick Stephenson
Role: Right-hand opening bat, right-arm medium bowler, county captain
Born: 14 March 1965, Stebbing, Essex
Height: 6ft 1in **Weight:** 12st 7lbs
Nickname: Stan
County debut: 1985 (Essex), 1995 (Hants)
County cap: 1989 (Essex)
Test debut: 1989
Tests: 1
1000 runs in a season: 5
1st-Class 50s: 65
1st-Class 100s: 19
1st-Class 200s: 1
1st-Class 5 w. in innings: 8
1st-Class catches: 128
One-Day 100s: 7
One-Day 5 w. in innings: 1
Place in batting averages: 187th av. 26.56 (1995 98th av. 34.30)
Place in bowling averages: 62nd av. 30.50 (1995 106th av. 36.35)

Strike rate: 56.11 (career 60.41)
Parents: Pat and Eve
Wife and date of marriage: Fiona Maria, 24 September 1994
Family links with cricket: Father was member of Rugby Meteors Cricketer Cup-winning side in 1973. Three brothers played in Felsted 1st XI; Guy played for Essex 2nd XI and now plays for Teddington
Education: Felsted Prep School; Felsted Senior School; Durham University
Qualifications: 7 O-levels, 3 A-levels, BA General Arts (Dunelm)
Off-season: Going on holiday
Overseas tours: English Schools U19 to Zimbabwe 1982-83; England A to Kenya and Zimbabwe 1989-90, to Bermuda and West Indies 1991-92
Overseas teams played for: Fitzroy, Melbourne 1982-83, 1987-88; Boland, South Africa 1988-89; Gold Coast Dolphins and Bond University, Australia 1990-91; St George's, Argentina 1994-95; Belgrano, Argentina 1994-95; Victoria CC, South Africa 1995-96
Cricketers particularly admired: Brian Hardie
Young players to look out for: Ben Hollioake
Injuries: Broken finger and pneumonia, out for three weeks
Relaxations: Watching cricket (*Sunday Telegraph*, *Wisden*, *The Cricketer*), reading, alternative music
Extras: Awarded 2nd XI cap in 1984 when leading run-scorer with Essex 2nd XI. Essex Young Player of the Year, 1985. Captained Durham University to victory in UAU Championship 1986 and captain of Combined Universities team 1987 in the first year that it was drawn from all universities. Called up to replace the injured Michael Atherton on England A tour to Bermuda and West Indies 1991-92 and was leading wicket-taker. Scored two not out centuries v Somerset at Taunton in 1992 and was on the field for the whole game (the first Essex player to achieve this). First Essex player to achieve 500 runs and 20 wickets in Sunday League season 1993. Took over the captaincy of Hampshire in 1996. Founded the One Test Wonder Club in 1996
Opinions on cricket: 'Leave the structure alone for a change.'
Best batting: 202* Essex v Somerset, Bath 1990
Best bowling: 7-51 Hampshire v Middlesex, Lord's 1995

1996 Season

	M	Inns	NO	Runs	HS	Avge	100s	50s	Ct	St	O	M	Runs	Wkts	Avge	Best	5wI	10wM
Test																		
All First	15	25	2	611	85	26.56	-	5	6	-	336.4	73	1098	36	30.50	6-48	3	
1-day Int																		
NatWest	3	3	0	142	107	47.33	1	-	-	-	23	0	118	3	39.33	2-49	-	
B & H	4	4	1	185	124 *	61.66	1	-	1	-	17.1	2	71	5	14.20	3-33	-	
Sunday	11	11	1	279	110 *	27.90	1	-	10	-	83	3	349	20	17.45	3-22	-	

Career Performances

	M	Inns	NO	Runs	HS	Avge	100s	50s	Ct	St	Balls	Runs	Wkts	Avge	Best	5wI	10wM
Test	1	2	0	36	25	18.00	-	-	-	-							
All First	220	379	38	11733	202 *	34.40	19	65	128	-	13109	7291	217	33.59	7-51	8	-
1-day Int																	
NatWest	21	20	1	769	107	40.47	1	7	7	-	689	598	12	49.83	3-78	-	
B & H	37	32	4	1274	142	45.50	2	9	7	-	1048	713	30	23.76	3-22	-	
Sunday	132	117	14	2967	110 *	28.80	4	13	56	-	3723	2845	113	25.17	5-58	1	

STEVENS, D. I.   Leicestershire

Name: Darren Ian Stevens
Role: Right-hand bat, right-arm medium bowler
Born: 30 April 1976, Leicester
Height: 5ft 11in **Weight:** 12st 7lbs
Nickname: Beetroot
County debut: No first-team appearance
Parents: Robert and Madeleine
Marital status: Single
Family links with cricket: Father and grandfather both played local cricket in the South Leicestershire League. Grandfather was awarded the Ernest Wright Award for his services to the Leicestershire league
Education: Mount Grange High School; John Cleavland College, Hinckley
Qualifications: BTEC in National Sports Studies
Off-season: Playing and coaching in South Africa
Overseas tours: Leicestershire U19 to South Africa 1994-95
Overseas teams played for: Wanderers CC, Johannesburg, South Africa 1995-97
Cricketers particularly admired: Graham Thorpe, Darryl Cullinan
Young players to look out for: Darren Maddy, Douglas Gain (captain of South Africa U19)
Other sports followed: Football (Leicester City)
Injuries: Right foot, out for one week
Relaxations: Going to the gym, reading and socialising
Opinions on cricket: 'Too much fixture congestion. Not enough time to practise.'

STEWART, A. J.   Surrey

Name: Alec James Stewart
Role: Right-hand bat, wicket-keeper
Born: 8 April 1963, Merton
Nickname: Stewie, Ming
Height: 5ft 11in **Weight:** 12st 10lbs
County debut: 1981
County cap: 1985
Benefit: 1994 (£202,187)
Test debut: 1989-90
Tests: 58
One-Day Internationals: 79
1000 runs in a season: 8
1st-Class 50s: 105
1st-Class 100s: 36
1st-Class 200s: 1
1st-Class catches: 387
1st-Class stumpings: 14
One-Day 100s: 14
Place in batting averages: 64th av. 42.00
(1995 78th av. 38.05)
Strike rate: (career 156.33)

Parents: Michael and Sheila
Wife and date of marriage: Lynn, 28 September 1991
Children: Andrew James, 21 May 1993; Emily Elizabeth, 6 September 1996
Family links with cricket: Father played for England (1962-64), Surrey (1954 -72) and Malden Wanderers. Brother Neil captains Malden Wanderers
Education: Tiffin Boys School
Qualifications: 'Street wise'
Off-season: Touring Zimbabwe and New Zealand with England
Overseas tours: England to India (Nehru Cup) 1989-90, to West Indies 1989-90, to Australia 1990-91, to Australia and New Zealand (World Cup) 1991-92, to India and Sri Lanka 1992-93, to West Indies 1993-94, to Australia 1994-95; to South Africa 1995-96, to Pakistan and India (World Cup) 1996, to Zimbabwe and New Zealand 1996-97
Overseas teams played for: Midland Guildford, Perth, Western Australia 1981-89
Cricketers particularly admired: Graham Monkhouse, Graham Gooch, Alan Knott, Geoff Arnold, K Gartrell
Young players to look out for: Ben Hollioake
Other sports followed: Football (Chelsea)
Relaxations: 'Spending as much time with my family as possible'
Extras: Captained England in a Test match for the first time v India at Madras 1992-93

and has acted as vice-captain to both Graham Gooch and Mike Atherton. First Englishman to score a century in each innings against West Indies, at Barbados 1994. He was the leading scorer in Test cricket in the 1996 calendar year (with 793 runs) ahead of Saeed Anwar (701)

Opinions on cricket: 'England players, especially bowlers, should be rested from county cricket when it is needed.'

Best batting: 206* Surrey v Essex, The Oval 1989
Best bowling: 1-7 Surrey v Lancashire, Old Trafford 1989

1996 Season

	M	Inns	NO	Runs	HS	Avge	100s	50s	Ct	St	O	M	Runs	Wkts	Avge	Best	5wI	10wM
Test	5	8	0	532	170	66.50	1	4	5	1								
All First	14	24	1	966	170	42.00	1	7	15	1	2	0	24	0	-		-	-
1-day Int	6	6	2	160	48	40.00	-	-	5	1								
NatWest	4	4	1	185	125 *	61.66	1	1	6	2								
B & H	5	5	1	297	160	74.25	1	2	5	-								
Sunday	9	7	2	296	112 *	59.20	2	-	11	-								

Career Performances

	M	Inns	NO	Runs	HS	Avge	100s	50s	Ct	St	Balls	Runs	Wkts	Avge	Best	5wI	10wM
Test	58	103	6	3935	190	40.56	8	20	70	5	20	13	0	-	-	-	-
All First	309	511	58	18197	206 *	40.17	36	105	387	14	469	417	3	139.00	1-7	-	-
1-day Int	79	74	7	2042	103	30.47	1	12	60	5							
NatWest	34	31	5	1240	125 *	47.69	3	8	37	2							
B & H	50	50	8	1937	167 *	46.11	3	13	34	4							
Sunday	154	138	15	3952	125	32.13	7	22	119	8	4	8	0	-	-	-	

Name: Paul Andrew Strang
Role: Right-hand bat, leg spin bowler
Born: 28 July 1970, Bulawayo, Zimbabwe
Height: 5ft 9in **Weight:** 11st 7lbs
Nickname: Stump
County debut: No first-team appearance
Strike rate: 39.50 (career 71.63)
Parents: Ronald Charles and Jennifer Joan
Marital status: Single
Family links with cricket: Father is a first-
class umpire. Brother Bryan plays for
Zimbabwe
Education: Falcon College, Esigodini,
Zimbabwe; University of Cape Town,
 South Africa
Qualifications: A-levels, BSoc Sc (Econ),
advanced coach
Overseas tours: Zimbabwe U19 to New
Zealand 1989; Zimbabwe to India and
Pakistan (World Cup) 1995-96, to Pakistan 1996-97
Cricketers particularly admired: David Houghton and John Traicos
Young players to look out for: Brian Murphy ('a young leg-spinner currently playing
for Zimbabwe B')
Other sports followed: Most international sport. 'Liverpool FC. I always keep an eye
on Nick Price and Byron Black (tennis).' Played hockey for Zimbabwe U19
Relaxations: 'I like to relax with mates watching sport'
Extras: Captained Zimbabwe U19 (1989-90). Shared all ten wickets with brother
Bryan in a local game. Played in the Birmingham league for Aston Manor (1989) and
Barnt Green (1996). Became only the 18th player to score a century and take five
wickets in an innings in a Test match against Pakistan at Sheikhupura. Made his first-
class debut in Zimbabwe against Kent
Opinions on cricket: 'LBWs for balls pitching outside leg would be nice!'
Best batting: 97 Mashonaland Country Districts v Matabeleland, Harare South 1994-95
Best bowling: 7-75 Mashonaland C D v Mashonaland U24, Harare South 1994-95

81. Which England batsman had three scores in excess of 150
and totalled 732 runs at 81.30 in the 1985 series?

1996 Season

	M	Inns	NO	Runs	HS	Avge	100s	50s	Ct	St	O	M	Runs	Wkts	Avge	Best	5wI	10wM
Test																		
All First	1	1	1	13	13 *	-	-	-	-	1	-	46.3	10	134	2	67.00	1-17	--
1-day Int																		
NatWest																		
B & H																		
Sunday																		

Career Performances

	M	Inns	NO	Runs	HS	Avge	100s	50s	Ct	St	Balls	Runs	Wkts	Avge	Best	5wI	10wM
Test	7	10	1	204	49	22.66	-	-	4	-	1170	548	7	78.28	3-65	-	-
All First	33	50	12	1027	97	27.02	-	5	28	-	6061	3118	86	36.25	7-75	6	-
1-day Int	17	15	7	221	28 *	27.62	-	-	3	-	895	648	24	27.00	5-21	1	-
NatWest																	
B & H																	
Sunday																	

STRAUSS, A. J. Middlesex

Name: Andrew John Strauss
Role: Left-hand bat
Born: 2 March 1977, Johannesburg, South Africa
Height: 6ft **Weight:** 12st 7lbs
Nickname: Johann
County debut: No first-team appearance
Parents: David and Dawn
Marital status: Single
Education: Caldicott Prep School; Radley College; University of Durham
Qualifications: 4 A-levels
Career outside cricket: Student
Cricketers particularly admired: Brian Lara, Allan Donald
Young players to look out for: Will House, Anurag Singh
Other sports followed: Rugby (plays for Durham University), golf
Relaxations: Any sport
Opinions on cricket: 'It's different from when it started'

STRONG, M.   Sussex

Name: Michael Strong
Role: Left-hand bat, right-arm
fast-medium bowler
Born: 28 June 1974, Cuckfield, West Sussex
Height: 6ft 1in **Weight:** 13st 10lbs
Nickname: Strongy, Strongblomqvist,
Stronglager
County debut: No first-team appearance
Parents: David and Gillian
Marital status: Single
Family links with cricket: 'My father, my
brother and I used to play in the same team,
giving scorers nightmares'
Education: St Peter's School, Burgess Hill;
Brighton College; Brunel University College
Qualifications: 9 GCSEs, 3 A-levels
Career outside cricket: Physical education
and geography teacher (training)
Off-season: Finishing off my degree course
Overseas tours: Brighton College to India 1991-92
Overseas teams played for: Multiquip Umbilo CC, Durban, South Africa 1992-93
Cricketers particularly admired: Allan Donald, Sachin Tendulkar, Rodney Malamba
(Umbilo CC 'changed my bowling action')
Young players to look out for: James Kirtley and Danny Law
Other sports followed: Rugby (England and Saracens), football (Chelsea and
Brighton), and hockey
Injuries: Sore shins and Achilles tendon, but missed no cricket
Relaxations: Sleeping, going to clubs and pubs with friends, 'lazing by my parents' pool'
Extras: 'Would like to thank master in charge of cricket at Brighton College, John
Spencer, for all the time he spent coaching me from the age of 10'
Opinions on cricket: 'Too much limited overs cricket. Poor structure to the game –
from schools through to county.'

SUCH, P. M.   Essex

Name: Peter Mark Such
Role: Right-hand bat, off-spin bowler
Born: 12 June 1964, Helensburgh, Scotland
Height: 6ft **Weight:** 11st 7lbs
Nickname: Suchy

County debut: 1982 (Nottinghamshire), 1987 (Leicestershire), 1990 (Essex)
County cap: 1991 (Essex)
Test debut: 1993
Tests: 8
50 wickets in a season: 4
1st-Class 50s: 2
1st-Class 5 w. in innings: 33
1st-Class 10 w. in innings: 6
1st-Class catches: 93
One-Day 5 w. in innings: 2
Place in batting averages: 262nd av. 16.00
Place in bowling averages: 34th av. 26.39 (1995 44th av. 26.80)
Strike rate: 56.46 (career 65.54)
Parents: John and Margaret
Marital status: Engaged
Family links with cricket: Father and brother both village cricketers
Education: Lantern Lane Primary; Harry Carlton Comprehensive, East Leake, Notts
Qualifications: 9 O-levels, 3 A-levels, advanced cricket coach
Off-season: Touring Australia with England A
Overseas tours: England A to Australia 1992-93, to South Africa 1993-94, to Australia 1996-97
Overseas teams played for: Kempton Park, South Africa 1982-83; Bathurst, Australia 1985-86; Matabeleland, Zimbabwe 1989-92
Cricketers particularly admired: Bob White, Eddie Hemmings, Graham Gooch, John Childs
Young players to look out for: Ashley Cowan, Robert Rollins, Andrew Harris
Relaxations: Gardening
Extras: Played for England YC v Australian YC 1983 and for TCCB XI v New Zealand, 1985. Left Nottinghamshire at end of 1986 season; joined Leicestershire in 1987 and released at end of 1989; signed by Essex for 1990. Played in one-day games for England A v Sri Lanka 1991. Joint winner with J.H. Childs of the Essex Player of the Year Award 1992 and shared the award again in 1993. Took 6-67 on Test debut v Australia 1993 – best figures by England Test debutant since John Lever in India 1976-77
Opinions on cricket: 'Present balance of one-day and four-day cricket is about right. NatWest should be 55 overs, B&H 50 overs, Sunday League 40 overs. Over rates in Championship are too high, 102 overs per day would be better. The quality of the pitches has improved this year but needs to be maintained. The TCCB needs to be very strict when monitoring the situation.'
Best batting: 54 Essex v Worcestershire, Chelmsford 1993
54 Essex v Nottinghamshire, Chelmsford 1996
Best bowling: 8-93 Essex v Hampshire, Colchester 1995

1996 Season

	M	Inns	NO	Runs	HS	Avge	100s	50s	Ct	St	O	M	Runs	Wkts	Avge	Best	5wI	10wM
Test																		
All First	19	22	11	176	54	16.00	-	1	12	-	771.4	190	2164	82	26.39	8-118	6	1
1-day Int																		
NatWest	5	2	0	0	0	0.00	-	-	1	-	57	3	206	8	25.75	3-56	-	
B & H	5	1	1	10	10 *	-	-	-	-	-	46	5	141	4	35.25	2-32	-	
Sunday	16	8	7	26	9 *	26.00	-	-	4	-	97.1	3	494	10	49.40	3-53	-	

Career Performances

	M	Inns	NO	Runs	HS	Avge	100s	50s	Ct	St	Balls	Runs	Wkts	Avge	Best	5wI	10wM
Test	8	11	4	65	14 *	9.28	-	-	2	-	2177	805	22	36.59	6-67	1	-
All First	218	218	70	1143	54	7.72	-	2	93	-	40571	18061	618	29.22	8-93	33	6
1-day Int																	
NatWest	17	7	3	14	8 *	3.50	-	-	2	-	1074	595	20	29.75	3-56	-	
B & H	27	10	5	28	10 *	5.60	-	-	3	-	1428	873	27	32.33	4-43	-	
Sunday	98	38	21	142	19 *	8.35	-	-	28	-	3915	3063	93	32.93	5-32	2	

SUTCLIFFE, I. J.   Leicestershire

Name: Iain John Sutcliffe
Role: Left-hand bat, leg-spin bowler
Born: 20 December 1974, Leeds
Height: 6ft 1in **Weight:** 12st
Nickname: Sooty, Bertie, Ripper
County debut: 1995
1st-Class 50s: 10
1st-Class 100s: 1
1st-Class catches: 12
Place in batting averages: 94th av. 36.91
(1995 54th av. 42.35)
Strike rate: 40.00 (career 48.00)
Parents: John and Valerie
Marital status: Single
Education: Leeds Grammar School; Oxford
University
Qualifications: 10 GCSEs, 4 A-levels, 2:1
PPE degree
Off-season: Selected on the NBC Denis Compton Scholarship to South Africa
Overseas tours: Leeds GS to Kenya
Cricketers particularly admired: David Gower, Brian Lara, Saeed Anwar
Young players to look out for: Gul Khan

Other sports followed: Boxing (Mike Tyson), football (Liverpool)
Relaxations: Listening to music, eating out
Extras: Played NCA England U14 and NCA Development Team U18/U19. Oxford boxing Blue 1994 and 1995, British Universities Light-middleweight Champion 1993. Highest partnership (283) with C. Gupte for Oxford University against a first-class county in which he scored 163 not out
Opinions on cricket: 'The NBC Denis Compton Scholarship scheme is a very good way of promoting the development of English cricketers. The county system should be more geared to Test cricket. At present, players play too much and have little time to practise and maintain sharpness.'
Best batting: 163* Oxford University v Hampshire, The Parks 1995
Best bowling: 2-21 Oxford University v Cambridge University, Lord's 1996

1996 Season

	M	Inns	NO	Runs	HS	Avge	100s	50s	Ct	St	O	M	Runs	Wkts	Avge	Best	5wI	10wM
Test																		
All First	8	12	0	443	83	36.91	-	5	1	-	20	1	86	3	28.66	2-21	-	-
1-day Int																		
NatWest	1	1	0	15	15	15.00	-	-	-	-								
B & H																		
Sunday																		

Career Performances

	M	Inns	NO	Runs	HS	Avge	100s	50s	Ct	St	Balls	Runs	Wkts	Avge	Best	5wI	10wM
Test																	
All First	27	40	5	1308	163 *	37.37	1	10	12	-	192	137	4	34.25	2-21	-	-
1-day Int																	
NatWest	2	2	0	83	68	41.50	-	1	1	-							
B & H	3	3	0	70	39	23.33	-	-	-	-							
Sunday	1	1	0	14	14	14.00	-	-	2	-							

82. Who bacame the third England wicket-keeper to score an Ashes hundred in Perth in 1986-87?

SWANN, A. J.   Northamptonshire

Name: Alec James Swann
Role: Right-hand opening bat
Born: 26 October 1976, Northampton
Height: 6ft 2in **Weight:** 12st
Nickname: Swanny, Ron
County debut: 1996
1st-Class 50s: 1
1st-Class catches: 1
Parents: Raymond and Mavis
Marital status: Single
Family links with cricket: Father has played
for Northumberland, Bedfordshire,
Northamptonshire 2nd XI and England
Amateurs. Brother Graeme has played for
England U14 and U15 and Northamptonshire
2nd XI
Education: Sponne Comprehensive,
Towcester
Qualifications: 9 GCSEs and 4 A-levels
Off-season: 'Hopefully working in Northampton and playing local football'
Overseas teams played for: Wallsend, NSW, Australia 1995-96
Cricketers particularly admired: Mark and Steve Waugh, Robin Smith, Russell
Warren
Young players to look out for: Graeme Swann, Ben Hollioake, James Ormond
Other sports followed: Football (Newcastle and Liverpool) and most other sports
except athletics
Relaxations: Listening to music, reading political thrillers, watching videos and films
and the odd bet
Extras: Played for England Schools U15 and U19. Opened batting for Bedfordshire
(with father in Minor Counties game). *Daily Telegraph* U15 Young Cricketer of the Year
1992. Midlands Club Cricket Conference Young Cricketer of the Year 1992. Played for
England U19 against New Zealand in 1996
Opinions on cricket: '2nd XI cricket should be played over four days, club cricket
could also be played over more than one afternoon. Tea interval should be half an hour
and there should be 15 minutes between innings. Batting gloves need to be reinforced,
there must be some foam or plastic available that could prevent hand/finger damage.
Practise facilities at most grounds need improving, especially where 2nd XI cricket is
played.'
Best batting: 76* Northamptonshire v Oxford University, The Parks 1996

1996 Season

	M	Inns	NO	Runs	HS	Avge	100s	50s	Ct	St	O	M	Runs	Wkts	Avge	Best	5wI	10wM
Test																		
All First	3	5	1	100	76 *	25.00	-	1	1	-	5	1	15	0	-	-	-	-
1-day Int																		
NatWest																			
B & H																			
Sunday																			

Career Performances

	M	Inns	NO	Runs	HS	Avge	100s	50s	Ct	St	Balls	Runs	Wkts	Avge	Best	5wI	10wM
Test																	
All First	3	5	1	100	76 *	25.00	-	1	1	-	30	15	0	-	-	-	-
1-day Int																	
NatWest																	
B & H																	
Sunday																	

SWANN, G. P.   Northamptonshire

Name: Graeme Peter Swann
Role: Right-hand bat, off-spin bowler
Born: 24 March 1979, Northampton
Height: 6ft **Weight:** 12st
Nickname: Swanny
County debut: No first-team appearance
Parents: Ray and Mavis
Marital status: Single
Family links with cricket: Brother on
Northamptonshire staff. Father has played
Minor Counties cricket for Bedfordshire and
Northumberland and also for England
Amateurs
Education: Abington Vale Lower School;
Sponne School, Towcester
Qualifications: 10 GCSEs
Off-season: Playing club cricket in Australia
or South Africa
Cricketers particularly admired: Mark
Waugh, John Crawley, Shane Warne, Carl Hooper
Young players to look out for: Alec Swann, Stephen Peters, Tim Roberts, David
Sales

Other sports followed: Football (Manchester United), rugby (Northampton Saints), golf
Relaxations: Listening to Oasis, going out with mates, watching sports, eating
Extras: Played for England U14, U15 and U17. Dual registered with Bedfordshire Minor County. *Daily Telegraph* regional bowling award winner in 1994. Gray Nicolls/Len Newbury Schools Cricketer of the Year in 1996
Opinions on cricket: 'Everything should be geared towards a strong national side. There are just as many high-class players in England as there are in Australia or South Africa, so it is not all doom and gloom for the future. Also, more turning pitches should be prepared.'

SWARBRICK, M.   Hampshire

Name: Matthew Swarbrick
Role: Right-hand bat
Born: 8 August 1977, Stockport, Cheshire
Height: 6ft 2in **Weight:** 13st
Nickname: Strawbs
County debut: No first-team appearance
Parents: Ian and Margaret
Marital status: Single
Family links with cricket: None
Education: St Walburgas; Cla111esmore; Exeter University
Qualifications: 6 GCSEs, 3 A-levels
Career outside cricket: Student
Off-season: Studying at Exeter University
Overseas teams played for: Glenwood Old Boys, Durban, South Africa 1995-96
Cricketers particularly admired: Robin Smith, John Crawley, Malcolm Marshall, Ian Botham
Other sports followed: Football (Manchester City, 'play for Exeter University') and rugby (Bath RFC)
Relaxations: Music, going out for a quiet pint
Extras: First player at Cla111esmore School to score 1,000 runs in a season in 1995. Captained the NAYC U19 in 1996. Southern League Young Player of the Year in 1996
Opinions on cricket: 'Have not played long enough to pass judgement on the game.'

SYMONDS, A.   Gloucestershire

Name: Andrew Symonds
Role: Right-hand bat, off-spin bowler
Born: 9 June 1975, Birmingham
Height: 6ft 1in   **Weight:** 13st 5lbs
Nickname: Roy
County debut: 1995
1000 runs in a season: 2
1st-Class 50s: 13
1st-Class 100s: 9
1st-Class 200s: 1
1st-Class catches: 19
Place in batting averages: 89th av. 37.82
(1995 11th av. 55.30)
Place in bowling averages: 65th av. 31.16
Strike rate: 59.25 (career 72.52)
Parents: Ken and Barbara
Marital status: Single
Family links with cricket: Father played
Minor County cricket
Education: All Saints Anglican School, Gold Coast, Australia; Ballarat and Clarondon
College, Gold Coast, Australia
Qualifications: Level Two coaching, professional fisherman
Off-season: Playing cricket in Australia
Overseas teams played for: Australian Cricket Academy 1993-94; Queensland Colts
1993-94; Queensland 1994-97
Cricketers particularly admired: Viv Richards, Shane Warne, Michael Holding
Other sports followed: Hockey, rugby, football (Norwich City, Newcastle United)
Injuries: Strained Achilles, out for one week
Relaxations: Fishing, camping and hunting
Extras: In his first season of first-class cricket he scored a century for Queensland
against England on their 1994-95 tour of Australia. Born in England, he has been
brought up in Australia and is a product of the Australian Cricket Academy. Hit a world
record number of sixes during his innings of 254 not out against Glamorgan in 1995.
Voted the Professional Cricketers' Association Young Player of the Year. Turned down
the invitation to tour with England A in 1995 so that he could remain eligible to play for
Australia. Became ineligible for Gloucestershire after being selected in the squad to play
for Australia A during the off-season against West Indies – he was ultimately 12th man
Best batting: 254* Gloucestershire v Glamorgan, Abergavenny 1995
Best bowling: 3-77 Queensland v New South Wales, Sydney 1994-95

1996 Season

	M	Inns	NO	Runs	HS	Avge	100s	50s	Ct	St	O	M	Runs	Wkts	Avge	Best	5wI	10wM
Test																		
All First	18	30	1	1097	127	37.82	3	4	9	-	118.3	25	374	12	31.16	2-21	-	-
1-day Int																		
NatWest	2	2	0	87	87	43.50	-	1	-	-	8	4	18	1	18.00	1-18	-	
B & H	5	5	0	111	67	22.20	-	1	3	-	4	0	23	0	-	-	-	-
Sunday	14	13	0	365	76	28.07	-	3	12	-	38	1	217	9	24.11	3-34	-	

Career Performances

	M	Inns	NO	Runs	HS	Avge	100s	50s	Ct	St	Balls	Runs	Wkts	Avge	Best	5wI	10wM
Test																	
All First	41	69	7	2859	254 *	46.11	9	13	19	-	1233	672	17	39.52	3-77	-	-
1-day Int																	
NatWest	5	5	0	166	87	33.20	-	1	-	-	102	63	1	63.00	1-18	-	
B & H	11	11	0	291	95	26.45	-	2	4	-	24	23	0	-	-	-	
Sunday	29	28	2	756	76	29.07	-	4	18	-	312	278	13	21.38	3-34	-	

TAYLOR, J. P.   Northamptonshire

Name: Jonathan Paul Taylor
Role: Left-hand bat, left-arm
fast-medium bowler
Born: 8 August 1964, Ashby-de-la-Zouch,
Leicestershire
Height: 6ft 2in **Weight:** 13st 10lbs
Nickname: Roadie, PT
County debut: 1988 (Derbyshire), 1991
(Northamptonshire)
County cap: 1992 (Northamptonshire)
Test debut: 1992-93
Tests: 2
One-Day Internationals: 1
50 wickets in a season: 4
1st-Class 50s: 4
1st-Class 5 w. in innings: 13
1st-Class 10 w. in match: 2
1st-Class catches: 38
Place in batting averages: 252nd av. 17.28
(1995 194th av. 21.82)
Place in bowling averages: 42nd av. 27.59 (1995 60th av. 29.03)
Strike rate: 51.50 (career 57.39)
Parents: Derek and Janet

Wife and date of marriage: Elaine Mary, 30 July 1993
Children: Christopher Paul, 8 July 1994
Family links with cricket: Father and brother played local league cricket
Education: Pingle School, Swadlincote, Derbyshire
Qualifications: 6 O-levels, NCA coaching certificate
Off-season: Coaching in Bedfordshire
Overseas tours: Midland Club Cricket Conference to Australia 1990-91; England to India and Sri Lanka 1992-93; Northamptonshire to Natal 1993, to Zimbabwe 1995, to Johannesburg 1996; England A to South Africa 1993-94
Overseas teams played for: Papakura, New Zealand 1984-85; Napier High School Old Boys, New Zealand 1985-86; North Kalgoorlie, Western Australia 1990-91; Great Boulder, Western Australia 1991-92
Cricketers particularly admired: Dennis Lillee, Bob Taylor, John Lever
Young players to look out for: Anthony McGrath, David Sales, Kevin Innes
Other sports followed: Soccer, rugby, basketball
Relaxations: Watching videos, eating out, 'looking after hyper-active little boy, if you can call that relaxing!'
Extras: Spent four seasons on the staff at Derbyshire 1984-87 and played Minor Counties cricket for Staffordshire 1989-90. Won Man of the Match in the Bain Clarkson Final in 1987 for Derbyshire, after being released. Played first game at Lord's in NatWest Trophy final 1992. Was voted Northamptonshire's Player of the Year in 1992. Called up as replacement during England A tour to South Africa 1993-94. Selected for England Indoor World Cup squad 1995
Opinions on cricket: 'More quality, less quantity.'
Best batting: 86 Northamptonshire v Durham, Northampton 1995
Best bowling: 7-23 Northamptonshire v Hampshire, Bournemouth 1992

1996 Season

	M	Inns	NO	Runs	HS	Avge	100s	50s	Ct	St	O	M	Runs	Wkts	Avge	Best	5wI	10wM
Test																		
All First	17	23	9	242	57	17.28	-	1	3	-	549.2	116	1766	64	27.59	7-88	3	1
1-day Int																		
NatWest	2	1	1	1	1*	-	-	-	-	-	22	1	84	2	42.00	2-40	-	
B & H	7	1	1	0	0*	-	-	-	-	-	64	6	279	15	18.60	5-45	1	
Sunday	16	4	3	14	9*	14.00	-	-	4	-	116.5	10	599	24	24.95	3-22	-	

Career Performances

	M	Inns	NO	Runs	HS	Avge	100s	50s	Ct	St	Balls	Runs	Wkts	Avge	Best	5wI	10wM
Test	2	4	2	34	17*	17.00	-	-	-	-	288	156	3	52.00	1-18	-	-
All First	116	124	52	981	86	13.62	-	4	38	-	20088	10437	350	29.82	7-23	13	2
1-day Int	1	1	0	1	1	1.00	-	-	-	-	18	20	0	-	-	-	
NatWest	24	8	4	22	9	5.50	-	-	6	-	1467	918	33	27.81	4-34	-	
B & H	23	9	7	23	7*	11.50	-	-	4	-	1275	736	32	23.00	5-45	1	
Sunday	83	28	13	127	24	8.46	-	-	15	-	3660	2872	99	29.01	3-14	-	

TAYLOR, N. R. Sussex

Name: Neil Royston Taylor
Role: Right-hand bat, occasional off-spin bowler
Born: 21 July 1959, Farnborough, Kent
Height: 6ft 1in **Weight:** 15st
Nickname: Map
County debut: 1979
County cap: 1982
Benefit: 1992 (£131,000)
1000 runs in a season: 10
1st-Class 50s: 84
1st-Class 100s: 42
1st-Class 200s: 2
1st-Class catches: 151
One-Day 100s: 5
Place in batting averages: 58th av. 42.10
(1994 38th av. 43.70)
Strike rate: (career 98.43)

Parents: Leonard and Audrey
Wife and date of marriage: Jane Claire, 25 September 1982
Children: Amy Louise, 7 November 1985; Lauren, 21 July 1988
Family links with cricket: Brother Colin played for Kent U19. Father played club cricket
Education: Cray Valley Technical High School
Qualifications: 8 O-levels, 2 A-levels, advanced cricket coach
Off-season: Coaching
Overseas tours: English Schools to India 1977-78; Kent to Canada 1978, to Zimbabwe 1992-93; Fred Rumsey XI to West Indies 1988
Overseas teams played for: Randburg, Johannesburg 1979-85; St Stithian's College, Johannesburg (as coach) 1980-85
Cricketers particularly admired: Chris Tavaré, Mark Benson, Mike Gatting, Robin Smith
Other sports followed: Rugby union, golf
Injuries: Broken finger/knuckle, out for four weeks
Relaxations: Music and reading (mainly biographies)
Extras: Made 110 on debut for Kent v Sri Lankans, 1979. Won four Man of the Match awards in his first five matches and scored three successive centuries in the B&H. Played for England B v Pakistan, 1982 and twice fielded as 12th man for England – v India in 1982 and v West Indies in 1988, both matches at The Oval. Holds Kent first and second wicket record partnerships with Mark Benson (300 v Derbyshire) and Simon Hinks (366 v Middlesex). Only Kent player to score 200 and 100 in a match twice (204 and 142 v Surrey, 111 and 203* v Sussex). Has scored 13 centuries at Canterbury,

beating Frank Woolley and Colin Cowdrey. Provides a weekly contribution to Radio Kent through the summer
Best batting: 204 Kent v Surrey, Canterbury 1990
Best bowling: 2-20 Kent v Somerset, Canterbury 1985

1996 Season (did not make any first-class or one-day appearances)

Career Performances

	M	Inns	NO	Runs	HS	Avge	100s	50s	Ct	St	Balls	Runs	Wkts	Avge	Best	5wI	10wM
Test																	
All First	303	515	68	17772	204	39.75	42	84	151	-	1575	891	16	55.68	2-20	-	-
1-day Int																	
NatWest	31	31	1	802	86	26.73	-	5	6	-	143	86	6	14.33	3-29	-	
B & H	51	48	2	1872	137	40.69	5	7	11	-	12	5	0	-	-	-	
Sunday	147	141	14	3887	95	30.60	-	24	37	-							

TERRY, V. P.   Hampshire

Name: Vivian Paul Terry
Role: Right-hand bat, right-arm medium bowler, slip and outfielder
Born: 14 January 1959, Osnabruck, West Germany
Height: 6ft **Weight:** 13st 10lbs
County debut: 1978
County cap: 1983
Benefit: 1994 (£143,277)
Test debut: 1984
Tests: 2
1000 runs in a season: 11
1st-Class 50s: 82
1st-Class 100s: 38
1st-Class catches: 332
One-Day 100s: 12
Place in batting averages: 88th av. 37.90
(1995 124th av. 30.66)
Parents: Charles Michael and Patricia Mary
Wife and date of marriage: Bernadette Mary, 4 June 1986
Children: Siobhan Catherine, 13 September 1987; Sean Paul, 1 August 1991
Education: Durlston Court, Hampshire; Millfield School
Qualifications: 10 O-levels, 1 A-level, advanced cricket coach, squash coach
Off-season: Playing and coaching in Perth

Overseas tours: English Schools to India 1977-78; English Counties XI to Zimbabwe 1984-85; Bournemouth Sports to Kenya 1986
Overseas teams played for: Northern Districts, Sydney 1979-80; Wakatu, Nelson 1980-81; Durban Collegians 1982-84; Perth 1986-88, 1991-92
Cricketers particularly admired: Chris Smith, Malcolm Marshall, Gary Sobers
Other sports followed: Most sports – golf, rugby, football
Relaxations: 'My kids and watching sport'
Extras: Released by Hampshire at the end of the 1996 season
Opinions on cricket: 'Heading in the right direction but still need to play less.'
Best batting: 190 Hampshire v Sri Lankans, Southampton 1988

1996 Season

	M	Inns	NO	Runs	HS	Avge	100s	50s	Ct	St	O	M	Runs	Wkts	Avge	Best	5wI	10wM
Test																		
All First	7	12	2	379	87 *	37.90	-	3	12	-								
1-day Int																		
NatWest	3	3	0	28	14	9.33	-	-	1	-								
B & H																		
Sunday																		

Career Performances

	M	Inns	NO	Runs	HS	Avge	100s	50s	Ct	St	Balls	Runs	Wkts	Avge	Best	5wI	10wM
Test	2	3	0	16	8	5.33	-	-	2	-							
All First	292	493	45	16427	190	36.66	38	82	332	-	95	58	0	-	-	-	-
1-day Int																	
NatWest	42	40	4	1509	165 *	41.91	4	9	17	-							
B & H	57	56	5	1874	134	36.74	2	13	24	-							
Sunday	201	187	25	5201	142	32.10	6	27	103	-							

THOMAS, A.   Leicestershire

Name: Anatole Thomas
Role: Right-hand bat, right arm fast bowler
Born: 26 March 1970, London
Height: 6ft 1in   **Weight:** 12st 7lbs
Nickname: Tolly, Rambo
County debut: No first-team appearance
Parents: James and Monica
Marital status: Single
Family links with cricket: Father and brother both played local cricket
Education: 'I went to primary school and secondary school in Dominique.'
Christopher Wren School, London

Qualifications: City and Guilds in Motor Mechanics
Career outside cricket: Hairdresser
Off-season: Resting and training
Cricketers particularly admired: Michael Holding, Viv Richards, Clive Lloyd, Dennis Lillee
Young players to look out for: Anatole Thomas, Owais Shah
Other sports followed: Football (Arsenal FC) and basketball (Chicago Bulls)
Injuries: Ankle ligaments, out from August till the end of the season
Relaxations: Music and videos
Opinions on cricket: 'If young players have the talent they should be given the chance in Test cricket.'

THOMAS, P   Worcestershire

Name: Paul Thomas
Role: Right-hand bat, right-arm fast bowler
Height: 5ft 9in **Weight:** 11st 8lbs
Born: 3 June 1971, Dudley
Nickname: Thommo
County debut: 1995
1st-Class 5 w. in innings: 1
1st-Class catches: 1
Place in batting averages: 310th av. 6.57
Place in bowling averages: 136th av. 47.91 (1995 139th av 47.09)
Strike rate: 60.50 (career 67.68)
Parents: Clifford and Myrtle
Marital status: Single
Family links with cricket: Father is a great fan of the game. Brothers play
Education: Broadway School
Off-season: Playing club cricket in Australia
Extras: Awarded 2nd XI cap in 1995
Best batting: 25 Worcestershire v Warwickshire, Edgbaston 1995
Best bowling: 5-70 Worcestershire v West Indies, Worcester 1995

1996 Season

	M	Inns	NO	Runs	HS	Avge	100s	50s	Ct	St	O	M	Runs	Wkts	Avge	Best	5wI	10wM
Test																		
All First	5	7	0	46	11	6.57	-	-	-	-	121	14	575	12	47.91	4-33	-	-
1-day Int																		
NatWest																		
B & H	2	1	0	3	3	3.00	-	-	-	-	18.4	2	85	1	85.00	1-34	-	
Sunday	1	0	0	0	0	-	-	-	-	-	6	0	30	0	-	-	-	

Career Performances

	M	Inns	NO	Runs	HS	Avge	100s	50s	Ct	St	Balls	Runs	Wkts	Avge	Best	5wI	10wM
Test																	
All First	19	22	4	103	25	5.72	-	-	1	-	3046	2129	45	47.31	5-70	1	-
1-day Int																	
NatWest	1	0	0	0	0	-	-	-	-	-	60	30	2	15.00	2-30	-	
B & H	2	1	0	3	3	3.00	-	-	-	-	112	85	1	85.00	1-34	-	
Sunday	1	0	0	0	0	-	-	-	-	-	36	30	0	-	-	-	

THOMAS, S. D. — Glamorgan

Name: Stuart Darren Thomas
Role: Left-hand bat, right-arm medium-fast bowler
Born: 25 January 1975, Morriston
Height: 5ft 11in **Weight:** 13st 3lbs
Nickname: Tomo, Dough Boy, Teddy, Ice
County debut: 1992
1st-Class 50s: 3
1st-Class 5 w. in innings: 5
1st-Class catches: 7
Place in batting averages: 269th av. 15.30 (1995 126th av. 30.09)
Place in bowling averages: 153rd av. 58.75 (1995 143rd av. 48.42)
Strike rate: 88.50 (career 58.98)
Parents: Stuart and Anne
Marital status: Engaged to Ceris
Family links with cricket: Dad played for local 1st XI
Education: Craig Comprehensive; Neath Tertiary College
Qualifications: 4 GCSEs, BTEC National Diploma in Sports Science, NCA coaching

certificate

Off-season: Playing and coaching in Bloemfontein, Orange Free State

Overseas tours: England U18 to South Africa 1992-93; Glamorgan to South Africa 1992-93, to Portugal 1994, to Zimbabwe 1995; England U19 to Sri Lanka 1993-94

Cricketers particularly admired: Steve Barwick, Steve Watkin, Phil Newport, Courtney Walsh, Matthew Maynard

Other sports followed: Rugby union and league (Warrington)

Injuries: Rib cartilage, missed six weeks

Relaxations: 'Spending a lot of time horseriding with my girlfriend. Surfing off the Gower coastline. Socialising with a few pints.'

Extras: Youngest player to take five wickets on debut v Derbyshire in 1992 and finished eighth in national bowling averages. BBC Welsh Young Sports Personality 1992. Played last U19 Test against India at Edgbaston 1994. Broke Alan Wilkins' (Glamorgan) best Benson and Hedges bowling record on his debut in the competition with six for 20 in 1995

Opinions on cricket: 'Enjoy coloured clothing in Sunday League. I think that third umpires should be used in all one-day games as there are so many close decisions made. Happy to see the four-day game. This has showed a bigger advance of young cricketers and gives more opportunities for the players as there is more time to play cricket.'

Best batting: 78* Glamorgan v Gloucestershire, Abergavenny 1995

Best bowling: 5-76 Glamorgan v Worcestershire, Worcester 1993

1996 Season

	M	Inns	NO	Runs	HS	Avge	100s	50s	Ct	St	O	M	Runs	Wkts	Avge	Best	5wI	10wM
Test																		
All First	11	16	3	199	48	15.30	-	-	2	-	295	33	1175	20	58.75	5-121	1	-
1-day Int																		
NatWest																		
B & H	6	3	1	27	27 *	13.50	-	-	4	-	46	1	244	7	34.85	4-51	-	
Sunday	5	4	3	30	20 *	30.00	-	-	-	-	18.4	0	136	0	-	-	-	

Career Performances

	M	Inns	NO	Runs	HS	Avge	100s	50s	Ct	St	Balls	Runs	Wkts	Avge	Best	5wI	10wM
Test																	
All First	35	50	15	628	78 *	17.94	-	3	9	-	5663	3808	96	39.66	5-76	5	-
1-day Int																	
NatWest	1	0	0	0	0	-	-	-	-	-	54	36	0	-	-	-	-
B & H	7	3	1	27	27 *	13.50	-	-	5	-	332	264	13	20.30	6-20	1	
Sunday	11	5	3	49	20 *	24.50	-	-	1	-	296	278	5	55.60	3-44	-	

THOMPSON, J. B.   Kent

Name: Julian Barton Thompson
Role: Right-hand bat, right-arm
fast-medium bowler
Born: 28 October 1968, Cape Town,
South Africa
Height: 6ft 5in **Weight:** 14st
Nickname: Thommo, Doc, Bambi
County debut: 1994
1st-Class 5 w. in innings: 1
1st-Class catches: 1
Strike rate: 60.88 (career 60.87)
Parents: John and Joyce
Marital status: Engaged to Tanya
Family links with cricket: Father played
club cricket
Education: The Judd School, Tonbridge,
Kent; Guy's Hospital Medical School,
London

Qualifications: MBBS
Career outside cricket: Doctor
Off-season: Senior House Officer, Kent and Canterbury Hospital
Overseas tours: University of London to India 1991
Overseas teams played for: Northern Districts, Sydney 1987-88
Cricketers particularly admired: Courtney Walsh, Ian Austin
Young players to look out for: Ben Phillips
Other sports followed: Golf, football (Liverpool)
Injuries: 'Wounded pride when hit three-quarters of the way up The Oval pavilion by
Ali Brown in the Sunday League'
Relaxations: Golf, relaxing with fiancée, cooking, eating and drinking
Extras: Dismissed Brian Lara twice for a duck in Kent's game against the West Indies
in 1995 – Brian Lara's only pair in first-class cricket. Dismissed three England captains
in first month of the 1996 season – Atherton, Gatting and Gooch
Opinions on cricket: 'Sunday League and/or B and H: for the first 20 overs, 8 x 6 feet
high stumps at each end, 20 fielders (no restrictions) and a 17-yard pitch.'
Best batting: 40* Kent v Cambridge University, Folkestone 1995
Best bowling: 5-72 Kent v Surrey, The Oval 1996

1996 Season

	M	Inns	NO	Runs	HS	Avge	100s	50s	Ct	St	O	M	Runs	Wkts	Avge	Best	5wI	10wM
Test																		
All First	5	5	0	89	37	17.80	-	-	-	-	91.2	16	336	9	37.33	5-72	1	-
1-day Int																		
NatWest																		
B & H	4	3	2	17	12 *	17.00	-	-	-	-	30	4	114	6	19.00	3-29	-	
Sunday	12	8	3	44	30	8.80	-	-	1	-	51	2	250	7	35.71	3-26	-	

Career Performances

	M	Inns	NO	Runs	HS	Avge	100s	50s	Ct	St	Balls	Runs	Wkts	Avge	Best	5wI	10wM
Test																	
All First	9	13	3	175	40 *	17.50	-	-	1	-	974	613	16	38.31	5-72	1	-
1-day Int																	
NatWest																	
B & H	4	3	2	17	12 *	17.00	-	-	-	-	180	114	6	19.00	3-29	-	
Sunday	16	10	5	47	30	9.40	-	-	2	-	438	374	9	41.55	3-26	-	

THORPE, G. P.   Surrey

Name: Graham Paul Thorpe
Role: Left-hand bat, occasional right-arm medium bowler
Born: 1 August 1969, Farnham
Height: 5ft 10in **Weight:** 12st
Nickname: Chalky
County debut: 1988
County cap: 1991
Test debut: 1993
Tests: 32
One-Day Internationals: 30
1000 runs in a season: 7
1st-Class 50s: 73
1st-Class 100s: 25
1st-Class 200s: 1
1st-Class catches: 142
One-Day 100s: 5
Place in batting averages: 9th av. 62.76 (1995 62nd av. 40.76)
Strike rate: 114.00 (career 90.04)
Parents: 'Mr and Mrs Thorpe'
Wife: Nicola

Family links with cricket: Both brothers play for Farnham, father also plays cricket and mother is 'professional scorer'
Education: Weydon Comprehensive; Farnham Sixth Form College
Qualifications: 7 O-levels, PE Diploma
Off-season: 'Touring Zimbabwe and New Zealand with England, before that resting and touching up on my golf'
Overseas tours: England A to Zimbabwe and Kenya 1989-90, to Pakistan 1990-91, to Bermuda and West Indies 1991-92, to Australia 1992-93; England to West Indies 1993-94, to Australia 1994-95, to South Africa 1995-96, to India and Pakistan (World Cup) 1996, to Zimbabwe and New Zealand 1996-97
Cricketers particularly admired: Viv Richards, Grahame Clinton, David Gower
Young players to look out for: Ben Hollioake
Other sports followed: Football (Chelsea FC), golf
Relaxations: Sleeping
Extras: Played for English Schools cricket U15 and U19 and England Schools football U18. Scored a century against Australia on his Test debut at Trent Bridge 1993. Arrived a few days late for the Zimbabwe leg of England's tour to attend the birth of his son. He scored hundreds in successive Tests during the winter tour to New Zealand
Best batting: 216 Surrey v Somerset, The Oval 1992
Best bowling: 4-40 Surrey v Australians, The Oval 1993

1996 Season

	M	Inns	NO	Runs	HS	Avge	100s	50s	Ct	St	O	M	Runs	Wkts	Avge	Best	5wI	10wM
Test	6	10	1	352	89	39.11	-	3	7	-	14	4	22	0	-	-	-	-
All First	16	29	4	1569	185	62.76	6	7	18	-	38	12	87	2	43.50	2-13	-	-
1-day Int	5	5	1	178	79 *	44.50	-	1	2	-	4	0	15	2	7.50	2-15	-	
NatWest	3	3	0	117	96	39.00	-	1	1	-								
B & H	5	4	0	130	41	32.50	-	-	3	-								
Sunday	7	5	1	122	36 *	30.50	-	-	8	-								

Career Performances

	M	Inns	NO	Runs	HS	Avge	100s	50s	Ct	St	Balls	Runs	Wkts	Avge	Best	5wI	10wM
Test	32	59	5	2194	123	40.62	2	18	29	-	132	37	0	-	-	-	-
All First	192	325	44	12377	216	44.04	25	73	142	-	2161	1210	24	50.41	4-40	-	-
1-day Int	30	30	4	1018	89	39.15	-	8	17	-	72	60	2	30.00	2-15	-	
NatWest	21	20	4	807	145 *	50.43	1	6	10	-	13	12	0	-	-	-	
B & H	29	28	2	912	103	35.07	1	5	12	-	168	131	4	32.75	3-35	-	
Sunday	102	93	13	2863	115 *	35.78	3	21	39	-	318	307	8	38.37	3-21	-	

THURSFIELD, M. J.   Sussex

Name: Martin John Thursfield
Role: Right-hand bat, right-arm
medium-fast bowler
Born: 14 December 1971, South Shields
Height: 6ft 4in **Weight:** 14st
Nickname: Thursy
County debut: 1990
1st-Class 5 w. in innings: 1
1st-Class catches: 1
Strike rate: 130.20 (career 76.20)
Parents: Anthony John and Maureen
Marital status: Single
Family links with cricket: Great-grandfather
played for Yorkshire, and father is a keen
club cricketer
Education: Boldon Comprehensive
Qualifications: GCSEs, NCA coaching
certificate
Overseas tours: England YC to New
Zealand 1990-91
Cricketers particularly admired: Robin Smith, Malcolm Marshall, Allan Donald
Other sports followed: Football, golf
Relaxations: Playing golf, watching football and sleeping
Extras: Bowled two balls with broken leg in first England YC One-Day International v
New Zealand 1990-91. One of the youngest golfers in the country to achieve a hole in
one, aged 10. Released by Hampshire at the end of the 1996 season and has joined
Sussex for 1997
Best batting: 47 Hampshire v Glamorgan, Southampton 1994
Best bowling: 6-130 Hampshire v Middlesex, Southampton 1994

1996 Season

	M	Inns	NO	Runs	HS	Avge	100s	50s	Ct	St	O	M	Runs	Wkts	Avge	Best	5wI	10wM
Test																		
All First	5	5	2	89	37 *	29.66	-	-	-	-	108.3	22	361	5	72.20	3-45	-	-
1-day Int																		
NatWest	1	0	0	0	0	-	-	-	-	-	10	2	34	1	34.00	1-34	-	
B & H	3	2	1	20	19	20.00	-	-	1	-	28	2	123	4	30.75	2-33	-	
Sunday	5	2	0	3	3	1.50	-	-	1	-	27	0	174	1	174.00	1-38	-	

Career Performances

	M	Inns	NO	Runs	HS	Avge	100s	50s	Ct	St	Balls	Runs	Wkts	Avge	Best	5wI	10wM
Test																	
All First	22	24	5	277	47	14.57	-	-	1	-	2667	1431	35	40.88	6-130	1	-
1-day Int																	
NatWest	1	0	0	0	0	-	-	-	-	-	60	34	1	34.00	1-34	-	
B & H	6	4	3	24	19	24.00	-	-	1	-	312	242	6	40.33	2-33	-	
Sunday	23	11	3	34	9	4.25	-	-	4	-	948	805	16	50.31	3-31	-	

TITCHARD, S. P. Lancashire

Name: Stephen Paul Titchard
Role: Right-hand bat, right-arm
medium bowler
Born: 17 December 1967, Warrington,
Cheshire
Height: 6ft 3in **Weight:** 15st
Nickname: Titch, Stainy, Tyrone
County debut: 1990
1st-Class 50s: 24
1st-Class 100s: 4
1st-Class catches: 50
Place in batting averages: 51st av. 44.71
(1995 116th av. 31.68)
Strike rate: (career 222.00)
Parents: Alan and Margaret
Marital status: Single
Family links with cricket: Father, uncle and
two brothers have played for Grappenhall 1st
XI in the Manchester Association League. Father also represented the Army
Education: Lymm County High School; Priestley College
Qualifications: 3 O-levels, NCA Senior Coaching Award
Career outside cricket: Coach
Overseas tours: Lancashire to Tasmania and Western Australia 1990, to Western
Australia 1991, to Johannesburg 1992
Overseas teams played for: South Canberra, Australia 1991-92
Cricketers particularly admired: Graham Gooch, Malcolm Marshall
Other sports followed: Football (Manchester City) and rugby league (Warrington)
Relaxations: Snooker, golf, 'most sports'
Extras: Played for England U19. Made record scores for Manchester Association U18
(200*) and Cheshire Schools U19 (203*)
Opinions on cricket: 'In Championship games, the day should comprise of three two-

hour sessions, with an extended tea break of at least ten minutes!'
Best batting: 163 Lancashire v Essex, Chelmsford 1996
Best bowling: 1-51 Lancashire v Warwickshire, Edgbaston 1996

1996 Season

	M	Inns	NO	Runs	HS	Avge	100s	50s	Ct	St	O	M	Runs	Wkts	Avge	Best	5wl	10wM
Test																		
All First	13	23	2	939	163	44.71	2	5	11	-	37	7	124	1	124.00	1-51	-	-
1-day Int																		
NatWest																		
B & H																		
Sunday	2	2	0	41	40	20.50	-	-	-	-								

Career Performances

	M	Inns	NO	Runs	HS	Avge	100s	50s	Ct	St	Balls	Runs	Wkts	Avge	Best	5wl	10wM
Test																	
All First	69	122	8	3765	163	33.02	4	24	50	-		222	124	1	124.00	1-51	-	-
1-day Int																	
NatWest	3	3	0	116	92	38.66	-	1	1	-							
B & H	3	3	0	101	82	33.66	-	1	1	-							
Sunday	29	29	3	705	96	27.11	-	3	4	-							

TOLLEY, C. M.   Nottinghamshire

Name: Christopher Mark Tolley
Role: Right-hand bat, left-arm
medium bowler
Born: 30 December 1967, Kidderminster
Height: 5ft 9in **Weight:** 12st
Nickname: Red'uns
County debut: 1989 (Worcestershire), 1996
(Nottinghamshire)
County cap: 1993 (Worcestershire)
1st-Class 50s: 4
1st-Class 5 w. in innings: 1
1st-Class catches: 29
Place in batting averages: 194th av. 25.50
Place in bowling averages: 151st av. 57.42
Strike rate: 92.57 (career 75.30)
Parents: Ray and Liz
Marital status: Single
Family links with cricket: Brother Richard

plays in the Birmingham League for Stourbridge

Education: Oldswinford Primary School; Redhill Comprehensive School; King Edward VI College, Stourbridge; Loughborough University
Qualifications: 9 O-levels, 3 A-levels, BSc (Hons) PE Sports Science & Recreation Management. Qualified teacher status and level 2 hockey coach
Career outside cricket: Teaching
Off-season: 'Hopefully abroad'
Overseas tours: British Universities Sports Federation tour to Barbados October 1989; Worcestershire to Zimbabwe and South Africa
Cricketers particularly admired: Ian Botham, Richard Hadlee, Graeme Hick
Young players to look out for: Jamie Hart
Other sports followed: Hockey
Injuries: Side strain, out for one week
Relaxations: Food and wine
Extras: Played for English Schools U19 in 1986 and for the Combined Universities in B&H Cup. Asked to be released by Worcestershire at the end of the 1995 season and joined Nottinghamshire for the 1996 season
Best batting: 84 Worcestershire v Derbyshire, Derby 1994
Best bowling: 5-55 Worcestershire v Kent, Worcester 1993

1996 Season

	M	Inns	NO	Runs	HS	Avge	100s	50s	Ct	St	O	M	Runs	Wkts	Avge	Best	5wl	10wM
Test																		
All First	9	14	2	306	67	25.50	-	1	2	-	216	37	804	14	57.42	4-68	-	-
1-day Int																		
NatWest	1	1	0	16	16	16.00	-	-	-	-	9	0	55	1	55.00	1-55	-	
B & H	4	4	0	90	66	22.50	-	1	-	-	28	0	132	2	66.00	1-29	-	
Sunday	15	8	3	112	20 *	22.40	-	-	8	-	92	1	476	19	25.05	5-16	1	

Career Performances

	M	Inns	NO	Runs	HS	Avge	100s	50s	Ct	St	Balls	Runs	Wkts	Avge	Best	5wl	10wM
Test																	
All First	72	88	23	1411	84	21.70	-	4	29	-	8525	4267	110	38.79	5-55	1	-
1-day Int																	
NatWest	6	3	2	37	16	37.00	-	-	-	-	306	203	7	29.00	3-25	-	
B & H	17	14	1	293	77	22.53	-	3	3	-	822	529	8	66.12	1-12	-	
Sunday	49	24	8	172	30	10.75	-	-	16	-	1576	1288	47	27.40	5-16	1	

TRAINOR, N. J.   Gloucestershire

Name: Nicholas James Trainor
Role: Right-hand bat, off-spin bowler
Born: 29 June 1975, Gateshead
Height: 6ft 2in **Weight:** 14st
Nickname: Big Red, Geordie
County debut: 1996
1st-Class 50s: 2
1st-Class catches: 5
Place in batting averages: 234th av. 20.07
Parents: Eric and Anna-Maria
Marital status: Single
Family links with cricket: Father played
club cricket for Gateshead Fell CC
Education: St Peters Primary School; St
Edmund Campion Secondary School
Qualifications: 9 GCSEs, BTEC in Business
and Finance
Off-season: Playing club cricket in South
Africa
Overseas teams played for: Triangle Rovers CC, South Africa 1994-95; Zoo Lake
CC, South Africa 1995-97
Cricketers particularly admired: Courtney Walsh, Jack Russell, Geoffrey Boycott,
Jonty Rhodes, Dean Jones, Ian Botham, Michael Atherton, Robin Smith
Young players to look out for: Chris Silverwood, Gary Butcher, Rob Cunliffe,
Kamran Sheeraz
Other sports followed: Golf, football (Newcastle Utd), squash, tennis, swimming
Relaxations: Socialising with friends and family. Spending time with girlfriend
Best batting: 67 Gloucestershire v Surrey, Gloucester 1996

1996 Season

	M	Inns	NO	Runs	HS	Avge	100s	50s	Ct	St	O	M	Runs	Wkts	Avge	Best	5wI	10wM
Test																		
All First	8	14	1	261	67	20.07	-	2	5	-	1	0	4	0	-	-	-	-
1-day Int																		
NatWest	1	1	0	14	14	14.00	-	-	-	-								
B & H	1	1	0	25	25	25.00	-	-	-	-								
Sunday	1	1	0	20	20	20.00	-	-	-	-								

	M	Inns	NO	Runs	HS	Avge	100s	50s	Ct	St	Balls	Runs	Wkts	Avge	Best	5wI	10wM
Test																	
All First	8	14	1	261	67	20.07	-	2	5	-	6	4	0	-	-	-	-
1-day Int																	
NatWest	1	1	0	14	14	14.00	-	-	-	-							
B & H	1	1	0	25	25	25.00	-	-	-	-							
Sunday	1	1	0	20	20	20.00	-	-	-	-							

TREAGUS, G. R. Hampshire

Name: Glyn Robert Treagus
Role: Right-hand opening bat
Born: 10 December 1974, Rustington, Sussex
Height: 5ft 10in **Weight:** 11st 3lbs
Nickname: Arthur, Alien
County debut: No first-team appearance
Parents: Bob and Annette
Marital status: Single
Family links with cricket: 'Dad was offered a place on the county staff as a fast bowler but declined'
Education: Oakmount; King Edward VI, Southampton; Brighton University
Qualifications: 9 GCSEs, 2 A-levels, certificate of Higher Education
Off-season: Sales executive for polythene extrusion company
Overseas tours: King Edward VI tour to South Africa 1993; Hampshire 2nd XI to Denmark 1996
Overseas teams played for: Queenstown, South Africa 1995-96
Cricketers particularly admired: Robin Smith, Malcolm Marshall
Other sports followed: Hockey, tennis, golf, football
Injuries: Haemorrhaged retina after being hit in the eye, out for two weeks
Relaxations: Going out with friends, watching MTV
Extras: *Daily Telegraph* U19 Batting Award (National). NAYC U19 and NCA YC U19 team 1994. Development of Excellence U19 XI in 1994
Opinions on cricket: 'I think the game is in a good way at the moment.'

TREGO, S. M.   Somerset

Name: Samuel Marc Trego
Role: Right-hand bat, off-spin bowler
Born: 7 June 1977, Weston-Super-Mere
Height: 6ft 1in **Weight:** 14st 10lbs
Nickname: Village, Fat Boy
County debut: No first-team appearance
Parents: Paul and Carol
Marital status: Single
Family links with cricket: Brother Peter
plays for England U15 and Somerset U17
Education: Worle School, Weston-Super-
Mare
Qualifications: 4 GCSEs, qualified lifeguard,
NCA coaching award
Career outside cricket: Lifeguard
Off-season: Working and training
Overseas teams played for: Stockton CC,
NSW, Australia 1995-96
Cricketers particularly admired:
Ian Botham
Young players to look out for: Peter Trego, Anthony McGrath
Other sports followed: Football (Manchester United), golf, swimming
Injuries: None
Relaxations: Reading and watching videos
Extras: Played for England U18 against South Africa U19 in 1995. Was voted the
Woodspring Sportsman of the Year in 1995
Opinions on cricket: 'There should be more cricket academies (like the one at Somerset
CC) to encourage the development of younger players.'

83. Apart from the Headingley Test, where was Australia's
other nightmare loss in 1981, when they were dismissed
for 121 chasing 151 for victory?

TRESCOTHICK, M. E.   Somerset

Name: Marcus Edward Trescothick
Role: Left-hand bat, right-arm swing bowler, reserve wicket-keeper
Born: 25 December 1975, Keynsham, Bristol
Height: 6ft 3in **Weight:** 14st 7lbs
Nickname: Banger
County debut: 1993
1st-Class 50s: 11
1st-Class 100s: 4
1st-Class catches: 42
One-Day 100s: 2
Place in batting averages: 178th av. 27.69 (1995 215th av. 18.95)
Strike rate: (career 67.20)
Parents: Martyn and Lin
Marital status: Single
Family links with cricket: Father played for Somerset 2nd XI; uncle played club cricket

Education: Sir Bernard Lovell School
Qualifications: 7 GCSEs
Off-season: Working, training and playing golf
Overseas tours: England U18 to South Africa 1992-93; England U19 to Sri Lanka 1993-94, to West Indies (captain) 1994-95
Cricketers particularly admired: Neil Fairbrother, Graham Gooch, Mark Lathwell
Young players to look out for: Stephen Peters
Other sports followed: Golf, football
Relaxations: Playing golf, repairing and renovating cricket bats and listening to music
Extras: Member of England U19 squad for home series against West Indies 1993. Man of the Series against India U19 in 1994, scoring most runs in the series. Whittingdale Young Player of the Month, August 1994. Took a hat-trick against Young Australia in 1995. Scored more than 1000 runs for England U19
Opinions on cricket: 'There should be some sort of retainer contract.'
Best batting: 178 Somerset v Hampshire, Taunton 1996
Best bowling: 4-36 Somerset v Young Australia, Taunton 1995

---

84. Which England nightwatchman scored 95 in the fifth Test in Sydney in 1982-83?

1996 Season

	M	Inns	NO	Runs	HS	Avge	100s	50s	Ct	St	O	M	Runs	Wkts	Avge	Best	5wI	10wM
Test																		
All First	15	26	0	720	178	27.69	1	2	11	-	23	1	97	0	-	-	-	-
1-day Int																		
NatWest	1	1	0	15	15	15.00	-	-	1	-	3	0	28	0	-	-	-	
B & H	1	1	1	57	57 *	-	-	-	1	-								
Sunday	13	10	1	171	61 *	19.00	-	1	4	-	9	0	55	2	27.50	1-13	-	

Career Performances

	M	Inns	NO	Runs	HS	Avge	100s	50s	Ct	St	Balls	Runs	Wkts	Avge	Best	5wI	10wM
Test																	
All First	41	74	1	2075	178	28.42	4	11	42	-	336	240	5	48.00	4-36	-	-
1-day Int																	
NatWest	4	4	0	189	116	47.25	1	-	2	-	18	28	0	-	-	-	
B & H	7	7	1	266	122	44.33	1	2	5	-							
Sunday	36	33	1	655	74	20.46	-	3	11	-	54	55	2	27.50	1-13	-	

TRUMP, H. R. J.   Somerset

Name: Harvey Russell John Trump
Role: Right-hand bat, off-spin bowler, gully/slip fielder
Born: 11 October 1968, Taunton
Height: 6ft 1in **Weight:** 14st
Nickname: Trumpy, Club Foot
County debut: 1988
County cap: 1994
50 wickets in a season: 1
1st-Class 5 w. in innings: 9
1st-Class 10 w. in match: 2
1st-Class catches: 76
Place in batting averages: 233rd av. 17.25 (1994 223rd av. 17.25)
Place in bowling averages: 129th av. 43.62 (1994 87th av. 33.57)
Strike rate: 64.50 (career 78.79)
Parents: Gerald and Jackie
Marital status: Single
Family links with cricket: Father played for Somerset 2nd XI and captained Devon
Education: Millfield School; Chester College of Higher Education
Qualifications: 7 O-levels, 2 A-levels, BA (Hons)

Career outside cricket: Teaching at Stamford School, Lincolnshire
Overseas tours: England YC to Sri Lanka 1986-87, to Australia (Youth World Cup) 1987-88
Cricketers particularly admired: David Graveney, John Emburey, Viv Richards
Other sports followed: Hockey, rugby and most other sports
Relaxations: Theatre, cinema, crosswords, reading
Extras: Played county hockey for Somerset U19. Qualified lifeguard, attaining bronze medallion life-saving award, and is preliminary teacher of disabled swimming certificate. 'He's the best fielder off his own bowling I've ever seen' – David Graveney 1991
Best batting: 48 Somerset v Hampshire, Taunton 1988
Best bowling: 7-52 Somerset v Gloucestershire, Gloucester 1992

1996 Season

	M	Inns	NO	Runs	HS	Avge	100s	50s	Ct	St	O	M	Runs	Wkts	Avge	Best	5wI	10wM
Test																		
All First	3	2	1	0	0 *	0.00	-	-	3	-	43	10	179	4	44.75	3-43	-	-
1-day Int																		
NatWest	3	1	0	3	3	3.00	-	-	1	-	35	4	104	4	26.00	3-15	-	
B & H	5	1	0	10	10	10.00	-	-	4	-	40	1	191	4	47.75	3-28	-	
Sunday	16	4	2	30	14 *	15.00	-	-	7	-	123	4	634	23	27.56	3-28	-	

Career Performances

	M	Inns	NO	Runs	HS	Avge	100s	50s	Ct	St	Balls	Runs	Wkts	Avge	Best	5wI	10wM
Test																	
All First	107	121	41	991	48	12.38	-	-	76	-	19146	9424	243	38.78	7-52	9	2
1-day Int																	
NatWest	10	6	2	19	10 *	4.75	-	-	4	-	547	342	7	48.85	3-15	-	
B & H	18	7	1	24	11	4.00	-	-	7	-	900	588	18	32.66	3-17	-	
Sunday	88	27	14	131	19	10.07	-	-	32	-	3548	2767	78	35.47	3-19	-	

TUDOR, A. J.   Surrey

Name: Alexander Jeremy Tudor
Role: Right-hand bat, right-arm fast bowler
Born: 23 October 1977,
West Brompton, London
Height: 6ft 4in **Weight:** 13st 7lbs
Nickname: Big Al, Bambi, Tudes
County debut: 1995
1st-Class 50s: 1
1st-Class 5 w. innings: 1
1st-Class catches: 1

Place in batting averages: (1995 261st av. 13.66)

Place in bowling averages: (1995 21st av. 22.85)

Strike rate: 35.78 (career 35.78)

Parents: Daryll and Jennifer

Marital status: Single

Family links with cricket: Brother was on the staff at The Oval

Education: Wandle Primary, Earlsfield; St Mark's C of E, Fulham; City of Westminster College

Off-season: Touring Pakistan with England U19

Overseas tours: England U15 to South Africa 1992-93; England U19 to Zimbabwe 1995-96, to Pakistan 1996-97

Cricketers particularly admired: Curtly Ambrose, Brian Lara

Other sports followed: Basketball, football (QPR)

Relaxations: Listening to music

Extras: Played for London Schools at all ages from U8. Played for England U17 against India in 1994. MCC Young Cricketer. Had to return home from the England U19 tour to Zimbabwe in 1995-96 through injury and subsequently missed the majority of the 1996 season through injury. He toured Pakistan with England U19 during the off-season to play an important role in England's series win including a match haul of seven wickets in the decisive first 'Test' win

Best batting: 56 Surrey v Leicestershire, Leicester 1995

Best bowling : 5-32 Surrey v Derbyshire, Derby 1995

1996 Season (did not make any first-class or one-day appearances)

Career Performances

	M	Inns	NO	Runs	HS	Avge	100s	50s	Ct	St	Balls	Runs	Wkts	Avge	Best	5wl	10wM
Test																	
All First	5	9	0	123	56	13.66	-	1	1	-	501	320	14	22.85	5-32	1	-
1-day Int																	
NatWest	1	0	0	0	0	-	-	-	-	-	60	27	1	27.00	1-27	-	
B & H																	
Sunday	2	2	1	40	29 *	40.00	-	-	2	-	42	48	1	48.00	1-19	-	

TUFNELL, P. C. R.   Middlesex

Name: Philip Clive Roderick Tufnell
Role: Right-hand bat, slow left-arm spinner
Born: 29 April 1966, Hadley Wood,
Hertfordshire
Height: 6ft **Weight:** 12st 7lbs
Nickname: The Cat
County debut: 1986
County cap: 1990
Test debut: 1990-91
Tests: 22
One-Day Internationals: 19
50 wickets in a season: 6
1st-Class 50s: 1
1st-Class 5 w. in innings: 35
1st-Class 10 w. in match: 4
1st-Class catches: 82
One-Day 5 w. in innings: 1
Place in batting averages: 243rd av. 18.12
Place in bowling averages: 12th av. 21.94 (1995 16th av. 22.08)
Strike rate: 64.55 (career 71.66)
Parents: Sylvia and Alan
Marital status: Divorced
Education: Highgate School; Southgate School
Qualifications: O-level in Art; City & Guilds Silversmithing
Off-season: Touring Zimbabwe and New Zealand with England
Overseas tours: England YC to West Indies 1984-85; England to Australia 1990-91, to New Zealand and Australia (World Cup) 1991-92, to India and Sri Lanka 1992-93, to West Indies 1993-94, to Australia 1994-95, to Zimbabwe and New Zealand 1996-97
Overseas teams played for: Queensland University, Australia
Cricketers particularly admired: Jason Pooley
Other sports followed: American football
Relaxations: Sleeping
Extras: MCC Young Cricketer of the Year 1984 and Middlesex Uncapped Bowler of the Year 1987. Was originally a seam bowler and gave up cricket for three years in his mid-teens. Recalled to the England squad for the winter tours after an absence of two years
Best batting: 67* Middlesex v Worcestershire, Lord's 1996
Best bowling: 8-29 Middlesex v Glamorgan, Cardiff 1993

1996 Season

	M	Inns	NO	Runs	HS	Avge	100s	50s	Ct	St	O	M	Runs	Wkts	Avge	Best	5wI	10wM
Test																		
All First	18	26	10	290	67 *	18.12	-	1	7	-	839.1	273	1712	78	21.94	7-49	6	1
1-day Int																		
NatWest	2	0	0	0	0	-	-	-	1	-	24	5	66	2	33.00	2-22	-	
B & H	3	1	1	3	3 *	-	-	-	1	-	22.5	2	90	4	22.50	2-31	-	
Sunday	1	0	0	0	0	-	-	-	-	-	5	0	28	0	-	-	-	

Career Performances

	M	Inns	NO	Runs	HS	Avge	100s	50s	Ct	St	Balls	Runs	Wkts	Avge	Best	5wI	10wM
Test	22	32	17	62	22 *	4.13	-	-	10	-	6378	2671	68	39.27	7-47	4	1
All First	196	204	84	1275	67 *	10.62	-	1	82	-	48946	20275	683	29.68	8-29	35	4
1-day Int	19	10	9	15	5 *	15.00	-	-	3	-	960	676	15	45.06	3-40	-	
NatWest	8	1	0	8	8	8.00	-	-	4	-	570	323	10	32.30	3-29	-	
B & H	13	6	4	44	18	22.00	-	-	2	-	713	519	13	39.92	3-32	-	
Sunday	31	9	5	23	13 *	5.75	-	-	3	-	1296	961	40	24.02	5-28	1	

TURNER, R. J. — Somerset

Name: Robert Julian Turner
Role: Right-hand bat, wicket-keeper
Born: 25 November 1967, Worcestershire
Height: 6ft 2in **Weight:** 13st 9lbs
Nickname: Noddy, Sniper, Cymbols, Marcus
County debut: 1991
County cap: 1994
1st-Class 50s: 14
1st-Class 100s: 4
1st-Class catches: 221
1st-Class stumpings: 34
Place in batting averages: 148th av. 31.80
(1995 120th av. 31.17)
Parents: Derek Edward and Doris Lilian
Marital status: Single
Family links with cricket: Father is
chairman of Weston-Super-Mare CC.
Brothers Simon and Richard play for and
have both captained the club and Simon is the
current captain. Simon played for Somerset 1st XI as a wicket-keeper
Education: Uphill Primary School; Broadoak School, Weston-Super-Mare; Millfield
School; Magdalene College, Cambridge University

Qualifications: BEng (Hons) in Engineering, Diploma in Computer Science
Career outside cricket: Maths teacher at Stanbridge Earls School, Hampshire
Off-season: Either teaching or playing in South Africa
Overseas tours: Millfield School to Barbados, 1985; Combined Universities to Barbados 1989, to Kuala Lumpur, Malaysia 1992, to Qantas, Western Australia 1993
Overseas teams played for: Claremont-Nedlands, Perth, Western Australia 1991-93
Cricketers particularly admired: Mushtaq Ahmed 'inspirational', Stuart Turner 'determination', Andy Brassington
Other sports followed: Golf, swimming, football ('The Villa'), rugby union
Relaxations: 'Reading books and magazines, playing the guitar and the piano, golf, meeting friends for beers and curry'
Extras: Captain of Cambridge University (Blue 1988-91) and Combined Universities 1991. Capped at end of 1994 season. Equalled Somerset record of six catches in an innings in 1995 against West Indies and eight dismissals in a match against West Indies and Durham
Opinions on cricket: 'Overseas players bring excitement, charisma and quality to the English game, as well as inspiring their team mates. I would be very wary of getting rid of them.'
Best batting: 106* Somerset v Derbyshire, Derby 1995

1996 Season

	M	Inns	NO	Runs	HS	Avge	100s	50s	Ct	St	O	M	Runs	Wkts	Avge	Best	5wl	10wM
Test																		
All First	18	27	6	668	100 *	31.80	1	3	64	3	1	0	3	0	-	-	-	-
1-day Int																		
NatWest	3	2	1	61	40	61.00	-	-	7	1								
B & H	5	5	2	224	70	74.66	-	1	4	-								
Sunday	16	12	2	172	39	17.20	-	-	14	3								

Career Performances

	M	Inns	NO	Runs	HS	Avge	100s	50s	Ct	St	Balls	Runs	Wkts	Avge	Best	5wl	10wM
Test																	
All First	102	158	33	3362	106 *	26.89	4	14	221	34	19	29	0	-	-	-	-
1-day Int																	
NatWest	7	5	1	85	40	21.25	-	-	14	1							
B & H	16	14	7	346	70	49.42	-	1	15	1							
Sunday	49	40	16	518	39	21.58	-	-	44	9							

85. Who were the three members of England's 1989 fourth Test side who had signed for a rebel tour of South Africa, and were subsequently dropped for the final two Tests?

TWEATS, T. A.   Derbyshire

Name: Timothy Andrew Tweats
Role: Right-hand bat, off-spin bowler
Born: 18 April 1974, Stoke-on-Trent
Height: 6ft 3in **Weight:** 13st
County debut: 1992
1st-Class 50s: 3
1st-Class catches: 12
Place in batting averages: (1995 201st av.
20.53)
Strike rate: (career 70.00)
Parents: Malcolm and Linda
Marital status: Single
Family links with cricket: Father and two
brothers, Jon and Simon, play for the local
club, Leek, for whom he played before
joining Derbyshire
Education: Endon High School; Stoke-on-
Trent Sixth Form College; Staffordshire
University
Qualifications: 5 GCSEs, 2 A-levels
Career outside cricket: Student
Overseas tours: Kidsgrove and District Junior Cricket League to Australia 1991
Cricketers particularly admired: Robin Smith, Phil Tufnell
Other sports followed: Football
Best batting: 89* Derbyshire v Cambridge University, Fenner's 1996
Best bowling: 1-23 Derbyshire v Surrey, Derby 1995

1996 Season

	M	Inns	NO	Runs	HS	Avge	100s	50s	Ct	St	O	M	Runs	Wkts	Avge	Best	5wI	10wM
Test																		
All First	4	7	2	130	89 *	26.00	-	1	4	-	3	0	14	0	-	-	-	-
1-day Int																		
NatWest																		
B & H	2	1	0	10	10	10.00	-	-	-	-								
Sunday	1	1	0	0	0	0.00	-	-	-	-								

86. Which two debutants shared the new ball for England
in the Trent Bridge Test of 1993?

603

Career Performances

	M	Inns	NO	Runs	HS	Avge	100s	50s	Ct	St	Balls	Runs	Wkts	Avge	Best	5wI	10wM
Test																	
All First	13	24	3	462	89 *	22.00	-	3	12	-	280	208	4	52.00	1-23	-	-
1-day Int																	
NatWest	1	1	0	16	16	16.00	-	-	1	-							
B & H	2	1	0	10	10	10.00	-	-	-	-							
Sunday	10	6	1	60	19	12.00	-	-	7	-	24	27	0	-		-	-

UDAL, S. D. Hampshire

Name: Shaun David Udal
Role: Right-hand bat, off-spin bowler, 'field in the deep'
Born: 18 March 1969, Farnborough
Height: 6ft 3in **Weight:** 13st 6lbs
Nickname: Shaggy
County debut: 1989
County cap: 1992
One-Day Internationals: 10
50 wickets in a season: 4
1st-Class 50s: 12
1st-Class 5 w. in innings: 20
1st-Class 10 w. in match: 4
1st-Class catches: 57
Place in batting averages: 225th av. 21.28
(1995 203rd av. 20.48)
Place in bowling averages: 132nd av. 46.52
(1995 88th av. 33.89)
Strike rate: 87.82 (career 68.55)
Parents: Robin and Mary
Wife and date of marriage: Emma Jane, 5 October 1991
Children: Katherine Mary, 26 August 1992; Rebecca, 17 November 1995
Family links with cricket: Father played for Surrey Colts and Camberley for 42 years; brother plays for Camberley 1st XI. Grandfather played for Leicestershire and Middlesex
Education: Tower Hill Infant and Junior Schools; Cove Comprehensive School
Qualifications: 8 CSEs, qualified print finisher
Career outside cricket: Director of Omega Print Finishers
Off-season: 'Running my business, hopefully successfully'
Overseas tours: England to Australia 1994-95; England A to Pakistan 1995-96
Overseas teams played for: Hamilton Wickham, Newcastle, NSW 1990-91

Cricketers particularly admired: Ian Botham, John Emburey, Robin Smith
Young players to look out for: Jason Laney, Anthony McGrath
Other sports followed: Football ('Aldershot Town in their quest for the ICIS championship'), golf, snooker
Injuries: Side strain, but continued playing
Relaxations: 'No time due to appearances in Robin Smith's benefit year!'
Extras: Has taken two hat-tricks in club cricket, scored a double hundred in a 40-over club game and took 8-50 v Sussex in the first game of 1992 season, his seventh Championship match. Man of the Match on NatWest debut against Berkshire 1991 and named Hampshire Cricket Association Player of the Year 1993
Opinions on cricket: 'Four-day game only good. Still feel our England players encounter far too strenuous tours which don't allow enough recovery time or a chance to work on your game. too many ra-ra's in the game.'
Best batting: 94 Hampshire v Glamorgan, Southampton 1994
Best bowling: 8-50 Hampshire v Sussex, Southampton 1992

1996 Season

	M	Inns	NO	Runs	HS	Avge	100s	50s	Ct	St	O	M	Runs	Wkts	Avge	Best	5wl	10wM
Test																		
All First	17	25	4	447	58	21.28	-	2	12	-	497.4	101	1582	34	46.52	5-82	1	-
1-day Int																		
NatWest	3	3	1	27	18	13.50	-	-	2	-	33	2	119	4	29.75	2-46	-	
B & H	2	2	0	42	32	21.00	-	-	-	-	20	0	101	0	-	-	-	
Sunday	14	9	5	100	54	25.00	-	1	3	-	88.5	1	476	13	36.61	3-36	-	

Career Performances

	M	Inns	NO	Runs	HS	Avge	100s	50s	Ct	St	Balls	Runs	Wkts	Avge	Best	5wl	10wM
Test																	
All First	108	156	27	2752	94	21.33	-	12	57	-	22074	11124	322	34.54	8-50	20	4
1-day Int	10	6	4	35	11 *	17.50	-	-	1	-	570	372	8	46.50	2-37	-	
NatWest	15	6	2	57	18	14.25	-	-	6	-	990	552	19	29.05	3-39	-	
B & H	25	11	4	102	32	14.57	-	-	4	-	1560	982	33	29.75	4-40	-	
Sunday	94	55	20	455	54	13.00	-	1	28	-	4049	3427	102	33.59	4-51	-	

VANDRAU, M. J.   Derbyshire

Name: Matthew James Vandrau
Role: Right-hand bat, off-spin bowler
Born: 22 July 1969, Epsom, Surrey
Height: 6ft 4in **Weight:** 12st 8lbs
Nickname: Cat, Luther
County debut: 1993
1st-Class 50s: 4
1st-Class 5 w. in innings: 7
1st-Class 10 w. in match: 2
1st-Class catches: 28
Place in batting averages: 249th av. 17.50
Place in bowling averages: 142nd av. 49.31
Strike rate: 84.75 (career 63.67)
Parents: Bruce and Maureen
Marital status: Single
Family links with cricket: Father played for
Transvaal in 1963, was Director of Cricket
between 1976 and 1991 and is now Vice
President. Brother Kevin plays for Durham University
Education: Craighall Primary School, Johannesburg; St Stithians College; St Johns
College; University of Witwatersrand, Johannesburg
Qualifications: JMB Matriculation, 3 A-levels, Bachelor of Commerce degree
Off-season: Playing club cricket in South Africa
Overseas teams played for: South African Schools 1986; South African Universities
1990; Transvaal 1991-95
Cricketers particularly admired: Clive Rice, Kim Barnett
Young players to look out for: Zander Debruin
Other sports followed: Golf, rugby (Transvaal), football (West Ham)
Injuries: Torn cartilage in left knee, missed one week
Relaxations: Golf, game parks, red wine, music, braaiis
Best batting: 66 Derbyshire v Kent, Derby 1994
Best bowling: 6-34 Derbyshire v Hampshire, Southampton 1996

---

87. Which two players were out for 99 at Lord's in 1993?

1996 Season

	M	Inns	NO	Runs	HS	Avge	100s	50s	Ct	St	O	M	Runs	Wkts	Avge	Best	5wI	10wM
Test																		
All First	10	16	6	175	34 *	17.50	-	-	4	-	226	30	789	16	49.31	6-34	1	-
1-day Int																		
NatWest	3	2	0	7	4	3.50	-	-	-	-	21	7	73	2	36.50	1-20	-	
B & H	3	3	1	23	12 *	11.50	-	-	1	-	20	1	112	2	56.00	1-53	-	
Sunday	7	1	1	21	21 *	-	-	-	3	-	40	1	225	10	22.50	3-30	-	

Career Performances

	M	Inns	NO	Runs	HS	Avge	100s	50s	Ct	St	Balls	Runs	Wkts	Avge	Best	5wI	10wM
Test																	
All First	54	86	17	1381	66	20.01	-	4	28	-	8150	4258	128	33.26	6-34	7	2
1-day Int																	
NatWest	7	5	1	55	27	13.75	-	-	-	-	294	163	7	23.28	2-36	-	
B & H	4	3	1	23	12 *	11.50	-	-	1	-	186	158	3	52.66	1-46	-	
Sunday	23	10	4	159	32 *	26.50	-	-	10	-	795	737	20	36.85	3-25	-	

VAN TROOST, A. P.   Somerset

Name: Adrianus Pelrus van Troost
Role: Right-hand bat 'specialist no 11 batsman', right-arm fast bowler
Born: 2 October 1972, Schiedam, Holland
Height: 6ft 7in **Weight:** 15st
Nickname: Flappie, Rooster
County debut: 1991
1st-Class 5 w. in innings: 4
1st-Class catches: 9
One-Day 5 w. in innings: 1
Place in batting averages: 316th av. 4.50 (1995 278th av. 10.25)
Place in bowling averages: (1995 115th av. 39.00)
Strike rate: 71.66 (career 58.60)
Parents: Aad and Anneke
Marital status: Single
Family links with cricket: Father plays for Excelsior in Holland; brother plays for Excelsior and Holland U23; grandfather played for Excelsior and Holland
Education: Spieringshoek College, Schiedam
Qualifications: Finished Havo schooling – specialised in languages

Career outside cricket: Works in a bank

Off-season: 'Playing for Holland again after five years of qualifying for England. Playing for them in South Africa and at the ICC Trophy in Malaysia'

Overseas tours: Holland to Zimbabwe 1989, to Namibia 1990, to Dubai 1991, to Canada, New Zealand and South Africa 1992

Overseas teams played for: Excelsior, Holland 1979-91; Alma Marist, Cape Town 1992-93; Griqualand West, South Africa 1994-96

Cricketers particularly admired: Eric Van't Zelfde, J.J. Esmeyer ('the best arm in the world')

Young players to look out for: K. Oosterholt, Eric Van't Zelfde

Other sports followed: Football, tennis and most other sports

Injuries: Groin strain, missed four weeks

Relaxations: Playing football and travelling

Extras: Played for Holland at age 15 and became third Dutch national to play professional cricket. Took 6-3 v Durham 2nd XI in 1992 season

Opinions on cricket: 'The best game in the world if things are going your way. Unless you are born in Australia or South Africa, qualifying for England seems impossible. Why?'

Best batting: 35 Somerset v Lancashire, Taunton 1993

Best bowling: 6-48 Somerset v Essex, Taunton 1992

1996 Season

	M	Inns	NO	Runs	HS	Avge	100s	50s	Ct	St	O	M	Runs	Wkts	Avge	Best	5wI	10wM
Test																		
All First	6	8	2	27	11	4.50	-	-	-	-	107.3	13	485	9	53.88	4-90	-	-
1-day Int																		
NatWest																			
B & H																			
Sunday																			

Career Performances

	M	Inns	NO	Runs	HS	Avge	100s	50s	Ct	St	Balls	Runs	Wkts	Avge	Best	5wI	10wM
Test																	
All First	60	70	23	380	35	8.08	-	-	9	-	7267	4702	124	37.91	6-48	4	-
1-day Int																	
NatWest	7	3	1	27	17 *	13.50	-	-	-	-	366	274	12	22.83	5-22	1	
B & H	3	3	1	19	9 *	9.50	-	-	-	-	172	172	4	43.00	2-38	-	
Sunday	17	6	3	29	9 *	9.66	-	-	2	-	639	532	17	31.29	4-23	-	

VAUGHAN, M. P. Yorkshire

Name: Michael Paul Vaughan
Role: Right-hand bat, off-spin bowler
Born: 29 October 1974, Eccles, Manchester
Height: 6ft 2in **Weight:** 11st 7lbs
Nickname: Virgil, Frankie
County debut: 1993
County cap: 1995
1000 runs in a season: 3
1st-Class 50s: 20
1st-Class 100s: 7
1st-Class catches: 25
Place in batting averages: 81st av. 38.70
(1995 110th av. 32.73)
Place in bowling averages: 125th av. 42.82
(1995 120th av. 39.81)
Strike rate: 66.17 (career 78.07)
Parents: Graham John and Dee
Marital status: Single
Family links with cricket: Dad played for Worsley CC and mother is related to the famous Tyldesley family (Lancashire and England)
Education: St Marks, Worsley; Dore Juniors, Sheffield; Silverdale Comprehensive, Sheffield
Qualifications: 4 GCSEs
Off-season: Touring Australia with England A
Overseas tours: England U19 to India 1992-93, to Sri Lanka 1993-94; Yorkshire to West Indies 1994, to South Africa 1995, to Zimbabwe 1996; England A to India 1994-95, to Australia 1996-97
Cricketers particularly admired: Peter Hartley, Michael Slater, Alex Morris, Glenn Chapple
Other sports followed: Football (Sheffield Wednesday), golf, squash, tennis, snooker
Relaxations: Playing golf, skiing, shopping, going out with friends, following Wednesday
Extras: Played club cricket for Sheffield Collegiate in the Yorkshire League. *Daily Telegraph* U15 Batsman of the Year, 1990. Maurice Leyland Batting Award 1990. Rapid Cricketline Player of the Month, June 1993. The Cricket Society Most Promising Young Cricketer 1993. AA Thompson Memorial Trophy – The Roses Cricketer of the Year 1993. Whittingdale Cricketer of the Month, July 1994. Scored 1066 runs in first full season of first-class cricket in 1994. Captained England U19 in home series against India 1994. Awarded county cap at the end of the 1995 season
Best batting: 183 Yorkshire v Glamorgan, Cardiff 1996
Best bowling: 4-39 Yorkshire v Oxford University, The Parks 1994

1996 Season

	M	Inns	NO	Runs	HS	Avge	100s	50s	Ct	St	O	M	Runs	Wkts	Avge	Best	5wI	10wM
Test																		
All First	18	32	2	1161	183	38.70	3	6	4	-	187.3	28	728	17	42.82	4-62	-	-
1-day Int																		
NatWest	4	4	0	87	64	21.75	-	1	2	-								
B & H	6	6	0	211	60	35.16	-	2	3	-	8	1	34	1	34.00	1-22	-	
Sunday	17	17	2	439	71*	29.26	-	2	4	-	1	0	13	0	-	-	-	

Career Performances

	M	Inns	NO	Runs	HS	Avge	100s	50s	Ct	St	Balls	Runs	Wkts	Avge	Best	5wI	10wM
Test																	
All First	62	114	4	3805	183	34.59	7	20	25	-	4372	2446	56	43.67	4-39	-	-
1-day Int																	
NatWest	10	10	0	163	64	16.30	-	1	2	-							
B & H	10	10	1	298	60	33.11	-	3	4	-	66	47	1	47.00	1-22	-	
Sunday	36	35	3	718	71*	22.43	-	2	7	-	42	44	0	-	-	-	

WAGH, M. A.   Warwickshire

Name: Mark Anant Wagh
Role: Right-hand bat, off-spin bowler
Born: 20 October 1976, Birmingham
Height: 6ft 2in **Weight:** 12st 7lbs
Nickname: Waggy
County debut: No first-team appearance
1st-Class catches: 4
Place in batting averages: 236th av. 19.80
Place in bowling averages: 155th av. 63.20
Strike rate: (career 112.50)
Parents: Mohan and Rita
Marital status: Single
Education: Harborne Junior School; King
Edward's School, Birmingham; Keble
College, Oxford
Qualifications: 12 GCSEs, 4 A-levels, basic
coaching
Off-season: At university
Overseas tours: Warwickshire U19 to South Africa 1992
Cricketers particularly admired: Carl Hooper, Brian Lara, David Gower, Daryll
Cullinan
Other sports followed: Hockey, snooker, football
Relaxations: Snooker and going out with friends

610

Best batting: 43 Oxford University v Hampshire, The Parks 1996
Best bowling: 3-82 Oxford University v Glamorgan, The Parks 1996

1996 Season

	M	Inns	NO	Runs	HS	Avge	100s	50s	Ct	St	O	M	Runs	Wkts	Avge	Best	5wl	10wM
Test																		
All First	11	13	3	198	43	19.80	-	-	4	-	187.3	31	632	10	63.20	3-82	-	-
1-day Int																		
NatWest																		
B & H	2	2	0	29	23	14.50	-	-	-	-	20	2	80	2	40.00	1-39	-	
Sunday																		

Career Performances

	M	Inns	NO	Runs	HS	Avge	100s	50s	Ct	St	Balls	Runs	Wkts	Avge	Best	5wl	10wM
Test																	
All First	11	13	3	198	43	19.80	-	-	4	-	1125	632	10	63.20	3-82	-	-
1-day Int																	
NatWest																	
B & H	2	2	0	29	23	14.50	-	-	-	-	120	80	2	40.00	1-39	-	
Sunday																	

WALKER, A.   Durham

Name: Alan Walker
Role: Left-hand bat, right-arm
medium-fast bowler
Born: 7 July 1962, Emley, near Huddersfield
Height: 5ft 11in **Weight:** 13st 7lbs
Nickname: Wacky, Walks
County debut: 1983 (Northants), 1994
(Durham)
County cap: 1987 (Northants)
1st-Class 5 w. in innings: 4
1st-Class 10 w. in match: 1
1st-Class catches: 39
Place in bowling averages: (1995 78th av.
30.90)
Strike rate: 240.00 (career 62.27)
Parents: Malcolm and Enid
Wife and date of marriage: Nicky, 2
October 1994
Children: Jessica, 3 March 1988

Family links with cricket: Grandfather played in local league
Education: Emley Junior School; Kirkburton Middle School; Shelley High School
Qualifications: 2 O-levels, 4 CSEs, qualified coal-face worker
Career outside cricket: Mining, building, coaching
Off-season: Landscape gardening
Overseas tours: NCA North U19 to Denmark; Northamptonshire to Durban
Overseas teams played for: Uitenhage, South Africa 1984-85 and 1987-88; Sunshine, Melbourne 1994-95
Cricketers particularly admired: Dennis Lillee, Richard Hadlee, Jeremy Snape 'for his ability to see the funny side of things when things are not going well'
Other sports followed: Football (Huddersfield Town and Emley), rugby league (Wakefield Trinity)
Injuries: Broken toe, out for ten days
Relaxations: DIY, drinking, gardening
Extras: Recorded best bowling and match figures by a Durham bowler in 1995 (eight for 118 and 14 for 177)
Best batting: 41* Northamptonshire v Warwickshire, Edgbaston 1987
Best bowling: 8-118 Durham v Essex, Chester-le-Street 1995

1996 Season

	M	Inns	NO	Runs	HS	Avge	100s	50s	Ct	St	O	M	Runs	Wkts	Avge	Best	5wI	10wM
Test																		
All First	3	6	3	25	20	8.33	-	-	-	-	80	13	277	2	138.50	1-50	-	-
1-day Int																		
NatWest	1	1	0	5	5	5.00	-	-	-	-	12	2	58	2	29.00	2-58	-	
B & H																		
Sunday	9	2	0	4	3	2.00	-	-	1	-	59.3	0	317	9	35.22	3-31	-	

Career Performances

	M	Inns	NO	Runs	HS	Avge	100s	50s	Ct	St	Balls	Runs	Wkts	Avge	Best	5wI	10wM
Test																	
All First	115	120	53	825	41 *	12.31	-	-	43	-	16503	8553	265	32.27	8-118	4	1
1-day Int																	
NatWest	21	7	1	52	13	8.66	-	-	5	-	1252	738	24	30.75	4-7	-	
B & H	33	15	10	52	15 *	10.40	-	-	7	-	1733	1259	39	32.28	4-42	-	
Sunday	134	39	16	253	30	11.00	-	-	30	-	5520	4347	154	28.22	4-21	-	

WALKER, L. N.   Nottinghamshire

Name: Lyndsay Nicholas Walker
Role: Right-hand bat, wicket-keeper
Born: 22 June 1974, Armidale, Australia
Height: 6ft 1in **Weight:** 12st 9lbs
Nickname: Max
County debut: 1994
1st-Class catches: 18
1st-Class stumpings: 3
Parents: Graham (deceased) and Barbara
Wife and date of marriage: Laurie, 17 June 1994
Children: Guy, 12 September 1995; another expected 10 April 1997
Family links with cricket: 'Dad and brother played good level of grade cricket in Australia. Mum was a great encouragement. My dog turns out in benefit games'
Education: Garden Suburb Primary School; Cardiff High School, New South Wales, Australia
Qualifications: High School Certificate, senior coaching certificate
Career outside cricket: 'Building, coaching, learning more in my journey for the Lord Jesus'
Off-season: Coaching and training at Trent Bridge. 'Going into schools and churches and sharing the experience of my faith in Jesus'
Overseas teams played for: Wallsend, Newcastle, Australia 1987-93; Johore, Malaysia 1993-94
Cricketers particularly admired: Mark Waugh, Bruce French, Allan Border, Alec Stewart, Shane Warne, Ian Healy
Other sports followed: Rugby league (Newcastle Knights), golf
Injuries: Ligament in thumb, missed six weeks
Relaxations: 'Anything to do with the Lord Jesus. Relaxing and spending time with my wife, son and dog'
Extras: Equalled the record for Nottinghamshire's most dismissals in an innings in 1996
Opinions on cricket: 'A great game but falling behind the times. One league, eight teams. The six Test grounds plus the two next best grounds. Therefore the best would be playing the best of this country. Need a Mr Packer or Mr Murdoch to invest millions, so that each ground had day/night cricket. These changes need to be made now, or cricket will never be able to attract the interest it deserves.'
Best batting: 36 Nottinghamshire v Northamptonshire, Trent Bridge 1996

1996 Season

	M	Inns	NO	Runs	HS	Avge	100s	50s	Ct	St	O	M	Runs	Wkts	Avge	Best	5wI	10wM
Test																		
All First	6	6	1	93	36	18.60	-	-	16	2								
1-day Int																		
NatWest	1	1	0	1	1	1.00	-	-	-	-								
B & H																		
Sunday																		

Career Performances

	M	Inns	NO	Runs	HS	Avge	100s	50s	Ct	St	Balls	Runs	Wkts	Avge	Best	5wI	10wM
Test																	
All First	8	10	1	136	36	15.11	-	-	18	3							
1-day Int																	
NatWest	1	1	0	1	1	1.00	-	-	-	-							
B & H																	
Sunday																	

WALKER, M. J.   Kent

Name: Matthew Jonathan Walker
Role: Left-hand bat, occasional right-arm medium bowler
Born: 2 January 1974, Gravesend, Kent
Height: 5ft 6in **Weight:** 13st
Nickname: Walkdog
County debut: 1992-93
1st-Class 50s: 3
1st-Class 100s: 2
1st-Class 200s: 1
1st-Class catches: 10
Place in batting averages: 13th av. 60.60 (1995 268th av. 12.46)
Parents: Richard and June
Marital status: Single
Family links with cricket: Grandfather played for Kent as a wicket-keeper and father was on Lord's groundstaff, having played for Middlesex and Kent 2nd XI
Education: Shorne Primary School; King's School, Rochester
Qualifications: 9 GCSEs, 2 A-levels, coaching certificates
Career outside cricket: 'Yet to be decided'

Off-season: Coaching hockey at King's School, Rochester. 'Winter tour to Dublin for Martin McCague's Stag Party XI'

Overseas tours: Kent U17 to New Zealand 1991; England U19 to Pakistan 1991-92, to India 1992-93; Kent to Zimbabwe 1992-93

Cricketers particularly admired: Aravinda De Silva, Carl Hooper

Young players to look out for: Eddie Stanford, Robert Key

Other sports followed: Rugby, hockey, skiing, football

Injuries: Lower back strain, out for two weeks

Relaxations: Music, watching films; 'like old pubs'

Extras: Captained England U15, U16 and U17 at hockey; represented Kent U18 at rugby; had football trials with Chelsea and Gillingham. Captained England U19 tour to India 1992-93 and v West Indies in 1993 home series which England U19 won 2-0 in one-day matches and 1-0 in 'Test' series. Received Sir Jack Hobbs award for best young cricketer 1989, and *Daily Telegraph* U15 batting award 1989. Selected for Kent U21 hockey team in 1993 and 1994. Woolwich Kent League's Young Cricketer of the Year 1994. Scored 275 not out against Somerset in 1996 – the highest ever individual score by a Kent batsman at Canterbury

Opinions on cricket: 'It's magnificent. I love the game and everything that goes with it.'

Best batting: 275* Kent v Somerset, Canterbury 1996

1996 Season

	M	Inns	NO	Runs	HS	Avge	100s	50s	Ct	St	O	M	Runs	Wkts	Avge	Best	5wI	10wM
Test																		
All First	8	13	3	606	275 *	60.60	1	2	2	-	1	0	19	0	-	-	-	-
1-day Int																		
NatWest	2	2	1	92	51	92.00	-	1	-	-								
B & H	6	6	1	139	41	27.80	-	-	2	-								
Sunday	16	15	3	169	27	14.08	-	-	4	-								

Career Performances

	M	Inns	NO	Runs	HS	Avge	100s	50s	Ct	St	Balls	Runs	Wkts	Avge	Best	5wI	10wM
Test																		
All First	23	36	5	1046	275 *	33.74	2	3	12	-	6	19	0	-	-	-	-
1-day Int																		
NatWest	2	2	1	92	51	92.00	-	1	-	-								
B & H	11	10	2	276	69 *	34.50	-	1	5	-								
Sunday	34	32	6	433	69 *	16.65	-	1	10	-								

WALSH, C. A.   Gloucestershire

Name: Courtney Andrew Walsh
Role: Right-hand bat, right-arm fast bowler
Born: 30 October 1962, Kingston, Jamaica
Height: 6ft 5½in **Weight:** 14st 7lbs
Nickname: Mark, Walshy, Cuddy, RP
County debut: 1984
County cap: 1985
Test debut: 1984-85
Tests: 82
One-Day Internationals: 162
50 wickets in a season: 9
100 wickets in a season: 1
1st-Class 50s: 8
1st-Class 5 w. in innings: 82
1st-Class 10 w. in match: 16
1st-Class catches: 89
One-Day 5 w. in innings: 3
Place in batting averages: 272nd av. 14.00
(1995 276th av. 11.10)
Place in bowling averages: 4th av. 16.84 (1995 58th av. 28.82)
Strike rate: 37.16 (career 46.55)
Parents: Eric and Joan
Marital status: Single
Education: Excelsior High School
Qualifications: GCE and CXL
Overseas tours: West Indies YC to England 1982; West Indies B to Zimbabwe 1983-84; West Indies to England 1984, to Australia 1984-85, to Pakistan, Australia and New Zealand 1986-87, to India and Pakistan (World Cup) 1987-88, to England 1988, to Australia 1988-89, to Pakistan 1990-91, to England 1991, to Australia and South Africa 1992-93, to Sharjah, India (Hero Cup) and Sri Lanka 1993-94, to India and New Zealand 1994-95, to Australia 1995-96, to India and Pakistan (World Cup) 1996, to Australia 1996-97
Overseas teams played for: Jamaica 1981-97
Relaxations: Swimming, reading and listening to music
Extras: Took record 10-43 in Jamaican school cricket in 1979. On tour, he has a reputation as an insatiable collector of souvenirs. David Graveney, when captaining Gloucestershire, reckoned Walsh was the 'best old-ball bowler in the world'. One of *Wisden*'s Five Cricketers of the Year 1986. Took hat-trick for West Indies v Australia in 1988-89. Captain of Jamaica 1991-92 and 1993-94. Cricketers' Association Player of the Year and Wombwell Cricket Lovers' Cricketer of the Year 1993. Took over captaincy of West Indies from Richie Richardson for Test series against India and New Zealand in

1994-95 and took full control in 1996. Was the leading wicket-taker in first-class cricket in 1996 with 85 wickets. Commitments with the West Indies side will prevent him from playing for Gloucestershire in the 1997 season

Opinions on cricket: 'Watch the changes.'

Best batting: 66 Gloucestershire v Kent, Cheltenham 1994

Best bowling: 9-72 Gloucestershire v Somerset, Bristol 1986

1996 Season

	M	Inns	NO	Runs	HS	Avge	100s	50s	Ct	St	O	M	Runs	Wkts	Avge	Best	5wI	10wM
Test																		
All First	15	24	13	154	25	14.00	-	-	7	-	526.3	145	1432	85	16.84	6-22	7	1
1-day Int																		
NatWest	2	2	0	0	0	0.00	-	-	-	-	16	3	64	1	64.00	1-23	-	
B & H	2	2	1	27	21 *	27.00	-	-	1	-	18.4	2	74	2	37.00	1-33	-	
Sunday	9	5	1	52	38	13.00	-	-	3	-	57.4	5	277	8	34.62	2-17	-	

Career Performances

	M	Inns	NO	Runs	HS	Avge	100s	50s	Ct	St	Balls	Runs	Wkts	Avge	Best	5wI	10wM
Test	82	108	32	712	30 *	9.36	-	-	12	-	17578	7739	309	25.04	7-37	11	2
All First	339	429	105	4020	66	12.40	-	8	89	-	65357	31023	1404	22.09	9-72	82	16
1-day Int	162	60	25	278	30	7.94	-	-	24	-	8554	5484	182	30.13	5-1	1	
NatWest	21	14	3	136	37	12.36	-	-	2	-	1314	712	42	16.95	6-21	2	
B & H	23	15	5	114	28	11.40	-	-	1	-	1367	819	26	31.50	2-19	-	
Sunday	109	69	11	545	38	9.39	-	-	23	-	4436	3002	143	20.99	4-19	-	

88. Four batsmen have scored triple centuries in Ashes Tests. Who were they?

WALSH, C. D.   Kent

Name: Christopher David Walsh
Role: Right-hand bat, leg-spin bowler
Born: 6 November 1975
Height: 6ft 1in **Weight:** 12st 7lbs
Nickname: Courtney, Spaceman
County debut: 1996
1st-Class 50s: 1
1st-Class catches: 2
Parents: David Robert and Carol Susan
Family links with cricket: Father played for
Oxford University 1967-69
Education: Yardley Court Prep School;
Tonbridge School; Exeter University
Qualifications: 11 GCSEs, 4 A-levels, 2AO-
levels, 2 S-levels
Off-season: Law student at Exeter University
Overseas tours: Tonbridge School to South
Africa 1992-93
Overseas teams played for: Swanbourne CC, Perth, Australia
Cricketers particularly admired: David Gower, Trevor Ward, Michael Atherton
Other sports followed: Hockey (University XI), Rackets (British U21 finalist),
squash, football (Tottenham Hotspur), Aussie rules (West Coast Eagles)
Relaxations: Cinema, skiing, listening to music, travelling
Extras: Scored three centuries in first 2nd XI championship season in 1995. *Daily
Telegraph* Batting Award in 1994. Woolwich Kent League Young Player of the Year in
1995. Kent CCC Blue Circle Award for The Most Improved Uncapped Player in 1995.
Member of the Kent U19 side which won the Hilda Overy Trophy at the
Oxford/Cambridge Festival in 1995
Opinions on cricket: 'Too much reluctance in the English game to throw young players
into high-pressure situations or matches. University cricket is in great need of re-
structuring (especially a need for better facilities) and more financial support needed.'
Best batting: 56* Kent v Oxford University, Canterbury 1996

1996 Season

	M	Inns	NO	Runs	HS	Avge	100s	50s	Ct	St	O	M	Runs	Wkts	Avge	Best	5wI	10wM
Test																		
All First	1	1	1	56	56*	-	-	1	2	-	12	0	64	0	-		-	--
1-day Int																		
NatWest																		
B & H																		
Sunday	1	1	0	0	0	0.00	-	-	-	-	8	3	20	1	20.00	1-20	-	

Career Performances

	M	Inns	NO	Runs	HS	Avge	100s	50s	Ct	St	Balls	Runs	Wkts	Avge	Best	5wI	10wM
Test																	
All First	1	1	1	56	56 *	-	-	1	2	-	72	64	0	-	-	-	-
1-day Int																	
NatWest																	
B & H																	
Sunday	1	1	0	0	0	0.00	-	-	-	-	48	20	1	20.00	1-20	-	

WALTON, T. C.   Northamptonshire

Name: Timothy Charles Walton
Role: Right-hand bat, right-arm
medium bowler
Born: 8 November 1972, Low Lead
Height: 6ft **Weight:** 12st 10lbs
Nickname: TC, Eric Spadge
County debut: 1992 (one-day),
1994 (first-class)
1st-Class 50s: 1
1st-Class catches: 2
Place in batting averages: 128th av. 33.55
(1995 230th av. 17.33)
Strike rate: 87.00 (career 85.50)
Parents: Alan Michael and Sally Ann
Marital status: single
Family links with cricket: Father and two
brothers, Jamie and Adam, play for local
village
Education: Leeds Grammar School;
University of Northumbria, Newcastle
Qualifications: 7 GCSEs, 3 A-levels, studying for Sports degree
Career outside cricket: Student
Overseas tours: England U19 to Pakistan 1991-92
Cricketers particularly admired: Phillip DeFreitas
Other sports followed: Rugby union and league
Relaxations: Running, raving and listening to music
Opinions on cricket: 'Appearance should be irrelevant if the cricketer is good enough,
i.e. long hair should be of no consequence. More commerciality and one-day games.'
Best batting: 71 Northamptonshire v Somerset, Taunton 1995
Best bowling: 1-26 Northamptonshire v Kent, Northampton 1994

1996 Season

	M	Inns	NO	Runs	HS	Avge	100s	50s	Ct	St	O	M	Runs	Wkts	Avge	Best	5wI	10wM
Test																		
All First	6	10	1	302	58	33.55	-	4	2	-	29	2	113	2	56.50	1-26	--	
1-day Int																		
NatWest	1	0	0	0	0	-	-	-	-	-								
B & H	3	2	1	98	70 *	98.00	-	1	-	-								
Sunday	14	11	3	167	40	20.87	-	-	1	-								

Career Performances

	M	Inns	NO	Runs	HS	Avge	100s	50s	Ct	St	Balls	Runs	Wkts	Avge	Best	5wI	10wM
Test																	
All First	12	19	2	422	71	24.82	-	5	4	-	342	237	4	59.25	1-26	-	-
1-day Int																	
NatWest	1	0	0	0	0	-	-	-	-	-							
B & H	5	4	1	133	70 *	44.33	-	1	1	-	36	27	1	27.00	1-27		
Sunday	34	29	5	658	72	27.41	-	4	11	-	240	197	6	32.83	2-27	-	

WAQAR YOUNIS   Glamorgan

Name: Waqar Younis
Role: Right-hand bat, right-arm fast bowler
Born: 16 November 1971, Vehari, Pakistan
Height: 5ft 11in **Weight:** 12st
Nickname: Wicky
County debut: 1990 (Surrey)
County cap: 1990 (Surrey)
Test debut: 1989-90
Tests: 41
One-Day Internationals: 128
50 wickets in a season: 3
1st-Class 5 w. in innings: 51
1st-Class 10 w. in match: 12
1st-Class catches: 33
One-Day 5 w. in innings: 9
Place in bowling averages: 10th av. 21.80
Strike rate: 39.03 (career 38.90)
Marital status: Single
Education: Pakistani College, Sharjah;
Government College, Vehari
Off-season: Playing for Pakistan
Overseas tours: Pakistan to India, Australia and Sharjah 1989-90, to England 1992, to

New Zealand, Australia, South Africa and West Indies 1992-93, to Sharjah 1993-94, to New Zealand 1993-94, to South Africa 1994-95, to Pakistan and India (World Cup) 1995-96, to England 1996, to New Zealand and Australia 1996-97
Overseas teams played for: United Bank, Pakistan
Cricketers particularly admired: Imran Khan, Wasim Akram, Geoff Arnold, Alec Stewart
Other sports followed: Football, badminton, squash
Relaxations: 'Sleeping and family get-togethers'
Extras: Made Test debut for Pakistan against India aged 17, taking 4 for 80 at Karachi. Signed by Surrey during the 1990 season on recommendation of Imran Khan who had first seen him bowling on television, and made his county debut in the quarter-final of the B&H Cup. Martin Crowe described his bowling during Pakistan's series with New Zealand as the best display of fast bowling he had ever seen. Named Cricketers' Association Cricketer of the Year 1991 and one of *Wisden*'s Cricketers of the Year in 1992. He has joined Glamorgan on a two-year contract from 1997
Opinions on cricket: 'There should be no over-rate fines'
Best batting: 55 Pakistan v Natal, Durban 1994-95
Best bowling: 7-64 United Bank v ADPB, Lahore 1990-91

1996 Season

	M	Inns	NO	Runs	HS	Avge	100s	50s	Ct	St	O	M	Runs	Wkts	Avge	Best	5wI	10wM
Test	3	3	1	11	7	5.50	-	-	1	-	125	25	431	16	26.93	4-69	--	
All First	7	7	2	19	8	3.80	-	-	2	-	195.1	42	654	30	21.80	5-42	1-	
1-day Int	3	2	1	4	4	4.00	-	-	-	-	26	1	131	4	32.75	2-49	-	
NatWest																		
B & H																		
Sunday																		

Career Performances

	M	Inns	NO	Runs	HS	Avge	100s	50s	Ct	St	Balls	Runs	Wkts	Avge	Best	5wI	10wM
Test	41	53	11	403	34	9.59	-	-	6	-	8483	4553	216	21.07	7-76	19	4
All First	132	147	40	1368	55	12.78	-	2	34	-	23877	12659	609	20.78	7-64	51	12
1-day Int	128	59	21	360	37	9.47	-	-	13	-	6408	4832	217	22.26	6-26	7	
NatWest	9	3	0	33	26	11.00	-	-	1	-	601	354	25	14.16	5-40	1	
B & H	6	5	2	15	5 *	5.00	-	-	1	-	341	222	8	27.75	3-29	-	
Sunday	40	16	4	104	39	8.66	-	-	7	-	1854	1298	78	16.64	5-26	1	

89. Who was the first England player to score a century in his first Ashes Test?

WARD, D. M.   Surrey

Name: David Mark Ward
Role: Right-hand bat, right-arm off-spin
bowler, occasional wicket-keeper
Born: 10 February 1961, Croydon
Height: 6ft 1in **Weight:** 'Fat'
Nickname: Cocker, Wardy, Jaws, Gnasher,
Fat Boy, Piano Man
County debut: 1985
County cap: 1990
1000 runs in a season: 2
1st-Class 50s: 32
1st-Class 100s: 16
1st-Class 200s: 3
1st-Class catches: 118
1st-Class stumpings: 3
One-Day 100s: 3
Strike rate: (career 53.50)
Parents: Tom and Dora
Wife and date of marriage: Ruth, 2 October
1993
Family links with cricket: 'Uncle (John Goodey) local legend with Banstead and
Temple Bar CC'
Education: Haling Manor High School; Croydon Technical College
Qualifications: 2 O-levels, Advanced City & Guilds in Carpentry and Joinery
Career outside cricket: Mortgage expert (Home Owners Advisory Service) and
carpenter
Off-season: 'Closing down benefit year and then a long holiday'
Overseas tours: Surrey to Barbados 1984, 1989, 1991; Lancashire to Mombasa 1990;
MCC to Bahrain 1994-95; England VI to Hong Kong 1996
Overseas teams played for: Caulfield, Melbourne 1984-87; Sunshine, Melbourne
1988-89; Perth, Western Australia 1990-91; St Augustine, Cape Town 1992-93
Cricketers particularly admired: Adam Hollioake, Graham Thorpe, Joey Benjamin,
Ian Austin, Andy Pick and Roger Thompson (Whalers Inn XI, Adelaide)
Young players to look out for: Ben Hollioake, Alex Morris ('both will be legends')
Other sports followed: Greyhound racing
Injuries: 'Selectionitis – apparently this affects your ability to play four-day cricket –
for most of the season'
Extras: In 1990 became first Surrey batsman since John Edrich to score 2000 runs in a
season and shared county record stand of 413 for third wicket with Darren Bicknell v
Kent at Canterbury. Hit century in 70 minutes for Surrey v Northamptonshire 1992.
Scored 294 not out against Derbyshire in 1994. Hit 44 off one over against Durham

University in 1995. Scored 108 against Durham in the Sunday League off 58 balls, the second 50 coming off just 13 balls. Released by Surrey at the end of the 1996 season
Opinions on cricket: 'Allow players to express themselves in their own way, we are all different people and characters. Play your own way.'
Best batting: 294* Surrey v Derbyshire, The Oval 1994
Best bowling: 2-66 Surrey v Gloucestershire, Guildford 1991

1996 Season

	M	Inns	NO	Runs	HS	Avge	100s	50s	Ct	St	O	M	Runs	Wkts	Avge	Best	5wI	10wM
Test																		
All First	2	4	1	81	64 *	27.00	-	1	2	-								
1-day Int																		
NatWest	2	2	0	27	20	13.50	-	-	1	-								
B & H	5	5	0	105	32	21.00	-	-	1	-								
Sunday	11	10	1	301	112	33.44	2	-	9	-								

Career Performances

	M	Inns	NO	Runs	HS	Avge	100s	50s	Ct	St	Balls	Runs	Wkts	Avge	Best	5wI	10wM
Test																	
All First	155	244	34	8078	294 *	38.46	16	32	120	3	107	113	2	56.50	2-66	-	-
1-day Int																	
NatWest	23	19	1	643	101 *	35.72	1	5	9	-							
B & H	39	35	6	778	73	26.82	-	4	13	2							
Sunday	160	142	23	3572	112	30.01	4	21	76	1							

Name: Ian Jerome Ward
Role: Left-hand bat, right-arm
medium bowler
Born: 20 September 1973, Guildford
Height: 5ft 8in **Weight:** 14st
Nickname: Stumpy, The Chimp, The Gnome,
Son of the Baboon, The All-American Kid
County debut: 1996
1st-Class catches: 1
Parents: Tony and Mary
Marital status: Single
Family links with cricket: Dad was a good
umpire and wicket-keeper
Education: Ripley Primary School; Millfield
School; 'Ben Holliolake's School of Life'
Qualifications: NCA coaching award and
'some A-levels'
Career outside cricket: 'Sloane No.1 of
White Horse'
Off-season: Playing for North Perth in Western Australia
Overseas tours: Surrey U19 to Barbados 1990; Millfield to Barbados 1991; Malden
Wanderers to Jersey 1994
Overseas teams played for: North Perth CC, Western Australia 1996-97
Cricketers particularly admired: Gregor Kennis, Ben Holliolake, Graham Thorpe
Young players to look out for: Ben Holliolake, Gregor Kennis, Richard Nowell
Other sports followed: Rugby, basketball, three-day eventing (The Olympic
equestrian squad)
Injuries: Hamstring, back, knee, ankle, wrist, out for one game 'but should have been
half a season according to medical advice'
Relaxations: Doing lunch
Extras: Surrey 2nd XI cap at the age of 23
Opinions on cricket: 'I'm just glad to be getting a second bite of the cherry. Better
filling in of footholes by groundsmen should be monitored.'
Best batting: 15 Surrey v South Africa A, The Oval 1996

90. Which English player scored four Test double centuries against Australia?

1996 Season

	M	Inns	NO	Runs	HS	Avge	100s	50s	Ct	St	O	M	Runs	Wkts	Avge	Best	5wl	10wM
Test																		
All First	1	2	0	19	15	9.50	-	-	-	-	9	2	49	0	-		-	-
1-day Int																		
NatWest	1	1	0	14	14	14.00	-	-	-	-								
B & H																		
Sunday	3	2	1	2	1 *	2.00	-	-	1	-	3.5	0	41	0	-		-	-

Career Performances

	M	Inns	NO	Runs	HS	Avge	100s	50s	Ct	St	Balls	Runs	Wkts	Avge	Best	5wl	10wM
Test																	
All First	2	3	0	19	15	6.33	-	-	1	-	102	84	0	-	-	-	-
1-day Int																	
NatWest	1	1	0	14	14	14.00	-	-	-	-							
B & H																	
Sunday	3	2	1	2	1 *	2.00	-	-	1	-	23	41	0	-		-	-

WARD, T. R.   Kent

Name: Trevor Robert Ward
Role: Right-hand bat, occasional off-spin bowler
Born: 18 January 1968, Farningham, Kent
Height: 5ft 11in **Weight:** 13st
Nickname: Wardy, Chikka
County debut: 1986
County cap: 1989
1000 runs in a season: 5
1st-Class 50s: 61
1st-Class 100s: 22
1st-Class 200s: 1
1st-Class catches: 150
One-Day 100s: 6
Place in batting averages: 65th av. 41.73 (1995 127th av. 30.06)
Strike rate: 27.00 (career 130.12)
Parents: Robert Henry and Hazel Ann
Wife and date of marriage: Sarah Ann, 29 September 1990
Children: Holly Ann, 23 October 1995
Family links with cricket: Father played club cricket

Education: Anthony Roper County Primary; Hextable Comprehensive
Qualifications: 7 O-levels, NCA coaching award
Overseas tours: NCA to Bermuda 1985; England YC to Sri Lanka 1986-87, to Australia (Youth World Cup) 1987-88
Overseas teams played for: Scarborough, Perth, Western Australia 1985; Gosnells, Perth 1993
Cricketers particularly admired: Ian Botham, Graham Gooch, Robin Smith
Other sports followed: Most sports
Relaxations: Fishing, watching television, golf
Extras: Was awarded £1000 for becoming the first player to score 400 runs in the Benson and Hedges Cup in 1995
Best batting: 235* Kent v Middlesex, Canterbury 1991
Best bowling: 2-10 Kent v Yorkshire, Canterbury 1996

1996 Season

	M	Inns	NO	Runs	HS	Avge	100s	50s	Ct	St	O	M	Runs	Wkts	Avge	Best	5wI	10wM
Test																		
All First	18	31	1	1252	161	41.73	2	9	12	-	9	3	29	2	14.50	2-10	-	-
1-day Int																		
NatWest	2	2	0	44	30	22.00	-	-	-	-	5	0	28	1	28.00	1-28	-	
B & H	6	6	0	300	98	50.00	-	3	1	-								
Sunday	17	17	1	424	65	26.50	-	3	3	-								

Career Performances

	M	Inns	NO	Runs	HS	Avge	100s	50s	Ct	St	Balls	Runs	Wkts	Avge	Best	5wI	10wM
Test																	
All First	168	288	17	10223	235 *	37.72	22	61	150	-	1041	609	8	76.12	2-10	-	-
1-day Int																	
NatWest	19	19	0	845	120	44.47	1	7	2	-	156	129	2	64.50	1-28	-	
B & H	37	37	3	1340	125	39.41	2	9	8	-	12	10	0	-	-	-	-
Sunday	127	126	5	3584	131	29.61	3	22	28	-	228	187	6	31.16	3-20	-	

WARNER, A. E. Derbyshire

Name: Allan Esmond Warner
Role: Right-hand bat, right-arm fast bowler, outfielder
Born: 12 May 1959, Birmingham
Height: 5ft 8in **Weight:** 10st
Nickname: Esis
County debut: 1982 (Worcestershire),
1985 (Derbyshire)
County cap: 1987 (Derbyshire)

Benefit: 1995
1st-Class 50s: 15
1st-Class 5 w. in innings: 8
1st-Class 10 w. in match: 1
1st-Class catches: 46
One-Day 5 w. in innings: 1
Place in batting averages: (1995 217th av. 18.92)
Place in bowling averages: 46th av. 26.92
Strike rate: 48.00 (career 63.24)
Parents: Edgar and Sarah
Children: Alvin, 6 September 1980
Education: Tabernacle School, St Kitts, West Indies
Qualifications: CSE Maths
Cricketers particularly admired: Malcolm Marshall, Michael Holding
Other sports followed: Football, boxing and athletics
Relaxations: Watching movies, music (soul, reggae and calypso)
Extras: Derbyshire Player of the Year 1993
Best batting: 95* Derbyshire v Kent, Canterbury 1993
Best bowling: 6-21 Derbyshire v Lancashire, Derby 1995

1996 Season

	M	Inns	NO	Runs	HS	Avge	100s	50s	Ct	St	O	M	Runs	Wkts	Avge	Best	5wI	10wM
Test																		
All First	1	0	0	0	0	-	-	-	-	-	8	0	41	1	41.00	1-41	-	-
1-day Int																		
NatWest																		
B & H																		
Sunday																		

Career Performances

	M	Inns	NO	Runs	HS	Avge	100s	50s	Ct	St	Balls	Runs	Wkts	Avge	Best	5wI	10wM
Test																	
All First	200	272	52	3763	95 *	17.10	-	15	46	-	26942	13399	426	31.45	6-21	8	1
1-day Int																	
NatWest	16	12	2	90	32	9.00	-	-	1	-	1011	656	17	38.58	4-39	-
B & H	50	29	12	213	35 *	12.52	-	-	5	-	2779	1768	70	25.25	4-36	-
Sunday	154	104	24	1018	68	12.72	-	2	23	-	6187	5100	183	27.86	5-39	1

WARREN, R. J.   Northamptonshire

Name: Russell John Warren
Role: Right-hand bat, occasional off-spin
bowler
Born: 10 September 1971, Northampton
Height: 6ft 2in **Weight:** 12st 4lbs
Nickname: Rabbit, Rab, Rab C
County debut: 1992
County cap: 1995
1st-Class 50s: 11
1st-Class 100s: 1
1st-Class 200s: 1
1st-Class catches: 63
1st-Class stumpings: 2
One-Day 100s: 1
Place in batting averages: 171st av. 28.58
(1995 60th av. 41.54)

Parents: John and Sally
Marital status: Single
Education: Whitehills Lower School;
Kingsthorpe Middle and Upper Schools
Qualifications: 8 O-levels, 2 A-levels
Off-season: Relaxing and training
Overseas tours: England YC to New Zealand 1990-91; Northamptonshire to Cape
Town 1993, to Zimbabwe 1995, to Johannesburg 1996
Overseas teams played for: Lancaster Park, Christchurch, and Canterbury B, New
Zealand 1991-93; Riverside CC, Lower Hutt, New Zealand 1994-95; Petone CC,
Wellington, New Zealand 1995-96
Cricketers particularly admired: Allan Lamb, Wayne Larkins, Graham Gooch
Young players to look out for: David Sales
Other sports followed: Football (Manchester United and Northampton Town), rugby
(Northampton Saints), golf, snooker and horse racing 'mostly Nick Cook and John
Hughes tips!'
Injuries: Broken thumb and inflamed tendon on left foot, missed a total of seven
weeks
Relaxations: Having a bet at Ladbrokes, listening to music and having a drink with
mates
Opinions on cricket: 'I believe the County Championship should be split into two
divisions with promotion and relegation, adding more interest to the supporters of each
county. It will also provide more "big" games for the players who are just cruising
through some games. I also believe there are too many players on full-time contracts at
most counties. Around 20 full-time players for the first-team squad, with the second XI
using locals and trialists when needed.'

Best batting: 201* Northamptonshire v Glamorgan, Northampton 1996

1996 Season

	M	Inns	NO	Runs	HS	Avge	100s	50s	Ct	St	O	M	Runs	Wkts	Avge	Best	5wI	10wM
Test																		
All First	11	18	1	486	201 *	28.58	1	1	19	1								
1-day Int																		
NatWest	2	1	0	13	13	13.00	-	-	4	-								
B & H	7	6	1	38	14 *	7.60	-	-	4	-								
Sunday	10	7	2	52	17	10.40	-	-	11	2								

Career Performances

	M	Inns	NO	Runs	HS	Avge	100s	50s	Ct	St	Balls	Runs	Wkts	Avge	Best	5wI	10wM
Test																	
All First	46	75	10	2049	201 *	31.52	2	11	63	2							
1-day Int																	
NatWest	10	8	2	248	100 *	41.33	1	-	14	-							
B & H	11	10	1	91	23	10.11	-	-	9	-							
Sunday	43	34	6	545	71 *	19.46	-	3	35	6							

WASIM AKRAM   Lancashire

Name: Wasim Akram
Role: Left-hand bat, left-arm
fast-medium bowler
Born: 3 June 1966, Lahore, Pakistan
Height: 6ft 3in **Weight:** 12st 7lbs
County debut: 1988
County cap: 1989
Test debut: 1984-85
Tests: 64
One-Day Internationals: 201
50 wickets in a season: 5
1st-Class 50s: 18
1st-Class 100s: 4
1st-Class 5 w. in innings: 62
1st-Class 10 w. in match: 14
1st-Class catches: 64
One-Day 5 w. in innings: 8
Place in batting averages: 191st av. 26.37
(1995 188th av. 22.26)
Place in bowling averages: 21st av. 24.59 (1995 6th av. 19.72)

Strike rate: 50.96 (career 47.99)
Education: Islamia College, Pakistan
Off-season: Playing for Pakistan
Overseas tours: Pakistan U23 to Sri Lanka 1984-85; Pakistan to New Zealand 1984-85, to Sri Lanka 1985-86, to India 1986-87, to England 1987, to West Indies 1987-88, to Australia 1989-90, to Australia and New Zealand (World Cup) 1991-92, to England 1992, to New Zealand, Australia, South Africa and West Indies 1992-93, to New Zealand 1993-94, to South Africa 1994-95, to Australia 1995-96, to India and Sri Lanka (World Cup) 1995-96, to England 1996
Overseas teams played for: PACO 1984-86; Lahore Whites 1985-86
Extras: His second first-class match was playing for Pakistan on tour in New Zealand. Imran Khan wrote of him: 'I have great faith in Wasim Akram. I think he will become a great all-rounder, as long as he realises how much hard work is required. As a bowler he is extremely gifted, and has it in him to be the best left-armer since Alan Davidson.' Hit maiden Test 100 v Australia 1989-90 during stand of 191 with Imran Khan. Signed a new four-year contract with Lancashire in 1992. Appointed captain of Pakistan 1992-93 and replaced by Salim Malik on tour to New Zealand 1993-94 but captained the tour to England in 1996. Alan Mullally became his 300th Test victim as the final wicket fell in the third Test at The Oval in 1996. Scored a career best 257 not out for Pakistan against Zimbabwe at Sheikhupura in 1996-97 – the highest score batting at No.8 in Test history
Best batting: 123 Pakistan v Australia, Adelaide 1989-90
Best bowling: 8-30 Lancashire v Somerset, Southport 1994

1996 Season

	M	Inns	NO	Runs	HS	Avge	100s	50s	Ct	St	O	M	Runs	Wkts	Avge	Best	5wI	10wM
Test	3	5	1	98	40	24.50	-	-	1	-	128	29	350	11	31.81	3-67	--	
All First	7	9	1	211	68	26.37	-	1	4	-	271.5	67	787	32	24.59	5-58	1-	
1-day Int	3	3	0	32	21	10.66	-	-	1	-	29.4	2	140	6	23.33	3-45	-	
NatWest																		
B & H																		
Sunday																		

Career Performances

	M	Inns	NO	Runs	HS	Avge	100s	50s	Ct	St	Balls	Runs	Wkts	Avge	Best	5wI	10wM
Test	64	98	12	1652	123	19.20	1	4	26	-	16034	6874	300	22.91	7-119	20	3
All First	187	265	30	5043	123	21.45	4	18	64	-	39022	17431	813	21.44	8-30	62	14
1-day Int	201	153	30	1838	86	14.94	-	2	40	-	10396	6556	291	22.52	5-15	5	
NatWest	17	14	3	192	50	17.45	-	1	5	-	1090	681	23	29.60	4-27	-	
B & H	28	21	4	454	64	26.70	-	2	2	-	1673	1088	54	20.14	5-10	2	
Sunday	91	73	19	1221	51 *	22.61	-	2	18	-	3922	2825	145	19.48	5-41	1	

WATKIN, S. L.   Glamorgan

Name: Steven Llewellyn Watkin
Role: Right-hand bat, right-arm
fast-medium bowler
Born: 15 September 1964, Maesteg
Height: 6ft 3in **Weight:** 12st 8lbs
Nickname: Watty, Banger
County debut: 1986
County cap: 1989
Test debut: 1991
Tests: 3
One-Day Internationals: 4
50 wickets in a season: 8
1st-Class 5 w. in innings: 22
1st-Class 10 w. in match: 4
1st-Class catches: 51
One-Day 5 w. in innings: 1
Place in batting averages: 291st av. 10.92

(1995 270th av. 12.42)
Place in bowling averages: 36th av. 26.82
(1995 49th av. 27.00)
Strike rate: 55.22 (career 58.73)
Parents: John and Sandra
Marital status: Single
Family links with cricket: One brother plays local cricket; 'older brother a good
watcher'
Education: Cymer Afan Comprehensive; Swansea College of Further Education;
South Glamorgan Institute of Higher Education
Qualifications: 8 O-levels, 2 A-levels, BA (Hons) in Human Movement Studies
Off-season: Development officer for cricket in West Glamorgan area
Overseas tours: British Colleges to West Indies 1987; England A to Kenya and
Zimbabwe 1989-90, to Pakistan and Sri Lanka 1990-91, to Bermuda and West Indies
1991-92; England to West Indies 1993-94
Overseas teams played for: Potchefstroom University, South Africa 1987-88; Aurora,
Durban, South Africa 1991-92
Cricketers particularly admired: Richard Hadlee, Dennis Lillee, Ian Botham
Young players to look out for: Alun Evans
Other sports followed: All sports except horse racing
Injuries: Knee, out for one game
Relaxations: Watching television, music, DIY, motor mechanics, 'a quiet pint'
Extras: Joint highest wicket-taker in 1989 with 94 wickets and took most (92) in 1993.
Sister Lynda has played for Great Britain at hockey. Players' Player of the Year and

Glamorgan Player of the Year 1993

Opinions on cricket: 'The amount of cricket must be reduced. It's not possible for players to perform at 100 per cent with present format. This surely affects Test performances as well.'

Best batting: 41 Glamorgan v Worcestershire, Worcester 1992

Best bowling: 8-59 Glamorgan v Warwickshire, Edgbaston 1988

1996 Season

	M	Inns	NO	Runs	HS	Avge	100s	50s	Ct	St	O	M	Runs	Wkts	Avge	Best	5wI	10wM
Test																		
All First	18	20	6	153	34	10.92	-	-	9	-	616.4	159	1797	67	26.82	4-28	-	-
1-day Int																		
NatWest	1	1	0	13	13	13.00	-	-	-	-	12	3	46	2	23.00	2-46	-	
B & H	6	1	1	2	2 *	-	-	-	1	-	58	12	246	12	20.50	4-31	-	
Sunday	15	6	2	25	9 *	6.25	-	-	2	-	108	10	430	13	33.07	2-9	-	

Career Performances

	M	Inns	NO	Runs	HS	Avge	100s	50s	Ct	St	Balls	Runs	Wkts	Avge	Best	5wI	10wM
Test	3	5	0	25	13	5.00	-	-	1	-	534	305	11	27.72	4-65	-	-
All First	193	216	71	1393	41	9.60	-	-	51	-	39058	19327	665	29.06	8-59	22	4
1-day Int	4	2	0	4	4	2.00	-	-	-	-	221	193	7	27.57	4-49	-	
NatWest	23	11	4	52	13	7.42	-	-	2	-	1458	735	30	24.50	4-26	-	
B & H	29	16	8	61	15	7.62	-	-	6	-	1731	1144	38	30.10	4-31	-	
Sunday	113	42	14	217	31 *	7.75	-	-	17	-	4958	3564	138	25.82	5-23	1	

WATKINSON, M.   Lancashire

Name: Michael Watkinson

Role: Right-hand bat, right-arm medium or off-spin bowler, county captain

Born: 1 August 1961, Westhoughton

Height: 6ft 1¹/₂in **Weight:** 13st

Nickname: Winker

County debut: 1982

County cap: 1987

Test debut: 1995

Tests: 4

One-Day Internationals: 1

1000 runs in a season: 1

50 wickets in a season: 7

1st-Class 50s: 46

1st-Class 100s: 9

1st-Class 5 w. in innings: 26

1st-Class 10 w. in match: 3
1st-Class catches: 139
One-Day 5 w. in innings: 3
Place in batting averages: 206th av. 23.88
(1995 102nd av. 34.11)
Place in bowling averages: 115th av. 40.56
(1995 65th av. 29.38)
Strike rate: 70.21 (career 64.64)
Parents: Albert and Marian
Wife and date of marriage: Susan, 12 April
1986
Children: Charlotte, 24 February 1989;
Liam, 27 July 1991
Education: Rivington and Blackrod High
School, Horwich
Qualifications: 8 O-levels, HTC Civil
Engineering
Career outside cricket: Draughtsman
Overseas tours: England to South Africa 1995-96
Cricketers particularly admired: Clive Lloyd, Imran Khan
Other sports followed: Football
Relaxations: Watching Bolton Wanderers
Extras: Played for Cheshire in Minor Counties Championship and in NatWest Trophy
(v Middlesex) 1982. Man of the Match in the first Refuge Assurance Cup final 1988 and
in B&H Cup final 1990. Appointed county captain for 1994 season
Best batting: 161 Lancashire v Essex, Old Trafford 1995
Best bowling: 8-30 Lancashire v Hampshire, Old Trafford 1994

1996 Season

	M	Inns	NO	Runs	HS	Avge	100s	50s	Ct	St	O	M	Runs	Wkts	Avge	Best	5wI	10wM
Test																		
All First	17	28	1	645	64	23.88	-	2	13	-	433	78	1501	37	40.56	5-15	1	-
1-day Int																		
NatWest	5	5	0	158	62	31.60	-	1	2	-	48	2	199	3	66.33	1-42	-	
B & H	8	6	0	120	56	20.00	-	1	6	-	71.5	3	329	17	19.35	5-44	1	
Sunday	16	15	1	486	121	34.71	1	2	6	-	104	1	592	21	28.19	3-40	-	

91. England's wicket-keeper in the 1980 Centenary Test at
Lord's played only one Ashes Test. Who was he?

Career Performances

	M	Inns	NO	Runs	HS	Avge	100s	50s	Ct	St	Balls	Runs	Wkts	Avge	Best	5wI	10wM
Test	4	6	1	167	82 *	33.40	-	1	1	-	672	348	10	34.80	3-64	-	-
All First	274	410	46	9701	161	26.65	9	46	139	-	44540	23132	689	33.57	8-30	26	3
1-day Int	1	0	0	0	0	-	-	-	-	-	54	43	0	-	-	-	-
NatWest	39	33	7	855	90	32.88	-	7	11	-	2369	1540	41	37.56	3-14	-	
B & H	70	50	12	785	76	20.65	-	4	21	-	3656	2565	86	29.82	5-44	2	
Sunday	202	158	37	2703	121	22.33	1	7	49	-	7980	6520	204	31.96	5-46	1	

WEEKES, P. N. Middlesex

Name: Paul Nicholas Weekes
Role: Left-hand bat, off-spin bowler
Born: 8 July 1969, Hackney, London
Height: 5ft 11in **Weight:** 13st
Nickname: Weekesy, Twiddles
County debut: 1990
County cap: 1993
1000 runs in a season: 1
1st-Class 50s: 18
1st-Class 100s: 7
1st-Class 5 w. in innings: 3
1st-Class catches: 66
One-Day 100s: 3
Place in batting averages: 95th av. 36.90
(1995 97th av. 34.31)
Place in bowling averages: 87th av. 33.81
(1995 147th av. 52.53)
Strike rate: 69.56 (career 82.94)
Parents: Robert and Carol
Marital status: 'Partner Christine'
Children: Cheri, 4 September 1993
Family links with cricket: Father played club cricket
Education: Homerton House Secondary School, Hackney; Hackney College
Qualifications: NCA cricket coach
Career outside cricket: Coaching for Middlesex CYT
Overseas tours: England A to India 1994-95
Overseas teams played for: Newcastle University, NSW, 1989; Sunrise, Zimbabwe 1990
Cricketers particularly admired: David Gower, Richie Richardson
Other sports followed: Boxing – 'middle and heavyweight especially'
Relaxations: 'Listening to music – ragga, soca. Chilling with the family'
Extras: Scored 50 in first innings for both 2nd and 1st teams. Took two catches whilst appearing as 12th man for England in the Second Test against West Indies at Lord's in 1995

Opinions on cricket: 'Lunch and tea intervals should be longer.'
Best batting: 171* Middlesex v Somerset, Uxbridge 1996
Best bowling: 8-39 Middlesex v Glamorgan, Lord's 1996

1996 Season

	M	Inns	NO	Runs	HS	Avge	100s	50s	Ct	St	O	M	Runs	Wkts	Avge	Best	5wI	10wM
Test																		
All First	19	35	2	1218	171 *	36.90	4	4	11	-	371	75	1082	32	33.81	8-39	2	-
1-day Int																		
NatWest	2	2	0	106	104	53.00	1	-	-	-	13.5	0	65	3	21.66	3-35	-	
B & H	5	5	0	113	52	22.60	-	1	1	-	38.2	0	205	5	41.00	2-39	-	
Sunday	16	16	1	535	119 *	35.66	1	5	9	-	94.1	1	497	21	23.66	4-29	-	

Career Performances

	M	Inns	NO	Runs	HS	Avge	100s	50s	Ct	St	Balls	Runs	Wkts	Avge	Best	5wI	10wM
Test																	
All First	88	133	15	3986	171 *	33.77	7	18	66	-	9456	4473	114	39.23	8-39	3	-
1-day Int																	
NatWest	9	9	1	334	143 *	41.75	2	1	3	-	533	358	11	32.54	3-35	-	
B & H	22	19	3	430	67 *	26.87	-	3	4	-	956	674	20	33.70	3-32	-	
Sunday	93	73	11	1698	119 *	27.38	1	8	39	-	3338	2837	102	27.81	4-29	-	

WELCH, G.   Warwickshire

Name: Graeme Welch
Role: Right-hand bat, right-arm
medium-fast bowler
Born: 21 March 1972, Tyne and Wear
Height: 6ft **Weight:** 13st
Nickname: Pop, Red Beard, Lalas
County debut: 1992 (one-day),
1994 (first-class)
1st-Class 50s: 4
1st-Class catches: 15
Place in batting averages: 276th av. 13.12
Place in bowling averages: 61st av. 30.44
Strike rate: 48.67 (career 57.58)
Parents: Robert and Jean
Marital status: Engaged to Emma
Family links with cricket: Dad plays club
cricket in Durham. Brother Barrie plays club
cricket for Olton in Birmingham

Education: Hetton Lyons Junior School; Hetton Comprehensive
Qualifications: 9 GCSEs, City & Guilds in Sports and Leisure, coaching certificate
Career outside cricket: 'Everything and anything'
Off-season: Playing club cricket in Wellington, New Zealand
Overseas tours: Warwickshire to Cape Town 1992 and 1993
Overseas teams played for: Avendale, Cape Town 1991-93; Johnsonville CC, New Zealand 1995-96
Cricketers particularly admired: Allan Donald, Dean Jones, Steve Waugh, Gladstone Small, Mike Burns, Dominic Ostler
Young players to look out for: Darren Altree, Tony Frost, Ashley Giles, Anurag Singh
Other sports followed: Football (Newcastle United)
Relaxations: 'Eating out with my fiancée Emma, playing Mortal Combat on Sega with brother Barrie'
Extras: Played for England YC v Australian YC 1991. Has taken two hat-tricks in the 2nd XI against Durham in 1992 and against Worcestershire. Axa Equity and Law Winners Medal 1994. Britannic Assurance Winners Medal 1994. Warwickshire's most improved player in 1994
Opinions on cricket: 'Lunch and tea should be extended by ten minutes. Third umpire is a good idea. 2nd XI facilities should be improved. 12-month contracts should be introduced.'
Best batting: 84* Warwickshire v Nottinghamshire, Edgbaston 1994
Best bowling: 4-74 Warwickshire v Yorkshire, Scarborough 1994

1996 Season

	M	Inns	NO	Runs	HS	Avge	100s	50s	Ct	St	O	M	Runs	Wkts	Avge	Best	5wI	10wM
Test																		
All First	13	17	1	210	45	13.12	-	-	9	-	275.5	42	1035	34	30.44	4-50	-	-
1-day Int																		
NatWest	1	1	0	14	14	14.00	-	-	-	-	5	2	11	1	11.00	1-11	-	
B & H	4	2	0	25	24	12.50	-	-	-	-	27	1	126	4	31.50	2-43	-	
Sunday	10	6	3	116	54	38.66	-	1	1	-	56.5	0	340	6	56.66	3-37	-	

Career Performances

	M	Inns	NO	Runs	HS	Avge	100s	50s	Ct	St	Balls	Runs	Wkts	Avge	Best	5wI	10wM
Test																	
All First	27	36	4	666	84 *	20.81	-	4	15	-	3455	2124	60	35.40	4-50	-	-
1-day Int																	
NatWest	3	2	1	14	14	14.00	-	-	-	-	126	52	1	52.00	1-11	-	
B & H	8	5	1	61	27 *	15.25	-	-	-	-	408	368	6	61.33	2-43	-	
Sunday	22	15	6	226	54	25.11	-	1	4	-	760	658	16	41.12	3-37	-	

WELLINGS, P. E.   Middlesex

Name: Peter Edward Wellings
Role: Right-hand bat, right-arm
medium bowler
Born: 5 March 1970, Wolverhampton
Height: 6ft 1in **Weight:** 13st 7lbs
Nickname: Wello, Action, Jarv
County debut: 1996
1st-Class catches: 1
Place in batting averages: 125th av. 33.85
Parents: John and Sandra
Marital status: Single
Family links with cricket: 'Uncle Keith
Worrall gave me bags of encouragement –
and still is. Dad has developed an interest.
Also big thanks to James While – the
infamous Goochie'
Education: Smeston Comprehensive,
Wolverhampton; Wulfrew College of Further
Education; Thames Valley University

Qualifications: 7 O-levels, 2 A-levels, BA (Hons) in Leisure Management, basic
coaching award
Career outside cricket: Sports development, coaching and club management
Off-season: Playing club cricket in South Africa for Coronations in Stellenbosch
Overseas tours: Harrow Chequers to South Africa 1993-94
Overseas teams played for: Pingrup, Western Australia 1991-92; Ongerup Green
Range, Western Australia 1991-92; Coronations, Stellenbosch, South Africa 1993-94
Cricketers particularly admired: Keith Brown, Graham Gooch, Angus Fraser,
Michael Bevan, Chris Cooper
Young players to look out for: Ian Blanchett, David Nash, Andy Strauss, Darren
Altree, Tim Walton
Other sports followed: Rugby union (Wolverhampton RFC), football (Wolves)
Relaxations: 'Science fiction, watching sport, reading, keeping fit, joining The
Nighttrain'
Extras: Scored 1,000 2nd XI runs on debut last year
Opinions on cricket: 'There is plenty of talent in British cricket but unlike Australia,
our system does not maximise its development. Having a one-day game in the middle of
the championship is ridiculous. 2nd XI cricket must become more competitive – not the
middle practise it often is. We play too much cricket at the expense of practice and
preparation. Unless we gear our system into producing top-class Test cricketers, we may,
quite seriously, not regain the Ashes for decades.'
Best batting: 48 Middlesex v Kent, Canterbury 1996

1996 Season

	M	Inns	NO	Runs	HS	Avge	100s	50s	Ct	St	O	M	Runs	Wkts	Avge	Best	5wI	10wM
Test																		
All First	4	8	1	237	48	33.85	-	-	1	-								
1-day Int																		
NatWest	1	1	1	9	9 *	-	-	-	-	-	5.5	1	20	1	20.00	1-20	-	
B & H	1	1	1	14	14 *	-	-	-	1	-	5.5	0	45	1	45.00	1-45	-	
Sunday	8	7	1	70	42	11.66	-	-	3	-	7	0	72	2	36.00	1-22	-	

Career Performances

	M	Inns	NO	Runs	HS	Avge	100s	50s	Ct	St	Balls	Runs	Wkts	Avge	Best	5wI	10wM
Test																	
All First	4	8	1	237	48	33.85	-	-	1	-							
1-day Int																	
NatWest	1	1	1	9	9 *	-	-	-	-	-	35	20	1	20.00	1-20	-	
B & H	1	1	1	14	14 *	-	-	-	1	-	35	45	1	45.00	1-45	-	
Sunday	8	7	1	70	42	11.66	-	-	3	-	42	72	2	36.00	1-22	-	

WELLS, A. P.   Kent

Name: Alan Peter Wells
Role: Right-hand bat, right-arm medium bowler
Born: 2 October 1961, Newhaven
Height: 6ft **Weight:** 'Going up'
Nickname: Morph, Bomber
County debut: 1981 (Sussex)
County cap: 1986 (Sussex)
Benefit: 1995
Test debut: 1995
Tests: 1
1000 runs in a season: 10
1st-Class 50s: 84
1st-Class 100s: 43
1st-Class 200s: 1
1st-Class catches: 204
One-Day 100s: 6
Place in batting averages: 97th av. 36.54
(1995 15th av. 54.42)
Strike rate: (career 104.50)
Parents: Ernest William Charles and Eunice Mae
Wife and date of marriage: Melanie Elizabeth, 26 September 1987

Children: Luke William Peter, 29 December 1990; Daniel Allan Christian, 24 June 1995
Family links with cricket: Father, Billy, played for many years for local club and had trial for Sussex. Eldest brother Ray plays club cricket; brother Colin played for Sussex and then joined Derbyshire and is now with Somerset
Education: Tideway Comprehensive, Newhaven
Qualifications: 5 O-levels, NCA coaching certificate
Career outside cricket: Family packaging business
Off-season: Senior World Cup in Bombay. Finishing off benefit and spending time with my family
Overseas tours: Unofficial England XI to South Africa 1989-90; England A to South Africa 1993-94, to India (captain) 1994-95
Overseas teams played for: Border, South Africa 1981-82
Cricketers particularly admired: Graham Gooch
Young players to look out for: Giles Haywood
Other sports followed: Football (Tottenham Hotspur)
Relaxations: Good wine, cooking, spending time with family, reading books and articles on wine
Extras: Played for England YC v India 1981. Banned from Test cricket for five years in 1990 for joining tour of South Africa, suspension remitted in 1992. Scored a century in each of his first two matches as acting-captain of Sussex and won both matches. Won top batting award for Sussex 1989-93, 'much to David Smith's annoyance'. Vice-captain on England A tour to South Africa 1993-94 and captain for the highly successful tour to India 1994-95. Scored a century in both innings against Kent at Hove in 1995, the first Sussex player to do so since C.B. Fry. This was followed by a pair against Glamorgan at Swansea ('Funny old game!'). Left Sussex after 15 years during the off-season and has joined Kent for the 1997 season
Opinions on cricket: 'Until groundsmen start producing the best possible pitch rather than pitches to suit their own attacks, I don't believe our game will improve. Four-day cricket may take a long time to bear its fruit, but it will only do so if played on good pitches. I think our game at international level will suffer if we don't play on good surfaces. We have to decide if county or country come first.'
Best batting: 253* Sussex v Yorkshire, Middlesbrough 1991
Best bowling: 3-67 Sussex v Worcestershire, Worcester 1987

1996 Season

	M	Inns	NO	Runs	HS	Avge	100s	50s	Ct	St	O	M	Runs	Wkts	Avge	Best	5wI	10wM
Test																		
All First	19	35	2	1206	122	36.54	2	6	13	-								
1-day Int																		
NatWest	3	3	0	145	113	48.33	1	-	1	-								
B & H	4	4	1	146	69	48.66	-	2	1	-								
Sunday	15	14	0	325	56	23.21	-	1	3	-								

Career Performances

	M	Inns	NO	Runs	HS	Avge	100s	50s	Ct	St	Balls	Runs	Wkts	Avge	Best	5wI	10wM
Test	1	2	1	3	3 *	3.00	-	-	-	-							
All First	321	537	77	18508	253 *	40.23	43	84	204	-	1045	765	10	76.50	3-67	-	-
1-day Int	1	1	0	15	15	15.00	-	-	-	-							
NatWest	34	31	6	952	119	38.08	3	4	13	-	6	1	0	-		-	-
B & H	54	51	7	1418	74	32.22	-	14	10	-	60	72	3	24.00	1-17	-	
Sunday	218	201	22	5482	127	30.62	3	34	60	-	62	69	4	17.25	1-0	-	

WELLS, C. M. Somerset

Name: Colin Mark Wells
Role: Right-hand bat, right-arm medium bowler
Born: 3 March 1960, Newhaven
Height: 6ft **Weight:** 13st
Nickname: Bomber, Dougie
County debut: 1979 (Sussex), 1994 (Derbyshire)
County cap: 1982 (Sussex)
Benefit: 1993 (£50,353)
One-Day Internationals: 2
1000 runs in a season: 6
50 wickets in a season: 2
1st-Class 50s: 67
1st-Class 100s: 24
1st-Class 200s: 1
1st-Class 5 w. in innings: 7
1st-Class catches: 110
One-Day 100s: 4
Place in batting averages: 85th av. 38.06 (1995 87th av. 36.14)
Place in bowling averages: av. 48.88 (1995 86th av. 32.60)
Strike rate: 109.33 (career 73.03)
Parents: Ernest William Charles and Eunice Mae
Wife and date of marriage: Celia, 25 September 1982
Children: Jessica Louise, 2 October 1987
Family links with cricket: Father, Billy, had trials for Sussex and played for Sussex Cricket Association. Elder brother Ray plays club cricket and younger brother Alan was captain of Sussex and has now joined Kent
Education: Tideway Comprehensive School, Newhaven
Qualifications: 9 O-levels, 2 CSEs, 1 A-level, intermediate coaching certificate
Overseas tours: England to Sharjah 1984-85

Overseas teams played for: Border, South Africa 1980-81; Western Province, South Africa 1984-85

Other sports followed: Football, rugby, hockey, basketball, tennis, table tennis

Relaxations: Sea-angling, philately, listening to music

Extras: Played in three John Player League matches in 1978. Was recommended to Sussex by former Sussex player, Ian Thomson. Appointed vice-captain of Sussex in 1988 and captain in 1992. Joined Derbyshire in 1994 but left at the end of the 1996 season to become the 2nd XI coach at Somerset

Best batting: 203 Sussex v Hampshire, Hove 1984

Best bowling: 7-42 Sussex v Derbyshire, Derby 1991

1996 Season

	M	Inns	NO	Runs	HS	Avge	100s	50s	Ct	St	O	M	Runs	Wkts	Avge	Best	5wl	10wM
Test																		
All First	12	19	3	609	165	38.06	1	3	4	-	164	40	440	9	48.88	2-20	-	-
1-day Int																		
NatWest	2	2	0	13	10	6.50	-	-	-	-	24	1	81	4	20.25	3-41	-	
B & H	5	4	1	62	56	20.66	-	1	-	-	20	2	93	6	15.50	4-36	-	
Sunday	9	7	2	94	39 *	18.80	-	-	4	-	56.3	1	252	10	25.20	4-20	-	

Career Performances

	M	Inns	NO	Runs	HS	Avge	100s	50s	Ct	St	Balls	Runs	Wkts	Avge	Best	5wl	10wM
Test																	
All First	318	510	78	14289	203	33.07	24	67	110	-	31257	14748	428	34.45	7-42	7	-
1-day Int	2	2	0	22	17	11.00	-	-	-								
NatWest	37	30	4	545	76	20.96	-	2	8	-	1737	855	22	38.86	3-16	-	
B & H	60	57	8	1442	117	29.42	3	5	13	-	2148	1390	44	31.59	4-21	-	
Sunday	216	188	30	4102	104 *	25.96	1	21	51	-	7305	4805	156	30.80	4-15	-	

92. Which keeper holds the record of 28 dismissals in an Ashes rubber?

WELLS, V. J.   Leicestershire

Name: Vincent John Wells
Role: Right-hand bat, right-arm medium
bowler, occasional wicket-keeper
Born: 6 August 1965, Dartford
Height: 6ft **Weight:** 13st
Nickname: Vinny, Both
County debut: 1987 (Kent), 1992
(Leicestershire)
1000 runs in a season: 1
1st-Class 50s: 22
1st-Class 100s: 6
1st-Class 200s: 2
1st-Class 5 w. in innings: 2
1st-Class catches: 65
One-Day 100s: 4
One-Day 200s: 1
One-Day 5 w. in innings: 1
Place in batting averages: 56th av. 44.36

(1995 142nd av. 28.43)
Place in bowling averages: 56th av. 29.42 (1995 24th av. 23.05)
Strike rate: 58.88 (career 52.87)
Parents: Pat and Jack
Wife and date of marriage: Deborah Louise, 14 October 1989
Children: Harrison John, 25 January 1995; Molly Louise, 2 June 1996
Family links with cricket: Brother plays league cricket in Kent
Education: Downs School, Dartford; Sir William Nottidge School, Whitstable
Qualifications: 1 O-level, 8 CSEs, junior and senior coaching certificates
Off-season: Coaching in South Africa at the Western Transvaal University
Overseas tours: Leicestershire to Jamaica 1993, to Bloemfontein, 1994 and 1995, to
Western Transvaal 1996
Overseas teams played for: Parnell, Auckland 1986; Avendale, Cape Town 1986-89,
1990-91
Cricketers particularly admired: David Gower, Robin Smith, Allan Donald, Phil
Simmons
Young players to look out for: Darren Maddy, Aftab Habib, Ben Smith
Other sports followed: Most sports especially football
Injuries: Side strain, out for three weeks
Relaxations: Spending time with family, bottle of wine, pint of Guinness
Extras: Was a schoolboy footballer with Leyton Orient. Scored 100 not out on NatWest
debut v Oxfordshire. Left Kent at the end of 1991 season to join Leicestershire. Missed
1992 NatWest final owing to viral infection. Hat-trick against Durham, 1994. Scored

201 not out against Berkshire in the 1996 NatWest Trophy

Opinions on cricket: 'The zonal Benson & Hedges games should be played straight off within the first two weeks of the season, leaving just the semi-finals and the finals to be played at a later date, then you can concentrate on four-day cricket. Over-rates are still much too high. Clubs should do more to help with winter employment or even offer longer contracts. Standard of pitches could still be better. Still dislike the fact of playing Sunday League in the middle of championship. Over-rates for 1996 much better. In favour of two divisions with promotion and relegation. Would like to see the introduction of evening cricket to see whether it would increase the crowds.'

Best batting: 204 Leicestershire v Northamptonshire, Leicester 1996
Best bowling: 5-43 Kent v Leicestershire, Leicester 1990

1996 Season

	M	Inns	NO	Runs	HS	Avge	100s	50s	Ct	St	O	M	Runs	Wkts	Avge	Best	5wl	10wM
Test																		
All First	20	30	0	1331	204	44.36	4	3	20	-	255.1	69	765	26	29.42	4-44	-	-
1-day Int																		
NatWest	2	2	0	201	201	100.50	1	-	-	-	6	0	22	2	11.00	2-22	-	
B & H	5	5	0	135	60	27.00	-	1	2	-	33	2	168	3	56.00	2-39	-	
Sunday	16	16	0	382	84	23.87	-	1	1	-	75.5	1	458	10	45.80	3-19	-	

Career Performances

	M	Inns	NO	Runs	HS	Avge	100s	50s	Ct	St	Balls	Runs	Wkts	Avge	Best	5wl	10wM
Test																	
All First	96	153	14	4466	204	32.12	6	22	65	-	8249	4126	156	26.44	5-43	2	-
1-day Int																	
NatWest	11	11	3	427	201	53.37	2	-	-	-	389	244	10	24.40	3-38	-	
B & H	24	21	3	398	60	22.11	-	1	8	-	876	697	20	34.85	4-37	-	
Sunday	78	72	12	1670	101	27.83	2	7	19	-	2503	2050	74	27.70	5-10	1	

93. Who was the first batsman given out by video evidence in an Ashes Test?

WELTON, G. E. Nottinghamshire

Name: Guy Edward Welton
Role: Right-hand bat
Born: 4 May 1978, Grimsby
Height: 6ft 1in **Weight:** 12st 7lbs
Nickname: Welts, Trigger
County debut: No first-team appearance
Parents: Bob and Diana
Marital status: Single
Family links with cricket: Father Bob a
well-known cricketer and coach in the
Lincolnshire area
Education: Healing Comprehensive;
Grimsby College of Technology
Qualifications: 8 GCSEs, BTEC in Business
and Finance, qualified cricket coach
Career outside cricket: Playing club cricket
in Johannesburg, South Africa
Overseas tours: England U17 to Holland 1995
Cricketers particularly admired: David
Gower, Viv Richards, Sachin Tendulkar
Young players to look out for: Usman Afzaal, Noel Gie
Other sports followed: Football (Grimsby and West Bromwich Albion)
Relaxations: Keeping fit, weights and listening to music
Extras: Completed a two-year YTS with Grimsby Town Football Club where he made
one first-team appearance as a substitute. Played cricket for England U14, U15 and U17.
Won the Lord's Taverners Young Player Award in 1993 and MCC Young Cricketer from
1994-95. Was 12th man for England at Lord's and The Oval against West Indies in 1995
Opinions on cricket: 'Tea intervals should be longer. Championship should be split into
two divisions.'

WESTON, R. M. S. Durham

Name: Robin Michael Swann Weston
Role: Right-hand bat, leg-break bowler
Born: 7 June 1975, Durham
Height: 6ft **Weight:** 12st 7lbs
County debut: 1995
1st-Class catches: 6
Strike rate: (career 145.00)

Parents: Michael Philip and Kathleen Mary
Marital status: Single
Family links with cricket: Father played for Durham; brother Philip plays for Worcestershire
Education: Bow School; Durham School; Loughborough University
Qualifications: 10 GCSEs, 4 A-levels, basic cricket coaching certificate
Career outside cricket: Student at Loughborough
Off-season: Loughborough University
Overseas tours: England U18 to South Africa 1992-93, to Denmark 1993; England U19 to Sri Lanka 1993-94
Cricketers particularly admired: Graeme Hick and Wayne Larkins
Other sports followed: Rugby and golf
Relaxations: Most sports, listening to music and socialising with friends
Extras: Youngest to play for Durham 1st XI, in Minor Counties competition, aged 15 in 1991. Played rugby for England U18
Opinions on cricket: '30 minutes for tea. Lower over-rate per hour.'
Best batting: 15 Durham v Pakistan, Chester-le-Street 1996
Best bowling: 1-41 Durham v Somerset, Chester-le-Street 1995

1996 Season

	M	Inns	NO	Runs	HS	Avge	100s	50s	Ct	St	O	M	Runs	Wkts	Avge	Best	5wl	10wM
Test																		
All First	3	5	0	29	15	5.80	-	-	1	-	2	1	6	0	-	-	-	-
1-day Int																		
NatWest																		
B & H																		
Sunday	1	1	0	13	13	13.00	-	-	-	-								

Career Performances

	M	Inns	NO	Runs	HS	Avge	100s	50s	Ct	St	Balls	Runs	Wkts	Avge	Best	5wl	10wM
Test																	
All First	6	11	0	44	15	4.00	-	-	6	-	145	76	1	76.00	1-41	-	-
1-day Int																	
NatWest																	
B & H																	
Sunday	1	1	0	13	13	13.00	-	-	-	-							

WESTON, W. P. C.   Worcestershire

Name: William Philip Christopher Weston
Role: Left-hand bat, left-arm medium bowler
Born: 16 June 1973, Durham
Height: 6ft 4in   **Weight:** 14st
Nickname: Junior, Sven, Reverend, Bambi,
Baby Giraffe
County debut: 1991
County cap: 1995
1000 runs in a season: 2
1st-Class 50s: 26
1st-Class 100s: 9
1st-Class catches: 51
Place in batting averages: 62nd av. 43.40
(1995 92nd av. 35.50)
Strike rate: (career 213.25)
Parents: Michael Philip and Kathleen Mary
Marital status: Single ('loved up')
Family links with cricket: 'Brother plays for
Durham. Father played for Durham. Mum

supports Durham. Wish I could play for Durham'
Education: Bow School, Durham; Durham School
Qualifications: 9 GCSEs, 4 A-levels, NCA Senior Coach
Career outside cricket: 'Quality controller on Cottesloe beach. Would like to work in Durham'
Off-season: 'On Cottesloe beach, Perth, Western Australia and playing grade cricket'
Overseas tours: England U18 to Canada; England YC to New Zealand 1990-91, to
Pakistan 1991-92 (captain)
Overseas teams played for: Melville, Perth 1992-94 and 1996-97; Swanbourne, Perth
1995-96
Cricketers particularly admired: Graeme Hick, Phil Newport, Tom Moody, Reuben
Spiring ('he pays me a ridiculously high rent') and 'most players who give 100% day
in day out'
Young players to look out for: Philip Weston
Other sports followed: Rugby union and football (Sunderland AFC)
Injuries: Back injury, out for one week
Relaxations: Travelling. Going to the beach. Wildlife. Spending time with family
Extras: Scored century for England YC v Australian YC 1991. Was appointed captain
of England U19 for their tour to Pakistan 1991-92 and told by Keble College, Oxford,
that he would not be accepted if he decided to tour; he chose to sacrifice his place at
Oxford. Downing College, Cambridge, offered him a place the following year, but by
then he was so disillusioned with universities that he turned down the offer and decided

to concentrate on his cricket. Played for Northamptonshire 2nd XI and Worcestershire 2nd XI in 1989. Cricket Society's Most Promising Young Cricketer 1992. Worcestershire Uncapped Player of the Year, 1992. Member of Whittingdale Fringe Squad 1993

Opinions on cricket: 'Four-day cricket is working but the pitches must improve to produce Test-quality players.'

Best batting: 171* Worcestershire v Lancashire, Old Trafford 1996

Best bowling: 2-39 Worcestershire v Pakistanis, Worcester 1992

1996 Season

	M	Inns	NO	Runs	HS	Avge	100s	50s	Ct	St	O	M	Runs	Wkts	Avge	Best	5wl	10wM
Test																		
All First	20	37	5	1389	171 *	43.40	4	7	20	-	7	0	36	0	-	-	-	-
1-day Int																		
NatWest	1	1	0	6	6	6.00	-	-	-	-								
B & H	4	3	0	50	20	16.66	-	-	2	-								
Sunday	15	14	4	416	80 *	41.60	-	2	2	-								

Career Performances

	M	Inns	NO	Runs	HS	Avge	100s	50s	Ct	St	Balls	Runs	Wkts	Avge	Best	5wl	10wM
Test																	
All First	88	151	15	4832	171 *	35.52	9	26	51	-	853	517	4	129.25	2-39	-	-
1-day Int																	
NatWest	7	7	0	97	31	13.85	-	-	1	-							
B & H	12	11	2	164	54 *	18.22	-	1	4	-							
Sunday	36	31	6	779	80 *	31.16	-	4	7	-	6	2	1	2.00	1-2	-	

94. Who was England's leading run-scorer in the 1994-95 Ashes series?

WHARF, A. G.   Yorkshire

Name: Alexander George Wharf
Role: Right-hand bat, right-arm
fast-medium bowler
Born: 4 June 1975, Bradford
Height: 6ft 4in **Weight:** 15st
Nickname: Gangster, Frank, River, Big'un
County debut: 1994
1st-Class 50s: 1
1st-Class catches: 1
Strike rate: 59.26 (career 70.85)
Parents: Derek and Jane
Marital status: Single
Family links with cricket: Father used to
play in local league cricket
Education: Marshfields First School;
Preistman Middle School; Buttershaw Upper
School; Thomas Danby College
Qualifications: 6 GCSEs, City and Guilds in
Sports Management
Career outside cricket: 'You name it, I do it'
Off-season: 'Resting and hopefully going on the pre-season tour to West Indies'
Overseas tours: Yorkshire to Cape Town 1994-95, to Guernsey 1996
Overseas teams played for: Somerset West, Cape Town 1993-95
Cricketers particularly admired: Wasim Akram, Curtly Ambrose, Ian Botham,
Bradley Parker, Anthony McGrath, Chris Burns (Undercliffe CC)
Young players to look out for: Anthony McGrath, Alex and Zac Morris, Gareth Batty
Other sports followed: Football (Manchester United)
Injuries: Groin, out for a month
Relaxations: Spending time with friends outside cricket
Opinions on cricket: '12- or nine-month contracts. Two divisions should be brought
into the game and we should also have a transfer system.'
Best batting: 62 Yorkshire v Glamorgan, Cardiff 1996
Best bowling: 4-29 Yorkshire v Lancashire, Old Trafford 1996

95. Who was England's leading wicket-taker in the 1994-95 Ashes series?

1996 Season

	M	Inns	NO	Runs	HS	Avge	100s	50s	Ct	St	O	M	Runs	Wkts	Avge	Best	5wI	10wM
Test																		
All First	4	4	1	121	62	40.33	-	1	1	-	59.4	18	221	6	36.83	4-29	-	-
1-day Int																		
NatWest																		
B & H	2	0	0	0	0	-	-	-	-	-	19	0	89	5	17.80	4-29	-	
Sunday	2	1	1	2	2 *	-	-	-	-	-	3	1	14	0	-		-	-

Career Performances

	M	Inns	NO	Runs	HS	Avge	100s	50s	Ct	St	Balls	Runs	Wkts	Avge	Best	5wI	10wM
Test																	
All First	5	6	1	167	62	33.40	-	1	1	-	496	299	7	42.71	4-29	-	-
1-day Int																	
NatWest																	
B & H	2	0	0	0	0	-	-	-	-	-	114	89	5	17.80	4-29	-	
Sunday	3	1	1	2	2 *	-	-	-	1	-	66	53	3	17.66	3-39	-	

WHITAKER, J. J.   Leicestershire

Name: John James Whitaker
Role: Right-hand bat, off-spin bowler,
county captain
Born: 5 May 1962, Skipton, Yorkshire
Height: 6ft **Weight:** 13st
Nickname: Jimmy
County debut: 1983
County cap: 1986
Benefit: 1993
Test debut: 1986-87
Tests: 1
One-Day Internationals: 2
1000 runs in a season: 10
1st-Class 50s: 76
1st-Class 100s: 34
1st-Class 200s: 2
1st-Class catches: 165
One-Day 100s: 6
Place in batting averages: 19th av. 54.65
(1995 55th av. 42.20)
Strike rate: (career 88.00)
Parents: John and Ann

Family links with cricket: Father is a local league player
Education: Malsis Hall Prep School; Uppingham School
Qualifications: 7 O-levels
Overseas tours: Uppingham to Australia 1980-81; England to Australia 1986-87, to Sharjah 1987; England A to Zimbabwe and Kenya 1990-91; Hong Kong Sixes 1991, 1992
Overseas teams played for: Glenelg, Australia 1982-83; Old Scotch, Tasmania 1983-84; Somerset West, Cape Town 1984-85
Cricketers particularly admired: Geoff Boycott, Dennis Amiss, Brian Davison, Maurice Hallam
Other sports followed: Football (Leicester City), golf, rugby (Leicester Tigers)
Injuries: Ankle ligaments, out for one month
Relaxations: Eating out, movies, watching sport
Extras: One of *Wisden*'s Five Cricketers of the Year 1986. Second in batting averages in 1986. Young Cricketer Award jointly in 1986. Voted the Brian Sellars County Captain of the Year by the Wombwell Cricket Lovers' Society in 1996. His 218 v Yorkshire in 1996 at Bradford was the highest score by a Yorkshireman against his native county
Opinions on cricket: 'Four-day game is ideal. The Sunday game in the middle is not. The over-rate and number of overs in a day are too high. Benson & Hedges cricket should be 50 overs, as in the World Cup. Keep pitches hard with true bounce and slightly green to start. Do not start a four-day game on a used pitch.'
Best batting: 218 Leicestershire v Yorkshire, Bradford 1996
Best bowling: 1-29 Leicestershire v Somerset, Leicester 1992

1996 Season

	M	Inns	NO	Runs	HS	Avge	100s	50s	Ct	St	O	M	Runs	Wkts	Avge	Best	5wl	10wM
Test																		
All First	16	23	3	1093	218	54.65	4	2	2	-								
1-day Int																		
NatWest	2	1	0	54	54	54.00	-	1	-	-								
B & H	5	5	0	143	70	28.60	-	1	2	-								
Sunday	12	11	2	192	60	21.33	-	1	5	-								

Career Performances

	M	Inns	NO	Runs	HS	Avge	100s	50s	Ct	St	Balls	Runs	Wkts	Avge	Best	5wl	10wM
Test	1	1	0	11	11	11.00	-	-	1	-							
All First	292	465	49	16034	218	38.54	34	76	165	-	176	268	2	134.00	1-29	-	-
1-day Int	2	2	1	48	44 *	48.00	-	-	1	-							
NatWest	28	27	2	1060	155	42.40	1	6	1	-	24	9	0	-	-	-	-
B & H	53	48	2	1375	100	29.89	1	8	9	-							
Sunday	169	157	18	4625	132	33.27	4	27	44	-	2	4	0	-	-	-	

WHITAKER, P. R.   Hampshire

Name: Paul Robert Whitaker
Role: Left-hand opening bat, right-arm
off-spin bowler
Born: 28 June 1973, Keighley, West
Yorkshire
Height: 5ft 10in **Weight:** 11st 7lbs
Nickname: Ticket, Chicken Tikka, Finger-
lickin'
County debut: 1994
1st-Class 50s: 8
1st-Class 100s: 1
1st-Class catches: 3
Place in batting averages: 174th av. 28.15
(1995 133rd av. 29.71)
Place in bowling averages: 123rd av. 42.30
Strike rate: 71.00 (career 70.09)
Parents: Robert and Maureen
Marital status: Single
Family links with cricket: Father played for
Bingley in Bradford League, and now coaches Yorkshire U15
Education: 8 GCSEs, 2 A-levels
Career outside cricket: PE teacher
Overseas tours: Represented England U17, U18 and U19
Overseas teams played for: Bedford, Perth, Australia 1992-93; Southern Hawkes
Bay, New Zealand 1993-94
Cricketers particularly admired: Ian Botham, Tim Tweats, Gary Streer
Other sports followed: Rugby league, football, horse racing
Injuries: Side strain, did not miss any cricket
Relaxations: 'A quiet meal in a restaurant drinking a bottle of Liebfraumilch 1982
wine.'
Best batting: 119 Hampshire v Worcestershire, Southampton 1995
Best bowling: 3-36 Hampshire v Oxford University, The Parks 1996

1996 Season

	M	Inns	NO	Runs	HS	Avge	100s	50s	Ct	St	O	M	Runs	Wkts	Avge	Best	5wI	10wM
Test																		
All First	12	22	3	535	67 *	28.15	-	4	4	-	118.2	26	423	10	42.30	3-36	-	-
1-day Int																		
NatWest	3	3	1	10	8	5.00	-		-	-	14	1	82	3	27.33	3-48	-	
B & H	4	4	0	74	53	18.50	-	1	-	-	27	1	92	4	23.00	2-33	-	
Sunday	13	12	1	218	54	19.81	-	1	1	-	31.2	0	182	7	26.00	3-44	-	

Career Performances

	M	Inns	NO	Runs	HS	Avge	100s	50s	Ct	St	Balls	Runs	Wkts	Avge	Best	5wI	10wM
Test																	
All First	27	46	3	1293	119	30.06	1	8	7	-	771	457	11	41.54	3-36	-	-
1-day Int																	
NatWest	4	4	1	23	13	7.66	-	-	-	-	120	99	3	33.00	3-48	-	
B & H	6	6	0	121	53	20.16	-	1	-	-	168	105	4	26.25	2-33	-	
Sunday	26	25	2	454	97	19.73	-	2	7	-	260	249	9	27.66	3-44	-	

WHITE, C. Yorkshire

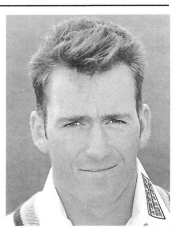

Name: Craig White
Role: Right-hand bat, off-spin bowler, cover fielder
Born: 16 December 1969, Morley, Yorkshire
Height: 6ft 1in **Weight:** 11st 11lbs
Nickname: Chalky, Bassey
County debut: 1990
County cap: 1993
Test debut: 1994
Tests: 6
One-Day Internationals: 10
1st-Class 50s: 26
1st-Class 100s: 6
1st-Class 5 w. in innings: 3
1st-Class catches: 66
One-Day 100s: 1
Place in batting averages: 139th av. 32.72 (1995 119th av. 31.21)
Place in bowling averages: 59th av. 29.72 (1995 110th av. 37.36)
Strike rate: 48.54 (career 54.07)
Parents: Fred Emsley and Cynthia Anne
Wife and date of marriage: Elizabeth Anne, 19 September 1992
Family links with cricket: Father played for Pudsey St Lawrence
Education: Kennington Primary; Flora Hill High School; Bendigo Senior High School (all Victoria, Australia)
Off-season: Touring Australia with England A
Overseas tours: Australian YC to West Indies 1989-90; England to Australia 1994-95, to South Africa 1995-96, to India and Pakistan (World Cup) 1995-96, to Zimbabwe and New Zealand 1996-97; England A to Pakistan 1995-96, to Australia 1996-97
Overseas teams played for: Victoria, Australia 1990-94

Cricketers particularly admired: Graeme Hick, Mark Waugh, Brian Lara
Other sports followed: Leeds RFC, motocross, golf, tennis
Injuries: Torn groin, out for five weeks
Relaxations: Playing guitar, reading, gardening and socialising
Extras: Recommended to Yorkshire by Victorian Cricket Academy, being eligible to play for Yorkshire as he was born in the county. 'Fred Trueman and I are the only Yorkshire players to debut in the 1st XI before the 2nd XI.' Had to fly home from the World Cup in 1995-96 with a side strain and was replaced by Dermot Reeve. Called up to England's tour to Zimbabwe and New Zealand after a successful A tour to Australia as cover for the injured Ronnie Irani
Best batting: 181 Yorkshire v Lancashire, Headingley 1996
Best bowling: 5-40 Yorkshire v Essex, Headingley 1994

1996 Season

	M	Inns	NO	Runs	HS	Avge	100s	50s	Ct	St	O	M	Runs	Wkts	Avge	Best	5wI	10wM
Test																		
All First	19	30	1	949	181	32.72	1	7	13	-	299.2	51	1100	37	29.72	4-15	-	-
1-day Int																		
NatWest	4	3	2	36	21 *	36.00	-	-	2	-	42	4	129	5	25.80	2-23	-	
B & H	6	5	2	94	57 *	31.33	-	1	-	-	49	1	284	7	40.57	2-56	-	
Sunday	17	15	1	249	45	17.78	-	-	3	-	101.1	6	443	20	22.15	4-21	-	

Career Performances

	M	Inns	NO	Runs	HS	Avge	100s	50s	Ct	St	Balls	Runs	Wkts	Avge	Best	5wI	10wM
Test	6	10	0	157	51	15.70	-	1	3	-	565	334	8	41.75	3-18	-	-
All First	110	169	26	4670	181	32.65	6	26	66	-	7516	4225	139	30.39	5-40	3	-
1-day Int	10	8	0	113	34	14.12	-	-	-	-	382	265	8	33.12	2-18	-	
NatWest	15	12	4	389	113	48.62	1	2	7	-	725	432	16	27.00	3-38	-	
B & H	16	13	3	218	57 *	21.80	-	1	3	-	594	490	12	40.83	2-30	-	
Sunday	75	64	14	1350	63	27.00	-	4	24	-	2006	1549	53	29.22	4-21	-	

96. Who was Australia's leading run-scorer in the 1994-95 Ashes series?

Name: Giles William White
Role: Right-hand bat, leg-break bowler
Born: 23 March 1972, Barnstaple
Height: 5ft 11in **Weight:** 12st
Nickname: Chalky, Giler
County debut: 1991 (Somerset), 1994
(Hampshire)
1st-Class 50s: 11
1st-Class 100s: 1
1st-Class catches: 39
Place in batting averages: 153rd av. 31.04
(1995 162nd av. 25.18)
Strike rate: (career 192.00)
Parents: John and Tina
Marital status: Single
Family links with cricket: Father played
club cricket in Devon
Education: Millfield School; Loughborough
University

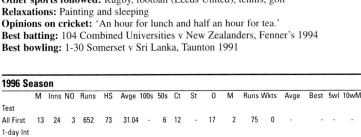

Qualifications: GCSEs, A-levels, BA (Hons)
Off-season: Playing in Cape Town, South Africa
Overseas tours: Millfield School to Australia 1989
Overseas teams played for: Waverley, Sydney 1990-91; Tigers Parrow, Cape Town
1994-95; Techs Mutual, Cape Town 1995-96
Cricketers particularly admired: Wayne Larkins, Brian Lara, Robin Smith, Mark
Lathwell, Paul Terry
Other sports followed: Rugby, football (Leeds United), tennis, golf
Relaxations: Painting and sleeping
Opinions on cricket: 'An hour for lunch and half an hour for tea.'
Best batting: 104 Combined Universities v New Zealanders, Fenner's 1994
Best bowling: 1-30 Somerset v Sri Lanka, Taunton 1991

1996 Season

	M	Inns	NO	Runs	HS	Avge	100s	50s	Ct	St	O	M	Runs	Wkts	Avge	Best	5wl	10wM
Test																		
All First	13	24	3	652	73	31.04	-	6	12	-	17	2	75	0	-	-	-	-
1-day Int																		
NatWest																		
B & H	3	3	0	32	30	10.66	-	-	-	-								
Sunday	9	7	0	207	56	29.57	-	2	2	-								

Career Performances

	M	Inns	NO	Runs	HS	Avge	100s	50s	Ct	St	Balls	Runs	Wkts	Avge	Best	5wI	10wM
Test																	
All First	40	69	6	1715	104	27.22	1	11	39	-	192	140	1	140.00	1-30	-	-
1-day Int																	
NatWest	3	3	0	12	11	4.00	-	-	2	-	72	45	1	45.00	1-45	-	
B & H	6	5	0	69	37	13.80	-	-	-	-							
Sunday	28	26	3	600	59	26.08	-	3	8	-							

WHITTICASE, P.   Leicestershire

Name: Philip Whitticase
Role: Right-hand bat, wicket-keeper
Born: 15 March 1965, Wythall, Birmingham
Height: 5ft 8in **Weight:** 11st
Nickname: Jasper, Tracy, Boggy, Rat
County debut: 1984
County cap: 1987
Benefit: 1997
1st-Class 50s: 17
1st-Class 100s: 1
1st-Class catches: 309
1st-Class stumpings: 14
Parents: Larry Gordon and Ann
Marital status: Single
Family links with cricket: Grandfather and
father played local club cricket (both were
wicket-keepers)
Education: Belle Vue Junior and Middle
School; Buckpool Secondary; Crestwood
Comprehensive
Qualifications: 5 O-levels, 4 CSEs, senior coaching certificate
Overseas teams played for: South Bunbury, Western Australia 1983-85
Cricketers particularly admired: Bob Taylor, Alan Knott, Dennis Amiss
Other sports followed: Football, rugby
Relaxations: Playing soccer, watching rugby and 'a good night out'
Extras: Played schoolboy football for Birmingham City. Was Derek Underwood's last
first-class victim. Lost seven teeth after being struck in the mouth by a bouncer from
Neil Williams in Leicestershire's game against Essex in April 1995
Best batting: 114* Leicestershire v Hampshire, Bournemouth 1991

1996 (did not make any first-class or one-day appearances)

Career Performances

	M	Inns	NO	Runs	HS	Avge	100s	50s	Ct	St	Balls	Runs	Wkts	Avge	Best	5wI	10wM
Test																	
All First	132	174	40	3113	114 *	23.23	1	17	309	14	5	7	0	-	-	-	-
1-day Int																	
NatWest	13	6	1	67	32	13.40	-	-	14	-							
B & H	29	19	7	313	45	26.08	-	-	29	4							
Sunday	69	45	9	413	38	11.47	-	-	56	4							

WILEMAN, J. R.   Nottinghamshire

Name: Jonathan Ritchie Wileman
Role: Right-hand bat, right-arm medium bowler
Born: 19 August 1970, Sheffield
Height: 6ft 1in **Weight:** 13st
County debut: 1992
1st-Class 100s: 1
1st-Class catches: 9
Place in batting averages: (1995 213th av. 19.16)
Strike rate: (career 142.50)
Parents: Peter and Joan
Marital status: Engaged to Nicole
Education: Malvern College; Salford University
Qualifications: 12 0-levels, 3 A-levels, BA in Modern Languages
Off-season: Playing in Sydney, Australia
Overseas teams played for: Gordon, Sydney 1995-96
Cricketers particularly admired: Ian Botham, Viv Richards
Other sports followed: Football (Sheffield Wednesday), skiing, tennis, baseball (Toronto Blue Jays)
Relaxations: 'Watching films, listening to music, being set on fire by Chris Cairns'
Extras: Scored 109 on first-class debut for Nottinghamshire against Cambridge University. Played for Lincolnshire and Minor Counties in 1994, did not play any first-team games for Nottinghamshire. Released by Nottinghamshire at the end of the 1996 season
Opinions on cricket: 'Required over-rate in first-class cricket is unrealistic.'

Best batting: 109 Nottinghamshire v Cambridge University, Trent Bridge 1992
Best bowling: 2-33 Nottinghamshire v Hampshire, Trent Bridge 1995

1996 Season

	M	Inns	NO	Runs	HS	Avge	100s	50s	Ct	St	O	M	Runs	Wkts	Avge	Best	5wI	10wM
Test																		
All First	1	0	0	0	0	-	-	-	-	-								
1-day Int																		
NatWest																		
B & H																		
Sunday																		

Career Performances

	M	Inns	NO	Runs	HS	Avge	100s	50s	Ct	St	Balls	Runs	Wkts	Avge	Best	5wI	10wM
Test																	
All First	12	21	6	447	109	29.80	1	-	9	-	570	217	4	54.25	2-33	-	-
1-day Int																	
NatWest	3	2	0	26	14	13.00	-	-	2	-	48	55	2	27.50	1-9	-	
B & H	2	1	0	0	0	0.00	-	-	1	-	18	15	0	-	-	-	
Sunday	16	13	8	226	51 *	45.20	-	1	9	-	488	476	17	28.00	4-21	-	

WILLIAMS, N. F.   Essex

Name: Neil FitzGerald Williams
Role: Right-hand bat, right-arm
fast-medium bowler
Born: 2 July 1962, Hope Well, St Vincent,
West Indies
Height: 5ft 10in **Weight:** 11st 7lbs
Nickname: Joe
County debut: 1982 (Middlesex),
1995 (Essex)
County cap: 1984 (Middlesex), 1996 (Essex)
Benefit: 1994
Test debut: 1990
Tests: 1
50 wickets in a season: 3
1st-Class 50s: 13
1st-Class 5 w. in innings: 21
1st-Class 10 w. in match: 2
1st-Class catches: 62
Place in batting averages: 255th av. 17.00

Place in bowling averages: 78th av. 33.14 (1995 100th av. 35.38)
Strike rate: 56.85 (career 55.65)
Parents: Alexander and Aldreta
Marital status: Single
Family links with cricket: 'Uncle Joe plays first division cricket in St Vincent and the Grenadines'
Education: Cane End Primary School, St Vincent; Acland Burghley School, Tufnell Park
Qualifications: School Leaver's Certificate, 6 O-levels, 1 A-level
Overseas tours: English Counties to Zimbabwe 1984-85; MCC to Leeward Islands 1992
Overseas teams played for: St Vincent 1982-92; Windward Islands 1982-92; Tasmania 1983-84
Cricketers particularly admired: Viv Richards, Desmond Haynes, David Gower
Other sports followed: Athletics
Relaxations: Music, 'useful DJ', cinema
Extras: Was on stand-by for England in New Zealand and Pakistan 1983-84. Joined Essex for the 1995 season
Best batting: 77 Middlesex v Warwickshire, Edgbaston 1991
Best bowling: 8-75 Middlesex v Gloucestershire, Lord's 1992

1996 Season

	M	Inns	NO	Runs	HS	Avge	100s	50s	Ct	St	O	M	Runs	Wkts	Avge	Best	5wI	10wM
Test																		
All First	12	16	3	221	39	17.00	-	-	2	-	331.4	59	1160	35	33.14	5-43	2	-
1-day Int																		
NatWest	3	2	2	17	11*	-	-	-	-	-	27.4	0	119	2	59.50	1-37	-	
B & H	1	0	0	0	0	-	-	-	-	-	10	0	67	2	33.50	2-67	-	
Sunday	2	1	0	12	12	12.00	-	-	-	-	11	0	71	2	35.50	2-56	-	

Career Performances

	M	Inns	NO	Runs	HS	Avge	100s	50s	Ct	St	Balls	Runs	Wkts	Avge	Best	5wI	10wM
Test	1	1	0	38	38	38.00	-	-	-	-	246	148	2	74.00	2-148	-	-
All First	242	281	56	4220	77	18.75	-	13	62	-	35398	19263	636	30.28	8-75	21	2
1-day Int																	
NatWest	22	12	5	66	11*	9.42	-	-	4	-	1079	737	17	43.35	4-36	-	
B & H	56	31	7	259	29*	10.79	-	-	7	-	2940	1879	58	32.39	3-16	-	
Sunday	125	55	20	455	43	13.00	-	-	31	-	5159	3860	137	28.17	4-39	-	

97. Who was Australia's leading wicket-taker in the 1994-95 Ashes series?

WILLIAMS, R. C. J.   Gloucestershire

Name: Richard Charles James Williams
Role: Left-hand bat, wicket-keeper
Born: 8 August 1969, Bristol
Height: 5ft 10in **Weight:** 11st
Nickname: Reg
County debut: 1990
County cap: 1996
1st-Class 50s: 4
1st-Class catches: 93
1st-Class stumpings: 14
Place in batting averages: 256th av. 16.62
(1995 166th av. 24.77)
Parents: Michael (deceased) and Angela
Marital status: Single
Family links with cricket: Father played
local club cricket
Education: Clifton College Preparatory
School; Millfield School
Qualifications: PE Diploma, NCA junior coaching award
Off-season: Gloucestershire Gypsies tour to South Africa
Overseas tours: Gloucestershire to Namibia 1990, to Kenya 1991, to Sri Lanka 1992-93; Romany CC to Durban & Cape Town 1993; Gloucestershire Gypsies to Zimbabwe 1994-95, to South Africa 1995-96
Overseas teams played for: Manicaland, Zimbabwe 1990-91
Cricketers particularly admired: Andy Brassington, Jack Russell, David Gower
Other sports followed: Football, hockey, squash, snooker
Relaxations: 'Eating out, pubs and clubs, strutting my funky stuff'
Best batting: 90 Gloucestershire v Oxford University, Bristol 1995

1996 Season

	M	Inns	NO	Runs	HS	Avge	100s	50s	Ct	St	O	M	Runs	Wkts	Avge	Best	5wI	10wM
Test																		
All First	5	8	0	133	44	16.62	-	-	12	1								
1-day Int																		
NatWest																		
B & H																		
Sunday	3	2	0	13	11	6.50	-	-	4	2								

	M	Inns	NO	Runs	HS	Avge	100s	50s	Ct	St	Balls	Runs	Wkts	Avge	Best	5wI	10wM
Test																	
All First	35	44	8	640	90	17.77	-	4	93	14							
1-day Int																	
NatWest																	
B & H																	
Sunday	17	6	2	76	19	19.00	-	-	19	4							

WILLIAMSON, D. Leicestershire

Name: Dominic Williamson
Role: Right-hand bat, right-arm medium-fast bowler
Born: 15 November 1975, Durham City
Height: 5ft 10in. **Weight:** 10st 7lbs
Nickname: Ewok
County debut: 1996
Strike rate: (career 174.00)
Parents: Gerard Williamson and Dorothy Smith
Marital status: Single
Family links with cricket: Father and brother both play in local leagues
Education: Easington C of E Primary School, Co. Durham; St Leonards RC Comprehensive, Co. Durham; Durham Sixth Form Centre
Qualifications: 7 O-levels, 3 A-levels
Career outside cricket: Accountancy
Off-season: Playing in South Africa
Overseas teams played for: Ashburton CC, Australia 1993-95; Klerksdorp CC, South Africa 1996-97
Cricketers particularly admired: Brian McMillan
Young players to look out for: Tim Mason
Other sports followed: Football (Newcastle United), tennis and golf
Injuries: None
Relaxations: Playing golf and going to the gym
Opinions on cricket: '2nd XI matches should be played over four days and not three.'
Best bowling: 1-32 Leicestershire v India, Leicester 1996

1996 Season

	M	Inns	NO	Runs	HS	Avge	100s	50s	Ct	St	O	M	Runs	Wkts	Avge	Best	5wI	10wM
Test																		
All First	1	0	0	0	0	-	-	-	-	-	29	8	95	1	95.00	1-32	-	-
1-day Int																		
NatWest																		
B & H	2	1	0	6	6	6.00	-	-	-	-	14	0	91	1	91.00	1-64	-	
Sunday	13	8	5	25	9	8.33	-	-	3	-	55.5	1	295	7	42.14	3-29	-	

Career Performances

	M	Inns	NO	Runs	HS	Avge	100s	50s	Ct	St	Balls	Runs	Wkts	Avge	Best	5wI	10wM
Test																	
All First	1	0	0	0	0	-	-	-	-	-	174	95	1	95.00	1-32	-	-
1-day Int																	
NatWest																	
B & H	2	1	0	6	6	6.00	-	-	-	-	84	91	1	91.00	1-64	-	
Sunday	13	8	5	25	9	8.33	-	-	3	-	335	295	7	42.14	3-29	-	

WILLIS, S. C.   Kent

Name: Simon Charles Willis
Role: Right-hand bat, wicket-keeper
Born: 19 March 1974, Greenwich, London
Height: 5ft 8in **Weight:** 12st 4lbs
Nickname: Wilco, Bruce
County debut: 1993
1st-Class 50s: 3
1st-Class catches: 23
Parents: Ray and Janet
Wife and date of marriage: Louise Clare,
12 October 1996
Family links with cricket: Father played in
the Kent League for many years
Education: Fleetdown Primary School;
Wilmington Grammar School
Qualifications: 9 GCSEs, NCA Junior
Coaching Certificate
Off-season: Coaching
Overseas tours: Kent U17 to New Zealand 1990-91; Kent to Zimbabwe 1993
Overseas teams played for: Scarborough, Western Australia 1992-93
Cricketers particularly admired: Alan Knott, Viv Richards, Robin Smith, Carl Hooper
Young players to look out for: Robert Key, Will House

Other sports followed: Golf, soccer (Arsenal FC), horse racing
Relaxations: 'Playing golf, listening to music and going out with my wife'
Best batting: 82 Kent v Cambridge University, Folkestone 1995

1996 Season

	M	Inns	NO	Runs	HS	Avge	100s	50s	Ct	St	O	M	Runs	Wkts	Avge	Best	5wl	10wM
Test																		
All First	5	6	1	141	78	28.20	-	1	11	-								
1-day Int																		
NatWest																		
B & H																		
Sunday	4	4	2	55	31 *	27.50	-	-	5	-								

Career Performances

	M	Inns	NO	Runs	HS	Avge	100s	50s	Ct	St	Balls	Runs	Wkts	Avge	Best	5wl	10wM
Test																	
All First	9	11	2	294	82	32.66	-	3	23	-							
1-day Int																	
NatWest	1	1	1	19	19 *	-	-	-	1	-							
B & H	1	0	0	0	0	-	-	-	-	-							
Sunday	7	6	2	80	31 *	20.00	-	-	11	-							

WILSON, D. G.   Essex

Name: Daniel Graeme Wilson
Role: Right-hand bat, right-arm
medium bowler
Born: 18 February 1977, Paddington
Height: 6ft 2in **Weight:** 13st
Nickname: OJ, Juice, Stan
County debut: 1996 (one-day)
Parents: Tony and Margaret
Marital status: Single
Family links with cricket: 'Dad played for
Trinidad Colts. Brother Rob, stepbrother Nick
and stepfather John play for the local village
team. Mum plays fantasy cricket'
Education: The Firs Primary School,
Bishop's Stortford; St Mary's RC School;
Cheltenham and Gloucester College of
Higher Education
Qualifications: 10 GCSEs, 3 A-levels

Career outside cricket: 'All aspects to do with college life'
Off-season: At university
Cricketers particularly admired: Michael Holding, Brian Lara, Phil Simmons, Nick Maley, Stuart Law
Young players to look out for: Robert Rollins
Other sports followed: Football (Liverpool FC), golf, snooker
Injuries: Ankle sprain, out for three weeks
Relaxations: 'Listening to sweet soul and smooth swing. Playing on my Playstation'
Extras: Father used to play in the 70s band Hot Chocolate
Opinions on cricket: 'Lunch and tea breaks should be ten minutes longer. Too much is stacked in favour of the batsman. Seams should be bigger and pitches a little more helpful to the bowlers. Spinners should be banned!'

1996 Season

	M	Inns	NO	Runs	HS	Avge	100s	50s	Ct	St	O	M	Runs	Wkts	Avge	Best	5wI	10wM
Test																		
All First																		
1-day Int																		
NatWest																		
B & H																		
Sunday	2	1	0	7	7	7.00	-	-	1	-	8	0	40	3	13.33	3-40	-	

Career Performances

	M	Inns	NO	Runs	HS	Avge	100s	50s	Ct	St	Balls	Runs	Wkts	Avge	Best	5wI	10wM
Test																	
All First																	
1-day Int																	
NatWest																	
B & H																	
Sunday	2	1	0	7	7	7.00	-	-	1	-	48	40	3	13.33	3-40	-	

98. Which Australian batsman scored centuries in his first two Test matches in 1994-95?

WILSON, E. J.   Worcestershire

Name: Elliot James Wilson
Role: Right-hand bat, 'bowls pies'
Born: 3 October 1976, London
Height: 6ft 2in **Weight:** 14st 7lbs
County debut: No first-team appearance
Parents: Alec and Fay
Marital status: Single
Family links with cricket: None
Education: Felsted Prep School; Felsted
School; University of Durham
Qualifications: 10 GCSEs, 3 A-levels
Career outside cricket: Student
Off-season: Studying at Durham University
Overseas tours: Felsted to Australia 1995-96
Overseas teams played for: Pinetown CC,
Durham, South Africa 1995-96
Cricketers particularly admired: Nick
Knight, Tom Jackson, Tom Moody
Young players to look out for: Stephen

Peters, Andrew Strauss, Tom Jackson, Tim Duke, Steve Molloy
Other sports followed: Rugby (England and Old Belly XV) and football (England)
Relaxations: 'Rixy's and Klute "chilling there"'
Extras: Took Felsted batting record off Nick Knight with 1200 runs in 16 innings
Opinions on cricket: 'Young players should be given every opportunity.'

WINDOWS, M. G. N.   Gloucestershire

Name: Matthew Guy Newman Windows
Role: Right-hand bat, left-arm bowler
Born: 5 April 1973, Clifton, Bristol
Height: 5ft 7in **Weight:** 11st
Nickname: Steamy
County debut: 1992
1st-Class 50s: 9
1st-Class 100s: 2
1st-Class catches: 28
Place in batting averages: 162nd av. 29.53 (1995 198th av. 20.86)
Strike rate: (career 25.50)
Parents: Tony and Carolyn

Marital status: Single
Family links with cricket: Father (A.R.) played for Gloucestershire (1960-69) and Cambridge University
Education: Clifton College; Durham University
Qualifications: 8 GCSEs, 3 A-levels, BA (Hons) in Sociology
Off-season: Playing overseas
Overseas tours: England U19 to Pakistan 1991-92; Durham University to South Africa 1992
Cricketers particularly admired: Graham Gooch, Mike Proctor
Young players to look out for: Vikram Solanki
Other sports followed: Rugby (Bristol RFC), rackets
Relaxations: Listening to music, sleeping, watching television, 'a couple of pints with my mates'
Extras: Played for Lincolnshire and in England U19 home series v Sri Lanka 1992. Public schools rackets and fives champion. 1994 Gloucestershire Young Player of the Year. Holds the record for highest individual score for Durham University (218 not out)
Opinions on cricket: 'We have to bowl too many overs in a day resulting in a heavy fine rate. The county circuit offers us great camaraderie.'
Best batting: 184 Gloucestershire v Warwickshire, Cheltenham 1996
Best bowling: 1-6 Combined Universities v West Indies, The Parks 1995

1996 Season

	M	Inns	NO	Runs	HS	Avge	100s	50s	Ct	St	O	M	Runs	Wkts	Avge	Best	5wI	10wM
Test																		
All First	9	17	2	443	184	29.53	1	1	4	-								
1-day Int																		
NatWest																		
B & H																		
Sunday	10	9	1	138	37	17.25	-	-	1	-								

Career Performances

	M	Inns	NO	Runs	HS	Avge	100s	50s	Ct	St	Balls	Runs	Wkts	Avge	Best	5wI	10wM
Test																	
All First	32	60	4	1695	184	30.26	2	9	28	-	51	39	2	19.50	1-6	-	-
1-day Int																	
NatWest	3	3	0	42	33	14.00	-	-	-	-							
B & H	1	1	1	16	16 *	-	-	-	-	-							
Sunday	33	32	2	597	72	19.90	-	2	7	-	48	49	0	-		-	-

WOMBLE, D. R. — Derbyshire

Name: David Robert Womble
Role: Right-hand bat, right-arm fast bowler
Born: 23 February 1977, Stoke-on-Trent
Height: 5ft 11in **Weight:** 12st 2lbs
Nickname: Wombz
County debut: 1996 (one-day)
Parents: Michael and Marjory
Marital status: Single
Family links with cricket: Father plays club cricket
Education: Parkhall County Primary; St Thomas More RC High School; Stoke-on-Trent Sixth Form College; Leeds Metropolitan University
Qualifications: Preliminary cricket award
Off-season: At university
Cricketers particularly admired: Ian Botham, Dominic Cork
Young players to look out for: Andrew Harris, Mike Longmore
Other sports followed: Football (Stoke City), rugby, squash
Injuries: Shin soreness, out for two months
Relaxations: Music and going out
Extras: Played for the National Association of Young Cricketers
Opinions on cricket: 'Brilliant, although maybe too much one-day cricket.'

1996 Season

	M	Inns	NO	Runs	HS	Avge	100s	50s	Ct	St	O	M	Runs	Wkts	Avge	Best	5wI	10wM
Test																		
All First																		
1-day Int																		
NatWest																		
B & H																		
Sunday	1	0	0	0	0	-	-	-	-	-	3	0	29	0	-		-	-

99. Who scored the only double century for England on their 1994-95 Australian tour?

Career Performances

	M	Inns	NO	Runs	HS	Avge	100s	50s	Ct	St	Balls	Runs	Wkts	Avge	Best	5wI	10wM
Test																	
All First																		
1-day Int																		
NatWest																		
B & H																		
Sunday	1	0	0	0	0	-	-	-	-	-	18	29	0	-	-	-	-

WOOD, J.   Durham

Name: John Wood
Role: Right-hand bat, right-arm
fast-medium bowler
Born: 22 July 1970, Wakefield
Height: 6ft 3in **Weight:** 16st
Nickname: Woody
County debut: 1992
1st-Class 50s: 2
1st-Class 5 w. in innings: 4
1st-Class catches: 10
Place in batting averages: 308th av. 6.92
(1994 267th av. 10.21)
Place in bowling averages: 138th av. 48.69
(1995 15th av. 21.64)
Strike rate: 67.26 (career 53.95)
Parents: Brian and Anne
Wife and date of marriage: Emma Louise,
30 October 1994
Children: Alexandra Mae, 7 April 1996
Family links with cricket: Father played and brother plays local cricket
Education: Crofton High School; Wakefield District College; Leeds Polytechnic
Qualifications: 6 O-levels, BTEC Diploma and HND in Electrical and Electronic
Engineering, senior coaching certificate
Off-season: 'Paying my mortgage off'
Overseas teams played for: Griqualand West Cricket Union, South Africa 1990-91;
TAWA, New Zealand 1993-95; Wellington, New Zealand, 1993-95
Cricketers particularly admired: Simon Brown, Andrew Pratt, Shaun Birbeck
Young players to look out for: 'Me'
Injuries: Rib injury, missed two months
Relaxations: Television, good food and pub, swimming
Extras: Played in the Bradford League. Made his debut for Durham (Minor Counties)
in 1991

Opinions on cricket: 'Crap game. Wish I could have been a football player.'
Best batting: 63* Durham v Nottinghamshire, Chester-le-Street 1993
Best bowling: 6-110 Durham v Essex, Stockton 1994

1996 Season

	M	Inns	NO	Runs	HS	Avge	100s	50s	Ct	St	O	M	Runs	Wkts	Avge	Best	5wl	10wM
Test																		
All First	9	16	2	97	35 *	6.92	-	-	4	-	291.3	46	1266	26	48.69	4-60	-	-
1-day Int																		
NatWest																		
B & H																		
Sunday	6	5	3	61	21	30.50	-	-	-	-	48	2	294	6	49.00	2-36	-	

Career Performances

	M	Inns	NO	Runs	HS	Avge	100s	50s	Ct	St	Balls	Runs	Wkts	Avge	Best	5wl	10wM
Test																	
All First	45	68	11	707	63 *	12.40	-	2	10	-	6367	4339	118	36.77	6-110	4	-
1-day Int																	
NatWest	5	1	0	1	1	1.00	-	-	-	-	228	168	4	42.00	2-22	-	
B & H	6	4	0	36	27	9.00	-	-	-	-	348	224	5	44.80	3-50	-	
Sunday	24	17	6	138	28	12.54	-	-	2	-	1008	913	21	43.47	2-26	-	

WOOD, M. J.   Yorkshire

Name: Matthew James Wood
Role: Right-hand opening bat
Born: 6 April 1977, Huddersfield
Height: 5ft 10in **Weight:** 11st 7lbs
Nickname: Chuddy, Woody, Forrest
County debut: No first-team appearance
Parents: Roger and Cathryn
Marital status: Single
Family links with cricket: 'Father played at local club Emley. Mother made the teas, sister was the scorer'
Education: Emley Primary School; Shelley High School; Shelley Sixth Form College
Qualifications: 9 GCSEs, 2 A-levels
Career outside cricket: 'None yet'
Off-season: 'Rest, stay at home, get fit and work hard on my game'
Overseas tours: England U19 to Zimbabwe

1995-96
Overseas teams played for: Somerset West CC, Cape Town 1995-96
Cricketers particularly admired: Martyn Moxon, Michael Slater, Anthony McGrath
Young players to look out for: Alex Morris, Alex Wharf
Other sports followed: Football (Liverpool FC)
Injuries: Pulled muscle in neck, out for 12 days
Relaxations: Socialising, listening to music, eating out, football
Extras: Played for England U17 against Sri Lanka in 1994. Yorkshire Academy 1994-95. Yorkshire Supporters Association Young Player of the Year 1995
Opinions on cricket: 'Players should get a nine- to 12-month contract, to reduce problems with winter employmennt.'

WOOD, N. T. Lancashire

Name: Nathan Theodore Wood
Role: Left-hand opening bat, right-arm
off-spin bowler
Born: 4 October 1974, Ossett, Yorkshire
Height: 5ft 7in **Weight:** 10st 7lbs
Nickname: Rodders, Precious
County debut: 1996
Parents: Barry and Janet
Marital status: Single
Family links with cricket: Father played for
Yorkshire, Lancashire, Derbyshire and
England; uncle (Ron) played for Yorkshire
Education: Altrincham Prep School; William
Hulme's Grammar School
Qualifications: 8 GCSEs, coaching awards
Off-season: 'Coaching young 'uns'
Overseas tours: England U18 to South
Africa 1992-93, to Denmark 1993; England
U19 to Sri Lanka 1993-94

Cricketers particularly admired: 'My father', David Gower, Michael Holding, Viv Richards
Other sports followed: Football (Manchester United)
Relaxations: Music and friends
Extras: Played in Junior One-Day Internationals against Zimbabwe, India, South Africa and Sri Lanka. Played in U19 Tests against West Indies and Sri Lanka
Opinions on cricket: 'Too many overs in a day.'
Best batting: 1 Lancashire v Essex, Chelmsford 1996

1996 Season

	M	Inns	NO	Runs	HS	Avge	100s	50s	Ct	St	O	M	Runs	Wkts	Avge	Best	5wl	10wM
Test																		
All First	1	1	0	1	1	1.00	-	-	-	-								
1-day Int																		
NatWest																		
B & H																		
Sunday																		

Career Performances

	M	Inns	NO	Runs	HS	Avge	100s	50s	Ct	St	Balls	Runs	Wkts	Avge	Best	5wl	10wM
Test																	
All First	1	1	0	1	1	1.00	-	-	-	-							
1-day Int																	
NatWest																	
B & H																	
Sunday																	

WREN, T. N.   Kent

Name: Timothy Neil Wren
Role: Right-hand bat, left-arm medium bowler
Born: 26 March 1970, Folkestone
Height: 6ft 3in **Weight:** 14st 7lbs
Nickname: Bear, Balou
County debut: 1989 (one-day), 1990 (first-class)
1st-Class 5 w. in innings: 3
1st-Class catches: 12
One-Day 5 w. in innings: 1
Place in bowling averages: (1995 89th av. 34.13)
Strike rate: 74.66 (career 62.06)
Parents: James and Gillian
Marital status: Single
Family links with cricket: 'Brother suicidal about his comeback!'
Education: Lyminge Primary; Harvey Grammar School, Folkestone
Qualifications: 6 O-levels, NCA coaching certificate
Career outside cricket: Plumbing and central heating engineer
Off-season: Working as a plumber, playing golf

Overseas teams played for: Universals, Zimbabwe 1989-90
Cricketers particularly admired: Aravinda De Silva, Carl Hooper, Curtly Ambrose
Other sports followed: Rugby, football (Lyminge)
Relaxations: 'Golf, reading, eating out, walking my dog'
Opinions on cricket: 'Too much talk of major changes. Not too much wrong with our cricket. Stop looking at other countries as a way to improve our cricket. Standard of pitches is not good enough, also sides are allowed to get away with sub-standard pitches.'
Best batting: 23 Kent v Sussex, Hove 1995
Best bowling: 6-48 Kent v Somerset, Canterbury 1994

1996 Season

	M	Inns	NO	Runs	HS	Avge	100s	50s	Ct	St	O	M	Runs	Wkts	Avge	Best	5wI	10wM
Test																		
All First	7	5	2	15	8	5.00	-	-	3	-	112	22	409	9	45.44	5-49	1	-
1-day Int																		
NatWest																		
B & H	2	1	0	0	0	0.00	-	-	1	-	5	0	53	1	53.00	1-21	-	
Sunday	13	6	3	19	7 *	6.33	-	-	1	-	83	3	429	6	71.50	2-32	-	

Career Performances

	M	Inns	NO	Runs	HS	Avge	100s	50s	Ct	St	Balls	Runs	Wkts	Avge	Best	5wI	10wM
Test																	
All First	29	33	12	130	23	6.19	-	-	12	-	3972	2394	64	37.40	6-48	3	-
1-day Int																	
NatWest	2	2	1	1	1 *	1.00	-	-	-	-	120	92	1	92.00	1-51	-	
B & H	7	3	1	11	7	5.50	-	-	2	-	324	256	13	19.69	6-41	1	
Sunday	32	12	9	34	7 *	11.33	-	-	5	-	1227	984	22	44.72	3-20	-	

---

100. Who, acting as a runner for Craig McDermott in the fifth
Test between Australia and England in Perth 1994-95,
was run out, leaving Steve Waugh stranded on 99?

WRIGHT, A. J.   Gloucestershire

Name: Anthony John Wright
Role: Right-hand bat, off-spin bowler
Born: 27 July 1962, Stevenage, Hertfordshire
Height: 6ft **Weight:** 14st
Nickname: Billy
County debut: 1982
County cap: 1987
1000 runs in a season: 6
1st-Class 50s: 65
1st-Class 100s: 18
1st-Class catches: 202
One-Day 100s: 3
Place in batting averages: 201st av. 24.41
(1995 36th av. 46.60)
Strike rate: (career 74.00)
Parents: Michael and Patricia
Wife and date of marriage: Rachel, 21
December 1986

Children: Hannah, 3 April 1988; Beth, 19
August 1992; Joseph, 29 November 1993
Education: Alleyn's School, Stevenage
Qualifications: 6 O-levels
Off-season: 'Working for IES Telecom, Bristol and preparing for my benefit. Also
creating chances for Bobby Dawson to score for Bristol North West FC'
Overseas tours: Gloucestershire to Sri Lanka 1987 and 1993, to Barbados 1980,
1985, 1988, to Namibia 1990, to Kenya 1991
Cricketers particularly admired: Mike Gatting, Malcolm Marshall, Dermot Reeve,
David Gower
Other sports followed: Soccer ('life-long Chelsea supporter'), rugby (Bristol RFC)
Relaxations: 'Celebrating any Arsenal defeat and hacking my way around a golf
course'
Extras: Captain of Gloucestershire for 1990-93. Awarded benefit for 1996
Opinions on cricket: 'I feel that it is vital that the game is introduced to as many
youngsters as possible. Unless kids are at private schools they are unlikely to get a
chance to participate – a shocking situation! I would like to see our Test team being
prepared specifically to beat the Aussies in the next series over here. I'm sick of hearing
them say how poor our game is.'
Best batting: 193 Gloucestershire v Nottinghamshire, Bristol 1995
Best bowling: 1-16 Gloucestershire v Yorkshire, Harrogate 1989

1996 Season

	M	Inns	NO	Runs	HS	Avge	100s	50s	Ct	St	O	M	Runs	Wkts	Avge	Best	5wI	10wM
Test																		
All First	9	17	0	415	106	24.41	1	3	11	-								
1-day Int																		
NatWest	2	2	0	12	7	6.00	-	-	-	-								
B & H	5	5	0	258	123	51.60	1	1	2	-								
Sunday	10	10	0	229	96	22.90	-	1	5	-								

Career Performances

	M	Inns	NO	Runs	HS	Avge	100s	50s	Ct	St	Balls	Runs	Wkts	Avge	Best	5wI	10wM
Test																	
All First	263	462	35	12679	193	29.69	18	65	202	-	74	68	1	68.00	1-16	-	-
1-day Int																	
NatWest	28	27	2	1082	142 *	43.28	2	9	10	-							
B & H	44	41	0	1274	123	31.07	1	8	10	-							
Sunday	171	160	17	3617	96	25.29	-	24	62	-	26	22	0	-		-	-

YATES, G. Lancashire

Name: Gary Yates
Role: Right-hand bat, off-spin bowler
Born: 20 September 1967,
Ashton-under-Lyne
Height: 6ft 1in **Weight:** 12st 10lbs
Nickname: Yugo, Pearly, Backyard, Zippy
County debut: 1990
County cap: 1994
1st-Class 50s: 3
1st-Class 100s: 3
1st-Class 5 w. in innings: 2
1st-Class catches: 17
Place in batting averages: (1995 177th av. 23.14)
Place in bowling averages: (1995 130th av. 44.90)
Strike rate: 112.00 (career 85.62)
Parents: Alan and Patricia
Marital status: Single
Family links with cricket: Father played in Lancashire Leagues
Education: Manchester Grammar School
Qualifications: 6 O-levels, Australian Coaching Council coach

Career outside cricket: 'Getting more involved in family business (Digical Ltd), selling diaries, calendars and business gifts.'

Off-season: 'Working in family business'

Overseas tours: Lancashire to Tasmania and Western Australia 1990, to Western Australia 1991, to Johannesburg 1992, to Barbados and St Lucia 1992

Overseas teams played for: South Barwon, Geelong, Australia 1987-88; Johnsonville, Wellington, New Zealand 1989-90; Western Suburbs, Brisbane 1991-92; Old Selbornian, East London, South Africa 1992-93; Hermanus CC, South Africa 1995-96

Cricketers particularly admired: Michael Atherton, Ian Botham, John Emburey

Other sports followed: All sports, especially football (Manchester City), golf, motor rallying

Injuries: Finger infection, out for four weeks

Relaxations: Playing golf, watching football and good films, eating

Extras: Played for Worcestershire 2nd XI in 1987; made debut for Lancashire 2nd XI in 1988 and taken on to county staff in 1990; scored century on Championship debut v Nottinghamshire at Trent Bridge. Rapid Cricketline Player of the Month April/May 1992

Opinions on cricket: 'Would like to see more points awarded for rained-off games or draws. This would hopefully help to abolish contrived matches. Hope four-day cricket is here to stay.'

Best batting: 134* Lancashire v Northamptonshire, Old Trafford 1993

Best bowling: 5-34 Lancashire v Hampshire, Old Trafford 1994

1996 Season

	M	Inns	NO	Runs	HS	Avge	100s	50s	Ct	St	O	M	Runs	Wkts	Avge	Best	5wI	10wM
Test																		
All First	3	5	1	21	16	5.25	-	-	2	-	93.2	20	325	5	65.00	3-91	-	-
1-day Int																		
NatWest	5	4	3	19	9	19.00	-	-	1	-	48	7	183	4	45.75	2-42	-	
B & H	8	5	0	46	26	9.20	-	-	-	-	55	4	222	7	31.71	3-65	-	
Sunday	17	9	3	92	38	15.33	-	-	3	-	99	0	492	18	27.33	3-18	-	

Career Performances

	M	Inns	NO	Runs	HS	Avge	100s	50s	Ct	St	Balls	Runs	Wkts	Avge	Best	5wI	10wM
Test																	
All First	55	74	31	1302	134 *	30.27	3	3	19	-	9247	4858	108	44.98	5-34	2	-
1-day Int																	
NatWest	10	6	4	35	9	17.50	-	-	1	-	648	369	9	41.00	2-42	-	-
B & H	21	6	1	65	26	13.00	-	-	4	-	960	648	22	29.45	3-42	-	
Sunday	58	21	9	167	38	13.91	-	-	15	-	2088	1760	61	28.85	4-34	-	

YOUNG, S.   Gloucestershire

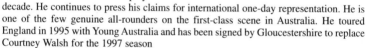

Name: Shaun Young
Role: Left-hand bat, right-arm
fast-medium bowler
Born: 13 June 1970, Burnie, Tasmania
County debut: No first-team appearance
1st-Class 50s: 23
1st-Class 100s: 6
1st-Class 5w. in innings: 6
1st-Class 10w. in match: 1
Strike rate: (career 71.73)
Off-season: Playing Shield cricket for
Tasmania
Overseas teams played for:
Tasmania 1991-1997
Overseas tours: Young Australia to England
1995
Extras: Has been rated as Tasmania's most
valuable non-international player of the
decade. He continues to press his claims for international one-day representation. He is
one of the few genuine all-rounders on the first-class scene in Australia. He toured
England in 1995 with Young Australia and has been signed by Gloucestershire to replace
Courtney Walsh for the 1997 season
Best batting: 175* Tasmania v Queensland, Brisbane 1995-96
Best bowling: 5-36 Tasmania v Pakistan, Devonport 1991-92

1996 season (did not make any first-class or one-day appearances)

Career Performances

	M	Inns	NO	Runs	HS	Avge	100s	50s	Ct	St	Balls	Runs	Wkts	Avge	Best	5wI	10wM
Test																	
All First	60	98	17	3418	175 *	42.19	6	23	43	-	10545	5100	147	34.69	5-36	6	1
1-day Int																	
NatWest																	
B & H																	
Sunday																	

THE UMPIRES

BALDERSTONE, J. C.

Name: John Christopher Balderstone
Role: Right-hand opening bat, slow
left-arm bowler
Born: 16 November 1940, Huddersfield
Height: 6ft 1in **Weight:** 12st 10lbs
Nickname: Baldy
Appointed to 1st-Class list: 1988
Appointed to Test panel: Stand-by
umpire in 1991
One-Day Internationals: 1
Counties: Yorkshire, Leicestershire
County debut: 1961 (Yorkshire),
1971 (Leicestershire)
County cap: 1973 (Leicestershire)
Test debut: 1976
Tests: 2
1000 runs in a season: 11
1st-Class 50s: 102
1st-Class 100s: 32
1st-Class 5 w. in innings: 5
One-Day 100s: 5
1st-Class catches: 210
Parents: Frank and Jenny (deceased)
Wife and date of marriage: Angela, January 1991
Children: Sally, 15 September 1970; Michael, 3 January 1973
Education: Paddock County School, Huddersfield
Qualifications: Advanced cricket coach, soccer coach
Career outside cricket: Professional footballer 1958-78
Off-season: Coaching cricket
Overseas tours: Leicestershire to Zimbabwe 1981, to Oman 1984
Cricketers particularly admired: Willie Watson, Brian Close, Fred Trueman, David
Gower, Ray Illingworth
Young players to look out for: Ben Hollioake
Other sports followed: All sports
Relaxations: Golf
Extras: 14 one-day Man of the Match Awards. Played a first-class cricket match and
football league game on the same day in 1975 (Leicestershire v Derbyshire, Doncaster
v Brentford).Was the first man to act as 'third umpire' in Test in England, in the second
Test against Australia at Lord's in 1993. Umpired first one-day International, England v
South Africa 1994
Opinions on cricket: 'Our first-class game is still good, despite all the critics pushing

the Australian academy players etc. We've got equally good young prospects pushing around our county cricket scene.'

Best batting: 181* Leicestershire v Gloucestershire, Leicester 1984
Best bowling: 6-25 Leicestershire v Hampshire, Southampton 1978

First-Class Career Performances

	M	Inns	NO	Runs	HS	Avge	100s	Ct	St	Runs	Wkts	Avge	Best	5wI	10wM
Test	2	4	0	39	35	9.75	-		1	80	1	80.00	1-80	-	-
All First	390	619	61	19034	181*	34.11	32	210	-	8160	310	26.32	6-25	5	-

BIRD, H. D.

Name: Harold Dennis Bird, MBE
Role: Right-hand opening bat
Born: 19 April 1933, Barnsley
Height: 5ft 10in **Weight:** 11st 7lbs
Nickname: Dickie
Appointed to 1st-class list: 1969
Appointed to Test panel: 1972
Appointed to International panel: 1994
Tests umpired: 68
One-Day Internationals umpired: 91
Counties: Yorkshire, Leicestershire
County debut: 1956 (Yorkshire),
1960 (Leicestershire)
County cap: 1960 (Leicestershire)
1000 runs in a season: 1
1st-Class 50s: 14
1st-Class 100s: 2
1st-Class catches: 28

Parents: James Harold and Ethel
Marital status: Single
Education: Burton Road Primary School; Raley School, Barnsley
Qualifications: MCC advanced cricket coach
Career outside cricket: 'Cricket is my life'
Off-season: After-dinner speaking and umpiring overseas
Cricketing superstitions or habits: Twitch of the shoulders, wears distinctive white cap
Other sports followed: Football
Cricketers particularly admired: Gary Sobers, Dennis Lillee, Viv Richards
Cricketers particularly learnt from: Gubby Allen, Johnny Wardle
Young players to look out for: Anthony McGrath (Yorkshire)
Relaxations: Listening to recordings of Barbra Streisand and Diana Ross

Extras: Has umpired 160 international matches to date, including three World Cup finals at Lord's (1975, 1979, 1983); also umpired at the World Cup in India in 1987. Umpired the Queen's Silver Jubilee Test, England v Australia 1977, the Centenary Test, England v Australia 1980 and the MCC Bicentenary Test, England v Rest of the World 1987. In 1982 he umpired the Women's World Cup final in Christchurch, New Zealand. During the mid-1980s he umpired several times in the various competitions staged at Sharjah, UAE. To date he has umpired 34 Cup finals all over the world, as well as the finals of other cricket events such as The Best All-rounder in the World, The Best Batsman in the World and the World Double Wicket competition. In 1977 he was voted Yorkshire Personality of the Year. He is an MCC member and author of three bestselling books, *Not Out*, *That's Out* and *From the Pavilion End*. Despite lucrative offers to join the 'Packer circus' and to visit South Africa with rebel tours, he remained loyal to the TCCB and to the established game on which he had been brought up in Yorkshire and which had given him so much in life. In June 1986 he received an MBE in the Queen's Birthday Honours List. With David Shepherd and Steve Bucknor became the first ICC officially-sponsored umpires in 1992, and was appointed to stand in Zimbabwe's first Test match (against India) in Harare. Subsequently, in Zimbabwe's second Test against New Zealand (also in Harare), he became the first umpire to officiate in 50 Test matches, having passed Frank Chester's world record of 48 Tests at Bulawayo six days earlier. Umpired all three Tests in West Indies home series against Pakistan in 1993. In 1994 he umpired Tests in New Zealand, England, Pakistan and India. Made Honorary Life Member of Yorkshire CCC in March 1994. Umpired in the Australia versus Pakistan Test series in 1996. Was voted the Yorkshireman of the Year in 1996. Awarded an honorary doctorate from Sheffield Hallam University for his outstanding services to cricket. Made an honorary Life Member of the MCC and of Leicestershire CCC. Retired from the Test scene after the second Test against India at Lord's in 1996

Opinions on cricket: 'The greatest game in the world. A game to be enjoyed by young and old. I have consistently advocated playing through all light unless the umpires are convinced that there is genuine physical danger to the batsman.'

Best batting: 181* Yorkshire v Glamorgan, Bradford 1959

First-Class Career Performances

	M	Inns	NO	Runs	HS	Avge	100s	Ct	St	Runs	Wkts	Avge	Best	5wI	10wM
Test															
All First	93	170	10	3314	181*	20.71	2	28	-	22	0	-	-	-	-

BOND, J. D.

Name: John David Bond
Role: Right-hand bat
Born: 6 May 1932, Kearsley, Lancashire
Nickname: Jackie
Appointed to 1st-class list: 1988
Counties: Lancashire, Nottinghamshire
County debut: 1955 (Lancashire),
1974 (Nottinghamshire)
County cap: 1961 (Lancashire)
1000 runs in a season: 2
1st-Class 50s: 54
1st-Class 100s: 14
1st-Class catches: 222
Education: Bolton School
Extras: Captain of Lancashire 1968-1972,
during which time Lancashire won the Gillette
Cup three years in succession (1970, 1971,
1972) and the John Player Sunday League in
1969 and 1970. He moved to Nottinghamshire

in 1974 and was a Test selector in the same year. He was appointed cricket manager at
Lancashire CCC in 1980 and held the position until 1986
Best batting: 157 Lancashire v Hampshire, Old Trafford 1962

First-Class Career Performances

	M	Inns	NO	Runs	HS	Avge	100s	Ct	St	Runs	Wkts	Avge	Best	5wl	10wM
Test															
All First	362	548	80	12125	157	25.90	14	222	-	69	0	-	-	-	-

BURGESS, G. I.

Name: Graham Iefvion Burgess
Role: Right-hand bat, right-arm
medium bowler
Born: 5 May 1943,
Glastonbury, Somerset
Appointed to 1st-class list: 1991
County: Somerset
County debut: 1966
County cap: 1968
Testimonial: 1977
1st-Class 100s: 2
1st-Class 5 w. in innings: 18
1st-Class 10 w. in match: 2
1st-Class catches: 120
Education: Millfield School
Extras: Played Minor Counties cricket for
Wiltshire 1981-82 and for Cambridgeshire
1983-84

Best batting: 129 Somerset v Gloucestershire, Taunton 1973
Best bowling: 7-43 Somerset v Oxford University, The Parks 1975

First-Class Career Performances

	M	Inns	NO	Runs	HS	Avge	100s	Ct	St	Runs	Wkts	Avge	Best	5wI	10wM
Test															
All First	252	414	37	7129	129	18.90	2	120	-	13543	474	28.57	7-43	18	2

CLARKSON, A.

Name: Anthony Clarkson
Role: Right-hand bat, right-arm off-spin
Born: 5 September 1939, Killinhall, North Yorkshire
Height: 6ft **Weight:** 14st
Appointed to 1st-class list: 1996
County: Somerset
County debut: 1963
County cap: 1969
1000 runs in a season: 2
1st-Class 100s: 2
1st-Class catches: 52
Parents: Joe (deceased) and Clarrie
Marital status: Engaged to Cheryl

Children: André, September 1964; Chantal, 27 May 1967; Pierre, 1 May 1969
Family links with cricket: Father was a league professional
Education: Killinghall C of E; Harrogate Grammar School; Leeds College of Building; Bradford Polytechnic; Brunel College, Bristol
Qualifications: 9 O-levels, past member of highway technicians
Career outside cricket: Architectural, Civil Engineering and Surveying Consultant
Off-season: Working and relaxing
Other sports followed: Golf and rugby ('especially league')
Relaxations: Golf, DIY, gardening and winemaking
Extras: First English player to score a century in the Sunday League

First-Class Career Performances

	M	Inns	NO	Runs	HS	Avge	100s	Ct	St	Runs	Wkts	Avge	Best	5wI	10wM
Test															
All First	110	189	12	4458	131	25.18	2	52	-	367	13	28.23	3-51	-	-

CONSTANT, D. J.

Name: David John Constant
Role: Left-hand bat, slow left-arm bowler
Born: 9 November 1941, Bradford-on-Avon, Wiltshire
Nickname: Connie
Appointed to 1st-class list: 1969
Appointed to Test panel: 1971
Tests umpired: 36
One-Day Internationals umpired: 30
Counties: Kent, Leicestershire
County debut: 1961 (Kent), 1965 (Leicestershire)
1st-Class 50s: 6
1st-Class catches: 33
Extras: County bowls player for Gloucestershire 1984-86
Best batting: 80 Leicestershire v Gloucestershire, Bristol 1966

First-Class Career Performances

	M	Inns	NO	Runs	HS	Avge	100s	Ct	St	Runs	Wkts	Avge	Best	5wl	10wM
Test															
All First	61	93	14	1517	80	19.20	-	33	-	36	1	36.00	1-28	-	-

DUDLESTON, B.

Name: Barry Dudleston
Role: Right-hand opening bat, slow left-arm bowler, occasional wicket-keeper
Born: 16 July 1945, Bebington, Cheshire
Height: 5ft 9in **Weight:** 13st 7lbs
Nickname: Danny
Appointed to 1st-class list: 1984
Appointed to Test panel: 1991
Tests umpired: 2
One-Day Internationals umpired: 1
Counties: Leicestershire, Gloucestershire
County debut: 1966 (Leicestershire), 1981 (Gloucestershire)
County cap: 1969 (Leicestershire)
Benefit: 1980 (£25,000)
1000 runs in a season: 8
1st-Class 100s: 32
1st-Class 200s: 1
One-Day 100s: 4
1st-Class catches: 234
Parents: Percy and Dorothy Vera
Wife and date of marriage: Louise, 19 October 1994
Children: Sharon Louise, 29 October 1968; Matthew Barry, 12 September 1988
Family links with cricket: Father was a club cricketer
Education: Stockport School
Qualifications: O-levels, junior coaching certificate
Career outside cricket: Managing director of Sunsport Ltd (tour operators)
Other sports followed: Most
Cricketers particularly admired: Gary Sobers, Tom Graveney
Cricketers particularly learnt from: Vinoo Mankad
Relaxations: Television, bridge, wine, golf
Extras: Played for England U25. Suffered badly from broken fingers, breaking fingers on the same hand three times in 1978. Played for Rhodesia in the Currie Cup 1976-80. Acted as 'third umpire' in the third Test against Australia at Trent Bridge 1993
Opinions on cricket: 'It is still the greatest test of skill and character – beautiful to

watch when played well. Am worried about the declining standards of behaviour.'
Best batting: 202 Leicestershire v Derbyshire, Leicester 1979
Best bowling: 4-6 Leicestershire v Surrey, Leicester 1972

First-Class Career Performances

	M	Inns	NO	Runs	HS	Avge	100s	Ct	St	Runs	Wkts	Avge	Best	5wI	10wM
Test															
All First	295	501	47	14747	202	32.48	32	234	7	1365	47	29.04	4-6	-	-

HAMPSHIRE, J. H.

Name: John Harry Hampshire
Role: Right-hand bat
Born: 10 February 1941,
Thurnscoe, Yorkshire
Height: 6ft **Weight:** 13st
Nickname: Hamp
Appointed to 1st-class list: 1985
Appointed to Test panel: 1989
Tests umpired: 11
One-Day Internationals umpired: 5
Counties: Yorkshire, Derbyshire
County debut: 1961 (Yorkshire),
1982 (Derbyshire)
County cap: 1963 (Yorkshire),
1982 (Derbyshire)
Benefit: 1976
Test debut: 1969
Tests: 8
1000 runs in a season: 15
1st-Class 50s: 142
1st-Class 100s: 43
1st-Class catches: 445
1st-Class 5 w. in innings: 2
One-Day 100s: 7
Parents: Jack and Vera
Wife and date of marriage: Judith Ann, 5 September 1964
Children: Ian Christopher, 6 January 1969; Paul Wesley, 12 February 1972
Family links with cricket: Father (J.) and brother (A.W.) both played for Yorkshire
Education: Oakwood Technical High School, Rotherham
Qualifications: City and Guilds in Printing
Off-season: Coach to Zimbabwe 1992-97
Overseas tours: MCC to Australia and New Zealand, 1970-71

Overseas teams played for: Tasmania, 1966-69, 1977-79
Cricketers particularly admired: Peter May, Gary Sobers
Other sports followed: Most sports
Relaxations: Gardening and cooking
Extras: Captained Yorkshire 1979-80. Played for Tasmania 1967-69 and 1977-79. Scored a century (107) in his first Test match, against West Indies at Lord's 1969. Appointed manager/coach of the Zimbabwe Test squad for their first Test matches against India and New Zealand. Umpired four Tests in Pakistan 1989-90
Best batting: 183* Yorkshire v Surrey, Hove 1971
Best bowling: 7-52 Yorkshire v Glamorgan, Cardiff 1963

First-Class Career Performances

	M	Inns	NO	Runs	HS	Avge	100s	Ct	St	Runs	Wkts	Avge	Best	5wI	10wM
Test	8	16	1	405	107	26.86	1	9	-						
All First	577	924	112	28059	183	*34.55	43	445	-	1637	30	54.56	7-52	2	-

HARRIS, J. H.

Name: John Henry Harris
Role: Left-hand bat, right-arm
fast-medium bowler
Born: 13 February 1936, Taunton
Appointed to 1st-class list: 1983
County: Somerset
County debut: 1952
1st-Class catches: 6
Extras: Made his debut for Somerset aged 16
years 99 days. Played Minor Counties cricket
for Suffolk (1960-62) and Devon (1975).
Third year as Chairman of the First-Class
Cricket Umpires Association
Best batting: 41 Somerset v Worcestershire,
Taunton 1957
Best bowling: 3-29 Somerset v
Worcestershire, Bristol 1959

First-Class Career Performances

	M	Inns	NO	Runs	HS	Avge	100s	Ct	St	Runs	Wkts	Avge	Best	5wI	10wM
Test															
All First	15	18	4	154	41	11.00	-	6	-	609	19	32.05	3.29	-	-

HOLDER, J. W.

Name: John Wakefield Holder
Role: Right-hand bat, right-arm
fast bowler
Born: 19 March 1945,
St George, Barbados
Height: 6ft **Weight:** 14st
Nickname: Benson, Hod
Appointed to 1st-class list: 1983
Appointed to Test panel: 1988
Tests umpired: 10
One-Day Internationals umpired: 14
County: Hampshire
County debut: 1968
50 wickets in a season: 1
1st-Class 5 w. in innings: 5
1st-Class 10 w. in match: 1
1st-Class catches: 12
Parents: Charles and Carnetta
Wife: Glenda
Children: Christopher 1968; Nigel 1970
Family links with cricket: None
Education: St Giles Boys School; Combermere High School, Barbados; Rochdale
College
Qualifications: 3 O-levels, MCC advanced cricket coach
Off-season: 'Idling'
Young players to look out for: Alex Tudor
Other sports followed: Football (Manchester United)
Relaxations: Keeping fit and helping coach the Rochdale Indoor Cricket Team which
plays in the National League in the winter
Extras: Umpired four Tests in Pakistan 1989-90
Best batting: 33 Hampshire v Sussex, Hove 1971
Best bowling: 7-79 Hampshire v Gloucestershire, Gloucester 1972

First-Class Career Performances

	M	Inns	NO	Runs	HS	Avge	100s	Ct	St	Runs	Wkts	Avge	Best	5wl	10wM
Test															
All First	47	49	14	374	33	10.68	-	12	-	3415	139	24.56	7-79	5	1

HOLDER, V. A.

Name: Vanburn Alonza Holder
Role: Right-hand bat, right-arm
fast-medium bowler
Born: 8 October 1945,
St Michael, Barbados
Nickname: Van
Appointed to 1st-class list: 1992
County: Worcestershire
County debut: 1968
County cap: 1970
Test debut: 1969
Tests: 40
1st-Class 50s: 4
1st-Class 100s: 1
1st-Class 5 w. in innings: 38
1st-Class 10 w. in match: 3
1st-Class catches: 98
Overseas tours: West Indies to England
1969, 1973, to India, Sri Lanka and Pakistan 1974-75, to Australia 1975-76, to
England 1976, to India and Sri Lanka 1978-79 (as vice-captain)
Extras: Made his debut for Barbados in the Shell Shield competition in 1966-67
Best batting: 122 Barbados v Trinidad, Bridgetown 1973-74
Best bowling: 7-40 Worcestershire v Glamorgan, Cardiff 1974

First-Class Career Performances

	M	Inns	NO	Runs	HS	Avge	100s	Ct	St	Runs	Wkts	Avge	Best	5wl	10wM
Test	40	59	11	682	42	14.20	-	16	-	3627	109	33.27	6-28	3	-
All First	311	354	81	3559	122	13.03	1	98	-	23183	948	24.45	7-40	38	3

JESTY, T. E.

Name: Trevor Edward Jesty
Role: Right-hand bat, right-arm
medium bowler
Born: 2 June 1948, Gosport, Hampshire
Height: 5ft 9in **Weight:** 11st 9lbs
Nickname: Jets
Appointed to 1st-class list: 1994
Counties: Hampshire, Surrey, Lancashire

County debut: 1966 (Hampshire),
1985 (Surrey), 1988 (Lancashire)
County cap: 1971 (Hampshire),
1985 (Surrey)
Benefit: 1982
One-Day Internationals: 10
1000 runs in a season: 10
50 wickets in a season: 2
1st-Class 50s: 110
1st-Class 100s: 35
1st-Class 200s: 2
1st-Class 5 w. in innings: 19
1st-Class catches: 265
1st-Class stumpings: 1
One-Day 100s: 7
Parents: Aubrey Edward and Sophia
Wife and date of marriage: Jacqueline, 12
September 1970
Children: Graeme Barry, 27 September 1972; Lorna Samantha, 7 November 1976
Education: Privet County Secondary Modern, Gosport
Overseas tours: International XI to West Indies 1982; England to Australia and New
Zealand 1982-83
Overseas teams played for: Border, South Africa 1973-74; Griqualand West 1974-77,
1980-81; Canterbury, New Zealand 1979-80
Cricketers particularly admired: Sir Garfield Sobers, Barry Richards
Relaxations: Watching football, gardening, golf
Extras: One of *Wisden*'s Five Cricketers of the Year 1982. Left Hampshire at end of
1984 when not appointed captain and offered the captaincy of Surrey for 1985 season.
Best batting: 248 Hampshire v Cambridge University, Fenner's 1984
Best bowling: 7-75 Hampshire v Worcestershire, Southampton 1976

First-Class Career Performances

	M	Inns	NO	Runs	HS	Avge	100s	Ct	St	Runs	Wkts	Avge	Best	5wI	10wM
Test															
All First	490	777	107	21916	248	32.71	35	265	1	16075	585	27.47	7-75	19	-

JONES, A. A.

Name: Alan Arthur Jones
Role: Right-hand bat, right-arm
fast-medium bowler
Born: 9 December 1947, Horley, Surrey
Height: 6ft 3in **Weight:** 14st
Nickname: Jonah, Buckets
Appointed to 1st-class list: 1985
One-Day Internationals umpired: 1
Counties: Sussex, Somerset,
Middlesex, Glamorgan
County debut: 1964 (Sussex),
1970 (Somerset), 1976 (Middlesex),
1980 (Glamorgan)
County cap: 1972 (Somerset),
1976 (Middlesex), 1980 (Glamorgan)
50 wickets in a season: 4
1st-Class 5 w. in innings: 23
1st-Class 10 w. in match: 3
1st-Class catches: 50
Parents: Leslie and Hazel
Wife: Marilyn
Children: Clare Michelle
Education: St John's College, Horsham
Qualifications: 5 O-levels, MCC advanced coach, NCA staff coach
Off-season: 'Recovering from the summer'
Overseas teams played for: Northern Transvaal 1971-72; Orange Free State 1976-77
Other sports followed: All sports
Cricketers particularly admired: Tom Cartwright, Brian Close
Young players to look out for: Darren Altree and Ashley Giles (Warwickshire), Jason
Laney (Hampshire)
Other sports followed: Golf
Relaxations: Reading, cooking and travel
Extras: Won two championship medals with Middlesex (1976 and 1977). He was the
first person to play for four counties – only one other player has done so since
Opinions on cricket: '110 overs in a day is too many. It should be reduced to 104 or
100. There is one one-day competition too many. Also, if we are to continue with four-
day cricket, it should be played from Wednesday to Saturday, so that if we do continue
with the Sunday League, it is not in the middle of the four-day match. There should also
be less 2nd XI cricket and more nets for younger players, with less significance on
fitness and more on skill.'
Best batting: 33 Middlesex v Kent, Canterbury 1978
Best bowling: 9-51 Somerset v Sussex, Hove 1976

First-Class Career Performances

	M	Inns	NO	Runs	HS	Avge	100s	Ct	St	Runs	Wkts	Avge	Best	5wl	10wM
Test															
All First	214	216	68	799	33	5-39	-	50	-	15414	549	28.07	9-51	23	3

JULIAN, R.

Name: Raymond Julian
Role: Right-hand bat, wicket-keeper
Born: 23 August 1936,
Cosby, Leicestershire
Height: 5ft 11in **Weight:** 13st 7lbs
Nickname: Julie
Appointed to 1st-class list: 1972
One-Day Internationals umpired: 1
County: Leicestershire
County debut: 1953
County cap: 1961
1st-Class 50s: 2
1st-Class catches: 381
1st-Class stumpings: 40
Parents: George Ernest and Doris
Wife and date of marriage:
Megan, 3rd April 1993
Children: Peter Raymond, 1 February 1958;
John Kelvin, 13 October 1960;
David Andrew, 15 October 1963; Paul Anthony, 22 September 1967
Family links with cricket: Father and two brothers all played local cricket. Two sons play local cricket
Education: Cosby Primary School, Leicestershire; Wigston Secondary Modern
Qualifications: Cricket coach, decorator and gardener
Career outside cricket: As above
Off-season: Watching the England tour in South Africa and holidays
Overseas tours: MCC to West Africa, 1975
Cricketers particularly admired: Gary Sobers, Keith Andrew
Young players to look out for: 'All players selected on U17 and U19 tours.'
Other sports followed: Football (support Taunton Town FC) , boxing, rugby
Relaxations: Gardening, holidays, travelling
Extras: Youngest player to make debut for Leicestershire (aged 15 years). Youngest wicket-keeper to play first-class cricket in 1953. Took six catches in an innings, Leicestershire v Northants, Kettering 1965. Played for the Army 1955-57. Gave eight LBW decisions in succession, Glamorgan v Sussex at Cardiff 1986. Has umpired three

B&H semi-finals and one Gillette Cup semi-final. Has just completed 25 years on the first-class list. Was awarded One-Day International between England and India at The Oval in 1996 and has been the stand-by umpire in three Tests

Opinions on cricket: 'Good now that we have four-day games. There is too much one-day cricket and too many overs in a day.'

Best batting: 51 Leicestershire v Worcestershire, Worcester 1962

First-Class Career Performances

	M	Inns	NO	Runs	HS	Avge	100s	Ct	St	Runs	Wkts	Avge	Best	5wl	10wM
Test															
All First	192	288	23	2581	51	9.73	-	381	40						

KITCHEN, M. J.

Name: Mervyn John Kitchen
Role: Left-hand bat, right-arm medium bowler
Born: 1 August 1940, Nailsea, Somerset
Appointed to 1st-class list: 1982
Appointed to Test panel: 1990
Appointed to International panel: 1995
Tests umpired: 13
One-Day Internationals umpired: 14
County: Somerset
County debut: 1960
County cap: 1966
Testimonial: 1973
1000 runs in a season: 7
1st-Class 50s: 68
1st-Class 100s: 17
1st-Class catches: 157
One-Day 100s: 1

Education: Blackwell Secondary Modern, Nailsea
Extras: Was third (replay) umpire for two Tests in 1994
Best batting: 189 Somerset v Pakistanis, Taunton 1967

First-Class Career Performances

	M	Inns	NO	Runs	HS	Avge	100s	Ct	St	Runs	Wkts	Avge	Best	5wl	10wM
Test															
All First	354	612	32	15230	189	26.25	17	157	-	109	2	54.50	1-4	-	-

LEADBEATER, B.

Name: Barrie Leadbeater
Role: Right-hand opening bat, right-arm medium bowler, slip fielder
Born: 14 August 1943, Leeds
Height: 6ft **Weight:** 13st
Nickname: Leady
One-Day Internationals umpired: 4
Appointed to 1st-class list: 1981
County: Yorkshire
County debut: 1966
County cap: 1969
Benefit: 1980 (joint benefit with G.A. Cope)
1st-Class 50s: 27
1st-Class 100s: 1
1st-Class catches: 82
Parents: Ronnie (deceased) and Nellie
Wife and date of marriage: Jacqueline, 18 September 1971

Children: Richard Barrie, 23 November 1972; Michael Spencer, 21 March 1976; Daniel Mark Ronnie, 19 June 1981
Education: Brownhill County Primary; Harehills Secondary Modern, Leeds
Qualifications: 2 O-levels
Career outside cricket: Coach driver
Overseas tours: Duke of Norfolk's XI to West Indies 1970
Overseas teams played for: Johannesburg Municipals 1978-79
Other sports followed: Table tennis, golf, snooker, football (Leeds United)
Cricketers particularly admired: Colin Cowdrey, Clive Rice, Richard Hadlee, Gary Sobers, Michael Holding
Cricketers particularly learnt from: Brian Close, Willie Watson, Arthur Mitchell, Maurice Leyland
Relaxations: Family, car maintenance, DIY, music
Extras: Acted as 'third umpire' in the fourth Test against Australia at Headingley 1993
Opinions on cricket: 'Disappointed in players who lack self-control and professional pride and set bad examples to young players and public alike. Public should be regularly and properly informed during stoppages in play. Stoppages for bad light cause more frustration for public, players and, not least, umpires and a change in regulations may be needed soon if the game is to retain its support and credibility. The recent theory of the wicket-keeper standing between the leg stump and the return crease when the slow left-arm bowler is operating over the wicket should be made illegal. It is grossly negative and against the spirit of the game.'
Best batting: 140* Yorkshire v Hampshire, Portsmouth 1976

First-Class Career Performances

	M	Inns	NO	Runs	HS	Avge	100s	Ct	St	Runs	Wkts	Avge	Best	5wl	10wM
Test															
All First	147	241	29	5373	140	*25.34	1	82	-	5	1	5.00	1-1	-	-

MEYER, B. J.

Name: Barrie John Meyer
Role: Right-hand bat, wicket-keeper
Born: 21 August 1931, Bournemouth
Height: 5ft 10in **Weight:** 12st 5lbs
Nickname: BJ
Appointed to 1st-class list: 1973
Appointed to Test panel: 1978
Tests umpired: 26
One-Day Internationals umpired: 23
County: Gloucestershire
County debut: 1957
County cap: 1958
Benefit: 1971
1st-Class 50s: 11
1st-Class catches: 707
1st-Class stumpings: 118
Parents: Deceased
Wife and date of marriage: Gillian,
4 September 1965

Children: Stephen Barrie; Christopher John; Adrian Michael
Education: Boscombe Secondary School, Bournemouth
Career outside cricket: Salesman
Off-season: Coaching and umpiring in South Africa
Other sports followed: Golf (handicap 9), football (was a pro footballer for Bristol Rovers, Plymouth Argyle, Newport County and Bristol City)
Cricketers particularly learnt from: Andy Wilson and Sonny Avery (coaches for Gloucestershire)
Relaxations: Golf, music, reading
Extras: Umpired 1979 and 1983 World Cup finals
Best batting: 63 Gloucestershire v Indians, Cheltenham 1959
        63 Gloucestershire v Oxford University, Bristol 1962
        63 Gloucestershire v Sussex, Bristol 1964

First-Class Career Performances

	M	Inns	NO	Runs	HS	Avge	100s	Ct	St	Runs	Wkts	Avge	Best	5wI	10wM
Test															
All First	406	569	191	5367	63	14.19	-	707	118						

PALMER, K. E.

Name: Kenneth Ernest Palmer
Role: Right-hand bat, right-arm
fast-medium bowler
Born: 22 April 1937, Winchester
Height: 5ft 10in **Weight:** 13st
Nickname: Pedlar
Appointed to 1st-class list: 1972
Appointed to Test panel: 1978
Appointed to International panel: 1994
Tests umpired: 22
One-Day Internationals umpired: 19
County: Somerset
County debut: 1955
County cap: 1958
Testimonial: 1968
Test debut: 1965
Tests: 1
1000 runs in a season: 1
50 wickets in a season: 6
1st-Class 50s: 27
1st-Class 100s: 2
1st-Class 5 w. in innings: 46
1st-Class 10 w. in match: 5
1st-Class catches: 156
Parents: Harry and Cecilia
Wife and date of marriage: Wife deceased
Children: Gary Vincent, 6 September 1961
Family links with cricket: Son played for Somerset, as did brother Roy, also a Test
umpire
Education: Southbroom Secondary Modern, Devizes
Overseas tours: Commonwealth XI to Pakistan 1962; International Cavaliers to West
Indies 1963-64
Other sports followed: Football and squash
Cricketers particularly admired: Gary Sobers, Richard Hadlee, Viv Richards, David
Gower, Michael Holding, Malcolm Marshall

Cricketers particularly learnt from: Father and Maurice Tremlett
Relaxations: Car enthusiast
Extras: Called into Test side while coaching in South Africa 1964-65. Umpired two B&H finals and two NatWest finals and was twice on World Cup panel in England. Won Carling Single Wicket Competition 1961. Did the 'double' in 1961 (114 wickets, 1036 runs). With Bill Alley holds the Somerset record for 6th wicket partnership.
Best batting: 125* Somerset v Northamptonshire, Northampton 1961
Best bowling: 9-57 Somerset v Nottinghamshire, Trent Bridge 1963

First-Class Career Performances

	M	Inns	NO	Runs	HS	Avge	100s	Ct	St	Runs	Wkts	Avge	Best	5wI	10wM
Test	1	1	0	10	10	10.00	-	-	-	189	1	189.00	1-113	-	-
All First	314	481	105	7771	125	*20.66	2	156	-	18485	866	21.34	9-57	46	5

PALMER, R.

Name: Roy Palmer
Role: Right-hand bat, right-arm fast-medium bowler
Born: 12 July 1942, Devizes, Wiltshire
Appointed to 1st-class list: 1980
Appointed to Test panel: 1992
Tests umpired: 2
One-Day Internationals umpired: 8
County: Somerset
County debut: 1965
50 wickets in a season: 1
1st-Class 50s: 1
1st-Class 5 w. in innings: 4
1st-Class catches: 25
Family links with cricket: Brother of Ken Palmer, Test umpire and former Somerset player; nephew Gary also played for Somerset
Education: Southbroom Secondary Modern, Devizes

Best batting: 84 Somerset v Leicestershire, Taunton 1967
Best bowling: 6-45 Somerset v Middlesex, Lord's 1967

First-Class Career Performances

	M	Inns	NO	Runs	HS	Avge	100s	Ct	St	Runs	Wkts	Avge	Best	5wI	10wM
Test															
All First	74	110	32	1037	84	13.29	-	25	-	5439	172	31.62	6-45	4	-

PLEWS, N. T.

Name: Nigel Trevor Plews
Role: Right-hand opening bat
Born: 5 September 1934, Nottingham
Height: 6ft 6in **Weight:** 16st 8lbs
Nickname: Plod, Sarge
Appointed to 1st-class list: 1982
Appointed to Test panel: 1988
Appointed to International panel: 1994
Tests umpired: 11
One-Day Internationals umpired: 16
Parents: Deceased
Wife and date of marriage:
Margaret, 24 September 1956
Children: Elaine, 1961; Douglas, 1964
Education: Mundella Grammar School,
Nottingham
Qualifications: School Certificate in
Commercial Subjects, RSA Advanced
Book-keeping

Career outside cricket: Nottingham City
police for 25 years (Det. Sgt in Fraud Squad for 15 years)
Off-season: National Grid International Panel Appointments
Other sports followed: Football, table tennis, swimming
Relaxations: Hill-walking, reading, travel, cricket administration
Extras: Played local league and club cricket in Nottingham. Toured as umpire with MCC to Namibia 1991. Has now umpired in 11 Tests and 16 One-Day Internationals

Did not play first-class cricket

SHARP, G.

Name: George Sharp
Role: Right-hand bat, wicket-keeper
Born: 12 March 1950,
Hartlepool, County Durham
Height: 5ft 11in **Weight:** 15st 7lbs
Nickname: Blunt, Razor, Sharpie
Appointed to 1st-class list: 1992
Appointed to International panel: 1996
Tests umpired: 1
One-Day Internationals umpired: 1
County: Northamptonshire
County debut: 1967
County cap: 1972
1st-Class catches: 565
1st-Class stumpings: 90
Parents: George and Grace
Wife: Audrey, 14 September 1974
Children: Gareth James, 27 June 1984
Education: Elwick Road, Hartlepool
Qualifications: NCA coach

Career outside cricket: Director of GSB Loams Ltd, suppliers of soil and turf for sports areas
Off-season: Working for GSB Loams Ltd
Overseas tours: England Counties XI to West Indies 1974
Cricketers particularly admired: Alan Knott, Bob Taylor, Keith Andrew
Other sports followed: Football (Newcastle and Middlesbrough)
Relaxations: Golf
Best batting: 98 Northamptonshire v Yorkshire, Northampton 1983

First-Class Career Performances

	M	Inns	NO	Runs	HS	Avge	100s	Ct	St	Runs	Wkts	Avge	Best	5wI	10wM
Test															
All First	306	396	81	6254	98	19.85	-	565	90	70	1	70.00	1-47	-	-

SHEPHERD, D. R.

Name: David Robert Shepherd
Role: Right-hand bat, right-arm medium bowler
Born: 27 December 1940, Bideford, Devon
Height: 5ft 10in **Weight:** 16st
Nickname: Shep
Appointed to 1st-class list: 1981
Appointed to Test panel: 1985
Appointed to International panel: 1994
Tests umpired: 30
One-Day Internationals umpired: 63
County: Gloucestershire
County debut: 1965
County cap: 1969
Benefit: 1978 (joint benefit with J. Davey)
1000 runs in a season: 2
1st-Class 50s: 55
1st-Class 100s: 12
1st-Class catches: 95
One-Day 100s: 2
Parents: Herbert and Doris (both deceased)
Marital status: Single
Education: Barnstaple Grammar School; St Luke's College, Exeter
Career outside cricket: Teacher
Off-season: Assisting brother in local post office/newsagent
Other sports followed: Rugby, football, most ball sports
Cricketers particularly admired: Gary Sobers, Mike Procter
Relaxations: All sports, philately, television
Extras: Played Minor Counties cricket for Devon 1959-64. Only Gloucestershire player to score a century on his first-class debut. Umpired the MCC Bicentenary Test, England v Rest of the World, at Lord's in 1987. With Dickie Bird and Steve Bucknor was one of the first umpires officially sponsored by the ICC. Known for his superstition regarding 'Nelson' score 111, and multiples – 222, 333 etc. Was England's umpire at the 1995-96 World Cup in India and Pakistan
Best batting: 153 Gloucestershire v Middlesex, Bristol 1968

First-Class Career Performances

	M	Inns	NO	Runs	HS	Avge	100s	Ct	St	Runs	Wkts	Avge	Best	5wI	10wM
Test															
All First	282	476	40	10672	153	24.47	12	95	-	106	2	53.00	1-1	-	-

STEELE, J. F.

Name: John Frederick Steele
Role: Right-hand bat, slow left-arm bowler
Born: 23 July 1946, Stafford
Height: 5ft 10in **Weight:** 11st 7lbs
Nickname: Steely
Appointed to 1st-class list: 1997
County: Leicestershire (1970-83),
Glamorgan (1984-94)
Parents: Alfred and Grace
Wife and date of marriage: Susan,
17 April 1977
Childen: Sarah Jane, 2 April 1982; Robert
Alfred, 10 April 1985
Family links with cricket: Uncle Stan
played for Staffordshire. Brother David
played for Northamptonshire and England.
Cousin Brian Crump played for
Northamptonshire and Staffordshire
Education: Endon School, Stoke-on-Trent;
Stafford College

Qualifications: Advanced cricket coach
Career outside cricket: Work study officer. Fireman with Staffordshire Fire Brigade
Off-season: Cricket coaching in South Africa and the UK
Overseas teams played for: Springs HSOB, Northern Transvaal 1971-73; Pine Town
CC, Natal, South Africa 1973-74, 1982-83; Natal, South Africa 1975-76, 1978-79
Young players to look out for: Anthony Cottey
Other sports followed: Soccer (Stoke City, Port Vale) and golf
Relaxations: Music and walking
Extras: Played for England U25. 1st wicket record partnership for Leicestershire of 390
with Barry Dudleston versus Derbyshire in 1979. Won 2 Man of the Match Awards in
the Gillette Cup and four in the Benson and Hedges Cup. Won the award for the most
catches in a season in 1984 and was voted Natal's Best Bowler in 1975-76.
Opinions on cricket: 'Would like to see two divisions in the County Championship.'
Best batting: 195 Leicestershire v Derbyshire, Leicester 1971
Best bowling: 7-29 Natal B v Griqualand West, Umzinto 1973-74
　　　　　　　　7-29 Leicestershire v Gloucestershire, Leicester 1980

First-class career performances

	M	Inns	NO	Runs	HS	Avge	100s	Ct	St	Runs	Wkts	Avge	Best	5wI	10wM
Test															
All First	379	605	85	15053	195	28.94	21	414	-	15793	584	27.04	7-29	16	-

WHITE, R. A.

Name: Robert Arthur White
Role: Left-hand bat, off-break bowler
Born: 6 October 1936, Fulham
Height: 5ft 9in **Weight:** 'Fluctuates'
Nickname: Knocker
Appointed to 1st-class list: 1982
Counties: Middlesex, Nottinghamshire
County debut: 1958 (Middlesex),
1966 (Nottinghamshire)
County cap: 1963 (Middlesex),
1966 (Nottinghamshire)
Benefit: 1974
1000 runs in a season: 1
50 wickets in a season: 2
1st-Class 50s: 50
1st-Class 100s: 5
1st-Class 5 w. in innings: 28
1st-Class 10 w. in match: 4
1st-Class catches: 190
Wife: Janice – 'still married, must be a record in the modern game'
Children: Robin and Vanessa
Education: Chiswick Grammar School
Qualifications: Matriculation and cricket coaching certificate
Career outside cricket: Fireworks salesman
Off-season: Working
Other sports followed: All sports – golf, football, ice-hockey and horse racing in particular
Cricketers particularly admired: 'Gary Sobers more than anyone else.'
Cricketers particularly learnt from: 'I tried to learn from everyone I encountered'
Young players for the future: 'All of them'
Relaxations: Theatre-going
Extras: Made independent coaching trips to South Africa 1959, 1960, 1966, 1967, 1968. Together with M.J. Smedley broke the Nottinghamshire seventh wicket record with 204 v Surrey at The Oval 1967
Opinions on cricket: 'There is so much verbal noise on the field these days (mainly in my opinion to distract the batsman), that I, if still a player, would wear earphones and carry a Walkman so that I could listen to soothing music and obliterate the verbals. Those people who saw me play would no doubt say that I would have had time just to hear the "Minute Waltz".'
Best batting: 116* Nottinghamshire v Surrey, The Oval 1967
Best bowling: 7-41 Nottinghamshire v Derbyshire, Ilkeston 1971

First-Class Career Performances

	M	Inns	NO	Runs	HS	Avge	100s	Ct	St	Runs	Wkts	Avge	Best	5wl	10wM
Test															
All First	413	642	105	12452	116*	23.18	5	190	-	21138	693	30.50	7-41	28	4

WHITEHEAD, A. G. T.

Name: Alan Geoffrey Thomas Whitehead
Role: Left-hand bat,
slow left-arm bowler
Born: 28 October 1940,
Butleigh, Somerset
Appointed to 1st-class list: 1970
Appointed to Test panel: 1982
Tests umpired: 5
One-Day Internationals umpired: 13
County: Somerset
County debut: 1957
1st-Class 5 w. in innings: 3
1st-Class catches: 20
Extras: Acted as third (replay) umpire in the
fifth Test against Australia at Edgbaston 1993
and in two Tests in 1994
Best batting: 15 Somerset v Hampshire,
Southampton 1959
Best bowling: 6-74 Somerset v Sussex,
Eastbourne 1959

First-Class Career Performances

	M	Inns	NO	Runs	HS	Avge	100s	Ct	St	Runs	Wkts	Avge	Best	5wl	10wM
Test															
All First	38	49	25	137	15	5.70	-	20	-	2306	67	34.41	6-74	3	-

WILLEY, P.

Name: Peter Willey
Role: Right-hand bat, off-break bowler
Born: 6 December 1949, Sedgefield, County Durham
Height: 6ft 1in **Weight:** 13st 4lbs
Nickname: Will, 'many unprintable'
Appointed to 1st-class list: 1993
Appointed to International panel: 1996
Tests umpired: 2
One-Day Internationals umpired: 2
Counties: Northamptonshire, Leicestershire
County debut: 1966 (Northamptonshire), 1984 (Leicestershire)
County cap: 1971 (Northamptonshire), 1984 (Leicestershire)
Benefit: 1981 (£31,400)
Test debut: 1976
Tests: 26
One-Day Internationals: 26
1000 runs in a season: 10
50 wickets in a season: 2
1st-Class 50s: 101
1st-Class 100s: 44
1st-Class 200s: 1
1st-Class 5 w. in innings: 26
1st-Class 10 w. in match: 3
1st-Class catches: 235
One-Day 100s: 9
Parents: Oswald and Maisie
Wife and date of marriage: Charmaine, 23 September 1971
Children: Heather Jane, 11 September 1985; David, 28 February 1990
Family links with cricket: Father played local club cricket in County Durham
Education: Seaham Secondary School, County Durham
Off-season: 'House husband'
Overseas tours: England to Australia and India 1979-80, to West Indies 1980-81 and 1985-86; with unofficial England XI to South Africa 1981-82
Overseas teams played for: Eastern Province, South Africa 1982-85
Cricketers particularly admired: Malcolm Marshall
Other sports followed: All sports
Relaxations: Gardening, dog walking
Extras: With Wayne Larkins, received 2016 pints of beer (seven barrels) from a brewery

in Northampton as a reward for their efforts in Australia with England in 1979-80. Youngest player ever to play for Northamptonshire at 16 years 180 days v Cambridge University in 1966. Banned from Test cricket for three years for joining England rebel tour of South Africa in 1982. Left Northamptonshire at end of 1983 and moved to Leicestershire as vice-captain. Appointed Leicestershire captain for 1987, but resigned after only one season. Released by Leicestershire at end of 1991 season to play for Northumberland in 1992. He was appointed to the first-class umpires list in 1993 and on to the International Panel in 1996. Umpired the Australia against West Indies series in Australia during the off-season

Opinions on cricket: 'I think the fun has gone out of the game for many of the players. Not enough hard work and practice is done to improve playing standards throughout the first-class game. Players of average ability are being paid silly money in the modern game, by clubs, so they may not need to try and improve their standards. Why does the English game need overseas coaches? Why do we also need team managers?'

Best batting: 227 Northamptonshire v Somerset, Northampton 1976

Best bowling: 7-37 Northamptonshire v Oxford University, The Parks 1975

First-Class Career Performances

	M	Inns	NO	Runs	HS	Avge	100s	Ct	St	Runs	Wkts	Avge	Best	5wI	10wM
Test	26	50	6	1184	102	*26.90	2	3	-	456	7	65.14	2-73	-	-
All First	559	918	121	24361	227	30.56	44	235	-	23400	756	30.95	7-37	26	3

ROLL OF HONOUR
1996

ROLL OF HONOUR 1996

BRITANNIC ASSURANCE CHAMPIONSHIP

		P	W	L	D	T	Bt	Bl	Pts
1	Leicestershire (7)	17	10	1	6	0	57	61	296
2	Derbyshire (14)	17	9	3	5	0	52	58	269
3	Surrey (12)	17	8	2	7	0	49	64	262
4	Kent (18)	17	9	2	6	0	47	52	261
5	Essex (5)	17	8	5	4	0	58	57	255
6	Yorkshire (8)	17	8	5	4	0	50	58	248
7	Worcestershire (10)	17	6	4	7	0	45	60	222
8	Warwickshire (1)	17	7	6	4	0	39	55	218
9	Middlesex (2)	17	7	6	4	0	30	59	213
10	Glamorgan (16)	17	6	5	6	0	50	43	207
11	Somerset (9)	17	5	6	6	0	38	61	197
12	Sussex (15)	17	6	9	2	0	36	58	196
13	Gloucestershire (6)	17	5	7	5	0	23	59	177
14	Hampshire (13)	17	3	7	7	0	41	56	166
15	Lancashire (4)	17	2	6	9	0	49	52	160
16	Northamptonshire (3)	17	3	8	6	0	36	57	159
17	Nottinghamshire (11)	17	1	9	7	0	42	52	131
18	Durham (17)	17	0	12	5	0	22	60	97

(1995 positions in brackets)

NATWEST TROPHY

Winners: Lancashire
Runners-up: Essex

BENSON & HEDGES CUP

Winners: Lancashire
Runners-up: Northamptonshire

AXA EQUITY & LAW LEAGUE

		P	W	L	T	NR	Pts
1	Surrey (9)	17	12	4	0	1	50
2	Nottinghamshire (11)	17	12	4	0	1	50
3	Yorkshire (12)	17	11	6	0	0	44
4	Warwickshire (2)	17	10	6	0	1	42
5	Somerset (14)	17	10	6	0	1	42
6	Northamptonshire (13)	17	10	6	0	1	42
7	Middlesex (17)	17	9	7	0	1	38
8	Worcestershire (3)	17	8	6	0	3	38
9	Lancashire (4)	17	8	8	1	0	34
10	Kent (1)	17	8	8	1	2	34
11	Derbyshire (8)	17	7	7	1	2	34
12	Leicestershire (7)	17	7	7	0	3	34
13	Glamorgan (6)	17	7	8	0	2	32
14	Sussex (10)	17	6	9	0	2	28
15	Hampshire (18)	17	4	10	0	3	22
16	Gloucestershire (15)	17	4	10	0	3	22
17	Essex (5)	17	4	12	0	1	18
18	Durham (16)	17	1	15	0	1	6

(1995 positions in brackets)

FIRST-CLASS AVERAGES
1996

1996 AVERAGES (all first-class matches)

BATTING AVERAGES - Including fielding.
Qualifying requirements : 6 completed innings at an average of over 35.

Name	Matches	Inns	NO	Runs	HS	Avge	100s	50s	Ct	St
S Ganguly	9	14	6	762	136	95.25	3	4	1	-
Saeed Anwar	10	19	1	1224	219*	68.00	5	4	6	-
G A Gooch	17	30	1	1944	201	67.03	8	6	18	-
H H Gibbs	8	14	1	867	183	66.69	2	5	10	-
A J Hollioake	17	29	6	1522	129	66.17	5	8	18	-
Inzamam-ul-Haq	9	14	2	792	169*	66.00	3	4	6	-
M G Bevan	12	22	3	1225	160*	64.47	3	8	6	-
S R Tendulkar	7	11	0	707	177	64.27	2	5	5	-
G P Thorpe	16	29	4	1569	185	62.76	6	7	18	-
M P Maynard	17	30	4	1610	214	61.92	6	6	20	-
S Lee	17	25	4	1300	167*	61.90	5	5	14	-
S G Law	15	26	1	1545	172	61.80	6	5	25	-
M J Walker	8	13	3	606	275*	60.60	1	2	2	-
K M Curran	15	28	7	1242	150	59.14	2	8	14	-
D N Crookes	7	11	1	566	155*	56.60	2	3	7	-
P V Simmons	17	24	2	1244	171	56.54	4	7	35	-
H Morris	18	32	2	1666	202*	55.53	6	9	14	-
W S Kendall	12	23	4	1045	145*	55.00	3	6	13	-
J J Whitaker	16	23	3	1093	218	54.65	4	2	2	-
N H Fairbrother	12	20	0	1068	204	53.40	2	8	10	-
C J Adams	20	36	3	1742	239	52.78	6	8	34	-
W J House	8	15	5	526	136	52.60	2	2	2	-
D M Jones	19	34	5	1502	214*	51.79	4	7	15	-
M A Butcher	18	34	3	1604	160	51.74	3	13	21	-
P A Cottey	20	36	6	1543	203	51.43	4	9	16	-
T M Moody	19	31	3	1427	212	50.96	7	4	12	-
R S Dravid	9	16	5	553	101*	50.27	1	4	6	1
D A Reeve	5	8	1	351	168*	50.14	1	-	7	-
J P Crawley	15	25	3	1102	112*	50.09	3	8	6	-
D Ripley	11	16	7	448	88*	49.77	-	3	23	-
G D Lloyd	15	25	1	1194	241	49.75	3	4	6	-
J B Commins	9	15	3	597	114*	49.75	1	5	2	-
M R Ramprakash	17	31	2	1441	169	49.68	4	8	7	-
I D Austin	10	12	3	437	95*	48.55	-	3	4	-
D M Cox	7	13	4	434	95*	48.22	-	4	2	-
R A Smith	17	31	2	1396	179	48.13	3	8	1	-
E T Smith	7	12	0	576	101	48.00	2	4	1	-
N V Knight	15	28	3	1196	132	47.84	4	5	18	-
B F Smith	20	29	3	1243	190	47.80	3	4	5	-
S P James	20	38	1	1766	235	47.72	7	6	15	-
C L Hooper	17	29	2	1287	155	47.66	3	9	33	-
Ijaz Ahmed	9	16	2	664	141	47.42	2	4	2	-
V Rathore	10	17	0	805	165	47.35	1	7	9	-

Name	Matches	Inns	NO	Runs	HS	Avge	100s	50s	Ct	St
C M Gupte	11	14	1	606	132	46.61	2	3	1	-
A C Ridley	7	9	0	417	155	46.33	2	1	1	-
N Hussain	18	31	1	1386	158	46.20	3	7	18	-
M B Loye	14	25	2	1048	205	45.56	2	5	5	-
K J Barnett	18	34	2	1456	200*	45.50	3	9	5	-
Salim Malik	9	14	4	450	104*	45.00	2	1	1	-
R T Robinson	17	31	2	1302	184	44.89	3	6	8	-
S P Titchard	13	23	2	939	163	44.71	2	5	11	-
Asif Mujtaba	10	16	6	445	100*	44.50	1	2	8	-
G A Hick	17	29	1	1245	215	44.46	5	3	19	-
J E R Gallian	15	29	3	1156	312	44.46	3	3	10	-
A D Jadeja	8	13	2	489	112*	44.45	2	2	6	-
V J Wells	20	30	0	1331	204	44.36	4	3	20	-
N Pothas	6	9	2	309	90	44.14	-	3	15	-
M Keech	12	21	3	793	104	44.05	1	7	9	-
M N Lathwell	18	32	4	1224	109	43.71	2	7	13	-
G F Archer	13	24	3	918	143	43.71	2	5	17	-
M D Moxon	14	25	3	961	213	43.68	2	5	5	-
W P C Weston	20	37	5	1389	171*	43.40	4	7	20	-
T L Penney	19	34	4	1295	134	43.16	3	8	14	-
A J Stewart	14	24	1	966	170	42.00	1	7	15	1
T R Ward	18	31	1	1252	161	41.73	2	9	12	-
K R Spiring	18	32	6	1084	144	41.69	3	7	9	-
K Greenfield	14	26	4	916	154*	41.63	3	3	10	-
S V Manjrekar	9	15	2	540	101	41.53	1	4	4	-
N Boje	7	9	2	289	89	41.28	-	3	5	-
P D Bowler	19	34	4	1228	207	40.93	2	7	5	-
H D Ackerman	7	11	0	447	99	40.63	-	4	3	-
K M Krikken	19	29	7	882	104	40.09	1	3	64	3
A N Aymes	19	32	12	801	113	40.05	2	2	42	3
P A Nixon	20	27	5	880	106	40.00	3	4	56	6
D J Sales	4	8	1	280	210*	40.00	1	-	4	-
M Azharuddin	8	13	2	439	111*	39.90	1	3	3	-
V S Solanki	14	24	3	828	90	39.42	-	6	9	-
C L Cairns	16	29	5	946	114	39.41	1	6	10	-
S J Rhodes	19	29	5	939	110	39.12	1	8	40	8
J S Laney	17	30	0	1163	112	38.76	4	5	13	-
M P Vaughan	18	32	2	1161	183	38.70	3	6	4	-
M A Atherton	15	26	1	963	160	38.52	1	7	8	-
R C Irani	19	31	4	1039	110*	38.48	1	7	10	-
N J Llong	14	22	2	763	130	38.15	2	5	12	-
C M Wells	12	19	3	609	165	38.06	1	3	4	-
R R Montgomerie	18	34	3	1178	168	38.00	4	4	17	-
G A Khan	13	18	2	608	101*	38.00	1	4	7	-
V P Terry	7	12	2	379	87*	37.90	-	3	12	-
A Symonds	18	30	1	1097	127	37.82	3	4	9	-
A W Evans	7	13	3	376	71*	37.60	-	2	5	-
W K Hegg	17	25	6	713	134	37.52	1	3	50	5
O D Gibson	9	15	3	449	97	37.41	-	3	6	-

Name	Matches	Inns	NO	Runs	HS	Avge	100s	50s	Ct	St
T J G O'Gorman	11	20	3	636	109*	37.41	1	6	7	-
I J Sutcliffe	8	12	0	443	83	36.91	-	5	1	-
P N Weekes	19	35	2	1218	171*	36.90	4	4	11	-
D L Hemp	8	13	2	405	103*	36.81	1	1	3	-
A P Wells	19	35	2	1206	122	36.54	2	6	13	-
N R Mongia	7	12	2	364	85	36.40	-	2	13	1
D J Roberts	4	7	0	254	73	36.28	-	2	-	-
B P Julian	16	23	2	759	119	36.14	2	3	9	-
N J Lenham	16	28	3	903	145	36.12	2	5	3	-
A J Moles	13	25	0	903	176	36.12	2	4	7	-
R J Bailey	12	22	2	722	163	36.10	1	3	8	-
M W Gatting	16	25	0	901	171	36.04	1	8	10	-
A Habib	16	24	2	792	215	36.00	1	2	10	-
A Singh	12	22	2	718	157	35.90	2	1	6	-
S L Campbell	16	29	0	1041	118	35.89	1	7	15	-
P C L Holloway	10	16	1	535	168	35.66	1	3	7	-
R J Harden	12	20	1	676	136	35.57	1	5	11	-
A S Rollins	19	36	5	1101	131	35.51	3	5	11	-
Shadab Kabir	7	12	1	390	99	35.45	-	3	6	-
K R Brown	18	31	5	917	83	35.26	-	8	60	1
D D J Robinson	12	23	2	738	97	35.14	-	8	6	-
A A Metcalfe	12	22	0	771	128	35.04	1	3	4	-

BOWLING AVERAGES
Qualifying requirements : 10 wickets taken at an average of under 30

Name	Overs	Mdns	Runs	Wkts	Avge	Best	5wI	10wM
Shahid Nazir	47	8	164	12	13.66	4-43	-	
Saqlain Mushtaq	166.5	43	456	29	15.72	6-52	2	-
C E L Ambrose	284.4	80	717	43	16.67	6-26	5	1
C A Walsh	526.3	145	1432	85	16.84	6-22	7	1
P V Simmons	364.4	87	1021	56	18.23	6-14	3	-
D A Mascarenhas	92	21	297	16	18.56	6-88	1	-
G M Gilder	95.1	29	243	13	18.69	8-22	1	1
Mushtaq Ahmed	325	85	861	41	21.00	7-91	5	1
M A Ealham	401.4	130	995	47	21.17	8-36	3	1
Waqar Younis	195.1	42	654	30	21.80	5-42	1	-
C A Connor	362.4	99	1071	49	21.85	9-38	2	-
P C R Tufnell	839.1	273	1712	78	21.94	7-49	6	1
N J Llong	80.5	23	249	11	22.63	5-21	1	-
D Gough	573.3	142	1535	67	22.91	6-36	2	-
J D Lewry	302	59	942	41	22.97	6-44	4	1
D J Bicknell	124.2	21	368	16	23.00	3-7	-	-
D J Millns	538.1	133	1659	72	23.04	6-54	2	1
S Lugsden	70.3	9	262	11	23.81	3-45	-	-
G D Rose	393.2	98	1218	50	24.36	7-47	3	1
M W Alleyne	458.1	123	1316	54	24.37	5-32	2	-
Wasim Akram	271.5	67	787	32	24.59	5-58	1	-
M P Bicknell	568.1	146	1633	66	24.74	5-17	3	-
M J McCague	590	120	1897	76	24.96	6-51	3	-

Name	Overs	Mdns	Runs	Wkts	Avge	Best	5wI	10wM
E S H Giddins	367.4	66	1204	48	25.08	6-47	2	-
B C Hollioake	65	12	252	10	25.20	4-74	-	-
A F Giles	633.3	191	1615	64	25.23	6-45	3	-
L Klusener	232.2	44	783	31	25.25	5-74	1	-
A D Mullally	628.5	166	1774	70	25.34	6-47	3	1
D Follett	147.2	26	589	23	25.60	8-22	3	1
T M Moody	319.5	86	956	37	25.83	7-92	3	1
A J Harris	379.1	76	1380	53	26.03	6-40	2	1
P A J DeFreitas	544.3	106	1687	64	26.35	7-101	4	-
P J Martin	427.4	106	1161	44	26.38	7-50	1	-
P M Such	771.4	190	2164	82	26.39	8-118	6	1
G J Smith	125.2	24	402	15	26.80	4-70	-	-
S L Watkin	616.4	159	1797	67	26.82	4-28	-	-
M V Fleming	168.3	32	484	18	26.88	3-6	-	-
A M Smith	487.3	114	1615	60	26.91	8-73	3	1
S J E Brown	642.1	109	2130	79	26.96	6-77	5	-
D W Headley	423	69	1387	51	27.19	8-98	2	1
R J Green	187.5	36	599	22	27.22	6-41	1	-
J P Taylor	549.2	116	1766	64	27.59	7-88	3	1
A R Caddick	604.1	131	2029	73	27.79	7-83	6	3
R J Kirtley	193.4	32	756	27	28.00	5-51	1	-
R C Irani	395	74	1320	47	28.08	5-27	1	-
S M Pollock	446.4	115	1183	42	28.16	6-56	1	-
G C Small	164	35	536	19	28.21	4-41	-	-
J P Hewitt	179.3	38	681	24	28.37	3-27	-	-
J A Afford	579.5	165	1471	51	28.84	6-51	2	-
B P Julian	447.4	86	1762	61	28.88	6-37	3	-
I D K Salisbury	505	109	1506	52	28.96	8-75	3	1
D R Law	320.4	45	1221	42	29.07	5-33	2	-
I D Austin	223.4	64	645	22	29.31	5-116	1	-
Venkatesh Prasad	252.3	59	734	25	29.36	5-76	1	-
K D James	301.1	57	882	30	29.40	5-74	1	-
V J Wells	255.1	69	765	26	29.42	4-44	-	-
K J Dean	144.1	32	471	16	29.43	3-47	-	-
P J Hartley	459.2	96	1602	54	29.66	6-67	2	1
C White	299.2	51	1100	37	29.72	4-15	-	-
C L Hooper	321.3	83	789	26	30.34	4-7	-	-
G Welch	275.5	42	1035	34	30.44	4-50	-	-
J P Stephenson	336.4	73	1098	36	30.50	6-48	3	-
C E W Silverwood	404.3	79	1442	47	30.68	5-72	2	-
P W Jarvis	168	27	592	19	31.15	4-60	-	-
A Symonds	118.3	25	374	12	31.16	2-21	-	-
T A Munton	404	116	1092	35	31.20	4-41	-	-
J E Benjamin	375.3	83	1217	39	31.20	4-17	-	-
N D Hirwani	115.3	24	375	12	31.25	6-60	1	-
J Srinath	233.3	68	628	20	31.40	4-103	-	-
M T Brimson	360.2	76	1106	35	31.60	5-12	2	-
D E Malcolm	639.1	99	2597	82	31.67	6-52	6	2
A L Penberthy	352.2	68	1077	34	31.67	5-92	1	-

Name	Overs	Mdns	Runs	Wkts	Avge	Best	5wI	10wM
V S Solanki	215.2	37	863	27	31.96	5-69	3	1
N W Preston	130.5	27	352	11	32.00	4-68	-	-
G J Parsons	555	170	1536	47	32.68	4-21	-	-
R D B Croft	955.4	237	2486	76	32.71	6-78	4	-
N M K Smith	486.4	115	1417	43	32.95	5-76	3	-
N F Williams	331.4	59	1160	35	33.14	5-43	2	-
D G Cork	589	121	1891	57	33.17	5-113	1	-
M C Ilott	550.2	118	1666	50	33.32	5-53	2	-
A R C Fraser	592.4	138	1636	49	33.38	5-55	2	1
G Chapple	477.1	94	1671	50	33.42	5-64	2	-
V C Drakes	454.3	79	1675	50	33.50	5-47	2	-
D J Capel	348.1	57	1181	35	33.74	4-60	-	-
R K Illingworth	717.1	208	1721	51	33.74	6-75	3	-
Mohammad Akram	128.2	21	473	14	33.78	7-51	1	-
P N Weekes	371	75	1082	32	33.81	8-39	2	-
D M Cox	306	87	883	26	33.96	5-97	2	1
S Ganguly	85.4	10	340	10	34.00	3-71	-	-
M J Saggars	101	12	443	13	34.07	6-65	1	-
K J Shine	276.3	44	1209	35	34.54	6-95	2	-
D A Leatherdale	106	21	384	11	34.90	4-75	-	-

WHYTE AND MACKAY RANKINGS 1996

BATTING

Rank	Player	Total
1	G.A. Gooch (Essex)	525
2	G.P. Thorpe (Surrey)	471
3	C.J. Adams (Derbyshire)	460
4	N. Hussain (Essex)	459
5	M.P. Maynard (Glamorgan)	447
6	M.R. Ramprakash (Middlesex)	443
=	K.J. Barnett (Derbyshire)	443
8	K.M. Curran (Northamptonshire)	442
9	M.A. Butcher (Surrey)	430
10	A.J. Stewart (Surrey)	427
11	A.J. Hollioake (Surrey)	422
12	R.A.Smith (Hampshire)	421
13	T.L. Penney (Warwickshire)	420
14	M.A. Atherton (Lancashire)	417
15	H. Morris (Glamorgan)	413
=	T.R. Ward (Kent)	413
17	P.A. Cottey (Glamorgan)	408
18	S.P. James (Glamorgan)	401
19	R.T. Robinson (Nottinghamshire)	398
=	N.V. Knight (Warwickshire)	398

BOWLING

Rank	Player	Total
1	D. Gough (Yorkshire)	526
2	R.D.B. Croft (Glamorgan)	510
3	A.D. Mullally (Leicestershire)	485
4	A.R. Caddick (Somerset)	481
5	M.P. Bicknell (Surrey)	479
6	S.J.E. Brown (Durham)	469
7	J.P. Taylor (Northamptonshire)	468
8	P.M. Such (Essex)	455
9	M.J. McCague (Kent)	449
10	D.G. Cork (Derbyshire)	448
11	S.L. Watkin (Glamorgan)	447
12	P.J. Hartley (Yorkshire)	411
13	P.A.J. DeFreitas (Derbyshire)	407
14	P.C.R.Tufnell (Middlesex)	400
15	A.M. Smith (Gloucestershire)	393
16	D.E. Malcolm (Derbyshire)	392
=	M.C. Ilott (Essex)	392
18	S.R.Lampitt (Worcestershire)	391
19	P.J. Martin (Lancashire)	390
20	D.J. Millns (Lancashire)	388

INDEX OF PLAYERS BY COUNTY

*denotes not registered for 1997 season. Where a player is known to have moved in the off-season he is listed under his new county.

DERBYSHIRE

ADAMS, C. J.
ALDRED, P.
BARNETT, K. J.
BASE, S. J.
BLACKWELL, I. D.
CASSAR, M. E.
CLARKE, V. P.
CORK, D. G.
DEAN, K. J.
DEFREITAS, P. A. J.
GRIFFITH, F. A.*
GRIFFITHS, S.
HARRIS, A. J.
JONES, D. M.
KHAN, G.
KRIKKEN, K. M.
MALCOLM, D. E.
MAY, M. R.
O'GORMAN, T. J. G.
OWEN, J. E.
ROBERTS, G. M.
ROLLINS, A. S.
TWEATS, T. A.
VANDRAU, M. J.
WARNER, A. E.
WOMBLE, D. R.

DURHAM

BAINBRIDGE, P.*
BETTS, M. M.
BIRBECK, S. D.*
BLENKIRON, D. A.
BOILING, J.
BOON, D. C.
BROWN, S. J. E.

CAMPBELL, C. L.
CAMPBELL, S. L.*
COLLINGWOOD, P. D.
COX, D. M.
DALEY, J. A.
FOSTER, M. J.
HUTTON, S.
KILLEEN, N.
LEWIS, J. J. B.
LIGERTWOOD, D. G. C.
LONGLEY, J. I.*
LUGSDEN, S.
MORRIS, J. E.
PRATT, A.
ROSEBERRY, M. A.
SAGGERS, M. J.
SCOTT, C. W.*
SEARLE, J. P.
SPEAK, N. J.
SPEIGHT, M. P.
WALKER, A.
WESTON, R. M. S.
WOOD, J.

ESSEX

ANDREW, S. J. W.
CHILDS, J. H.*
COUSINS, D. M.
COWAN, A. P.
DERBYSHIRE, N. A.*
FLANAGAN, I.
GOOCH, G. A.
GOODWIN, G. J. A.
GRAYSON, A. P.
HIBBERT, A. J. E.
HODGSON, T. P.

HUSSAIN, N.
HYAM, B. J.
ILOTT, M. C.
IRANI, R.
LAW, D. R. C.
LAW, S. G.
PETERS, S. D.
POWELL, J.
PRICHARD, P. J.
ROBINSON, D. D. J.
ROLLINS, R. J.
SUCH, P. M.
WILLIAMS, N. F.
WILSON, D. G.

GLAMORGAN

BARWICK, S. R.*
BUTCHER, G. P.
COSKER, D. A.
COTTEY, P. A.
CROFT, R. D. B.
DALE, A.
DALTON, A. J.
DAVIES, A. P.
EDWARDS, G.
EVANS, A. W.
GIBSON, O. D.*
JAMES, S. P.
JONES, S. P.
KENDRICK, N. M.*
MAYNARD, M. P.
METSON, C. P.
MORRIS, H.
PARKIN, O. T.
SHAW, A. D.
THOMAS, S. D.

WATKIN, S. L.
WAQAR YOUNIS

GLOUCESTERSHIRE

ALLEYNE, M. W.
AVERIS, J. M. M.
BALL, M. C. J.
BODEN, D. J. P.*
CAWDRON, M. J.
COOPER, K. E.*
CUNLIFFE, R. J.
DAVIS, R. P.
DAWSON, R. I.
HANCOCK, T. H. C.
HEWSON, D. R.
LEWIS, J.
LYNCH, M.
READ, C. W. M.
RUSSELL, R. C.
SHEERAZ, K. P.
SMITH, A. M.
SYMONDS, A.*
TRAINOR, N. J.
WALSH, C. A.
WILLIAMS, R. C. J.
WINDOWS, M. G. N.
WRIGHT, A. J.
YOUNG, S.

HAMPSHIRE

AYMES, A. N.
BENJAMIN, W. K. M.*
BOTHAM, L. J.
BOVILL, J. N. B.
CONNOR, C. A.
DIBDEN, R. R.
FRANCIS, S. R. G.
GARAWAY, M.

HAYDEN, M. L.
JAMES, K. D.
KEECH, M.
KENDALL, W. S.
KENWAY, D.
LANEY, J. S.
MARU, R. J.
MASCARENHAS, D. A.
MILBURN, S.
MORRIS, R. S. M.*
RENSHAW, S. J.
SAVIDENT, L.
SMITH, R. A.
STEPHENSON, J. P.
SWARBRICK, M.
TERRY, V. P.*
TREAGUS, G. R.
UDAL, S. D.
WHITAKER, P. R.
WHITE, G. W.

KENT

COWDREY, G. R.
EALHAM, M. A.
FLEMING, M. V.
FORD, J. A.
FULTON, D. P.
HEADLEY, D. W.
HOOPER, C. L.
HOUSE, W. J.
LLONG, N. J.
MARSH, S. A.
McCAGUE, M. J.
PATEL, M. M.
PHILLIPS, B. J.
PRESTON, N. W.
SPENCER, D. J.
STANFORD, E. J.
THOMPSON, J. B.

WALKER, M. J.
WALSH, C. D.
WARD, T. R.
WELLS, A. P.
WILLIS, S. C.
WREN, T. N.

LANCASHIRE

ATHERTON, M. A.
AUSTIN, I. D.
BROWN, C.
CHAPPLE, G.
CHILTON, M. J.
CRAWLEY, J. P.
ELWORTHY, S.*
FAIRBROTHER, N. H.
FLINTOFF, A.
GALLIAN, J. E. R.
GREEN, R. J.
HARVEY, M. E.
HAYNES, J. J.
HEGG, W. K.
KEEDY, G.
LLOYD, G. D.
MARTIN, P. J.
MCKEOWN, P. C.
RIDGEWAY, P. M.
SHADFORD, D. J.
TITCHARD, S. P.
WASIM AKRAM
WATKINSON, M.
WOOD, N. T.
YATES, G.

LEICESTERSHIRE

BRIMSON, M. T.
CROWE, C. D.
DAKIN, J. M.

INDEX OF PLAYERS BY COUNTY

HABIB, A.
MACMILLAN, G. I.
MADDY, D. L.
MASON, T. J.
MILLNS, D. J.
MULLALLY, A. D.
NIXON, P. A.
ORMOND, J.
PARSONS, G. J.
PIERSON, A. R. K.
REMY, C. C.*
ROBINSON, P. E.
SIMMONS, P. V.
SMITH, B. F.
STEVENS, D.
SUTCLIFFE, I. J.
THOMAS, A.
WELLS, V. J.
WILLIAMSON, D.
WHITAKER, J. J.
WHITTICASE, P.

MIDDLESEX

BLANCHETT, I. N.
BLEWETT, G. S.
BROWN, K. R.
CARR, J. D.*
DUTCH, K. P.
EVANS, M. R.
FAY, R. A.
FELTHAM, M. A.*
FRASER, A. R. C.
GATTING, M. W.
GOODCHILD, D.
GOULD, I. J.*
HARRISON, J. C.
HEWITT, J. P.
JOHNSON, R. L.
LARAMAN, A. W.

LYE, D.
MOFFAT, S. P.
NASH, D. C.
NASH, D. J.*
POOLEY, J. C.
RAMPRAKASH, M. R.
RASHID, U.
SHAH, O.
STRAUSS, A. J.
TUFNELL, P. C. R.
WEEKES, P. N.
WELLINGS, P.

NORTHAMPTONSHIRE

AMBROSE, C. E. L.*
BAILEY, R. J.
BAILEY, T. M. B.
BLAIN, J. A. R.
BOSWELL, S. A. J.
BROWN, J. F.
CAPEL, D. J.
CURRAN, K. M.
DAVIES, M. K.
DOBSON, M.
EMBUREY, J. E.
FOLLETT, D.
FORDHAM, A.
HUGHES, J. G.
INNES, K. J.
LOGAN, R.
LOYE, M. B.
MALLENDER, N. A.
MONTGOMERIE, R. R.
PENBERTHY, A. L.
RIPLEY, D.
ROBERTS, A. R.*
ROBERTS, D. J.
SALES, D. J.
SNAPE, J. N.

STEELE, M. V.
SWANN, A. J.
SWANN, G.
TAYLOR, J. P.
WALTON, T. C.
WARREN, R. J.

NOTTINGHAMSHIRE

AFFORD, J. A.
AFZAAL, U.
ARCHER, G. F.
BATES, R. T.
BOWEN, M. N.
BROADHURST, M.*
CAIRNS, C. L.
DOWMAN, M. P.
EVANS, K. P.
FRANKS, P.
GIE, N. A.
HART, J. P.
HINDSON, J. E.
JOHNSON, P.
METCALFE, A.A.
MIKE, G. W.*
NEWELL, M.
NOON, W. M.
PENNETT, D. B.*
PICK, R. A.
POLLARD, P. R.
ROBINSON, R. T.
TOLLEY, C. M.
WALKER, L. N.
WELTON, G. E.
WILEMAN, J. R.*

SOMERSET

BATTY, J. D.*
BATTY, J. N.

INDEX OF PLAYERS BY COUNTY

BOWLER, P. D.
BURNS, M.
CADDICK, A. R.
DIMOND, M.
ECCLESTONE, S. C.
HARDEN, R. J.
HAYHURST, A. N.*
HOLLOWAY, P. C. L.
KERR, J. I. D.
LATHWELL, M. N.
LEE, S.*
MORGAN, H.
MUSHTAQ AHMED
PARSONS, K. A.
REEVE, D. A.
ROSE, G. D.
SHINE, K. J.
TREGO, S.
TRESCOTHICK, M. E.
TRUMP, H. R. J.
TURNER, R. J.
VAN TROOST, A. P.
WELLS, C. M.

SURREY

BENJAMIN, J. E.
BICKNELL, D. J.
BICKNELL, M. P.
BROWN, A. D.
BUTCHER, M. A.
DE LA PENA, J.
HOLLIOAKE, A. J.
HOLLIOAKE, B. C.
KENLOCK, S. G.*
KENNIS, G. J.
KNOTT, J. A.
LEWIS, C. C.
NOWELL, R. W
PATTERSON, M. W.

PEARSON, R, M.
PIGOTT, A. C. S.*
RATCLIFFE, J. D.
SALISBURY, I. D. K.
SHAHID, N.
SMITH, A. W.*
STEWART, A. J.
THORPE, G. P.
TUDOR, A. J.
WARD, D. M.
WARD, I. J.

SUSSEX

ATHEY, C. W. J.
BATES, J. J.
DRAKES, V. C.
EDWARDS, A.
GREENFIELD, K.
HALL, J. W.*
HUMPHRIES, S.
JARVIS, P.W.
KIRTLEY, R. J.
KHAN, A. A.
LENHAM, N. J.
LEWRY, J. D.
MARTIN-JENKINS, R. S.
MOORES, P.
NEWELL, K.
NEWELL, M.
PEIRCE, M. T. E.
PHILLIPS. N. C.
PYEMONT, J.
RAO, R. K.
STRONG, M.
TAYLOR, N. R.
THURSFIELD, M. J.

WARWICKSHIRE

ALTREE, D. A.
BELL, M. A. V.
BROWN, D. R.
DONALD, A. A.
EDMOND, M. D.
FROST, A.
GIDDENS, E. S. H.
GILES, A. F.
HEMP, D. L.
KHAN, W. G.
KNIGHT, N. V.
McDONALD, S.
MOLES, A. J.
MUNTON, T. A.
OSTLER, D. P.
PENNEY, T. L.
PIPER, K. J.
POLLOCK, S. M.*
POWELL, M. J.
SINGH, A.
SMALL, G. C.
SMITH, N. M. K.
SMITH, P. A.*
WAGH, M.
WELCH, G.

WORCESTERSHIRE

AMJAD, M.*
BRINKLEY, J. E.
CHAPMAN, M.
CHAPMAN, R. J.
CHURCH, M. J.*
CURTIS, T. S.
DAWOOD, I.
D'OLIVEIRA, D. B.
ELLIS, S. W. K.
HAYNES, G. R.
HICK, G. A.

YORKSHIRE

ANSWERS TO QUIZ

1. Sachin Tendulkar
2. Anil Kumble
3. Dean Headley
4. Shahid Afridi of Pakistan
5. Geoff Marsh
6. Darren and Martin Bicknell, Adam and Ben Hollioake
7. James Whitaker (Leicestershire), 218 at Bradford 1996 and Geoff Cook (Northamptonshire), 203 at Scarborough 1988)
8. Raman Subba Row, 300 Northamptonshire v Surrey, The Oval 1958 (he was born in Streatham)
9. Phil Simmons, Leicestershire v Gloucestershire
10. Ireland beat Holland
11. Ian Austin
12. J.B. Commins
13. Millfied School
14. Bradfield Waifs
15. Kevan James, Hampshire against India
16. Warren Hegg, Lancashire (134) and Paul Nixon, Leicestershire (106)
17. Alan Mullally
18. Imran Khan, Wasim Akram, Abdul Qadir, Waqar Younis
19. Devon beat Norfolk
20. Saurav Ganguly, av. 95.25
21. Graham Gooch, av. 67.03
22. Shahid Nazir, av.13.66
23. Dimitri Masceranhas, av. 18.56
24. Glamorgan: Tony Cottey, Stephen James, Matthew Maynard and Hugh Morris
25. Hassan Raza of Pakistan
26. Wasim Akram, 257* v Zimbabwe, Sheikhupura 1996-97
27. Andrew Harris
28. Steve Rixon
29. India beat South Africa
30. Graham Gooch, Tim Curtis, Mike Gatting, Graeme Hick
31. Danny Morrison
32. Julian Thompson of Kent who dismissed Graham Gooch, Mike Gatting and Michael Atherton
33. Shaun Pollock for Warwickshire against Leicestershire
34. Andy Flower
35. Emily Drumm
36. Sachin Tendulkar (23 yrs 228 days) beat Javed Miandad (24 yrs 280 days)
37. Graeme Fowler
38. John Crawley, Alec Stewart and Graham Thorpe
39. Steve Waugh and Glen McGrath
40. Peter Willey and Bob Willis, 171 minutes, England v West Indies, The Oval 1980
41. Phil Tufnell
42. Jack Russell
43. Sir Donald Bradman
44. Taslim Arif, 210 v Australia, Faisalabad 1979-80
45. Les Ames, 149 v West Indies, Kingston 1929-30
46. Viv Richards, 11 Tests
47. Pakistan beat West Indies
48. Brian Lara
49. Michael Atherton, Lord's 1994
50. Ben Hollioake
51. Chris Tavaré
52. Jeff Thompson
53. He scored three Test centuries on tour
54. David Boon
55. Phil Tufnell
56. 1980 Centenary Test
57. 227 runs
58. Geoff Lawson
59. 1982-83
60. Arnie Sidebottom
61. Peter Sleep
62. David Constant
63. Andrew Hilditch
64. Richard Ellison
65. John Morris
66. Paul Downton
67. Bruce Yardley
68. Dirk Welham
69. Tim Robinson
70. Bruce Reid and Merv Hughes
71. Don Bradman and Walter Hammond
72. Graham Gooch
73. 1981
74. David Gower
75. Wayne Phillips
76. None
77. 22 runs
78. Mike Valetta and Tony Dodemaide
79. Paul Allott
80. Tim Zoehrer and Greg Dyer
81. David Gower
82. Jack Richards
83. Edgbaston
84. Eddie Hemmings
85. John Emburey, Tim Robinson and Neil Foster
86. Mark Ilott and Martin McCague
87. Mark Waugh and Michael Atherton
88. Don Bradman, Bobby Simpson, Bob Cowper and Len Hutton
89. W.G. Grace
90. Walter Hammond
91. David Bairstow
92. Rod Marsh
93. Robin Smith in 1993
94. Graham Thorpe, 444 runs at 49.33
95. Darren Gough, 20 wickets at 21.25
96. Michael Slater, 623 runs at 62.30
97. Craig McDermott, 32 wickets at 21.09
98. Greg Blewett
99. Mike Gatting
100. Mark Waugh